A BIOGRAPHY

TOM NOLAN

SCRIBNER

SCRIBNER
1230 Avenue of the Americas
New York, NY 10020

SCRIBNER and design are trademarks of Simon & Schuster Inc.

DESIGNED BY COLIN JOH

Set in New Baskerville

Manufactured in the United States of America

1   3   5   7   9   10   8   6   4   2

Library of Congress Cataloging-in-Publication Data
Nolan, Tom.
Ross Macdonald : a biography / Tom Nolan.
p.   cm.
Includes index.
1. Macdonald, Ross, 1915– . 2. Novelists,
American—20th century—Biography.
3. Detective and mystery stories—Authorship.
PS3525.I486Z79   1999
813'.52—dc21
[b]   98-48225
CIP

ISBN 0-684-81217-7

All quotations from unpublished letters and other unpublished writings by Kenneth
Millar and all quotations from unpublished letters by Margaret Millar are used with
the extremely kind permission of the trustee of the Margaret Millar Charitable
Remainder Unitrust, owner of the books, copyrights, and materials related to the
collected works of Kenneth Millar (Ross Macdonald) and Margaret Millar. The trustee
has also kindly allowed use of lengthy excerpts from the published Ross Macdonald
essays "The Scene of the Crime" and "The Writer as Detective Hero," and from the
published Kenneth Millar poems "Wild Goose" and "If Light Were Dark."
Permissions continued on page 422.

For my father

INTRODUCTION
by Sue Grafton

The contrast between Ken Millar the man, Ross Macdonald the novelist, and Lew Archer the fictional private detective is one that will doubtless fascinate scholars and psychologists for years to come. What Tom Nolan accomplishes in this meticulous biography is to detail the connections between Ken Millar's personal odyssey and his professional pursuits. Fair-minded, evenhanded, Tom Nolan's account of the life of Ken Millar gives depth and dimension to a man who tended to say little about himself. This biography provides the basis for a renewed appreciation of the man and his achievement. Ken Millar's struggle for success, the pleasure he took in the trajectory of his career, and the complexities of his marriage to mystery writer Margaret Millar are related with a balance and a grace of which Millar himself would have approved.

Nolan has the confidence to let Millar's life stand without speculation, though the darker aspects of the writer's history must have provided a powerful temptation. From Millar's troubled adolescence to his only daughter's clashes with the law, Nolan locates Millar's work within the context of his life and allows these events to speak for themselves.

I was privileged to meet Kenneth Millar twice here in Santa Barbara. This was sometime in the late sixties, long before my career as a mystery writer was launched. Introduced by mutual acquaintances, we did no more than shake hands in passing. I was, at that point, a lowly creative-writing student in an adult-education class, and he had already achieved near legendary status. Even as an avid reader of his work, I knew little of the man. I would love to report that he made some cogent comment that shaped my aspirations and gave impetus to my ambition. Alas, he did not, though his unwitting influence on my career was profound. One gathers that Ken Millar wasn't often given to casual or hasty comment, though he afforded other writers his unfailing support. He was, by all reports, a man of intelligence and reserve, whose observations about writing were neither haplessly assembled nor carelessly disseminated. Quiet, courtly, and unprepossessing, Millar was the quintessential intellectual in a genre formerly reserved for men of more flamboyant style and more inflammatory imagination.

ROSS MACDONALD

Ken Millar was intrigued by the hard-boiled detective genre. Taking the reins from Dashiell Hammett and Raymond Chandler, he handled the form with mounting confidence. Where Hammett and Chandler wrote only a scant few novels each (five in Hammett's case, seven in Chandler's), Ross Macdonald's eighteen Lew Archer novels were written over a span of some twenty-five years, allowing the writer a narrative range and breadth in which to hone his skills. Millar incorporated into the Lew Archer novels his own maturing worldview and thus imbued the series with a melancholy, hard-won wisdom.

More poetic than Hammett, less cynical than Chandler, what Ross Macdonald demonstrated many times over was that the hard-boiled detective novel was no longer the exclusive domain of the whiskey-drinking gumshoe, fists flying, guns blazing, blonde bombshell perched on the edge of his desk. Like his creator, Lew Archer was a man with a finely honed sensibility, whose passion for fairness permeated everything he did.

From Ross Macdonald, we learned to see southern California as we'd never seen it before. From him, we finally understood that the crime novel could be as challenging, as astute, and as rarefied as the sonnet . . . precise, perceptive, and passionate . . . even while its fundamental subject matter remained rooted in crime and violent death. If Dashiell Hammett can be said to have injected the hard-boiled detective novel with its primitive force, and Raymond Chandler gave shape to its prevailing tone, it was Ken Millar, writing as Ross Macdonald, who gave the genre its current respectability, generating a worldwide readership that has paved the way for those of us following in his footsteps.

Sue Grafton
Santa Barbara, California
July 28, 1998

Ten years ago, while nobody was watching—or, rather, while every-one was looking in the wrong direction—a writer of detective stories turned into a major American novelist.

—John Leonard, *The New York Times Book Review*

. . . the Archer books, the finest series of detective novels ever writ-ten by an American.

—William Goldman, *The New York Times Book Review*

In 1969, when most literate readers thought detective stories beneath consideration and mystery fiction rarely appeared on best-seller lists, a handful of New York journalists conspired to push a California writer of private-eye novels to the front rank of American letters.

The writer was Ross Macdonald, a mystery novelist who didn't so much transcend the genre as elevate it, showing again (like Hammett, Faulkner, Collins, Dickens, Greene, and many others since Poe) how the crime story can at any time become art.

The conspiracy worked.

Front-page celebrations in the *New York Times Book Review* and a cover story in *Newsweek* turned Ross Macdonald's books about detective Lew Archer into national best-sellers. Movies and a television series were made. Millions of Macdonald's books were sold. After twenty years in the mystery field, Ross Macdonald was an overnight success.

The world at large discovered a writer already well known to mystery fans. Crime-fiction reviewers had long hailed Macdonald as the hard-boiled successor to Dashiell Hammett and Raymond Chandler. His influ-ence on a generation of mystery writers was profound. In such classic works as *The Doomsters, The Galton Case, The Chill, Black Money, The Goodbye Look, The Underground Man,* and *Sleeping Beauty,* Macdonald opened fresh thematic territory and set a new literary standard for his genre. Vital trends in modern crime fiction drew impetus from Macdonald's work. Writers as diverse as Sara Paretsky, Jonathan Kellerman, Jerome Charyn, and James Ellroy have called Macdonald an influence. Simply as a best-selling mystery author he broke ground; his success, before a time when genre authors routinely became household names, showed the way for the future Parkers, Graftons, Hillermans, Cornwells, and Mosleys.

Ross Macdonald's appeal and importance extended beyond the mystery field. He was seen as an important California author, a novelist who evoked his region as tellingly as such mainstream writers as Nathanael West and Joan Didion. Before he died, Macdonald was given the *Los Angeles Times*'s Robert Kirsch Award for a distinguished body of work about the West. Some critics ranked him among the best American novelists of his generation.

By any standard he was remarkable. His first books, patterned on Hammett and Chandler, were at once vivid chronicles of a postwar California and elaborate retellings of Greek and other classic myths. Gradually he swapped the hard-boiled trappings for more subjective themes: personal identity, the family secret, the family scapegoat, the childhood trauma; how men and women need and battle each other, how the buried past rises like a skeleton to confront the present. He brought the tragic drama of Freud and the psychology of Sophocles to detective stories, and his prose flashed with poetic imagery. By the time of his commercial breakthrough, some of Macdonald's concerns (the breakdown between generations, the fragility of moral and global ecologies) held special resonance for a country divided by an unpopular war and alarmed for the environment. His vision was strong enough to spill into real life, where a news story or a friend's revelation could prompt the comment "Just like a Ross Macdonald novel."

It was a vision with meaning for all sorts of readers. Macdonald got fan mail from soldiers, professors, teenagers, movie directors, ministers, housewives, poets. He was claimed as a colleague by good writers around the world, including Eudora Welty, Andrey Voznesensky, Elizabeth Bowen, Thomas Berger, Marshall McLuhan, Margaret Laurence, Osvaldo Soriano, Hugh Kenner, Nelson Algren, Donald Davie, and Reynolds Price.

When he died in 1983, Ross Macdonald was the best-known and most highly regarded crime-fiction writer in America. But (despite dozens of articles, two documentary films, and two critical studies) not much was known about the author of "the finest series of detective novels ever written by an American."

It was no secret Ross Macdonald was the pseudonym of Kenneth Millar, a Santa Barbara man married to another good mystery writer, Margaret Millar. But his official biography was spare: born in northern California of Canadian parents, raised in Ontario and other provinces, he earned a doctorate at Michigan, served in the U.S. Navy, and moved with wife and daughter to California in 1946. In a handful of autobiographical essays, Millar seemed to conceal as much as he told.

Hiding things came second nature, to protect himself and spare his family. Like the people in his fiction, Millar had secrets, and he persuaded sympathetic journalists to collaborate in keeping them.

Yet he believed in the writing of candid biography and expected to be its subject. He valued works that made connections between a novelist's life and his fiction. Millar preserved much material that proved helpful in explicating the books of Ross Macdonald, who admitted he was one of those authors who strew their novels with personal clues, "like burglars who secretly wish to be caught." Among the revealing documents Millar left future literary detectives were a candid notebook memoir, an unpublished autobiographical novel, and thirty years' correspondence.

Now—after the deaths of his widow, their only child, and their only grandchild; after unrestricted examination of the Kenneth and Margaret

Millar Papers at the University of California, Irvine, as well as other archives' material; and after hundreds of interviews with those who knew Millar—a fuller picture emerges of this admired American writer.

Ross Macdonald came to crime writing honestly. Virtually fatherless and growing up poor, Kenneth Millar broke social and moral laws: having sex from the age of eight, getting drunk at twelve, fighting violently, stealing. "I'm amazed at some of the chances I took as a boy," he admitted. Worse than the things he did were those he imagined. Mad at the world and at his lot in life, he sometimes felt angry enough to kill. As a youngster he read Poe and Hawthorne and Dostoyevsky: writers who wrestled with the good and the bad angels he too was assaulted by. When he wrote his own mystery stories, Millar saw himself in his tales' wrongdoers. "I don't have to be violent," he said, "my books are."

By his own reckoning, he barely escaped being a criminal. When he stopped breaking laws before starting college, he fashioned a code of conduct for himself (and others) as unyielding as the formal religious creeds he had rejected. Millar put himself in a behavioral box as if his life or mental health depended on it, though his psyche often strained against the box's walls. He stayed over forty years in an often rancorous marriage, putting its tensions to use as he turned his wife and himself into published authors. He stayed in the box of detective fiction, determined to provide for his family and avoid the failures of his irresponsible father.

"The Split Man" was a title Macdonald often played with. Millar himself was a man split along national, cultural, intellectual, professional, and even sexual fault lines. Born in California, raised in Canada, as a young man he thought of moving to England. All his life he felt on the wrong side of whatever border he'd most recently crossed. The roots of Macdonald's tales of troubled families in a corrupted California lay in Millar's bleak Ontario childhood with its "long conspiracies of silent pain."

The man who created the hard-boiled Lew Archer was one of the most brilliant graduate students in the history of the University of Michigan. While Macdonald's private-eye stories were being published in *Manhunt* magazine next to Mickey Spillane's (which he detested), Millar was writing a Ph.D. dissertation on the psychological criticism of Samuel Taylor Coleridge. His academic colleagues disparaged or despaired of his detective fiction; his fellow crime writers were puzzled or intimidated by his university work.

In the sunshine of Santa Barbara, California, Kenneth Millar dressed like a Midwesterner and spoke with a Scots-Canadian accent. In the wealthy heart of Nixon and Reagan country, he was a Stevensonian Democrat; even as a beach-club member, he still felt like an underdog.

He was a gentle man with a frightening temper, an intellectual who went to murder trials, a person of great pride and startling humility. Once or twice he nearly broke under his complexities. Like Oedipus (a recurring archetype in Macdonald's fiction and Millar's psyche), he seemed to bring about the tragedies he tried to avoid. Determined to be the good parent his own were not, Millar fathered an only child whose life was scarred by emotional and legal trauma. Obsessed with not causing fatal harm, he saw his daughter become entangled in the sort of headline-making events he'd always dreaded, incidents his own stories seemed to eerily foretell. At his daughter's darkest hours, Millar acted like his books' hero Lew Archer; then turned her crises into the fiction from which they might have sprung.

In his novels, Millar resolved his contradictions: there he hid and revealed an aching loneliness, a melancholy humor, and a lifetime of anger, fear, and regret. These singular works changed their genre and changed the way readers saw the world. In these stories, ordinary families became the stuff of mystery; and there was always guilt enough to go around. We recognized ourselves as characters in Ross Macdonald's novels. And the most interesting Macdonald character of all was Kenneth Millar.

The Mariner tells how the ship sailed southward with a good wind and fair weather, till it reached the line.	The ship was cheered, the harbour cleared, Merrily did we drop Below the kirk, below the hill, Below the lighthouse top.

The Mariner   The ship was cheered, the harbour cleared,
tells how the   Merrily did we drop
ship sailed   Below the kirk, below the hill,
southward   Below the lighthouse top.
with a good
wind and fair   The Sun came up upon the left,
weather, till it   Out of the sea came he!
reached the   And he shone bright, and on the right
line.   Went down into the sea.

—S. T. Coleridge, "The Rime of the Ancient Mariner"

Before Alzheimer's disease put an end to his writing, Millar recorded his earliest memories: recollections formed in the final months of World War One, in Vancouver, British Columbia. His father was a harbor-boat pilot there, and Millar recalled the "unforgettable" occasion when his dad took him to sea: "I stood beside him in the offshore light, with his hands and my hand on the wheel." At the age of sixty-three, he judged this "the happiest day of my childhood if not my life."

Millar's parents separated when he was four, and his mother took him to a harsher province. As a troubled child and an uneasy adult, Ken Millar mourned the loss of that moment of bliss and belonging, of being loved and protected. The fiction he wrote was informed by the painful knowledge of the difference between the way life was supposed to be and the way it was. In his books, people looked obsessively for lost parents and vanished birthrights; children took dangerous paths; a detective tried to discover when and where and why it all went wrong.

Vancouver wasn't the first paradise he lost. Millar's birthplace was California, something his parents never let him forget. In his youth that state took on a golden aura: the Great Right Place where he should be but wasn't. He was born in Los Gatos, near San Francisco, during a heavy rainstorm at three in the morning of Monday, December 13, 1915.

The Bay Area was celebrating that year, with a Panama-Pacific Exposition in San Francisco to mark completion of the Panama Canal and the city's recovery from the 1906 earthquake and fire. This Millar baby also became news of a sort: his father wrote a poem about him that was printed in the *Los Gatos Mail*. The poet-father was John Macdonald "Jack" Millar, a forty-two-year-old Canadian who'd edited newspapers in British Columbia and Alberta settlements for the past several years. Defying its spelling, the family name was pronounced "Miller," an ambiguous touchstone for a son who'd spend a lifetime pondering questions of identity.

The dad had his own obsession with such matters, having lived with Indians in the Northwest Territories, befriended Japanese fishing families in Vancouver, and for years written poems in the dialect of a Scotland he'd never seen.

John Macdonald Millar's Scottish connection came through his father, another John Millar, who had emigrated from Galashiels (near Edinburgh) to southern Ontario, Canada, in 1856. The senior John Millar was a solid citizen, serving at different times as reeve (mayor), township clerk, postmaster, police magistrate, and justice of the peace. He and his Scots-Canadian wife had nine children, seven of whom survived; the sixth was Jack Millar, born in 1873. After teaching school and keeping a general store, the senior Millar started the *Walkerton Herald,* a newspaper that stayed in business for at least a century. Printer's ink was in the Millar blood, some said: the first successful Scottish printer, around 1506, was a Millar. This "fatal predisposition to words" was passed on to Jack—along with a youthful rebellion. Jack Millar adopted his father's Liberal politics but rejected his Presbyterian faith, becoming an admirer of Robert Green Ingersoll, "the Great Agnostic." Like John Millar, who'd sailed from Scotland as a teenager, the teenaged Jack Millar left the family home early to strike out on his own.

Jack Millar was medium sized but powerfully built, a good wrestler and strong swimmer. He made his way to the western Canadian provinces, then south into the United States, where he mined for silver in Colorado. Back in Canada, he lived for close to a year with Indians around Great Slave Lake. In 1899, the territory-wise Jack Millar joined two Toronto newspapermen, John Innes and J. P. McConnell, on a six-week pack-train journey across Alberta and British Columbia.

Jack was in Vancouver, British Columbia, in 1907, when young William Mackenzie King, federal deputy minister of labor, came to investigate anti-Japanese riots there. Millar, friendly with the port's Japanese fishermen, informally helped the future prime minister in his inquiries.

A year later, in Red Deer, Alberta, the thirty-four-year-old Millar met a tall, attractive, thirty-three-year-old former nurse named Anna Moyer. Jack courted Annie on horseback and read her his Robbie Burns–like poems. Born in Walkerton, the town whose newspaper Jack's dad had started, Annie had turned down several youthful suitors in order to study and work in Canada and the States. Typhoid fever caught from a hospital patient had ended her nursing. She was ready to accept Jack's proposal. Before they married, John Macdonald Millar, like his father before him, became a newspaper editor-manager, taking over a monthly in the copper-mining town of Greenwood, British Columbia; then starting his own paper in Granum, Alberta. Jack and Annie were married in Calgary, Alberta, in September 1909.

Millar put out three other papers in his first four years of marriage, trekking with Annie to frontier mining, logging, and shipping towns in British Columbia and Alberta. It was a rough haul. Annie had two stillbirths before she and Jack moved to San Diego, California, in 1913. They hoped the California climate would give them a healthy baby. But in San Diego, in 1913, they buried another infant.

Annie had family living in Escondido, near San Diego, including her married sister Adeline, a Christian Science convert. Adeline told Annie, raised Methodist like her, that if she joined Mary Baker Eddy's church, she'd have a healthy baby. Annie converted. From San Diego, the Millars went north to Los Gatos, where Annie Millar gave birth to Kenneth. This baby was healthy—twelve and a half pounds—with eyes that were an almost violet blue: his mother's eyes.

The Millars returned to Canada. After a mild stroke, Jack Millar gave up newspaper work. In Vancouver, he earned sea captain's papers and, with the First World War on, became pilot of a harbor boat. The family lived in upper-floor rooms of a downtown waterfront hotel, and here Kennie first became aware of the world around him. His mother read him fairy tales and other stories. She took him bathing at English Bay, a busy beach where a huge black lifeguard kept watch like Neptune over hundreds of youngsters.

Jack took his boy to the studio of painter John Innes, one of the Toronto newspapermen he'd helped guide from Alberta to Vancouver in 1899. Innes was now a dramatically whiskered artist, capturing on canvas the already vanishing frontier of his and Jack's journey. His studio, full of pack saddles, riding boots, and other Western gear, was a haven for old cronies like Millar. Innes at work in his lair made a big impression on Jack's wide-eyed son.

Kennie showed some artistic ability of his own. Given a slate, he drew chalk pictures, including a pretty good one of Charlie Chaplin, whom he'd seen at the silent pictures. On his slate, Kennie learned numbers and letters. He seemed a bright boy, full of curiosity. At rest, the boy looked serene, with big, wise-seeming eyes and the half-smile of an oriental prince.

But his parents quarreled. After nine years, their differences now eclipsed what they'd had in common. Annie gave thanks to God and to Christian Science for the good things in life; Jack, the freethinking atheist, put his faith in the social theorist Henry George. In love with the West he'd known when young, Jack was glad to spend the day explaining Indian signs or listening to tall tales told by the snow-blind prospector who lived in the hotel basement; Annie was sick of their unsettled life and of her husband's fruitless "hobbies."

In November 1918, the Great War ended. Mobs of celebrants jammed Vancouver's streets. Returning troops marched in dress uniform on the avenue near the Hudson's Bay store. The world had made peace—but not Jack and Annie.

Around this time Jack took his boy for that boat ride along the Vancouver coast.

The boy later remembered a less happy incident: when he looked through a hotel balcony grating and saw a body spread-eagled in the alley below. The man wasn't dead, only dead drunk; but the frightening image stayed in his mind. For the four-year-old, his parents' separation was as sudden and awful as the sight of that body. Like a child in a fairy tale, he blamed himself. His father's absence marked him forever. The world, it seemed, was a place that took full payment for an hour of perfect bliss.

I must be the only American crime novelist who got his early ethical training in a Canadian Mennonite Sunday School.
—Ross Macdonald

When the Son of man comes in his glory, and all the angels with him, then he will sit on his glorious throne. Before him will be gathered all the nations, and he will separate them one from another as a shepherd separates the sheep from the goats.
—Matthew 25:31–32.

Kitchener, Ontario, half a continent away from any ocean, was where Kenneth and Annie Millar went in 1920. Unlike Vancouver, haven of freethinkers, Kitchener was a practical place, founded by Mennonite farmers and settled by German merchants. Instead of sea salt in the air, here there were fumes from three rubber factories. The city had been called Berlin until the recent war, and over half its twenty-two thousand people still spoke German. Black-clad Mennonites came to town in horse-drawn buggies. Annie Millar grew up a few miles from here with eight sisters and brothers, all living above father Aaron Moyer's Mildmay general store. The Presbyterian Moyer, married to the Mennonite Veronica Bowman, raised his children Methodist. An ex-schoolteacher, Aaron Moyer encouraged his seven daughters and two sons to sing harmony, play instruments, write letters, and draw pictures.

But Aaron Moyer was dead, buried on the Saskatchewan prairie where he'd gone with his family to homestead at seventy-three. When his widow came back to Ontario, she joined the reformed branch of the Mennonite Church of her youth. No cardplaying or other sinful pursuits were allowed in the two-story, brick bungalow at 32 Brubacher Street where Grandma Moyer lived with Annie's sister Adeline (who'd wired the money for Annie's and Ken's train fares). This was the forbidding house Ken Millar and his mother moved into.

Grandmother Moyer at seventy-four was a strong-willed woman who demanded obedience. She insisted that five-year-old Kennie attend Sunday school at her New Mennonite church. There he learned about Judgment Day, when the sheep would be separated from the goats. The boy sensed his grandmother and her Bowman kin already placed him with the latter. It was as if his brow bore some mark of Jack Millar's curse. "My original sin, so to speak," he later judged, "was to be left by my father." There was fear and pain now in his blue eyes. His mother changed too. At forty-five, she looked like an old woman. Her and his presence at 32 Brubacher caused problems, and in 1921, Anna and Kennie moved out of Grandma

Moyer's house and into furnished rooms. The boy blamed himself for this, as he'd blamed himself for his father's having gone away.

Too weak to work, Annie ran out of funds. Sometimes she took Ken into the street and begged for food. Finally she brought the six-year-old to an orphanage and filled out papers to have him admitted. The iron gates of the orphanage were branded in his memory like the gates to the Mennonites' hell. At the last minute, as in one of the fairy tales his mother read him, he was rescued. Rob Millar, a cousin of Jack's who lived ninety miles north of Kitchener, said he and his wife, Elizabeth, would take Ken into their home. Life was full of surprises and sudden reversals. Instead of an orphanage, Ken Millar was sent to live in the town of Wiarton, on the idyllic banks of Georgian Bay.

Most of the detective work that accomplishes anything is due to the use of good common sense, and much of the remainder is just luck.
—William A. Pinkerton, quoted in the *Canadian Echo*, Wiarton, 1922

"The Mystery of the Silver Dagger," by Randall Parrish . . . Here is a double-riveted mystery story as thrilling as anything this great master of mystery, adventure and romantic tales, ever has produced. It is compounded of love, intrigue, a million dollars and mysterious criminals in a most unusual combination . . . *Soon to Appear in These Columns*. READ IT!
—*The Canadian Echo*, Wiarton, 1922

Millar was a common name in Wiarton, where Jack Millar once won a two-mile swimming race across Colpoys Bay. Nearby was a bump in the road called Millarton, where many of Jack's Scots-Canadian cousins had settled. A local legend involved the *Jane Millar*, a passenger steamer that vanished with nary a trace in 1881.

Kenneth's "uncle" Rob (actually his second cousin) was the town's electrical engineer. Having lost two daughters to fatal illness, he and his wife, Elizabeth, welcomed six-year-old Kennie like a son into their George Street house. Elizabeth gave Kenneth an uncomplicated love much easier to accept than his own troubled mother's. Rob became the first of several father substitutes Kennie found throughout and beyond his childhood.

Rob Millar's skills exposed Kennie to new excitements. Over the radio Rob built, Ken heard songs from the States such as "Yes! We Have No Bananas" and "There'll Be Some Changes Made." On Saturdays, Rob ran the Wonderland moving picture theater, where Ken watched the silent adventures of Robinson Crusoe and the athletic doings of Pearl White, an androgynous heroine young Ken half fell in love with.

In Wiarton he started the lifelong habit of reading the newspaper. Rob and Elizabeth Millar were mentioned often in the weekly *Canadian Echo*'s local columns. Kenneth's own name began appearing regularly on the *Echo*'s front page, in monthly school standings that showed him rising to near the top of his elementary school class.

Through the *Echo*'s syndicated features and serialized novels, Ken Millar got his first tastes of crime fact and fiction. During 1922 and '23, the *Echo* carried interviews with William A. Pinkerton ("head of the greatest detective agency in the world") and detective-story writers Arthur B. Reeve and Sir Arthur Conan Doyle. Adventure stories printed in the *Echo* included Randall Parrish's "The Mystery of the Silver Dagger," Conan Doyle's "The Great Shadow," and Canadian writer Hesketh Prichard's "November Joe: The Detective of the Woods."

Loved and protected by Rob and Elizabeth, Kenneth Millar found safe haven. But it was tainted by his fear and anger at being parted from his father and mother, and he showed some disturbing behavior. In the schoolyard, Kenneth bullied younger classmates. At his guardians' home, he initiated frequent sexual play with a mentally retarded teenaged maid. And for the first time, he stole: taking a shiny dime from an Indian basket filled with mementos of Rob and Elizabeth's dead daughters. With the dime the future crime writer bought a pencil—then deliberately broke the pencil in two.

Despite these acts, he was happier in Wiarton than he'd been since Vancouver. And as in Vancouver, life took payment in full. In October 1923, fifty-one-year-old Elizabeth Millar went to nearby Owen Sound for a gall-bladder operation. She died on the surgeon's table. A grieving Rob Millar said he could no longer look after his "nephew." Like a character in one of the Wonderland Theater's serials, Kenneth Millar was catapulted again into an uncertain future.

The heart felt sympathy of the community goes out to Mr. Millar . . .
and to little Kenneth, in the great loss they have sustained.
—The Canadian Echo, October 31, 1923

Anna Moyer had moved back to her mother's house at 32 Brubacher. That's where Kenneth joined her in late 1923, a month before his eighth birthday. Also living in the two-story brick bungalow were his thirty-seven-year-old bachelor uncle Edwin, who worked in a commercial laundry; and his recently widowed aunt Adeline, head of filing at the Mutual Life Assurance in neighboring Waterloo.

Jack Millar too was in Kitchener in 1923, clerking a while for Mutual Life (probably thanks to Adeline), then employed at the Kitchener Gas Works. He and Annie, never divorced, tried twice to reconcile—living together briefly and arguing sometimes violently about money and sex. The reconciliations didn't take.

Jack lingered in Ontario for a few years, in rented Kitchener rooms or at an uncle's Caledon East farm. Kennie spent bits of summer with his dad but for the most part was in his mother's company. Annie and her boy, poor to the bone, moved from one rooming-house address to another: 124 Krug Street, 43 Ellen Street East, 52 Francis Street North. One place they stayed was run by a Mrs. Funk. Sometimes they stopped with relatives, such as Sylvia Vollick, one of Annie's married sisters, in Mildmay. All the Moyers felt sorry for them, but no one had room or money to spare.

Kenneth went away from both parents some summers, to the farm of another married aunt. When he was eight, two young male cousins there introduced him to "homo-sex," which excited and shamed him. At this same farm, he speared his groin walking a picket fence and had to be taken to the hospital.

Without a father around, he was vulnerable to temptations and dangers. His overemotional mother couldn't protect him. In cramped rooms in Kitchener, Annie and her son slept in the same bed, long after he felt right about it. He sensed he'd taken his father's place in his fractured family. The woman once ready to give him to an orphanage was devoted to him in ways that seemed unhealthy. She expected him to do what Jack Millar couldn't: rescue them from their wretched state. Sometimes Annie was sentimentally loving, other times violently critical. Her son learned to gauge her moods and manipulate them.

She came up with pathetic schemes to earn money—such as going door-to-door selling homemade dusting cloths—that he was afraid his Suddaby classmates would learn of. Ken didn't speak of his mother unless he had to. Nor did he mention his dad. Few Kitchener people even knew of Jack's existence. Many took it for granted Annie was a widow. Ken Millar learned early to keep family secrets.

He escaped by reading and could often start a book at dawn and finish it by breakfast. He devoured the adventure serials (Edgar Wallace's *Sanders of the River* and *The Green Archer*) in British boys' magazines such as *Chums*. He loved the Tarzan stories. And at ten, he was bowled over by Charles Dickens's *Oliver Twist*, a tale of a workhouse boy fallen among thieves. He read it for so many hours at a time that his mother worried he'd damage his eyes. Ken Millar identified with Oliver, his grinding poverty, the dangers that menaced him. Oliver's workhouse reminded Kenneth of the orphanage he'd escaped. Dickens wrote of a world the Kitchener boy recognized: violent and frightening, full of rescues and snares, of instant enemies and unknown relatives. *Oliver Twist,* like the scary Pearl White serial in Wiarton, was something you could put your fears into and feel better for.

In 1927, Kenneth's life took another Dickensian turn. His father's sister Margaret, an aunt he'd never met, invited her eleven-year-old nephew to come live with her in Winnipeg, Manitoba, and attend a private school at her expense.

No doubt Jack Millar was behind this (as he'd probably been behind cousin Rob's bringing Kennie to Wiarton). Annie Millar could hardly refuse this generous offer. Again Kenneth was sent off by himself, this time by train, to another province and a world different from any he'd known.

An education that aims not merely at instruction in sound knowledge, but at the building up of a manly Christian character under
religious influence—that is the ideal of St. John's.

—St. John's College School, Winnipeg, Class and Honor List, 1928

K. Millar: Who's the best business man in the world?
Byng: John D. Rockefeller.
Millar: No. A man who can buy from a Jew and sell to a Scotchman
at a profit.

—*The Black and Gold*, St. John's College School, 1929

S t. John's was an Anglican school, a college prep academy founded in
1820 and modeled on English lines; most of the masters were English.
There were playing fields, a skating rink, and a gymnasium. The
curriculum here was rigorous: Latin, French, English, geography, math, algebra, geometry, physics; British, Canadian, and general history; religion. Daily
chapel and military drill were compulsory. Ken Millar sang in the St. John's
church choir and competed in gym, hockey, and team equestrian events.

The other St. John's boys were sons of well-to-do merchants and ministers from several provinces and even U.S. cities like Chicago—a much different bunch from the ragtag "Five Points gang" Millar played street
hockey and "run sheep run" with in Kitchener.

During the week, he boarded at school. After dorm bedtime, he'd rig a
mirror to reflect hall light on his pillow so he could read into the night.
Ken Millar liked stories of heroes who worked outside the law, righting
wrongs and making the rich pay: gentleman-thief Jimmie Dale, written by
Canadian-American Frank L. Packard; O. Henry's safecracker Jimmy
Valentine; best of all Falcon Swift, "the Monocled Manhunter," who
starred in an English boys' magazine Millar bought on Saturdays at a store
on North Main.

Weekends he stayed at his aunt Margaret's apartment at 109 Devon
Court, on Broadway, across from the provincial capitol. His father's sister
was a "sophisticated" woman who smoked cigarettes and drove an automobile. Aunt Margaret had worked as a Detroit bookkeeper, then married
a Chicago florist who died and left her well-off. In Winnipeg, she apparently supervised a string of beauty parlors and played the stock market. She
was married to a Winnipeg man named Ed, with an adopted son (younger
than Millar) whose middle name was Ross; this boy too went to St. John's.

Aunt Margaret gave weekend parties at her apartment, where paintings
of nudes hung on the walls and a Pianola cranked out hits of the day like
"In a Little Spanish Town." Her party guests were active on the stock and

grain exchanges and in Winnipeg politics. Millar, used to damp Kitchener rooming houses where rats sometimes scurried in the walls, got a taste of how the other half lived.

There were odd things about his aunt's household, though. Uncle Ed kept a heavy handgun in his Packard glove box: an odd accessory for someone listed in the Winnipeg directory sometimes as a dentist and sometimes as a chiropractor. Millar in time concluded that his uncle managed a Winnipeg slot machine racket, one with ties to a Detroit crime syndicate.

Kenneth kept out of Uncle Ed's way. Aunt Margaret, who "smiled like a lioness," bought Millar school clothes and took him to see touring English plays *(The Pirates of Penzance)* and his first "talking pictures."

One day his father, shy and uncertain, showed up at Devon Court and proposed that his boy come with him out West, where Jack was bound for one last journey. His son didn't want to leave school and go West. Jack departed Winnipeg alone.

The visit was a painful reminder of Kenneth's father's failures, and it made the twelve-year-old ashamed and angry. He got into fistfights with some of his classmates, and homosexual episodes with other boys. He stole. He filched drinks from his aunt's parties and got drunk.

But he worked hard at St. John's. He spent his evenings in the gym, practicing on the uneven and horizontal bars and the sawhorse, and earned a drill medal in mid-1928. He also won honors in English, mathematics, and Bible study. "An *excellent scholar,*" his headmaster wrote on his midsummer report. Millar placed second in his class and was given a scholarship.

In Kitchener for the summer, Kenneth saw his father again, returned from the West where Jack had shipped out as a common seaman. Jack Millar had done a brave thing: jumped into icy waters to rescue a comrade fallen overboard. But the act broke what was left of his health. Jack had come back to Ontario to die.

On July 1, 1928, a few weeks shy of his fifty-fifth birthday, John Millar of 72 Ontario Street West wrote a two-page letter of advice to his twelve-year-old son: "Be kind, industrious and independent. Keep up physical exercises. Practice writing and public speaking. Don't quarrel with anyone. It is futile. Don't fight unless you have to—then fight like hell." Jack appended a reading list: Robert Burns, Luther Burbank, Thomas Paine, Clemenceau, Jefferson, Ingersoll, Henry George, Adam Smith, Karl Marx. "Without humanity," he wrote, "all religion is as 'sounding brass.' It is the 'tinkling cymbal' of the glad-handers and that's what most religionists and politicians are. (Propagandists.)" Jack told his boy to be considerate of other people's rights and opinions, and to make the most of his life. " 'Knowledge has power,' and both money and the pen are mightier than the sword." He signed himself, "Daddy."

"Throughout my life," Millar wrote in late middle age, "I remained my father's son."

*   *   *

Jack Millar's testament sent his boy back to St. John's with new purpose. He applied himself aggressively to his studies, and by Christmas he was at the head of his class.

Millar had decided he wanted to be a writer. For years reading had been his best escape from unpleasant reality, his chief entertainment and source of information. Books were the most important thing to him, except people; writing seemed almost sacred. In stories (as in movies, which he also loved) you could shape things in ways that let you make sense of them, get them under control.

Kenneth wanted to be a writer like Dickens, whose *Oliver Twist* set his heart and mind racing. Dickens was a writer anyone could appreciate; he wrote classics for common people.

There were writing models on both sides of Millar's family. His mother's people expressed themselves well in letters; and his mother's brother Stanley Moyer, the artist, wrote poems and articles for magazines. Ken's grandfather had started the Walkerton newspaper. And there was his father, who worked all his life with words, for profit and for pleasure.

During his hours alone at St. John's, Kenneth labored on poems and stories. One was a ballad of Bonnie Prince Charlie, the Scottish Pretender, who fled to France with the help of a woman named Macdonald.

Millar didn't neglect his studies, though, and was first in his form again at midsummer 1929. "A most promising young Scholar," his headmaster wrote. "He will go far if he gets the chance."

But he wouldn't. When the term ended, he learned he'd be leaving St. John's. His aunt had lost money in the stock market and couldn't afford his fees: that's what he was told. But for all Kenneth knew, he was getting the boot because of something wrong done at school or in the apartment. His life was starting to seem like some mean game of snakes and ladders.

He spent the summer in Kitchener, until another aunt volunteered to take him: his mother's sister Laura in Medicine Hat, Alberta. Now thirteen, Kenneth again boarded the transcontinental train.

In Alberta, the coldest and most cheerless place he'd seen, he went through tenth grade at Medicine Hat's Alexandra High School. Ken Millar liked Aunt Laura but never warmed to Uncle Fred, a school inspector and amateur naturalist with a collection of tens of thousands of dead beetles. Millar kept up his grades in Medicine Hat and didn't steal, but there were homosexual incidents with other boys, and he thought his aunt and uncle learned of one, though they didn't say so. When spring term ended, though, he was told he'd be leaving Medicine Hat.

Back he went to Kitchener, to his grandmother's red-brick bungalow. Uncle Edwin with the cleft palate was still there, and hardworking Aunt Adeline, and disapproving Grandma Moyer. Hardest of all for Millar to deal with was his pitiable mother, who was coming apart emotionally, either raging at him or expecting him to restore the family fortunes. He took to hitchhiking, to get away from the house. In Wiarton he looked up Rob Millar, half-hoping for an invitation to come live here again. But Rob Millar was remarried and had a real son. Ken stayed the night and left the next day, rejected again.

He hitched to the Bruce Peninsula to see his father on a run-down farm where Jack was staying with a sick male cousin. "Old Jack" was unable to speak after his most recent stroke, but the poet kept writing and still had a spark in his eye.

With no place else to go, Millar enrolled for eleventh grade at the Kitchener-Waterloo Collegiate Institute: KCI. To ease the sting of being a poor relation, he got an after-school job as stockboy and handyman in a "groceteria." Working two hours each schoolday and all day Saturday, he earned two and a quarter dollars a week: pretty good wages considering Canada, like the States, was now in the grip of a great financial depression that looked as if it could last forever.

DASHIELL HAMMETT writes a superior mystery novel because for many years he was a Pinkerton detective. He is probably the only "bull" who has ever turned his experience into the writing of crime stories. To Hammett, plot is not the main thing in the story. It is the behavior of the detective attacking a problem which intrigues him.
—Dust jacket, *The Maltese Falcon,* 1930

The ambitious young investigator, Herlock Sholmes, yawned behind his false moustache and poured for himself a cocaine-and-soda.
—Kenneth Millar, "The South Sea Soup Co.," *The Grumbler,* 1931

In Kitchener, Millar continued to steal and to have sex with other boys, though guilt over both things made him miserable. He also kept making poems and stories, training to be a writer. Wanting encouragement but not trusting the KCI teachers, he showed his poetry to his mother's cousin Sheldon Brubacher, a Toronto high school instructor with a university degree. Brubacher said Kenneth's poems reminded him of early work by Byron and Shelley (a flattering exaggeration, Millar much later realized). This praise gave him the confidence to continue.

At KCI, he made friends with half a dozen male students who also wrote. The boys showed their pages to one another and discussed books. Wanting to learn more than what was taught at school, they read and analyzed works by Aristotle and the pre-Socratic philosophers. Millar spent a lot of time at the Kitchener Public Library, where the woman in charge was B. Mabel Dunham, a published author of local-historical novels.

Miss Dunham (a practicing spiritualist who claimed she communed with the deceased she wrote about) had reason to take note of Millar. She knew his artist uncle Stan Moyer, whom Millar sometimes hitchhiked to visit in Toronto. Moyer's articles were printed in magazines that the library stocked; eventually Stan Moyer painted Mabel Dunham's portrait.

Millar's uncle was a gentle-looking man with dry Canadian wit. Uncle Stan stirred memories of Ken Millar's visits to John Innes's Vancouver studio, and his work showed Ken how to see with a painter's eye: a crucial thing for the writer he hoped to become. Stan Moyer was an essential emblem: a member of Millar's own family who was a real artist. Stan's sister (Ken's Aunt Louisa) had married an American architect named Albert Wood; their household, full of artistically gifted kids, was another hopeful beacon to Millar. The novelist-librarian Mabel Dunham was important in a similar way. The achievements of these people Millar knew personally encouraged him to think he too might accomplish such things.

Miss Dunham's library became Ken Millar's second home. He checked its "recent arrivals" section often, alert for books from New York publisher Alfred A. Knopf, whose well-printed volumes Kenneth thought were always the best. Millar read every Knopf "Borzoi Book" he could find. Each Saturday, he also read the new issues of all the English and American magazines. When he discovered the *American Mercury,* an outstanding U.S. journal edited by H. L. Mencken and with strong ties to Knopf, Kenneth hunted in secondhand-book stores for back issues.

All this was to prepare himself for a writing career. But Millar read for pleasure too: lots of science fiction and (his special favorite) detective stories. Vowing to read every mystery in the library, he went through hundreds of British and American books by such writers as Allingham, Bentley, Chesterton, Christie, Conan Doyle, and S. S. Van Dine. Mabel Dunham saw what he was up to and stocked the mystery section creatively. "I had read all of *Crime and Punishment,*" he later wrote, "before I realized I'd been conned by an expert."

Another KCI student often at the library was Margaret Sturm, the brightest girl at school. Witty, popular, and a good pianist, she was the daughter of alderman Henry Sturm, manager of the Conger-Lehigh Coal Company. Like Ken Millar, Margaret Sturm liked to read mysteries and liked to write stories and poems. She submitted a Maugham-like tale to KCI's 1931 student annual, the *Grumbler,* where Millar was literary editor. He accepted it for the issue's lineup, along with a sketch of his own: a Sherlock Holmes parody in the style of Canadian humorist Stephen Leacock. It was Millar's first printed story, a small step toward his goal of becoming a professional.

He kept that dream to himself. It wasn't smart to speak openly at the Brubacher house, in the face of his grandmother's Pennsylvania Dutch mutterings that he was bound to come to a bad end. His mother on the other hand was sure he was destined for greatness, and her pipe dreams were just as difficult to bear. Anna tried to inspire her boy with stories of their distant Bowman cousin who'd helped found Johns Hopkins, and of Kenneth's great-grandfather who walked to Canada from Pennsylvania with only a quarter and died a rich man, and of his grandfather the newspaper publisher who'd also been justice of the peace. Often Anna reminded her son he'd been born in California, a golden land she hoped he'd return to.

Millar spent as little time as possible in the Brubacher Street house, whose every inch—the leaded-glass fanlight above the front door, the faded wallpaper, the stains in the sink—seemed depressing. Using his gymnast skills, he shinnied up and down the drainpipe to come and go as he pleased. He'd sneak into movie theaters without paying to see pictures like *The Return of Dr. Fu Manchu.* Downtown he discovered McCallum's Cigar Store, a billiard parlor on King Street West.

McCallum's had a barbershop and a rental library. There were slot machines of the sort found in stores and restaurants all over town. A constant poker game went on upstairs. But the big lure were the smooth green pool tables, lit by overhead lamps and hazed in blue tobacco smoke. The teenaged Millar was accepted in McCallum's, no questions asked. Playing pool and smoking cigarettes under the pressed-iron ceiling, he felt like a man. The pool hall became as much a haven as the public library.

He was being pulled in two directions. The split within him had grown since he was a kid, when he'd learned to keep facts and feelings to himself. Now he had vices to hide: smoking, drinking, stealing, sex. He was leading a double life: in public he was a well-mannered, soft-spoken, bookish young person; roaming the town on his own, he was a fellow full of shame and envy.

He wanted to make something of himself but wasn't certain he could. He lived in poverty, went to school in a tattered windbreaker, wore the same sweater all year. He knew he was smart, but he sensed his potential for evil. When he saw a well-fed, well-loved boy somewhere—at the train station, say, fussed over by loving parents—part of him wanted to be that youngster, part of him wanted to smash the kid.

He was always aware of the gulf between haves and have-nots. His father was in a charity ward ("the poorhouse"), where Anna went and nursed him at his worst: another painful family secret.

All over Canada, young people were angry about the financial depression that saw families living on pennies. Millar was angrier than most. He was mad at his mother for being ignorant of life, mad at his father for causing their situation, mad at a town that looked down on a fatherless boy, mad at a world that allowed such things. He was angry at himself and his own self-pity. If he'd still believed in God, he'd have been angry with Him.

The teenager turned his discontented attention on the hidden life of the city. What secret deals allowed some people to pay for nice houses and clothing and cars? The slot machines all over town drew his special scrutiny. "Mint machines," they were called, but they paid off in twenty-dollar jackpots. There was a machine in the lunchroom across from school; lots of boys lost money in it, but school authorities never acknowledged its presence. These slots probably took in thousands of dollars, but city fathers ignored this thriving racket in a kind of conspiracy of silence. Maybe police were paid to look the other way. Maybe gangsters from the States were involved.

Other betting went on in Kitchener. The poker room was easy to find, as was the floating dice game. Horse bets were taken in cigar stores and pool halls. Bookmakers did business out of private houses. All these things were open secrets, and it irked Millar that you never encountered this sort of real life in fiction.

But that changed. Browsing the rental library at McCallum's, he found a novel by a man called Dashiell Hammett. It was fitting he see it here, where money was gambled and deals were made. (Alderman Henry Sturm, Marg Sturm's father and soon to be the mayor of Kitchener, was a former McCallum's manager.) This Hammett novel was just the sort of book Millar sought: one that told the truth about how the world worked. It was a mystery novel, supposedly, but unlike any mystery Millar had ever read: set in a tough town, with real-seeming crooks, cops, politicians, and other types tangled together. *Hard-boiled* was the word for this new kind of crime story. "As I stood there absorbing Hammett's novel," he later wrote, "the slot machines at the back of the shop were clanking and whirring, and in the billiard room upstairs the perpetual poker game was being played. Like iron filings magnetized by the book in my hands, the secret meanings of the city began to organize themselves around me."

This novel confirmed his sense of how things worked, not only in Kitchener but in other cities such as Winnipeg, scene of a violent general strike and home of his scary uncle. He read most of the Hammett book in one standing. It was printed by Alfred A. Knopf, his favorite publisher. But Millar hadn't seen this important work at the public library, where Knopf books were stocked as a matter of course. Why wasn't it there?

It *was* there, he discovered—but along with other new and old titles, it was hidden. Library staff kept certain books out of sight of the public in whose name they'd been purchased. Exploring the library, Millar came upon these restricted books and was outraged at being denied things he thought vital to his education. At night, when the library was closed, Millar climbed its fire escape and entered the building through an unlocked window. He went to the room with the uncirculated books and read his fill of Dashiell Hammett, Ernest Hemingway, Rabelais, Flaubert, and William Faulkner. When he left, he took revenge, like a literary Falcon Swift, on those who would rob him of such essential writing. He stole an armful of best-selling fiction from the open shelves: the sort of false-to-life stuff he considered trash. On the way back to his bed at 32 Brubacher, Millar dropped this junk down a manhole and into the Kitchener sewer.

It is generally agreed by doctors that a school pupil should sleep at least 10 hours a day. Harvey Bacher is "sleeping" up to this fact in 102.

Mr. Archer on the other hand, prefers the policy of Lafontaine's "to let the sleeping dog lie."

—"Form News," *The Grumbler,* 1931

Visitor: "Doctor can you help me? My name is Archer."
Doctor: "No, I'm sorry I can't do a thing for you."

—*The Grumbler,* 1931

Shoplifting, stealing money from school cloakrooms and YMCA lockers, boosting cars for joyrides, rolling drunks: these were crimes a grown-up Millar ascribed to teen males in autobiographical fiction he drafted. In real life, the teenaged Millar certainly stole. He knew pimps, prostitutes, and other low types from his pool-hall rambles. A scheme for the blue-eyed Millar to work a homosexual badger game, luring adult males into compromising situations, may well have been proposed to him; such a hustle also turned up in later fiction notes. At fifteen, Millar looked handsome but haunted, a boy hovering between sexual orientations, chased by furies of good and evil.

He nursed a crush on Margaret Sturm and secretly followed her home after classes. He loved her sharp humor, her self-assurance (she was nearly a year older), her intelligence, her coltish legs. "Someday I'm going to marry that girl," he told a buddy (echoing a man in Hammett's *The Glass Key* who's smitten with a politician's daughter). But to Margaret, Kenneth said not a word.

Millar felt insecure in nearly every way and craved knowledge of how to live in the world. He felt himself pulled along dangerous paths. It was as if two sides of his nature were in a race: sometimes the sensitive, studious boy was leading; sometimes the angry, destructive boy dashed ahead. For the first time in his life, Millar did poorly in school. Then he was caught in a crime, something serious enough to warrant calling the police. But police were not called. Whoever nabbed Millar (perhaps a KCI teacher, a store employee, or a YMCA worker) meted out their own punishment—possibly forcing Kenneth to run behind a moving automobile he was tied to, a penalty mentioned in later Millar notebooks. Whatever happened had the desired effect: Ken Millar resolved to stop his downward slide.

Some teachers helped him. One was Cyril Phelp, his debate-team coach, who gave him firm guidance and good counsel. And there was a Mr. Archer, who taught at KCI in 1931. With good father figures encouraging him, Millar did well in his senior year's finals—but not well enough to cancel a poor early-semester showing. Ken Millar graduated in the middle ranks of a class he'd headed the previous term. There'd be no university scholarship. His change of heart had come too late.

Canada was still frozen in a bad financial depression. Millar couldn't afford college, and without a degree he'd be scuffling for work with the rest of the unemployed. His aunt Adeline, who'd already done a great deal for the family, got him an interview for an office job at Mutual Life in Waterloo, a position that paid ten dollars a week and that once secured could be his for life. But Ken Millar didn't want to work in an office forever, or even a year. He wanted to be a writer, and he knew this job would prevent it. He purposely botched the interview. Not long after, Aunt Adeline died.

Millar's future was as uncertain as his past was unsettled. At sixteen, he counted the number of rooms he'd lived in and got fifty. He'd been frightened, bored, or intellectually insulted by Mennonites, Christian Scientists, Methodists, Episcopalians, and Presbyterians (the Anglicans were okay, he thought), and he turned his back on all of them. But he believed in his potential, and he refused to be a criminal.

He bought himself time by working for room and board on the Snyder family's Oxbow farm, six miles outside Kitchener. Here he continued his self-education, reading Schopenhauer and Kierkegaard into the night. The Snyders liked Millar and tolerated his late risings. Farm life agreed with him; he put on fifty pounds, bringing his weight to 180. He enjoyed being away from his mother and other relatives. Alone, he could set his own rules and goals. He gave up stealing. An affair with an older girl confirmed his heterosexuality and helped him renounce the homosexual acts that had shamed him since he was eight. He drew a moral code for himself to follow, using Western thought from the Greeks to Freud. Philosophical ideas weren't mere abstractions to Ken Millar but words to live by. Though he rejected formal religion, the standards he set for himself were as strict as the Mennonites'. "Hell lies at the bottom of the human heart," he later wrote, "and you find it by expressing your personality." Millar dealt with the worst impulses of his own personality—rage, self-pity, the urge to do harm—by suppressing them. He'd keep himself under rigid control. This was as serious to him as life or death, for he knew he had the strength and the anger to kill. Thoughts of succumbing to evil terrified him.

While Ken Millar wrestled with such matters, his father Jack (thanks to Annie Millar's efforts) was admitted in September 1932 to Toronto's Queen Elizabeth Hospital for Incurables, a good facility where he'd get decent care. Millar went to see him there. Jack Millar was unable to speak, barely able to move, but he still scrawled lines on paper. "His writing was so shaky that I couldn't make out the words," Millar wrote later. "But I could see that it was written in rhymed couplets."

Ken Millar had been at the Snyder farm for fourteen months when his father died in Toronto. John Macdonald Millar, fifty-nine, was buried in Kitchener on May 24, 1933. A quarter century later, his son penned this tough appraisal: "The best of his talents were wasted on bad verse à la Burns, Ingersoll atheism, the company of masculine friends who loved him truly but stupidly. 'Poor Jack' was a futile Ulysses, a Jack London with more heart and less brains. His son has spent his life trying to forgive him his bad luck."

Some good luck now came Millar's way. Unbeknownst to his wife and son, Jack Millar had a life insurance policy, no doubt thanks to Aunt Adeline, who apparently arranged for its premiums to be paid even after her death. Anna Millar received $2,212 and used it to buy an annuity for her son. Two thousand dollars would pay for four years of college. Millar would get his degree.

A parent's death, a sudden windfall: linkages of bad and good fortune would plague and bless Millar's life and occur often in his fiction. In the fall of 1933, seventeen-year-old Kenneth Millar entered Waterloo College, a Lutheran seminary with a liberal arts section. Primed by self-imposed study and the fear of failure, he was ready to excel.

Thou sad-voiced sky-born Fury, thou storm-child of the North;
Swift arrow of His vengeance, what Bowman launched thee forth?
—Kenneth Millar, "Wild Goose," *The College Cord,* 1934

Ken Millar has a reflection on ice-breaking:
Candy is dandy. But liquor is quicker.
—*The College Cord,* 1934

In his first Waterloo semester, Millar earned ten A's and moved to the head of the thirty-six-member class. Second semester he went out for sports and won seven track events. He became a reporter for the *College Cord* and published fiction and poetry in that school paper. All the energy that had once gone into furtive rebellion was now channeled into achievement and study.

Socially he was less adept and used alcohol to fight his shyness. He kept company with a blue-eyed brunette named Gretchen Kalbfleisch, a smart scholarship student who found him intense but withdrawn. He talked easily about literature though and was excited by *Esquire,* an American magazine publishing stories by Hemingway, Fitzgerald, Hammett, and Canada's Morley Callaghan. Millar submitted some things of his own to this New York monthly; when they were rejected, he wrote and informed the magazines editors that someday Esquire *would* publish his work.

Ken Millar was alive to all great writing, new or old. He loved the modern verse of T. S. Eliot, but when he found Coleridge's unfinished 1800 poem "Christabel," he so fell under its spell that he tried to complete it. What he wanted most was to be a writer, but he also wanted to do the right things: to be responsible, and not to be selfish or destructive. He wanted for instance to repay his mother for his college education. The best way to do that, he decided, was to become a high school teacher, which would let him support her and at the same time begin a writing career. He wasn't going to do what his father had done and walk away from family duty. In the fall of 1934, Millar transferred to the University of Western Ontario in London, Ontario, to pursue a five-year honors course with history and English majors, after which he'd get his teaching certificate.

At Western too he was an outstanding student. But his writing plans got revised after one of the school's best instructors, Frank Stiling, introduced Millar to the work of D. H. Lawrence. He could never write fiction as good as Lawrence's, Millar decided, so the novel as a form was closed to him— because whatever sort of writing he did, he wanted to be the best at it. He'd have to make his mark elsewhere. Since he liked modern drama (Ibsen, Strindberg, O'Neill, Pirandello), maybe he'd be a playwright. To acquire stagecraft knowledge, Millar got cast in the university production of *Lady Windermere's Fan*.

He also went out for sports and made Western's wrestling and swimming teams (his dad's events). And he made some good friends, notably Robert Ford, son of the managing editor of the *London* (Ontario) *Free Press*. With girls, though, Millar was still ill at ease. Craving sex but unwilling or unable to seduce coeds, he went to prostitutes, assuring himself these encounters were "truly human."

After one semester at Western, Millar asked his mother in Kitchener to come live with him. He saw it as a formal reconciliation: the two hadn't stayed under the same roof for three years. In late 1935, mother and son moved into a small apartment on Askin Street in London. Though Ken and Anna Millar still clashed, she stopped nagging him to attend her church services; their months together were fairly peaceful. Millar felt he'd come a long way toward forgiving his mother his childhood.

One day around Christmas, Kenneth came home and found Annie Millar lying naked and helpless. At the hospital she was diagnosed with a brain tumor. She lay delirious for weeks, having conversations with the past. Millar visited his mother but didn't keep vigil at her bedside. He wasn't present when Anna Moyer Millar died on January 26, 1936.

Guilt and depression hit him hard. He hadn't realized she might suddenly die, but he sensed he may have stayed away to punish her for not making a good marriage—and for those orphanage gates. In time he'd appreciate all that she'd done for him when he was young, how she'd encouraged his talents and kept his spirit alive. He'd struggle for years with her memory and the knowledge that he'd failed her.

Anna Millar was buried in Kitchener's Woodland Cemetery, in the same plot as the husband she'd never divorced. Millar had lost both parents, as well as the aunt who'd made his education possible. He drank a lot of beer and felt miserably lost, though he soldiered through the school term, keeping his grades up and drawing "roars of laughter" as a bourgeois American businessman in Noël Coward's *The Young Idea*. But in June, he arranged to drop out of Western for a semester. With a bit of money from his mother's death (Anna's share of Adeline's estate), he booked steamship passage for Ireland, where one of his aunts lived.

After visiting her, he bicycled all around Ireland, Scotland, and England, ending in London, where he stayed a month in a youth hostel. Half-raised on English books and journals, Ken Millar saw London as the capital of the civilized world. In the reading room of the British Museum, he caught up on new English writers such as W. H. Auden and Christopher Isherwood. At the Duchess Theatre he saw Emlyn Williams's *Night Must Fall*. The city was full of political ferment; Millar threw himself into it: marching in an antifascist demonstration, getting chased by mounted police. He met English university people, and German Jews who'd fled to

London. With Hitler, Mussolini, and Franco in power or gaining it, the Continent was about to explode. Millar wanted a firsthand look at the prelude. He tried and failed to get to Spain, then went to Munich for eight weeks in Hitler's Reich.

Thanks to his German friends in London, he made good Munich contacts: a teacher whose father was a Nazi general, the daughter of a Reichstag deputy, Jews who'd stayed in the city. He had an affair with a melancholy German girl. He had his English pipe knocked from his mouth while watching a military parade. He acquired enough anecdotes to last a decade, the sort of stories from which first novels are made (as his would be). Millar spent his twenty-first birthday in Munich, two days after Edward VIII abdicated the English throne, then went to Paris and saw in the New Year. He had what he wanted from his trip: he'd shaken the worst of his depression and gotten some kind of grip on manhood.

During these months Millar flirted with possible futures. He considered staying in England to study, but that meant "going British"—a badly regressive move for a Canadian, he felt. He thought of chucking school and going to sea, like his dad; but despite a strong romantic bent, he wasn't really willing to give up normal life and culture—though he was pretty sure he'd never marry, so as not to pass on his mother's emotional problems to any children. With a school term approaching, Millar took the sensible course of returning to Ontario to resume classes at Western. He'd banished the ghosts of his childhood, it seemed. But time, Millar learned, is a closed circuit. His ghosts would reappear.

MILLAR SPEAKS OF RECENT JOURNEY
Last evening the Hesperian Club met at the home of Professor and
Mrs. W. F. Tamblyn, 973 Waterloo Street, and conducted one of its
most successful meetings. The feature of the evening was Kenneth
Millar's sketch of his recent sojourn in Europe, with special reference to Germany. Mr. Millar's talk, delivered in his usual droll
manner, was sprinkled with lively anecdotes, and did not fail to provide humour and interest for the large number of students present.
    —*University of Western Ontario Gazette,* March 1937

> I came after Armageddon,
> And it's very heavy sleddin'
> —Kenneth Millar, 1937

M ost of Western's undergrads and many teachers wouldn't acknowledge Millar's news of impending world war; they laughed at his
picaresque vignettes but yawned at his warnings. He felt more iso
lated than ever in provincial Canada.

The costume he'd acquired in Europe set him farther apart. Millar
strode campus in an English trench coat and a green Bavarian fedora with
white cable-cord trim. He cut a romantic figure, but some peers were wary
of this traveler from the newsreel continent. Donald Ross Pearce, a junior,
kept his distance from Millar. "I thought he was not only sort of sinister,"
remembered Pearce, "but probably a dangerous person. Someone who'd
been to the Third Reich? Who knew what he'd been up to there?"

But Pearce and Millar were thrown together in rehearsals for *Twelfth
Night,* in which the lean Pearce was cast as Feste the clown opposite Millar's
stolid Duke Orsino. The two stood side by side in the wings one day, listening to a sea captain's first-act speech about a shipwrecked comrade.
"Isn't that magnificent!" Pearce exclaimed. " 'I saw him hold acquaintance
with the waves, so long as I could see!' " Millar retorted, " 'S'not magnificent atall, that's just rhetoric, Elizabethan rhetoric." Shocked, Pearce took
issue. A friendship began.

Pearce found the physically imposing Millar was also a person of great
verbal and mental strength. "There was a kind of awful force that you
quickly came to recognize," he said. "He could really and truly, without
any brutality, put a sort of conversational headlock on you. At the same
time there was something enormously gentle about him. He used to blink
bashfully, with almost a fluttering of the eyelids, whenever he was moved
to say something of a critical nature; then these great baby eyes would
stare at you while he expounded. So there were two sides: a moral

wrestler's strength—he *wrestled* with problems—and something very vulnerable, because he was so open to people."

Thanks to his wrestling and swimming, not to mention bicycling around Europe, Millar was a handsome human specimen: tall and powerfully built, with an unusually deliberate manner. He walked with a long, slow stride: frame erect and well positioned, never hurrying, never turning rapidly, but going ahead with force and purpose. And the way Millar moved, Donald Pearce saw, was much the same way he expressed himself in speech and on paper. Physically and mentally, Millar was of a piece; the Cartesian mind-body split didn't seem to exist for him—in fact, Millar deplored that Cartesian idea and blamed it for most of civilization's woes.

Pearce became a close observer of Millar. "He loved and was terribly skillful at making careful and obvious distinctions you had never noticed before," Pearce saw. "Like a poet, like Baudelaire, he could find connections between apparently disparate things. Ken created pedagogical symposiums whenever he was present! The level of the conversation would rise after Ken was in the room. He wouldn't be trying to do that. He somehow caused it. It always mystified me. I think there was something mystical about him, not just mysterious.

"He loved perspective. Distant connections. Loved the narrative among events that tied things historically. Loved to know what went before, so that he could understand what was coming after. He was a structuralist about life, and he used an X ray on it. It's no surprise he should have been a history major too. And then the English poetry and so on was the love of the immediate texture of an actual work of art or piece of writing: savoring it in and of and for itself. There were two sides, and they came together."

Complementing Millar's intellectualism was a playful sense of humor, Pearce said: "He could make up interesting aphorisms and little witticisms. Sometimes he would really let himself go and become a sort of boisterous and cavorting comic. On the other hand, he had this need to have rational control at all times. And there was a dynamic struggle between his emotional, passionate self and the intellectual, rational self. They really were in primal contradiction, keeping that volcano capped. Yet that force underneath the rational Ken was what gave his reason such passion and feeling. He could see the truth of situations or people or fictions better than anyone. He knew his own value, knew he had superiority; on the other hand he was dogged by humility, ill at ease and self-conscious with people—though he was marvelous at seeing through them or into them, interpreting them. God, he was good on people."

Millar dubbed Pearce a "golden boy," said he was "doomed to success." It was an affectionate tag, but it carried a wisp of envy of the middle-class background that took Pearce to college as a matter of course. Millar worked hard for what he got, and success was never certain.

But he and Pearce had more in common than not. So it was with the tall, thin, patrician-seeming Robert Ford. All three loved culture and the intellect and one another's company. They were joined in camaraderie by a fourth student, John Lee, whom Pearce thought "an unbelievably happy man, full of laughter and anecdotes." Millar prized Lee's "graceful warmth," Pearce said. "What mattered to Ken was sincerity, honesty, and uncluttered warmth of person. It seems to me that's a need that went away way back, to something he wanted and never got maybe as a child."

With these friends Millar was at ease, in his eccentric way. "He liked silence between people," Pearce said. "His silence was not unpleasant, because he always smiled. He was like a Buddha. Something profoundly magnetic about him. But it was unnerving too: that strong, warm, listening, scrutinizing, weighing presence. There was a saintly aspect to his nature. His personality, mind, and character were profoundly ballasted by moral concerns. Nothing offended him more than slippery or unsavory conduct. It shocked him when wrong things occurred. He was always coming into contact with life almost for the first time. In a sense he lived in the Garden of Eden—but a garden that had been visited by all the devils too.

"In a way he was maybe a very concealed kind of person, with a lot of pain and sadness and strain. He was also the most open and unprogrammed person you could imagine. And yet you felt that when Ken was being normal, he was working at it. It was conscious and deliberate normalcy—which of course makes it abnormal. He was an abnormal man who succeeded in converting his traumas and neuroses into positive forces."

Not everyone was comfortable in the presence of such a willed personality. When Pearce praised his new friend to the dean of the university, the dean said, "Yes, yes, brilliant of course—but there's a screw loose somewhere in that man."

Some teachers at Western, intimidated by Millar's knowledge, actually seemed afraid of him. For his part, Millar couldn't take seriously any instructor who hadn't heard of Maxwell Anderson or other figures well known to anyone who read the *New Yorker.* But the better Western instructors admired and even loved Millar as an outstanding student. One man spoke Millar's name with undisguised awe, Pearce recalled: "'Ken,' he would say, and almost roll his eyes." Millar was treated almost as an equal by some of these men. "Professors held him in great regard and predicted fine things for him," Pearce said, "though nobody knew just what."

Millar himself was unsure what to do with his gifts. He wanted to be a writer, but of what? His botched attempt to complete "Christabel" and his acquaintance with Bob Ford (obviously a real poet) ended his verse pursuit (though he'd write occasional poems all his life). After his exposure to theater in London and (coming back from Europe) New York, the notion of being a playwright seemed impractical: Canada had no theater scene. Becoming a novelist seemed unlikely, after the intimidating example of Lawrence, whose heavy influence he still fought to shake.

Millar's English instructors urged that he go to graduate school and there develop his gift for literary analysis; this was what he decided to do. Creative writing could wait until he established himself at a university. He wasn't going to follow Jack Millar's aimless footsteps into a life of fruitless scribbling. Millar's excellent grades almost guaranteed him a fellowship from a good American school. Bob Ford, whose grades were about as good, was applying to Cornell. A department head who was a Harvard grad talked Millar into writing to Harvard, with the implicit understanding that the professor would smooth Millar's admission with a strong letter of recommendation.

Pearce arranged for Millar to room during his last Western semesters at Huron College, a nearby Anglican residence house where Pearce had digs. Late in 1937, Ford also moved into Huron, a two-story, English-style, small-college structure full of dim corridors and creaking stairways. Each morning, Ford, Millar, and Pearce walked the mile and a quarter to the Western campus along roads often slippery with ice. Ford, who had a degenerative muscle disease and was afraid of breaking bones, strode behind Millar and held on to the belt of his trench coat; Millar, clutching a bulging briefcase, kept up the aesthetic banter. The two made an arresting sight, thought Pearce, like something straight out of James Joyce. "Ken had a very warm and pleasant and valuable final year at Huron," Pearce said. "He needed warmth, and he got it there. It made him believe again in the existence of a loving community, so to speak. Because he had a very clear vision too of the way things could or should or *ought* to be, different from what they often are. This was the happiest year of his life to that point, I'm sure."

Not all Western students felt so warmly toward Millar. Some seemed to envy or resent his intelligence. Several considered his (or anyone's) creative writing unscholarly, even ungentlemanly. Millar and Ford caused a stir when they coedited the university's year-end literary supplement in December 1937. Judging most of the submissions (except those by Pearce and some others) too pedestrian to publish, the editors, with faculty approval, wrote most of the section themselves, under their own and assumed names ("Kerith Mill" and "George Beale" were Millar's pseudonyms). When irate undergraduates complained, "Mill" and "Beale" responded jauntily in print.

Through act and attitude, Millar stood out. Western's yearbook printed a candid photo of him in three-piece suit and tie, cigarette dangling from a half-clenched fist, glaring intelligently; the taunting caption: "'S matter, Ken?"

One noon two seniors, pets of the poli-sci and economics professors, publicly baited him into a lunchroom debate on the nature of certainty. Millar held the position that certainty couldn't exist, since all things are subjective. His inquisitors said he was dead wrong: science is certain; the solar system moves in a given way whatever you think about it. Millar couldn't quote a theory to defend his thesis, and the two pushed him into a philosophical corner. It was the one time at college he'd felt frustrated and humiliated, he confessed to Pearce. Millar went hunting for ammunition and found what he sought in Hume's work on causality, which said perception of cause and effect is entirely subjective, a preference of our thinking apparatus imposed on the world; there's no logical reason for previous arrangements to obtain in the present or future—all we can know is that they once did. "Ken was *thrilled* to find this argument," Pearce said. " 'I *knew* I was right,' he said, 'but I didn't have the terminology. Had I known this statement, I could have *slain* them.' " When you were an underdog like Millar, the chips were always down.

> Sin is despair.
> —Søren Kierkegaard

> There is a force in men like him which causes them to seek out the best and the most difficult; it is the essential human force, at least in the Christian West, and it is both strength and weakness.
> —Kenneth Millar

As Millar finished his studies at Western, growing "rich on the heritage of the Christian West" as he put it without irony, he began a personal relationship that would last his lifetime and be crucial in shaping him as a man and a writer.

He encountered Margaret Sturm, his high school crush, in London, Ontario, after returning from Europe in early 1937. Millar had also bumped into Margaret before he left for Europe and quite seriously ("He was *always* serious," she said) invited her to go with him to Ireland. This meeting was different, though. Margaret was in a bad way, and soon Ken Millar learned all about it. She'd won a classics scholarship to the University of Toronto, but after her mother's death had washed out of college, had a "nervous breakdown," and moved in with a London aunt. She'd enrolled in a business course, dropped out of that, then suffered through an unhappy affair, a mild schizophrenic episode, and a suicide attempt. Now she was studying psychiatry on her own, trying to understand her problems, and writing stories and poems. Like Ken Millar, Margaret Sturm hoped to become a writer.

"He knew his fate when he saw it" was how Millar would put it. He began seeing Margaret daily. Within weeks they were lovers. Millar, sensing the relationship's difficulties and potential, chose to let Margaret become "the greatest of his monumental images": an inspiration, a challenge, a test of strength, and his own hope for a useful life. He believed in mind and heart that one man plus one woman equaled civilization; choosing Margaret as partner, he thought, was the best and most difficult thing he could do. They shared "a true Kierkegaardian view of a tragic world, fed by ancient tragedy and by modern sensibility": the Greeks, and Freud. They'd be each other's salvation, he hoped.

In the spring of '38, as Millar's graduation neared, his and Margaret's future hinged on Harvard's response to his fellowship application. Each morning Millar looked on the downstairs table at Huron for an envelope from Massachusetts. At last Harvard's letter came: Millar had been rejected. He read the bad news without expression (Pearce was watching) and went about his business. But later (Pearce never knew how) Millar got hold of the letter written about him by the professor who'd talked him into applying to

Harvard. It enraged him. The man described Millar not as a brilliant student but as a colorful eccentric: "The most impressive thing he said I think," Pearce recalled, "was that he was a very *picturesque* figure with his green hat and his flowing scarf, which *infuriated* Ken as being certain to undo his credit as a scholar. 'He just pictured me as a Bohemian!' " The unfairness shocked him (no one said such things about Ford, who got his Cornell fellowship without a hitch); and his resentment would linger for decades.

Millar determined to pursue the Ph.D. part-time and arranged to take summer classes at the University of Michigan, across the Canadian border. In a way it was just as well; he was afraid if he left Margaret Sturm on her own while he went off to school, she'd sink into despair and maybe again attempt suicide. Now they could get married right away. After his first summer in Michigan, he said (in a revamp of his plan to support his mother), he'd attend the Toronto teaching college and then get a job as a high school instructor. Margaret was against the idea—she wanted them to become writers right now—but Millar was adamant. It was a "bitter choice," but he was determined not to fail like his father; he admitted he lacked the courage to try to make it as a writer immediately.

Practical as it was, his decision required cash. Again, as with his father's insurance, a sudden inheritance came to his rescue. Millar was willed two thousand dollars by an uncle in Oregon he'd never met. Before receiving the money, though, he got entangled with another uncle he knew all too well: his Aunt Margaret's husband, Ed, who wrote to say Aunt Margaret had died and he needed Millar's power of attorney to settle her estate. After sending his power of attorney, Millar learned from other relatives that Uncle Ed claimed he hadn't been able to contact Kenneth; he said Millar's inheritance should be sent to *him* for forwarding. After consulting a Toronto lawyer, Millar wrote Ed a terse note ("Dear Mr. J_____") rescinding the power of attorney, demanding a personal meeting, and threatening legal action: "So you better snap out of it." His furtive uncle wrote to arrange a Toronto rendezvous ("Will meet you in the lobby of the Ford Hotel next Wednesday at 8 P.M. Be on time as I am leaving shortly after 9 o'clock") where he blamed "business connections" in the States ("the boys in St. Louis") for holding things up. Millar got his money, with fictional interest: twenty years later, Uncle Ed would slither chameleonlike into some of Millar's best books.

When his Western friends learned of his involvement with Margaret Sturm, they were amazed. Don Pearce had met Margaret years earlier at a Kitchener party and remembered her vividly, he said: "Long hair hanging low, and a smile that completely engulfed her face: I think her eyebrows went up, I think her *forehead* smiled; her cheeks swelled, her eyes got big and laughing, and her teeth became prominently apparent, uppers *and* lowers—it was a neon experience of some sort, that smile. She played the piano, not all that well but with a certain abandon. Very slender. Handsome, you know. Big eyes, with impressively clear whites. A prominent and strong nose, which Ken told me she hated. Very social, very outgoing, very witty, very self-confident, with this *strong* laughter when she was pleased, affectionate laughter that was musical and rich." After knowing Margaret better, Pearce could add, "She was unforgettably charming when she felt like being, and a totally intolerable neurotic of the worst kind when she wanted to be. Hard to handle." Pearce said Bob Ford "deplored" the idea of two such egotistical people marrying each other and predicted nothing but strain.

But Millar's mind was made up and his course inflexible, as Pearce found when he tried to joke about the impending wedding. "I was as usual showing off in some way or other," he said, "quoting I think Shelley about the injustices of things like the marriage institution: that it was an intolerable abuse that laws should bind the wanderings of passion, and why should a grown man be constrained by the choices of an immature youth? And Ken said, 'That is a foolish and confused statement. For one thing I am *not* an immature youth, I am a *mature* youth. And I am not *making* the kinds of mistakes you are referring to. That's typical of Shelley, he's not in touch with reality. Maybe *he* was immature; I am not.' And stamped off."

Only two years after his mother's death, Millar was about to commit himself to an equally formidable and demanding relationship. How badly he must have craved structure, companionship, and the anchor of duty. When Margaret, the teetotaling sister of alcoholic brothers, insisted he give up liquor, the beer-loving Millar instantly complied.

An incident one night at Huron College showed Ken Millar's almost childlike dependence on his fiancée's approval. Millar, Pearce, Ford, and Lee were in Pearce's room when the subject of Millar's wrestling career came up. Millar said with some pride that all the time he'd been on Western's team no one had gotten a hold on him he'd been unable to break. Lee, a good athlete, asked if he might try. As Pearce and Ford watched, Lee got Millar in a full nelson. A tremendous struggle ensued; with a violent effort, Millar broke Lee's grip. In doing so he'd strained the capillaries above his neck; his face was bloodshot purple. "Oh my God, I'm seeing Margaret tomorrow!" Millar exclaimed when he looked in the mirror. "What will I tell her? What will she say?"

If light were dark
And dark were light,
Moon a black hole
In the blaze of night,

A raven's wing
As bright as tin
Then you, my love,
Would be darker than sin.
—Kenneth Millar, Toronto *Saturday Night*

Millar barked: "Hey, you! Are you the house dick here or the house cat?"
—Raymond Chandler, "The King in Yellow," 1938

They were too young; he saw that later. But at twenty-two, Millar was eager to embrace his fate. On June 2, 1938, the day after graduating with first-class honors from the University of Western Ontario, Kenneth Millar married Margaret Sturm in London, Ontario, with a Church of England minister from Huron College presiding.

Things were bumpy from the start. The two honeymooned for eight days at Millar's dentist's cabin on a Georgian Bay island filled with bugs and poison ivy. "When the boat came back for us," Margaret said, "I decided I intended to get a divorce as soon as I hit land." Divorce was an option Millar's bride didn't rule out for years, if ever. "A woman feels funny when she's married," she explained later, "especially a very independent type like me. You feel trapped. 'What have I done with my life?' " Early on, offering Millar a second helping of food and meaning to say "Would you like a little more?" Margaret asked, "Would you like a little divorce?"

Millar was as determined to make a success of his marriage as he was to pursue his studies. Two weeks after their honeymoon, the Millars went to Ann Arbor, Michigan, where Kenneth enrolled for three summer classes in the University of Michigan graduate school. They rented rooms in a house near campus. Margaret hated her husband's student routine and suffered migraines. The newlyweds slept in separate rooms whenever possible, ostensibly because he snored and she was nervous. The Millars slept apart their entire marriage.

After his summer courses (he earned two A's and an A-plus), they moved to Toronto (first to Hepbourne Street, then to Spadina Avenue), and in the fall of '38, Millar started a year's study at the Ontario College of Education. The course was tough, with a lot of drillwork he found distasteful; but Millar stuck with it. His goal was to head his class and obtain one of the few available teaching jobs. He and Maggie lived cheaply, paring his inheritance into a ninety-dollar monthly budget (twenty-five for rent). They couldn't afford movies. Instead, they listened to the radio and read secondhand books he brought home by the two-dollar armful. In the evening they bought day-old éclairs, three for a nickel. Margaret hand-rolled their cigarettes.

The Millars were affectionate between clashes and worked well as a team, pulling together at a moment's notice. In bed late one Saturday morning, they saw the dean of Millar's college approaching their door on a social call; by the time he knocked, they'd put up the folding bed, thrown on robes, straightened the room, and were ready to greet him: *Why, Dean, come in, would you care for coffee?*

Moments of pressure were more common, though. The pressure increased when Margaret got pregnant. She blamed her poor knowledge of birth control. The Millars hadn't planned on a child (Margaret wanted a career; Kenneth was afraid of passing on his mother's emotional problems), and they considered abortion. But a doctor talked them out of that, and the Millars accepted their baby-to-be—Millar more happily than his wife.

Nearly all their cash was gone. Millar topped his class as planned and lined up a teaching job for the fall: at his and Margaret's old Kitchener high school. But the Millars needed money immediately.

This June, Millar went to hear a high school commencement address by the governor general of Canada, better known as John Buchan, Scottish author of several thrillers including *The Thirty-Nine Steps*. Buchan told the familiar fable of the race between tortoise and hare—but in Buchan's version, the hare won. The race didn't always go to the slow, Buchan said. Millar took this to heart. He had said he'd make money someday by writing; with a baby due, now it was time to get off the starting block.

A radio quiz announced it would award an Underwood typewriter to the listener answering the most questions about books and publishing. Millar declared that he'd win that typewriter—and he did.

In the past his critical faculty had made him self-conscious of his creative writing and impeded his output, but now the need for funds freed him from being hypercritical. Scribbling longhand in pen or pencil on pulp tablets, school notebooks, and any other available scraps of paper, he wrote dozens of stories, sketches, and poems in the next weeks: mock memoir in the Leacock mode, parodies of Ogden Nash and Edgar Lee Masters, a six-thousand-word horror tale, versions of "Little Miss Muffet" in the styles of moderns T. S. Eliot, W. H. Auden, and Gertrude Stein. The shortest thing was a four-line poem; the most ambitious was a short story, "The Yellow Dusters," done under the influence of Toronto author Morley Callaghan, a worthy model to replace D. H. Lawrence. Callaghan's stories of ordinary Canadians were a bit in the "hard-boiled" Hemingway manner but also akin to Chekhov. "Morley Callaghan was the one that we all most admired and wanted to emulate," Millar said later of his generation of aspiring Canadian writers. In the powerful "The Yellow Dusters," an auto-biographical vignette of a boy and his mother, Millar showed himself an able Callaghan disciple.

On June 18, 1939, Margaret gave birth at Toronto's Women's College Hospital to a daughter the Millars named Linda Jane. The baby had Millar's violet-blue eyes: his mother's eyes. Millar was thrilled by the infant. Margaret, though, was upset. "That's when you really feel the entrapment," she said later. " 'Here I am—*stuck.*' " She had her worst migraine ever, with nausea. Home from the hospital, she was happy to let her sister or an aunt tend the baby while she went to the Underwood. Millar couldn't type; Margaret could. In the first six weeks of Linda Jane's life, Margaret prepared thirty-five Millar manuscripts for submission on spec to American magazines, from the *New Yorker* and *Esquire* to *Strange Stories.*

No U.S. publication wanted Ken's stuff, but the half dozen stories he wrote for "the Sunday School papers"—five youth magazines (*The Canadian Boy, The Canadian Girl, Onward, Explorer, Jewels*) printed in Toronto by the United Church of Canada—were bought by an editor named Archer Wallace. Millar earned over a hundred dollars: enough to pay Margaret's hospital bill.

The first piece of his that saw print, though, was a comic verse taken by *Saturday Night,* a slick Toronto weekly where his uncle Stan Moyer published. *Saturday Night* took several other things, including "The Yellow Dusters." Soon Kenneth Millar was a familiar byline on *Saturday Night's* popular "Back Page." He was a pro. "*Saturday Night* came out on Saturday morning," he recalled, "and we used to walk up Bloor Street to see if anything of mine had been printed that week. Payment was just a cent a word, but the early joys of authorship were almost as sweet as sex."

A buoyant Millar moved with wife and daughter in mid-1939 from the big and impersonal city of Toronto to the small and all-too-familiar town of Kitchener, first to Frederick Street and then to a building on Louisa. In September, his husky bulk buttoned into a three-piece suit and his blue eyes blurred behind clear-glass spectacles from Woolworth's, Millar became a colleague of the men who'd taught him at KCI not many years before. Heraclitus, a pre-Socratic philosopher Millar was fond of, said you couldn't step into the same river twice. Millar, though, seemed to have waded upstream into the river of his adolescence. Not for the last time, he felt the odd sensation of the present pulling him into the past.

He began the job with enthusiasm, loving the tough English and history courses he was given to teach and looking forward to helping teenagers clear some of life's hurdles, as he had been helped. "He was a *born* teacher," Margaret said. "He never really got over it. And he took no nonsense. Because he was big and strong, you know, people didn't misbehave. Boys didn't cut up the way they did for some other teachers, because he'd just take and carry them into the hall."

But if Millar could make his pupils pay attention, he couldn't force them to learn. The average student didn't share Mr. Millar's keen interest in history; the ordinary boy's mind was on hockey or girls or what job he'd get after graduation. The prospect of facing 350 bored students each year ate at Millar's resolve. And he wasn't popular with the other instructors, who found him aloof and thought he spoke above most students' level. By rights Millar should have been in graduate school with the brightest minds of his generation; instead he was teaching high school in Kitchener—for the excellent reason it paid $1,450 a year, in a lingering Depression when many workingmen were grateful for five bucks a week.

Millar didn't intend to spend the rest of his life as a high school instructor. In the summer of 1940 he was back at Michigan's grad school (having missed the summer Linda was born). He made one A and two A-pluses this time, while continuing his freelance *Saturday Night* work. With teaching, studying, and writing, Millar hadn't much time for his wife and daughter. Margaret, still his typist, accused him of ducking family duties. Part of him thought she might be right. Like his wife, he felt trapped. Both of them were unhappy, and he sensed the baby suffered for it.

The Millars argued over how to treat Linda. Margaret the self-taught psychologist wanted to raise her daughter "scientifically." The scientist whose rules she followed (seven years before Dr. Benjamin Spock's commonsense child-care manual) was behaviorist John Broadus Watson, who said not to kiss or hold children and to ignore their crying. Millar thought these notions were nuts, but Margaret insisted, "Mother knows best."

They fought about other things. Margaret wanted him to stop studying and get on with his writing. Millar, haunted by memories of his father in the charity ward, was bound to get that Ph.D. He wanted sex more often. She was cold and remote for long periods. He shouted, pounded walls, broke things. With their child as witness, the Millars formed a twisted hybrid of the fractured families that had produced the two of them.

His happy college days now seemed far in the past. Proof they were gone forever came late in 1939, when Royal Air Force pilot John Lee, Millar's friend from Western, died in a training accident, one of the first Canadian casualties of the world war Millar had warned was coming. Ken Millar went to Highgate, Ontario, for John Lee's funeral: a somber event to begin the new decade.

Margaret also faced a depressing 1940. Her life as wife and mother felt empty, and she hated being in Kitchener. She wanted to be a writer, but her bid to review movies for a Toronto newspaper was turned down. She found more neurotic means of expression. Don Pearce called on the Millars one night and found them engaged in a weird contest: "Ken was home sick with a flu, and Margaret was developing a serious headache. Each seemed to be struggling to outdo the other. Ken said very wryly and disgruntedly to me, in her presence, 'We are having a little competitive illness, tonight.' "

Margaret's ailments escalated. A doctor diagnosed toxic myocarditis—inflammation of the heart muscle ("Probably just nerves," she conceded later)—and confined her to bed. Millar saw his wife slipping into the role of part-time semi-invalid. To distract her, he brought home library books, thirty or forty at a time, most of them mystery novels.

He chose wisely. Margaret had loved detective stories since childhood. "I was brought up with mysteries," she said. "That was because of my two brothers, six and eight years older. I'd see them bringing home these magazines: *Black Mask, Detective Fiction Weekly, Argosy.* They used to hide them underneath the mattress. Now for a girl like me, that is a temptation. I never missed a copy."

Mystery stories surged in popularity in 1940, a century after Edgar Allan Poe had invented the form. Newspaper and magazine articles scrutinized the craze: Were mysteries a mental challenge or a mindless escape? Did mystery addicts seek sanctuary from harsh reality or moral affirmation in a time of growing evil? Whatever the answers, publishers couldn't print detective stories fast enough to meet demand. Nearly three hundred mystery novels came out in the United States in 1940. Many major presses had separate detective lines: Simon & Schuster's Inner Sanctum Mysteries, Dodd, Mead's Red Badge books, Doubleday Doran's Crime Club. Ellery Queen, Rex Stout, and Erle Stanley Gardner were among the field's star writers, but a raft of newcomers made waves in 1940.

One was Raymond Chandler, whose 1939 book *The Big Sleep* was followed in 1940 by *Farewell, My Lovely.* Both featured private detective–narrator Philip Marlowe, a romanticized Los Angeles version of Dashiell Hammett's San Francisco op Sam Spade; like Hammett, Chandler was published by Alfred A. Knopf. Chandler's style was vivid and highly entertaining. Margaret urged that Millar read him.

Few detective novels were as good as Chandler's, though. There was more dross than gold in the dozens of mysteries Margaret scanned in early 1940. One book was so bad she threw it across the room, shouting: *"I could do better than that!"*

Go ahead, her husband urged.

She'd need a plot, she said.

He said he'd give her one, and he quickly came up with two. One was a murder mystery with a high school setting. Margaret liked the second one better: a story with a bunch of suspects cooped up in an old house waiting to see who gets knocked off. As her sleuth, Margaret dreamed up a six-foot-five movie-star-handsome psychiatrist, Dr. Paul Prye. She could *do* this, Margaret thought. Unlike the poems and short stories she'd strained to create, mysteries were something she *knew.* Once she had her plot and setting, the sentences flowed.

Working in bed, she wrote sixty thousand words in fifteen days, then rewrote the whole manuscript two or three times. "I had to do something to get out of that bed," she said later. "To get out of that *town.*" Millar was essential to her enterprise. In addition to plotting and editing (and perhaps giving Paul Prye his bad habit of quoting William Blake), he looked after Linda and did household chores. If KCI colleagues or students smirked at the sight of Mr. Millar hanging out the laundry, let them. He did everything he could to help his wife reach her goal—*their* goal.

The Invisible Worm (a Blake quote) was the title they gave Margaret's mystery. The book wasn't half-bad: a fast-moving mix of harum-scarum, psychology, wisecracks, and the screwball humor of the *Thin Man* movies. They had *The Invisible Worm* professionally typed and mailed unsolicited copies to two of the top U.S. mystery lines. Margaret's "heart ailment" vanished.

Months later Millar was called out of his KCI classroom to take a telephone call. A jubilant Margaret read him a wire from Isabelle Taylor, mystery editor at Doubleday Doran: MANUSCRIPT ACCEPTED. PUBLICATION CRIME CLUB. CONGRATULATIONS. LETTER FOLLOWS. He was as thrilled as she was, she said: "We both almost had a conniption fit."

Doubleday's letter said they'd pay $250 for this book and an option on another. Margaret immediately began writing a second mystery. She'd have liked to publish the first under her maiden name, but "*The Invisible Worm* by Margaret Sturm" simply would not do. Reluctantly she accepted "Margaret Millar" as her byline. Though her name alone would be on the book, Doubleday's contract listed Margaret and Kenneth Millar as coauthors, with royalties to be divided equally.

She wanted her freedom to be his freedom too; he could stop teaching now and be a full-time writer, she said. Millar was ready to leave KCI, all right, but for a different reason: the English professors at the University of Michigan, dazzled by his A-plus average, had offered him a teaching fellowship for 1941. Here in effect was the opportunity Harvard had denied him. Michigan's six-hundred-dollar fellowship was a thousand dollars less than KCI was paying him, but with the Doubleday money and his freelance work, Millar thought they could make it. Margaret was against the idea but gave in. They would each get something they wanted, and both would leave Kitchener: scene of too much past and not enough future. As a girl, Margaret's ideal had been Houdini, who got out of tight places. Millar's boyhood idol was Pearl White, who leapt clear of disasters. Now, daughter in tow, the Millars imitated their childhood heroes: they escaped.

Auden . . . is the peculiarly modern man, finding images and impli-
cations in the detective story, exploring Dante's territory in a New
York bar.

—Chad Walsh, *Today's Poets*

I was leaning against the bar in a speakeasy on Fifty-second Street . . .
—Dashiell Hammett, *The Thin Man*

If Ross Macdonald was the only American crime writer to receive early
ethical training in a Canadian Mennonite Sunday school (as Ken Millar later proposed), he was also the first private-eye novelist to get a
friendly shove toward the genre from the greatest English poet of his generation.

The poet was Auden; the shove began in a class Millar took at Michigan
in 1941: Fate and the Individual in European Literature, a daunting
course surveying Western writing from Shakespeare to Kafka. Its forty-
five-book reading list chased many registrants from the class—but not Millar, of course, and not Donald Pearce, who had also opted to do his
graduate studies at Michigan.

W. H. Auden, internationally famous at thirty-four, cut a strikingly odd
figure. Fair-skinned, long-faced, and with unkempt reddish hair, he
moved sideways like a skittish colt; his laugh was a whinny. He made no
eye contact with students in class, staring out the window while lecturing as
if in contact with the dead writers of whom he spoke. Auden played opera
records to make literary points, analyzed Shakespeare's characters from a
Jungian point of view, and spoke about people (Rimbaud, Freud, Valéry)
largely unknown to American grad students. Millar, Pearce, and others
were electrified by his brilliance. Millar dubbed Auden "a young Socrates
and an old Ariel rolled into one." Auden was impressed with Millar too
and graded his essays (and Pearce's) A-plus.

One paper Millar wrote compared Dante's *The Divine Comedy* to Kafka's
The Castle. In lieu of a final, Auden had students memorize any six Dante
cantos. Millar's close study of the *Comedy* for Auden's class heightened his
appreciation of Dante's epic. Pearce recalled Millar analyzing the poet's
technique: "Ken would talk about how the imagery in the Inferno was
heavy and concrete and specific and dark: 'so like the place that's being
described.' Then he said, 'If you look at the imagery in the Purgatorio,
what a change that is: it's clear, rational, careful, and calculated—exactly
what ought to occur in a place where you get cleansed of all your mud and
error and sin and guilt. Then see what he does with the Paradiso imagery:
it's all light and high-musical and lyric.' "

Millar later put these stylistic lessons to good use. *The Divine Comedy* would be a frame of reference for Ross Macdonald's southern California, whose many-leveled populace evaded or were exposed by or struggled toward a harshly clarifying light. Millar asked Pearce, "Did you ever notice how people in hell engage in conversation all the time?" Dante seemed to be saying hell *consists* largely of conversation, self-justification, accusation. Macdonald's Lew Archer would prove an expert Dantesque interrogator, eliciting many testimonies, self-deceptions, lies, and alibis. And Archer, like Millar, would value merciful silence.

Auden clearly saw Millar's ability and especially encouraged the twenty-five-year-old. He said Millar should be writing for the *New Republic* and offered to introduce the young man to the magazine's editors. Millar attended Auden's Friday-evening student "at-homes" on Pontiac Trail; Auden, with companion Chester Kallman, came to dinner at the Millars' rented place at 1020 Hill Street.

"It was strange," Margaret recalled. "My daughter took a terrible dislike to his voice, but he was very interested in the raising of children and making sure they went to Sunday school." (Auden dumbfounded a number of contemporaries by proclaiming himself a Christian before coming to Michigan.) Maggie was put off by Auden's appearance and manner, but she didn't fail to hear him compliment her work, a compliment she often repeated. "He read one of my books and he thought it was terrific," she said. (Margaret had published four books by the time Auden came to dinner.) "He laughed himself sick about this certain scene I'd written," in which a character uses his trouser cuff as an impromptu ashtray. "I was of course flattered."

Auden, one of the world's great poets, was a compulsive detective-story reader and not ashamed of it, something unusual in a year when most intellectuals sneered at mysteries. ("With so many fine books to read," Edmund Wilson would famously write, "so much to be studied and known, there is no need to bore ourselves with this rubbish.") Auden's first published prose had been crime-fiction reviews for London newspapers. Fellow poet Cecil Day-Lewis (under the pseudonym Nicholas Blake) used Auden as the model for his fictional detective Nigel Strangeways. Auden not only liked mystery fiction (he was a particular fan of Hammett and Chandler) but took it seriously; and while Millar didn't buy his theories on the genre (after reading Auden's essay on detective fiction, "The Guilty Vicarage," Millar told Pearce that Auden simply didn't know what he was talking about), the poet's imprimatur on the form was as heartening to Millar as his praise of Millar's talent. Auden thinking well of Millar allowed Millar to think well of himself; Auden approving of mystery fiction reinforced Millar's growing belief that it might be a worthwhile thing to write.

Ken Millar would later judge meeting W. H. Auden one of the four or five crucial events in his life. Auden had been "a remarkable kind of saint," he'd say; and Millar had "really loved him." Perhaps Auden was one of those surrogate fathers that Millar had a knack for finding, or perhaps a surrogate older brother (one whom Millar would caricature in an early Archer book, and then feel guilt at "betraying"). But in Michigan, Millar (perhaps at his wife's urging) kept a certain distance from Auden. He didn't take up the poet's offer to introduce him around Manhattan, partly because Millar didn't care to go to New York then, but more because he didn't think it a good idea to go there under the auspices of a well-known homosexual. No, given Ken Millar's blue-eyed looks and the boyhood habits he'd abandoned, not a good idea at all.

> The man in the black shirt and yellow scarf was sneering at me
> over the *New Republic*.
> "You ought to lay off that fluff and get your teeth into something
> solid, like a pulp magazine," I told him.
> —Raymond Chandler, *The Little Sister*

Millar's Michigan studies (including a doctoral dissertation on Samuel T. Coleridge) and teaching duties (four sections of freshman English) took up nearly all his time. He was anxious to establish himself at the university and drew quick attention by doing spectacularly well on an intelligence and aptitude test taken by all grad students. The dean of the grad school said no one else in the history of the test had scored as high as Millar: no doubt her husband was a genius, he told Margaret. The remarkable thing was that Millar did as well on the math and engineering side as on the verbal, so well that it was suggested he might wish to change his major.

Millar stayed with English, but his math and engineering aptitude would find expression in the algebraic complexity of the novels he'd write. The rigors of study made him postpone creative work, though. Grad school and creativity seemed pretty antithetical.

Not that he didn't have writing chores. He'd assumed the task of cowriting a column of current-event quips for Toronto's *Saturday Night* for two and a half dollars a week, a sum that made a difference to the cash-strapped Millars. Though he did most of "The Passing Show," Millar's name didn't appear on the anonymous column; that way (Millar guessed) its coauthor, the magazine's new literary editor, Robertson Davies, could take credit for its best lines. Millar's copy was politically sharp and full of witty puns:

> The Australian pilot who successfully landed two planes which had locked together in mid-air simply refused to admit the gravity of the situation.

> Mussolini says that Italy and Germany will march on, side by side, to the end. That's what we hope.

> It has been rumored that Vichy discharged several "non-Aryan" professors of psychology on Hitler's orders. But a vegetarian like Adolf should have no objection to French Freuds.

"The Passing Show" was popular; Millar's unsigned quips were reprinted in newspapers throughout Canada. He wrote his weekly quota on Saturdays in Angell Hall, when the campus was all but deserted because of the varsity football game.

Millar's other writing responsibilities involved his wife's mystery books. Ken was an active participant in Margaret's fiction career, so active he sometimes felt like a full collaborator. When her first book was published in June 1941, she'd already finished a second (*The Weak-Eyed Bat*) and part of a third, as well as a long magazine novelette. The *Bat* contract again named Margaret and Kenneth Millar as "authors and proprietors" of the work and stipulated all monies be divided evenly between them. A Michigan newspaper piece on Margaret described Millar's role as "silent partner":

> He helps to devise plots, and he uses his red pencil as though she were a freshman student and he a stern professor of composition. "Omit or alter," he scrawls on her portion of her manuscripts. "Sometimes I rebel against that red pencil," she sighs. "But on *The Weak-Eyed Bat*, I disregarded two of his orders, and the publisher suggested two alterations in the manuscript. Yes, you guessed it."

The Millars' efforts paid off with good notices from mystery reviewers in the top U.S. journals. The *Saturday Review of Literature* pronounced *The Invisible Worm* "commendable," the *New Yorker* noted its sound plot, and Will Cuppy in the *New York Herald Tribune* called Margaret Millar "a mystery find of considerable voltage." When *The Weak-Eyed Bat* was printed, Cuppy declared, "Margaret Millar is a humdinger, right up in the top rank of bafflers, including the British."

To their contemporaries at Michigan, the Millars seemed a pretty colorful couple: the husband-and-wife mystery writers, very wrapped up in their work. At Margaret's insistence, Millar stopped wearing his dime-store spectacles, leaving his handsome face open to the world. "Ken was very impressive, both in size and intellect," said Georgia Haugh, wife of a Michigan grad student. "Well built, very affable. Ken was very smooth: I mean that in a complimentary fashion." Margaret was a presence too, her long hair parted in the middle and sometimes pulled back in a bun, her shrewd eyes sizing you up. Marianne Meisel, wife of German-born professor James "Hans" Meisel, recalled, "They both at that time spent all their main thought and all their minor thought on what would make a good detective story. He would use one of the old can openers that cut a triangular hole, thoughtfully feel the edge: 'These things are amazingly sharp!' And they would both give it this meaningful look: How fast could you kill somebody with *that*?" To Mrs. Meisel, who wrote a novel published by Scribner's, Millar seemed quite single-minded, with a clear sense of his potential: "Margaret's success was showing him the way. She was an impressive person, working with a certain fierceness." Millar *watched* people, as if collecting them for future books, and loved when they spoke candidly. After listening to a refugee friend of the Meisels' talk of a tempestuous love affair, Millar exclaimed, "Oh, Europeans are wonderful, they *tell* you things!"

He was the gregarious one, eager to have people over to Hill Street. Margaret tolerated gatherings and took part if she wasn't writing, but she refused to do any "entertaining," not even putting out cheese and crackers. Once a hungry grad student asked if there wasn't something to *eat* around here, and Millar shushed him, "For God's sake be quiet, or Margaret will throw you out." She rescinded her ban on alcohol, though, one sweltering Ann Arbor night. When Maggie suggested a nice cold beer, Millar raced to a liquor store and brought back several bottles before she could change her mind. At twenty-six, Margaret Sturm Millar drank her first alcohol; from then on, beer fueled the Millars' social life.

Housing was famously scarce in Ann Arbor. The three Millars lived in a one-floor converted garage, with two tiny bedrooms and a long, enclosed corridor that served as a walk-in closet. Set back from the street and hidden by shrubs, the mock cottage looked like something from one of Margaret's spooky mysteries. Twenty-five dollars from the Millars' tight budget went for an old black piano; when guests came Margaret could sometimes be coaxed to play hit-parade tunes or some of her own things such as "Mad at the Moon." Millar loved Maggie's playing; he'd grin hugely and twist his body into pretzel-like shapes when she got off a jazzy or bluesy lick. Frequent visitors to Hill Street included Don Pearce, with his new wife, Mary; Chad Walsh, a budding poet and dawning Christian who debated faith and morals with the "agnostic" Millars; and the young African-American poet Robert Hayden, who delighted Millar by bringing over jazz records, including 78s of Billie Holiday with the Teddy Wilson orchestra. Hayden and Walsh, like Millar, were crazy about Auden and benefited from his encouragement. Walsh and Hayden also liked detective fiction.

Millar was intrigued to learn that another professional mystery writer, H. C. Branson, lived in Ann Arbor. Branson's first book, *I'll Eat You Last,* was published the same week as Maggie's *Invisible Worm,* and the two authors were favorably reviewed together in the mystery-roundup columns. Millar got Henry Clay Branson's number from the directory and invited himself over to visit the Bransons on Catherine Street.

A round-cheeked man in rimless spectacles, Branson had studied at Princeton and gotten a B.A. at Michigan, then spent time in Paris mingling with expatriate Americans. He knew a lot about American history and classical music. Henry and his wife, Anna, a wonderfully friendly woman, both played the piano; they had two young daughters.

Millar instantly enjoyed the Bransons' company, and he greatly admired Branson's writing: the clarity of his prose and the adult nature of his stories. Branson's mysteries (*The Pricking Thumb* came out in 1942) weren't gimmicky whodunits but realistic tales that addressed the nature of evil, as Millar felt mysteries should. His spare style (which purposely avoided simile and metaphor) was very different from Millar's, but other Branson characteristics—strong plots, a story that made a circle (something Millar knew went as far back as the Greeks), a present-day crime with roots in the past—would become typical of Millar's books. Branson personally was an inspiration: like Auden, a man of intelligence and education who considered the writing of mystery fiction a worthwhile pursuit.

With the Bransons, Millar was often cheerfully physical, Anna Branson said: "If something struck him as funny, he would give a very raucous laugh, and every once in a while he'd sort of *cavort* about the room." On one occasion former gymnast Millar picked up a startled Branson and spun him around in the air.

Another instance of Millar's antic euphoria took place in Don and Mary Pearce's third-floor apartment: holding forth on modern man's inability to demonstrate sheer joy ("For instance, we can't do *this* anymore—"), Millar opened a window and flung himself outside to hang by his fingers three stories above the street—then pulled himself back inside, laughing like mad.

Margaret's social athleticism was limited to playing charades ("shar-*ahds*"). She and Millar were agile conversationalists, though, something that could make for a peculiarly unsettling evening, according to Don Pearce: "You never knew when an innocent remark of yours was going to set off a scoffing response. Ken would be more understanding, but Margaret was really quite like a lighted fuse. When Ken and Margaret were in the room, I'm telling you, it was like walking through a minefield. You felt you had to be careful always of what you said, especially around Margaret, unless it happened to coincide with her range of opinions. She could be a delightful laughing companion for an evening—half an evening, anyway. Other times: nerve-racking."

The Millars seemed to Pearce in many ways opposites: "I don't think she entertained abstractions easily, and she was living with a person who was very comfortable with abstractions. Hers was a very concrete and practical mind, full of passionate and outspoken hates. She was interested in people as a novelist, and she talked a lot along those lines: rapidly constructed theories about how they live and what they live for; a kind of expert gossip that wasn't lowbrow. Loved to recite her latest clever opening to a chapter. Needed praise; didn't want competition. For all her strength of mind and rhinocerine will, she had a fragile ego. Someone who was compulsively difficult and never can be cured of that. In other words she was neurotic. She was a problem, for him. And yet, who knows? They certainly hammered out between them a pretty tough and maybe dynamic polar relationship. They were a spectacular pair. Not very many friendships survived that sort of domestic intensity, though."

The Millars played an excellent if often unpleasant game of conversational Ping-Pong, Pearce said. Anna Branson long remembered this volley: "One time we were all arguing about something and Maggie turned to Ken and said, 'You wouldn't know your ass from a hole in the ground!' And very quietly he replied, 'But I'd know *your* ass from a hole in the ground.' She topped him though, she said, 'Oh, now you're being crude.' We all howled at that."

No one could be around the Millars much without being aware of the tensions built into their relationship. "There was a lot of fighting going on," said Marianne Meisel. "Both of them were very much *there* and didn't let the other one get away with anything. I think they must have had a very difficult time because she told me that she *had* to be top dog, the center of attention. She said, 'If there are three people walking down the street, I *have* to be the one in the middle'—which stayed in my mind, because it seemed very *odd* to me."

Their daughter was a frequent source of friction between the Millars. "Ken was enormously attached to Linda, really truly was, and always took her side," said Don Pearce. "If ever I saw anybody who was wrapped up in a child, it was Ken when Linda was brand-new; he couldn't believe this had happened to him. He was the softie in the whole thing. Margaret was always revving Linda's engine as it were, stepping on the accelerator of her personality, making her *do* all sorts of things, making her a bit of a show-off. I can remember Linda sitting at the dinner table, no older than three, confronted with a dish she didn't want, tomato soup or something, and being not exactly hysterical but getting on for it, saying, 'I *can't* eat that, it's in-*ed*-ible, it's in-*ed*-ible, Mother, I will not *touch* it!' I'm not kidding, she was in command of that household, and sounding exactly like Margaret shrunk to about two and a half or three years old; and she would get her way.

"Another time Margaret was going to demonstrate to me how clever Linda was, how she understood long words, for instance the word *nevertheless*. 'She doesn't like *nevertheless*,' Margaret said, 'because that's when I get my way, when I say *nevertheless*.' So she said to Linda, 'Well, it's time for you to go to bed, Linda.' 'But I don't want to go to bed now,' Linda said. And Margaret said, 'Nevertheless!' 'Oh, not *nevertheless*,' Linda cried, 'not *nevertheless*, Mummy!' 'Nevertheless!' 'Mummy, not *nevertheless!*' And so on. And Margaret was doing this to *show* me, you see. I mean, those parents never gave that child a moment's peace. Not that they tortured her, but with Linda the box was always open, as it were, with people looking in, expecting, commenting, constantly stimulating in ways that somehow or other make for a nervous youngster. I think they were both simply astonished that they *had* a child."

Millar contributed to Linda's repertoire of routines by teaching her the names of her body parts, then cuing her with finger-pointings in an innocent litany: "What's this called, Linda?" "Foot." "What's this, Linda?" "Knee." "Linda, what's this?" "Vulva." "And what's this, Linda?" "Elbow." His favorite times with Linda were on weekday mornings when he wheeled her in a "go-cart buggy" across the mile-long, tree-lined Michigan-campus diagonal to her nursery school. Focused on his daughter's unblinking gaze, oblivious to anything else, Millar in a big, deep voice sang "King Joe," Richard Wright's blues to boxer Joe Louis that Paul Robeson had recorded with the Count Basie band.

For several Ann Arbor residents, including Anna Branson, the sight of a devoted Ken Millar steering Linda along as he boomed out the slow Joe Louis blues was a high point of the morning. To glimpse Millar then, all wrapped up in his daughter's wide-eyed presence, you wouldn't think he had a care in the world.

For what is the sensibility of our age? Is there any one sensibility? Do we respond to T. S. Eliot, Dashiell Hammett, Mary Roberts Rinehart, or Tiffany Thayer? The objective answer must be that some of us respond to one and some to another.

—Cleanth Brooks, *The Well Wrought Urn*

If you come from a fiery-furnace home . . . God, usually pictured as a cosmic policeman, was the invisible guest at every meal; His name was invoked to keep you from doing the things you wanted to do; He seemed the private detective employed by your parents.

—Chad Walsh, *Campus Gods on Trial*

Lighthearted Michigan moments were the exception for Millar, though. He was under increasing pressure on campus and at home. The winter of '41 was especially tough. With no money for coal, the Millars kept warm by burning packing crates. Millar borrowed fifty dollars from Pearce to buy Christmas presents. When the United States entered the world war after Pearl Harbor, things became even more somber. Many colleagues left school for the armed forces or government jobs. Working on a dissertation about an eighteenth-century poet didn't seem so important when the fate of the globe was at stake—and Margaret Millar wasn't shy about saying so.

Margaret had hated Ann Arbor from the first day. Millar wasn't crazy about it either, but he had a near-paranoid determination to "make something of himself" and somehow justify his parents' marriage. His hard work was paying off: A-plus was his usual grade, and he was the rising star of the English department if not the whole humanities division. But he didn't like what came with the territory: the brutalization of his sensibility, the academic politics, the frivolous attitudes of certain contemporaries.

The latter was crystallized in a poetry seminar taught by guest lecturer Cleanth Brooks in the summer of '42. Brooks, coeditor of the influential "little magazine" the *Southern Review,* was using this seminar to refine theories of the "new criticism" he would expound in *The Well Wrought Urn,* a 1947 book he'd dedicate to this Michigan class. Unity in a work of art was the main idea: each element in a poem pulling equal weight in balance with the others—a Coleridgean scheme, and something Millar already knew a lot about. Also in the class, at Brooks's suggestion, were some philosophy students, who were supposed to add an extra dimension to the discussion. Instead, Millar thought, they merely spouted precepts of this or that ism as if philosophy were a game for show-offs. "To me," an offended Millar told Pearce, "philosophy is the *hinge* of the world." It was like the occasion at Western when Millar clashed with those smart-aleck students over the nature of the universe. But this time Millar was pre-pared. Having read and absorbed an Aristotle work these sophists glibly misquoted, Millar publicly nailed them.

Margaret played on Millar's discontents and urged he leave the acad-emy, do what she'd done, be a full-time writer. Having dropped out of uni-versity herself, she seemed to see his college career as a prolonged evasion of responsibility. Maybe she was right: Millar was ashamed of his lack of courage, his failure to assume "true headship" of the family. The more he achieved at Michigan, the more Margaret hammered away. Shortly after he won a Rackham Predoctoral Fellowship (which carried a sum of $875), Margaret burst in on a conversation he and Pearce were having at the Hill Street house. "We were talking," Pearce recalled, "a bit too loudly it seems, about some of the things he'd been reading or that had been taught by some of the teachers; it was the kind of conversation Margaret could sim-ply not *endure*. She came in and shouted at him, 'Einstein! Einstein!' He'd just got the highest university fellowship they gave; she couldn't forgive him for that. We left soon, and as we walked toward school together, I being a bit embarrassed, he said to me—and this was the only negative thing he ever said about her in my presence—he said, 'You know, I don't think Margaret respects me as much as she should.' "

Alone with his wife, Millar wasn't so placid. He and Margaret shouted, broke dishes, shoved and slapped each other. Maggie blamed Ken for his rot-ten temper, but she had one to match. Once she threw an egg at him; when he ducked, it splattered on the wall, where she left it to dry. Another time she dropped a typewriter from a second-story window. Mornings were touchy as Millar readied Linda for school and Margaret supervised from bed, often telling him he was doing things all wrong. One such morning he threw a rub-ber doll at Margaret, and its detachable head came off. She accused him of breaking his daughter's toy. He hit her and caused a cut over her eye. They called a doctor and made up something about an accident. Linda saw it all. To his lifelong shame, Millar sometimes shook or slapped Linda, in mis-placed anger at her mother. Linda was the prize her parents fought for. The family was deranged somehow, and all three knew it.

Millar's tensions sometimes came out in spooky fashion. Talking late one night to Pearce on an Ann Arbor street, Millar said calmly, "A specter has been standing beside us all during this conversation. I think it was my mother." Another time when Pearce knocked at the Hill Street door unex-pectedly one afternoon, Millar slowly opened it only an inch and peered warily with one eye through the crack. "I don't know what he was nervous or anxious about," Pearce said, "but it was as if he was a *pursued* person."

Margaret had her own odd fears. "She was always nervous when there were other women around," said Marianne Meisel. "She was always afraid I was going to *snatch* Ken. And Ken was *not* flirtatious." Anna Branson agreed: "I really think he trod the straight and narrow. He *liked* to think of himself as a boulevardier, a philanderer, something like that—but he wasn't!" Margaret's anxieties weren't restricted to women, Pearce recalled: "Margaret was talking about W. H. Auden having been over to the house. 'Oh, I just *hated* his black teeth, and his self-importance,' she said. 'Moreover, his pant leg slid up his shin, and here was this bare stretch of absolutely hairless leg. It was terrible!' And she said, 'Pearce, pull your pant leg up.' I pulled my pant leg up. She said, 'That's ex*actly* what a man's leg should look like!' Well, a few years later I learned in a letter from Bob Ford that Margaret thought I was a latent homosexual in love with Ken, because I was so devoted to him in many ways. Apparently she had been uneasy with me for a long time, from the first time she set eyes on me I think. But when she asked me to exhibit my leg and saw that it was adequately hairy, that relieved her of any problem that she had regarding me, and I was a *welcome* person after that."

And Margaret Millar has just presented to the many campus "who-done-it" bugs her fourth thriller, an ingenious mystery, full of psychological analysis and sly satire. Only the other day we caught Ken Millar in front of the Arcade newsstand anxiously scanning the *New Yorker*'s book review column. If we may judge by his expression, the review was favorable.

—University of Michigan English Department Newsletter,
September 7, 1943

MYSTERY AND CRIME
WALL OF EYES, by Margaret Millar.
. . . Inspector Sands works out a very neat solution and, in his quiet way, turns out to be the kind of detective it would be nice to meet more often. Highly recommended.

—The New Yorker, September 4, 1943

Things had gone well for Margaret: the *Toronto Star* paid to serialize two of her books, and reprint editions brought the Millars a few more hundred dollars. Sales of her third title were twice those of her second, and reviewers especially liked her. Doubleday's Isabelle Taylor told Margaret she had "a definite reputation and standing in mystery fiction."

All that seemed in doubt, though, when she submitted *Wall of Eyes* to Doubleday Doran in late 1942. Margaret had dropped her psychiatrist-sleuth Dr. Prye for a dour Toronto police detective, Inspector Sands. Instead of a light semicomedy, *Wall of Eyes* was a grimly realistic and sometimes shocking tale of neurotic characters. Taylor and staff were not pleased with this radical departure. The editor's verdict was blunt: "It doesn't come off." She advised Margaret Millar to chalk this one up to experience and quickly write another lighthearted tale.

But Margaret believed in *Wall of Eyes,* as did Millar. She'd begun corresponding with romance novelist Faith Baldwin, a mystery addict who'd written Maggie after seeing her name mentioned in *The Weak-Eyed Bat.* Margaret told Baldwin of her trouble with Doubleday, and the best-selling Baldwin said she should get an agent. Baldwin recommended her own: Harold Ober, a well-known New York rep whose clients included William Faulkner and the late F. Scott Fitzgerald. Ober read Margaret's published books, signed her, and immediately sold *Wall of Eyes* to Bennett Cerf's Random House for an advance of five hundred dollars—twice what Doubleday had been giving her. What was nearly a setback had become a career move. *Wall of Eyes* was scheduled for publication in September 1943.

Margaret complained even more now of Millar's domestic failings. She

scolded him for not spending enough time with his family, especially Linda. Margaret herself did her best for their daughter, but with her constant writing she didn't have time for Linda either. And Linda seemed to need extra attention these days. Things weren't good for the three-year-old in her new nursery school, with its "progressive" policy of letting kids fight out their differences. Linda became withdrawn and distrustful. A disturbing thing happened while she was home sick with a cough: she swallowed a pint of codeine syrup and had to have her stomach pumped.

Margaret also criticized Millar's college career, an expensive endeavor that (no matter how many fellowships he won) Margaret's mysteries were bankrolling. He was done with his courses for the doctorate by mid-1943 and would finish grad school with an A-plus average; all he needed to get his Ph.D. was to write a dissertation. But Millar was depressed by the academic game and restless and guilty on campus with so many men gone off to war. Encouraged by Margaret, he came up with a plan to postpone his dissertation: he'd try for a U.S. Navy commission, which would fulfill his urge to take part in the war effort and (not incidentally) earn an officer's wage that could stake him later to a year's writing.

Margaret's Random House signing may have played a part in his decision. With her serious new book and her fine new publisher, Maggie was bounding ahead in their writerly competition. "While we were very very proud of each other," she said, "I *think* there was an element of keeping *up* with the other guy that was very helpful."

In spring 1943, Millar went to the Book Tower Building in Detroit to secure his commission in the Naval Reserve. He didn't get it. A nervous stomach and an ulcer (the results, he figured, of grad school stress) caused the navy to turn Millar down. He wouldn't be leaving Michigan after all. Reluctantly, he resumed teaching duties. In the summer of '43 these included a section of premeteorology for air force officer candidates: the same sort of commissioned men whose ranks he'd been kept out of. The irony couldn't have pleased Ken Millar.

Frustration inspired him to turn rejection into opportunity. After helping plot and edit Maggie's books, Millar felt he'd gotten the hang of writing mysteries. He'd steal time this summer to write his own thriller.

Having no spare hours during the day, he took time from the evenings. Telling almost no one what he was about, he hid for two hours each night in his office in Angell Hall, which was otherwise empty. He'd be Mr. Hyde, exploring his "dark side" after the day's Dr. Jekyll–like work. His goal was ten pages a night, for a book in a month. It was a race (within the larger one with Margaret) to the start of the new school term, and publication that month of *Wall of Eyes*.

John Buchan, whose Toronto talk inspired Millar to start writing for magazines (and gave him his tortoise-and-hare metaphor for his and Margaret's careers), influenced Millar's first book *The Dark Tunnel:* a spy story that bore some resemblance to Buchan's classic *The Thirty-Nine Steps.*

Another writer, Raymond Chandler, had an equally powerful effect on this work.

Chandler had become a favorite of Millar's (and of any number of other smart readers, Auden included). Whenever a new Chandler book with private detective Philip Marlowe was published (for instance, *The High Window*, in August 1942), Millar hastened to the Ann Arbor rental library to reserve it. He loved Chandler's colorful style and the excited revulsion with which Chandler described the sins and perils of southern California. After being drilled for years in dry scholarship, Millar found Chandler's exuberance liberating. The effect of Chandler can be seen in *The Dark Tunnel*'s rough-and-ready humor, its extravagant similes, and its more lurid events and descriptions (such as the egg-cracking sound of a skull hitting pavement).

Millar's mystery, like Chandler's most recent one, had a victim being thrown from a high window. In Millar's tale the window was the type in Angell Hall, and he devised an inventive murder method that took advantage of this window's tip-up design.

Millar adapted other aspects of the Michigan campus for his story, a domestic-espionage tale set at "Midwestern University" in "Arbana," near Detroit. A major sequence took place in a network of underground steam tunnels like the one that connected several U of M buildings. Access to these tunnels was forbidden to all but engineers; wartime sabotage was a concern. A night watchman patrolled the locked entryways. Millar made up his mind to explore these passages as research for his book. Timing the watchman's route and using skills acquired as a Kitchener teenager, the assistant professor and would-be novelist got into the tunnels, took his notes, and escaped. The fearful thrill he must have felt found its way palpably into the scenes he immediately wrote.

The Dark Tunnel took shape as a hybrid of old-fashioned puzzle-mystery, Buchanesque spy adventure, and Chandleresque exposé of sexual perversion. Its professor hero, Robert Branch, like Millar, is a democratic intellectual who appreciates all sorts of culture: Norse myth, Shakespeare, T. S. Eliot, W. C. Handy. Like his creator, Branch straddles social worlds and contains contradictions: a Ph.D. who can jimmy a Yale lock, a Heraclitus quoter who trades quips with cabdrivers. A hard-boiled egghead, Branch cracks wise in a brainy way—as when he tells a dull-witted cop, "I want to talk to a detective who isn't moribund above the coccyx." The physically manic side of the Millar who could hang outside a third-story window or twirl someone above his head found prose expression in Branch's words and deeds.

When Millar's manuscript was done and typed, he sent it to Ivan von Auw at the Harold Ober Agency; without any difficulty, von Auw placed the book with Dodd, Mead, to be published in 1944 in its Red Badge mystery line. The secretive Millar now told friends and colleagues what he'd been up to. "He was rather smug and pleased," Marianne Meisel said, "because the darn thing got bought immediately! That was pleasant to see." Wasting no time, Millar began another novel, a collaboration with

James Meisel about a con man in Nazi Germany. The men finished a manuscript of one hundred thousand words, which von Auw also represented. Although it didn't sell (interest in Germany was waning even before the end of the war), it received flattering rejections (from Houghton Mifflin and Knopf) and boosted Millar's confidence.

Buoyed by his achievements, he applied again for a navy commission. His health hadn't changed, but the service's standards had; this time Millar made it. When Margaret's *Wall of Eyes* was published to fine notices (the *New York Times Book Review* made it a "New Books for Christmas" recommendation), Millar had things of his own to be proud of: a first novel sold, and a job to break him out of academe. Millar's life would never be the same.

Everyone else looks pretty shoddy to me, darling. Saps & weak-
lings & dumbbells & liars & hypocrites. You can't realize what you
mean to me . . . what you don't know is how I *admire* you, & respect
you & look up to you.

—Margaret to Kenneth, 1945

The waiter just brought me my third bottle of beer. It tastes very
good indeed when you get it only Saturday night. Don't tell me values aren't conditioned by environment.

—Kenneth to Margaret, 1944

Millar was at Harvard when his novel came out—not working
toward a Ph.D., as he'd once hoped to be doing there, but studying to be a naval communications officer. It had taken a world
war to get Millar into the school that had rejected his fellowship application in 1938. However tangential his stay, Millar was eager to make the
most of the opportunity. The new ensign threw himself into his work as
wholeheartedly as he had in an earlier two-month stretch at Princeton.
Though he hated typing, he forced himself to achieve the required profi-
ciency; and he managed to master Morse code in fifteen minutes instead
of the regulation fifteen days.

Margaret and Linda relocated with him to Massachusetts, as they'd first
followed him (with Linda's good Ann Arbor nursery school teacher and
Margaret's sister, a nurse on leave from the Canadian Army) to Princeton.
During that New Jersey posting, the Millar entourage stayed on Mercer
Street in the rented house of Listerine manufacturer Gerard Lambert, a
few doors away from the genius whose name Margaret sometimes took in
vain: Albert Einstein. When Millar transferred to Harvard, the Millars
moved to an apartment in Belmont, Massachusetts, an hour's trolley ride
from the Cambridge campus. That's where they were in September 1944
when Dodd, Mead brought out *The Dark Tunnel*.

Millar's first book got its share of praise in the special review columns
and roundups to which 1940s mystery fiction was consigned. The *New York
Times* called it "a thrilling story told with consummate skill," the *Chicago
Sun* praised its "politically progressive views" and "anti-reactionary
ironies," and the *New Republic* (one of Millar's favorite magazines) said it
was "a humdinger—and well written to boot." In December, the *Saturday
Review*'s mystery critic judged *The Dark Tunnel* "the best 'suspense' yarn of
the year."

By then Millar was not only a published author but a naval communications officer. Ensign Millar traveled with his wife and daughter by Santa Fe
train from Michigan to the West Coast. Given his pick of postings, he'd

chosen the Eleventh Naval District, headquartered in San Diego, where his parents once lived. Primed by his mother's stories, Millar would finally see California.

After he'd reported for duty, the Millars stayed a month in the ocean-front town of La Jolla, at the Cabrillo Hotel. Ken and Margaret enjoyed themselves thoroughly: swimming in the Pacific, watching seals frolic on the beach, dancing at night to the Cabrillo's orchestra, taking day trips to Tijuana. They met La Jolla writer Max Miller, author of *I Cover the Water-front* and other best-sellers, who showed them his second-floor office with its mesmerizing ocean view. These California weeks made a strong impression on Millar. He didn't feel he'd "come home" exactly, but he did think this was a place he could live with pleasure. His wife and daughter liked it too. Margaret wanted to move to La Jolla.

Such a notion, unthinkable a year ago, was actually an option. Margaret Millar's latest manuscript, a psychological thriller called *The Iron Gates*, had caused a stir at Random House, which planned an optimistic first printing of eighty-five hundred copies. If the book did well, the Millars might earn enough to live here. Margaret couldn't imagine a better place than California for Millar to be a writer.

Margaret and Linda stayed on the West Coast when a British ship took Millar in February to Pearl Harbor to join the crew of the USS *Shipley Bay*, an aircraft carrier making regular runs from Hawaii to Samar and Luzon. Ensign Millar would be in charge of all ship's coding, but he planned to start a second thriller for Dodd, Mead in his spare hours. When he began a book in March, his mind was still filled with La Jolla and San Diego. He wrote Margaret, "The only place I imagine with automatic ease is Southern California."

Blending with Millar's firsthand California impressions were ones he'd gotten from Raymond Chandler's writing; Millar's interest in Chandler was still keen (he urged Margaret to mail him a new Chandler book if one came out). Now Chandler's vision filled the movie screen, in a film of James Cain's *Double Indemnity*, written by Chandler with director Billy Wilder. The *Shipley Bay*'s crew saw *Double Indemnity* in March, and Millar thought it "really first-class." A few weeks later he got another shipboard shot of Chandler in *Murder, My Sweet*, a movie of Chandler's *Farewell, My Lovely* that starred Dick Powell as detective Philip Marlowe. Millar took a break from his thriller writing to watch it ("I couldn't miss that show") and found it "*good*, though not so good as *Double Indemnity:* didn't have the drama and was a bit confusing. But lots of good violence and cynicism and stuff, and funny dialogue: they told it the same way as *Double Indemnity*—I could stand to see more of the same."

As for his own work in progress, Millar warned, "It's going to be a strange book. I don't *like* it but I'm sort of fascinated by it—a mixture of sex, action, the negro problem, love, tragedy, melodrama, about five murders, in some places quite good writing, and farce." He claimed to have broken free of his strongest influence: "I can't be bothered cleaving to the Chandler line any more." But when he wrote a final sequence filled with "poetically" graphic violence, he admitted his Chandler manner was back: "Please don't tell me I'm too completely Chandlerized, though I know I bear his mark still (The Red Badge of Chandler). But from page to page I write as I please. . . . If Raymond and I get excited about the same things, O.K., O.K." Except for his author wife, Millar said, Chandler was "the only one that carries me away."

After reading the chapters he mailed her, Margaret told him, "It does sound Chandlerish of course; but you can write rings around him and you know it. He's not *various* enough." Though she was the one who'd steered him to Chandler in the first place, her own enthusiasm for Chandler's work had cooled. But she did try telephoning Chandler when she spent a March day in LA, she wrote Millar: "Just did it so I could report to you." (No one answered at Chandler's end.)

Margaret spent weeks traveling up and down the coast by rail, from San Diego to Carmel, scouting communities for a rental house where she and Millar could work, "slinging crap at a few cents a word." Her first choice to live was La Jolla, but prices there were too high; anyway, nothing was available. Wherever they ended up, she assured Millar, "you will *not* have to, and you will *not* go back to teaching of any kind unless you feel compelled to by urge divine: rather doubt you will."

Meanwhile, Millar got a finished copy of *The Iron Gates* by mail on the *Shipley Bay*. He read it again and wrote Margaret, "I think it's excellent. I don't think you have to worry about its success. A fine piece of writing, and it makes me envious. You don't get that far with style without working on it steadily for years, which is what I plan to do after the war." Her book was "an extraordinary piece of writing," he told her, "it will go down as a classic of its kind, and I mean it."

Early reviews bore him out. A Book-of-the-Month-Club critic said *The Iron Gates* was no mere detective story but "a good novel built around a murder." Dorothy B. Hughes, herself a noted mystery writer, called *Gates* "one of the finest psychological mysteries of all time," a book that achieved "the status of literature." Unicorn Mystery Book Club chose *Gates* as a member selection, which meant five hundred dollars for Margaret. A reprint edition brought her another five hundred. On the strength of the *Gates* showing, Ivan von Auw got Random House to advance Margaret a further two thousand dollars, which she put to quick use.

In mid-April, Margaret Millar notified her husband he would soon be co-owner of a home in Santa Barbara, California, a city she'd found almost by chance while passing through by train. "There are mountains and the sea, and Santa Barbara is between; and the trees are lovely and the city not too small. . . . It is not as *pretty* as La Jolla but it is more beautiful, I think. And I, personally, Margaret Millar, *love* it." Their new home at 2124 Bath was "a *good solid* Spanish structure," she said, priced at $6,750. Margaret and Linda would be moved in by the end of the month, with Linda enrolled in a school across the road. "We can live here for *years,* see?"

No one could say she hadn't acted decisively. However pleased (or startled) he was, Millar couldn't help but see how completely all this had been Margaret's doing, and how it was her success that made it possible. "Sweet, darling *Gates,*" as she wrote proudly, "it bought us a house!"

Chandler is undoubtedly one of the best of mystery story writers and it is my belief that if he had not been subject to the blind pigeonholing which has affected all mystery stories, his novels might well have appeared on the best-seller lists. . . . The first publisher who senses this, who chooses the right man and the right book, might well be surprised, may find that instead of a four to ten thousand sale there may be a forty to a hundred thousand sale. Does it seem ridiculous? But has any publisher tried to see if it is ridiculous?

—D. C. Russell, "Raymond Chandler, and the Future of Whodunits," *New York Times Book Review,* 1945

Now a publisher with a promising manuscript—a manuscript, say, like Margaret Millar's *The Iron Gates*—will naturally hesitate to call it a detective story and so, almost infallibly, limit its sales. Random House called *The Iron Gates* "a psychological novel" and from the evidences of its advertising, must have sold a good many more copies than would have been sold without such merchandising.

—James Sandoe, "Dagger of the Mind," 1946

The Millars expected good things from Margaret's sixth book, but what happened with *The Iron Gates* exceeded their most optimistic daydreams.

Advertised in the *New York Times* and the *Saturday Review,* its first printing of eighty-five hundred copies sold out, as did a second of two thousand; Random House ordered a third printing. Two reprint editions (hard- and softcover) vied to bring *The Iron Gates* to an even wider audience. The book was condensed in *Liberty* magazine. In New York there were two nibbles for stage rights: one from producers associated with Lillian Hellman, another from actor Raymond Massey. Margaret's agents stalled these theater people because Ober's Hollywood contact H. N. Swanson thought he could make a movie deal for *Gates.*

Swanson's instinct was good. Mysteries of all types were hot in Hollywood, and the studios were especially impressed by books that were well promoted by publishers. On June 12, Margaret wrote Millar with this stunning news: Warner Bros. had bought movie rights to *The Iron Gates* for fifteen thousand dollars, and she was being hired to write its script for seven hundred fifty dollars a week. She'd be supervised by senior producer Henry Blanke, who hoped Bette Davis would star in the film. "I am excited, scared and miss you like hell," Margaret told Millar. "What I feel so damn *marvellous* about is that when you get out of the navy, you won't have to go job-hunting or asskissing or nothing. You'll just come home & we'll write."

Ensign Millar's delight was unmitigated. He drew a cartoon of himself leaping with joy and enclosed it in a message filled with congratulations and happy advice. He told Margaret, "I know you won't go Hollywood. I wouldn't give a damn if you decided to work there steadily."

The same week Millar got his wife's news, Okinawa fell to U.S. forces, in the only major battle the *Shipley Bay* took part in; at its conclusion, Millar's ship left the Pacific theater. In mid-July, Millar saw San Francisco come into view. No city had ever looked better to him. Margaret was there to meet Ken, and they spent a day and a night's leave together before he put back to sea and she took the train to Hollywood.

As soon as she hit the Warner lot, Margaret was sending her husband daily bulletins:

> Hello my darling, Here I am. And all those books on Hollywood were so much *crap*. I am working like mad; I am the cynosure of all eyes, especially Mr. Blanke's; & I am the *sole* writer on the script. . . . I have an office as big as our whole house, + a desk I could float to Pearl on top of. . . . Lunched with Mr. B. in a small room containing, among others, Cary Grant, Charles Boyer, & Bette Davis. Ha ha ha! They look exactly as they look on the screen, but older, especially Davis.

The new screenwriter was in fast company. Among other authors under contract at Warners were fellow Ober client William Faulkner, W. R. Burnett *(Little Caesar, High Sierra)*, John Collier, Elliot Paul, Jo Pagano, Kurt Siodmak, and young Chris Isherwood. "All writers lunch together *except* Faulkner who is so pathologically shy that he *once* came to lunch, couldn't eat with so many people, left. Glimpsed him today. Nice-looking, gray hair, black moustache. No one ever *sees* him unless they go to his office." Margaret got up the nerve to speak to Faulkner: "I then tried to tell him what I tho't of Light in August, got *tonguetied* & left with an abrupt 'Well, that's all.' No doubt Faulkner thinks I'm as crazy as he is." A few mornings later "Bill" Faulkner telephoned to invite Margaret to his office for coffee. "He was perfectly charming in his shy way, using the most extraordinary words in his Mississippi drawl. We talked of books and stories." Faulkner expressed great admiration for Melville, and he and Margaret agreed Faulkner was a much better writer than Hemingway. "I stayed for an hour and a half. It is THE FIRST TIME Faulkner has ever approached another human being on the lot and I felt most flattered."

As part of her duties Margaret saw a screening of Warners' just-completed version of Raymond Chandler's *The Big Sleep* (done from a script by Faulkner and Leigh Brackett), starring Humphrey Bogart and newcomer Lauren Bacall. Margaret reported, "It's *not* good. Bacall can't act for beans & whole thing is muddled but fairly *enjoyable*." There were other duties: "WE ALL had to listen to J. [Jack] Warner make a speech last night about his experiences in Europe. It lasted nearly as long as his trip. I had the sorest ass this side of paradise. Arrived at hotel at NINE oclock, hungry, thirsty and bitter."

While working weekdays and half-Saturdays at the Burbank studio, Margaret lodged "over the hill" at the Hollywood-Roosevelt, while six-year-old Linda in Santa Barbara was looked after by her old Ann Arbor nursery school teacher. Margaret had arranged for this woman to come "take over the house and Linda" for the summer. The separation would do both mother and daughter good, Margaret rationalized; and they *would* see each other most weekends. Millar agreed no harm would be done. In any case, Margaret said, it couldn't be helped: "I'm so busy I can't turn around. I mean, I'm a career gal now."

Decked out in a new wardrobe, Margaret was enjoying her studio labors. She felt camaraderie with the other writers and enjoyed the attentions of such slick types as British playwright Barre Lyndon ("He said, 'Good God it isn't Iron Gates Millar, is it? It's just a kid.' He's a *smooth* customer. I like him") and Hollywood agent H. N. Swanson ("Tall [very], handsome [very, very], 46, suave; I can hardly take him seriously, he's too ultra"). But she resisted Swanson's efforts to get her to sign several long-term contracts. Margaret vowed not to stay long at the studios. "Encourage me in this," she urged Millar, "for I think Hollywood is a bad place & can do only bad things for people. I am not joking. I have always felt the presence of evil, strongly, & this place has it more than I dreamed of. . . . For us, for our marriage, for our family life, I want to get out of here."

Millar soon saw Hollywood for himself. When the *Shipley Bay* put into San Diego in August, Ensign Millar went to LA on extended leave. He met Margaret at the Chapman Park, a bungalow-style Wilshire Boulevard hotel where she was now staying. The next day they went to the Warners lot in Burbank.

A visit to a major studio would have been a big event for any movie-mad American in 1945, but Millar's trip to Warners on Tuesday, August 14, 1945, became unforgettable. At four that afternoon, word broke of Japan's unconditional surrender. Hidden bottles of liquor came out of desk drawers in the writers' building. Margaret Millar had her first shots of hard liquor toasting the end of World War II.

The Millars had earlier invited Elliot Paul and his wife for dinner, and the couples carried on as planned. They drove in the Pauls' car from Warners across the Cahuenga Pass, through Hollywood streets jammed with riotous celebrants, to the Chapman Park. After dinner, Mrs. Paul drove the four of them slowly through even more crowded streets back to the Valley, to the Toluca Lake home of MCA agent Johnny Hyde (who in a few years would get Marilyn Monroe her first movie roles). From Hyde's they traveled once more over the hill to the Pauls' house in Hollywood. Elliot Paul, a sad-faced man with soft-boiled eyes and a thick gray goatee, was the Random House author of the 1942 number one best-seller *The Last Time I Saw Paris* and several humorous mysteries. His wife was a senator's daughter.

("I don't know how she got stuck with *him*," Margaret said.) Paul was fond of liquor and had applied for a license to found something called Alcoholics Incorporated. He invited the Millars to be charter members; they declined. Nonetheless, Millar recorded, "Everybody got gloriously tight" this raucous evening. The Pauls had two pianos in their front room, and Elliot and Margaret played them for two hours, with Paul giving a marathon display of boogie-woogie. Margaret woke the next morning with her first (and she claimed last) hangover.

Another highlight of Millar's Hollywood stay was a brief meeting with William Faulkner, who told the Millars of his concern for a foaling mare he'd given his daughter in Mississippi. (Not long after, Faulkner checked into a sanitarium to dry out from alcohol.)

Millar was intrigued by these glimpses at the inner workings of an industry whose product had entranced him since he was a kid in Wiarton. But he was appalled by Hollywood. Beneath the studio writers' high jinks lay the despair and self-pity of people who sold themselves into long-term slavery and then whimpered about betraying their art. The studio world seemed a mecca of corruption. Millar wasn't sorry to leave the garish sprawl of LA in late September for sea duty.

His ship became a troop transport shuttling combat vets back from the Pacific zone. Millar's next return to the States on October 9 brought him to San Francisco, where he and Margaret stayed four days. His last night in port, Millar and his wife met someone whose effect on his life and career would be nearly as great as W. H. Auden's.

Thirty-four-year-old Anthony Boucher, an owlish-looking man in horn-rimmed spectacles, came to the Millars' hotel for several rounds of drinks. A graduate of USC with a master's from Berkeley, Boucher (a pseudonym for William A. P. White) was making his name on the mystery scene as a novelist, short-story writer, editor, and radio scriptwriter *(The New Adventures of Sherlock Homes, The Adventures of Ellery Queen)*. It was as a reviewer, though, that "Tony" Boucher would be most influential, writing about mysteries in regular review columns for the *San Francisco Chronicle* and later the *New York Times*.

Millar, who thought Boucher's critique of *The Iron Gates* had been that book's best, noted, "He has a knack for many-sided concentrated praise which no writer could fail to appreciate." Boucher liked Millar's work too; he said *The Dark Tunnel* showed great promise and joked it was unfair that one family should have so much writing talent.

The unwritten rule that reviewers and authors don't mingle wasn't much observed in the genre communities, where writers and critics felt united in common cause to promote higher standards, bigger sales, and more respect for books that the mainstream sneered at. As Boucher and the Millars got pleasantly tight, Tony invited them to join the newly formed Mystery Writers of America, whose motto was "Crime does not pay—enough." And Boucher urged both Millars to enter the *Ellery Queen's*

Mystery Magazine short-story contest, which was offering five thousand dollars prize money.

"I liked Boucher," Millar wrote Margaret from the *Shipley Bay*, "even tho' I disapprove of the professional anything, and he's the professional Mystery Man. But a good guy, and intelligent enough for keeps." (He was also an influential person to cultivate; Millar soon initiated a lifelong correspondence with the critic.) Boucher's few words of praise, as distilled as one of his choice printed paragraphs, spurred Millar to immediate action. In his cramped cabin below the waterline, he began a short story for the *EQMM* contest. He set it partly in Hollywood, and for its detective he concocted a private eye named Joe Rogers. Millar seemed to have an instant affinity with the private-eye form. "I really *enjoyed* writing for the first time in ages," he told Margaret. He quickly did a second story with Rogers and informed his wife, "I'm developing a detective (successor to Marlowe) and a style I think with which I'll go on for a bit till I hit pay dirt." Even dashing off stories for a magazine contest, Millar set his sights at the summit. Believing (erroneously) that Raymond Chandler was about fifty, the nearly thirty Millar told Margaret, "Give me another twenty years, baby." He wondered though whether these first stories were good enough to submit, but Margaret declared them "marvellous" and in November had them entered (by Ober) in the contest. A month later she sent good news to the *Shipley Bay:* Millar's "Find the Woman" won a $300 fourth prize. Whether he knew it or not, the course of Millar's career was set.

The dandified esthete and the noble savage thus united their anti-social instincts to produce the detective—a combination of school-boy athletic hero and sadistic sophisticate.

—Herbert Marshall McLuhan, "Footprints in the Sands of Crime," 1946

I make a point of noticing people who make a thousand a week. I do that because a thousand a week is fifty thousand a year.

—Kenneth Millar, "Find the Woman"

Whatever the future might bring, right now Margaret was the family's big breadwinner. The couple's 1945 income was thirty thousand dollars, with Ken Millar contributing only five thousand of that. Millar didn't like living on a woman's earnings, even if the woman was his wife—especially if. It made him feel outclassed.

Their first clash over the Hollywood money had to do with buying the Bath Street house. Millar advised paying off the mortgage, but Margaret preferred to put cash in savings. He gave in quickly, saying, "It's your own business"—and indeed it was. Now that Millar was writing his own books, Margaret's contracts no longer bore his name. *The Iron Gates* was her first work under the new arrangement, and the big money it earned underscored how far Millar had "fallen behind."

His resentment boiled over when Margaret made a will (with the help of a bank estate expert) in which half her money would go to him and half to Linda in trust. In a January 1946 letter from the *Shipley Bay,* he expressed deep offense:

You stated quite bluntly that if you died I'd probably (the probability being underlined by your will . . .) come under the influence of some woman, a blonde, who would force me to steal Linda's money; also that you evidently preferred the probity of the notorious Bank of America to mine. . . . I realized (for the first time in months if not years) your unfaith in me; hypothetical because all the factors I can think of, hereditary, biological and medical, indicate that you'll outlive me. I hope you do anyway. I wouldn't want to go on living without you. Even if you don't trust me. It's funny, isn't it, how men like Dr. Prichard or G. J. Smith (multiple murderers both) can gain the trust of any number of women in a few weeks, while a man who has made a religion of fidelity (myself: that sounds pretentious and egotistic but it's literally true) can't get the trust of his wife in nine years. Maybe you see deeper into my nature than I do. If you do, don't tell me about it. . . . I thought everything between us was on a high lyrical level, and I found out that in your eyes I was just another middleclass American with an incurable money itch and a wandering eye. . . .

You were fundamentally right in opposing my academic activities, *but* I had no way out until the Navy, and then your books, gave me a way out. The resulting conflict was insufferable. I went into teaching in the first place to make a living, and economic necessity kept me there. Sure, I could have written. But I had no assurance that it wouldn't be financially a waste of time. I had seen too many others waste their time and ruin their chances trying to be writers. Sure, I lacked assurance. That's the weakness I spoke of, the weakness I'm ashamed of. But remember that Steinbeck's first book sold 1500, Hemingway couldn't make a living writing for years, Joyce died in abject poverty, and so on. I felt that I had to stick with teaching and scholarship and make a go of them, until the last year, when I gave up for good. You were fundamentally right but I still think impractical. How pleasant now to be able to be both right and practical.

The money question kept nagging at Millar. In February he wrote Margaret another long letter about it:

I've been trying to reconcile myself to the idea of letting you support me for a year while I write a novel, and I haven't been able to. What I'll do is make enough money to *support myself,* and then write my novel. If it turns out that I can't make a living writing (it won't) I'll make a living teaching, even if it means separation from you (it shouldn't). The present time does seem a rather peculiar time to start worrying about whether I'll be a complacent gigolo. . . . Don't you see that a man whose wife makes more money than he (during the last eight months your income was as much as I could make teaching in fifteen to twenty years at my prewar rate) is in a difficult dilemma? I can't possibly support you and Linda at your present standard of living, and I am not the one that sets the standard. Yet just because you've made a lot of money is no reason why I should strain my life all out of shape to do the same (though I suppose I'll try). There's the dilemma, which I have seen with perfect clarity from the beginning. Sympathy, cooperation and love are the way out. You'll have to not do things that I can't share in, financially speaking. For example, as I said, I can do without a car. If *you* can, wait to buy one until I have the money to pay my half. Don't buy me any more expensive gifts. Don't spend so much money on Linda that I'm outclassed. Save your money for the long future. Every unnecessary dollar you spend sells you personally into slavery (that's why writers stay in Hollywood—it's not *really* because their husband can't or won't support them). And I will write considerable wordage (I don't *have* to start now, even if I haven't written a book for a month). . . . (I love you very much—if I didn't, I could play you for a sucker, but wouldn't.)

Margaret Millar read her husband's concerns as criticisms (which made her feel like "a failure") and ultimatums (which she resented). "If we live here we're going to live nicely," she wrote from Santa Barbara. "(My soul is not ennobled by floor stains. Nor, I believe, is yours?) Who pays for the niceties I don't care & don't think about, & wish you didn't. Wish it most hard." She pointedly signed herself "Margaret Mil*lar*," underlining the mispronunciation she'd gotten used to at Warners. She liked this way of differentiating herself from her husband. He was "Miller," she was Mil*lar*. Margaret would insist on Mil*lar* for the rest of her life, while he went on being "Miller."

They'd cleared the air, sort of; but Millar clung to the notion of paying his own way. Some of his angrier money feelings turned up in the thriller he was finishing in February 1946.

Trouble Follows Me had as its first-person narrator Ensign Sam Drake, ex–Detroit newspaperman on leave after a year's battle duty. He learns of an Oahu spy ring leaking classified information out of Pearl Harbor. The death of a woman disc jockey seems connected to the spies. Drake follows his suspicions to Detroit and there investigates a militant Negro organization. After a second killing, he pursues a likely suspect by train to Santa Barbara—to 2124 Bath Street. Information he gets there leads him to San Diego and then Tijuana.

The book's final shocks involve the revelation that the spy ring's ultimate villain is female: an amoral creature whose abnormal ego allows her to kill without conscience. This temptress offers Drake marriage and a chance at a fortune, in a proposition similar in sum to the studio contracts being dangled before Margaret Millar:

> ". . . We could make more money than you've ever dreamed of."
> "How much?"
> "A hundred thousand dollars in six months." Her eyes glittered like glass, and I saw what her central emotion was. She loved money so passionately that she couldn't imagine how cold her numbers left me. . . .
> "I'd rather go into business with a hyena and make love to a corpse."

Like *The Dark Tunnel*, *Trouble Follows Me* was an often awkward blend of graceful passages and bizarre locutions, well-evoked scenes and wild improbabilities. Maybe the most improbable thing was that the book got written at all under such cramped conditions. During his twelve months on the *Shipley Bay*, Millar also wrote a children's story ("Seabag," illustrated by a fellow crew member), four short stories (two of which got published), a lot of poetry, hundreds of letters to his wife, other business and personal correspondence, dozens of plot ideas, and one song lyric ("The Stateside Blues"), all while performing demanding duties as a communications officer. Millar put all the hours he could find toward becoming a professional writer. When his wife said he was wasting his time and talent on mysteries, he retorted, "Better mysteries than nothing at all." Financial security was essential to his being a freelancer, he told her: "That is because I used to visit my father in the poorhouse."

Sex was another contentious issue Millar addressed in letters from the *Shipley Bay*. He told his wife:

> The main cause of trouble between us (apart from economic pressure) has been this: you've wanted to go to bed with me about every two weeks. The rest of the time you've found it necessary to keep pretty well away from me, lest I get excited. . . . I've never told you how wretched it is for me to be with you and not be able to touch you, to sleep under the same roof with you but always by myself. . . . Is it strange that I should get angry thoughts.

When physical passion occurred (as it did during a San Francisco leave), Millar celebrated:

> That wild strange marvellous night we had together . . . how perfectly wonderful you were . . . we had a lovemaking as total as any war. I worship you. . . . The way other people believe in God, I believe in you. . . . The sweet and powerful language of your body, your loving movements, your loving looks (your talk, too . . .) is the only language my loneliness can hear. I'm talking now not only of this special loneliness of a sea-voyage, but of all the loneliness I've ever felt, and which you alone have freed me from . . . nothing before I met you and we became lovers, ever touched my loneliness. That's truer than you could ever believe. . . . I feel humble and grateful towards you. I value your love beyond everything else. . . . I cling desperately to the thought of you and our future.

The things he asked were "so simple," he said, "merely to cohabit with my wife, work my head off at the hardest job I can think of (except playing the piano), and watch my daughter grow up."

With civilian life in sight ("I'll be resuming the headship of the family—ha ha—by April Fools' Day"), newly promoted Lieutenant (junior grade) Kenneth Millar made the most of a March weekend's leave in New York City, where he stuffed himself with art: seeing paintings at the Met, going to plays on Broadway, and hearing jazz in the Fifty-second Street clubs. Jazz was without doubt his favorite music now, and he saw several of its star players on "Swing Street": Art Tatum, Coleman Hawkins, J. C. Higginbotham, Lionel Hampton, Dizzy Gillespie. "Those hours, Friday & Saturday night, in the 52nd St. dives were as pleasant and stimulating as any I've spent not in your company," he wrote his wife:

> There's something very austere and single-minded about advanced jazz, I think—almost no erotic element—it's athletic, technical and imagina-

tive. Some time quite soon you and I must come to New York (in the fall or the spring) and spend two weeks. It takes two weeks to begin to cover the things you want to cover: 12 or 15 plays, 15 or 20 orchestras, ballet, etc.—does it sound exhausting? The air of the Broadway region is as intoxicating as any drink. Nope, I didn't spend a hell of a lot of money. About 40 bucks, including hotel room, meals, and train fare; also Gertrude Lawrence. Gertie was superb in *Pygmalion*, Massey excellent. A lovely play. For sheer acting, *Anna Lucasta* was just as good: a wonderful cast, and all Negro (nearly all the best jazzmen are Negro too, apparently. Did you ever hear of Dizzy Gillespie's trumpet?) Did I tell you I sat in on a very uninhibited jam session after closing hours in the Onyx Club? Also Benny Field saxophonist of Lionel Hampton's band sat in with a clarinet and did surrealistic improvised dementia praecox for an hour and a half for the fun of it. Wonderful. But I'm not trying to make you jealous. I want you to come to New York with me.

Millar returned to Manhattan ("Can't get enough of jazz") for a "swell" Eddie Condon concert at Symphony Hall, where pianist Joe Sullivan played especially well: "*best I ever heard.*" With these exciting sounds fresh in his memory, Millar was discharged from active duty and flew west, to California and into his postwar future.

> Between the mountains and the sea,
>> Walled by the rock, fringed by the foam,
> A valley stretches fair and free
>> Beneath the blue of heaven's dome.
>> —Francis Fisher Browne, "Santa Barbara"

> When I was a boy, Santa Barbara, like the French Riviera, had a
> reputation as a sunny place for shady people.
>> —Marshall Bond Jr.

I f New York was as intoxicating as a cocktail, Santa Barbara was as calming as a tranquilizer.

The oceanside city where Millar joined his family in the spring of 1946 smelled like a seaport but at night was as quiet as a prairie village. The town was a fantasy of a Spanish past that never was: Hispanic plazas with fountains, neat streets of stucco buildings and red-tiled roofs, spic-and-span patios; it was all like one big movie set. Apparently there was no middle class in this city of twenty-five thousand: only the rich in their botanically lush estates, and a lower class who served them. And the unchanging climate was eerie: it was disconcerting to have summer weather all year long.

Millar liked it here, but he didn't trust it: the seductive heat, the easy pace, and the make-believe architecture that tricked you into not seeing sin, sickness, and death. You risked your reality in southern California. His mother had raised him to think the Golden State was a magical place where the light came from. Now that he lived in that light's daily glare, it seemed artificial and unsettling. Like a man in a novel he'd soon write, "he couldn't help thinking of himself as a black-and-grey character who had involuntarily wandered into a Technicolor movie. . . . His ear was permanently cocked for the director's outraged bellow to the assistant director, to get that man off the Southern California scene, we're going to start shooting." Millar felt more Canadian in California than he ever had in Canada.

The place he lived in by the grace of Maggie was a four-room house on Bath Street in a humble neighborhood near the train tracks. When the Southern Pacific went by on its way to LA, the Millar house rattled like a cold-water flat in a movie comedy. The house was neat and clean, but there was no central heating. On chilly days—fog often made mornings and evenings cold in Santa Barbara—Millar put on his overcoat before he sat down to write.

He worked in his bedroom, which Margaret had had furnished for him with custom-made pieces bought with Hollywood money: a red-leather armchair and matching ottoman (both piped in ivory leather), a leather-topped table-desk and an ivory-and-red dresser. It was "a very manly room," as Millar mordantly wrote in one of his books, "the kind of room a hopeful mother might furnish for her son."

The Millars weren't alone in their place on Bath. Margaret's sister had come to Santa Barbara, gotten a job as an X-ray technician, and moved in temporarily with Maggie and Linda. Millar accepted this arrangement with fairly good grace; he liked Maggie's sister, and the situation had its advantages: seven-year-old Linda could often be tended by her aunt while the Millars in separate rooms scribbled longhand in spiral-bound note-books.

Linda had a hard time grasping what her parents did for a living, and why it took so much time and silence and privacy. She felt out of place in her own house and for a while attached herself to a neighbor's family. She didn't fit in well at school either. Her favorite pursuits were solitary: making crayon and watercolor pictures, banging at the piano for hours, swinging on gym rings until her hands were bloody. Her parents, proud of her talents, left Linda mostly to her own devices. They had work to do. As Margaret would say, "No writee, no eatee."

Maggie turned down all those Hollywood contracts she and Millar knew would make her unhappy, so it was back to book writing. For her that meant a mainstream novel she'd put aside when Warners hired her. Millar had a "real" novel planned too, but he wouldn't allow himself to begin before doing some more commercial books. He gave himself a year to see if he had what it took to make a living as a writer; if not, he'd go back to teaching. His first effort was a thriller, *Blue City*, which he called "a tough mystery in the Hammett tradition."

It was set in a corrupt Midwestern town (purposely unnamed, but a wildly exaggerated Kitchener, crossed with the wide-open Jacksonville, Florida). Millar felt the hard-boiled tradition existed to show the underside of society. So too in a way did jazz, a music of and for the people. Jazz grew out of the blues' folk poetry, and its history paralleled hard-boiled fiction's. Both told the story of the modern city in the city's own rhythms.

Millar was much taken with *Really the Blues*, a jazz-celebrating 1946 memoir by Mezz Mezzrow (with Bernard Wolfe) published by Random House. Mezzrow, a self-proclaimed "voluntary Negro," called jazz an expression of the human spirit. That struck a chord with Lieutenant (j.g.) Millar. Listening to jazz records had allowed white officers and black stewards on the *Shipley Bay* some limited social contact. Millar had been greatly upset by the 1943 Detroit race riots, and he thought jazz could provide a bridge between black and white citizens. He declared of a Chicago jam session he saw where a Caucasian and a Negro player traded phrases joyously for several choruses, "It was the brotherhood of man!"

Millar learned a good deal about writing and attitudes toward writing from jazz musicians, he'd later guess. The ideal image for an artist was jazz variations, he'd say: the awareness that instead of just one way to express something, there were infinite possibilities; and that differences in style or tone between voices that were profoundly similar—Charlie Parker's and Lester Young's, for instance—could be at once minor and of great importance. Painters were as strong an influence on him as jazz musicians. "They really *spoke* to me, directly," he'd recall, "and they taught me things to do in writing that you couldn't learn from other writers, you had to learn from musicians and painters. At least *I* did."

Millar wanted to do in prose what jazzmen did in music. One way might be to have tones and motifs recur in a book, as chords and phrases would repeat in a jazz piece or solo; he tried to sound "a strong blue note" through *Blue City*. A grander scheme could be to build a book on one or more earlier works (a Greek myth, a Romantic poem, another man's novel), as Duke Ellington created new compositions on age-old chord sequences such as "I Got Rhythm"'s or the blues's. Nelson Algren's *Never Come Morning* and several Hammett stories (*Red Harvest, The Glass Key,* "Nightmare Town") were works Millar used as templates in writing *Blue City*.

The book was narrated by twenty-two-year-old John Weather Jr., who returns from the service and finds his hometown much changed. His political-boss father has been murdered, the police force is run by thugs, and gambling and prostitution flourish. A wrathful Weather vows to bring the town's villains to heel. Millar channeled a lot of his own emotions into this tough thriller: his still-raw anger at Kitchener, where he'd felt alone and vulnerable; the strain of trying to adjust to civilian life (new house, new town, new job); the pressure to equal his wife's achievement. Later he'd say this book and its quick successors were "a substitute for a postwar nervous breakdown." Writing in a lean, jazz-influenced style, working in cold fury, he finished *Blue City* in only a month.

The novel was a tough stew of civics lectures and two-fisted justice. Weather was another "roughneck intellectual" in the Millar mode, spouting an unlikely mix of brilliant prattle and tough-guy banter. Margaret Millar, usually the recipient of her husband's critical counseling, now gave him some advice. "I loved writing dialogue," she said. "He could not write dialogue; he liked writing action. In his first two books especially, all the characters talked like Ken! I don't even *know* anybody who talks like Ken. And I told him he had to *listen.* He just had to *listen.* We went around to a lot of places. We'd go to pawnshops, *low* bars. And he realized how different people talk."

Getting around by bus and bike in this postwar year when cars were scarce, the Millars made field trips to different neighborhoods. At night they went bar-crawling along lower State. Millar liked Santa Barbara's small-town feel. He enjoyed riding his bicycle the twenty-one blocks from Bath to the ocean and back. The town didn't have or need traffic lights; there were so few cars he could cruise down the center of the narrow main street (past the art museum, the library, and the Lobero Theater, and around the "old California" courthouse) with the Millars' black mutt, Skipper, running behind.

The people who strolled State, including newspaper publisher Tom Storke (as tall as his name, and always wearing a high-crowned ranger's hat), all seemed to know each other. Millar's favorite Santa Barbara place was the coastline, where ocean and beach met and made something better than land or sea. He and Margaret took daily swims, whatever the water temperature. Margaret adored their new town. "When you grew up in Kitchener, Ontario," she said, "where you had to pass the slaughterhouse on the way to school every day, Santa Barbara seemed like paradise."

Evenings when they didn't barhop, the Millars stayed home and played gin rummy, read, listened to records. Millar had a growing collection of jazz discs, heavy on piano players: Mary Lou Williams, Fats Waller, Meade Lux Lewis, and (thanks to 78s sent from Canada by Don Pearce) a Montreal fellow named Oscar Peterson, whose version of Ellington's "C Jam Blues" was a special favorite. Ellington showed what you could do in popular art: make uncommonly good work from common materials. Thus did the crowd-pleasing Elizabethan revenge play become "The Tragedy of Hamlet: Prince of Denmark."

For his part, Millar hoped "to rise through mysteries to the serious novel," he wrote Henry Branson, "but at the moment I'd rather write good commercial tripe than unpublished serious stuff, and that's what I'm doing." In June he started his second book in two months: a "psychothriller" about an amnesiac naval lieutenant hunting his wife's killer in LA. For plot reasons it would be told in the third person, a voice that didn't come naturally to him (though Maggie used it exclusively). Millar put a lot of himself into the alienated naval man and a lot of Margaret into his screenwriter girlfriend. *The Three Roads* took Millar's fresh impressions of many Hollywood types: the witty, alcoholic studio people; the opportunistic hustlers; all the sunbaked souls in anxious misery. Halfway through his manuscript, Millar wrote Branson this was becoming "the first book of mine I'm not ashamed of, though I suppose I shall be by the time it gets into print."

As he penned the last chapters of this "psychiatric mystery," Dodd, Mead published *Trouble Follows Me*, the spy story finished aboard the *Shipley Bay*. The book got kind notices (the *New Republic* called it "literate and exciting," and Boucher said it showed "a God-given ability to write which has no business striking twice in the Millar family"), but Millar knew he could do better, had already done better, and felt it time he broke away from Dodd, Mead and its elementary Red Badge line.

Millar had agent Ivan von Auw submit *Blue City* as a one-book option deal, so if Dodd, Mead rejected it, von Auw could take it—and Millar—elsewhere. The ploy worked. Dodd, Mead turned down *Blue City*, despite von Auw's getting them to give it a second read. The agent next tried *Blue City* on Henry Branson's publisher, Simon & Schuster; they passed on it too. (Random House was out: the house said at the time of *The Dark Tunnel* its policy was not to publish spouses of Random authors.) Millar made a bold suggestion: send *Blue City* to the best publisher in America, Alfred A. Knopf. As the imprint of Hammett, Chandler, and James M. Cain (three of the "toughest" writers in U.S. letters), Knopf wouldn't be put off by Millar's violent Midwestern fable; and Knopf would be ideal for the better books Millar hoped to write soon. Von Auw agreed to send "Alfred" the manuscript.

The anxious tension of the next several weeks was relieved by the arrival of the car Margaret had ordered back in 1945: a fourteen-hundred-dollar Chevrolet sedan. It was the first automobile either Millar ever had. "I owned a house before I owned a car," Margaret said. "Ken had forgotten how to drive. Our neighbor at that time started him driving again, but I never got the feeling that he was quite at *home* behind the wheel of a car." Nonetheless Millar took off on solo excursions, exploring out-of-the-way beaches and mountain passes, even getting as far as Las Vegas, Nevada, where mobsters (colleagues perhaps of the ones who might have put slots into Kitchener and kept tabs on his Winnipeg uncle) were to Millar's disgust decreeing neon-lit pleasure domes in the desert.

The good news came in November: if Millar would polish the ending and take out a few scatological words, Knopf would be pleased to publish *Blue City*. An overjoyed Millar swiftly agreed. His Dodd, Mead gamble had paid off. Knopf taking his book made him feel he was on the way up. Probably Knopf would take *The Three Roads* too. It looked as if Millar's one-year race to be a professional writer was won five months early.

The family celebrated by trimming a Christmas tree the night before Millar's December 13 birthday. Now it was time for the next test: writing that "real" novel. In late December he took the plunge.

"Just what is your business? You're not an artist?"
"Hardly. I'm a private detective."
—Kenneth Millar, "The Bearded Lady"

Whenever I am asked what kind of writing is the most lucrative, I have to say, ransom notes.

—H. N. Swanson

Sitting in Santa Barbara in the red-leather armchair, Millar imagined a sixteen-year-old high school senior named William, living, in this postwar year, in Rockfield, Ohio. In most respects, though, William was in Kitchener, Ontario, in 1931: his story was Millar's own.

"I'm having my fling at serious fiction," Millar told Anthony Boucher, with a book "about an adolescent boy being shoved into delinquency by social and economic pressure. That may sound familiar in summary, but I think I'm writing it fresh." It was close to the bone, anyhow. William lived with his mother, grandmother, aunt, and unmarried uncle in a tall, old house that loomed "like something left over from a sad and dingy past." Every dreary detail is pressed into William's mind: "the fanlight of purple glass over the front door . . . each sliver of peeling softwood floor, the thousand faded roses stencilled on the walls, the long bruise of water across the ceiling." Wearing baggy pants and a plaid windbreaker he's outgrown, William shunts between his suffocating home, the school where he's snubbed, and the pool hall. His stroke-crippled father is in the charity ward of the public hospital; his mother's a pathetic creature whose illusions he resents and protects: "He lived in a world which she didn't realize existed. . . . He played pool, lusted after women, read dirty books, ran wild in the streets at night, suffered under the eyes of the well-heeled every day and hated them for it, carried the guilt of his father's poverty. He didn't even believe in God anymore. And his mother didn't even know he smoked cigarettes. She had enough troubles of her own. . . . Silence and trickery were his only recourse."

This was *Winter Solstice,* the serious novel Millar felt he owed himself but postponed until his thrillers paid some bills. It was put-up-or-shut-up time now, but Millar was having trouble turning his past into fiction. To shape your material you needed to be objective, and the things he was writing about made him angry and upset.

As he wrestled with fact and fiction, his first Knopf book was readied for publication. *Blue City* would be presented in fine style, with a handsome dust jacket and ads that linked Millar to Cain, Hammett, and Chandler. Alfred Knopf himself wrote to welcome Millar to the house: "I was much intrigued by the discovery of how very different our opinion of this book is from that held by your former publishers. We will do our best to prove Dodd, Mead wrong." Millar later learned Tommy Dodd had contacted Knopf angrily, certain Millar and his agent had sold Knopf a different manuscript from the one Dodd's editors had twice turned down.

"I prize your imprint," Millar candidly told Knopf. It wasn't an imprint you took for granted, he learned. Knopf's thousand-dollar contract for *Blue City* omitted the standard option giving the firm first crack at the author's next book; Knopf wanted to see that book before he bought it. Millar's trick with Dodd, Mead was being played back on him.

In June 1947, von Auw submitted *The Three Roads*. The three Knopfs (Alfred; wife and partner, Blanche; son Alfred "Pat" Jr.) all liked it, but they thought the novel slow in starting and that it should be cut by two hundred pages. Millar sent a revision outline and said he'd start rewriting immediately; but he told Knopf, "If you should decide to go ahead *pari passu* with the preparation of the contract, I'd feel happier about the whole thing." Knopf did not so decide; Millar went ahead on faith.

Blue City's reviews were far from cheering. "Very, very tough," the *New Yorker* summarized, "and a little silly, too." The *Saturday Review*'s unappetizing assessment: "Raw meat." Boucher in the *San Francisco Chronicle* was kinder: "Routine enough in concept and in much of its plot; but Mr. Millar is to be congratulated on his sharp prose, his absorbing tempo, and above all on his ability to create a hardboiled hero who is not a storm trooper."

That was in response to another "hero" debuting this season: Mickey Spillane's Mike Hammer, in the very violent *I, the Jury*. With his comic-book plot and his thuggish protagonist, Spillane hijacked the hard-boiled tradition, looting its lurid aspects and tossing out its stylistic and moral controls. (Millar would privately refer to Spillane as "the poet laureate of sexual psychopathy.")

James Sandoe, the *Chicago Sun*'s mystery man, also gave *Blue City* credit for being "a good deal less offensive" than Spillane's "shabby and rather nasty little venture," but Sandoe (a Chandler partisan and a Margaret Millar booster) took umbrage at Knopf's comparing Millar to Chandler, Hammett, and Cain. Of *Blue City*, Sandoe said, "Its plot is as transparent as its ingredients are familiar, and it lacks any distinguishing force of character."

These discouraging words didn't bother Millar much once he'd seen the *Philadelphia Inquirer* review by Nelson Algren, whose *Never Come Morning* partly inspired *Blue City*. Algren was generous: "*Blue City* retains its own pattern, stands on its own legs all the way, and is written without the pell-mell haste with which this sort of thriller is so commonly turned out. Kenneth Millar never uses two words where one will do; and when he wants you to see a thing, you see it." The Chicago novelist rated Millar's descriptive prose just short of Stephen Crane's and said *Blue City* was "a whacking good thriller." It was the first important review of Millar's career, all the more meaningful coming from someone he was a fan of. "Unless one or two things like that happen in the course of your life," he said later, "you don't go *on.*"

He needed encouragement. The *Three Roads* revisions dragged through summer and into fall. While Millar admitted his novel read better for being shorter, he resented having to cut "ten thousand good words." More changes were requested in September, and he made those too. Finally, after three months of rewrites, on September 26, Knopf drew up a contract with a thousand-dollar advance for *The Three Roads.* By then the firm had shipped some forty-five hundred copies of *Blue City* to bookstores; in a regretful tone that Millar would grow to know well, Knopf wrote, "I am not delighted with this sale," though he said neither of them "should feel too disappointed."

Millar responded with the laconic hope that a reprint deal might reimburse Knopf's expense. His confidence was badly shaken. What he'd thought was his best book *(Roads)* barely got published, reviewers had mocked *Blue City,* and *Winter Solstice* was bogged down. Millar now learned he had gout, the first of several postwar ailments he thought were his body's way of coping with psychic distress. As if in sympathetic (or competitive) misery, Margaret developed a bad cold and Linda broke an arm. Millar added medical bills to his worries.

The couple's income had fallen sharply after the Warners windfall. Their combined earnings in 1947 would be under twelve thousand dollars (with Millar bringing in only two thousand). Warners never made a movie of *The Iron Gates* (no leading actress, including Bette Davis, wanted a role that ended two-thirds through the picture), but Margaret kept her studio contacts open. She wrote a fifteen-page critique of another writer's treatment of the James Cain novel *Serenade* for director Mike Curtiz and discussed a screenplay of Knopf author Forrest Rosaire's *East of Midnight* for producer Mark Hellinger, but no assignments came.

Millar also sought Hollywood work through agent H. N. Swanson. Hellinger, needing a Humphrey Bogart vehicle, requested a copy of *Blue City,* and director Allan Dwan asked how much the book's film rights would cost. Swanson (who it turned out was Raymond Chandler's Hollywood agent) said twenty-five thousand dollars, then shrugged when Dwan balked; "I feel we can get a much better setup elsewhere," Swanson wrote Millar, but nothing happened. Millar was leery of "Swanee," this sauve Sunset Strip smoothie with the slick Hollywood backchat ("As far as the job situation is concerned, blood is running in the streets here, hip deep"), but the Millars seemed stuck with him as Ober's West Coast op.

Millar needed to do another book, for money and to keep his career going. *Winter Solstice* was in no shape to submit. "By God I'll fall back on my thrillers rather than not be published," he vowed to Branson. "Writing badly is only the second sin in my book; not being published is the first." After the *Three Roads* experience, Millar thought his next Knopf manuscript should be a quick, colorful, salable piece of goods.

He consulted the plot notebooks he'd started keeping and found several ideas there involving hit-and-run. "Man chases hit-run slayer of his child all over," read one, "forgives him when he catches him." Another had a district attorney fatally running down his wife and forcing a garageman to repaint the damaged car. Hit-and-run engaged Millar's fictive imagination early: *The Dark Tunnel*, written in Michigan, contained a reference to "a bad hit-run case on the other side of town." In California, where cars seemed a cultural imperative, he saw many story possibilities involving auto crime. Late in 1947, Millar wrote eighteen pages of a tale called *Hit and Run* in which a boxer kills a man in a fistfight, then conspires with the man's wife to make the death look like a hit-run accident.

But Millar put *Hit and Run* aside in favor of another plot. At the back of a spiral-bound pad he made four pages of notes for *The Snatch*, a mystery about the missing Benedict Swain, a famous author working under poor terms at a Hollywood studio. Swain resembles Faulkner (and his name is like Faulkner's movie agent "Swanee" Swanson's). Swain may be on a bender or he may have been abducted, or perhaps he chose to disappear à la Ambrose Bierce. In any case the studio wants him back. Hired to find him would be "Rogers, or a similar man under another name," Rogers being the private detective in the Hollywood-oriented "Find the Woman," written shortly after Millar met Faulkner at Warners.

Private eyes were having a boom year in 1947. There seemed a great postwar yearning for the type of tough, capable figure popularized by Hammett and Chandler. Hammett wasn't writing books, and Chandler didn't often (his most recent was in 1943); but movies and radio were full of private investigators, and several book writers (Frederick Brown, Thomas B. Dewey, John Evans, Wade Miller) started new PI series. Millar revived his idea of creating a successor to Marlowe. *The Snatch*, though its outline changed a lot, was the "quick, colorful, salable" mystery Millar would write.

To do so, he needed privacy. The pressure he felt to match Margaret's success, along with the *Solstice* setback, made things tense at 2124 Bath. Millar wanted someplace else to write. Margaret's sister had moved to an apartment on Sola; she said Millar could use her place when she was at work. In the last months of 1947, he bicycled there each day and wrote chapters of his first private-eye novel.

Millar had it in mind to do a series of books with this detective, who needed a better name than Joe Rogers. A dozen years earlier, in a poem for the Waterloo college paper, he'd used his mother's mother's maiden name, Bowman, to symbolize a divine archer ("What Bowman launched thee forth?"). In naming this book's lead, he now leapt from Bowman to Archer; nice too, he thought, because the archer stood for Sagittarius, Millar's astrological sign. (His detective, though, was a Gemini, with the birthdate of June 2: the Millars' anniversary. In the first Archer book, an astrology buff tells Lew that the Gemini male "often marries a woman older than himself." Margaret was ten months older than Millar.) He had no conscious thought of Miles Archer, Sam Spade's murdered partner in Hammett's *The Maltese Falcon*. When he later saw the similarity of names, Millar drew attention to it and sometimes claimed it had been intentional; still later, he admitted it wasn't. If he'd been thinking consciously of anyone, it may have been the Mr. Archer who taught at his Kitchener high school. The real link though was with Millar himself. "I'm not Archer, exactly," he'd say famously, "but Archer is me." From birthday to family tree, Archer and author are twinned.

Archer's first name seems to have come on a chain of mental associations. The United Church magazines editor who bought Millar's first professional stories was Archer Wallace. Detective Archer, another beginning for Millar, might have brought Archer Wallace to mind, which in turn may have prompted thought of author Lew Wallace. Millar, who'd always liked the name Lew, would say, "Lew Archer was actually named after General Lew Wallace, who wrote *Ben-Hur*." Bowman to Archer, to Archer Wallace, to Lew Wallace, to Lew Archer. Significantly or not, Archer shares initials with the city of Los Angeles, where he works from an office at 8411½ Sunset Boulevard, a few blocks east on the Strip from H. N. Swanson's agency at 8523.

While writing his Archer novel, Millar found a couple of sources of quick income. Seeing in the Mystery Writers of America newsletter that *Esquire* was in the market for mysteries, he had von Auw submit *Blue City* there, and the monthly bought serial rights to his book for five hundred dollars. Millar thus made good on his college vow that he'd be published in the magazine of Hammett, Fitzgerald, and Callaghan. He also learned that the *American* (a general-interest monthly and no relation to the *American Mercury*, to which he sold a mainstream short story around this time) paid well for mystery "novelettes" by popular writers such as Erle Stanley Gardner, Rex Stout, and even Graham Greene. The glossy *American* favored formula fiction with colorful settings and romantic endings; Margaret Millar had been unable to please its editors with a novelette commissioned six years ago. Millar tried now to cut a tale to its slick pattern and came up with "The Bearded Lady," a story of art theft and murder in San Marcos, a Santa Barbara–like California city. Its hero-narrator was newspaperman Sam Drake, the lead from Millar's second Dodd, Mead novel. "Bearded Lady" was tightly plotted and smoothly written, and its downbeat ending was offset by the promise of romance for Drake and a beautiful nurse. Crafting a novelette for this market made Millar uneasy; he called his story "very bad" and didn't expect to sell it. He wrote Henry Branson: "I did it to prove to myself once and for all that the slicks aren't for me, thus setting my mind at rest." After sending "Lady" to von Auw, he turned his attention back to *The Snatch*.

Millar's detective in the book, Lew Archer, was thirty-five (three years older than Millar), a former Long Beach police officer, married but being divorced. As a first-person narrator, he resembled Chandler's Marlowe; in being morally implicated (or seeing himself so) in the corruption he investigates, he was more like Hammett's Spade.

Certainly the territory he works (for fifty to sixty-five dollars a day), the rancid West Coast paradise, brings Chandler to mind. But Archer's California is postwar: faster, glitzier, and greedier than Marlowe's. And Archer's first client doesn't live in the Chandlertowns of West Hollywood or Pasadena but in placid Santa Teresa: a Santa Barbara–like city a hundred and twenty miles (at least in this first book) north of LA. The missing man in the case isn't the novelist of Millar's early outline but an alcoholic oil millionaire named Ralph Sampson, who's a bit like the eccentric inventor who drops from sight in Dashiell Hammett's *The Thin Man*.

Like a jazzman, Millar played variations on Chandler's and Hammett's themes, nervily putting his book forward as the next step in the PI tradition. When his client (the millionaire's wife) offers him a drink, Archer refuses: "I'm the new-type detective." Archer's first meeting with his client evokes and inverts Marlowe's entrance in *The Big Sleep*. There the client was the paralyzed and likable General Sternwood, clinging to life in a literal hothouse. Archer's disagreeable Mrs. Sampson is paralyzed too, but youthful; she plans to outlive her husband and spend his money. Her main sickness is spiritual, and the insufferable heat here isn't from a greenhouse but from the hammering California sun.

There's another nod to *The Big Sleep*. The psychopathic daughter in Chandler's book was named Carmen. Sampson's daughter is called Miranda. Together they recall Carmen Miranda, the movie spitfire who wore outlandish fruit headdresses. Millar's Miranda isn't crazy like Chandler's Carmen, but her head's full of fruity ideas. She tells Archer she speeds her car when she's bored, rushing to meet something "utterly new. Something naked and bright, a moving target in the road." He says, "You'll meet something new. A smashed head and oblivion." Like a lay analyst, Archer advises, "Find out what you feel about this business, and have a good cry, or you'll end up schizo." Miranda half-rhymes with Linda: maybe the author projected onto this ingenue some fears concerning his own daughter, growing up in a state full of new moral dangers.

Millar subscribed to Wyndham Lewis's idea of the writer as shaman: the one who endures by choice what others avoid, who experiences fear and evil for the rest of the tribe. That's what artists did, Millar thought; and even a humble mystery writer could aspire to the role. As Archer seeks the missing millionaire, he sees the sickness in California society. And as Millar imagined the years to come, he couldn't help but be concerned for his daughter's future. Archer's often afraid for females in this modern world. Afraid of them too: at one point it seems to him evil is "a female quality, a poison that women secreted and transmitted to men like disease." Evil's omnipresent in the Southland that Archer prowls, from the seemingly benign Santa Teresa to the movie lots where (recalling Margaret's intuition) evil "hung in studio air like an odorless gas."

His first case took Archer to many scenes of LA's postwar excess: an oak-paneled insiders' restaurant near Hollywood and Vine, a louche jazz dive on the Strip, a mountaintop temple of a crackpot religion, a pueblo hotel off Wilshire. Disorder and perversion are everywhere. Mores break down as jaded citizens seek thrills and grifters look for a faster buck. In this amoral world, people want what they shouldn't have. The aging lawyer wants the pretty girl who's young enough to be his daughter (and rich enough to be his boss). The pretty girl wants excitement, "the moving target" in the road. The targets want to lash back in violence or blot out their pain with kicks.

Archer's not immune to the moral sickness. Sometimes he doubts his own identity in this "fairy-tale world" of false fronts and fake egos. His intellectual knowledge that life isn't black-and-white is at odds with his ex-cop urge to split the world into good and bad and punish the bad. "I'm fouled up," he admits. But if Archer's no saint, he's a good private eye: he unravels the kidnapping, uncovers a racket in exploited Mexican workers, and fights a thug named Puddler to the death.

Though deriving from Chandler and Hammett, *The Snatch* had its own tone and point of view: tough but not repellent, smart but not smug. The dialogue was crisp, the descriptions vivid. (Claude, the bogus prophet, by day "looked like the rayed sun in an old map"; at night, "a moonlit caricature of a Roman senator.") There were sharp glimpses of soundstages and of nightlife dens. One ten-page sequence, from discovery of a ransom note through a fog-shrouded money drop to the finding of a corpse, was especially well done. What seemed most fresh was the book's social conscience. Archer knows why the exploited Mexicans are treated like objects: "It makes it easier to gouge people if you don't admit they're human." He sees how a town like Santa Teresa is divided into the rich and those who serve them, and how trying to leap from the latter to the former can destroy someone.

Millar worked on the book for nearly a year, rewriting it from start to finish, forging his own voice and style to compete with postwar Chandler imitators (and with Chandler himself). He checked technical aspects with people at the FBI and the Justice and Immigration Departments, and he was pleased when a Santa Barbara lawyer read the manuscript and claimed it captured "the basic evil of this place (which is the book's real subject) better than it has ever been done before." Millar had dramatized some of his worst misgivings about California, and the result seemed to him and to other readers (including Margaret) pretty satisfying. He didn't consider *The Snatch* a "literary" book; it was another bread-and-butter mystery, to keep his career going until he pulled his real novel into shape. But he was proud of *The Snatch* for what it was, and all but certain it would win quick favor at Knopf.

"Life is full of constant sordid surprises."
—Alfred Knopf, quoted in the *New Yorker*, 1948

"*Son* of a bitch!"
—Kenneth Millar, 1948

I f Alfred Knopf was America's most imposing publisher, Bennett Cerf was perhaps its most charming. The urbane Cerf, head of Random House, had a flair for genially promoting his firm's books through such outlets as his *Saturday Review* "Trade Winds" column. Visiting southern California in early 1948, Cerf sent readers this postcard of Margaret and Kenneth Millar:

> Beside the Santa Barbara Biltmore's Olympic Pool I found Margaret Millar sunning her shapely torso while her husband, Kenneth Millar, took time out from a new whodunit for Knopf to give a diving exhibition that brought exclamations of wonder from Ed Corle and a Flicka of the eyelashes from Mary O'Hara. Margaret Millar's new book, *It's All in the Family*, is the most delightful story I have read in months. I laughed so hard over the galleys that I wired home to triple the print order.

Margaret's latest was a fictionalized account of her twenties girlhood. While Millar struggled with a depressing novel about his wretched Kitchener youth, his wife wrote a comic account of her more privileged upbringing in the same town. Random House hesitated before buying the book, then geared up to promote it heavily, predicting a minor best-seller.

However well *It's All in the Family* might do, though (it was excerpted in the May issue of *Ladies' Home Journal*), there'd be no royalties until 1949. As of May 31, the Millars' '48 income was only two hundred dollars. Monies were due from other sales (a Dell reprint of *The Iron Gates*, a British edition of *Blue City*), but no telling when they'd arrive. The Millars lived on dwindling savings, budgeting almost as tightly as they had in Ann Arbor. Millar was depending on the thousand dollars Knopf would likely pay for his private-eye book.

By the time of Cerf's trip, the Millars were a bit more at home in Santa Barbara. They'd made friends: children's book author Don Freeman and his artist wife, Lydia; humorist-screenwriter M. M. Musselman; ragtime-piano-playing English professor George Hand; a bookstore-owning couple. Millar was delighted to learn F. Scott Fitzgerald wrote part of *The Last Tycoon* near Santa Barbara's Miramar Beach. (*Gatsby*'s Daisy honeymooned in Santa Barbara.) Millar collected such scraps of proof that the town wasn't quite the intellectual backwater it first seemed, but he still felt isolated. The Santa Ynez mountain range he saw from his yard looked to him like the Great Wall of China, cutting him off from the cultural currents of America.

While his old college chum Bob Ford, now chargé d'affaires at the Canadian embassy in Moscow (and the dedicatee of *Blue City*), sent him fascinating bulletins via diplomatic pouch about meetings with Arthur Koestler and Fernand Léger and Vladimir Horowitz, Millar attended minor-league baseball games, drank rounds with *Santa Barbara News-Press* staffers, and took daily swims in the Pacific. Only the occasional visiting fireman like Cerf enlivened his quiet routine.

Nobel Prize winner Sinclair Lewis, a Random House author, was another celebrity who called on the Millars during a Santa Barbara stay. "He was off the sauce that whole summer," Margaret Millar recalled, "and very very pleasant. He would come to our house and bring a bottle of booze for us, I don't know why, and soda water for himself. He was really trying hard. (Of course that changed, and he became a drunk again later.) At first you thought how ugly he was, but after a while you didn't notice. He was just so pleasant to us, with not particularly any reason why he should be. He autographed our *walls*." Lewis told Santa Barbara writer Barnaby Conrad (another Random House author) he envied the Millars. "Their talent?" asked Conrad. "No," said the unlucky-in-love Lewis, "their marriage."

The Millars of course didn't show Lewis any sign of the strains they were under. The book Margaret was writing in 1948, *The Cannibal Heart,* gave sharper glimpses into an edgy union that seemed based on her own:

> In the past week Mark had become less nervous and tense, but at the same time increasingly critical of her. She blamed it partly on herself and partly on the circumstance of their isolation. Mark had always been surrounded by people. . . . Whatever they wanted Mark always tried to give them, but eventually he reached the point where his nerves began to crack and he had to get away for a while by himself. Once he was away from people, though, he began almost immediately to miss them. It seemed to Evelyn that she was expected to make up the loss and she couldn't do it.

One way Millar could be around people was to pay daily visits to the Coral Casino Beach Club. Across from the Biltmore Hotel, the beach club was the site of Cerf's poolside snapshot. The Millars joined the Coral Casino partly to have a place to entertain people like Cerf; using it for business purposes also let them deduct a third of their three-hundred-dollar yearly dues. A gray, wooden, barrackslike building, the club had two dining areas and a tiered complex with about a hundred cabanas arranged horseshoe-style around an outdoor pool. There was beach access; the Millars ate lunch at the club before or after their half-mile ocean swims. Here Millar studied privileged Santa Barbarans at close range, watching and listening at will. The Coral Casino was his laboratory, his spyhole: an essential source of information for his southern California books. The club would appear under aliases in many Kenneth and Margaret Millar novels.

Millar taught himself to high-dive off the Coral Casino platform tower after studying an Olympic team at practice. Don Pearce, who later moved to Santa Barbara, witnessed him in action: "He would go up there—this was a pretty good tower, twelve meters, approximately thirty-six feet—and stand at the far end, studying the board. Then he would walk forward deliberately and slowly, turn around—and stand in statuesque stillness for an unconscionable length of time. It was perfectly clear he was rehearsing or imagining every movement of the dive he was about to take. Then he would go up, and out, and over, and down, doing a jackknife or something like it. The legs were frequently not together properly, so the entry was spoiled a bit; it was clear he was a self-taught rather than an instructed diver. But he simply determined to *do* that, and succeeded in doing it, by *thinking* it over so thoroughly—and then did it. Why?" To conquer his fear of it—not that he told anyone. "He was a great man for testing himself," said Hugh Kenner, another Santa Barbara friend.

Millar's life seemed to be one test after another, or the same test prolonged. When *The Three Roads* was published in mid-1948, he felt he was failing. The new book got some nice notices: "highly recommended" was the *New Yorker*'s verdict; "distinguished" judged the *Saturday Review*, with that magazine's mystery expert nominating *Roads* best thriller of the year. James Sandoe of the *Chicago Sun*, who'd scorned *Blue City*, thought *Roads* "an astonishing stride beyond" the previous book. But Howard Haycraft in *Ellery Queen's Mystery Magazine* said *Roads* suffered "from overmuch psychiatry." Helen B. Parker in the *New York Times Book Review*, on the other hand, could have done with *more* psychiatric content and lamented Millar's choosing "the Hitchcock fork rather than the Jungian curve." The negative reviews loomed larger; Millar thought them wrongheaded, but they discouraged him.

Also oddly discouraging was the news that the *American* was buying his spec novelette for five thousand dollars. That was much more than he'd made from any book, and it would solve the Millars' cash-flow problem; but the sale depressed him, since he thought the story awful. "It took me months to make it bad enough," he wrote the Bransons, "and nearly cost me my precarious sanity." To learn he had a knack for creating the trash he'd once thrown down the Kitchener sewer, when his best book met with critical apathy and he couldn't bring off his work in progress, made him think he'd never be a decent writer. Maybe he should pack it in.

In this downbeat mood Millar took the train in July to Chicago and the Midwestern Writers Conference, where he'd earn three hundred dollars critiquing manuscripts and conducting the novel workshop. Linda and Margaret came with him (Margaret took part in a panel); afterward they'd go on to Canada for a long-anticipated visit "home." The last thing Millar did before leaving was send the finished draft of his Lew Archer mystery, *The Snatch,* to New York for submission.

Nelson Algren was also attending the Chicago writers conference. Millar looked forward to meeting the author who'd been so nice to *Blue City* (Algren also singled Millar out in a Chicago speech as a writer to watch), but the best the two managed was a wave and a shout across a crowded room. Millar spent his free time in Chicago bookstore-browsing with Nolan Miller, a writer he'd known in Michigan, and Feike Feikema, a burly novelist whose publisher billed him "the Thomas Wolfe of the Midwest."

With her book *It's All in the Family* just out, Margaret did a radio interview in Chicago and three more in Toronto, where Millar joined her and Linda after a stop in Ann Arbor to visit the Pearces, the Bransons, and his old professor Thorpe. In Toronto, Random House of Canada gave Margaret Millar a luncheon in a dining room overlooking the university she'd once attended. On this return to the country of their youth, Margaret was clearly the star of the household, as she'd been the star three years earlier when Millar returned to his "home state" of California at the time of her *Iron Gates* success. As *Roads* got a second round of mixed reviews, *Family* drew raves and climbed on the *New York Herald Tribune* best-seller list. Margaret still relied on Ken's editing and plotting advice, but Millar considered her the more naturally gifted writer. With this best-seller she'd outpaced him again in their "friendly and healthy" career competition.

Millar wanted to write good fiction for the general reader. His background made him a common man, and that's whom he hoped to reach (without speaking down to). Though he loved "mandarin" authors such as Joyce and Proust, he didn't aim to be one. He aspired to enter the excellent mainstream of Fitzgerald, Hemingway, Farrell, Faulkner, Algren. But Millar feared he wouldn't make enough money, and he feared becoming a hack. He didn't want to ruin his talent and abandon his goal; he didn't want to be like Hollywood writers, earning big cash for bad work and mourning lost ideals.

He was ripe for a course of action Professor Thorpe urged during his Ann Arbor visit: return to university, finish the dissertation, get the doctorate. It made sense, Millar told himself, to wrap up his Ph.D. before he lost the academic habit. With the doctorate he could get a part-time teaching post, maybe at Santa Barbara College, and be free to write fiction without pressure to do bread-and-butter mysteries or magazine novelettes.

The more he thought about it, the better the solution seemed—not only to his career "crisis" but to the constant tensions he felt from a daughter he didn't know how to father, a wife whose moods got on his nerves, and a town he couldn't adapt to. Frustrated in California, he'd escape to Michigan.

As he and Margaret drank Black Horse ale and enjoyed the Ontario countryside, Millar found his wife sympathetic; she said she might even be willing to spend the winter in Ann Arbor. Margaret had a better understanding now of a freelance writer's problems and accepted her share of the blame for their shaky situation; the Millars were now down to their last three thousand dollars.

By the time they got back to Santa Barbara, Millar's plan had taken shape. He'd drive the Chevrolet to Ann Arbor in September and find a furnished house, after which Margaret and Linda would join him. But the plan changed. Margaret, revising a novel and afraid she couldn't write in Ann Arbor, said she and Linda would stay in Santa Barbara for the first of his two semesters; he'd be on his own for half a year at least.

Millar expected to spend August in Santa Barbara revising his Archer manuscript to Knopf's specs, but August passed with no comment from New York. Then on the first Saturday in September, as he packed for his Michigan trip, Millar got a hand grenade of a letter from Alfred Knopf.

"Cut it any way you like," Knopf wrote, this new book was "a big comedown for Kenneth Millar, not only from THE THREE ROADS but even from BLUE CITY. The latter was outstanding as a hard-boiled tough story, the former lifted itself right out of the run-of-the-mill thriller category. But THE SNATCH—a perfectly impossible title of course, as I am sure you will understand—goes right back to ordinary, average, fair-to-middling run-of-the-mill stuff." The book was well written, Knopf conceded, but how could its publisher expect to do "anything out of the way" with it? The firm expected to keep him as an author, Knopf said—"we've put far too much time and money into your work to want to drop it at this stage"—but he advised Millar to forget the current work: "take your courage in both hands and put this book to one side, writing it off as a bad debt." (A bad debt to whom? Knopf hadn't paid an advance.)

Millar quickly wrote a long, forceful letter to von Auw, telling the agent he wanted by all means to keep his affiliation with Knopf: "I have a serious novel on the fire, half-a-dozen more in my head, and I hope that Knopf will publish them. . . . Beside that hope for the future, and the books I am going to write, THE SNATCH is not of major importance." In fact, given this reaction, he doubted he'd ever do any more straight mysteries like *The Snatch* (one of his least accurate predictions). Yet he didn't agree that this private-eye work was mediocre. "I think it's an interesting book, and rather well-constructed. . . . I wrote hard on it, and wrote it twice. It wasn't thrown together, by any means. The 'twist' at the end was planned for and prepared from the beginning. I admit it's unconventional to end a murder novel with the main murder, but I'm not a wholly conventional writer, nor do I consider my book 'average' or 'ordinary.' George Harmon Coxe, who is 'ordinary,' couldn't touch it. Ray Chandler can, but doesn't. If it isn't saleable, I miss my guess, and Margaret misses hers."

Every publisher had his blind spots, Millar reminded his agent: Dodd, Mead had rejected *Blue City,* Doubleday had turned down Margaret's *Wall of Eyes,* and Random House had hesitated over *It's All in the Family,* a book now doing quite well for that firm. Millar didn't want to quit Knopf, but he didn't want to scrap this "really very interesting" book either. "I can't easily afford to throw away six months' work," he said (actually more like a year's), "especially when I honestly believe that the book stands up and that people, if not critics, will like it—as my very persnickety wife does." Millar had a solution: von Auw could submit the book elsewhere, under a pseudonym.

It was an impassioned and persuasive fifteen-hundred-word "hasty note" Millar penned on the eve of his long car journey. Included were detailed plans for revisions von Auw thought necessary. He'd be happy to make these or other changes, Millar said—but not until some publisher actually *bought* the book. In a later letter, Millar proposed a new title for the work: *The Moving Target* (a suitable challenge for an Archer); and as a pseudonym he suggested "John Macdonald," the first two names of his father, John Macdonald Millar.

He was shocked and shaken by Knopf's rejection, which made a hard departure to Michigan all the more painful. Keeping the speedometer at a strict fifty-five (as he'd promised Margaret), Millar reached Salt Lake City September 6 and telephoned his wife. After they spoke, he wept a bit, he wrote her: "Utah will always be my personal landscape of grief." Driving fourteen or fifteen hours a day, he got to Ann Arbor late on a Friday evening and went to the Bransons, where he'd arranged to stay briefly. Hank and Anna welcomed him with beer, but Millar didn't feel festive. Waiting for him was a letter from von Auw, forwarded by Margaret, in which the agent reiterated how "bitterly disappointed" both the Knopfs were by Millar's book. "Son of a bitch!" he swore as he read the letter. "*Son* of a bitch!"

A gloomy Millar moved into rented rooms two and a half miles outside town. It seemed strange being back on the campus he'd worked so hard to escape. "Crossing from California to the middle west," he wrote Maggie, "is like living a brief lifetime in reverse." To Blanche Knopf, he said, "My drive across the country got me nowhere." Millar enrolled in a creative writing course, to get academic credit for his *Winter Solstice* revisions; he hoped to enter the manuscript in competition for one of the university's annual Hopwood Prizes, and started referring to *Solstice* as "the Hopwood novel."

He faced a grinding regimen: dissertation research and writing in the mornings, teaching freshman English three days a week at noon, revising *Solstice* at night. He didn't expect to see his family except at Christmas and Easter visits to Santa Barbara. After only a week Millar was "bitterly lonely," holding back tears as he paced his rooms, needing beer or wine to sleep. "I love you better than I love myself (or I wouldn't be here)," he wrote Margaret. "I feel almost trapped by my sense of duty or something." Maggie, also "terribly heartbreakingly lonely," wrote him, "You're everything I want; I've found that out in the past 2 years. No yachts, no swimmingpool, no big house, no diamonds, no furs."

On September 20, Millar got some "peculiar news" to lighten his mood.

In a letter thanking Millar for his "understanding" and "wonderful spirit," Alfred Knopf told him that *Knopf itself* would publish "THE MOVING TARGET by John Macdonald," providing Millar made revisions already discussed. The announcement surprised and cheered him, and he told his agent to take Knopf's offer: "Why not?" Whatever money deal von Auw worked out was okay with him.

Knowing how much Millar valued his imprint, Knopf offered stiff terms. *Target*'s advance would be five hundred dollars, half what Knopf had paid for Millar's earlier books. After Millar and von Auw accepted this cut rate, Knopf reduced the author's royalty from 17 to 15 percent. Von Auw grumbled but agreed. Thus the first entry in what the *New York Times* would twenty years later call "the finest series of detective stories ever written by an American" slunk inauspiciously into the Knopf catalog.

Millar was glad the *Target* matter was resolved, but his isolation and sink-or-swim schedule were still getting him down. In October he proposed to return to California next semester and finish his dissertation at UCLA. "It's weak of me," Millar told his wife, "but I really can't help it," though he promised, "I'll do whatever I have to to insure our future." A desperate-sounding Margaret ("I could never stand another separation, I'd rather kill myself") begged, "PLEASE don't stay the second semester, no matter What. It's a whole year out of our lives practically." She had a counterproposal: since her writing was going better than expected, she'd rent out the Bath Street house and come with Linda to Ann Arbor right now. Millar seconded the idea and thanked her profusely: "I feel like weeping but must work instead." He added, "I couldn't have survived the winter without you."

Hard as it sometimes was to cohabit, the Millars found it impossible to be apart. "There's no one I feel completely at home with but you," Millar told Margaret. "You're not only the woman I love, but the most decent person I know, and the best thing in my life is being able to live with you (most of the time)." Margaret responded, "I love you awfully! I don't feel worthy of you, & I'm not." She said Millar felt like "my other, better half, my miraculous twin."

Millar rented a roomy house in Ann Arbor at 204 Burwood Place. Soon he had extracurricular chores, as the once-scorned *The Moving Target* was hurried toward print as part of Knopf's 1949 spring list.

Knopf himself stopped in Ann Arbor in November 1948, during one of his periodic trips around the country to touch base with bookstore owners and librarians. Ken and Margaret Millar met the fifty-six-year-old living legend for the first time. The *New Yorker* ran a three-part profile of Knopf this month ("The only advantage of living in Ann Arbor," Millar said, "is that you get the *New Yorker* four days sooner"); writer Geoffrey T. Hellman conveyed the dramatic impression made by the bald publisher: "Knopf is at once Olympian and dressy; few literary men can stare him down. His aspect is bold and piratical. He has bushy black eyebrows; a bristling moustache, once jet and now gray; reproachful liquid brown eyes; and an expression at the same time intolerant and long-suffering."

This bold pirate brought Millar good news: Doubleday's fledgling Mystery Guild book club was snagging *The Moving Target* as an early selection, for two thousand dollars, which Millar and his publisher would split. Knopf had already doubled his five-hundred-dollar investment in *Target*.

His wife, Blanche, shepherded the manuscript toward publication, coaxing Millar (who didn't need coaxing) through a last-chapter rewrite by mail. Mrs. Knopf came up with what she thought an "amusing and fun" idea for an author portrait of "John Macdonald": a full-length photograph taken from behind. Such a gimmick, she thought, might well stir reader and reviewer interest. Millar was doubtful and conveyed his misgivings in a letter whose careening idioms reflect the schizoid perspective of a man involved simultaneously with a doctoral dissertation, a mainstream novel, and a private-eye yarn: "While I hesitate to disagree with you in a matter that you know a great deal more about than I, and while I very much appreciate your suggestion as a mark of your interest in selling the book—I do wonder whether its pseudonymity should be underlined. And wouldn't a picture taken *a tergo* have that effect? I don't mean to be refractory, and I have no personal objection to the gag. . . . I simply have a feeling that a thing of this kind either goes over with a bang or falls as flat as a pancake."

Mrs. Knopf persisted, arguing that the alternative to presenting "a mythical Macdonald" was to pretend John Macdonald was a real person and concoct a fake biography. Millar took her point. He arranged a session with an Ann Arbor photographer on December 14, the day after his thirty-third birthday. Don Pearce, sworn to secrecy, accompanied him. Wearing his own trench coat and soft-brimmed fedora, Millar was photographed in full-length silhouette, smoking a cigarette. The image of a pensive watcher in the urban shadows seemed to loom out of a Warners crime movie, the type the French would call *film noir.* "It's a specter, a ghost figure becoming real," said Pearce. "Kenneth Millar lost his identity in North America; Ross Macdonald acquired one. And Archer became more real than Macdonald, a distillation of Ken." This moody shot would be used for a decade to picture a pseudonymous author whose persona was fused from the start with his leading character's. Millar wore several masks in his fragmented and uneasy life: Canadian, American, delinquent, academic, husband, father. In Macdonald he found his most fitting role.

The next chapter will attempt to show how the Aristotelian theory of Imitation was used by Coleridge to free poetry from scientism, and completed by his conception of imagination. This conception arose, as Chapters III and IV will demonstrate, from the dynamic theory of cognition and creation which constituted Coleridge's answer to the eighteenth-century machine psychologies, and from the principle of unity which he opposed to the seventeenth-century dualistic philosophies described in Chapter V.

—Kenneth Millar, "The Inward Eye: A Revaluation of Coleridge's Psychological Criticism"

Even theses end.
—Kenneth Millar to Blanche Knopf

This would be one of their *good* years, Millar insisted when Maggie joined him in Ann Arbor. He made sure they socialized at night and saw a good deal of the Pearces and the Bransons. As usual, beer fueled the festivities. Millar bought bottled brew by the case and saved the empties to return; at one point there were twenty-one cases of empty beer bottles stacked in the Millar rec room. Music was another constant in Millar get-togethers. Maggie could still be coaxed to play the piano. "I'd Like to Get You on a Slow Boat to China" was a new number her husband especially liked her to do, one that made him writhe with pleasure.

Strangely, music could also bring out the odd mean streak in Millar, Anna Branson said: "We had a copy of the Berlioz Requiem. This record had a special significance for me, because it was recorded in France at the time of the Occupation of Paris. The musicians when they recorded it were in this church with all the doors and windows closed. Anyway I was moved by the music, and the one thing I especially liked was the Sanctus, where this tenor's voice really *soars* out. As usual I got tears in my eyes, you know? So Millar comes over to me and says, 'Does that *send* you?' And I said, 'Yes, it does.' He said, 'Well, it shouldn't.' "

Don Pearce recalled trying to introduce Millar to another classical piece: "I figured he ought to hear something on the phonograph, a piece I was overwhelmed with but wasn't exactly sure why: Sibelius's *Finlandia*. I tried to convey why the concluding sections were so impressive; I must have been taking a long time, and at last he said, 'I know, I know, it's hope in a context of despair'—and of course that is *precisely* what that piece is all about. Another instance of that succinct defining power he had, the critic's power to nail something down neatly."

That power found irritating expression in Millar's frequent phrase *What you mean is*. "I used to hate that secretly," Pearce admitted. " 'What *you* mean is'—then he would rephrase what you were saying and you'd have to privately admit maybe that *was* it, but you'd also lose track of what you wanted to say. He had this liability built into his nature, the need to clear things up for other people. Margaret and he were great at doing that: straightening out other people's lives. Forthrightly and candidly, explicitly and angrily, telling you where the hell you're wrong about everything."

Both Millars liked to point out the "real" reasons behind your behavior. "They were great ones for explaining things through psychology," Anna Branson said. "Once I was griping about some forty-dollar pharmacy bill I'd forgotten to pay, and very seriously Ken said, 'That's because you didn't *want* to pay it.' See? There was always a little *explanation*, something that *made* you do what you did. I got to the point where I decided, I'm just gonna be careful what I say."

The Millars became more of a trial for their friends as the winter wore on. As feared, Maggie was unable to write in Ann Arbor. She often suffered bronchitis and sinusitis, and her presence at any event was problematic. One evening when Anna Branson made a special meal for both Millars, he arrived alone, bearing an extravagant peace offering. "Ken was really grave," Anna said, "because Maggie had been invited and she wouldn't come. He handed me a book. It was F. Scott Fitzgerald's *The Crack-Up*. Ken and I both loved Fitzgerald's work; it was a special *bond* between us. And this was Ken's own copy of *The Crack-Up* from when he was in the navy; it had his name and the name of his ship written in it. I said, 'Oh, Ken! These are hard to come by, and they cost a lotta money!' He said, 'I know. That's why I'm giving it to you.' " He didn't tell Anna the book was a wartime present to him from Margaret.

It wasn't just other people's events Maggie ducked. Anna Branson recalled a night at Burwood Place when Margaret failed to come to her *own* dinner party: "The tables were set up and everything, but Maggie never showed. Ken just took over; he didn't bat an eye."

Evenings with the Millars could be "unpredictably gruesome," Don Pearce found. He was present for one especially awkward event at the Millar place attended by several U of M people, including the dean of the graduate school. "For some reason or other the conversation didn't exactly get off the ground," Pearce said, "and Ken went and stood by the mantel, and holding out a glass of beer, he said, 'Excuse me, would you all mind if we shifted to another topic? I can't quite get my *hooks* into what you're talking about, and I feel completely left out.' He suggested another subject for discussion. And that one didn't get very far. After a while Ken disappeared from the room. And he stayed disappeared. After a bit Margaret went after him—and came back alone. The party went on and it got not too bad, but—Ken had simply gone to bed! Eventually everyone decided to go home. I was the last to leave. Margaret sat there, putting cigarette after cigarette into her long cigarette holder, with a smile that never came off her face; she sort of loved the way the whole evening had fallen apart and eventually vanished."

Despite her and his peculiarities, Millar showed an affection for his wife that was rooted deep. Anna Branson remembered, "Ken was waiting at our place for Maggie to show up one day, and we looked out the window. It was wintertime, and there were snowdrifts out there. And here she was coming up from Division Street towards our house; she had these beautiful, long legs, and she was jumping over the snow piles. And Ken says, 'Oh, Mar-gee, my sweet Mar-gee,' with all that affection in his voice. He was the only one she allowed to call her that."

Some of Millar's other attitudes could seem old-fashioned. "Ken was a very moral sort of person," Anna Branson said. "*Very* moral. In a sense you got the impression he was out to *protect* women. I was talking to him about doing the hula. And, you know, the hula is suggestive. I said, 'I've been teaching that to Annie,' " the Bransons' young daughter. "He says, 'Oh, *don't* do *that!* ' "

The Millars had a rather more relaxed attitude toward their own daughter's upbringing, though. "All she needs is the barest of supervision," Maggie claimed of nine-year-old Linda, enrolled this winter at Ann Arbor's Bach School. Her parents always gave Linda the benefit of the doubt. A year before, when she'd stolen money "almost innocently" from the top of a dresser, it was enough for Millar that Linda surrendered the money without fuss. "Her candor has always been lovely," he thought. Others saw her less idealistically. "Linda was a terror, she really was," said Anna Branson. "Very pretty girl, and bright. But she rode over people roughshod. She took situations over, Linda did." One afternoon Anna came home to find Linda Millar playing horsies with seven-year-old Annie Branson: "Linda had made a harness out of a rope and had it around Annie's arms and was saying, 'Giddyap!' Annie turned and saw me, opened her mouth, and just started to bawl."

Linda's play sometimes took a bizarre turn. The black-hatted snow-woman in the Millar's front yard this frosty winter of 1948–49 had an icicle dagger stabbed in her chest and red nail polish leaking from the frozen wound. (Surely Maggie had a hand in this; an identical snowwoman turned up in the text and on the jacket of a book she later wrote.) When Anna Branson looked closely at the several dolls in the dollhouse in Linda's attic bedroom, she saw something out of a Charles Addams cartoon: "Every single one of those dolls was sitting in a chair, bound and gagged."

The Millars placed few restrictions on their daughter's reading. After racing through Grimms' tales and Louisa May Alcott, Linda turned to adult fare like Carson McCullers's *The Heart Is a Lonely Hunter* and her parents' works. Soon Linda Millar was writing her own "strange misspelt tales of madness and retribution," as her father described them. "Boy, this is really gruesome," her mother overheard her as Linda scribbled, "just like *The Three Roads.*"

A couple of things happened to Linda and Margaret Millar in Ann

Arbor that ruined the year for them. Both incidents were accidents—but the psychologists, and the Millars, didn't believe in "accidents."

The first occurred one noon after Margaret dropped Ken off at the university. The two had a tense exchange before Maggie drove away. A few minutes later she ran their car into a truck. A pair of ice skates on the dashboard hit her forehead, causing a cut that needed stitches. Millar thought this must have reminded Linda of the time she'd seen him hit Maggie's brow and draw blood—and that this new wound set the psychic stage for what happened the next day.

Linda was looking forward to a visit from her old Ann Arbor teacher, the woman who'd been her Santa Barbara nanny. At the last minute the woman canceled. A dejected Linda climbed the stairs to her bedroom, slipped on a doll, fell downstairs, and broke her left arm—the same arm broken the year before. She was brought to the university hospital where, without consulting her parents, doctors took bone from her hip to repair a cyst found in the broken arm. The operation was botched and had to be repeated later in California. Linda's arm was in a cast for months, and Margaret blamed Ken: if he hadn't caused them to be in Ann Arbor, these things would never have happened.

Adding to this year's disappointment was Millar's acknowledgment that *Winter Solstice* was stillborn. He shelved the novel rather than suffer the pain of having Mr. or Mrs. Knopf reject it.

On the other hand, his Coleridge dissertation was being called a triumph. Thorpe and others were certain "The Inward Eye" was Millar's ticket to any university post he wanted.

He was 250 pages into the dissertation when, in March 1949, Knopf mailed Millar an advance finished copy of John Macdonald's *The Moving Target*. Anthony Boucher, about to start covering mystery fiction for the *New York Times Book Review,* also received an early copy of the Archer novel. Without naming *Target,* Millar had earlier tipped Boucher that he'd done a pseudonymous book for Knopf. Boucher picked *Target* to review, then wrote Ann Arbor and asked if "Macdonald" was Millar. Boucher enclosed his forthcoming *Book Review* piece on *Target,* which began, "Just at the time that the tough genre in fiction needs revitalizing, John Macdonald turns up." Boucher praised the book's "outstanding freshness" and said its author, "as a weaver of words and an observer of people, stands head and shoulders above . . . his competitors." Macdonald and Archer, he concluded, "have given the tough tec a new lease on life."

Millar had gone out of his way to cultivate Boucher, corresponding with him, revealing his high-minded goal to use the detective story as an instrument of moral good, trading ribald limericks. Millar hand-carried a copy of the *American Mercury* with his mainstream short story to San Francisco so Boucher would be sure to see it; he was quick to thank Boucher for all printed kindnesses to his and Maggie's books. Boucher encouraged Millar with private comments and suggestions. He was impressed with Millar's abilities and seemed his biggest fan. After reading *The Moving Target,* critic told author, "You can write like a son of a bitch." As Boucher became the country's most influential mystery reviewer, his support would prove crucial to Macdonald's reputation.

Yes, Millar now told Boucher, of course he was "Macdonald." The pseudonym had been Knopf's idea, he disingenuously claimed: "I fell in with the plan because I want to try a serious novel . . . and if I let Macdonald do the mysteries, there won't be any interference (as there has been in Maggie's case)."

When Boucher's review was published in April, Knopf capitalized by taking a *Times* ad quoting it in full. Boucher found more occasions to praise *Target.* In a summer *Times* roundup he called it "the most human and disturbing novel of the hard-boiled school in many years." In *Ellery Queen's Mystery Magazine,* he said *Target* was for him "the high point of recent American books. . . . You can put this on your Hammett-Chandler shelf; it won't be at all out of place in that company."

Boucher wasn't the only critic impressed by *The Moving Target.* His colleague James Sandoe (winner of a 1949 Edgar Allan Poe Award from the Mystery Writers of America for his *Chicago Sun-Times* reviews) thought enough of *Target* to bring it to Raymond Chandler's attention. "An astonishing book has come from Knopf," Sandoe wrote Chandler in La Jolla (where the Chandlers had moved in 1946, becoming near neighbors of Max Miller), "it's pure pastiche and Macdonald has clearly read you with scrupulous care for it's the nearest thing to your fairly striking manner that I've met for all the boys that have tried to manage it." The book "must, fundamentally, be a phoney," Sandoe said, but "it disguised the fact better than I could possibly have anticipated." He asked what Chandler thought of it.

Raymond Chandler claimed not to mind *Target*'s similarities to *The Thin Man* and to his own *The Big Sleep,* but he said he found the "pretentiousness" of its phrasing "rather repellant." The book's author affected a strained prose in order to seem literate, Chandler told Sandoe: "A car is 'acned with rust,' not spotted. Scribblings on toilet walls are 'graffiti' (we know Italian yet, it says); one refers to 'podex osculation' (medical Latin too, ain't we hell?). 'The seconds piled up precariously like a tower of poker chips,' etc. The simile that does not quite come off because it doesn't understand what the purpose of the simile is." This, Chandler said, showed "the stylistic misuse of language, and I think that certain writers are under a compulsion to write in recherché phrases as a compensation for a lack of some kind of natural animal emotion. They feel nothing, they are literary eunuchs, and therefore they fall back on oblique terminology to prove their distinction. It is the sort of mind that keeps avant garde magazines alive."

Chandler's quibbles ring hollow. *Graffiti* is not so obscure; it holds up better than *recherché.* *Podex osculation* wasn't pretentious; it was code for an earthy phrase Alfred Knopf wouldn't print. For all its youthful flaws, *Target* fairly throbs with emotion; and its similes are no more off-center than many of Chandler's ("acned with rust" seems fine). Clearly, the old master, faced with Sandoe's praise of *Target,* was at pains to find fault with the young pretender. Significantly, Sandoe wasn't put off; he reviewed *The Moving Target* positively, calling it "the most creditable [Chandler] imitation I have read and a narrative that keeps one steadily absorbed."

After such strong reviews and the Mystery Guild sale, *Target* was bought for softcover reprint by Pocket Books (Chandler's own paperback publisher), which meant another two thousand dollars for Millar and Knopf to share. This "run-of-the-mill" work Alfred Knopf at first refused to publish had become Millar's most successful book. He was back in the writing game, and eager to get out of the academy. Getting his doctorate would take another semester, and none of the Millars wanted to stay in Ann Arbor for that. In June 1949, Kenneth, Margaret, and Linda packed up the Chevy and once more headed West.

All I really want is to be able to write about twenty books in about twenty years.

—Kenneth Millar to Blanche Knopf

The picaresque or something like it is about the only convention you can use to describe Southern California life as she is lived.

—Kenneth Millar to Pat Knopf

With *The Moving Target*, Millar was beginning to make a name for himself: the assumed name of John Macdonald. He was nonplussed then to hear from another thriller writer with a similar byline: one John D. MacDonald, of Utica, New York. *This* MacDonald said he'd been publishing for three and a half years and had sold dozens of stories to slick magazines and detective pulps. *The Moving Target* was causing him professional confusion, MacDonald claimed in a letter to Harold Ober: "Even my mother bought a copy, thinking I wrote it." A "bit of gumshoe work" led him to guess *Target*'s author might be "a Mr. Kenneth Millar—whose work I admire very much by the way." If Ober's Millar *was* Macdonald, Utica's MacDonald said, would he please pick a new pseudonym pronto. "For the life of me," concluded John D. MacDonald (not a pseudonym), "I can't understand why he, or anyone, should choose to write under such a thoroughly undistinguished name anyway."

Millar hardly needed this problem. Privately he blamed the Ober agents for not having checked authors' indexes. With the good press ink he'd earned as "John Macdonald" and a second Lew Archer tale already half-done, Millar wasn't about to give up his alter ego. What he *would* do, he told Ober, was add a middle initial; he'd be John R. Macdonald. Together with the difference in their last names' spelling, that ought to keep the two writers separate. John D. MacDonald (who'd also have a long and successful career) agreed that this should do the trick. "Please thank Mr. Millar for me," he wrote Ober, "and also tell him that I have consistently enjoyed his work, particularly BLUE CITY and THE MOVING TARGET."

Millar was now decisively launched, professionally and psychologically, on a Lew Archer series. Though he felt guilty at postponing more serious writing, the private-eye books would let him master the mystery form and make a living at the same time. He could match Margaret in royalties if not in art. And the detective genre held an appeal more basic and immediate for him as a writer than mainstream fiction: he felt the hard-boiled tradition in general, and the private-eye form in particular, were still open to development—that he could still *do* things with it, even if all he ended up doing was making it a bit more medium-boiled. "I wanted to write as well as I possibly could," he'd explain in 1953, "to deal with life-and-death problems in contemporary society. And the form of Wilkie Collins and Graham Greene, of Hammett and Chandler, seemed to offer me all the rope I would ever need."

He didn't feel a bit handicapped as a non-Californian trying to write private-eye stories set in the Golden State. Crime was crime, wherever it took place, and he'd seen or heard about plenty of it since he was a kid. His mother's father's family had been all but ruined once by a defaulting store employee. Margaret's kin had suffered from a family member's forgeries. While in the navy, Millar later obliquely told a journalist, "I took the confession of murder by someone I knew." The trauma of his own mother's death was something Millar could incorporate into his mystery stories. When a new Santa Barbara friend, a fellow Canadian named Hugh Kenner, asked where Millar had found out so much about Americans, Millar told him, "In *Ontario.*"

Which wasn't to say Millar didn't give California's denizens his closest scrutiny. He viewed the Santa Barbara natives with a novelist's curiosity and an outsider's wariness. Among the most restless natives were those in the wealthy adjacent village of Montecito. This was a dangerous social set: witty and accomplished, but reckless in pursuit of pleasure. "Montecito was a hotbed of hard drinking, wife-swapping, and all kinds of scandalous stuff," said magazine writer Al Stump, another new friend of the Millars'. "I suppose it was a little like Hollywood in the twenties: you couldn't go to a party there without having coke thrown at you. Montecito was kind of a disgrace to the rest of the town." The second Lew Archer book, *The Drowning Pool,* was full of Montecito types.

The novel began with a visit to Archer's Hollywood office by Mrs. Maude Slocum, who's concerned about an anonymous letter sent her husband from Quinto, sixty miles north of LA. The letter (intercepted by Mrs. Slocum) accuses her of adultery. She fears more such letters may cause scandal and divorce; Maude wants to protect her teenaged daughter. Archer agrees to help.

Soon he's in the Santa Barbara–like town of Quinto, "Jewel of the Sea," population twenty-five thousand. Quinto's quaint Spanish architecture seems an unreal stage setting to Archer. The artificiality heightens when he sees Mrs. Slocum's dilettante husband, James, rehearsing with a semiprofessional theater troupe. Slocum's a thin, sensitive fellow in a yellow turtleneck; Archer loathes him at first sight. The private eye watches Slocum and cast run through "the kind of play that only a mother or an actor could love, the kind of stuff that parodied itself," in a witty vignette that skewers fake sophistication. To wash off the psychic residue, Archer goes for a swim in Millar's beloved Pacific: "They had jerrybuilt the beaches from San Diego to the Golden Gate, bulldozed super-highways through the mountains, cut down a thousand years of redwood growth, and built an urban wilderness in the desert. They couldn't touch the ocean. They poured their sewage into it, but it couldn't be tainted." So it seemed in 1949.

Tom Nolan

In ugly contrast to the refreshing sea is the corrupted paradise of Nopal Valley, where the Slocums live. Nopal stinks of the oil and sulfur gas responsible for its tumorous growth. "A quiet town in a sunny valley had hit the jackpot hard," Archer observes, "and didn't know what to do with itself at all." On a mesa far above the herd dwell the Slocums in a house that hums with tension. James's mother rules the roost with "enough ego to equip a dictator" and keeps her son on a short-money leash. Sixteen-year-old Cathy Slocum, intellectually precocious but emotionally vulnerable, has her jealous mother cowed and her high-strung father acting like an incestuous suitor. The family order is badly awry.

Intruding further between husband and wife is Francis Marvell, an Oxford-educated poet-playwright who's usurped James Slocum's affections. With his skittish walk and "his Adam's apple bobbing like a soft egg caught in his throat," Marvell (namesake of a famous English poet) is the image of Wystan Auden. When he crosses his legs, Marvell shows thin legs "pale and hairless above the drooping socks." Marvell and several other acidly sketched types chatter through a set piece of a cocktail party. Like the most jaded Montecito-ites, they drop a litany of trendy names (Capote, Gide, Anaïs Nin, Djuna Barnes) and are obsessed with sex: "Sex solo, in duet, trio, quartet; for all-male chorus; for choir and symphony; and played on the harpsichord in three-fourths time. And Albert Schweitzer and the dignity of everything that lives."

Providing social if not comic relief is Pat Reavis, the Slocums' vainly handsome chauffeur, with whom Archer has drinks. Thumbnail sketch of a California phony: "He told me how he was promoted in the field on Guadalcanal, to become the youngest captain in the whole Pacific. How the OSS heard of his prowess and gave him a hush-hush assignment tracking down spies and saboteurs. How the *Saturday Evening Post* offered him several thousand dollars for an article about his personal experiences, but he was sworn to secrecy." When the police come with news of a murder at the Slocums', Reavis disappears.

In search of the chauffeur, Archer seeks out seventeen-year-old Gretchen, a "fallen angel" who works the Romp Room, a dive even more depraved than *The Moving Target*'s Wild Piano. Gretchen preserves a kind of innocence in her sordid surroundings but pays for it with early-morning "screaming meemies." Archer feels like a pander coaxing information from her. As in *Target*, the detective catches a sleazy glimpse of himself: "the shadow-figure without a life of his own," peering "through dirty glass at the dirty lives of people in a very dirty world." Millar's private eye, with his unflattering self-knowledge, is sharply different from Chandler's Marlowe, whose romantic loneliness tends to self-pity.

The Drowning Pool moves like a fast movie, with scenes set from the San Fernando Valley to Las Vegas; half the book's action occurs in a single day and night. The novel's a bit spoiled by a heavy-breathing subplot involving Archer with a dubious businessman's wife. Maggie Millar didn't care for this part, nor for the bloody fistfight that ended the book, but Millar thought the hard-boiled form and its readers demanded such chapters. He put them to his own good use. We learn the businessman, owner of a controlling interest in Nopal Valley's oil company, acquired his first fortune peddling black-market cars in Detroit. Success makes him legitimate; now he's "grand old California stock." Such revelations of "the way things work" updated the insights a teenaged Millar gleaned reading Hammett in Ontario, and they dramatized the unreality of life in the Golden State.

Archer tracks California fakery to a primary source when he visits a Hollywood movie studio (unnamed, but obviously Warners). Gazing at a hagiographic gallery of the studio's stars, the detective imagines how easily two of the good-looking people in this case might have entered that pantheon—except one is dead on a slab, the other in police custody. "The happy endings and the biggest oranges," he reflects, "were the ones that California saved for export."

Archer's more sensitive to the people around him in *Pool* than he was in *Target*. He's especially aware of the California perils that menace young females. The fallen Gretchen shows one way a girl can go wrong in this land of sun and shadows. Mavis Kilbourne, an evil man's kept wife, shows another. Then there's Cathy Slocum, whose near-genius IQ doesn't bring wisdom. Archer muses, "The night was murmurous with the voices of girls who threw their youth away and got the screaming meemies at three or four A.M."

Surely some of Archer's concern for young women came from Millar's worries about his ten-year-old daughter, whose adjustment to California life was shaky. Linda seemed more out of place in Santa Barbara after the family's most recent Michigan stay. She felt different from other kids here and thought she was ugly. For years she'd loved art; one of her drawings was bought by the Santa Barbara museum, and a good critic said her work showed great promise. Yet when an elementary school teacher insisted she enter an art contest, Linda went into a rage and refused ever to make another picture.

Millar thought Linda's personality problems would work themselves out in time, but he was forming the habit of turning his immediate concerns—including his daughter's problems—into fiction. In *The Drowning Pool*, which twists patterns from Greek drama and Freudian psychology into a postwar Electra tragedy, Millar and his wife and daughter are the actors behind the grotesque masks of the Slocum family.

Millar thought *Drowning Pool* was a good cut above *Moving Target*—more sensitive and subjective, and with a better plot. Since Raymond Chandler had apparently stopped writing books, Millar felt *Pool* gave him (or "Macdonald") a shot at being the best private-eye novelist going. Chandler surprised him in 1949 with *The Little Sister,* the first Marlowe in six years, published not by Knopf (whom Chandler had left after four books) but by Houghton Mifflin. Millar didn't read the new Marlowe (wanting to avoid further Chandler influence), but he read its mixed reviews. Boucher's *New York Times* piece was harsh; it said *Sister* showed "the spectacle of a prose writer of high attainments wasting his talents in a pretentious attempt to make bricks without straw—or much clay, either." The Chandler was conspicuously absent from Boucher's *Times* list of 1949's dozen best mysteries. Notably present there was John Macdonald's *The Moving Target,* of which Boucher said, "Human compassion and literary skill returns the much-abused hard boiled detective story to its original Hammett-high level." Even with Chandler still writing, it seemed Macdonald's Archer might be halfway to becoming what Millar imagined four years ago on the *Shipley Bay:* a "successor to Marlowe."

Millar wrote Knopf shortly after submitting *Pool,* "I have an idea that Archer as he becomes known will do quite well for both of us. I hear on all sides, though I refrain from reading Chandler myself, that Chandler's last book wasn't good, which leaves a bit of a vacuum in the field." Knopf, who *had* read *The Little Sister,* replied, "Chandler's last was just as well written as ever, but it exposed clearly his weakness and satisfied me that there were quite sound reasons why we had never sold him as he thought he ought to be sold. He just can't build a plot; in fact I don't think he even tries. The result is that the book sparkles and is brilliant in parts, but simply doesn't hang together or build up to the necessary climax." In any case, Knopf was sold on *The Drowning Pool;* the firm was "very glad indeed" to publish the book, he said: "It's a good job." Knopf settled with von Auw on a thousand-dollar advance for *Pool* (twice the bargain rate paid for *Target*), and the firm's contract included an option on the next two Millar novels. The publisher now told his Santa Barbara author, who was still calling him "Mr. Knopf," "For Heaven's sake don't go on being so formal." From now on it should be "Ken" and "Alfred."

Through hard work, good prose, and a cooperative attitude—and by making money—Millar had earned Knopf's respect. As a rule the publisher didn't read his firm's suspense or mystery manuscripts, but he always read Millar's. Alfred and Blanche Knopf believed Millar was a serious novelist on a par with Cain and Hammett and Chandler. "He was one of the few authors my father dealt with directly," Pat Knopf said. In early 1950, Alfred told Ken, "I . . . quite agree that we ought to get somewhere with Archer." Neither of them perhaps guessed how far, nor how long it would take.

You haven't let me down at all after the limb I went & climbed out on with your first Macdonald. You're still right up there on top of the hardboiled field. . . . I'm especially struck with the way you turn the Chandlerism, the colorful unlikely metaphor or simile, into legitimate novelistic indication of character, rather than trick writing for its own sake.
—Anthony Boucher to Kenneth Millar, regarding *The Drowning Pool*

You seem to have committed yourself to one of the most parochial and overworked fields of writing there is—a style so desperately overdone that in some of its recent manifestations (for instance, *The Drowning Pool* by John Ross MacDonald) it has become a burlesque. There are pages in this book which are pure parody. The man has ability. He could be a good writer. Yet everything in his book is borrowed, and everything in it is spoiled by exaggeration.
—Raymond Chandler to James M. Fox

It was an extraordinary occasion for Ken and Margaret Millar, formerly of Kitchener, Ontario: a Saturday-evening dinner party in February 1950 at the Palm Springs estate of Darryl F. Zanuck, the cigar-chomping boss of the Twentieth Century–Fox film studio. The stellar company at Zanuck's included playwright-director Moss Hart and wife, Kitty Carlisle; veteran performers Jack Oakie, George Jessel, and Louis Jourdan; Fox director Jean Negulesco; various well-endowed females and assorted males; and Mr. and Mrs. Bennett Cerf: the Millars' hosts for a weekend at the nearby resort of La Quinta. Millar thought his wife's urbane publisher the most engaging man he'd ever met, and this glimpse Cerf allowed him of a movie mogul's desert palace proved invaluable to his fiction.

"Anything that fantasy can invent will find its real-life counterpart in California," Millar wrote Alfred Knopf; he described some of the events at Zanuck's: "George Jessel made a series of wonderful speeches in dialect and a cowboy suit. He informed me that he too was a potential Knopf author, on religious themes, and on the strength of this rather tenuous bond we had our picture taken together by Moss Hart, who was wildly enthusiastic about a new thousand-dollar camera he had bought. There Zanuck himself was shaved in public by a barber in the middle of his living room, and afterwards took off his shoes and sat with his bare feet twinkling aloft on the table. Sic sedet gloria mundi. John Macdonald was all eyes and ears." He wasn't kidding. Five years from now Millar would weave memories and fantasies of this night into a long party sequence in Macdonald's Hollywood-oriented *The Barbarous Coast*. Before that, he'd insert expressionist sketches of Zanuck into a couple of Archer short stories.

Exotic outings like this were rare for the Millars. In 1950, Millar found a more accessible source of inspiration. Alone or with Margaret, he went regularly to the Santa Barbara county courthouse, a Spanish Revival structure whose tower clock dominated the downtown skyline. The Millars would attend dozens of murder and other trials here over the years. Millar's impressive gift for reading character (honed in a childhood depending on quick assessments) was sharpened in the courtroom. Journalist Brad Darrach captured Millar in action:

> A fierce old man sits sputtering in the witness box. . . . "See the eyes, the forehead, the nose?" Millar whispers. "Dominated by reason. But the mouth is completely appalled! As if all his life the mouth had been dragged, protesting, by the will." Frail and exhausted, the old man's wife sits blankly at the litigant's table. "The suit was his idea," Millar whispers. "When she was injured, he was walking beside her. Now he has to prove he wasn't to blame. He'll prove it if it kills her!" Under cross-examination, the old man makes careless admissions that damage his wife's case. "See? He doesn't really want to win the suit. Having failed with his wife, he's demanding satisfaction from society." Millar sighs. "That's the story of all reformers."

Santa Barbara lawyer Harris Seed, who became friends with the Millars in 1951, said the writers were constant presences at most major Santa Barbara trials for a quarter century: "He and Margaret sat through the big ones, whether they took a week, a month, or two months. They *participated* in those trials. And most of the time, if you knew what you were looking for, eventually you could find the thread of the heinous murder or whatever crime led to the trial in *one* of their books."

The Millars grew friendly with prosecutors, judges, and clerks, who'd alert them to interesting cases. Millar learned early not to base fiction too closely on fact. At the first murder trial he attended in Santa Barbara, an alibi witness dropped dead of a heart attack right after testifying. Such melodrama would seem absurd in a novel. Millar felt he'd marred *The Drowning Pool* with a hydrotherapy torture scene based on a real Santa Barbara incident. He'd become better at balancing truth with invention. He wrote Pat Knopf, "It's rather fun to see how much stuff I can get a detective story to carry without going completely haywire."

With his academic mentors, Millar took a more apologetic tone toward his "bread-and-butter" work, describing his private-eye novels to Thorpe as "pseudonymous books written, too quickly, for the rather rigid requirements of the commercial market." But there was one brilliant scholar with whom Millar felt free to show his enthusiasm for detective fiction: young Hugh Kenner, a new member of the UCSB English faculty. The bespectacled Kenner, extremely tall and thin, was a native of Peterborough, Ontario. "I grew up in a part of southern Ontario he knew," Kenner said, "and I think he thought there was some kind of bond between us. He seemed to regard Canada as a country to make wry jokes about, but it was not something he ever went into. He was a very complicated man, and you observed more than you understood. Even though I saw him a lot, I never felt I knew him very well. I don't know anyone who did."

Kenner met Millar at the home of George Hand, the ragtime-piano-playing Santa Barbara College dean. Soon Kenner was paying frequent visits to the Millars' Bath Street cottage. "Ken was a guarded, laconic man," Kenner found. "He spoke few words, carefully chosen, but the carefully chosen words were always to the point. In his monosyllabic way he could be extremely good company, and when he was talking about something he understood—for example, knowledge of literary technique—I never met anybody to surpass him. His intelligence was obviously of a very high order."

Kenner's own intellect was formidable. Twenty-seven when he met Millar, Kenner was on the brink of a dazzling career as a critic specializing in the revolutionary moderns (Joyce, Pound, Eliot, Beckett). Listening to Kenner talk, Millar said, was like taking several graduate courses at once.

As knowledgeable as Kenner was, he saw he could learn a thing or two from Millar. He began bringing essays and other works in progress to Bath Street, where Millar helped the scholar see that exposition and narrative were not separate things. "Ken was quietly persuasive," Kenner said. "*All* was narrative. When hard to follow, it was *bad* narrative." Recommending an ABA "sonata" or "sandwich" framework, Millar helped Kenner organize his study of Wyndham Lewis, a work Kenner calls his "first good book." Kenner would be known as a notably readable academic; his writing always followed the approach Millar devised for this Lewis book. "He was immensely valuable to me," said Kenner.

In turn Kenner read the galleys of Millar's books to catch errors of detail or logic. Like Auden, Kenner wasn't ashamed of enjoying mysteries. He encouraged Millar's effort to fill his novels with meaning and predicted, "You will write the *Ulysses* of the tecs yet, i.e., the book that exhausts the form and simultaneously brings it to the realization of all of which it is capable."

Kenner said, "Ken's working quota I think was five pages a day. That meant getting that five pages into a pretty quasi-final form. He said the economics of mystery writing really required that you produce two books a year, and between them Ken and Margaret could do that. He pointed out that a number of other mystery writers after World War II began to overproduce out of necessity. A good example is John Dickson Carr, also known as Carter Dickson. He reached a point where he was doing like three and four a year, and they got to be pretty poor. It was simply that you could no longer live on the rate of production that had worked in the 1930s. So that arrangement of Ken and Margaret's was what kept them going."

Al Stump, a sports journalist for magazines like the *Saturday Evening Post*, had a different sort of friendship with Millar than Kenner's. "We never talked a lot about writing," Stump said. "We'd talk mostly sports. I had a studio office in that courtyard on State called the Streets of Spain. Ken used to flop into my big easy chair, pick up a magazine, and say, 'I only came for a minute'—then stay maybe an hour but never speak, never interrupt my work. I think he was just lonesome for someone to be with: kind of the occupational disease of the fiction writer." Stump sometimes kept Millar company when Ken took his daily dip in the Pacific. "He used to go out in the ocean off the Biltmore Hotel and swim for a couple three miles every day, parallel to the shore. I'd sit on the sand and watch him; I wasn't about to go into that cold chop. He'd go out in any kinda weather, except hard rain."

Millar sometimes invited Stump to eat at the Coral Casino, where Millar paid. Stump would reciprocate with drinks at a downtown bar. "He had a grave way about him," Stump said, "a silent way. Very introspective. You only had to be with him for five minutes to know you were talking to a damned intelligent man. But he'd let others speak for the most part; he'd sit and observe. He studied mankind, and he remembered. I don't think he ever went to bed at night without having contemplated a number of serious things during the day. Not just fun things, but life around him. He was curious about everything that moved. Great eye for detail. Fantastic memory. Go down to the yacht harbor with him and be looking at boats—ask him a week later and he could tell you the names of most of the boats in the harbor."

Stump and Millar enjoyed exploring Santa Barbara on foot. "It was really more of a village than a town then," Stump remembered. "You could walk up and down the street and meet people you knew! Like Don Freeman; he and his wife were two of the nicest people to ever walk the earth. Freeman did children's books, and she illustrated them. Some of 'em were national prizewinners. He did the famous one called *Chuggy and the Blue Caboose*. Don Freeman was the kind of a guy who'd come downtown to buy some pipe tobacco and go home with a Ping-Pong table, a surfboard, and more stuff than he could carry—have to hire a cab and have all this stuff sticking out of it; Ken thought that was the funniest thing he'd ever seen. They were good friends."

Santa Barbara's population was about twenty-six thousand in 1951, roughly the same as Kitchener's when Millar was a teenager. "Santa Barbara then was the ideal place to be," said Stump, "if you overlooked the fact that it was snobbish as hell in some areas. I miss the seals barking at night out my bedroom window, the sound of the surf on the beach just below my house—a lotta things." The town drew Hollywood celebrities, Stump said. "The stars liked to come because there was an unwritten law that you didn't go up and ask for an autograph; there was sort of a Santa Barbara pride in not acting like fans. Dana Andrews took the booze cure up there. There were famous people living there too, good solid citizens: that Australian actress Judith Anderson. Barry Fitzgerald. Ronald Colman had a restaurant up there when he was doing *The Halls of Ivy,* a popular radio show."

The town's placid facade hid a reality more lurid than city fathers liked to acknowledge, Stump said. "To show you how wild the town was, all this happened in a period of about three months: The president of the university was in New York and got picked up for soliciting a young boy. Shortly after that, the football coach was thrown in jail when they raided his apartment and found it full of electrical appliances swiped outta stores. Then the professor of criminology—this made headlines all up and down California—he was lecturing on crime in the daytime, and at night he was a sneak thief; he had a girlfriend who liked fur coats, so he'd go out and rob people's houses. That's the kind of a town it was, somethin' crazy always goin' on. But the paper's policy was, bury it on the back page. Yeah, you have a big story like that crime professor, which made page-one headlines in the *LA Times*—in the *News-Press,* it went back with the truss ads. The people who owned the *News-Press* were old-timers, old Santa Barbara, reluctant to let any bad news at all creep out; it just wasn't done. Ken and I laughed about that a lot."

Avery Brundage, head of the International Olympic Committee, was a prominent Santa Barbara resident in the fifties. "He was the kingpin of the Olympic Games," said Stump, "widely disliked for his stand on amateurism; he kicked a lotta guys off the Olympic team if they took one dime. Ken saw me writing a story on him I think for *Liberty* magazine and said he'd like to meet Brundage. But I was afraid he might say something like, 'I notice you live in a mansion in Santa Barbara, while some of these poor athletes are starving to death. You can't put a dollar price on the muscle, and why should they bother?' They might get into a hot argument, so I didn't arrange that they meet."

Stump did get Millar together with former world welterweight boxing champion Jimmy McLarnin, he said: "Ken was thrilled. McLarnin had won his title in LA at a big fight at Gilmore Field back in 1933. Now it's the fifties, but Ken's still as enthused as a little kid going to meet Babe Ruth. And Jimmy—God bless the little guy, he took terrible beatings in the ring, but he held on—Jimmy was a Canadian too, born in Ireland but raised in Vancouver and Victoria. They had a lot in common, and they had a good talk. Jimmy showed Ken a couple professional moves, how to slip a punch for instance: instead of ducking it, you just move your head left or right and it goes by your ear." This head dodge would help Lew Archer through many fistfights.

Millar was well into the writing of his third Archer manuscript—a work he promised would be "a more human book than either of the others, more original, not so slick, and a truer picture of our very messed-up society"— when *The Drowning Pool* was published in July 1950. *Pool* was dedicated "TO TONY," by way of covertly thanking Anthony Boucher for his kindness to *The Moving Target* (which had no dedicatee). *The Drowning Pool* went a step further in separating Millar's work from the prolific John D. MacDonald's: on this second Archer, the pseudonym changed to John Ross Macdonald. Ross was a name Millar liked; his life was full of Rosses. His Winnipeg aunt Margaret's adopted son's middle name was Ross. Maggie had a brother named Ross. One of Millar's oldest friends was Donald Ross Pearce, middle-named for Pearce's godfather, Canadian House of Commons Speaker Ross Macdonald.

Pool was praised in the magazine and newspaper mystery roundup columns. "As it's a long time since Hammett and a long time between Chandlers," wrote Chandler correspondent James Sandoe in the *Chicago Sun-Times,* "it is more than agreeable to have fastidious prose set forth upon a hardboiled framework." Knopf promoted *Pool* with eye-catching little ads in the major book reviews, but the book didn't do well. By late September, when Millar was writing the final pages of its successor, *The Drowning Pool* had sold less than four thousand copies.

The average hardcover mystery sale in 1950, even for first novels, was about three thousand, as Millar learned from the Mystery Writers of America newsletter. Detective fiction was increasingly popular: one in four Americans claimed to be a mystery fan, according to a Gallup poll; and over half the country's college grads said they liked crime fiction. But these readers more and more preferred mysteries in pocket-size softbound editions rather than hardcover. Paperback printings jumped from 66 million in 1945 to 214 million in 1950, with mysteries being more than a quarter of that 1950 output.

Millar benefited from these trends. A softcover house called Lion reprinted his two first Dodd, Mead books in 1950. Dell did a paperback edition of *Blue City*, which proved such a good seller that Dell also did *The Three Roads.* And Pocket Books of course had the Lew Archer titles.

Millar's work was also available in Europe. "He told me he was a bestseller in France," said Hugh Kenner. "His early books would translate into French very easily, into an idiom related to that of Baudelaire." Millar's *À feu et à sang (Blue City)* was the thirtieth book in Gallimard's hugely successful Série Noire line, which also reprinted Chandler, Cain, and Hammett; each of these hardbound thrillers (which cost less than a dollar) sold a minimum of forty thousand copies, with some selling as many as one hundred thousand.

Still it was hard to make a living. In 1950 the Millars' total combined income was $8,428. Their joint adjusted gross for 1951 would be $6,266. With Margaret following her muse where it led, Millar thought he needed to keep his "dependable" Archer series going. "Being a woman and less responsible economically," he complained mildly to Thorpe, "she can afford greater artistic responsibility, I suppose." He felt pressure to write more, faster, better. The mental strain expressed itself, as he saw it, through physical illness. Gout periodically crippled his writing arm. In 1950 he had a hemorrhoidectomy. As a longtime reader of Freud, Jung, Horney, Menninger, et al., he interpreted these ailments as a substitute for psychosis. The Korean crisis added to his psychic imbalance: there was a chance Millar would be called to active duty, maybe as a code instructor (though it seemed just as likely his gout would keep him home). Millar's drinking was steady these days and a bit worrying; he attended at least one Alcoholics Anonymous meeting around 1950 and took notes of the guest speaker, later using some of her turns of speech ("muscadoodle" for muscatel) in his books.

The Millars' eleven-year-old endured her share of physical and mental ordeals this season, including an arm operation to rectify the botched bone graft done the last year in Ann Arbor. Linda handled this with stoic good grace, but her aunt's 1951 marriage upset her unduly. Maggie's sister had been a kind of surrogate mother to Linda for the past five years; now Linda felt deserted and betrayed. She stole a key one morning and snuck into her aunt's apartment before dawn, then fled without being seen. When the couple woke, they thought burglars had broken in. When Millar questioned Linda in private, she confessed. He said he understood, that he'd done wrong too when he was her age. He didn't tell the newlyweds Linda had been their intruder.

Her school problems grew worse, and in June 1951 she and her parents met with a counselor to discuss Linda's "maladjustment" due to "negativistic" traits. Millar defended his daughter, saying "he thought it was normal for Linda to show an interest in morbid subjects, in that he himself had similar interests." Maggie acknowledged using Linda as a basis for characters sometimes, especially the nine-year-old in 1949's *The Cannibal Heart*, whose mother notes, "The clothes, without Jessie in them, were somehow very sweet; they conjured up a Jessie without faults, a sleeping child innocent as heaven. It was a shock to come unexpectedly on the real Jessie, looking a little sullen, holding her hands behind her back, her eyes brooding with secrets." Linda Jane (a habitual reader of her parents' novels) was made uncomfortable by such portraits. Perhaps just as unsettling would be to see her parents in characters who argue and are unhappy: " 'We're not a *family*—you know what I mean?—and sometimes I think, I can't help thinking, that Jessie knows that, and that she hates us both.' " Her school counselor concluded Linda Millar was "still disturbed" and needed "careful handling."

Millar left his family again in 1951 for Ann Arbor and the final work on his Ph.D. He wasn't the only one wanting to get away. Linda asked if she could go to Michigan too and "keep house." Her father left town without her of course, boarding the train on Monday, June 18. It was Linda's twelfth birthday.

THE WAY SOME
PEOPLE DIE
John Ross Macdonald
(Knopf: $2.50)
Summing Up
The coastal scene and its
underworld at last treated
by someone who can *write* . . .
Verdict
Subtle hard-boiled gem
—Kathleen Sproul, *The Saturday Review,* 1951

The problem is the age-old one of how to convert literary or sub-literary excellence into a living income.
—Ken Millar to Alfred Knopf, 1951

Having published eight books in the past seven years, Millar was more a novelist than a graduate student in 1951—how much more so was apparent in the opening moments of the defense of his dissertation, a marathon event in a room at the University of Michigan's Angell Hall.

"The chairman of the graduate committee introduced Ken by saying various things about him as a student and the things he'd done at the university," said Michigan faculty member Don Pearce, present for the occasion. "It was a pleasant but stiff and pedantic sort of introduction—and he ended by saying, 'And he also writes murder mysteries.' " The chairman's perfunctory tag failed to do Millar's fiction justice. Called by the *New York Times* the best writer of hard-boiled prose since Dashiell Hammett, Millar hardly needed condescension from a Midwestern academic. "He did have this pride, you know, mixed up with an inordinate sort of humility and modesty," said Pearce. "He had no egotistical side to him atall unless he was rubbed the wrong way, and then he knew his value. And I think Ken was offended by this tiny little mention his writing career had been given, in comparison to his obsolete and by then kind of irrelevant scholarly career." Millar stood and thanked the chairman and said, "I'd just like to point out that my most recent book"—here Millar slammed a notebook down with a bang—"is called *The Way* Some *People Die.*" In the silence that followed, Millar stared significantly at each man present. His meaning seemed clear: certain people were so out of touch they were half-dead already.

Millar joked to Boucher that he nearly called his dissertation "The Way Some People Die, Volume Two." Later he'd say what convinced him to be a full-time writer was not wanting to be like the men on his doctoral committee. Surely it would be hard to imagine a tenured fifties Michigan Ph.D. writing as vital a book as *The Way Some People Die*, which was at once a vivid tableau of postwar southern California and a stylish retelling of certain Greek myths.

The novel starts with Lew Archer summoned to Santa Monica by Mrs. Lawrence, a gray-haired, black-clad woman speaking the pious phrases of the self-righteously devout and shielding her eyes from the harsh glare of LA reality. Her decaying house with its purple-glass fanlight over the door and its front room stuffed with oppressively heavy pieces might have been transported straight from the Kitchener of Millar's youth. As Archer sits in her shadowy parlor, he feels himself dragged unpleasantly into the past, assailed by mental images of his own grandmother "in crisp black funeral silks." Mrs. Lawrence lives "within rifleshot of the sea," and Archer looks toward the Pacific to chase away unbidden memories; but the ocean in this book delivers not solace and purity but doom.

Mrs. Lawrence wants Lew to look for her twenty-four-year-old daughter, Galatea, a hospital nurse missing for two months. Galley is frighteningly beautiful, Archer sees from a photo, with "fierce curled lips, black eyes and clean angry bones." Her chill perfection is worthy of classical sculpture. Greek myth tells of two Galateas, and Galley Lawrence evokes both. One is Pygmalion's statue come to life: apt symbol for the stone-hearted Galley. The other Galatea is a sea nymph who lures lovers to watery death. *Way* is drenched in marine imagery, and the ocean is central to its characters: yearning, grasping types who wait for ships (symbolic and real) to come in. Scheming to wreck and pillage those vessels is a merciless nymph hatched in the California heat.

The mythological allusions needn't be noticed for *The Way Some People Die* to be enjoyed as hard-boiled adventure. Where *The Drowning Pool* and *The Three Roads* make classical sources explicit, this work plants clues. Millar here put into sophisticated practice his theory of a democratic literature that could be liked on different levels by all sorts of readers.

From its strong opening in Mrs. Lawrence's claustrophobic Santa Monica house (matched by a similar scene at book's end), *Way* moves south to the La Jolla/San Diego–like Pacific Point, then north to Hollywood. Archer learns Galley's hooked up with handsome hood Joe Tarantine. At Joe and Galley's empty apartment off Sunset, Archer's surprised by a gun-toting thug and driven to a hilltop lair near Pacific Palisades.

There he meets Mr. Dowser, a short, broad-shouldered mobster in a double-breasted blue suit, whose eyes look "as if they had been dipped in muddy water and stuck on his face to dry." Grotesque as he is, Dowser seems real, like the porcine Mickey Cohen, an LA crime boss famous in tabloids. Dowser says Tarantine stole something from him; he wants Archer to find Joe and Galley. Archer takes his money to buy his trust. By 10 P.M. (twelve hours after meeting Galley's mother) Lew's in Palm Springs, where Galley's been sighted.

In a Wild West–themed bar, he finds unemployed actor Keith Dalling, Joe and Galley's West Hollywood neighbor, who leads him to a house where Galley's supposed to be—and where Archer's knocked out. By morning the detective's back in West Hollywood, at Dalling's apartment, where he takes in the scene with a camera's (or painter's) eye:

> The living-room was dim behind closed Venetian blinds. I jerked the cord to let the morning in, and looked around me. A scarred prewar radio-phonograph stood by the window, with piles of records on the floor beside it. There was a shallow fireplace in the inside wall, containing a cold gas heater unnecessarily protected by a brass fire-screen. On the wall above the fireplace Van Gogh's much reproduced sunflowers burned in a bamboo frame. The mantel held some old copies of *Daily Variety* and *Hollywood Reporter,* and a few books: cheap reprints of Thorne Smith, Erskine Caldwell, the poems of Joseph Moncure March, and *The Lost Weekend.* There was one handsome book, a copy of *Sonnets from the Portuguese* bound in green tooled leather. Its flyleaf was inscribed: "If thou must love me, let it be for naught except for love's sake only.— Jane." Jane wrote a precise small hand.
>
> The most conspicuous piece of furniture was a Murphy bed standing on its hind legs in a doorway across the room. I had to push it aside before I could get through the door. I did this with my elbow, instead of my fingerprint surfaces. I suppose I smelled the blood before I was conscious of it.

This third Archer book is full of such color glossies of California interiors circa 1950. Archer is as good at reading character through decor as through physiognomy, and his photomurals include just the right trompe l'oeil details.

In later years Millar would be less concerned with documenting the California scene and more rooted in timeless themes of personal guilts, but much of the vitality of the early Archers comes from the immediacy with which they describe "the endless city" from San Diego to Santa Barbara to San Francisco. Like a hard-boiled Balzac, Archer travels high and low, cruising ritzy Strip cribs, seedy waterfront fleabags, movie factories, squalid nightclubs. *The Way Some People Die* was one of his greatest tours, a dark Technicolor travelogue filled with striking scenes: a wrestling match in a stifling arena, a face-off with a repellent drug peddler, a violent fight with a murderer.

Way had a lot going for it: an exciting plot in which Archer solves murders and foils a heroin racket, a host of well-drawn characters, and a surreal "death by water" that fast-froze Greek myth to West Coast consumer culture. Again Archer went out of his way to help a troubled female teenager, an addict headed down a sordid road.

Way was written with great assurance and style. In moving away from his "personal neuroses" (as he saw it) and more into hard-boiled terrain, Millar reached a new level of achievement. To many crime-fiction critics and writers, *The Way Some People Die* became the book to match or beat. It was a knockout, a humdinger. With his third private-eye novel, Millar—"John Ross Macdonald"—wrote a genre classic.

It drew raves this summer of 1951. James Sandoe, reviewing now for the *New York Herald Tribune,* said, "Macdonald can write really well and his book follows the hard-boiled pattern with a rare freshness and originality." Lenore Glen Offord assured her *San Francisco Chronicle* readers, "The tough ones don't come any better than this." Boucher, as usual the most eloquent and extravagant champion, stated, "Macdonald has the makings of a novelist of serious caliber—in his vivid realization of locale; in his striking prose style, reminiscent of Chandler and yet suggesting the poetic evocation of Kenneth Fearing; in his moving three-dimensional characterization; and above all in his strangely just attitude toward human beings, which seems incredibly to fuse the biting contempt of a Swift with the embracing love of a Saroyan." This new Macdonald, he wrote, was "the best novel in the tough tradition that I've read since *Farewell, My Lovely . . .* and possibly since *The Maltese Falcon.*"

Sending thanks from Ann Arbor, Millar wrote Boucher (now president of the Mystery Writers of America), "An element of smugness enters in from the fact that I've finished [*Way*'s] successor . . . and you ain't seen nothing yet. No kidding."

The fourth Archer (working title *The Split Woman,* published as *The Ivory Grin*) was done under the conscious influence of Nelson Algren's *The Man with the Golden Arm,* and Millar felt it his "biggest" novel yet. One night at his rented Ann Arbor apartment, Millar held forth to Don Pearce on the book's serious theme.

"He spent quite a bit of time explaining to me the nature of the Miltonic split, as he called it," said Pearce, "and the damage that Milton had done to English-speaking civilization by driving home the notion that woman was the bearer of evil in our culture: you know, 'It was Eve's fault.' Ken said women as a result of this disparagement and devaluation are uncompleted beings, and as a result of *that,* men are incomplete too—because it's a very close symbiotic polar relationship between the sexes, and if one of them is denied full identity and freedom, the other inevitably suffers. You know this sounds very modern, but he was saying it real early, long before I'd ever heard it from anyone else in any serious way. And he had a real theory and thesis about all this, backed up by a good deal of reading and observation."

Millar had a thick typescript of *The Ivory Grin* with him, and he read its final lines to Pearce: " 'I do feel grief for her. I loved her. There was nothing I wouldn't do.' He started down the veranda steps, his short black shadow dragging and jerking at his heels." "And Ken said, 'What that means, Don, is that the incomplete man in this culture is the broken shadow of the uncompleted woman.' That's what that scene was supposed to be saying! I don't know how many readers would pick it up, but that's what he was illustrating." By way of dramatic emphasis, Millar with a sweep of his hand strewed his typescript all over the floor. "I jumped up to help him," Pearce said, "thinking he had done it by accident. 'No, no,' he said. 'Just part of the act!' "

Millar was acting more oddly than usual as he worked to finish his dissertation. In grappling with Coleridge, Millar was wrestling with thoughts and concepts that had preoccupied him for twenty years. "It's not just a subject he happened to turn up that could satisfy the requirements for the Ph.D.," said Pearce. "This was a life-and-death matter with him in some ways. It's no mystery that he should have done a dissertation on Coleridge, because Ken resembled Coleridge. Both of them had profound awareness of the chief intellectual currents of their time—the subtle intellectual philosophical side of life—and wanted to synthesize them; and on the other hand both Coleridge and Ken had serious knowledge and experience of the dark side of human life in their time, the nightmare side. That's a pretty powerful similarity when you get right down to it. You could see why a person would do a dissertation on a father figure of that kind. He's Ken's ancestor in many ways."

The anxieties Millar struggled with were both global and personal. On another evening this summer, at Pearce's house, Millar expounded on some of these. "He spoke of how the great encyclopedic syntheses of everything known in the world had formerly been shaped by men," Pearce said, "how Hegel and Kant and other eighteenth-century philosophers attempted to erect great conspectuses so that everything could have relationship to everything else and there could be coherence to the world. *Men* produced these systems. And with the collapse of those things during the disastrous nineteenth century, men dropped the ball and have never been able to get it back. He went on in this fashion: now it is women who are beginning to produce the new synthesis, but because they are different psychological beings, it's probable they will restore flux rather than order. He was very worried about the subject, he really was. One thing that worried him more than anything else along this line was the presence and emergence of the homosexual. I can remember his telling me that a new kind of anarchy would result from the increasingly dominant presence of homosexuals in institutions of higher learning and in various other responsible organizations. Ken had this tendency to construct a universal generalization out of very few compass points; for all his stress on objectivity and fact and information, he was profoundly intuitive. Anyway he had these nightmare things."

What Millar feared would emerge in society he was afraid was within himself. The "homo-sex" of his youth was a shameful memory. Some of his books showed homosexuals as evil grotesques (in the hard-boiled tradition, be it noted, of Hammett and Chandler). Millar was concerned that a homosexual tendency ran deeper in him than he'd imagined.

He told Pearce of a disturbing experience he had had on the train from

California. "There was a young man sitting opposite him," Pearce said. "They'd been talking, and eventually the young man took a blanket and went to sleep. Ken got sort of drowsy too. And every now and then his eyes would open, and when he looked over, he saw that the young man appeared to have turned into a young woman. Ken said that was one of the most shocking things that had ever happened to him. I said, 'Ken, for heaven's sake, what's so shocking about that? You just sort of normally misread the features for a moment.' He said, 'Don't tell *me* what psychology was involved. I *wanted* to see that young man that way.' He wanted an opportunity to view him in a permissibly feminine form, I think is the way he put it; he wanted to see him as a young woman, in order to make it possible for him to feel the way he did about him. And he seemed shocked and horrified by it. He said, 'I wonder if I'm not a covert homosexual,' words to that effect."

Pearce and Millar spoke until four or five that morning. When Pearce saw him to the door, Millar embraced him. "After a second I backed off normally," said Pearce. "He said, 'Don't draw away, don't be afraid,' and he just very lightly held me. It wasn't unpleasant. I don't think it was a kind of homosexual hug; that would have felt different, I'm sure. But it wasn't called for. It was strange. There was this peculiarly tender side to him. I think Ken believed physical friendship between men was not easy in our culture, and he was trying to overcome that."

Millar's long summer culminated on an August Saturday in a room at Angell Hall, with his oral examination for the doctorate. The Michigan orals were a daunting ordeal, something like an academic wrestling match with the challenger facing a tag team of opponents. One heckling assistant professor seemed especially bent on making trouble for candidate Millar.

"The whole thing was a discussion of poetical and human knowledge," said Pearce, to whom Millar described the occasion. "Ken was maintaining that all we can have is symbolic knowledge of something, since you can never *be* it, and so on; and this fellow was upsetting the discussion in gratuitous ways. 'He played a dirty trick on me,' Ken said, 'he tried to trip me two or three times with peculiar references. So I just began playing into his hand, I decided to risk it. I fed him along and fed him along—and then eventually I said, "In that case, what do you make of Shakespeare's *The Tempest*?" He had to admit that he didn't know how what he had said applied to *The Tempest* and didn't think he could come up with an answer without a lot of thought. I just let him hang there, and hang there.' This fellow disgraced himself, and Ken sailed free. Apparently the oral was tremendously successful—partly because of that event!"

An exhausted Millar took the train to California the next day. It had been a tough season in a tough year, during which it sometimes felt that the combined weight of writing a novel and rewriting a thesis might break his back ("1000 pages longhand since January 2"). Five days after leaving Ann Arbor, Millar walked into a Santa Barbara household in turmoil.

Margaret had been upset by his leaving but had done her best to put a good face on things ("Please don't worry about me going to pieces. I know I am an emotional problem to you, but I can *try*, & I am trying"). Her brave facade didn't last. While he was gone, she had an operation to remove a benign tumor ("But how can a tumor be benign?" Millar wondered), something he thought probably a physical manifestation of her anxiety; and she had some "hysteria." In his absence, Margaret and her sister got word of the bizarre death in Canada of their brother Ross. "The accident was pretty ghastly and mysterious," Margaret wrote. "He was killed by a train on Fri & so mangled he wasn't identified until Sun. & then only by the drain tube he was wearing in his chest—he'd just been released from the hosp. after a pneumonia siege. Apparently he'd been wandering around or something—details are vague." Margaret didn't feel she could afford to fly back for the funeral. "I feel bad about it all, of course," she told her husband. "Had stomach cramps etc, but my greatest feeling was that thank God, it wasn't you."

She was in poor shape when Millar returned. So was Linda, with mother and daughter often brawling. Abetted by her mother and a good teacher, Linda was practicing the piano furiously these days, substituting music for social interaction. Approaching puberty and the start of junior high, the lanky twelve-year-old was ogled now by teenaged boys at the beach club pool; but she still shared a bedroom with her mother. Their room, their house, their family, seemed too small to contain two such strong-willed people—not to mention a couple of frisky dogs and the sometimes explosive Millar. As Maggie said of herself and Linda, "We're getting bloody sick of each other, I guess."

Millar had held himself together through several difficult seasons since the war—since his marriage—but faced with this situation, he gave way. Ken Millar "attempted suicide." The quote marks are his, the details unknown. What occurred was serious enough that Maggie and her sister urged Millar to have himself committed. He refused all professional help and was grimly determined to solve his own problems. He'd write of himself, "Grant's words were much in his mind: 'We'll fight it out on this line if it takes all summer' . . . perhaps an ill-chosen motto for a man faced with the irrevocable past, the built-in past." For weeks he wrestled his demons, later judging he'd escaped hospitalization by the skin of his teeth.

Several things vexed him. Millar blamed Margaret for making his academic career impossible, though he acknowledged his own ambivalence in the matter. He felt trapped in Santa Barbara—a Canadian adrift in California, an intellectual in a land of hedonists, a democrat in a town of aristocrats. He believed in equality of the sexes but doubted his wife's wisdom and was ashamed of his reluctance to be the head of the family. Most of all "he saw the necessity for incorporating into himself, instead of rejecting à la Hemingway, the feminine forces which had been so strong in forming him."

Unable to work, he grappled with depression and anger, though in a let-

ter to Boucher he claimed to be "happily rusticating and vegetating."
Santa Barbara friends sensed his inner struggle, but the closemouthed Millar spoke not a word. Hugh Kenner recalled a day when Millar came to his
house on Bluff Drive and silently drank a can of beer: "He was sitting in a
chair, holding an empty beer can"—in a year when beer cans were made of
thick metal—"and suddenly he just crushed the can in his hand and said,
'Strangler's hands.' *Strangler's hands*. That was an eerie moment."

Though he lacked the energy to start a new book, Millar had to attend to
the already written *The Ivory Grin*. Alfred Knopf said he'd read the manuscript "with a good deal of pleasure" but thought it lacked something crucial: "Archer never in the book finds himself on a really hot spot—physically
speaking I mean. . . . Doesn't the reader expect to be kept for a while every
now and then on the edge of his chair wondering how the devil the hero is
going to get out of this one." In Knopf's opinion such scenes were desirable
in "whodunits" (a word Millar hated). "We didn't as you know do too well
with THE DROWNING POOL," Knopf reminded the author, adding the
outlook for *The Way Some People Die* wasn't "too rosy" either. "Perhaps what
I have pointed out is a factor worth considering."

Millar didn't appreciate this second-guessing of what he thought was his
best novel, one in which he'd tried to ease away a bit from the tough-guy
school. But he promised he'd see what he could do about "injecting some
fear into it," assuring Knopf, "I am quite as eager to produce saleable books
as you are to sell them." He drafted a scene with Archer menaced by a gunman, but decided it didn't work. Margaret didn't like it either, and they
both thought it a bad idea to fiddle around with his carefully structured
narrative. "With all due respect for Alfred's opinion and the hard-boiled
convention," Millar wrote Knopf's ad manager Dave Herrmann, "and all
due humility, I think the book has an imaginative and moral impact which
is pretty independent of physical violence or terror, and which might be
damaged by an attempt to have one's bloody meat and eat it too." Yet Millar also was discouraged by his novels' disappointing sales, and he couldn't
blame Knopf: the publisher had promoted *Way* with nice ads and clever
bookstore teaser cards. "You'd think a book like that, with such good backing, would sell five thousand anyway," he wrote Herrmann. "Maybe it even
will. In the meantime, I'll write another good one. It's either that or have a
prefrontal lobotomy so I can write like Mickey Spillane."

Spillane, whose crude tales of brutal private eye Mike Hammer sold in
the millions, had apparently drained or scared away many readers who
might otherwise be buying books in the literate Hammett-Chandler
mode. "Is the hardboiled mystery on the way out, or having a bad interlude, or what?" Millar asked Boucher plaintively. Maybe he should drop
Archer and try his hand at something else—except his Santa Barbara
bookseller friends told him the Archer series was just starting to catch on
and it would be a big mistake to stop it now.

Ivan von Auw, knowing his client's concerns, prodded Knopf to meet with Millar during a West Coast visit. On a September Tuesday, Millar drove south to the Bel-Air Hotel for a one-hour conference with his publisher. He had no real gripes, Millar said; and after his recent run in "the doctoral rat-race," he was more certain than ever that he wanted to be a writer. He worried about money, was all, what with a daughter who said she hoped to go to medical school; Millar would only make about five thousand this year, his wife less than three thousand. On the other hand, it was heartening that Pocket Books had agreed to reprint *The Drowning Pool* and would probaby also take *The Way Some People Die*. Surely paperback exposure would cause greater hardcover sales? And while Millar knew critical praise didn't sell books, he did feel the high opinion of his work expressed by Boucher, the dean of mystery reviewers, meant eventually "Macdonald" and Knopf *were* going to hit it— if "it" existed anymore.

It was a useful meeting, Millar thought, and one that reached some conclusions. Knopf agreed it was unnecessary to inject violence and fear into his books when what Millar wanted was to emphasize greater psychological range. Since the Archer books didn't sell well under the hard-boiled label, Knopf (starting with *Grin*) would stress the quality of their prose. Let Spillane have the kick-'em-in-the-teeth crowd; "Macdonald" would lure a more literate bunch. To ease Millar's money woes, a novel scheme was hatched: The author would do an annual "Kenneth Millar" in addition to "Macdonald"'s Archer, thus doubling his income. A deadline of February 1952 was fixed for the first "Millar" book.

Things improved at home too. The Millars took a mortgage on the Bath Street place, which they kept as rental property, and bought a bigger house where Linda could have her own room. In October, three Millars and two dogs moved into a white stucco ranch house at 2136 Cliff Drive, on the mesa above the business part of town. Their new residence (once the horse barn of the Meigs Ranch, a historic spread) wasn't in the best neighborhood, but it overlooked the ocean. Maybe here the volatile family would find more domestic tranquillity. Hopeful but broke, Ken and Margaret Millar each began writing a book.

After the first ten books they come a bit harder.
　　　　　　　　　　—Kenneth Millar to C. D. Thorpe

The annual bash at the estate of detective-fiction enthusiast E. T. "Ned" Guymon Jr. was a much anticipated fifties event among West Coast members of the Mystery Writers of America. "He had a mansion in the old part of San Diego," recalled Bob Wade, half of the writing team Wade Miller, "and everybody'd come there and get drunk." Guymon, an affiliate member of the MWA who had begun collecting mystery fiction in 1930, had the country's biggest library of detective books, some eight thousand volumes (the collection eventually quadrupled), including rare Doyle and Poe items.

The affair the Millars attended in December 1951 was specially themed: invitations were mock court summonses commanding one and all to arrive in costume as the title of a well-known detective, mystery, or horror book. Some traveled long distances to Guymon's gathering: Fredric Brown, writer of the "Ed and Am" mysteries, came from Taos, New Mexico. Stuart Palmer (of the "amazing Miss Withers" books) drove down from LA, as did James M. Fox. Raymond Chandler, who lived next door in La Jolla (and who summered with his wife in 1951 at a dude ranch near Santa Barbara), had come to Guymon's party the previous year but (busy with a new book) skipped this year's. William Campbell Gault of Pacific Palisades showed up, though, in company with Hal Braham, who published in *Black Mask* under the name Mel Colton.

The forty-one-year-old Gault, born in Milwaukee, had written dozens of short stories for the waning pulps and was about to bring out his first novel (which would win the MWA's Edgar Allan Poe Award). Gault was impressed by his first sight of Guymon's spread, with its lawns and tennis courts: "God, they got black guys, servants, all around, you know, big foyer—oh, a rich guy." The feisty Gault had ignored his host's command to come in costume: "I thought it was kinda corny, kinda high school. I'm not about to go around with a funny hat on at a party; I'll leave that to the Rotary people, and if they didn't like it, they could lump it." Plenty of others went along with the gag, though, including Lawrence G. Blochman, who wore a turban in honor of his own book *Bombay Mail*. Millar had a gold-colored plastic sheath over one jacket sleeve: *The Man with the Golden Arm*. Bill Gault introduced himself: " 'Are you Ken Millar?' I says. 'That's Nelson Algren's book, isn't it?' He said, 'I'm surprised you should know about a man of that caliber, how would *you* know that book?' Pretty snotty, right? So I said, 'Well, I'd like you to meet the fellow who came up with me: this is Nelson Algren's *cousin*.' Hal Braham, yeah. I said, 'I'll tell you something else: your wife writes better than *you* do.' I thought she did. Maggie's in the toilet and overhears me. When she comes out, she says, 'Some little son of a bitch out there says I write better than Ken!' So we got to be, not enemies but—frictional."

The Millars were unique among married mystery writers: they didn't collaborate, and their works were equally praised by critics. Margaret's books made Boucher's and Sandoe's best-of-year lists nearly as often as John Ross Macdonald's. In 1952, when Maggie published both *Rose's Last Summer* (from a plot given her by Ken) and *Vanish in an Instant* and Macdonald had *The Ivory Grin*, Millar could rightly tell their Hollywood agent, "Between us we've had about the best critical receptions of the year in the mystery field."

Though several other good writers were working the private-eye street in 1952 (such as Wade Miller, Thomas Dewey, and Bart Spicer), Macdonald and his Archer novels received the lion's share of reviewers' praise. As the tough style grew dumber and more brutal after Spillane, and as Boucher continued to hail Macdonald as the successor of Hammett and Chandler, Millar tried to make his books less violent and more individualized, and (not so incidentally) to distance himself from Chandler.

The book he began in 1952 was a further step removed: it had as its hero-narrator not Lew Archer but a young county probation officer called Howard Cross. This was meant as the first "Kenneth Millar" novel the author and Knopf thought would alternate with the Archer books. Millar made friends with people in the Santa Barbara probation office, who vetted his manuscript for authenticity. The story (a variation on Millar's fatal-hit-and-run theme) involved analysis of car paint and headlight evidence. To get these details right, Millar called on the leading expert in such matters: LA forensic chemist Ray Pinker, the "test-tube detective" famous from his portrayal on the radio and television police drama *Dragnet*.

Jack Webb's *Dragnet* was one of many shows the Millars watched regularly in 1952 on a TV bought in February for four hundred thirty dollars. The writers' viewing was partly research: Maggie told Ken she intended to earn enough money writing television scripts to buy a new car. "He wasn't *keen* on my doing it," she said, "but he went along with it, of *course*."

Millar's own writing was stopped in early '52 by painful gout attacks that froze his right elbow and swelled his hands and feet. He was confined to a rented wheelchair for weeks. Here (to his mind) was another ailment triggered by an anxious psyche, a somatic attempt perhaps to soften a too rigid personality. Dependent on Margaret for weeks and months at a time, he came to value her help and friendship more than ever.

Except for the gout, Millar was happier in the spring of '52 than he'd been in a long time. When a team from the *Santa Barbara News-Press* came in March to do a flattering story about these accomplished Cliff Drive dwellers, the Millars looked the picture of southern California success: Kenneth grinning bashfully like the cat that swallowed the Ph.D., his two women beaming at him with something close to adoration, the three of them seated in front of shelves filled with books written by husband and wife. "To many Santa Barbarans," wrote reporter Verne Linderman, "Margaret and Kenneth Millar might be regarded as the town's most enviable couple."

The third Millar wasn't having such an enviable time, though. Nearly thirteen, Linda was ill at ease in junior high, where the lessons were dull and where rowdy kids ruled the roost. At home she felt cowed by her parents' IQs and achievements. She'd given up piano, as she'd given up art. Though she said she planned on medical school, her fondest wish was to grow up and have children. Millar wrote Branson, "It's a long wait between puberty and adulthood in this society, and Algebra, French and swimming don't quite fill the gap."

In her insecurity Linda was prey to bad influences; an older girl taught her to smoke. More worrisome were the young hoods among her classmates. Two boys with police records followed her and a girlfriend home one day, bent on sex. Millar sent the punks packing as swiftly as he'd dealt with troublemakers when he was a Kitchener high school teacher, but this was the last straw. He wouldn't have his daughter menaced. He and Margaret would take Linda out of public school at the end of term and enroll her in Laguna Blanca, an excellent private prep school. It would be expensive, but their peace of mind (and Linda's safety) would be worth it.

As almost always, the Millars needed cash (they'd make about eleven thousand dollars in 1952, with him bringing in nine thousand of it). Millar's television-watching gave him ideas. He talked up the notion of a thirteen-week Lew Archer TV series with H. N. Swanson (working title: *The Moving Target*). As the basis for a possible leadoff episode, Millar wrote an Archer short story ("The Guilty Ones") structured like a TV play, and he cooked up plots for another dozen *Target* episodes. Millar reminded Swannie there'd be a strong new Archer novel *(The Ivory Grin)* out soon: "If it makes the splash I expect it to, it should help to sell an Archer television series." Millar's non-Archer novel in progress also presented a good TV prospect, he told Swannie: "It seems to me a probation officer, with the freedom of a private eye, and the reality and responsibility of a *Dragnet* cop, would make a great character to string crime dramas on. In what form should that idea be presented for sale? One audition play and summaries of the rest? Please let me know what you think of it. I have a number of ideas for it, and have been offered access to official files in which there are plenty more."

The probation officer book was sent to New York in late July, and Alfred Knopf told Millar, "I like it immensely. I think it is one of your best." Millar thought he might do more books with this Howard Cross hero. He and Knopf agreed that since the new book was no great departure in style from the Archer novels and since the publisher had worked hard to build the Macdonald name (with some success: *The Ivory Grin* went into a second printing), they might as well bring out this book as by "John Ross Macdonald" and not "Kenneth Millar."

The agents sold the Cross book to *Cosmopolitan* magazine for condensation: a nice $5,000 surprise. All was well on the publishing front until

August, when Knopf passed on disquieting comments from Pocket Books: the paperback house had strong misgivings about this new non-Archer.

Knopf quoted the Pocket Books honcho: "Reading the manuscript left me once again puzzled about the author and his works. He is a very good writer and a fairly capable plotter, but for some reason all the books lack the kind of punch which should go with the sort of story he writes. Maybe the author is just too nice a person, but his bad characters somehow or other aren't believably bad. The sharp contrast between good and evil, so noticeable in Chandler's books and so important to this kind of story, is simply missing, at least for me. I wonder if some one of your [Knopf's] experts couldn't somehow sharpen both the characters and the action."

Millar was offended and angered by the suggestion that a Knopf editor rewrite his work to make it more like Chandler's. He wrote Knopf a five-page letter that was part defense, part attack, and part statement of artistic principles:

> Do you think the book needs rewriting? It's already had a lot. While I'm perfectly willing to rewrite places where the action drags or characters fade out—just show me the places—and to concede that any of my books is improvable, I think that perhaps a main difficulty arises from Pocket Books' assumption that this is a hardboiled novel, which it is not, and more specifically that this is an imitation of Chandler which fails for some reason to come off. I must confess I was pleased with the characterization—the characters are more human than in anything I've done, closer to life—and more than pleased with the plot. Plot is important to me. I try to make my plots carry meaning, and this meaning such as it is determines and controls the movement of the story. I know I have a tendency to subordinate individual scenes to the overall intention, to make the book the unit of effect. Perhaps this needs some correction, without going to the opposite extreme. This opposite extreme is represented by Chandler, one of my masters with whose theory and practice I am in growing disagreement. For him any old plot will do—most of his plots depend on the tired and essentially meaningless device of blackmail—and he has stated that a good plot is one that makes for good scenes. So far from taking him as the last word and model in my field, which Pocket Books thinks I should do, it would seem—I am interested in doing things in the mystery which Chandler didn't do, and probably couldn't.
>
> His subject is the evilness of evil, his most characteristic achievement the short vivid scene of conflict between (conventional) evil and (what he takes to be) good. With all due respect for the power of these scenes and the remarkable intensity of his vision, I can't accept Chandler's vision of good and evil. It is conventional to the point of occasional old-maidishness, anti-human to the point of frequent sadism (Chandler hates all women and most men, reserving only lovable oldsters, boys and Marlowe for his affection), and the mind behind it, for all its enviable

imaginative force, is uncultivated and second-rate. At least it strikes my mind that way. I owe a lot to Chandler (and more to Hammett), but it would be simple self-stultification for me to take him as the last word in the mystery. My literary range greatly exceeds his, and my approach to writing will not wear out so fast.

My subject is something like this: human error, and the ambivalence of motive. My interest is the exploration of lives. If my stories lack a powerful contrast between good and evil, as Pocket Books points out, it isn't mere inadvertence. I don't see things that way, and haven't since *Blue City*. Even in *Blue City*, you may recall, the victim of the murder and the father of the "hero" was also the source of corruption in the city. Because my theme is exploration, I employ a more open and I think subtler set of values than is usual; its background is sociological and psychological rather than theological. I chose the hardboiled convention in the first place because it seemed to offer both a market, and a structure with which almost anything could be done, a technique both difficult and free, adapted to my subject matter, and a field in which I might hope to combine the "popular" and the "sensitive" hero, and forge a style combining flexibility, literacy and depth with the solidity and eloquence of the American-colorful-colloquial. These have been my literary aims; my hope is to write "popular" novels which will not be inferior to "serious" novels. I have barely started.

In spite of the Spillane phenomenon which has nothing much to do with the mystery but which probably has unsettled paperback publishers' notions of what a mystery is, I think the future of the mystery is in the hands of a few good writers like myself. The old-line hardboiled novel with its many guns and fornications and fisticuffs has been ruined by its practitioners, including the later Chandler. Spillane pulled the plug. I have no intention of plunging after it down the drain. My new book, though it is an offspring or variant of the hardboiled form, is a stage in my emergence from that form and a conscious step towards the popular novel I envisage. That very tone to which Pocket Books objects, and which I have tried to make literate without being forbidding, human without being smeary, and let us face it adult, is what distinguishes it from the run-of-the-gin-mill mystery. It isn't as if I were out on a limb by myself. The critics and my colleagues know what I am doing. Some of my fellow mystery-writers, and they are the real experts, think that my last two books are the best that have ever been done in the tradition that Hammett started. While I don't think myself that I possess Hammett's genius—and that's a hard thing for me to admit—I do think the talent I have is flexible and durable. My rather disproportionate (for a fiction writer) training in literary history and criticism which tended to make me a slow and diffident starter also operates to keep me going and I think improving. I do know I can write a sample of the ordinary hardboiled mystery with my eyes closed. But preferring as I do to keep my eyes open, I've spent several years developing it into a form of my own, which nobody can imitate. When the tough school dies its inevitable death I expect to be going strong, twenty or thirty books from now. As I see it, my hope of real success as a writer, both artistic and commercial, resides in developing my own point of view and narrative approach to the limit. If I overvalue my point of view and the work I do from it, that is the defect of the virtue of believing in what I am doing. I believe in the present book, though it's not by any means as good a book as I am sure I can write.

Knopf certainly hadn't meant to prompt such a long and impassioned document. The publisher assured Millar, "I am all for the writer who wants to go his own way. . . . So I say more power to your pen and typewriter!" But they did need a new title for the probation officer book, Knopf insisted. Millar called it *Message from Hell,* which Knopf nixed. Pocket Books (who bought the book without revisions) wanted *The Convenient Corpse,* which Millar couldn't abide. The author halfheartedly countered with *Meet Me at the Morgue,* which Knopf seized on: "And good luck to all of us."

If Knopf hadn't known how seriously Millar took his writing, he certainly knew now. Millar brought the same sense of purpose to the civic sphere this presidential election season. He and Margaret were both energized by Democratic candidate Adlai Stevenson. As Millar's gout receded under cortisone treatment (he was on crutches by August, walking unaided by October), he participated fully in Stevenson's Santa Barbara campaign: doing two weeks of precinct work, penning a speech for Woodrow Wilson's daughter, and writing a hard-hitting radio response to Senator Joe McCarthy's Stevenson attack.

Most but not all of Ken's and Maggie's friends were Democrats. Millar accommodated himself to Republican chums (though bad feelings over this election wrecked the Millars' relationship with a couple they'd each dedicated books to). One good Republican friend was Harris Seed, a young lawyer who met the Millars when he and his wife rented the Bath Street house. Harris and Nancy Seed spent occasional evenings at the Millar house on Cliff Drive, drinking beer and playing Scrabble. (As Seed recalled, Margaret memorized the dictionary's X and Z words.) He and Millar valued frank discussions of legal and social matters, said Seed: "We talked about all the current issues of the time: the death penalty, things of that character. We didn't feel the need to hide our emotions, we had at it. Who better than a brilliant antagonist to argue with? Not much fun talking to a dummy."

The politically conservative Hugh Kenner (later good friends with William F. Buckley Jr.) ducked discussion of U.S. electoral matters by invoking his Canadian citizenship. Millar was more interested in talking literature with Kenner anyhow. Maggie was the one for whom Kenner was a trial. "Margaret and I always had a very guarded relationship," Kenner said. "She was intensely antiacademic, and I think she suspected that I had a bad influence on Ken by dragging him in that direction." You could see Margaret's dislike of Kenner in her body language, said Don Pearce, whom Kenner looked up in Michigan at Millar's urging: "She would *roll* her cigarette holder, as if she were getting ready to *throw* a remark like a javelin. But he never gave her a chance, he always would talk *on* in a way that was impregnable because it was backed up with information that she didn't have. He'd discovered how to do that after being made uncomfortable by her for quite a while." "My God that guy has crust," Maggie groused to Millar of Kenner. "Only two people inhabit his strange world, himself and his alter ego, the kid."

The Millars invited all their friends to a post-Halloween costume party the Saturday night before the election. Taking a leaf from Ned Guymon, Margaret insisted they all come as book titles. Al Stump's wife, Claire, said, "I flunked sewing, so I put a brain on a plate and that was *Peace of Mind.* I remember when I arrived, Harris Seed was out front hiding behind a bush, feeling like a fool in his costume, and Nancy was kind of flailing him on into the house; I think he was *The Rains Came.*" Kenner wrote Pearce in advance: "M. J. [Mary Jo], who is seven months pregnant, is going to be *The Man Within* without benefit of costume; I'm going to pin a watch to my lapel along with a drawing of two holes in the ground (wells) and be *The Time Machine.* I like doing these things simply, if only to annoy Maggie."

The Millars threw another party for Democrats only the night of Tuesday, November 4, to view the election returns on TV. Dwight Eisenhower's crushing defeat of Stevenson took Ken and Maggie completely by surprise. Two days later, Millar wrote an emotional letter of support to the defeated candidate: "We saw a civilization taking shape at last here under your hand, an age of Stevenson. Your speeches made politics real to us for the first time, and your integrity promised to hold back the slipping reality of life itself. . . . If a majority of our people turned their backs on you and the future, they did it out of simple childishness and fear. Which only proves that we need you more than I thought. . . . Like many others in the last few months I have come to love you, you will excuse the word: no weaker one will do."

Millar didn't do things by half. His commitments—to a wife, a candidate, a genre—were total. He brought the idealism of his politics to the writing of detective stories. Millar told Michigan professor Dick Boys, "I see the mystery in all its varying degrees of contemporary consciousness as a symbolic attempt to grapple with the American fear of death, for which our culture makes such meager provision, and to fit it into life." It was one of his aims, he said, to purge the Chandler-Hammett hero of his current aggressions, "fed raw to us by such practitioners as Spillane the poet laureate of sexual psychopathy," and restore him "to a practical relation with ethics and the community." To his old professor Thorpe, Millar wrote he wanted "to impart first-class standards into the standardless mass of popular culture, somewhat along lines laid down by Poe and [Robert Louis] Stevenson and Graham Greene." Family, politics, a decent home, the ocean: these all gave Millar's life meaning and pleasure, but it was work that brought real satisfaction. Now, Millar told Thorpe, after twelve books in nine years, "I think I know where I'm going and will find ways to take my readers with me."

The audience in Angell Hall the first Wednesday of July 1953 stirred
in anticipation of Ken Millar's four-thirty lecture titled "The Scene
of the Crime: Social Meanings of the Detective Story"—part of an
ambitious summer symposium on the popular arts in America, whose
other participants included W. C. Handy, cartoonist Milt Caniff, and film
historian Kenneth MacGowan. Interest in Millar's talk ran high, said Don
Pearce: "He was a hot number right then, and there were three hundred
and fifty people present, which absolutely filled that main auditorium."
The lecture was publicized on the front page of the campus paper ("Ace
Writer of Mysteries Talks Today") and would be broadcast later over an
educational radio network to several states and parts of Canada.

Millar was keyed up for the event. "I'll do my damnedest to squeeze out
some first-rate doctrine," he promised organizer Richard Boys. His long
paper was a serious exploration of the detective story from its roots in the
Romantic tradition through its definition at the hands of Poe and Doyle to
its present possibilities. "I'm a *writer*, not a speaker," Millar warned. He would
read straight from the page: no concessions to the audience, almost no eye
contact. Such performances made Millar nervous all his life; by the end of
this one, his white shirt and tan pants would be soaked with sweat. "The last
occasion I had not so long ago to address a group in Angell Hall was my oral
examination for the doctorate," he began, "and I feel—to misquote Synge—
that there isn't anything more that Angell Hall can do to me."

He approached his topic with a few words on a Nobel Prize winner who once wrote scripts for Warner Bros. "William Faulkner is not usually thought of when mystery authors are mentioned," Millar said, but Faulkner's *Intruder in the Dust* was "probably our most ambitious American mystery novel." Millar wasn't claiming this great novelist was just a detective writer but that "the mystery tradition is available for the purposes of the highest art."

The form originated, he said, in the nineteenth century's freedom "to know evil as well as good," and the tales of Poe ("our first completely aware nineteenth-century man") expressed the urge to evil, "which modern man accepted as part of the bargain when he took entire command of his own will." Poe invented the detective story, Millar thought, "in order to grasp and objectify the nature of the evil and somehow to place the guilt. That is probably the function of all good detective stories: to confront us imaginatively with evil, to explain it in the course of a narrative which convinces us of its reality, if possible to purge the evil." Yet "the very best detective stories," Millar said, "present a true vision of evil to which there is no rational counterstatement, and leave a residue of terror and understanding pity, as tragedy does, which can't be explained away." Among such works he included Faulkner's *Sanctuary,* Hammett's *The Glass Key,* Chandler's *Farewell, My Lovely,* the "remarkable" *The Leaden Bubble* by H. C. Branson (in the audience today), and *Vanish in an Instant*—"written by a former Ann Arborite who shall be nameless" (Margaret Millar, of course).

Among the "first-rate and tormented geniuses" who'd put crime fiction to its most serious use were Dostoyevsky and Dickens. The line continued to the present, with many modern writers choosing to undergo "the sharpest pains and bitterest moral dilemmas of our society," voluntarily submitting themselves to "the involuntary anguish of the criminal, the insane, the dispossessed." Unfortunately, Millar thought, the traditional detective story with its "brilliant" sleuth-hero (Sherlock Holmes or Nero Wolfe) didn't lend itself to such explorations. "It is the murderer rather than the detective who must be the center of attention," he contended, "if the mystery is to have a genuine tragic interest."

He and other writers who didn't choose to hold the problem of evil at arm's length preferred "the so-called hard-boiled mystery," he said (getting a laugh by admitting he'd prefer it be called something like "the American colorful mystery"). Millar caused an excited ripple by stating, "I don't speak for the current truants from the school—the semiliterate unreconstructed Darwinian men, and the kindergarten Krafft-Ebings"—naming no names but obviously meaning Spillane and crew—"the less said about them the better." No, Millar went on, "I speak for the respectable and quite serious literary tradition founded by Dashiell Hammett and less brilliantly I think by Raymond Chandler, but he should be mentioned too; he's been very important as a master to me, in my way." The difference between them and their apostates, Millar said, was "moral control, which expresses itself in stylistic control, as it doesn't in the ones I object to."

Dashiell Hammett's books, hidden by libraries thirty years ago due to racy content, were now being yanked from U.S. shelves abroad because of their author's politics. Millar spent eleven minutes telling this Ann Arbor audience of Hammett's literary aspects and virtues, focusing his remarks on *The Maltese Falcon* in what was probably the most serious critical analysis of that book since its publication. "This novel has astonishing imaginative energy after more than twenty years," Millar claimed of the work he'd first read as a teenager in Kitchener. "I believe it can still express contemporary truth and comes close to tragedy, if there can be such a thing as deadpan tragedy."

Hammett's hard-boiled road was one viable path to an understanding of modern reality, Millar said—a quest we needed to take to wean ourselves from the patronizing attitude of the Holmesian superinvestigator who looked at evil and commented complacently, "There, but for the grace of God, go I." Staring his audience in the face for the first time, Millar concluded, "There is more humility and redemptive virtue in the contemporary hero-as-defendant, who says, 'There go I, in *spite* of the grace of God.' "

An instant of stunned silence was followed by a wave of heavy applause. It had been a powerful talk, nearly an hour in length, and Millar was proud of his performance. He paid ten dollars for a transcription disc of the lecture, which he'd take back to Santa Barbara and insist on playing for friends such as Hugh Kenner. "He was awfully pleased to have that on record," said Donald Pearce, "especially that storm of applause at the end—which must have meant more to him than I would be willing to speculate in terms of righting the injustices of his academic connection with the University of Michigan."

In town without Margaret, Millar stayed on in Ann Arbor a few days. Perhaps he enjoyed the break from his Santa Barbara routine, some aspects of which struck Michigan friends as bizarre. "He told me," said Pearce, "he and Margaret had a reputation in Santa Barbara for being fastidious about eating when they went to people's homes, and everyone wondered how they managed to get along on the little bit they'd put on their plates. 'The secret,' he said, 'is whenever we have an invitation to go anywhere, we always eat first at home.' I thought, 'What a grotesque and strange thing to do.' He explained Margaret found eating with other people disgusting: to watch them chew and salivate and talk while munching, and be aware of the food being swallowed down the gullet and into the stomach—it was barbarous. She thought people should eat alone." Her rationale masked an eating disorder that had begun in childhood. Millar went along with her, as he accommodated her reluctance to go out at night (ostensibly because she developed respiratory problems and headaches after dark).

He and Maggie were getting along better than ever, he thought, and it was a matter of honor to him that he'd never strayed into affairs. "Ken was proud of the fact that when he was a navy officer, he was never unfaithful," Hugh Kenner said, "which I gather was not always typical of navy officers. He was a strictly good and faithful husband and father." But the marriage had its strains at the best of times (some of the best lines in their books came from their fights, the Millars told friends; in Margaret's *Do Evil in Return,* for instance, a man named Lew says, "No, I haven't been drinking, much. Just enough to keep me from strangling my wife"); and Millar did have tender feelings toward other women. During this Ann Arbor stay he went to some lengths to express one such fondness.

"He had a real affection for the wife of someone at Michigan," said Pearce. "She and her husband invited Ken over one night and he asked if he could bring me along. Ken was in *very* good humor and obviously very happy to be there. He and I were talking quite spontaneously to each other, and this woman said, 'Oh, when I see the immediate responsiveness that you two have in conversation, I really *envy* that'—almost like saying, 'I wish I had something in my life like that'; it was like dropping a pretty strong hint of some sort. Anyway, this served to fan the evening a little bit. And Ken—he was really quite cunning in some ways—insisted I sing. I'm sure he wanted me to sing something like 'The Man I Love,' but I couldn't think of anything except 'Old Man River'! After a while the rest of them joined in, and that made the evening even looser and more pleasant. And then a question was asked of Ken as to how Margaret was, and he said, 'You know, you've no idea how much pluck and strength she has; when she's fond of somebody, she'll risk anything for that person.' " Millar told of visiting their friend M. M. Musselman the previous year in a Santa Monica hospital before his death from pancreatic cancer. ("Mussey was my darling," Maggie remembered. "We both really loved that man. He was in hideous pain. He had a blockage, and he was actually at the point where his feces were coming up through his throat.") "And Ken said, 'On leaving that evening, Margaret went over to him'—and here Ken raised his voice—'and *kissed* him on the *mouth!*' And he said, 'That took a *lot* to do, and that's the kind of person she is.'

"Later as we were hanging around the door saying good-night, Ken made a little move toward this woman—and she and he had a nice kiss, on the mouth. And her husband in a kind of rough, austere sort of tone said, 'Well, the only difference between me and Ken is that *I'm* staying the *night.*' Anyway we left, and afterwards Ken explained the psychology of that evening to me, how he had planned it, and how I was to come along in order to provide some assistance and loosen things up. No kidding. He *planned* that he would kiss her openly and she would respond, and his way of doing it was to drop in the emphasized statement *and kissed him on the mouth,* almost like a push-button command. And he was proud of the way that had worked out; this had been a successful evening for Ken. Okay. Colorful guy."

He loved that woman, Millar explained in a letter to Branson, as he also loved Anna Branson and Mary Pearce and Hank and Don and other males and females: "But I don't mean sexual love by all this, which is something you've never understood. With women even, it's only the potentiality of sexual love. I'm strictly monogamous, and with the help of God and advancing age I'll stay that way. Just so you won't think I'm the wolf I sometimes appear to be. I enjoy people so much my enjoyment sometimes runs away with me, but never to the point I am talking about. Which may be why women are able and willing to show me affection, that I value above all else."

"There was a great deal of warmth in him," said Pearce. "And he was grateful for small warmths, if they were genuine; he loved that. I can't imagine a more lonely person down deep, really lonely. Looking for the person whom he could freely and without concentration *be* with, somebody who didn't constantly keep him in a state of self-definition—in other words a real affection or friendly relationship. I don't think he ever had it. And don't think he didn't long for it. He did."

Millar's aesthetic ideals might be as elevated as any Knopf author's this side of Sartre ("I should like to see [the mystery's] philosophic possibilities explored, as Pirandello developed the problem drama for philosophic purposes or Kafka the psychological novel for theological ends"), but his career took him where the market led. In 1953 it led into the pages of *Manhunt,* a digest-sized New York crime-fiction magazine. Here Millar's work (and that of James M. Cain, David Goodis, William Irish, and Evan Hunter) appeared cheek by bloody jowl with Mickey Spillane's, whose crude fantasies Millar and most of his MWA colleagues loathed. *Manhunt* aimed to combine the hard-boiled style of classic pulps like *Black Mask* with the commercial appeal of Spillane ("the largest-selling writer in the world today"). Its first issue included a Spillane story and sold a whopping half million copies; Millar was in that issue with "Shock Treatment," a "Kenneth Millar" tale dashed off aboard the *Shipley Bay. Manhunt*'s second issue, in which Spillane also appeared, had Macdonald's Lew Archer novelette "The Imaginary Blonde." Millar/Macdonald published four stories in *Manhunt* in 1953, each (except "Shock Treatment") about fifteen thousand words long and paying the author about seven hundred fifty dollars. As the Archer novels were influenced by movie technique, so these short stories seemed written with TV in mind; in fact "The Guilty Ones" was constructed for possible television adaptation. For a Macdonald author picture, Millar sent *Manhunt* a frontal X ray of his skull (taken with his nurse sister-in-law's help), and the gag scored a big hit with *Manhunt* readers, he was told.

The same picture was used on the jacket of *Meet Me at the Morgue.* That non-Archer book got good reviews, and though it didn't do well in hardcover ("the present state of the fiction market . . . is unbelievably bad," Knopf told Millar, "and nothing is really selling"), it was bought after all for reprint by Pocket Books; and the Mystery Guild paid two thousand dollars to do its own edition. Better yet, the book sold to *Cosmopolitan*. All this was encouraging and lucrative, but it did seem that for every career step forward there was some unforeseen price.

Millar's pleasure in the Cosmo sale for instance was mitigated by an unexpected complaint from John D. MacDonald, last heard from in 1949.

MacDonald, now a prolific author of paperback "originals," telegraphed his agent (who forwarded the wire to Millar): THROUGH HAROLD OBER IN 1949 I GAVE KENNETH MILLAR LIMITED APPROVAL TO USE JOHN MACDONALD PSEUDONYM MERELY BECAUSE HE HAD ALREADY CONTRACTED UNDER THAT NAME FOR LEW ARCHER SERIES. I HAVE THE CORRESPONDENCE. REGISTER STRONGEST POSSIBLE PROTEST OVER CURRENT COSMO NOVELETTE. I WANT IT STOPPED. MacDonald's agent wrote von Auw that his client would seek an injunction to prevent Millar from using the Macdonald pseudonym on anything other than Archer stories.

Millar responded to this "shocking surprise" with a long letter to von Auw:

An "agreement" to which Mr. MacDonald refers, limiting my Macdonald publications to Archer novels, never, in fact, existed, as you know. . . . I have never made any agreement whatever with him. At this advanced stage in my career . . . I cannot possibly enter into an agreement to limit my production in accordance with his desires. The suggestion seems to me inordinate, and the statement that I "infringe on his identity," the implication that a writer of my standing seeks or would seek to trade on his reputation, gratuitous and insulting. . . . What Mr. MacDonald demands would convert a minor annoyance to both of us into a major disaster to my career. . . . Mr. MacDonald writes as a man with a grievance. I do not understand how I have harmed him. . . . I had always supposed that there was room for all of us. When Mr. MacDonald . . . also emerged as a mystery novelist under the name MacDonald, it did not occur to me that his success could be a threat to mine. I have always taken pleasure in another writer's success. But I cannot take pleasure in an attempt to use such success as a stick to beat me with.

MacDonald thought this "objectionable" and "snotty" and wrote Millar to say so, in a letter Millar nonetheless claimed put things "on a friendlier footing." In a five-page reply, he asked:

Could you have mistaken a letter of explanation for an agreement? My point is that I don't use the name J.R.M. with or by your permission. But before you get sore as hell again, let me hasten to add that I'm not trying to go legalistic and evasive on you. I seem to be in your hair, and I want to get out of your hair. . . . Look at my side of it for a moment. I've spent five years building the name J.R.M. into an important name in my field. . . . Perhaps my original choice of the name was stupid, though it didn't seem so at the time. Certainly it was an unlucky choice. . . . The similarity of my father's name to yours was a damned unlucky coincidence, more unlucky for me than for you, as I think you'll admit if you think about it. The most depressing aspect of the thing is that you seem to believe . . . that I am trading on the similarity of my pseudonym to your name—now that you have emerged as a big name—in order to sell fiction to your markets. To put it as quietly as possible, this is not the case. . . . Give me credit for honesty at least, and stick to the facts.

Cosmo certainly hadn't helped matters, he agreed, by misspelling his pseudonym as "MacDonald" (an already common error), but he assured MacDonald, "I am incapable of trying to trade on your reputation. I have a perfectly good reputation of my own to trade on." He couldn't afford to ditch the name and start all over, he said, but:

> What I can do—and this is not an agreement or a contract but a statement of intention . . . I can do my best to shift away from the name Macdonald wherever and whenever possible. That's vague, I know. Writing's a chancy business, and I can't tie myself up with any hard and fast agreement. . . . On the other hand, if I go into paperback originals, as I may, I wouldn't want to do it under the name Macdonald. . . . I've given the thing some days of anxious thought, and this seems to be the best I can come up with. . . . I hope this doesn't strike you as another snotty letter. . . . I am going to do my damnedest to lean as far over in your direction as I can without falling flat on my face.

Millar closed with some ambiguous praise: "Your letter caught me in the midst of reading *The Neon Jungle*"—MacDonald's most recent paperback original—"and wondering how you write so much so well so fast." MacDonald answered in mollifying fashion:

> I was not implying that *you* per se were trading on or attempting to trade on my ill gotten gains. Only implying that all publishers are, in essence, bastards, and if they could trade on the similarity of names at this point at your expense or mine, they would. . . . Look, don't sweat it at this point. Writing is rough enough all over, and there are few enough of us living at it. (This is living?) I accept it from here as an accomplished thing, about which little can be done. About which maybe nothing should be done . . . maybe, God knows, we're even helping each other. . . . Thank God, if this had to happen, at least it happened with somebody who can write. . . . If you want to chill your blood, sit down some time and ponder the fact that your father's name might have been Michael Spillane MacDonald.

This trouble was minor compared to what Millar faced in September. Alfred Knopf and others at the firm thought the new Archer novel, *Find a Victim*, was disappointingly weak; Mystery Guild declined the book; and Pocket Books said it wouldn't reprint it. Millar had lost his paperback house. Given publishing economics, Knopf was unlikely to do the book in hardcover without being assured of a softcover sale. This was a potential disaster.

Fortunately a solution was at hand. Bantam Books senior editor Saul David, a fan of Millar's since reading *Blue City* in *Esquire*, had for three years been telling his friend Pat Knopf that Bantam should be Macdonald's reprint house, saying Bantam could do much better by him than Pocket. In October 1953, Pat Knopf informed David that Macdonald would finally make the move. The Bantam people were delighted. There was one hitch, Alfred Knopf informed Millar: Bantam wanted reassurance that Millar meant to keep on writing mysteries. "I'm sure you can understand their point of view," he wrote, "they don't want to start with you unless they can look forward to a continuing, profitable association." Knopf urged him to say yes: "It doesn't seem to me at this stage that you can afford to give up Macdonald." Millar was pleased (if puzzled) to state his intentions clearly: "I expect to write a mystery novel every year or so for the rest of my life. And I have twenty notebooks, believe it or not, filled with plots. . . . I don't know where the idea arose that I was planning professional harikari."

Though Bantam seemed happy with *Find a Victim* and Knopf agreed to buy it, Alfred still didn't like the manuscript (too talky, not dramatic enough) and instructed Millar to finish revisions already begun: "If we like them, we will show them to Bantam; if we don't, we will stick, after all, to the original text."

Knopf's dissatisfaction with *Victim* took Millar by surprise, since he'd kept Knopf's advice about "action and general menace" in mind as he'd written the book ("parts of it as often as five times"). But he conceded its effects maybe got muffled when he tried to tone down the blood-and-guts parts in favor of character and psychology. "I leaned over backwards a bit in the face of the Spillane phenomenon, and will now lean forward again." The book was too intricately constructed for him to do a major rewrite, he said, but he'd try to cut wordy passages, sharpen dramatic scenes, and bring out the suppressed sex and violence. "Believe me," he assured Knopf, "I'm grateful for your interest and concern, in spite of the attendant pains of the situation. I believe this jolt—everyone needs an occasional jolt, damn it—will turn out to be beneficial in the long run. It strengthens my desire to become the world's best mystery writer." Millar outlined his plans for several sequences. Would Knopf oblige him by saying where and how the story seemed inadequate?

Knopf would not. "We're in a somewhat awkward three-cornered situation now," he maintained. "We have a book which we don't like too well, but which we are willing to publish. Bantam is willing to publish it. You see ways of improving it." Given these complexities, Knopf said, "I somehow feel I ought not to put in my oar." Instead he passed Millar's proposals to Saul David. Let David and Millar hash it out.

The Bantam editor thought Millar's ideas were fine, but he asked that the author add one more scene: "We'd like to see Kerrigan beaten up before he's killed. . . . We're agreed that the reader feels an aching need to lay hands on this guy." Millar, who'd in the past rejected such suggestions from Knopf and Pocket Books, could hardly refuse his new softcover savior. Bantam, a younger house with a leaner roster, seemed thrilled to have Macdonald joining its ranks; David spoke with unabashed enthusiasm: "I'd like to say how pleased we are here at becoming your reprinter . . . extremely pleased . . . because—among other reasons—we get to read your books quicker this way." How different this was from the mood at Pocket, where they had their pick of established stars and had acted as if they were doing Macdonald a favor. As "a crowning stupidity" (which Millar resented "like hell" but could do nothing about), Pocket announced that their reprint of *The Ivory Grin* would be called *Marked for Murder.*

Millar was glad to get away from Pocket Books, where he'd always been in Chandler's shadow. Having Chandler and Macdonald at the same reprint house was nearly as bad as if Chandler and Macdonald had both been at Knopf. Interestingly, Alfred Knopf wrote Raymond Chandler this year and asked if he was on strike against publishing methods (Chandler, now with Houghton Mifflin, hadn't done a novel since 1949). Perhaps Knopf was sick of the hypersensitive Millar, with his anemic sales and his paperback snafus, and hoped to lure Chandler back to Borzoi. Chandler admitted to Knopf that "in a way I regret that I was ever persuaded to leave you. . . . But I did, and a man can't keep jumping about from publisher to publisher. Anyhow, you have your hard-boiled writer now, and for a house of your standing one is enough." (Was Chandler hinting that if Knopf were to drop Macdonald though . . . ?)

Through October, November, and December, Millar revised *Find a Victim,* trying to please both of his publishers in hopes of better sales all round. He tired of the effort and was getting a bit sick of Lew Archer, he told Hank Branson: "I'd like to ditch that character, at least temporarily . . . but he seems to be my bread-and-butter, and I can't afford to be bored with that." The poor showing of the Archerless *Meet Me at the Morgue* confirmed Millar's need to stick with his private eye.

In December, Knopf had new cause to find fault with his lone hard-boiled author. The year-end *Wilson Library Bulletin* included a biography (with photograph) of Kenneth Millar that revealed his identity as John Ross Macdonald. Millar had agreed to the disclosure (the piece wouldn't have been printed if he hadn't) and supplied the disingenuous information he'd taken a pen name "partly because there were so many Kenneth and Margaret Millar titles on the market." The Macdonald "secret" had been told before (in the MWA newsletter, and on the broadcast of his Michigan talk), but the *Wilson* article (reprinted in *Current Biography*) shouted it. A querulous Knopf wrote von Auw, "I don't suppose any harm has been done, but I do wish he had told me whenever he made up his mind that he didn't care who knew that Millar and Macdonald were one and the same." Now they'd have to figure out how to deal with it on the jacket of the new Archer book.

If there ever was a new book. Millar sent the second half of the revised

Victim to New York the day after New Year's, 1954, telling Knopf he felt the text was much better now, literarily and commercially: "I wouldn't have redone the book if you had liked it in the first place, but now I'm glad I did. As I wrote to Saul David . . . I'm willing to do whatever I can to secure for my talent the audience we all feel it deserves." Knopf agreed the book was in good shape, but he wasn't done with demands. He wanted Millar to take out or tone down several semi-explicit sex references in the new pages: "I think this sort of thing should not appear in books of this kind. They do no particular good and they do offend a great many of the kind of readers on whom you and we have to count." Millar seemed to be getting mixed signals from the old man: prodded by paperback houses, Knopf suggested Millar spice up Archer; faced with what he found to be overly frank prose, Knopf drew back. A tired Millar said he'd make the requested deletions: "I've no wish to offend anyone of course, and actually prefer the pages as altered."

All this second- and third-guessing and re-rewriting was getting him down. He tried to look on the bright side: Bantam would pay better money than Pocket Books, and foreign sales were good. Cassell in England and Les Presses de la Cité in France sold more hardcover Archers overseas than Knopf did in the United States (though Millar hardly wanted that publicized). Also heartening was a review in the London *Times Literary Supplement* (unsigned, but written by Julian Symons) that said, "Mr. John Ross Macdonald must be ranked high among American thriller writers. His evocations of scenes and people are as sharp as those of Mr. Raymond Chandler. . . . Mr. Macdonald's unusual merit is the ability to make an implicit social comment on the world he describes. *The Ivory Grin* uses many of the thriller's standard ingredients, but it is not at all a standard product." Millar was encouraged at being favorably compared with Chandler in the most important book paper in England, a country where Chandler was considered a serious novelist. Millar for one felt no one charged the hard-boiled form with more life and meaning than he himself. If only he could get book buyers to see that—not to mention the capricious Alfred A. Knopf.

REASONABLE FACSIMILE

. . . With Dashiell Hammett no longer producing and Raymond
Chandler showing signs of weariness, Macdonald is just the man
for fans who like those original brands.

—*Time*, July 1954

ANNUAL EVENT

As of now, John Ross Macdonald (the alias of Kenneth Millar) is
the best hardboiled mystery writer cooking. His yearly novels are a
sort of Churchilliana among the knife-and-knucks memoirists.

—*Newsweek*, September 1954

In search of material for the next Archer, Millar spent the first weeks of
1954 in the company of psychiatric social worker Stanley Tenney, visiting juvenile halls and state hospitals (including Camarillo) up and
down the coast. Millar also attended Civil Service Commission hearings
on the firing of a veteran detective accused of paying informers with nar-
cotics; the cop's friends insisted he was framed by a local sheriff.

What affected Millar most in all his research were the damaged young
people: kids who strayed into theft or drugs and got in over their heads.
He often saw himself in such youngsters and recalled some fates he'd
barely escaped. "Most people don't know what it is they've been saved
from," said Don Pearce. "He did. And he spent his life understanding it,
and reliving it in a way in his books."

While Millar made field trips to see victims of bad luck and poor
choices, his own teenaged daughter was headed for trouble. Linda had
done well the past year at her private prep school; coached by good teachers, she'd come into her own as an excellent student. But she still couldn't
adjust socially and saw herself as an ugly duckling. Her parents tried to
encourage a compensating superiority—she was *smarter* than the other
kids, *better* than they were—but that didn't help much. Gripped by "the A
fever," Linda used studies as a substitute for friends. The Millars were glad
when she started earning pocket money baby-sitting for the Kenners and
the Seeds; it seemed to make her feel better about herself.

"Linda was an interesting girl," Hugh Kenner recalled, "a little shy, a little strange, a little aloof. There was a stubborn, rebellious streak in that
girl. Something happens when you're an only child and you're brought up
by two parents who are always working." In Kenner's opinion, "Something
unbalanced in Margaret I think got accentuated in Linda—really accentuated—and she just went over the edge."

Some of the Millars' friends were disturbed by Linda's precociousness.
One woman complained that Linda brought "very bad reading material"

(*Studs Lonigan*) to her home and discussed contraceptives and other sex matters with her children. Margaret brushed such criticisms aside; the Millars wouldn't ever stifle Linda's intellectual curiosity.

But Linda craved more than mental stimulation. "I think she was mainly interested in experiencing life in the raw, that's the impression I got," said Geoff Aggeler, a Laguna Blanca classmate. "She was an extremely, extremely, extremely bright girl; she'd read a helluva lot. But she wanted excitement. She kind of intimidated me a bit." Aggeler, later a professor at the University of Utah, was drawn to Linda partly because neither was popular at prep school. "Most of the kids who went there were little richies from Hope Ranch and Montecito," he said, "kids who spent their weekends at places like the Coral Casino, the Biltmore Hotel. We weren't part of that in group. She and I were sort of rivals as English types in the school. She was extremely gifted. Had her parents' brains, obviously; they were, you know, these brilliant people. But I guess she got a little bit on the wild side. One of the first times I ever got drunk actually was over at her house when I was about thirteen."

The Millars didn't know of her drinking, Aggeler said. "I dunno what that girl's problem was, but it certainly wasn't a lack of concern on the part of her parents. They seem to have been devoted to her. I remember seeing them on Sundays out riding bicycles together: Ken and Margaret Millar, Linda and another girl. I can remember going to a party with other kids our age at a neighbor's house, and Ken driving us all home. He was an absolutely devoted father. It really impressed me. He did the best he could; in retrospect I can see he really must have had his hands full. I guess Linda was a little bit unstable."

Linda was terrified at the prospect of going to public high school in the fall of 1954. All the right kids would hate her, she knew, and she'd be stuck with the misfits. Millar told her high school was a necessary evil, that things would be better in college; she'd come into her own there, as he had. To get Linda to college sooner, the Millars devised an accelerated study plan in which she'd do three years of high school in two.

Millar blamed some of his daughter's problems on the vacuous California culture. He too felt disconnected here, despite his civic and social activities, which included an every-other-Wednesday lunch with other Santa Barbara writers (Paul Ellerbe, Willard Temple, John Mersereau, Al Stump, city librarian John Smith) that Millar had helped establish. Millar blamed Hollywood and the fake dreams it pandered for a lot of the displaced values, or lack of values, in this empty paradise. When he wrote the next Archer story, it drew as much on his disgust with Hollywood as it did all of his dogged research.

Millar refreshed his impressions of the studio world by helping Maggie make good on her vow to buy a new car. H. N. Swanson got Margaret together with producers at Revue (the TV arm of MCA), with her husband as part of the package. The Millars went south and into the San Fernando

Valley for story meetings at Republic Studios with the makers of *City Detective,* a syndicated police series starring Rod Cameron (of whom *TV Guide* said, "Most of his acting ability is in his fists"). They pitched ideas sifted from Millar's notebooks and drew assignments for two scripts. One involved a man hiding from the aftermath of a hit-run accident that killed a teenaged girl; Margaret wrote the half-hour teleplay (alternately titled "Blind Justice" and "Blindman's Buff"), and the Millars got a joint payment of seven hundred dollars. They earned another seven hundred with a story and script called "Like a Fox." Margaret got sole credit (and the seven-hundred-dollar payment) for "Black Pearl," a thirty-minute anthology episode for Revue. After more story sales by Maggie to *The Web* and *Kraft Television Theatre,* the Millars had enough for their car: a three-thousand-dollar eight-cylinder, black Ford. She picked the color, he the make and model: a limited-edition convertible with extra-heavy undercarriage. Millar took "laconic but very visible pride" in the new Ford, Pearce said: "He was proud that it was stronger and more powerful and much *safer* than any other convertible. Ken was a very cautious man. He did not take risks." After Linda's fifteenth birthday, in June 1954, Millar started teaching her to drive: a significant test of tolerance for both, given their mutual tempers.

This same summer, as Millar worked his way into a new Lew Archer manuscript, the fifth Archer novel was published. Despite Millar's rewrites, *Find a Victim* found no friends at Knopf. "As far as the future is concerned," one editor there wrote of Millar, "I do think that it should be suggested to him that his characters are getting more and more sordid and twisted and that he might advantageously let up on them a bit." After von Auw sent Knopf a soft-soaping note about *Find a Victim* ("probably the handsomest and smartest all round production job I have ever seen in a novel of this category . . . a model of good taste and fine designing"), the agent received a sharp-seeming response: "My best thanks. Now, if you will only send up this way a manuscript that will be fully worthy of not only our best efforts in design and production, but in promotion and selling, we'll all be glad." The firm "promoted" this novel with a tiny three-and-a-half-inch "walking footprints" ad in the *New York Times* that made *Find a Victim* look like the most frivolous whodunit of the year. Knopf's sales force placed orders for a mere twenty-seven hundred copies.

For the first time in many seasons, some of the country's top mystery reviewers were moved to utter a discouraging word about a Millar book: "Falls somewhat below his best work," ventured Lenore Glen Offord in the *San Francisco Chronicle. Kirkus Reviews* was more blunt: "A long haul here." *Find a Victim* was a hard book to like. Set around a small northern California town, it began in exciting fashion, with Archer finding a dying man by the side of a highway and being drawn into a scenario involving hijacked trucks, embezzled cash, and several murders. But as Millar later acknowledged, great starts can lead to muddled middles. *Victim* bogged down in scenes of domestic unpleasantness that seemed to belong in someone else's bad play. Little sunlight brightened a plot filled with adultery, drug-taking, and incest.

Paradoxically, the problematic *Find a Victim* brought Millar more national attention than any previous book. Apparently spurred by the dust-cover revelation that John Ross Macdonald was really Ken Millar, the country's leading newsweeklies both ran favorable reviews of *Victim,* the first time Millar or Macdonald had been noticed by *Time* or *Newsweek; Time* also printed a photo of Millar, pipe in gout-swollen hand. Both magazines echoed the Boucher line on Macdonald as heir apparent to Hammett and Chandler. Boucher himself didn't fail to come through for this book, calling it "the best yet of the novels about . . . Lew Archer—which means that it is about as good as the hardboiled detective story can get." Millar, in an effusive letter of thanks, told Boucher the review brought tears to his eyes. "I had difficulties with publishers over the book which it would be tedious and painful to describe. . . . Your opinion makes me feel, know, that I'm not off in the wilderness by myself."

Raymond Chandler had a new book out this quarter too: *The Long Goodbye,* the first Philip Marlowe novel in five years and, many thought, the best ever. Boucher praised *Goodbye* as "probably the definitive" private eye novel and (unlike Chandler's *The Little Sister*) included it in his *New York Times* best-of-the-year list. But on that same list, not at all eclipsed by Chandler's effort, was John Ross Macdonald's *Find a Victim.*

Another sort of book demanded Millar's quick attention in the summer of 1954. Bantam, demonstrating its pleasure at signing Macdonald ("Bantam at least seems solidly behind me," Millar wrote Boucher, now that Knopf seemed lukewarm), made a deal for a collection of Lew Archer short stories. The paperback would combine the five Archer novelettes done for *Manhunt* and *Ellery Queen's Mystery Magazine* with two Millar stories written with other protagonists ("Find the Woman"'s Joe Rogers, "The Bearded Lady"'s Sam Drake) who'd both become Archer in this book. Saul David said Bantam's salespeople were "vastly enthusastic about the prospect." The firm wanted to print the collection immediately so it could be on newsstands in time for Bantam's edition of *Find a Victim* in early 1955.

Though Bantam didn't request revisions, Millar wanted to rewrite the stories a little before committing them to a book, even a paperback. He took out violent bits that now seemed too Spillane-like, but in place of a romantic subplot in "The Bearded Lady" (whose sale to the *American* had so depressed him) Millar inserted a fight scene.

He mailed the book to Bantam in late August. Saul David pronounced the revised stories "grand," and from Millar's list of proposed titles he chose *The Name Is Archer.* Bantam billed this collection "the case-book of a tough private eye" and wrapped it in a dramatic cover with a charcoal sketch of an ashen-faced Lew Archer holding a revolver at the ready.

A lot of readers discovered Macdonald through this attention-grabbing "paperback original." The book had a profound effect on at least one of them: Joe Gores. "One of the great turning points in my life was *The Name Is Archer*," Gores recalled. "I was a student at Stanford when I read that, and I just went out of my fucking skull. Here was this *vital* kind of writing—something that had a beginning, a middle, and an end and wasn't about some ponytailed graduate student who was gonna kill herself because she got a D. Here were stories that were *about* something: that gray-faced man on the cover, with the big gun. I devoured anything I could get by Macdonald." Inspired by his reading, Gores became a private investigator in 1955; two years later he sold a short story to *Manhunt* and began a successful career as a crime-fiction writer.

The Name Is Archer, conceived by Saul David as a way to earn a few dollars for Millar (and for his paperback house), would have sixteen Bantam printings in the next thirty-two years and be recognized as a classic in its field. Bill Pronzini, first president of the Private Eye Writers of America, in 1986 ranked Macdonald's anthology "with Hammett's Continental Op collections and Chandler's *Simple Art of Murder* as the finest volumes of so-called hard-boiled crime stories." Critic Douglas G. Greene went further, putting *The Name Is Archer* on his 1993 list of the Fifteen Greatest Detective Short Story Volumes Since Poe.

After sending *The Name Is Archer* to New York, Millar went into the hospital for an operation to remove a thyroid tumor: another manifestation, he believed, of psychological stress. The tumor was benign, and Millar surprised the doctors and his wife by driving himself home two days after surgery. Maybe the "softening-up process" such ailments induced had a positive side. Certainly he and Maggie got along better these days. After sixteen years, Millar wrote the Bransons, he and Margaret had reached "the joint conclusion—believe it or not—that we've come into some kind of maturity in our marriage. Haven't had a fight for months, just plain seem to enjoy each other's company."

Millar could still give his wife literary assistance. In 1954, Margaret was well into the writing of a contemporary tale of a mentally ill woman, inspired in part by the Beauchamps case (the first recorded instance of schizophrenia in the United States), when the CBS-TV series *Studio One* aired a Gore Vidal play based on the same subject. The story was so similar and the show so well done that Margaret wanted to junk her manuscript. But Millar came up with a twist that saved his wife's plot. Margaret finished her book, *Beast in View*, which became her best-known work.

It was not without cost. Margaret so identified with her disturbed character, she wrote, that she shared her nightmare: "Every sound was a threat. . . . The telephone no longer rang, it shrilled. People didn't talk, they screamed. A dog's bark would make me jump out of my chair." Doing the book "nearly killed" Maggie, Millar told friends. It took four months, she said, for her to recover.

As his wife explored her worst imaginings for *Beast in View*, Millar was "drowning himself" in an Archer manuscript that also dealt powerfully with mental illness and violence. Both these writers specialized in turning trauma into fiction; they'd made careers out of wrestling their demons. Soon they'd be pitched into real-life nightmare by the one Millar family member who was unable to escape into art.

We had to pioneer a novel land
And track the darkling wood behind the eyes.
But who was Psyche? who analysand?
Who is the hero of our mysteries?
                    —from "To M.," Kenneth Millar

Later he'd call it the biggest mistake of his life, but at the time it seemed to make perfect sense. On March 21, 1955, at a Ford dealership on North Ann Arbor Street in Saline, Michigan, Ken Millar bought a used six-cylinder, 1953, light-green Ford Tudor sedan for $1,175, as a present for his daughter, who'd be sixteen in June.

It was a reward for good grades. Her parents felt Linda deserved a morale booster. High school had turned out as bad as she'd feared. Being good-looking and popular was what counted the most there, and the peers who made the rules thought Linda was neither. The school counselor said she looked "dumpy." Classmates tagged her "Brains." Linda couldn't play their social game.

Millar was sickened and angered by what went on at his daughter's school, "a place where our cultural conflicts are worked out, often at the expense of human souls. . . . Between the sheep and the goats, the squares and the rowdies, there seems no middle ground." The lack of options turned Linda "boy crazy," he felt; and her choice of males was poor. "Where boys were concerned," he admitted, "she never learned much." Some "pretty odd specimens" showed up at the Millar house, several of whom her parents banned, "literally for the girl's safety." When Linda admitted that one good-looking fellow had given her alcohol (she swore it was the first she'd had, and her father believed her), the Millars not only forbade her to see him again but took care to instruct her thoroughly on the dangers of drinking.

Alcohol was a sore subject. Millar felt he and Margaret set their daughter a poor example. Maggie still enjoyed her Miller High Life; with friends she'd sometimes have six brews in a single evening. Millar, who'd switched from beer to Scotch because of his gout, depended on Johnnie Walker to help him get to sleep. He didn't *have* to drink, he insisted; but he took care to ration himself (only after 10 P.M., only a quarter of a fifth per night). He knew his drinking was a problem, a poor substitute for a more active social life.

But the culture in general depressed him. Wherever he looked things were coming apart, especially among young people. All sorts of delinquency—sexual, criminal, narcotic, vehicular—were on the rise, as dramatized in this year's hit movie *Blackboard Jungle* (from a novel by Millar's *Manhunt* stablemate Evan Hunter). Here were the citizens of tomorrow: mindless and boorish spawn of a lowbrow populace that preferred Ike to

Adlai. When a nasty strain of flu swept the country this winter, Millar equated it with the influenza that accompanied World War I: "the somatic expression of a spiritual malaise which is rocking this country to its foundations." His fears weren't just metaphor. Two of Linda's best "friend-boys" were killed in car accidents early in 1955. Millar was afraid for his daughter's safety, so much so that he thought of getting a teaching job and moving the family to Michigan or Ontario. He too felt unfulfilled in California: isolated, bored, often ill, somewhat stalled in his career.

Which brought him to Michigan in the spring of 1955, where he bought Linda a good secondhand Ford. Until the Millars left Santa Barbara, at least she wouldn't have to depend on the wretched local bus system. And having her own car would distance her from the dangerous hot-rod crowd.

Millar drove the sedan (which he dubbed Honeybug) on a two-week solo trip through Michigan and Canada. Ostensibly he was scouting a suitable place to relocate, but the drive soon became a sentimental journey. He visited the Bransons and the Pearces in Ann Arbor, then went to Kitchener and bought himself a sharp Harris Tweed jacket at a department store owned by a former KCI classmate. Through an unseasonable spring blizzard, Millar drove to Ottawa, where he looked up Bob Ford, now head of the Canadian foreign-service European division. Ford, married to a Brazilian woman, was about to have his first book of poetry published (it would win the Governor-General's Award). He hadn't seen Millar in seventeen years, but the two resumed talking as easily as if they were still living across the hall from each other in Huron College.

From Ottawa, Millar drove to London and the University of Western Ontario, where former colleague Frank Stiling rolled out the red carpet. In Toronto he hooked up with his artist uncle Stan Moyer; the two motored to Montreal and back, visiting other relatives along the way.

Maggie and Linda were due to join Millar in Kitchener. Before flying there, both wrote him with bloodcurdling news from Santa Barbara: two more horrible auto accidents, one involving teenagers Linda knew from school. His daughter filled Millar in on the gory details: "3 were killed, Richard F——, Dorothy G—— and some guy called Dick who was decapitated and 3 were very seriously injured, Loretta F—— had her face all mangled and the 2 others may die. I knew Loretta because she rode our bus and she was a friend of mine. The way it happened was that the guy, an 18 yr. old who's getting about 7 yrs. in the clink, who was driving stopped the car on the railroad tracks on purpose. The idea is that they stay on the tracks when a train is coming as long as they can without getting hit by the train. Whoever says to start the car is called 'chicken' which is the name of the 'game.' Well, the guy couldn't start the car and they all got hit. Awful isn't it? Next night there was an article in the paper about the high insurance rates for driving by teenagers and I wrote a letter to the editor about how that only applied to boys. It should be in the editorials demain soir, and I'll sure make enemies by it."

In Kitchener, the three of them visited Maggie's father and sat for a newspaper photographer, who snapped a dour-looking Maggie, a "gussied-up" Linda, a bemused Millar. After more family visits, the Millars and Honeybug hit the road for California. In Boulder, Colorado, near where Jack Millar mined for silver, they lunched with James Sandoe, the mystery critic and university librarian. Sandoe predicted big sales for Bantam's just-published collection of Archer short stories. Millar scoffed at the notion, but by the time he got back to Santa Barbara, *The Name Is Archer* was already in its third printing.

Linda had behaved poorly at the Sandoes'; Millar apologized by letter ("Linda is usually a cheerful soul, but had been under the weather physically and spiritually"). Her father often had cause to made excuses for Linda. When she was wan with what were probably hangovers, he said she had "scholar's pallor" from hitting the books too hard. When she was caught smoking or drinking, it was the other kids' fault. Linda always had some plausible story, and her father always believed it. He knew she never lied.

Millar sent his newest Archer manuscript to New York in August. As usual after finishing a book, he felt it was the best he'd ever done, and for once Alfred Knopf agreed, saying this book was "first rate—the best we have had from you in a long, long time. We have no suggestion for changes of any kind. Congratulations."

This sixth Archer, strongly written and exciting, gave a private eye's view of the corrupt doings behind the scenes at Helio-Graff Studios, an independent movie lot run by Simon Graff, a "short, broad-shouldered" mogul modeled physically on Darryl Zanuck.

Graff's executive fixer is a spooky security chief named Leroy Frost. Taken to Frost's office under duress, Archer endures a smarmy sermon on professional friendships and capitalist family values:

> ". . . I want you to take me seriously, Lew, it offends my sense of fitness when you don't. Not that I matter personally. I'm just another joe working my way through life—a little cog in a big machine." He lowered his eyes in humility. "A *very* big machine. Do you know what our investment is, in plant and contracts and unreleased film and all?"
>
> He paused rhetorically. Through the window to my right, I could see hangarlike sound stages and a series of open sets: Brownstone Front, Midwestern Town, South Sea Village, and the Western Street where dozens of celluloid heroes had taken the death walk. The studio seemed to be shut down, and the sets were deserted, dream scenes abandoned by the minds that had dreamed them.
>
> "Close to fifteen million," Frost said in the tone of a priest revealing a mystery. "A huge investment. And you know what its safety depends on?"
>
> "Sun spots?"

Archer's drawn into this world of fake fronts and false glamour by George Wall, a Toronto sportswriter in search of his estranged wife, Hester, who's taken up with the dangerous Helio-Graff crowd. As Lew uncovers some of the dark secrets covered up by Frost and others, he finds the seedier side of the Hollywood myth: stage mothers bent on using their kids to secure their own futures, screenwriters whose self-respect goes the way of all first drafts, moguls surrounded by so many yes-men they've forgotten the sound of no.

The Icarus myth is one reference point for this ambitious private-eye novel; Hawthorne's *The Scarlet Letter* is another. Millar used all that good Zanuck party material in a bravura sequence set at the fictional Channel Club in Malibu (the first of his many transformations of Santa Barbara's Coral Casino). The Millars' late friend M. M. Musselman seems to stand behind Sammy Swift, Archer's disenchanted scriptwriter pal:

"I came out here for the kicks, going along with the gag—seven fifty a week for playing word games. Then it turns out that it isn't a gag. It's for keeps, it's your life, the only one you've got. And Sime Graff has got you by the short hairs."

In this extended party scene (of which Millar was justly proud), the author skewers a slew of Hollywood types as lethally as he satirized the Montecito set in *The Drowning Pool*. In the club's drinking room, Archer observes:

There were actresses with that numb and varnished look, and would-be actresses with that waiting look; junior-executive types hacking diligently at each other with their profiles. . . . Some of their eyes were knowing previews of that gray, shaking hangover dawn when all the mortgage payments came due at once and the options fell like snow.

Such are the folk who fuel the machine that spreads the corruption that spills to Nevada, where types like Graff front for mob bosses building "legitimate" vice palaces in Vegas. In addition to sociology, satire, and sharp writing, this Archer novel had action. Despite the stand he'd taken with Pocket Books, Millar wasn't oblivious to publishers' wants. He wrote plenty of "hero in danger" scenes of the sort Alfred Knopf thought desirable, and there were enough moments of Archer manhandling bad guys to gladden Saul David's heart. Such passages weren't add-ons but integral parts of a book as vital as *Find a Victim* was dreary. This was a terrific return to form: Macdonald's best book since *The Way Some People Die*.

Though Knopf didn't ask Millar to change a word of it, he did have a perversely disquieting comment for its author: "I do find myself wondering, however, if you are not continuing to work what has become a decreasingly profitable market. I begin to suspect that you ought to attempt a serious novel rather than continuing to sweat blood over what the trade looks on as whodunits for which the market is automatically limited." No doubt Knopf was dismayed at the prospect of not selling more copies of this fine Macdonald than he had of its predecessor, but he seemed to be sending conflicting signals. Knopf had insisted Millar reassure Bantam he wouldn't stop writing mysteries; now he implied Millar was wasting his time on them.

Actually, Millar's career finally seemed to be hitting some sort of stride. *Cosmopolitan* bought his new book for abridgement (as they had Margaret's latest); their forty-five-hundred-dollar fee allowed the Millars to pay off the Cliff Drive house's second mortgage. The producers of *Climax,* a new sixty-minute CBS-TV show (whose debut play was a live dramatization of Chandler's *The Long Goodbye*), expressed interest in adapting something by Macdonald; Millar chose instead though to get involved with a proposed Mystery Writers of America series, for which he did a script of his "Bearded Lady" novelette. His two Dodd, Mead novels were issued again in softcover, bringing extra found money. With good foreign royalties (especially from France), 1955 would be Millar's most profitable year yet as a freelance writer; he'd gross nearly fourteen thousand five hundred dollars (to Margaret's seven thousand).

So while he thanked his publisher for his "thoughtful and friendly warning that I may be mining a dwindling vein," Millar wasn't about to abandon mysteries on the dubious advice of the mercurial Alfred Knopf. Of course he admired Knopf enormously, Millar told von Auw, and well knew his imprint's value; but he wasn't sure the publisher was 100 percent in his corner. Millar was still sore from the pain Knopf put him through with Pocket Books. "If [the new book] has enough success to change his attitude to my work in an up-beat direction," Millar wrote his agent, "that will solve *my* problem." But Millar thought Knopf had real problems of his own: "I know this because Margaret who never kids me regards Alfred as a troubled and a troubling man."

Ray Bond, his old Dodd, Mead editor, had been in touch with Millar. After apologizing for his "stupidity" in turning down *Blue City,* Bond floated the idea of the author doing more "Kenneth Millar" books for Dodd, Mead. This scheme appealed greatly to Millar. But the task at hand was seeing the new Archer into Knopf print.

Millar submitted it with the title *The Dying Animal,* which Knopf rejected as unattractive. Someone at the firm made a list of scarcely more appealing suggestions: *Skull Crasher, Cut the Throat Slowly, My Gun Is Me, The Dead Don't Cry, The Hardboiled Angel, A Gun for Lew Archer, Kill Hard!, A Doll for the Butcher, Slaughterhouse, The Blood Pit, Blood on My Knuckles, Blood on the Velvet, The Naked Kill, His Head in the Gutter, A Fist in the Guts,* and *A Handful of Guts.* Knopf spared his author this Spillanesque litany, suggesting only *The Wrong Way Out.* Millar countered with something he thought possessed "wit, impact, and the all-important element of class": *The Barbarous Coast.* "Agreed," said Knopf.

With *Coast*, Millar put final distance between his pseudonymous self and the prolific John D. MacDonald. Millar suggested *Coast* be bylined "J. Ross Macdonald," in transition toward an eventual "Ross Macdonald"; but Knopf said they should take the bull by the horns and go straight to "Ross Macdonald" now. Millar said yes. With his agent he celebrated "the dissolution of my marriage of inconvenience to John D., whose writing fails to improve with time, I'm afraid." This twelfth book—"my most important," he was certain—would bear the name Millar signed to his work for the rest of his life. The new byline would happen to coincide with events that would change both Millar and Macdonald forever.

My imaginative identification with the outcast children of nineteenth-century English society enlarged my sympathies and incidentally prepared them for a world which doesn't change as much as we like to think. Children are still being deprived, in India, in the Central Valley, and in the lower depths of our own city.

—Ken Millar, Santa Barbara Library talk, 1956

That made me think of a half-built life—and of my parents. I was mad when I thought they did not show me how to build my life. . . . I was mad at being forced to grow up—without help—I tried . . . but I didn't do well.

—Linda Millar, Rorschach test reaction, 1956

As time passed and new books took their attention, the Millars forgot about their idea of moving away from Santa Barbara. Linda seemed happier at school now, and she loved the Ford Tudor. At first she was a careful driver, but early in 1956 she started speeding. She was cited by the Highway Patrol for running a stop sign and for not carrying her license. When Millar went with her to the Santa Barbara Probation Department, she was let off with a reprimand.

Her father always defended Linda; his friends feared he idealized his daughter. For instance, he was proud that she never lied to him, but librarian John Smith knew this was not the case: when he caught Linda smoking, she begged him not to tell her folks. Linda assured her parents that she didn't drink—but she bragged of her hangovers to a family friend's daughter and said she snuck vodka out of the house or bought it at a grocery store that sold liquor to teens.

Millar often blew up at his daughter about the poor company she kept, and how it would hurt her reputation. He didn't know the half of it: Linda secretly met boys he'd forbidden her to date and had sex with them. Al Stump sensed enough about what went on to ban his own daughter from seeing Linda, he said: "We knew what Linda was up to, sneaking out the back window at night, running around with these kids who only wanted one thing. And then drugs were just starting to come in, dope and all. I had to tell Ken his daughter wasn't the little angel he thought she was. He didn't like it a bit, and it took him a long time to forgive me. Eventually he took it seriously, I guess, and tried to straighten her out, but maybe by then it was too late."

Despite what his friends thought, Millar was concerned about Linda in all sorts of ways. He was saddened by the cheap look she affected (short haircut, long fingernails, heavy makeup) trying "to be loved on any terms, by anyone." He knew her bad behavior, whatever it was, was in angry rebellion against her parents, especially him. Her long ocean swims were another cause for alarm. It pained and grieved him to see what was happening with Linda. Badly wanting a boyfriend, she got involved with oddballs: an overweight misfit who fastened on her for support, then rejected her nastily when she wouldn't marry him; effeminate fellows who weren't much use to her; car-crazy kids who encouraged her recklessness; a handsome lady-killer who dropped her after one date. Meanwhile no one suitable asked her to the school dance, and her bid to join a "Y" club was ignored. It all added up, Millar feared, to a crushing emptiness.

He tried his best to be a good father *and* a good husband, but there were problems. The roles sometimes seemed contradictory. Maggie had a need for "a jealous and exclusive love," and he thought his wife hypersensitive to "the fairly normal incestuous content in the father-daughter relationship." On the other hand, Linda was unhealthily aware of her parents' sex life, and jealous of it. "It is hard to know," Millar wrote, "where normality ends."

In February 1956 the Millars took a week's break from work and school for a vacation that turned memorably awful. At an out-of-state snow resort, Linda got angry and afraid at her first try on skis. A ride on a ski lift had her weeping with fright. Their last night at the resort, her parents allowed Linda to go out alone; when she came back wearing someone else's coat, her father accused her of drinking and slapped her. Crying, she ran barefoot into the snow. Driving home the next day, Millar let her take the wheel on the desert highway to California, and Linda speeded into a dust storm. They stopped in Anaheim at the recently opened Disneyland, where Linda gleefully went on Mister Toad's Wild Ride twice, which (given its emphasis on out-of-control driving) alarmed her father. Millar was appalled by the amusement park's "organized childishness and emptiness" and felt his daughter must be disappointed too in the banality this culture expected young people to settle for. The family drove to Long Beach for an overnight visit with relatives of Margaret's, where Linda went for Cokes with a sixteen-year-old boy cousin; they didn't get back until 1 A.M. Millar, who'd been out searching for her, lectured his daughter angrily about her indiscreet and dangerous behavior. Nevertheless Millar insisted to friends the vacation had been "most successful" and immediately made plans for another such trip.

Meanwhile Linda's big and little problems mixed together in an adolescent jumble. She and her parents were highly strung individuals unable to coexist in their pressure cooker of a family. Linda was mad at her father and mother for not helping her put life together. She said she hated them, but she craved their attention. She did forbidden things to get noticed. She hung around with "bums" so she could feel superior. Her phony front got mixed up with her real self, until she couldn't tell which was which. She didn't feel she had control of the part of herself that did things her father said not to: the Linda who didn't give a damn. She couldn't imagine a future where things turned out well. She thought about running her car into a train. She kept drinking.

The stage, as Freud or Sophocles or Millar might say, was set for tragedy.

"It isn't true that there's no such thing as bad publicity."
—Kenneth Millar, "Find the Woman," 1946

"I have only one daughter, Mr. Archer, only the one child. It was my duty to defend her, as best I could."
"Defend her from what?"
"From shame, from the police, from prison."
—John Ross Macdonald, "Gone Girl," 1953

At 5:30 P.M. Thursday, February 23, 1956, a girlfriend of Linda's whom the Millars trusted phoned and asked if Linda could come to her house and play cards. The Millars said yes, if Linda's chores and homework were finished. After doing the dishes and feeding the three dogs, Linda drove away from Cliff Drive in the green Ford Tudor. It was six o'clock, and a light rain was falling.

She'd told her friend to expect her at seven. At ten to seven the friend got a call from Linda saying she'd be late, she "had some business to take care of." Linda never made it to her friend's.

It had stopped raining at seven-thirty, but the road was still slick as the Millar Ford drove past the intersection of Alisos and the oddly named Indio Muerto, where the streets merged in a curve near Highway 101. There were no sidewalks on Alisos (something residents had complained of), and the lighting was poor. Three thirteen-year-old boys, eighth-grade students from Our Lady of Guadalupe, were walking south on Alisos in the dark after leaving a dinner celebrating their school's victory in a basketball tournament. The boys ate popcorn from a paper sack as they strode on the road shoulder or maybe in the street, since the dirt shoulder was muddy from the rain. They didn't hear or see the Ford as it came up behind them. Two boys were struck and thrown seventy feet. The Ford, screeching brakes, rammed a concrete retaining wall, then sped away, leaving a churn of skid marks. The third boy, who'd only been grazed, ran for help.

Less than five minutes later, at the junction of Cota and Laguna Streets a few miles away, the same Ford with Linda Millar at the wheel slammed the rear of a Buick stopped with parking lights on. The Buick and its male occupant were knocked more than sixty feet. The Ford rolled left and onto its roof, then came to rest on its right side.

A youngster burst into the nearby Mom's Italian Village restaurant where a Safety Council dinner was being held and shouted there'd been an accident. One man there hurried out and found Linda Millar sitting on a curb, weeping and screaming. He tried to console her, saying this could have happened to anyone. "Yes," Linda said, "but *God damn*, what will I tell my parents?"

A teenaged bystander fetched a blanket from his house and put it around Linda's shoulders. He sat next to her and tried to calm her. "God damn," she repeated, "what will I tell my folks?" Several times she asked was the Buick's driver all right, was he walking around. (He was.) Once she tried to break away, saying she was going to kill herself. The boy put his arms around her and held her. Linda was sobbing hysterically when patrolmen arrived. The teenager rode with her in the police car that took her to Cottage Hospital. On the way, Linda tried to open the squad car door and jump out. Again the boy restrained her.

She got to Cottage at seven-forty. A few minutes later, the two victims from Alisos Street were brought in. The surgeon on duty certified one thirteen-year-old dead on arrival. The same doctor briefly examined a loudly weeping Linda Millar. He gave her Luminal to quiet her, then went to attend the second thirteen-year-old, who seemed to have a concussion and a fractured leg. X rays were ordered, and the boy was admitted to the hospital. The surgeon then looked at Linda more thoroughly. Her injuries were minor, but she kept saying, "It was all my fault." The doctor asked, "What was?" "The car," she said. "It's all smashed." Don't worry about the *car*, the doctor told her; you're lucky to be *alive*. But until the Luminal took effect, Linda talked on and on about the shame she was going to bring her family. By then Millar was at the hospital, with Margaret's sister. At nine o'clock Linda was released to their care.

That night's TV and radio news told of a statewide alarm issued for "the hit-run killer" who'd fled the scene of the fatal Alisos Street accident. Santa Barbara police stopped and inspected over seventy-five automobiles. Gas station and garage operators were told to be on the lookout for a late-model, metallic-green car with damaged right front fender and bumper. Privately, authorities thought the car they sought was already found.

A pair of cops came to the Cliff Drive house Friday afternoon with Santa Barbara D.A. Vern Thomas, who knew Ken and Margaret Millar well from their frequent attendance at the courthouse. With her parents present, Thomas advised Linda Millar of her rights and asked what she'd done Thursday evening. Linda said after leaving the house she'd driven around aimlessly for ninety minutes, then crashed into the Buick. She said she'd been alone the whole time and denied being on Alisos Street. Thomas pressed her: Did she think a person involved in an incident in which a boy was killed and another injured should as an act of good citizenship stop and render assistance? Linda said they certainly should. Thomas asked directly if she'd been involved in the Alisos collision or had knowledge of it. Linda said no. The police impounded the Millars' Ford Tudor.

The front-page headline of Friday afternoon's *News-Press* read, "Police Have Suspect Car in Hit-Run Death of Boy." The car owner's identity was withheld pending further investigation, the paper said. The Alisos accident was the lead story in Saturday's *News-Press* too, under the banner headline "Expert Examining Hit-Run Vehicle." Called specially to Santa

Barbara to inspect the car was the most famous police chemist in the country: Ray Pinker, the same "test-tube detective" who'd helped Millar with his hit-run research and who played a cameo part in *Meet Me at the Morgue*.

Serious trouble had found the Millars. They retained Harris Seed as Linda's lawyer; he called in John Westwick, an experienced criminal attorney, to assist.

By Saturday, Pinker had positively matched paint particles from the concrete wall at Alisos with paint from the Millar Ford's bumper and headlight rim. He also matched a fabric pattern mark embedded in the grime of the Ford's bumper guard with the gray trousers worn by the boy who had died. A warrant was issued late Saturday night for Linda Millar's arrest. Police came to Cliff Drive to serve it. Millar told the officers Linda was sedated, under a doctor's care. He promised to bring her to the police station himself in the morning.

"Girl, 16, Faces Arrest After Hit-Run Death" was the headline in Sunday's *News-Press*, which printed the names and address of Linda and her parents ("well known writers of mystery and suspense novels"). The revelation that Thursday night's hit-run driver was apparently a teenager focused the city's outrage over all the recent youthful car wrecks. The perceived contrast between the accident's victims (working-class kids from parochial school) and the alleged perpetrator (daughter of folks with a house on the Mesa, never mind that the Millars lived in a poor neighborhood) sparked resentment in the blue-collar community. Better-off Santa Barbarans, more likely to know the Millars' joint income only equaled a high school teacher's salary, spread a different sort of gossip.

Millar delivered Linda to the police as promised on Sunday. The Millars posted her twenty-five-hundred-dollar bail, putting up both their houses as security. Monday, Linda was arraigned on two felony counts of hit-run driving. The *News-Press* evening edition had a photo of her striding somberly into municipal court. Monday was also the day of the funeral for the youngster killed. His parents were said to be too grief-stricken to attend, but over five hundred fifty others (including the boy's classmates and delegations from four other Catholic schools) went to his requiem mass. The subsequent procession was said by Santa Barbara traffic officers to be "one of the longest in many years."

Both wire services carried stories on the accident and arraignment, identifying the Millars (and "Macdonald") as successful writers. United Press gave Linda's IQ as 127 and said she was pretty.

As Linda was a minor, the judge in her case certified the charges against her for juvenile court and ordered an investigation by the Santa Barbara probation office. Following her lawyers' advice, though, Linda refused to discuss the accident with probation people or court-appointed doctors. She did speak with apparent candor to a local psychiatrist her father got her, a man who also counseled Ken and Margaret Millar at this time. The psychiatrist saw Linda daily for weeks and recorded what she said of that

Thursday evening: "She had been planning to go to a girlfriend's house, but before going there had stopped and had something to drink, and that the next she remembered was that she had crashed into a car. She stated that she couldn't exactly remember hitting the boys, but she thought she probably had." In her most emotional moments, Linda called herself a murderer. These guilt-provoked statements were what caused her lawyers to forbid her to talk to police or probation officers.

Her parents were also advised to keep quiet. All an "obviously distraught" Millar could tell the *Santa Barbara Star* was that "we are filled with grief for all the children. I hope and pray that the situation may be worked out." To von Auw, Millar wrote bravely, "We look to the future without fear. Our community is reasonably civilized; Linda remains what she always was, a dear good girl without a mean bone in her body; we and everyone who knows her are with her, fully. And Maggie is stronger than I ever dreamed."

Linda took the prescribed sedatives Seconal and Placidyl nightly. Though she stopped going to school, she saw a home tutor. Incredibly, the Millars thought Linda could still graduate from high school in September.

As part of the probation department investigation, a psychologist administered tests to Linda, whom she diagnosed: "very superior intelligence. Schizoid personality type."

Hoping to sharpen Linda's memories of February 23, her psychiatrist gave her sodium pentothal. A fuller account of that Thursday evening emerged. At a store where high school kids could get wine without showing ID ("Not forever, I hope," Millar commented), Linda bought a half-bottle of 20 percent alcohol port, she said, drank it in the car, then bought another half-bottle and drank it too. This scenario puzzled Millar: "One-fifth gallon in an hour, yet within a few minutes of this no signs of intoxication were detected by trained people, doctor, policemen, aunt." Was Linda lying or holding things back under pentothal?

With the psychiatrist, Linda acted unnaturally flip, denying regret about anything except not having a car. She noted her lack of remorse and said she must be a psychopath or a sadist. The doctor felt she was trying to hide her true feelings; her tension and anxiety seemed apparent. Linda became dependent on the psychiatrist. When he was unable to see her the last week of March, she grew fearful and depressed and stayed in bed all day. She spoke to her parents of her terrible guilt and her pity for the boys and their families. Over and over she said she wanted to die.

Margaret was able to resume work on a novel, doing a page or two a day; but for Millar, fiction was out of the question until Linda's problems were resolved. Alarmed by his daughter's condition, he stayed awake nights on suicide watch. During these sleepless hours, Millar wrote a candid autobiographical document, "Notes of a Son and Father." In third-person voice, he filled a spiral-bound notebook with frank revelations of his life as a child, teenager, husband, and father. He aimed to show how his and his wife's actions adversely affected their child ("we are interested in the moral mechanisms of family life, and when the machine broke down"), with the larger purpose of aiding Linda's treatment. In a belated attempt to save his daughter, the intensely private Ken Millar bared his soul.

Linda knew her father was staying up on her account, and that both parents checked her room at all hours. On the last Saturday night in March, she told a court-appointed psychiatrist, she felt more hopeless than ever: "Nothing seemed to matter. I felt, 'So what if I go to a reform school?' It looked as if I might. I was so depressed about the night of the accident, and my bad life. I wanted to hurt my parents and myself." Crying, she got out of bed and slashed her wrists with a razor. The next time Maggie came to her room, Linda held out her bleeding wrists and said, "Look what I've done." On her psychiatrist's recommendation Linda was admitted to Dani Rest Home, to be closely watched and treated with Thorazine. Her April juvenile court hearing was postponed, and the home tutoring ended.

A week after Linda went in the rest home, Margaret Millar's *Beast in View* won the Mystery Writers of America's Edgar Allan Poe Award as best novel of 1955. (Raymond Chandler's *The Long Goodbye* was the 1954 winner.) This wasn't the first or last time the Millars experienced extremes of good and bad fortune at once. Random House editor Harry Maule accepted the Edgar in New York on his author's behalf. Soon a small ceramic bust of Poe nestled among the teacups at 2136 Cliff Drive. Circumstances dampened Maggie's pleasure in winning the Edgar, but they didn't extinguish it. Nonetheless the grim irony of being honored for a story of schizophrenia, sudden death, and suicide while living through similar events couldn't have escaped her. "Ironies," Margaret said years later, "one's life is filled with them. When you get old enough you collect 'em. Most of 'em are—not too good."

There were plenty of ironies for Millar too: The irony that Linda, rebelling against her father by doing the things he'd forbidden, brought about what Millar himself had feared and been able to avoid at her age: scandal, tragedy, death. The irony that the car he'd bought to keep her out of trouble had driven her into it. The irony that Millar had sought out and knew the man whose expertise tied Linda to trouble. The irony that the world Millar researched for fiction—juvenile courts, mental health clinics, probation departments—was now his reality: he and his family were living the sort of story Millar and his wife got paid to make up.

Greatest of all was the eerie irony that so many things that had happened were foreshadowed in Millar's books and notebooks. Time and again Millar had shuffled plot pieces involving hit-run accidents (often with young victims), hunts for a "killer car," civic outrage, ambiguous guilt, mental breakdown.

Since college, he'd subscribed to Wyndham Lewis's notion of the artist as shaman or scapegoat of the culture. "Artists are people who voluntarily undergo what other people undergo involuntarily," Millar had said as an undergraduate. Three years ago at Ann Arbor he'd lectured, "Many modern writers have felt the need to undergo and imaginatively express the sharpest pain and bitterest moral dilemmas of our society." Through Linda, Millar was experiencing moral pain and mental anguish in a way more real than he'd ever imagined. Maybe these awful confluences of art and life were what prompted the semi-Delphic warnings Millar would utter in later years, such as, "As a man writes his fiction, his fiction is writing him. We can never change ourselves back into what we were. . . . So we have to be careful about what we write."

The worst of Linda's ordeal seemed over by May, when she was moved from the rest home to the California branch of the Devereux Schools, though Millar guessed it would take a year's hospitalization for her to recover from her "severe breakdown." He wrote von Auw May 4, "Life seems to come in tidal waves, with long stretches of calm between. Well. Reality has its compensations, too."

There was more reality to come. The Millars expected Linda to be granted probation at her closed juvenile court hearing May 10, with bail vacated and psychiatric treatment continued. But because of her refusal (under lawyers' orders) to discuss the accident, the judge declared Linda an unfit subject for juvenile court and remanded her for arraignment and trial as an adult. If convicted on both counts, she could get ten years in prison. Her parents wept.

Money was a problem now. Legal and medical expenses were running over a thousand dollars a month, and the Millars' property was still tied up as bail bond. The Millars borrowed a thousand (with interest) from George Hand and his wife. Other friends made cash loans or gifts. Millar was forced to write von Auw a letter he'd hoped to avoid: "I am prompted by the moral and practical necessity of retaining for Linda, who is being held on the verge of a schizophrenic break, the best psychiatric treatment available, and incidentally lawyers who can see her through the courts to further treatment. . . . Will Bantam or Knopf pay me the full paperback advance for *Barbarous Coast* now? Failing that, will Knopf give me a general advance of say $1500 on future earnings? Failing that, will Knopf advance $1250 on an unwritten novel? Failing that, will your office advance us a thousand or more, with the understanding that it will be repaid within three months, if not from earnings, then from money realized on our property as soon as it can be liquidated? This is a rough series of questions to throw in your lap. If none of them can be answered affirmatively, don't feel that there will be any sense of personal letdown. . . . M. is holding her own emotionally very well, and is back at work on the conclusion of her book. Linda is a little better than holding her own, and the ultimate prognosis is encouraging. The fact and degree of her illness need not be kept secret from someone like Alfred. You can also tell him if you like that in and through this situation I've taken a step towards becoming the writer he would like to see me be. . . . Whatever happens, don't feel anxious for us. I imagine most families have this one great crisis, and in the deepest sense we have passed through the worst of ours."

Von Auw immediately sent Millar a check for a thousand dollars from agency funds. Knopf hurried the sale of *Coast* to Bantam and a week later sent two thousand dollars (the author's half of the paperback advance) to von Auw, which the agent forwarded to Millar after deducting Ober's thousand-dollar loan. This was enough to tide Millar over. He gratefully informed von Auw the money would enable him "to move immediately to get for Linda perhaps the top adolescent-psychosis man in the country."

But things got worse. Linda's doctors thought it advisable she be voluntarily committed by her parents to the State Hospital in Camarillo, sixty miles from Santa Barbara. Millar tried to look on the bright side: "Happily it's no snake pit but a well-organized institution where she seems to feel secure and where we have plenty of opportunity to visit her." It was a blow though. In California, people said "Camarillo" to mean "loony bin," and in fact there were such references in *The Barbarous Coast* and *Beast in View*. Camarillo was a place to keep out of. "Maggie's a grief-stricken woman," Ken reported to von Auw, "but she's holding on. So am I."

Linda returned briefly to Santa Barbara the last Friday in May, when all three Millars were summoned to a closed Superior Court session of the county grand jury.

Linda's 2 P.M. turn on the stand was brief: on advice of her attorneys, she refused to testify or give evidence and was allowed to step down. Her father was sworn in.

Millar had cooperated fully with authorities since February 23. Belief in the principle of law was a cornerstone of his being. Claire Stump recalled an example of his integrity: "One of my children picked up several golf balls at a putting range and brought them home, and I made my child take them back. Some people said, 'Oh, you'll just make the child feel *guilty*.' But Ken said, 'Well, that's the beginning of her moral life.' " Lydia Freeman said Millar insisted his daughter face whatever legal penalty came her way in 1956: "He was determined that Linda should go through with whatever the law demanded." At the same time he got his daughter good lawyers, and the lawyers told him not to repeat what Linda had said about the accident.

A visibly distressed Millar ("I appreciate you are under some strain," the district attorney apologized) answered Vern Thomas's questions with polite "Yes, sir"s and "No, sir"s until they reached the heart of the matter: Millar's conversations with his daughter.

"What did the girl have to say about this collision?" Thomas asked.

"I refuse to answer."

"You say you refuse to answer?"

"Yes, sir."

"On what grounds, sir?"

"On the advice of Mr. Seed."

"Well, the advice of Mr. Seed, as far as this proceeding is concerned, Mr. Millar, would be immaterial. It is my understanding that a person who is charged with an offense has a right to refuse to answer on the grounds—constitutional grounds that the answer or answers given might incriminate him. You are not seeking to exercise any constitutional privilege here, are you?"

"I don't know the law, sir. I refuse to answer for the reasons that I gave you."

"Isn't it a fact that your daughter has admitted being involved in this collision on Alisos Street and striking down these kids and running away from the scene?"

"I refuse to answer."

"On the same grounds, the advice of Mr. Seed, your counsel?"

"Yes. Mr. Seed is the attorney who is representing my daughter."

"When your daughter left the house, she was driving the car, was she?"

"Yes, sir."

"You saw her drive out of the premises? Correct?"

"I heard her. I assume that she was driving. I know that she was."

"Do you appreciate that you might be cited for contempt to the Superior Court for refusing to answer these questions that I place to you, Mr. Millar?"

"Yes, sir."

"You appreciate that?"

"Yes, sir."

"You refuse to answer any and all questions, as I understand it, that I may place to you regarding anything the girl may have said about this Alisos Street collision; is that correct?"

"Yes, sir." The threat of being held in contempt of Superior Court didn't budge him.

Margaret Millar, after confirming that Linda had left the house that night driving the Ford Tudor, wasn't much help to the D.A. either. "I have never been present when Linda has discussed the accident with anyone," she told Thomas. All she'd done, she said, was reassure Linda: "I said that I had more faith in the case and they would discover the truth, and that she need not be worried about it." Margaret wept.

"I appreciate, Mrs. Millar—"

"It is horrible."

"—you are under a great deal of strain, but I am under the unfortunate obligation of fulfilling certain duties."

"Why, sure."

"This is not at all pleasant for me, Mrs. Millar," said Thomas, used to seeing the Millars under friendlier circumstances. "We meet, but I must go into these matters." He asked if she had at any time spoken with Linda about the Alisos Street incident.

"Her father took over all that," Margaret said. "They were trying to— He has always spared me things, because I get upset."

The D.A. didn't need more from the Millars. There were enough other witnesses for the grand jury that day (including Ray Pinker) to establish the rough outlines of a case. A two-count felony indictment was returned that night against Linda Jane Millar. Three days later she was arraigned. On June 11, Linda returned from Camarillo to plead not guilty. A jury trial was set for July 10.

The February accident had become a focus of civic concern in Santa Barbara, prompting public forums and proposed actions. There was a petition drive to install sidewalks on Alisos. A town hall meeting at the Lobero Theater on the problems of young adults cited the lack of a city program "to aid and reclaim young people who actually get into serious trouble."A teenage traffic-safety conference organized by kids from Linda's school was hailed by town fathers as a worthy effort by Santa Barbara's responsible youth. At another teenage panel sponsored by the American Legion, one young spokesman insisted "ninety-five percent of America's teenagers want to be helped by their elders, want to 'do the right thing,' but the remaining five percent has given today's youth an unjustified reputation for irresponsible, reckless conduct." (Linda told her father some of these meetings' "youth leaders" were among her school's worst drunks.)

The Millars were targets of nasty gossip. Some said Ken and Margaret were alcoholics who fought constantly and neglected Linda. Others speculated the Millars' jobs as mystery writers somehow induced morbid tendencies in their child. There were rumors Linda ran down those kids intentionally; others said someone else had been driving the car. A young man who'd taken advantage of Linda's drunkenness in a movie house two nights before the accident to make a pass at her (she'd slapped his face) came to the Millar house after her arrest to upbraid her. ("Nice person," Millar dryly noted.) "It was just a ghastly experience for the Millars," Claire Stump said.

The *Santa Barbara Star* referred to "bitterness" in some quarters over supposed special treatment of Linda Millar. (Her father meanwhile feared the judge would be swayed to make an example of her, a scapegoat for all the teen accidents.) Geoff Aggeler, Linda's friend from Laguna Blanca, witnessed the bitterness: "I was at the Catholic high school, which was attended by some of the richest kids in town and some of the poorest. There was a lotta resentment about Linda among my classmates; the kids who weren't so well off were *really* hostile. It was perceived that because her father was so prominent as a writer and with his connections that she would get off in a way that maybe they wouldn't in that same situation. It was a red-hot topic at my school, and it gives you an idea of the shock wave that went around. The nun in our creative composition class actually assigned us to write an essay on the subject of what should be *done* with this girl. Yeah, it was real heavy. Most of my classmates were really denouncing her, but I wrote an essay being very sympathetic to Linda and saying this was a lot of hypocrisy. Nobody knew I was a friend of hers, and I didn't mention it. I wasn't terribly popular there anyway so I didn't care. Actually I began with a Scripture text: 'Let he who is without sin cast the first stone.' They hadn't had that kind of perspective on it; I think maybe they *thought* about it a little bit after that."

Adding to the controversy was a story Linda's lawyers went public with. The *News-Press* banner-headlined it with skeptical quotes on June 13: " 'Witness' in Hit-Run Case Here Sought." The woman operator of a "doll hospital" had contacted Linda's attorneys and told of a female customer in her shop the day after the Alisos crash saying she'd seen a man jump out of the driver's side of "the death car" and flee on foot before a young woman drove off in the Ford. "I have suspected something like this was involved from the very beginning," John Westwick said. Linda's lawyers hired an LA private investigator (a real Lew Archer, as it were) to canvass homes near the accident site with the shop woman in search of her vanished customer, but they had no luck. "Linda is not in a competent mental condition to confirm or deny the story of a man being in the car," said Westwick, who revealed that Linda was confined at Camarillo. He hoped *News-Press* coverage would locate the witness.

Meanwhile the latest Macdonald book made its way into stores and onto reviewers' desks. The leading mystery critics outdid themselves in praising *The Barbarous Coast.* Anthony Boucher told his *New York Times* readers that "no rational enthusiast of the detective story (or indeed of the novel) should think of missing a word of Ross Macdonald," and that this Archer was "written as admirably as one can ask from a novelist in any genre." James Sandoe in the *New York Herald Tribune* hailed *Coast* as "an admirable, thoroughly absorbing piece of work" and thought it appropriate it appear under the new "Ross Macdonald" name, because it showed this writer had gone beyond "clever pastiche" to "a manner that is quite admirably his own. . . . The consequence is a nightmare of shocking lucidity and exceptional terror with a dawn of relief such as we usually experience after nightmare."

Given such a solid book and no doubt wanting to boost Millar's fortunes and spirits, Knopf took a fine-looking *New York Times Book Review* ad for *Coast,* proudly showing the Borzoi medallion and declaring this to be "Macdonald's masterpiece!" Despite the ballyhoo, *Coast* got off to a slow start, shipping only thirty-two hundred copies in its first weeks and prompting a stiff-upper-lip note from publisher to author: "You know how much I like THE BARBAROUS COAST. . . . I am not giving up hope by a long shot."

Millar, caught in his own nightmare of shocking lucidity, and no doubt hoping for a dawn of relief, took little notice of his novel's fate. But he couldn't ignore his paperback publisher when Oscar Dystel, head of Bantam, came to Santa Barbara in late June and lunched for the first time with Kenneth and Margaret Millar. Dystel happily reiterated that *The Name Is*

Tom Nolan

Archer had sold phenomenally well. Margaret Millar would soon be a Bantam author too: Dystel and company had acquired reprint rights to her Edgar-winning *Beast in View.*

There were other business matters to attend to in June, mainly the signing of foreign contracts. The Ober agents, aware of the Millars' needs, seemed to have overseas associates step up efforts on both authors' behalf. New deals were done this summer for quite a few Millar titles with publishers in Japan, Sweden, Italy, Spain, England, and France.

A jury pool was already drawn for the *People of the State of California vs. Linda Millar* when the defendant's lawyers made a surprise move: they asked that charges against her be judged without trial on the basis of grand jury testimony. This would bounce the matter back to juvenile court, with its more lenient penalties. The judge permitted it. After five months' controversy and with no advance notice, Linda Millar's case came close to resolution in a brief proceeding in Judge Ernest Wagner's courtroom on July 11, with less than a dozen people (including Linda's parents) present. After having read the grand jury testimony several times, the judge said, he believed "there can be no other logical conclusion" than that Linda Millar was at fault; he found her guilty of both felony charges.

Westwick and Seed quickly requested probation for Linda, who'd just turned seventeen. The judge said he'd consider it but warned he'd need greater cooperation. Westwick assured him, "There has been a change in the attitude of the defendant." Linda was ready to talk. Later that day she met with a probation officer and handwrote an account of what had happened five months ago:

After I had dinner on the night of February 23rd, Thursday, my girl-friend . . . called me up and asked me if I could come over to her house to play cards. I asked my parents and they said it was alright if I went. While I was doing the dishes I decided to do some drinking before I went there. So after I finished the dishes I got 39¢ and left the house and drove directly to the Victoria Grocery Store where I bought a 39¢ bottle of wine. It was after 6:00 P.M. at this time but I don't remember exactly what time. I drove from the store to the little side street across from the S.B. high school tennis courts where I drank the bottle very rapidly. I put the bottle under one of the trees. Then I decided I wanted some more wine so I went back to the same store again. I asked the proprietor if I could charge a bottle of wine and told him if he didn't trust me to pay him I would give him my name and address. I gave him the false name of Alicia Morrison and the address of 117 or 217 Equestrian Ave. He said alright and I bought the wine. I also asked him if I could use the phone. I didn't want [my girlfriend] to be suspicious about my being late. (On either my first or second trip I bought some dentine [Dentyne] gum which I chewed while drinking the wine.)

ROSS MACDONALD

I phoned [my girlfriend] and told her I had a few things to do and that
I'd be over soon. I left the store and drove to the Jr. High (Santa Barbara
Jr. Hg) where I drank the second bottle of wine. It was 39¢ too. I then
decided to go cruising some more, not realizing I was so drunk and
incompetent to drive. I drove around the Milpas area but I didn't know
what streets I was on. I drove down Alisos Street not knowing it was Alisos
Street and I was driving fast. Suddenly the next thing I knew there were
two boys—I wasn't sure if it was one or two boys) right in front of me and
a second later I ran into them. It was too late to do anything by the time
I saw them. I saw a boy in a light-colored jacket fly up in front of me and
I remember hitting him with the wheels of the car after he hit the
ground. I don't remember putting on the brakes or hitting the wall. I
panicked and drove away from the scene of the accident without stopping. Right after the accident I turned to the left & up another street I
don't know the name of. I stopped the car quite a ways up the block. I
didn't know if it was 1 or 2 boys I'd hit. I got out and saw the two huge
fender dents. It was then that I decided to kill myself. I drove around still
not knowing where I was, and trying to think how to commit suicide.
Then I saw a car with its parking lights on on the right side of the road
which I thought was parked. I also didn't know anyone was in it. With the
intention of dying, I swerved the car to the right and crashed headlong
into the car. The rest of the story you know. The reason it happened was
because I was driving recklessly and didn't see them and the reason I
didn't stop was because I panicked.

Linda's statement had some interesting inclusions and omissions. That
false name given the store owner (and remembered all these months later)
added novelistic specificity: "Alicia Morrison" could be a character in a
Lew Archer tale; women with the initials A.M. were ubiquitous in the tales
written by Anna Moyer Millar's son. The gum chewed while drinking wine
addressed the question raised in her father's mind of how Linda could
consume that much alcohol and not have it on her breath. Did Millar
coach Linda? It wouldn't be the first time he'd helped a family member fill
gaps in a tricky plot.
   The girlfriend who invited her to play cards told investigators Linda
had in the past used her as a cover to meet a boyfriend. Had something
similar happened that Thursday night?
   Linda's written confession wasn't subject to cross-examination and
became the official last word. The officer in charge of Linda's case recommended probation. The judge went along, setting her term at eight years
and imposing several conditions: Linda's license would be revoked, she
would undergo psychiatric treatment, she would continue regular school-
ing, and she would "refrain absolutely from any intoxicating liquor." No
frequenting of bars, no gambling, no associating with "idle, dissolute or
criminal persons." Should she violate these terms, Judge Wagner was

174

empowered to sentence her to the Women's Prison at Corona. Linda signed the probation agreement August 27, ending her three months' confinement in Camarillo.

Santa Barbarans learned of the case's resolution in the evening's *News-Press*. Several were mad enough to telephone Judge Wagner and threaten physical harm. "Many of the callers were laboring under the misapprehension that this was a homicide case," the judge told the *Santa Barbara Star*. Both the town's newspapers printed nearly all of Linda's confession, but the upstart *Star* also quoted liberally from other documents in the fifty-one-page probation report. Juicy excerpts from school counselors' records, friends' statements, and doctors' summaries showed Linda and her parents in the worst possible light: "Mr. and Mrs. Millar have failed to provide a normal home environment for Linda. . . . Linda has had considerable insecurity because her parents have used her as 'material' in their novels. . . . She has been morbid in introspection and attitudes. By reading books of her parents, one may realize how such feelings materialize. . . . When questioned directly as to why, in her opinion, she was prevented from making a statement to the Probation Officer or the Court earlier, she stated that it was because she was mentally ill and believed that she had committed murder, but since in her own statements she is now improved, she knows that this is not so. . . . Miss Millar's difficulties stem from 'a serious personality disturbance of the schizoid type.' " A sidebar described Linda's suicide attempts.

Having their anguish displayed in public was the excruciating conclusion of a gruesome six months for the Millars. Margaret was especially upset by this unpleasant finale, which underscored something Linda's probation officer wrote: "It has been obvious to all parties that the possibilities of Linda making any sort of an adjustment in Santa Barbara are extremely remote."

The Millars sold their two houses and bought one in northern California. Another irony: their departure would coincide with the move to Santa Barbara from Michigan of one of Millar's oldest friends, Don Pearce, whom Hugh Kenner, new head of the UCSB English department, had (at Millar's urging) looked up and then tapped to become his lieutenant. A saving grace: the Pearces bought the Millars' Cliff Drive house, sight unseen.

The Millars' legal troubles were far from over. A $65,000 wrongful death suit was filed against them by the parents of the boy killed in the accident (with papers served by a deputy for Sheriff John D. Ross, whose name seemed to splice Millar's byline with that of his Florida near-namesake). Another civil suit was brought by the injured boy's family (with those summonses served by a deputy with the unforgettable name of Marlowe). But, as John Smith told a probation officer, the Millars were "not panicky about the future in spite of great financial drain." With the criminal case closed, the worst really was over.

Yet there'd always be cause to wonder: Was Linda's account completely truthful? Had she lied to protect someone? Harris Seed said his client had a willful nature: "She was a headstrong young lady. Certainly had her own concepts and did things pretty much her own way." Forty years later, Seed still thought it possible Linda hadn't been alone that night. "Everybody knew it was that car—but was Linda driving it? Lotta doubt about that. Was she covering up for somebody? Lotta doubt about that. Yes, she pled guilty and received probation, after a very long procedure in which part of the time Linda was in a mental hospital. It was entirely possible to believe for a long time, or maybe forever, that Linda was shielding someone, and difficult if not impossible to find out. It was not an easy period. So it wasn't open and shut, night and day. It wasn't like, 'Well, my daughter did it and she should serve her time,' or some other damn thing; it was never black-and-white. Not easy to deal with no matter *what* side of that case you were on or who you were—doctor, lawyer, parent, defendant—difficult all the way. Even the court: problems. You could write a whole book about that case, believe me. I think that's about all that I know, or all I'm gonna talk about, Linda's difficulty."

"When there's trouble in a family, it tends to show up in the weakest member. And the other members of the family know that. They make allowances for the one in trouble, try to protect her and so on, because they know they're implicated themselves. Do you follow me?"

"I learned it long ago in the course of my work."

—Ross Macdonald, *Sleeping Beauty*, 1973

On the eve of Memorial Day, I stared at my wife in helpless pride and longing. . . . She railed at me, saying that I was sick, would always be sick. I held myself in silence for the most part, but there was trouble and the shadow of blackmail. Linda slammed a door.

—Kenneth Millar, "Memorial Day," 1957

*C*learing a space in another part of the forest was what Millar started doing when he and Margaret and Linda moved into their new home in Menlo Park, California. It wasn't just a figure of speech: he got a city permit allowing him to burn kindling on the lot at 518 Bay Road. The Millars' place stood at the edge of the Peninsular oak woods that Scottish-born naturalist John Muir had written of, around the time of Millar's birth in Los Gatos, forty-one years and twenty-five miles away. Millar, who savored slow revolving turns of fate in life and in fiction, saw an oblong sphere being traced on his biographical chart: a four-decade loop that started in northern California, went up to British Columbia, east to Ontario, south to Michigan, west to southern California, then north to where it began.

His daughter helped chart the last part of the journey. In a way, Millar felt, Linda had taken on his curse, the one his grandmother had uttered long ago in Ontario when she predicted he'd come to a bad end. Linda relieved him of that by becoming the scapegoat. The sins of the father (and mother) were visited on the child, another pattern that occurred and recurred in Millar's books. Linda's trouble was a fulcrum for the rest of Millar's life and art. He'd do his belated best to help her back to health.

Remarkably, she already seemed well on her way. Out of Santa Barbara and free from the threat of reform school, Linda made what her Menlo Park psychiatrist called surprising progress. In September 1956 she enrolled in a Menlo Park high school. "Things are working out better than we'd dared to hope," Millar said. "In the end there will be no scar on her. We can't complain." Dorothy Olding, von Auw's Ober colleague, was encouraged by Linda's cheerful demeanor when the agent saw the three Millars during a San Francisco visit.

Millar liked Olding immediately. Although he doubted either of Ober's chief agents, with their dazzling client roster (J. D. Salinger's 1953 book,

Nine Stories, was codedicated to Olding), took him quite seriously, Millar felt a rapport with Olding that over the years grew into something like love. For her part, the big-boned, handsome, unmarried Olding thought of Millar, now and in future crises, as the bravest man she knew.

Surely it took courage to confront his most painful memories through the psychiatric treatment he began in 1956. For a year Millar had weekly sessions with a Menlo Park analyst, therapy he described as "a watershed event" in his life. In a sense he'd been prepping for it since college, through extensive reading of Freud and his followers. The perceptions of modern psychiatry were central for him. It didn't much matter which school or discipline an analyst subscribed to, he said; the important thing was having a sympathetic doctor who'd stay one jump ahead of you. His therapist helped him put things in perspective, Millar said, helped him "get the genie back into the bottle."

The very hardest thing for him to face, he found, wasn't his daughter's deeds or his parental failings but his own painful childhood. His struggle to reconcile with it would last a lifetime. Don Pearce said Millar proved a fine analysand, though: "He was very good at honestly digging up and articulating things about himself, and wanted to do it—not just to feel better, but to have more of himself available for use in his work. 'I want to get the most out of myself that I can,' he said." Millar's therapy and Macdonald's fiction developed a synergistic relationship through an oeuvre in which the writer repeatedly explored themes and events intimately meaningful to him. Jerry Tutunjian, who interviewed Macdonald in 1972, said, "I asked him about the accusation that he was writing the same book twenty-four times. He said, 'No. Every time you do it, you dig deeper. It's like going to a shrink: you're telling the same story every time, but at the same time you're discovering different aspects of it, and of yourself.' "

It took Millar a while to make peace with the analytical process. In his early months of wrestling with the demons and angels of his past and present, his mood swings were dramatic. Pearce was alarmed by the change in his friend's personality when a somber and edgy Millar visited him in Santa Barbara early in 1957.

To begin with, Pearce said, Millar predicted dire things for America after its second rejection of Adlai Stevenson in the recent presidential election. " 'The whole country has just slipped backwards one big cog,' Ken said, 'and it'll be two hundred years before we can get it back up to the level Roosevelt left it at.' " Pearce had looked forward to a pleasant evening with his friend in the Cliff Drive house he'd bought from the Millars, but things went awry: the harder Pearce tried to put Millar at ease, the more tense and prickly he got. When Pearce made reference to the ebullient Ken Millar of college days, Millar cut him short: "Don't try to appeal to that Ken Millar, that Ken Millar is *dead*." Millar stared at his cigarette and repeated dourly, "Dead." A neighbor couple Pearce had invited over, former friends of the Millars', made matters worse. "They began talking about how much Santa Barbara had changed since Ken had left," Pearce said, "the awful traffic, and how dangerous it was to walk across the street. Ken became *livid*. He told them, and me, that he couldn't stay in the *room* with people so undiplomatic and thoughtless as to bring up questions of traffic and accidents to him, and he simply left the house." Pearce hurried after him. "He was in his car, backing out the driveway, and he flicked the headlights off—didn't want to *see* me, even."

When Pearce sent a conciliatory letter to Menlo Park, an upbeat Millar responded with a telephone call: " 'A letter like that deserves not a letter back but a conversation,' he said, 'I want to *talk* to you.' And he went on in a way that seemed much too generous and hubristic and euphoric. He'd been up all night writing poetry, he said, and he wanted to read it to me. And he did. It sounded like a very bad translation, at sight, from some German introspectionist."

Millar wrote a lot of poetry in his year in Menlo Park, much of it in rambling blank verse, most of it more therapeutic than lyric. His best creative efforts went into a new Lew Archer novel, begun in the bleak autumn of 1956 and finished in the promising spring of 1957.

Circumstances required the new book be an Archer: given Millar's legal and medical bills, this was no time to risk something new. The author used an already written manuscript to start from: an unpublished Archer novelette ("The Angry Man") done in his best *Manhunt* manner. Onto this sketchy framework he built *The Doomsters*, a novel full of insights gained during his and Linda's recent ordeal. The book became such a personalized fiction that Millar called it his "diary of psychic progress."

The Doomsters is suffused with pain and remorse. Its characters (including Archer) are damaged people: puppets jerked by neurotic or psychotic impulses, automatons propelled by greed and lust, hollow husks with false faces. Despite this heavy psychological freight, *The Doomsters* moves as swiftly as a Santa Fe Super Chief. From Archer's opening line, the book declares itself a most unusual mystery:

> I was dreaming about a hairless ape who lived in a cage by himself. His trouble was that people were always trying to get in. It kept the ape in a state of nervous tension. I came out of sleep sweating, aware that somebody was at the door.

Archer's early-morning caller is Carl Hallman, as tall and blue-eyed as Kenneth Millar—and an escapee from the state mental hospital. Son of a deceased rancher and political boss in the valley town of Purissima, Carl claims he was railroaded into the asylum by his brother, who Carl says covets their father's estate. He makes further charges implying the senior Hallman was murdered. Reluctant to help his uninvited guest, Archer realizes, "It was one of those times when you have to decide between your own convenience and the unknown quantity of another man's trouble." The detective agrees to look into Hallman's case if Hallman will go back in the hospital. On their way there, Hallman knocks Archer out and takes his car. The detective makes his way alone to the state hospital—and into a world Linda Millar had lived in for months.

A sympathetic doctor tells Archer the disturbed Carl is at heart naive and idealistic: potentially a valuable citizen. While in the hospital, Hallman helped care for some of the less able patients, including a heroin addict named Tom Rica, with whom he escaped. Archer knows Rica, a delinquent youth whom Lew once tried to straighten out. Obviously Rica steered Hallman to Archer. The private eye feels guilty ghosts stirring, specters that haunt this most subjective of all the Archer books.

Lew goes to the run-down house where Hallman's wife, Mildred, lives with her mother. Like Millar's childhood home, this place has a fanlight of colored glass over the door, like a window on faded grandeur. There's a feel here of decades overlapping, of generations feeding on each other. Lipstick stains on the teeth of Mildred's mother, the alcoholic Mrs. Gley, gleam like blood; we think of a deranged animal eating its young. "Mrs. Gley," Archer observes, "looked like the wreck of dreams." Her name brings to mind a line from Jack Millar's favorite poet, Bobby Burns: "The best-laid schemes o' mice and men gang aft a-gley." The self-pitying Mrs. Gley lives in the squalid dark, nursed by drink, soothed by the unreal world of television. Archer glimpses a TV play in which a woman can't choose between career and children so "settles" for both. In real life, Archer/Millar knows, the children are sacrificed.

Like Jack Millar, Mildred's father was an impractical dreamer who left wife and child to fend for themselves. Like Ken Millar, Mildred senses unpleasant feelings sealed in the rooms where unhappy people live: "They're in the cracks in the walls, the smokestains on the ceiling, the smells in the kitchen."

Archer and Mildred go to the Hallman ranch, where modern trappings clash with old oak and adobe in chambers that have the unlived-in feel of natural-history exhibits. The people here—Carl's brother, Jerry; Jerry's brassy wife, Zinnie; Grantland, the family doctor—all have false fronts, phony expressions, mask faces. Archer sees his own falseness and failings reflected in theirs.

In these ranch scenes, Millar scatters more autobiographical fragments. Zinnie and Jerry's three-year-old, Martha, is a portrait of Linda at that age, speaking clearly ("I want to ring for him, Mummy"), showing irritability ("Don't spell! You mustn't spell!"), being tugged at by grown-ups competing for moral custody of a human trophy.

Details from the Millars' more recent past were strewn throughout *The Doomsters*. There are references to pentothol, Thorazine, the cutting of wrists. Mildred, like Linda, twice attempts suicide. "She was a human being with more grief on her young mind than it was able to bear," Archer says. (In early notes for the novel Millar had Mildred living on "Alisos Street.") When a distraught Mildred begs, "Leave me alone," Archer responds, "A lot of people have. Maybe that's the trouble." Hidden beneath *The Doomsters'* canvas, like a picture visible only by X ray, is a group portrait of three generations of Millars.

As the seeming price of their wealth and power, the Hallmans carry a "family curse": a hereditary emotional illness that contributed to the suicide of Carl's mother, who felt plagued by tormenting "doomsters." After her death Carl became the family scapegoat, with his father predicting Carl would inherit "his mother's trouble" and "come to a bad end." When brother Jerry's shot dead in the greenhouse, Carl is named chief suspect. Archer tries to find Hallman ahead of a corrupt sheriff and salvage some truth from the family's web of schizophrenic guilt.

The Doomsters is bold in its complex design. Part of it unfolds as slow as a stage play; other sections race like a movie thriller. Scenes of realistic violence alternate with sequences that wouldn't be out of place in a "country house" mystery. Like earlier Macdonalds, this seventh Archer stops at compass points all over the California map. One of its most memorable sets is a motel-cottage bordello with a panoramic Hollywood photomural. The book flashes with many deft Macdonald images: the pink-satin whorehouse bedroom that looks "like the inside of a coffin"; the drug addict whose eyes are "puddles of tar"; coffee grounds stuck in a glass percolator "like black sand in a static hourglass that wouldn't let time pass"; the Japanese servant whose protective coloration lets him fade into the background, "remote as a gardener bent in ritual over flowers in a print."

With its sure pace and crisp prose, *The Doomsters* belonged with the best of the previous Archers. What was new was its more complex view of behavior. In this book Macdonald said good-bye to the simplistic views and solutions of the hard-boiled school. Archer, in contrast to the title of Chandler's story *Trouble Is My Business*, states, "Protection is my business."

Encouraged by a woman psychiatric social worker (something Linda once aspired to be), Archer moves away from his too easy good-versus-evil stance and toward a mature understanding. Good and bad, the woman tells Archer, are terms we use to torment ourselves; not living up to them leads to self-hatred: "We think we have to punish somebody for the human mess we're in, so we single out the scapegoats and call them evil. And Christian love and virtue go down the drain." Love is the grail that eludes most of the book's characters. Guilt fills the vacuum of its absence.

In *The Doomsters*, Archer strives to give and receive saving love. He doesn't deny the murderer's responsibility, but he perceives "an alternating current of guilt" through which the killer's blame flows "in a closed circuit" to many others, including himself.

Lew's plugged into the circuit through Tom Rica, the addict he once tried to help, then gave up on. When Rica turned up again trying to avert disaster, an unthinking Archer showed him the door. It was his own younger self he'd been trying to banish, Lew sees:

> When Tom stood in my office with the lost look on him, the years blew away like torn pieces of newspaper. I saw myself when I was a frightened junior-grade hood in Long Beach, kicking the world in the shins because it wouldn't dance for me. I brushed him off.
>
> It isn't possible to brush people off, let alone yourself. They wait for you in time, which is also a closed circuit.

In spurning Rica, Archer committed a mortal sin of omission and allowed a murderous cycle to start. Lew's revelations stun the reader like a boxer's combination. They stun Archer too; he says he's nearly ready to believe in the dead Mrs. Hallman's doomsters: "Perhaps they existed in the sense that men and women were their own doomsters, the secret authors of their own destruction. You had to be very careful what you dreamed."

Some of Millar's worst notebook dreams had come true through his daughter's troubles. In this novel he'd transformed some of his and her trauma back to fiction—to comprehend it, to exorcise it, and maybe to atone for it.

Millar sent the typed *Doomsters* manuscript air express to his agents May 27, 1957. The same day, flush with pride at what he'd achieved, he wrote von Auw:

> *The Doomsters*, by Ross Macdonald, is in my opinion, always subject to correction; and the opinion of M. and another good writer who read it, the culminating book (though not the last) in the Archer series. For that reason and others, I like the fact that it runs close to 100,000 words and resist in advance the notion of cutting it down to standard size, or writing it down to standard style. So far as my American hard books are concerned, such Procrustean maneuverings have proved fruitless in the past, and are even more likely to prove so in the future. The mystery and the novel are tending to merge—the tendency is noticeable all over the lot, including my book, and is the most encouraging and will be the most profitable trend in my field. I've talked to Boucher about it. Saul David tells me that the most saleable books in his soft-cover department are longer books of some literary standing. Length I have; standing is still in the future; but I'm on my way. I'd borrow money rather than knuckle under to Knopf on this issue. The tendency in the mystery is definitely towards the literary, the psychological, the non-athletic, and incidentally the *detective*-story. My book is intended to close off an era—rather a big word, but I'm feeling my oats a little—in the "hardboiled" field, and probably will. — My longtime and ultimate project is to find a place to stand from which I can fling some tenderizing salt on the tail of, con-

ceivably, a small new Canadian or North American Karamazov or Quixote. Well, I am feeling my oats. For the present, of course, I'd like to make some money, and I'd like to make it out of *Doomsters*. The sale of *Barbarous Coast,* a lesser but good book, was disgusting. I say this without personal feeling against Alfred, and with some knowledge of *his* problems. I'm sure he was just as disgusted as I was. But if all he sees in my new book is problems, rather than creative opportunities for a publisher, I'm not eager for him to handle it. Maybe we can find a better label than hardboiled, better sponsors than Hammett and Chandler. They're my masters, sure, but in ways that count to me and a lot of good readers I'd like to sell books to, I'm beginning to trace concentric rings around those fine old primitives.

Millar's high spirits were nearly matched by his wife's. Margaret followed her award-winning *Beast in View* with another strong book, *Vanish in an Instant* (partly written during Linda's crisis), which won top marks from genre reviewers; and her peers elected Maggie president of the Mystery Writers of America. During a ten-day solo stay in New York, she presided with flair at the MWA's Edgar Awards dinner at Toots Shor's and gave several newspaper interviews. Both Millars went to Bay Area MWA gatherings this year of her presidency; and on a June Sunday a week before Linda's eighteenth birthday, the Millars hosted forty-five guests (including Anthony Boucher) at an MWA open house at 518 Bay Road.

Linda's continued progress heartened her parents. Millar wrote von Auw, "Things look green after the drought . . . Linda is blooming again." She graduated high school in the top 30 of a 454-member senior class and would start UC Davis in September. Both civil suits from her accident were settled by midyear: one, the case for damages brought by the parents of the boy killed, was dismissed with prejudice; the other, which sought $45,000 in compensatory damages for the injured boy, ended in a jury awarding $10,800 plus $343 in costs (which Millar paid in full immediately).

Don Pearce encountered a lively Linda Millar when he drove a new car to Menlo Park this summer. "Linda immediately liked my car," Pearce said. "It was a real good one. We'd all met somewhere, and Ken said, 'Okay, Linda, I'm going to give you a special treat: you can ride home with Don Pearce.' She directed me to their house, and I drove the car a little too fast—not for her, though, she loved it; she said, 'Let's make Dad eat some rubber!' I was at the house a minute before Ken got there in the black Ford convertible, and he was in quite a severe and subdued mood. He thought I'd drive a great deal more slowly, and I can see the reason for it: he'd had enough of fast automobiles for a while. But she was just as happy as could be. I'm sure she would have loved to have *driven* the car, but . . ."

With Linda departing soon for college, her parents now considered *their* leaving Menlo Park too. Despite being close to the Bouchers and to first-rate San Francisco jazz clubs, the Millars never felt quite settled in the

Bay Area. An exotic plan began forming, inspired by Millar's friend (and Linda's godfather) Bob Ford being Canada's ambassador to Colombia. After Linda's first Davis semester, the three Millars would move to Bogotá, where Linda could attend a good university. Margaret was willing, and the Fords were enthusiastic. But that idea was trumped by an even more daring one: returning to Santa Barbara. Margaret thought of that town as her home, and leaving it made Millar see how much he liked it too. Being away was like living in exile.

So in August 1957, the Millars—accompanied by a Scotty pup named John Ross Macdonald Jr.—ended their northern exile by quietly moving back to the city they'd fled only twelve months before.

"Ever since the days of Francis Galton psychologists have been concentrating on the importance of individual differences. . . ."
—Margaret Millar, *The Invisible Worm*

The leased house the Millars moved into, 1843 Camino de la Luz, was on Santa Barbara's mesa only a few blocks from their old Cliff Drive home. Small but charming, it overlooked the ocean; a lighthouse was a hundred fifty feet away. Both Millars loved the house. (By September, Linda was living at UC Davis, near Sacramento.) There was beach access by a wooden, cliffside staircase, and Millar's bedroom-study picture window had a terrific view of the Pacific; on lucky days you saw whales swimming. Millar, pulled toward the ocean all his life, thought this a perfect setting for the start of what felt like a new chapter in his work and history. He wrote Knopf, "It looks like an interesting decade coming up."

Gazing at the Pacific, Millar often thought of his sea-captain father. Jack Millar's son now continued a family tradition by renting a sailboat for three dollars a day from the Santa Barbara marina. "It was an eighteen-footer, I think, with a nice mainsail and jib," said Don Pearce, who sometimes crewed for Millar. "Ken taught me what to do: how to handle the line and how to bring sail over at the call of 'Ready about'; then the next command, 'Helm's alee,' when the helm goes over. You learn very quickly, it's no big deal. But Ken always took things very very importantly; there was never anything halfhearted about him. So here'd be the two of us way out in the ocean, or just clearing the harbor for that matter, and he'd say, 'Rea-deee! A-booout!' And then: 'Helllm's! A-leee!' We were just turning the boat forty-five degrees or something, but he would have a very serious look—this was a great, important public occasion: the Boat, is being Turned, in its Course! Nobody else in the wide wide world would do that. But that's what one loved about him."

Pearce had twenty years' experience tempering his sail to Millar's moods. Newer acquaintances weren't always so sure what to make of him. Writer Robert Easton at first thought Ken Millar was one of the rudest fellows he'd ever met. Tall and gentlemanly, Easton had been a rancher, a radio station owner, and an oil company engineer; his 1940 book, *The Happy Man: A Novel of California Ranch Life*, was called a minor classic. He met Millar at the writers' lunch at Harry's El Cielito and later wrote, "Hostility toward life apparently including me seemed to seethe just beneath his surface." But Millar invited him for a sail, and the two men hit it off. Still, Millar took getting used to, Easton said: "He could maintain long silences. I mean monumental ones." Sometimes he'd show up without warning at Bob and Jane Easton's house (Jane was the daughter of author

Max Brand) and sit without speaking, "until one of us asked if he had anything on his mind. He'd smile, say, 'Yes,' sit there for a while longer, then get up and leave."

English poet and critic Donald Davie, a bluffly handsome Yorkshireman teaching for a year at UCSB, was at first put off by Millar's demeanor. "Ken was an unusually *con*trolled person," Davie recalled. "He radiated a sort of calm which seemed *un*natural, you know? I was a little daunted. There was suspicion on my part to begin with; he was taking very seriously the Freudian understanding of psychological life, and I was much more skeptical about psychoanalytic techniques. Then of course I hadn't read his books, and, yes, I must admit I *had* a snobbish prejudice against the detective thriller as a genre."

But the Ph.D.'s got past their wariness and onto common ground. Davie read and praised Millar's Coleridge dissertation and encouraged him to revise it for publication; Millar tried to interest Knopf in Davie's poetry. Don and Doreen Davie, living this year of Kenner's sabbatical in the nearby Kenner house on Bluff Drive, for a while called frequently at the Millar place. "Looking back, it seems we were a little tactless," Davie allowed. "I'm not blaming his wife for after a while resenting the extent to which we took their hospitality for granted, but a certain tension built up between us and Margaret. I think this was common among Ken's friends. Almost from the very first, Margaret made it plain that her life was different, and that, although she was perfectly civil to us, there was a distance to be maintained. After the *very* first couple of times, I don't even believe that Ken and Margaret and my wife and I were part of the same conversation. Margaret used to go to bed, you know?"

"M. is more chipper than she's been for years," Millar maintained to von Auw. Margaret was indeed glad to be back in Santa Barbara, but she kept a low profile. "I got the sense that Ken and Margaret were sort of testing the waters," said Davie. "If they'd made themselves conspicuous, then the whole thing about Linda might have blown up again." Harris Seed said, "Margaret didn't want to go through things that reminded her of Linda's difficulties. She did not care to be around many people very much. Ken honored that. For a while they became quite reclusive."

Still Margaret exercised her prerogative to criticize her husband publicly when she felt he deserved it—as on the day he recited a Lorca poem to Don Pearce. "He was saying it out in a chantlike way," Pearce recalled, " '*Green,* I want you, *green* . . .' Margaret came into the room and just made him *stop* it, said he was absolutely making some sort of fool of himself and this was not the way for a person of any maturity to behave. She left after having said some other disapproving things; and he said to me, out loud so that she could hear, 'Well, that just goes to illustrate the fact that in the modern world, a man cannot be a *poet* and live in pleasure with his *wife.*' It was all pretty controlled on the surface, I guess, but there was a volcano in that relationship at the bottom. Ken tried to romanticize their verbal violence by saying that Frieda and D. H. Lawrence fought 'like ravening tigers, like sporting serpents.' The truth is he was under constant strain."

Millar and Davie took to meeting out of Margaret's presence. One day the two sat in the kitchen at Camino de la Luz and spoke of works in progress. Millar was in the early stages of an Archer book, one begun as a mainstream novel, another run at the autobiographical *Winter Solstice*. At first he'd tried to tell the tale of a Toronto delinquent lured into a scheme to defraud a wealthy California woman. When that story fizzled, he turned it into an Archer and approached it the other way round, with Lew tracing a California heir back to hidden Canadian roots. Questions of personal and cultural identity were central to the book, which was obliquely patterned on Millar's biography. Davie then talked of *his* current project: *The Forests of Lithuania*, a translation of Polish poet Adam MicKiewcz's *Pan Tadéusz*, about the search for a lost father. Surprisingly, this epic poem sounded nearly identical to Millar's detective novel. "What we realized," Davie said, "was that these two so dissimilar-appearing pieces of work turned upon basically the same plot: the boy who has lost his father and in finding him finds his own and his national identity. From there you get into talking about whether it's true that there are only eight or eleven or however many archetypal plots in literature, and that the lost father is one of them. This thrilled both Ken and me very much."

Millar returned to his wayward-son book with new energy, buoyed by the knowledge that Davie, in another cliffside house two hundred yards east, was busy on *his* lost-father saga. Engaged in this "shared" labor, pleased that his daughter and wife were well, Millar worked happily through what he knew was the best winter of his life.

To make extra money and to exercise his urge to teach, Millar moonlighted as a creative-writing instructor for a community college adult-ed course. He took the job with characteristic seriousness, and for at least a few of his nineteen students he'd be a lifelong influence.

One so affected was Herb Harker, a tall, broadly built former cowboy from Alberta. Millar used both published stories and student work for class discussions, Harker said: "Sometimes he would read aloud a short story such as D. H. Lawrence's 'The Horse Trader's Daughter' and then go over it in detail. For instance, he mentioned there were sexual intonations in the passage where the horse was described; I said, yeah, that's right! I'd noticed that when I read it, but I didn't have enough confidence to suppose my impressions were accurate; Ken spelled it out. Another story he read was 'A Bottle of Milk for Mother,' by the Chicago writer Algren; that one just breaks your heart. So he picked a few really fine stories and walked us through 'em, showed us what was possible." Millar analyzed students' stories in similar fashion. Class member Noel Young (later founder of Capra Press) marveled at Millar's knack of juxtaposing amateur work with that of great writers in a way that elevated the students' efforts: "I'll never know how he achieved that—it must have been in his tone, his astute selection—I think of this as one of his great gifts and contributions. . . . I'll never forget that class, Ken's command and the quiet intensity that inspired us all."

A story is a circle, Millar told them, drawing blackboard diagrams to prove it. "He taught so much with just a few words here and there," Harker said. "He was generous in using his time to work on individual manuscripts, and that meant a lot." Millar's written commentaries on submissions were often longer than the works themselves. "I liked the way he moved you to do things that needed to be done," said Harker. "He'd point out problems and maybe suggest ways to approach them, but he left the work up to you. I remember how eagerly I used to watch for his comments. One day he returned a manuscript of mine and at the bottom he'd put, 'Your talent requires that you become a writer.' "

Millar thought enough of Harker's potential that he offered to tutor him informally after the school term. "The first time I went to his house I was just floating, that he would give me such a privilege," Harker said. "He took me to where he had spread books all over the couch; he said, 'We need to have something to talk about.' He was giving me suggested reading, primarily. He said, 'The place to start is with Ibsen; he's the grandfather of us all.' "

Millar's night school students mostly didn't read Ross Macdonald's books. These serious people only cared about *real* writing. But no one was more serious about writing than Ken Millar, who saw Ibsen's relevance to the detective story, at least the kind Millar tried to write: one that moved beyond simplistic formulas. "The hiss-and-boo villain died in the nineteenth century," Millar said. "You know who killed him? Ibsen blamed everybody."

What Millar strove toward, he wrote Anthony Boucher, was "what we both desire, the mystery as a standard and serious novelistic form." A step in that direction, he thought, was *The Doomsters,* published in February 1958. Millar read its reviews carefully, attentive as always to the mystery critics who mattered. The verdict on his adventurous effort was mixed. Boucher was firmly supportive, saying *The Doomsters* exemplified how "the hardboiled private detective story can become literature, as satisfying (and as subtle) as any less violent, more 'literary' study of character as revealed in crime." James Sandoe liked *The Doomsters* too ("a milieu evoked with singular and precise imagination"). But others were put off by Macdonald's "snake-pit" subject matter and his efforts to stretch the genre's conventions. Lenore Glen Offord (a guest at the Millars' 1957 Menlo Park open house) confessed in the *San Francisco Chronicle* she was "kind of homesick for the days when detectives such as Lew Archer didn't search their own consciences as much and murderers weren't allowed long, case-history autobiographies at the end." The *Saturday Review* turned up its nose at the book's "generally unpleasant personnel" and graded *The Doomsters* only "medium."

Of more concern was the word from Knopf. Bookstores ordered less than four thousand copies of *The Doomsters*—not much of an improvement over the thirty-two hundred hardcovers shipped of *The Barbarous Coast*. Knopf wrote Millar, "I am worried and distressed as I always am when we publish a book by you at our failure to put it over as it deserves to be put over." Knopf's mysteries, like other publishers', were priced cheaper than its mainstream fiction; *The Doomsters* sold for $2.95, not $3.50. This was a boon to genre fans, but it segregated the better mystery writers such as Macdonald and seemed to diminish the value of their work. Knopf people considered pricing the next Macdonald as "a novel" at $3.50, with a corresponding increase in ads; but some wondered if it would make much difference. One Knopf editor (a Macdonald fan) told the boss he thought the answer might be a book without Archer to peg it as a "hard-boiled" item, a book in which the characters didn't seem sordid: "He writes like an angel but I personally feel that his view of the world as hopeless and degraded is what predicates against a better sale than we get." Knopf passed these words on to Millar, and the author responded with clarity, courtesy, pride, and panic:

Dear Alfred:

I thank you for your letter, though the news that my book has not been doing well is naturally even more distressing to me than it must be to you. While I don't feel able to solve this problem quite unilaterally—and indeed you have always given of your publishing best to my books—I have been giving serious thought to the idea of changing my pen somewhat, and will continue to. I have no desire to expend my powers on a form which does not seem, for one reason and another, to have attained the status I'd hoped for it; in this country, at least.

My new book, which is three-fourths done and should be in your hands later this Spring, was planned as a transition out of the "hard-boiled" realm—which I have felt as a limitation for some years—and seems to me to be coming off successfully. It is, however, an Archer novel, and I am naturally concerned whether your letter is to be taken as a rejection of any future Archer novels, including this one. The economic facts of life, let alone this book's intrinsic merit, if I am any judge, would hardly permit me to scrap it. Perhaps I had better finish and submit it; and then our discussion can proceed from that point.

May I add that my ambition for these coming years is to write on serious themes, not necessarily lugubrious ones, with a simplicity and speed and perhaps bravura which all of my books have had in some degree. I aim at narrative beauties, which seem to be rather rare these days. So much for my aims. The proof of the pudding is in the eating.

Perhaps the intent of The Doomsters *is somewhat at odds with its form. I can't really regret the book, though. Some people who have called or written about it see it as I tried to write it, otherwise than as an exploration of sordor; rather as a work of tolerance trying to reach beyond tragedy. I am glad you published it.*

> *Sincerely,*
> *Ken*

"Don't, for heaven's sake, get it into your head that we don't want to go on publishing you," Knopf reassured his author. "We most certainly do expect to do the next book, and if Archer is in it, Archer is in it, and we'll do our best."

Millar submitted the book in May 1958 as *The Enormous Detour.* The same editor who had lamented the "degraded and sordid" nature of earlier works had nothing but praise for this one: "This is a fine Archer. As usual it is exciting, well-paced, interesting and exceptionally well-written. In addition Macdonald has 'gotten off the doomsday kick' . . . and made half a dozen or more of his characters exceedingly sympathetic. . . . Another plus to this is that it ends on a high note, i.e. has a happy ending. . . . My general feeling about this is 'hurray!' " Knopf himself, though, thought the book's ending too ambiguous and its second half weak. He wasn't demanding a rewrite, Knopf insisted, saying he'd read the manuscript "with great enjoyment." In any case publisher and author could discuss all this in person: Knopf was coming to the West Coast and planned a lunch with Millar for Monday, July 21, at the Beverly Hills Brown Derby.

Millar still had mixed feelings about Knopf and only dropped the idea of doing "Kenneth Millar" books for Dodd, Mead after von Auw said it was unlikely Alfred would stand for such a thing. Millar's main problem was still not being sure Knopf was completely in his corner.

But their LA meeting went exceedingly well. The two spoke frankly of matters vital to each: of a publisher's duty to nurture a writer throughout a career (something Knopf had done for Joseph *Conrad*), of the artist's debt to his talent. The lunch marked a new phase in Millar's relationship with Knopf, as if he'd rounded a corner and left his doubts behind. The old man was so gracious and full of friendly encouragement; maybe he'd come to believe more in Millar. The writer found himself agreeing with Knopf's gently voiced qualms about the new Archer, and he resolved to improve the manuscript. When they left the Derby, the publisher (a longtime amateur photographer) took several pictures of his California detective novelist on Wilshire Boulevard, close to where Knopf had photographed Raymond Chandler in 1940. Crew-cut and beaming, Millar seemed to be looking forward to his future.

Living in Santa Barbara had a lot to do with his newfound contentment. Millar felt different about the place than he had when he'd first moved there. The town had everything other towns did, and a bit more: an ocean with dolphins and whales, the Channel Islands visible from shore, birds in great numbers, a green profusion of plants and trees. It was a civilized place in a gorgeous setting, and there was more cultural activity here than first met the eye. Millar now saw his corner of California not as an outpost cut off from the rest of the country but as a vital center in its own right.

Santa Barbara seemed especially exciting this summer of 1958, thanks to the presence at UCSB of a number of good guest lecturers invited by the on-sabbatical Kenner. There was Jesuit poet Walter Ong, Shakespeare-festival director Homer Swander, Greek city-planner Constantin Doxi-ades, and the magnetic Donald Davie (who showed Aldous Huxley around Santa Barbara in 1958). Two new English department members, Don Pearce and Marvin Mudrick, also elevated the atmosphere. The most stim-ulating summer presence by far though was Herbert Marshall McLuhan, a Toronto academic and cultural critic who in ten years would be world-famous in the global village he'd name. Millar already knew McLuhan's work well and arranged to audit his summer-school class. "Marshall was at his most brilliant," said Davie, who also sat in on McLuhan's course. "He was sort of crazy brilliant, you know? All the things that were subsequently to appear in his books which made him a great guru of the world, he was in fact trying out there in lectures to the Santa Barbara students; they—they—they—turned your head around!"

Millar was an enthusiastic, note-taking, hand-raising participant in McLuhan's four-times-a-week class. He and McLuhan struck up a friendship. "They recognized each other's originality and valued each other a lot," Pearce said. McLuhan was one of the few academics Margaret Millar could abide; he and wife Corinne were always welcome at the Millars'. "She was madly in love with him," Maggie said of Corinne. "We got to know him quite well. Marshall was a pretty fascinating guy." Davie too enjoyed McLuhan's company: "Marshall was a perfectly human man; I mean he wasn't just a dis-embodied mind, a 'crazy professor' sort. He was a nice, easy guy that liked to drink beer and go on the beach with his family and my family."

Millar gave McLuhan a typescript of his new novel to read, and the pro-fessor praised it. "This was not your ordinary whodunit," Pearce heard him say, "this was a *novel*. Deserved to be studied on the university curriculum, he thought." Whether or not McLuhan spoke in hyperbole, *The Galton Case* (as the novel would be titled) and other Macdonald books would be taught on the college level a dozen years from now. Loren D. Estleman, a fine private-eye novelist of the 1980s, would call *The Galton Case* Macdon-ald's "major contribution to the form." Millar himself rightfully saw this eighth Archer novel as a turning point in his work.

The seed of *The Galton Case* was a sentence in one of his notebooks: "Oedi-pus killed his father because he banished him from the kingdom." Millar's contemporary reinvention of the ancient tale dropped clues to its origins through references to Athens, a character named Cassandra, an invocation of the Fates. Also half-hidden were allusions to the theories of Sir Francis Galton, the nineteenth-century father of scientific psychology. First to juxtapose the terms *nature* and *nurture*, Galton said eminence ran in families and mental traits were inherited; he began the study of individual differences and introduced fingerprinting. A Galtonesque scrutiny of generational habits runs through *The Galton Case*, a mystery that turns upon multiple questions of inheritance and identity. Using Oedipus and Galton, Macdonald fashioned a fictional twisting of Ken Millar's history.

In it, Archer's hired by a sleek lawyer named Sable (a smooth fantasy of the Winnipeg uncle who tried to fiddle Millar out of an inheritance) to find what became of the long-lost son of a Santa Teresa matron. Anthony Galton walked away from college and a good social position in 1936 for a proletarian existence as "John Brown," accompanied by a lower-class wife who gave birth to John Brown Jr. "I'm afraid my son had a *nostalgie de la boue*—a nostalgia for the gutter," the Galton matriarch tells Archer. (Millar's inspiration for Brown was a Western classmate, a "golden boy" who abandoned a life of privilege to go underground as a radical organizer.)

In the Bay Area where Galton-Brown was last seen, the detective finds a link between past and present in the person of Chad Bolling, a San Francisco poet who once printed some verse by Brown. (The poem offered in evidence, "Luna," was one of Millar's own early efforts.) Archer sees Bolling perform at the Listening Ear (similar to a San Francisco club Millar had been to, the Hungry Eye), where the poet recites over jazz played by musicians who "smiled and nodded like space jockeys passing in the night."

Chad Bolling was inspired in part by Kenneth Rexroth, a northern California bard Millar saw in performance at the Lobero Theater, where Rexroth chanted poems a bit abashedly to the accompaniment of prerecorded jazz. Rexroth was a father figure to beat poets. Millar, an artistic conservative in matters of craft, was turned off by the beatniks' sloppy aesthetics and angered by the destructive "philosophy" of beat fellow travelers like Norman Mailer. The trouble with the beats, Millar told Don Pearce, was they thought it was more important to *have* life experiences than to write well about them. He lambasted half a dozen beatnik standard-bearers including Rexroth in a book review ("Passengers on a Cable Car Named Despair") for the *San Francisco Chronicle* in the summer of 1958. Through Bolling, one of his most memorable minor characters, Macdonald continued his California satire:

> " 'Death Is Tabu,' " he said, and began to chant in a hoarse carrying voice that reminded me of a carnival spieler. He said that at the end of the night he sat in wino alley where the angels drink canned heat, and that he heard a beat. It seemed a girl came to the mouth of the alley and

asked him what he was doing in death valley. " 'Death is the ultimate crutch,' she said," he said. She asked him to come home with her to bed.

He said that sex was the ultimate crutch, but he turned out to be wrong. It seemed he heard a gong. She fled like a ghost, and he was lost, at the end of the end of the night.

Bolling is one of several semi-impostors Archer encounters in *The Galton Case*. But Lew also sees things to admire in Bolling: the poet, however compromised, still believes in his art.

Archer drives with Bolling to Luna Bay near San Francisco (and Los Gatos), where construction work has turned up a skeleton thought to be Galton-Brown's. Coincidentally a young man calling himself John Brown Jr. has been asking about someone he claims was his father.

The friendly, angry, volatile fellow claiming to be John Brown's son bears intentional resemblance to Millar. His life history is a fun-house reflection of the author's. He shares Millar's birthdate and northern California origins. Like Millar, he "never had a father." His mother, he says, placed him in a Midwestern orphanage (a fate Millar narrowly escaped); the orphanage's iron gates have an ironic counterpart in the fortresslike gates at the Galton estate. John Jr. was the virtual ward of a Michigan teacher (a man like the Kitchener teachers who took Millar in hand), lived at 1028 Hill Street in Ann Arbor (quite near the Millars' residence at 1020), and paid for college with two thousand dollars left by his (substitute) father. (Unlike Millar, John Brown Jr. kept faithful vigil at his "parent"'s hospital deathbed.) "I'm bright, and I'm not ashamed of it," John proudly declares—a variation on a Millar epigram: "An intellectual is someone who's smart and insists on it." Now John's returned to the Golden State of his birth, a place with a fairy-tale aura: the prince is back from the poorhouse to reclaim his kingdom.

What happened to John Brown Sr. and whether this man is his son are the matters of fact with which *The Galton Case* is concerned. But for Millar, the novel's central events were John Brown Jr.'s crossing of geographical and psychological borders; they represented Millar's entering into his estate as an American citizen, "rejoining" a life he'd been told he belonged in. Millar created once-removed emotional autobiography. As Archer probes the early life of this possible faker, and as John Jr. confronts the same problematic past, Millar in a way faces down his own history and makes peace with his angry young self.

Another character also stands in for Millar: Tommy Lemberg, the apprentice hood who steals Archer's car at gunpoint. (Having his car stolen was becoming a habit for Archer.) Violent, easily manipulated, desperate for approval, Tommy's another there-but-for-fortune picture of what Millar might have become without good guidance and his own strong will. The second time Archer encounters Lemberg is at the desert lair of mobster

Otto Schwartz. The suave lawyer Sable is one fictional projection of Millar's Winnipeg uncle; Schwartz is an alternative fantasy of the same uncle as a low-echelon crime boss. The living room of Schwartz's place near Reno is fitted with slot machines (like the slots Millar thought his uncle supervised for U.S. crooks) and an electric player piano (like the one in his aunt's apartment). When Lemberg activates the machine, it plays "In a Little Spanish Town," a song popular when Millar lived with Aunt Margaret and Uncle Ed in 1927.

Alternate aspects of Linda Millar are presented in Sheila Howell and Alice Sable. Sheila's nineteen (like Linda in 1958), healthy but morose, not yet at home in the world: "Her eyes were candid, the color of the sky," Archer observes, as she sits "with a pale, closed look, undergoing the growing pains of womanhood." In love with the enigmatic Galton heir, Sheila "seemed to be moving heavily and fatally out of her father's protective control." If Sheila seems headed for trouble, borderline psychotic Alice Sable has emerged on its other side, her psyche fractured by a death she's either caused or witnessed. Doctors shield Alice from police questioning while trying to help her sort memory from delusion.

By twisting his and others' experience into fictional Möbius strips, Millar transmuted the messy stuff of life into fiction without succumbing to overemotional prose (as he had in the botched *Winter Solstice*) and without overtly invading his own or others' privacy. And he did it in the context of a tightly plotted detective novel. Images are often joined to make two sides of an ironic coin: Archer says of a woman yearning for the long-gone Galton, "Cassie's emotion was like spontaneous combustion in an old hope chest"; later, when Archer's shown the bones of the late John Galton, they're in "a metal box about the size of a hope chest."

The most evocative objet trouvé yet found by Lew Archer is a murdered man's suitcase: "It was a limp old canvas affair, held together with straps, which looked as if it had been kicked around every bus station between Seattle and San Diego. . . . Its contents emitted a whiff of tobacco, sea water, sweat, and the subtle indescribable odor of masculine loneliness." Millar eventually revealed, "These were the smells, as I remembered and imagined them, of the pipe-smoking sea-captain who left my mother and me."

Galton gathers momentum and excitement as it unfolds, moving beyond Kierkegaardian bleakness toward forgiveness and hope. "I know it sounds wild," Sheila says of her boyfriend's strange story, "but it's only as wild as life." Archer's perception of young Galton shifts as he sees the young man first as genuine, then phony, now as a true heir, now a fraud. Finally he's all of these. As Archer and he comprehend this, the reader feels the author accepting equivalent truths of himself.

The Galton Case, in conception and style, was several cuts above even *The Doomsters*. It was the first of Macdonald's mature works: a dozen or so books that belong with the best American mystery fiction. *Galton* would hold special meaning for those who knew Millar when he wrote it. "I still think *The Galton Case* is the finest thing he ever did," Donald Davie said thirty years later. "Very very profound and moving fiction indeed." Millar, though, was already looking ahead. "Now let's see if I can write a better book," he proposed to Alfred Knopf. "This one doesn't satisfy me by a long shot."

Harold Brodkey's collection is simply dumbfounding, not fiction but a cosmetic application of the limberest and most knowing *faux-naif* manner to the most elementary preoccupations of women's-magazine maudlin. . . . If you go for chromium melancholy and like to think of life and art as essentially uncomplicated by anything more than the need to turn a phrase, Mr. Brodkey is your man. . . .

[T]he glassy glitter of the style and the patness of plot-making seem to testify as surely to Mr. [Angus] Wilson's boredom and distaste as to the characters'. Stories like Mr. Wilson's and Mr. Purdy's make one wonder about the relation of the artist, not to society necessarily, but to the human race. . . .

Albert Camus, at least, is concerned with such large issues as the dignity of man and the need for compassion. . . . Nevertheless, serious and humane as Camus clearly appears in these stories, the stories themselves are as solemn and restricted as philanthropy, with none of the true storyteller's gaiety of impulse. . . .

—Marvin Mudrick, "Is Fiction Human?"
The Hudson Review, Summer 1958

Kenneth Rexroth, a poet of more scholarly attainments who knows the long case history of hobohemia, seems out of place at first on this cable car named despair. But this manifesto of beatmanship comes blandly to the conclusion that the current generation of young people may have to kill themselves off, "voluntarily, even enthusiastically," to make way for he doesn't know what. . . . The currency of such inverted values suggests that a failure of humane leadership, in and out of school, has exposed an eager body of adolescent and semi-literate readers, and writers, to the addled pretensions of poolroom mystics and nihilists posing as saviors. The self-enclosed contemporaneousness, without history or future, which Mailer praises and his beat ones enact, is a special circle of hell reserved for stone-age savages, the mentally ill and retarded, and writers who have succumbed to intellectual and moral sloth.

—Kenneth Millar, "Passengers on a Cable Car Named Despair,"
San Francisco Chronicle, 1958

When Oscar Dystel and Saul David of Bantam Books came to Santa Barbara on a blustery day in September 1958, they brought splendid news: Ross Macdonald was now Bantam's number one mystery writer, with highest sales and lowest rate of return. (Other crime authors currently on the Bantam list included Rex Stout, Georges Simenon,

John Dickson Carr, Eric Ambler, Julian Symons, Bart Spicer, and Margaret Millar.) Bantam was eager for more Macdonald. In October they'd bring out Millar's *Blue City* under the Macdonald byline; Dystel and David proposed reissuing all the Millar/Macdonald books. "It appears that the market is there if we can reach it," the author told Knopf, as he sought help getting reprint rights to his earlier titles back from Dell and Pocket Books.

Hearing of Bantam's plans, though, Pocket Books decided *they* wanted to bring out new editions of five Macdonald works. This miffed Bantam ("Pocket Books didn't care until we did," David complained), but it worked to Millar's (and Knopf's) benefit: Pat Knopf negotiated a new fifteen-thousand-dollar contract with Pocket. Millar was delighted with the deal, further proof of Macdonald's commercial potential. "I've always believed there was mileage in my work," he wrote Alfred. "Things do appear to be looking up, don't they?"

There was television interest too. Producers of another proposed MWA anthology wanted to option the non-Archer *Meet Me at the Morgue* (as well as Margaret Millar's *Vanish in an Instant*). MCA-TV asked about adapting the Archer novelettes for *Mickey Spillane's Mike Hammer.* More flatteringly, Millar was approached about doing a Lew Archer series. He proceeded with caution in all cases; Millar didn't trust TV people and didn't want to spoil any chance of a movie sale. He did agree (for $750) to sell his 1945 story "Find the Woman" to an upcoming hour-long, live CBS show, *Pursuit,* on condition the play's private eye be called not Archer but Rogers.

Millar thought this TV interest and the paperback deals might mean Macdonald was about to break big. He urged Knopf give *The Galton Case* all feasible help "going over the hump." Encouraged by Bantam, Millar toyed again with the idea of doing a separate "Kenneth Millar" series, and maybe even (à la Graham Greene) dividing future work into serious "novels" and mystery "entertainments." He still hoped to do things outside the genre; after reading Camus's guilt-obsessed novel *The Fall,* he informed Knopf (Camus's U.S. publisher), "I have the ambition to undertake an office of that sort for the American conscience."

The open intellectual range Millar roamed was reflected in the growing bunch of writers he got to attend the alternate-Wednesday lunches at Harry's El Cielito on State Street: there were *Saturday Evening Post* and *Argosy* veterans, academic-quarterly contributors, *News-Press* reporters, crime novelists, the occasional screenwriter. When William Campbell Gault (met memorably by the Millars at Ned Guymon's 1951 bash) moved to Santa Barbara in 1958, he became a luncheon regular. Breaking bread and drinking beer this year at the same El Cielito table as the raspy-voiced Gault, writer of *The Bloody Bokhara* and *The Convertible Hearse,* was the suave Donald Davie, author of *Purity of Diction in English Verse* and *Articulate Energy: An Inquiry into the Syntax of English Poetry.*

Davie also liked gathering with Millar and others at Bob Easton's house, where talk could be about anything from early American literature to the ideal death: Millar, with his small smile, said he wanted to die "in the act of love." Easton recalled, "All agreed with Ken's hopes."

Davie again urged Millar to revise his Coleridge dissertation for publication, something Millar undertook now in spare nighttime hours. "It's not a book that will make money," he acknowledged to von Auw, "but it's likely to become a 'standard' work of scholarship, and I'm eager to have it published for a number of reasons." It was a way to show he was a serious writer. Also toward that end, he stayed up late doing free book reviews for editor Bill Hogan at the *San Francisco Chronicle*. If his literary reputation was going to be made, Millar thought, it had better be in the coming ten years. He'd be forty-three at the end of this one. "It's not a case of now or never," he wrote Knopf, "but now is beginning to look like a good time."

The notion was underscored by Macdonald's *The Ivory Grin* being included in late 1958 on a London *Sunday Times* list of "The 99 Best Crime Stories" from 1794 to the present. The list's compiler was Julian Symons, the rising crime novelist and man of letters who (as the *Times Literary Supplement*'s anonymous mystery reviewer) was England's equivalent of Anthony Boucher or James Sandoe. Symons in fact consulted Sandoe and Boucher when making this list; he also invited suggestions from Agatha Christie, Rex Stout, Ellery Queen, and Raymond Chandler.

The seventy-year-old Chandler was in London at the time, Symons later wrote: "While we talked about the idea, he . . . sat back with his diluted whisky talking pontifically. It was clear that he didn't like being contradicted, at least by me, although he kept saying that I was a critic and had read twenty times more crime stories than he had even heard of, so why come to him, and so on." Symons thought America had three important private-eye writers: Hammett, Chandler, and Macdonald. Chandler praised Hammett but not Macdonald, Symons wrote: "This lack of generosity to another writer was untypical, but something about Macdonald's work rankled." When Chandler sent Symons suggestions for his London *Times* list (none of which Symons used), "he remarked that he had 'omitted numerous gentlemen who have paid me the compliment of imitation,' and this was principally a hit at Macdonald." On the *Times* list, Symons noted Macdonald's early debt to Chandler but said he'd since "developed a personal style and feeling" that was "wholly individual"; in addition to *Grin*, Symons cited *The Way Some People Die* and *The Barbarous Coast*. ("Less surprisingly," Millar modestly noted to von Auw, "he listed M's *Beast in View*.")

Given his rising critical and publishing stock, Millar resurrected a favorite plan: if he taught creative writing at a university, he'd have the financial freedom to write books without Archer. The chance for such employment seemed obviously present in Santa Barbara. Millar's friend Kenner (still on sabbatical) was head of the UCSB English department; Pearce, who'd idolized Millar for twenty years, was acting chairman. Millar's rapport with guest lecturers McLuhan and Davie gave him even more reason to think UCSB was ideal for him. Late in the year he started lobbying for a job.

The English department was a treacherous place in Kenner's absence, though, with hard-fought turf scuffles and (in Claire Stump's phrase) "a dagger behind every velvet curtain." Pearce supported Millar's bid for employment but was opposed by Marvin Mudrick, who'd also blocked UCSB from hiring Marshall McLuhan. Notorious for his scathing fiction critiques in the *Hudson Review,* Mudrick was not among those who thought Millar made literature out of the detective story. He told Pearce he regarded Ken Millar as a man trapped and victimized by an inferior art form. "Marvin loathed Ken," Pearce said. "Loathed, hated, and despised him." "Oh, *sure,*" Mudrick said sarcastically of Millar to Donald Davie, "I *love* to associate with the ruins of once-great minds."

Davie felt caught in the middle between the pro- and anti-Millar factions, he said: "I had a bad time as sort of the visiting character, with both sides trying to enlist me to say yea or no. I think I was used by the anti-Ken lobby in a way that I wasn't aware of at the time. I seem to remember that at their instigation I actually spoke to him and said, 'Back off, Ken.' Didn't like it. That rather spoiled the end of the year."

Mudrick next went to work on Pearce, who agreed with Mudrick that the English department needed drastic overhaul. But Millar was friendly with teachers who had to go, Mudrick said; if hired, he'd polarize and destroy the department, trying to play peacemaker between the forward-thinking newcomers and the targeted "dinosaurs." Pearce was forced to concede: "If Ken had a social friendship with somebody, he wasn't going to falsify it when he became a colleague; it would have been impossible." In a maneuver worthy of a Shakespearean intriguer, Mudrick used Millar's integrity against him in persuading his best friend to deny him a job.

Pearce brought the bad news. Millar took it angrily. Walking Hendry's Beach with Pearce, he spurned the university that spurned him. Face contorted in rage, he declared, "I hereby re-*nounce* that institution!"

Proving Mudrick correct, though, Millar wouldn't renounce his friends. He didn't break with Pearce, not over this. And when Davie left town for his next academic post, Millar alone among his Santa Barbara chums showed up at the bus station to see him off.

That sort of unannounced generosity was typical of Millar, Dick Lid learned. Lid, another new UCSB faculty member hired by Kenner, came with wife Betty to Santa Barbara from Michigan in 1958, when Lid was thirty; after renting awhile, the Lids bought a small house. "Not having much money," Lid said, "I was getting a trailer to move everything myself over a very long day. Ken knew what day it would be, and my God, he just showed up to help me."

Lid first met Millar at the Pearces', where Lid recognized Millar as author of the best Ph.D. dissertation he'd ever read. Seeking a model for his own doctoral work a year or so earlier in Ann Arbor, Lid had found

"Coleridge and the Inward Eye" among dozens of otherwise dismal theses in the Michigan stacks. "It was so beautifully written," Lid recalled. "I went back over to Angell Hall to the person in the English department I was doing my dissertation under and said, 'Who *is* this Kenneth Millar?' And they said with a lotta contempt, 'Oh, he's a *mystery* writer.' " Millar became one of Lid's first California friends, and a guide to his new town.

"Santa Barbara was a strange community to live in," Lid said, "at least in those days. Had that kind of crazy small-town feel. Tom Storke, who gave the land for UCSB, was the owner of the town newspaper; he'd walk down main street wearing his Boy Scout or Highway Patrol–type peaked cap, and you could say, 'Hello, Mr. Storke'—and he would stop and *talk* to you! It wasn't like living in Canoga Park or one of these other nameless, sprawling communities; if you were living in Santa Barbara, you were someone *special*. It was full of seeming Bohemians with money who lived up in the hills. I'd never conceived of anyone having such wealth as the sort of money-people I encountered in Santa Barbara. Walking near the Biltmore with Ken one time, we stepped over the bodies of two multimillionaires on the beach: both of them dead drunk at ten-thirty in the morning."

The Millars were happy in their snug house on Camino de la Luz, but their lease was expiring, and the house was not for sale. Having lived here a year without incident and finally able to sell their Menlo Park property (it's nice to note a Mrs. Hammett played a part in that Bay Area deal), they made their Santa Barbara move permanent by buying a home in the wooded, low-rent section of high-class Montecito.

Chelham Way, their new street, was off Sycamore Canyon. The house at 840 was small but nice enough, with a narrow garden in back and a ravine that became a creek in summer. The Millars moved in on December 1, 1958. Millar built himself a downstairs apartment with bath in part of the garage, laying the plumbing himself. As if to publicly declare his presence in town, Millar put his name, address, and telephone number in the Santa Barbara Yellow Pages, where it stayed listed for years, the sole entry (between "Wrecking Contractors" and "X-Ray Apparatus") under "Writers."

Like all the Millars' houses, Chelham Way was modestly furnished; for Ken and Margaret, the only essentials were bookcases. "Material things never mattered to them," Betty Lid said. "The sofa would look like it belonged in an office anteroom. But they had a great sense of place because they worked at home, and you just didn't call during those hours."

"They weren't together that much," noticed Dick Lid, who visited often. "Maggie was a very early riser, and she'd be through writing by noon; Ken didn't write until after noon. So they had their days organized that way; it was a very circumscribed life. Her path in the afternoon was to the Coral Casino and then home. She wanted to shield herself. I usually went to Chelham Way alone and at night. There was a lower lanai level that was enclosed; Ken and I used to sit down there and talk, drink beer or whisky, play Ping-Pong. It was a very relaxing type of evening. We spoke a lot about Fitzgerald, and some about Hemingway. And Faulkner. I remember Ken saying, 'If you want to see great structuring of a book, look at *Sanctuary:* he saves the story of Popeye's life for the final chapter. Now that takes skill.' "

The Millars had been at Chelham Way a month and a half when CBS-TV's *Pursuit* broadcast its one-hour, live version of "Find the Woman." Michael Rennie starred as Rogers, with Rick Jason, Sally Forrest, Joan Bennett, and Rip Torn in support. Millar thought the show poorly done; when its woman producer hinted she might want to do an Archer series, he was noncommittal. A query from New York intrigued him, though: a theater producer affiliated with Dashiell Hammett's friend Lillian Hellman had read *The Galton Case* and told von Auw that Archer would be great for TV ("he thinks that this is the most imaginative character, etc., etc. since Sam Spade"). Millar spent a couple months working up story ideas, but this New York operator's conditions proved so onerous the author finally cut off talks. West Coast nibbles at Archer from Screen Gems and MCA-TV also came to naught, reinforcing Millar's caution.

"His opinion," said Pearce, "was that Hollywood people were not to be trusted; that you had to scrutinize, with the help of a good lawyer, every sort of dealing with them because they just wanted to get their mitts on your material and exploit it any way they could. And he said there was nobody worse in the whole commercial entertainment industry than these television people." Pearce witnessed Millar "negotiating" by phone with one such type: "He was sitting on his living room sofa, chewing out this person in the most sarcastic terms. Ken was getting *wryer* and *wryer:* 'So that is *all* you are going to offer me, is it? Here I am a writer of a *dozen* books, and you think I will fall all *over* you and be thrilled and delighted to have you *milk* everything you can *get* out of me? I know the kinds of terms you people set up, and they've gotta be an awful lot better than they are right *now* before you will interest *me.*' He got much rougher than that, ending up sort of firmly nasty before hanging up the receiver with a harsh *clack.*" As visions of a Lew Archer show vanished, ABC (as Millar read in the MWA newsletter) planned production of a series based on Chandler's Philip Marlowe.

Raymond Chandler was elected president of the Mystery Writers of America in February, succeeding Rex Stout (who'd succeeded Margaret Millar). The honor came just in time. Chandler died of bronchial pneumonia in March. His affairs were in disarray. Hasty arrangements led to his being buried at San Diego in a virtual pauper's grave. Only seventeen mourners (including Ned Guymon) were present as Raymond Chandler was put to rest in Mount Hope, the same cemetery where Jack and Annie Millar buried a stillborn daughter in 1913.

Three days after Chandler's death, James Sandoe (the critic who'd first brought Macdonald to Chandler's disapproving attention) reviewed *The Galton Case* in the *New York Herald Tribune;* Sandoe wrote, "There has been a singularly involving excitement about Ross Macdonald's recent novels that is difficult to describe save by saying that the last page leads one back to the first all over again. It is a curious, provocative, often unattractive milieu but one compulsively present and quite possibly more real, in its pinch and propulsion, than every day. Whatever the condition of the spell, gritty and compassionate, angry and dismayed, it is a proper enchantment."

Other reviewers, from the *San Francisco Chronicle* to the *New Yorker,* gave *The Galton Case* ringing endorsements. Oddly, though, Tony Boucher, usually Macdonald's biggest fan, was less than enthusiastic about *Galton,* apparently because of its cover notes: "For the jacket of Ross Macdonald's new novel, *The Galton Case,* his publisher has supplied ecstatic blurbing: 'a novelist of explosive excitement . . . a rising master of a complex and colorful art . . . speaks to people of all sorts, powerfully and imaginatively, about the basic hopes and dreads of life.' Such remarks are not mere blurb-burbling but perfectly true; and my only complaint is with, 'We feel that this book achieves a new maturity'—Macdonald has been this good for ten years now, and I'm glad his publisher has finally noticed it. . . . Some of Archer's other cases (notably last year's *The Doomsters*) have seemed to me to impinge more directly on 'the basic hopes and dreads.' " Shockingly, Boucher omitted *Galton* from his 1959 "best of the year" lists in the *New York Times.*

Knopf promoted *Galton* with a good ad in the *Times Book Review,* but a week after publication Alfred reported only thirty-five hundred copies had been shipped: a decline even from *The Doomsters*'s disappointing advance sale. "For some reason this struck me as laughable," Millar wrote von Auw. "So did Boucher's review, probably because I wrote that blurb myself. If Boucher ever found out, he'd have a cat-fit. He probably got mad because he wasn't, for once, quoted on the jacket," while Sandoe and others were. "We'll have to remember that next time."

Despite *Galton*'s poor showing, Millar was in no mood to complain. As he told von Auw, "One way and another, I do feel my name is being made, and the hard way is really more interesting than the easy way. Am I getting wise, or punchy?" He had a new non-Archer manuscript under way, Margaret's latest novel *(The Listening Walls)* was getting fine notices, and thanks to his Pocket Books deal Millar was out of debt for the first time in three years. Best of all, as Millar wrote von Auw in March, "Lin's doing extremely well at school—head student in her Psychology course, for instance, and a very interesting person all around. I believe we're all over the hump, and trust that isn't hybris."

But the doomsters were waiting in the wings.

"What is man?" the tragic poet asks through a Lear or a Hamlet, and answers: A being who can learn through suffering. Suffering does not teach, perhaps; it does induce a willingness to learn.
—Kenneth Millar, *San Francisco Chronicle*, July 1959

To paraphrase an old line from THE GREEN HAT, the Millars are never let off anything.
—Ivan von Auw, July 1959

It was true that Linda was doing well academically at UC Davis: she earned entry to an honor society in her freshman year. But within two months of taking up residence on the conservative Davis campus, she violated the school's behavior code. After partying one night in town with a couple of air force fellows, she came back to school drunk and was campused ("I can assure you that's the last time I'll ever miss my lockout," she wrote her parents, who weren't told the worst of it). In January 1958 (near the accident's two-year anniversary), Linda was again drunk at school and put under official censure. Once more she promised to behave and on her own initiative began consulting a Sacramento psychiatrist. In May 1959, though, as finals week approached, she was seen drinking beer in a dorm stairwell and reprimanded by the dean, who scheduled the incident for disciplinary committee review. Linda was sure (despite the dean's reassurance) she'd be expelled, causing her to violate probation and be sent to jail. Her psychiatrist thought a desire to be punished caused her to get into trouble; then when trouble occurred, she panicked. In May a schoolfriend told the dean that Linda was "falling apart." Her Sacramento doctor warned that if that hearing wasn't canceled, Linda would likely run away or commit suicide; she was already asking him to "hide her out."

Her parents didn't know much of this, partly because Linda begged the dean not to tell them, partly because her doctors felt it crucial she keep some psychological distance from her folks. Don Pearce recalled an occasion before she went to college when Ken Millar seemed to smother Linda with fatherly concern: "I was driving the two of them somewhere, with Linda in the backseat and Ken in the front, when Linda made some fairly routine little self-disparaging reference to 'my typical way of goofing up.' Ken turned around immediately and grabbed her hand and held it and talked over anything she was saying, and kept on talking, about how it wasn't her fault, how everything was fine, she was perfectly okay, he understood better than anybody and she was back with him and it was all swell again, and she need not feel any guilt and he knew *why* she would feel that way. It came in waves, and it just kept on coming as he held her hand tightly, turned fully around in his seat. His concern was understandable enough, but in my opinion she did not *need* that much assurance. She had only made a simple remark, something a teenager might ordinarily say, especially one who'd been through something; but it seemed to have opened oceans of concern for Ken. I felt he was overdoing it; it should have been just a pat on the shoulder. Instead she then had to handle *his* concern, so to speak, inside of herself."

On the other hand, once Linda was at Davis, the Millars perhaps over-estimated how well she was coping. But as parents in more than one Macdonald book say, *You can't live their lives for them; you can't lock them in their rooms forever.*

In her intensifying anxiety fugue, Linda accepted a spur-of-the-moment invitation on Saturday, May 30, to drive with a nonstudent she knew and his male friend to the Harrah's casino at Stateline on the Nevada border, a hundred miles east. Signing out of her dorm, she lied and said she was going to Sacramento. At 7 P.M. Linda drove off in a white Simca sports car. Like the other Hughes Hall residents, she was expected back by 2:30 A.M.

When she hadn't returned by Sunday morning, her house mother informed the dean of women and telephoned Linda's parents. Linda had missed lockout before; campus people honored the Millars' request not to publicize her absence. But probation officials had to be told. The Santa Barbara judge in Linda's case issued an all-points bulletin for her as a probation violator, which the *News-Press* reported. Monday came, then Tuesday (the Millars' twenty-first anniversary), with no sign of Linda. On Wednesday, Ken Millar took a United flight to Sacramento, bound to find his daughter.

At the Davis campus, Millar spoke with Linda's girlfriends, learned of her disturbed frame of mind and of the quick departure to Harrah's. He went to Stateline, Nevada, checked in at the El Dorado Motel, and contacted law enforcement officers in Stateline and the nearby towns of Lake Tahoe, Reno, and Carson City. Millar got a Reno doctor to monitor admissions at psychiatric hospitals: maybe Linda would find her way to such a clinic—if she hadn't taken off with someone in a car or met with foul play. "S.B. police should forward full teletype with description marked Attention Reno P.D.," Millar noted in a daybook, "(and I think too Salt Lake City, Las Vegas, & San Francisco). *Also* fingerprints to all interested stations. Maggie send *all available pictures* to me by special delivery at El Dorado Motel, Stateline Calif."

Lew Archer's creator needed a private eye. Police and casino security referred Millar to Armand Girola of Reno's National Detective Agency: a two-person team of Girola and wife Thelma, also a licensed PI. During the week the Girolas tracked down losers who ducked out on casino debts; on weekends they held a pro bono people's court for their working-class neighborhood. Girola was short and nondescript: "good and gentle," Millar noted, "profoundly offended by violence." (Macdonald later based the semi-recurring character of Archer's Nevada colleague Arnie Walters on Girola: "He was a short broad man in his early fifties who looked like somebody you'd see selling tips at a race track. But he had the qualities of a first-rate detective: honesty, imagination, curiosity, and a love of people. Ten or twelve years in Reno had left him poor and uncorrupted.") Millar hired him. The writer and the detective went together to Sacramento; and on Friday, June 5, at Woodland, near Davis, interviewed one of the men who'd taken Lin to Stateline.

This fellow told them what he'd told police: he and his friend had picked up Linda at 7 P.M. Saturday and driven in the friend's Simca toward Nevada, stopping en route to buy two six-packs of beer, which they drank in the car. They reached Stateline around eleven and went straight to Harrah's. At eleven-thirty Linda was anxious to start back for her lockout; the driver was gambling and put her off. Linda grew upset. When her friend wouldn't hot-wire his buddy's car and take her back alone, she left to find another ride. Around 5 A.M. one of the men finally went looking for Linda but didn't find her.

Millar was disgusted with Linda's "friend" (a married man) and hoped to press charges, but that could wait. He paid Girola a hundred sixty dollars cash, and the detective returned to Reno-Tahoe to search for Linda Millar stayed in Sacramento, to convince the university people Linda was absent through no fault of her own; he hoped to counter stories in the Santa Barbara press implying she was a runaway.

Saturday morning he met with Linda's Sacramento psychiatrist, who told him school officials had ignored his pleas that they hospitalize Linda. Her Santa Barbara psychiatrist suggested that Linda, acting on a "self-debasing tendency," might be looking for work as a waitress or chambermaid. The Girolas followed up several such leads: the young woman with brown hair and a slight stutter who asked for a maid's job at the Totem Pole Motel on Tahoe Vista, the "Lin" who applied as a waitress at a Truckee restaurant, the lone female who turned up at the Tahoe Tavern. None panned out. Millar was relieved when nothing came of a more awful chance: the Girolas viewed the nude corpse of a young woman found near Lake Mead and reported it wasn't Linda.

It was seven days since she'd left Davis. A frantic, frustrated, angry Millar showed up at eight o'clock Saturday night at the Yolo County sheriff's office in Woodland and confronted Lieutenant James L. Gorman, who wrote, "Mr. Millar (missing girl's father) came into this office stating he was quite dissatisfied with the progress the authorities were making in the search for his daughter. He was informed that we were trying to keep her disappearance as quiet as possible to save the girl any undue publicity. He disagreed, stating he wanted it publicized, because he definitely believed there was possibility of foul play. He stated why keep it quiet here when it is in all the Santa Barbara and Los Angeles papers. I told him it was O.K. if he wanted it that way and I turned Mr. Millar over to a newspaper

reporter, Mr. Bob Slayman, who was in the sheriff's office at the time."
Slayman, of the *Woodland Democrat,* had time to write and file a brief piece
for his Sunday paper. Millar then had Gorman phone the head of the
Santa Barbara probation office at home at 9:30 P.M. and advise him that as
far as the Woodland police knew, Linda had had no intention of not
returning to Davis when she left.

Millar continued his campaign for press coverage Saturday night, calling Reno and Sacramento papers and TV stations. Bill Hogan, the *Chronicle* book editor, was startled to get a late-night call from Millar at his home
in Mill Valley: "He said, 'Look, can any of your people try and get a line on
Linda?' He thought she was somewhere between Santa Barbara and Reno.
I said, 'Ken, what about the Highway Patrol?' He says, 'Oh, yeah yeah, I've
done all that.' He was hoping some *journalist* might track down this girl. I
thought to myself, 'My God, this sounds like a Ross Macdonald novel'—
you know: 'Get a *newspaper* guy on this.' "

In fact it was like two specific Macdonald novels: *The Barbarous Coast,* in
which Archer combs a casino town for a missing young woman, and the
current *The Galton Case* (set partly in Reno), where a distraught father waits
word of a daughter last seen in a northern California city. A couple of Macdonald short stories also involved vanished girls: the recently televised
"Find the Woman" had a missing daughter, "The Suicide" a sister missing
in Nevada. Current events in Millar's life were even more eerily similar to
ideas in recent plot notebooks, where the teenager-gone-from-college
notion had replaced the hit-and-run theme as the story Millar now most
often toyed with. Some of Margaret's books foreshadowed Linda's new
trouble too: 1952's *Rose's Last Summer* had a daughter named Lora who
vanished; her latest, *The Listening Walls,* involved a missing woman.

Don Pearce came to Sacramento to give Millar moral support. Millar
especially wanted Pearce with him for a Sunday-morning meeting with the
UC Davis chancellor and the college's public relations officer; the presence of UC professor Pearce would show Millar's standing and give weight
to his demands. "Ken was his usual darkly defensive self," Pearce recalled.
"He said, 'What have you *done* here at the university to *find* Linda? What
have you done to *cause* this thing to happen to her, anyway?' And the chancellor said to him, 'I have to point out to you, Mr. Millar, sorry as we are
about all this, you can't *a priori* consider the university at fault in this
instance.' It depended what a person meant by 'at fault' and so on, and he
said, 'And that is a question of semantics.' And Ken said, 'Don't try using
expressions like *semantics* on me! I know what semantics are, I took a whole
year of *study* in semantics, I know *all* about it! Don't try using fancy terms
on *me!*' And he said, 'If my daughter is not found, and if the university
proves to be guilty in this matter, *you will never get over the day that I will make
for you.*' "

The meeting lasted ninety minutes. Millar insisted the chancellor
approve a statement saying the university didn't hold Linda responsible

and wouldn't punish her. The chancellor agreed to this—once Millar assured him that Linda wouldn't be returning to Davis as a student. Millar handwrote the school's "press release" himself: "Linda is not a runaway from college as we thought at first, and she will be welcomed back to the university without disciplinary action. Having knowledge of her medical condition, we are deeply concerned for her safety and anxious to have any word of her." Later Millar had Pearce pen a detailed account of the meeting. "He was really considering suing the University of California for gross negligence," Pearce said. "Oh, he was beside himself, beside himself. I remember him saying to me in low, tense, slow, enraged tones, 'If Linda ends up *bumped off,* I will *shake this university* to its *foundations.*'"

Armed with his press release, Millar went to work getting coverage of the disappearance. He gave interviews on Sunday to half a dozen print reporters, including wire service reps. On Monday the story broke. The case of the missing coed made front-page headlines from Sacramento to Hollywood. Even New York papers picked it up: "Mystery Writer's Toughest Case—Daughter Vanishes."

Linda was described as a vulnerable, guilt-haunted girl who'd panicked when she didn't get back on time. Millar told of the accident and his daughter's emotional state; many stories quoted her Sacramento psychiatrist. All papers published a ghostly head shot of Linda in which she seemed to stare blankly into the uncertain future: *She is 5 feet 6 inches tall, weighs 135 pounds, has medium length brown hair with an artificial reddish tinge and has dark hazel eyes. When last seen she was wearing a black sweater and black skirt and high-heeled, light-colored, plastic shoes and was carrying a white basket-type purse.*

More information came in about Linda's actions on Saturday night and Sunday morning. A Sacramento man who'd known Linda at Davis telephoned Lieutenant Gorman and told of being with her from 1 A.M. until 3 A.M. in a casino and then at a motel party. She was drinking heavily, angry at the men who'd brought her to Stateline, and asked this fellow to drive her to Davis; when he said no, she asked if he'd take her to Wyoming. When he said no again, she left to find some cowboys she'd seen at a gambling table; maybe *they'd* take her to Wyoming.

Another call tipped Gorman to the Sun and Sands Motel in Tahoe, where an employee described a girl fitting Linda's description being with a party of three Salt Lake City insurance men until checkout time Sunday. The girl placed three phone calls from their room, including one to the Matson steamship line in San Francisco. Linda's panicky urge to flee must have been escalating.

Millar theorized scenarios: she may have tried to hitchhike to Davis on Highway 50 or gotten on a free bus returning casino customers to the Bay Area. "She could be anyplace in the United States," he told a reporter, "if she is still alive."

The newspaper stories and photograph caused a deluge of calls to the

Woodland sheriff's office on Monday, June 8. People all over the country claimed to have seen Linda Millar. Many were cranks, but Monday afternoon, with Millar there, a Teletype message came into Gorman's office from the Hollywood LAPD that looked like a real break. An employee at the Hollywood Ranch Market on Vine Street claimed to have cashed a ten-dollar check for Linda on Friday. It was the first indication in nine days she was alive. Millar wept.

There were problems with this story: supposedly Linda showed a UCLA ID and a California driver's license; Millar thought he'd destroyed her license under court order. But this was their only lead, and Millar would follow it. He made several calls: to a Sacramento lawyer, arranging to cover any and all checks Linda wrote; to friends in Santa Barbara, for help in LA; to an airline and to a Hollywood hotel. "You know," he told Slayman of the Woodland paper (who wrote that Millar was "obviously fatigued by the more than five days and nights of personal investigation"), "there haven't been many pleasant things about this past week, but I'll never forget the sincere concern and help of so many strangers." He especially praised Gorman.

Before leaving Woodland, Millar drafted an impassioned message to Linda, which was printed and broadcast throughout California and Nevada on Tuesday:

> Come home, dear, if you read this. You have nothing to fear from anybody. Everybody involved in this just wants to see you safe. The situation was misunderstood at first. But now the various authorities, college and otherwise, recognize that your apparent runaway was due to circumstances beyond your control. I cried with joy and relief when I learned you are alive. You're the person we love most. Did you ever doubt it? You're afraid; you must be afraid, or you'd have come home long since. Believe me, there's nothing to be afraid of. We need your help, too. The best help you could give would be to call me at the Knickerbocker Hotel, or call Maggie at home. Faith can move mountains, you know, but most of the mountains you may feel you have to climb alone are mole hills under a magnifying glass and you're not going to have to climb them alone. I am one hundred per cent for you and I wouldn't trade you for any other daughter in the world.

Millar took a 7:10 P.M. Convair flight from Sacramento to Burbank, then a cab to the police station in Hollywood where Dick and Betty Lid waited. Lid had driven the Millars' black Ford convertible from Santa Barbara, with Betty following in the Lids' white Chevrolet. "I had to teach the next day," Lid said. "We spent a few hours with him at the police station, staying as late as we could. I talked with the detectives a bit, although Betty and I hadn't even met Linda." Millar gave the police names of Southland acquaintances his daughter might contact, and the cops told him which

Hollywood clubs drew young people: Cosmo Alley, the Lamp, Sancho Panza, Pandora's Box (that one jumped out at him).

Millar stayed at the Hollywood Knickerbocker, one of the hotels Maggie'd lived in when she worked at Warners. Al Stump found him pacing the floor there when Stump showed up with two hundred dollars Millar had asked him to bring: "He was almost out of his mind, because people kept phoning and saying they'd seen Linda." The check-cashing tale, Millar's open letter to Linda, and his flight to LA kept "the mystery of the mystery writer's daughter" statewide front-page news on Tuesday: "Missing Coed in LA," "Hunted Girl in Hollywood," "Dad's Plea to Missing Girl." The story was on every TV and radio news broadcast in southern California.

Hundreds of alleged sightings were reported all over LA. A bartender in a saloon on Western thought Linda Millar had been a weekend customer. Workers in a Santa Monica appliance store said they'd consoled a depressed young woman who looked like Linda. Someone at a Thrifty's on North Vermont recalled a patron who might have been the Millar girl. Five staff members at the Santa Monica YWCA insisted she'd registered there under another name; Millar saw the application card and said it wasn't her writing. "There were a lot of disappointments like that," Stump said. "It was agonizing for Ken."

Millar had gone a week without sleep. The *Hollywood Citizen-News* published an alarming front-page photo of him: unshaven, heavy-lidded, and ashen-faced, he looked near death. Still he pushed himself: coordinating with Hollywood police, consulting by phone with lawyer Jerry Geisler (who'd defended Lana Turner's teenaged daughter for stabbing hoodlum Johnny Stompanato) about suing the *LA Mirror* for libel, giving more interviews. "I'm afraid she is trying to sink out of sight," he told one reporter, "after a long, mounting emotional crisis in which she was not given assistance by anyone, probably including myself."

Officers searched the Southland "from Santa Monica to Torrance" for Linda Millar, but the best lead remained the Vine Street check-cashing that had swung the search from Stateline to Hollywood. That market photographed all check customers. The *Citizen-News* arranged to examine a huge roll of film showing four thousand patrons. Millar and Stump waited while it was scrutinized. Linda wasn't on it. The lead was false. There was no reason now to believe Linda had ever been in Hollywood—or was even alive.

Stump stayed by the Knickerbocker telephone Tuesday afternoon while a devastated Millar went to TV station KTLA for one last attempt at reaching his daughter. Granting an LAPD request, Channel 5 was interrupting its regular programming ("Skipper Frank"'s 4 P.M. cartoon show) for an appeal to be carried by special hookup over several California stations. After a brief introduction, Millar pleaded for Linda's return.

When he came off camera, he was handed a message: telephone Mr. Stump at the Knickerbocker immediately. From there, Stump gave him an urgent instruction: call Maggie at home right away. Millar was put through to Santa Barbara, where Margaret and her sister had been taking turns keeping vigil by the telephone. A near-hysterical Maggie spoke with Ken. Millar scrawled on the back of a Channel 5 logsheet:

> *The Stag*—a bar
> Reno, Nevada
> FA 39665
> wants to come home

As he told it later, Millar reached Armand Girola and gave him the location, then phoned the Reno bar and talked to Linda until the Girolas got to her.

His relief was enormous, but the crisis wasn't over. Earlier this day the Santa Barbara judge, because of Linda's supposed presence in LA, ordered a bench warrant for her arrest—"for Linda's own protection," he insisted; it didn't mean she'd be punished for violating parole. Millar didn't buy that. There was a warrant out for Linda; if police found her, she'd be arrested. He wanted his daughter in a doctor's care, not a jail cell.

Millar made plans with the Girolas, then enlisted Stump's aid. He'd leave his Ford with Stump and sneak on a flight to Santa Barbara. If asked, Stump would say Millar went home for a family emergency.

Exiting the hotel room on his way out of town, Millar was surprised by a TV film crew. "They were standing in the corridor outside," Stump said, "waiting to grab some footage as soon as he opened the door; that's how they did it back then. Ken got a flash look at them, and he went out that door like a tiger; I've never seen anyone move so fast. He took this guy by the crotch and the front of the shirt and threw him down the hall, sent him crashing into all his equipment." LA papers did what they could with Millar's sudden departure ("Mystery Writer Disappears, Adds to Confusion Over Missing Girl"), but his secret held.

Linda spent a restless Tuesday night at the Girolas' Reno home while her father flew to Santa Barbara and stayed out of sight. Five-thirty Wednesday morning Millar called Dick Lid from a pay phone on a street corner not far from Lid's house in the San Roque area and asked if he'd drive him to pick up Linda.

"The answer of course is yes," Lid recalled. "I pick him up on upper State Street—I don't even know how he got there—and off we go in the Chevy. Ken was very very scared that the Highway Patrol would discover Linda in Nevada, or even in California, before we could return to Santa Barbara where there was a friendly probation officer to help her, and that she'd be incarcerated. I think that was the reason for the secrecy; it was as if I was being sworn not to reveal the event. We took back roads, at least they were to me. I remember Castaic, and changing roads to go into the desert; remember, there was no inland 101 at this point in time. I was driving our 1956 Chevy convertible, white, with continental rear; God I loved that car! I had no desert or semidesert experience—California was new to me—so I didn't even know where I was, but I thought for sure the radiator would explode, or we'd boil over or blow a tire. I was surprised my Chevy took the beating so well, because I drove between eighty and ninety miles per hour the whole way."

They reached Girola's prearranged meeting place on the outskirts of Bishop, California, before noon. "It was at a park or a grove, or what in the Middle West we call a forest preserve," said Lid. "The detective and Linda were already there. Ken and the detective talked for maybe five minutes, then Linda transferred to the backseat of my car, then Ken. They sat there and talked very quietly for ten, maybe fifteen minutes. Then Ken says, 'Let's go.' We were back in Santa Barbara around five-thirty or six P.M. I must have driven close to a thousand miles that day. I went into the house with the two of them, at Ken's request; I think he didn't know what to expect at the mother-daughter reunion. It became embarrassing, and I left."

Linda and Maggie were both sedated under a doctor's care; Thursday night Linda entered UCLA Medical Center for ten days' psychiatric treatment. On Thursday, Millar met with reporters and said his daughter had suffered "some kind of psychic break": "She doesn't remember anything well for a period of a week or more. She has a rather dim memory of having been wandering around." As he related it, Linda was in "deep depression" when she heard a description of herself on the radio and said, "That's me." Later she read a newspaper account of her disappearance, which caused her to call home. The problem now, Millar said, "is to convince her that authorities and the world in general are not against her."

The warrant for her arrest was withdrawn after the Millars posted a twenty-five-hundred-dollar cash bail (mostly borrowed from friends). The judge ordered a probation department investigation into her disappearance, in the course of which Linda handwrote a statement (never publicly released) setting forth events as she recalled them:

> I do know I tried my hardest to get back to Davis on time and I know I had every intention of returning. I was pretty upset . . . and I was panicky. I never even thought of phoning in. If I had been thinking clearly I would have.
>
> Sometime during the evening I met someone who I think gave me some silver dollars. . . . The next memory I have is of being in someone's car—an elderly man's. I might have asked him to take me to Davis but I don't remember. But we ended up somewhere along the lake in his cabin which was very isolated. I think I was hysterical but I'm not sure. I think I remember being terribly afraid to return to Davis but this was after I'd failed to get a ride back. I must have lost my head after being stranded. I didn't mean to run away I'm sure of that.

When we got to his cabin he tried to make love to me but I refused and he didn't press the issue. The next day he said I could use his cabin for a while while he went away on business. I don't know how long I was there—probably 4 to 6 days. It seemed as if I were in a dream or a nightmare there. I didn't know quite what I was doing there, nor do I remember thinking about home, parents, or friends or school. I was afraid to leave the cabin, because I kept thinking things were coming in after me. . . . I knew I had to get out of the cabin. . . . I walked to a store and asked the proprietor for a ride to state line. Why I didn't ask for a ride to Sacramento I don't know. . . . I'm not sure how this was all arranged but he did take me to Carson City. I don't think I was there long before someone with dark hair took me to Reno. I remember wandering around Reno a lot—in and out of places. . . . I remember the click click of slot machines and hundreds of people.

It must have been when I first entered Reno that I met a blond young man. I was probably desperate for a place to sleep so I let him take me to his hotel room. He tried to make love to me that night but I refused to let him. I had a bad case of hysteria. I guess it was the next day that I let him make love to me. My resistance must have been down or I wouldn't have. Afterwards he left me and never came back. I stayed in that room for maybe two days without leaving, without eating.

When I'd almost lost all my strength I knew I had to eat something or I'd be very sick. I remember buying a meal somewhere, and wandering around Reno for a while, and meeting a nice old man. I can't remember what I told him but he knew I was alone without money or friends. He bought me a room in his hotel. I think he fixed up an arrangement of some sort with the landlord whom he knew. It seemed as if I were there for a very long time but I think it was just for a few days. One night I heard my description over the radio and it didn't seem real. But after I heard it I think I got very upset and told this man my name and that I was missing. I always knew who I was and that I was gone but it didn't really seem real to me until I heard my description.

The next day when he brought me food he brought a newspaper and I saw a picture of me on the front page as well as headlines. All of a sudden my mind cleared and it hit me: what was I doing alone in a room in Reno. The first thing I thought of doing was running to the nearest police station and turning myself in, but the man thought that wouldn't be a good idea. He even offered to buy my plane ticket home but I thought it would be better to notify my parents immediately, tell them I was all right, and ask them how I should come home.

So I got to the nearest telephone which was at the back of a bar and phoned my mother. I told her I'd stay there until she found out what to do from my father. So I sat there until my father phoned me and told me to wait there until a private detective and his wife picked me up. . . .

It's hard for me to write this and I keep getting confused as to some of the things that happened. . . . But I do know I didn't do anything wrong while I was gone. Oh and I wasn't in Los Angeles. There would have been something about it I would have remembered if I had.

The probation people didn't press Linda further, nor did the judge at the brief hearing in which he gave her a suspended sentence and extended and modified her probation, allowing her to discontinue college, live in Los Angeles, work as an aide at a Santa Monica hospital, and get psychiatric treatment at UCLA. It's possible to believe Millar helped his daughter with her story, as he may have coached her with her accident account. Lid said, "I personally don't believe Linda called home. Girola found her, or his wife did, in Reno; they initially placed the call, then Linda talked to Ken or Maggie or both." Her seeing a newspaper with an account of her disappearance is strikingly similar to an incident in *The Barbarous Coast*. Yet things may have happened exactly as the court was told, in ironic counterpoint to the Millars' fiction.

Certainly Millar's frantic odyssey took the same sort of acute trajectory as Lew Archer in breaking a case: from Santa Barbara to Davis and Sacramento, to Stateline and Tahoe and Reno, to LA, to Santa Barbara, to Bishop, back to Santa Barbara to close the circle. He covered two states, and the enormous publicity he generated was at least partly responsible for Linda's return. He'd been at his desperate best, and everyone he encountered (cops, reporters, doctors, lawyers) was moved by his devotion and grit. Millar for his part was moved by the kindness of strangers; he told Margaret's Random House editor, "Trouble can help to solidify one's relationship with the human race."

He paid a high price for those ten days. Millar's blood pressure soared alarmingly, and he was hospitalized for two weeks in June. Doctors diagnosed severe hypertension, kidney stones, and heart damage; he'd suffered a sort of stroke. When Bob Easton saw him in the hospital, he thought Millar was about to die. But, taking nine medicines a day, Millar came back to health. He'd stopped his ocean swims when he moved up north, but he vowed to resume them. Even before he left the hospital, he was back at work, revising the Coleridge book.

He couldn't afford to stop writing; he was in financial straits again. His and Linda's medical expenses were running five hundred dollars a week. Millar had to get money. He'd resolved never to deal with Hollywood agent H. N. Swanson again, but now, "on the spur of a rather desperate moment," he called Eddie Carter of the Swanson agency and asked if any movie or TV interest could be drummed up. Several private-eye shows were on the air or in the works this year (*Richard Diamond, Peter Gunn, 77 Sunset Strip, Markham, Mr. Lucky, Johnny Staccato*, not to mention *Philip Marlowe* and *Mike Hammer*); wouldn't this be an ideal time for a series based on the critically acclaimed Lew Archer books? The best Carter could come up with, though, was the chance of selling some Archer short stories as one-shots to *General Electric Theater.* Coincidentally, an Ober agent in New York was negotiating for an Archer series with Jaemar, Bob Hope's TV producers. The Ober people didn't want their efforts jeopardized by Carter's, so Millar called Carter off. When Jaemar's offer was deemed inadequate, Millar was back where he'd started: broke and in need of cash.

"I have to make some money writing this year," he penned plaintively to Ivan von Auw. It seemed "almost incredible" to him that *The Galton Case* hadn't even earned back its Knopf advance. He'd written the best book he could write, it had got great reviews, but no more than four thousand people had paid three dollars to read it in hardcover. It galled Millar that certain hacks earned fortunes churning out the sort of trash he once threw down the Kitchener sewer. His only way to get more money was to write more novels: for instance, the non-Archer manuscript put aside when Linda had disappeared. Millar finished it and on September 18, mailed to New York the typed text of what would be his fifteenth published book: *The Ferguson Affair.*

Mystery: You say that you've known detectives?
Ross Macdonald: Over the years I've known detectives, yes.
Mystery: Did you go out on investigations with them?
Ross Macdonald: Oh yes.

—Mystery, 1979

THE FERGUSON AFFAIR, by Ross Macdonald (Knopf). Another insanely complicated but rationally resolved chapter in the author's spirited history of night-town southern California—its plethora of journeyman crime (adultery, arson, blackmail, kidnapping, robbery, murder), its population of grotesques (alcoholic millionaires, degenerate starlets, giggling male nurses, psychopathic lifeguards, menopausic lunatics), and its sunbaked, drag-race, leatherette culture. Thoroughly up to standard.

—The New Yorker, 1960

The narrator of Macdonald's first book without Archer in seven years was Bill Gunnarson, a young married attorney and expectant father in the city of Buenavista (not unlike Santa Teresa/Santa Barbara). Gunnarson's court-appointed client is a nurse named Ella, accused of being part of a burglary ring. Gunnarson believes she's essentially innocent, that fear keeps her from saying what she knows. When a pawn-shop owner connected to the thieves is killed, Gunnarson investigates. He looks for Larry Gaines, a country club lifeguard whom Ella dated. Gaines was also involved with one of the club members' wives: an ex-movie actress named Holly May who's married to the blustering, distraught Colonel Ian Ferguson. Gunnarson and Ferguson learn Holly's been kidnapped, apparently by the burglary ring.

Searching for Holly May and Larry Gaines, lawyer Gunnarson proves as able as any Archer at uncovering guilty secrets and family skeletons. He caroms from Beverly Hills to the hinterlands of the Santa Ynez Valley to the equally remote (to him) Hispanic neighborhood of his own town. As Gunnarson explores Buenavista's less privileged sector—"the wrong side of the tracts"—he finds inhabitants united by class, geography, parochial school, and ethnic pride. He's made aware of the gulf between the city's rich and poor, and the wall of distrust separating "the suits" from "the serfs."

On a private level, *The Ferguson Affair* reads like an apologia to the Santa Barbara sector most upset by Linda Millar's accident and the court's apparent refusal to "punish" her. The book pleads forgiveness for the unintended sins of the young. "Everybody's entitled to one big mistake," Gunnarson assures his client; he says of Ella, "Her only crime was lack of judgment." A cop reminds Gunnarson, "You don't judge a man by what he did in his crazy teens. You judge him by his contribution over the long hike." So Millar wished to be judged and to have his daughter judged. A hospitalized Gunnarson almost religiously merges with the lower town's "others" when he receives a blood transfusion from a Hispanic cop.

The question of identity is central to this book too, and Millar draws upon his own past in reconstructing Larry Gaines's. Here again is the suffocating, female-dominated household gripped by religiosity and teetering on hysteria. Gaines is another autobiographical fantasy of what might have become of Millar if his better nature hadn't asserted itself.

Colonel Ferguson, the Scots-Canadian oilman from Alberta, is a quite different imaginary persona of the author's. Like Millar, the colonel's an ex–school gymnast, stubborn, with a bad temper, susceptible to a gloomy view of life; a man who feels like a foreigner in southern California, and who's further alienated through the melodramatic crisis of having a loved one disappear. The colonel sums up his feelings toward his wife with a quote from Catullus, *"Odi et amo. Excrucior":* "I hate her and I love her, and I'm on the rack"—a tag that turns up in so many Ken and Margaret Millar books as to seem their personal motto. In the Fergusons' odd sexual dynamic (the colonel may inadvertently have married his illegitimate daughter), there's the threat of incest.

Ferguson also stands in for Linda Millar. At the height of his despair, the colonel rams his blue Imperial into a truck, laying down two hundred feet of skid marks; when Gunnarson finds him sitting on a curb, nose bleeding, Ferguson confesses that he hit the truck deliberately in a suicide attempt.

In the book's small-town girls gone bad, the author imagines his daughter's future if she'd kept keeping company with "bums." A mother says how hard it is to manage such a child: " 'Have you been lapping up liquor?' . . . She denied it and denied it. . . . I dunno, you can't beat a girl to death. Or lock her up in her room. She would have jumped out the window anyway, that's how wild she was. Drinking and tearing around in cars and shoplifting in the stores and probably worse." There seems to be a lot of Linda Jane in sisters Hilda and June.

The real-life currents shaping Millar's story gave it the subliminal resonance of felt experience, but the "facts" were sealed into a fast book filled with fine descriptive touches. At a talent agent's office, the occupant's name "was tastefully printed on one of the doors in lower-case letters, like a line from a modern poem." At sundown in the barrio, "Evening light ran in the alley like red-stained water. The berries on the Cotoneaster tree were the color of nail polish and blood." Gunnarson, socially ill at ease at the country club, notes, "Some kind of cooked-meat smell was emanating from the clubhouse. Prime ribs of unicorn, perhaps, or breast of phoenix under glass." Of a driver who's just run someone down in the road: "His eyes were headline black." Millar included a private joke about his own headline-making hunt for Linda, having a show-biz type mock Gunnarson: "I've been following your adventures in the newspapers. Greatest thing since Pearl White in *Plunder*." In a different sort of private gesture, Millar dedicated this book written in the quick wake of Linda's recent trouble to someone who had helped him through some of its most desperate hours: Al Stump.

Millar's strength returned in autumn; his blood pressure went back to normal, and the heart damage was reversed. "I am now one of those health bugs who swim a half-mile daily, rain or shine, and never felt better in my life," he informed Knopf in October. Maggie joined Ken in his swimming and lost twenty pounds. Linda was well too, living in a Westwood apartment, working at a Santa Monica hospital, having psychotherapy and hoping to return to college the next year.

Millar began a new decade by starting a new Lew Archer book *(The Wycherly Woman)* on January 4, 1960. When Dorothy Olding visited Santa Barbara in May, Millar took advantage of his agent's presence to unburden himself of several things that had bothered him for years. Walking the beach with Olding, he said he felt like a poor relation on the Ober roster: undervalued and underattended. He needed to be taken more seriously— by readers, by critics, by the agents—and he needed to make some money! He'd be forty-five in December; it was close to now-or-never time. He was doing *his* part: writing better books (let Olding be the judge), "legitimizing" himself with serious reviews for the *San Francisco Chronicle* (and he hoped soon to break into a New York paper), scrambling to get his dissertation between hard covers. Now he wanted Ober to pull their weight. Olding, who handled magazine sales, could be especially helpful: *Cosmopolitan* hadn't bought a novel from him in four years.

Another gripe: Millar felt hamstrung by the ambiguous relations between Ober and their Hollywood rep. For years the Millars thought they were obliged to let H. N. Swanson peddle their work to the studios, lest they jeopardize their Ober relationship. Now the reverse seemed true: Ober's East Coast efforts conflicted with Swanson's, and no one was directing traffic.

Olding took Millar's complaints to heart. She greatly liked Ken Millar (her opinion of him soared during his hunt for Linda), and she admired his work. After reading *The Wycherly Woman* she wrote him, "This may seem like an odd simile, but to me your writing is like delicate porcelain or glass, bright, sharp, clear, yet inherently beautiful. In spite of the fact that your excellent mystery plotting goes on steadily, holding the reader fascinated as the sentences follow each other with an impelling rhythm so suitable to the subject matter, there are underlying cadences of beauty, dropped lightly into the paragraphs. That was what fascinated me so when I first read *The Doomsters*, that while you pulled the reader along with you relentlessly to the end of the mystery, still you managed to show great empathy for your people, for their tragedies and triumphs."

Olding and Millar grew closer. In coming years, the agent would seek both Millars' counsel on key decisions regarding the Ober agency's future; and Millar allowed Dorothy Olding to become an important person in his life. He paid her his highest compliment, said Herb Harker: "Ken said, 'You can *depend* on Dorothy,' in a way that made me realize that was one of the measures by which he gauged people. Because I suppose—I'm just surmising here—some of the key people in his life he'd found he could *not* depend on; there just seemed to be an open wound there."

Millar's allies came through for him strongly in 1960, as if to make up for the nightmare of 1959. When *Ferguson* was published in July (with, as Millar suggested, a Boucher quote prominent on its jacket), Tony Boucher delivered a rave in the *New York Times Book Review,* perhaps his strongest praise yet for Macdonald; Knopf placed an ad in the *New York Herald Tribune* reprinting it in its entirety. And for whatever reasons—a book priced (at $3.50) and perceived as a "novel," the coattail effect of the successful *Perry Mason* TV show, possibly all that publicity from Linda's disappearance—this book with the lawyer hero sold much better than any Archer hardcover. By the end of August, seven thousand books had shipped, with ninety-five hundred in print. The Detective Book Club paid two thousand dollars for *Ferguson.* King Features bought newspaper serialization rights. And the book struck unexpected pay dirt on the West Coast: H. N. Swanson (supervised long-distance by von Auw) peddled film rights to *The Ferguson Affair* for $16,500: Millar's first movie sale. He used the money to pay off a second mortgage ("Happy Day!").

There was more. Von Auw wrote Millar in mid-August with this "rather staggering piece of news": the English house of Collins (Agatha Christie's publisher) agreed to pay a thousand pounds each for British rights to Macdonald's next four books; helping clinch the deal was Knopf's ad quoting Boucher on *Ferguson,* which von Auw had sent to London during negotiations. Still more good news: Macdonald would be published again in France, after a tiff between rival presses had kept him out of print there for the last several years. (Less lucrative but more exotic foreign deals were also made, allowing it to be said that Macdonald's work was available "from Finland to Japan.") Von Auw told his client, "This begins to look like your lucky year."

Millar agreed it was "almost laughably good." His new novel's Colonel Ferguson spoke of the book of life as a giant ledger: "Your good actions and your bad actions, your good luck and your bad luck, balance out. Everything comes back to you. The whole thing works like clockwork." It seemed this was Millar's payback time, with the lucky turns of fate falling into place like tumblers on a winning slot machine.

In October an invigorated Millar went with Margaret on his first trip to New York since 1946. She had a book about to be published (*A Stranger in*

My Grave), and he'd been named a director of the Mystery Writers of America. The Millars stayed at Manhattan's Beckman Tower and attended to business matters. Von Auw said everyone was pleased with *The Wycherly Woman* manuscript. After Macdonald's good *Ferguson* sales, Knopf raised his *Wycherly* advance from $1,500 to $2,500 ($500 more than Margaret Millar was now getting from Random House). Alfred Knopf, disappointed by his son Pat's defection from the family business to cofound Atheneum, staggered the publishing world this year by merging his firm with Bennett Cerf's Random House, a move Millar said was as surprising "as if England had joined the European Community."

The Millars gave joint interviews with several New York book-page writers, chats in which Millar carried the ball with his gentle, dry wit. Maurice Dolbier of the *Herald Tribune* recorded this exchange regarding the Knopf–Random House merger: " 'Talk about togetherness!' says Mrs. Millar. 'We are putting,' says Mr. Millar, 'both our egos in one basket.' " *Publishers Weekly* reported, "The Millars do not collaborate in their writing, nor do they intend to; it would be, says Mr. Millar, 'like trying to hitch up a unicorn and a mule. I'm the mule.' " To Martha MacGregor of the *New York Post,* Millar said, "I don't think I write escape fiction, although it contains some escape hatches." MacGregor showed the Millars' differing reactions to the fare at the tony Four Seasons restaurant, with Margaret exclaiming, " 'Will you look at this? Tiny noodles—for four dollars I want *big* noodles.' . . . Mrs. Millar ordered plain old steak. Mr. Macdonald ordered Turban of Sole Four Seasons—a dish as complicated as one of his plots. . . . Mr. Macdonald said he wished she would learn to cook Turban of Sole Four Seasons when they got back to Santa Barbara, California. Mrs. Millar said she wouldn't, because Mr. Macdonald was on a diet and should be eating lamb chops and baked potato." MacGregor's piece, with the married writers' dialogue on their life and work habits ("SHE: We live in a split level house, one part is his and the other part is mine. HE: We occasionally meet on the stairs"), was used by S. J. Perelman as the jumping-off point for a comical *New Yorker* sketch about rival husband-and-wife Civil War writers in Santa Barbara; Millar claimed to be delighted with the publicity: nothing was going to faze him during this good year.

The Millars extended their trip with a jaunt to Ontario, visiting Maggie's father and Ken's Canadian publisher, Jack McClelland. Millar would happily have kept traveling, but (he wrote von Auw) "Maggie's a hard girl to keep away from home for more than two weeks at a time." The authors were back home for John Kennedy's November election as president, an event they greeted with joy. ("We'll have a man in the White House who can read and write," Margaret crowed to James Sandoe. "Yippee!")

There was soon more for Millar to celebrate: *Cosmopolitan* bought *The Wycherly Woman* for condensation, which meant another five thousand dollars to help pay the doctors. Olding surely had done her job for Millar this year, and the author asked his agent's permission to dedicate *The Wycherly Woman* to her, "as a token of affection and with the wish that it were a better book."

Millar had again drawn on recent experience in writing *The Wycherly Woman*, which had Lew Archer hired by a rich heir to find his missing daughter, Phoebe: a name in Greek myth, someone points out, for Diana of the hunt. This hunted girl also carries a hint of a Dreiser story, "The Lost Phoebe." But the girl Phoebe brought most to mind for Millar was of course Linda, whose face looks at Archer dolefully from a photograph: "Her mouth was wide and straight, passionate in a kind of ingrown way. She looked like one of those sensitive girls who could grow up into beauty or into hard-faced spinsterhood. If she grew up at all."

Phoebe's divorced father, Homer Wycherly, learns she's gone only when he returns from a long cruise. Through Wycherly, Millar mocks the way he acted at Davis, having Wycherly threaten in a similar manner, "They're going to admit that they're at fault. . . . They're going to know who they're dealing with before I'm through with them." Archer observes, "I suspected they knew already: a foolish man full of passions he couldn't handle."

But Homer Wycherly—smoothly charming but tense beneath the surface—actually looks and acts a lot like Alfred Knopf: "He wore imported-looking tweeds buttoned over his stomach. On his face he wore a home-grown expression of dismay." Homer uses Knopf-like expressions like "heavens, no" and "stir up the animals." His best effort at friendliness is a fierce grin; he keeps his real self hidden.

Harding "Pete" Lemay, Knopf's publicity manager, witnessed the fascination that Alfred Knopf held for Millar. "Ken and I would talk about Alfred," said Lemay, whom Millar met in New York. "Alfred was bigger than life, like a pirate. And I think Ken, who was a modest man, found that rather amusing. Alfred wasn't like anything *he'd* grown up with, any more than he was like anything *I'd* grown up with. Alfred was a great *character,* and to somebody like Ken—a very observant, quiet man who sat back and *watched* people—he was I suppose a source of inspiration."

Wycherly lives in Meadow Farms, an edge-of-the-desert town like Bishop. His Phoebe is missing from Boulder Beach College, a northern California school where Archer finds Phoebe's roommate, Dolly, typing a sociology paper on a twenty-year-old Royal suspiciously like the machine Millar won in Toronto the year Linda was born. "The *e*'s were out of alignment," he notices. "Maybe it was a clue." This is a nicely wry joke on Archer as sleuth—but later it turns out the typewriter *is* a clue.

Wycherly speeds up the Bay Area Peninsula and into the heart of Sam Spade's *Maltese Falcon* turf; Macdonald tips his fedora by describing a fellow in a San Francisco office with a telephone receiver "perched like a black bird against his short neck." Lew encounters the usual coterie of sharply observed types. Some folks Archer sums up in a single line, such as this aging employee in a third-rate hotel: "Forty years as a bellhop hollows a man out into a kind of receptacle for tips." Not that Lew spares himself: "Twenty years as a detective works changes in a man, too."

Archer undergoes chameleonic change while hunting Wycherly's daughter and (not incidentally) Wycherly's ex-wife. Posing as Homer, the better to ask after his missing women, Lew takes on Homer's emotional attachments: "I was beginning to feel his load of grief, as if I'd assumed it magically with his name." Macdonald thus draws directly on Millar's sense memories of his 1959 ordeal. This creates a weird vertigo: a view at once close-up and distant. In an essay Macdonald said his detective gave him a protective disguise in which to approach autobiographical ore, "a kind of welder's mask . . . to handle dangerously hot material." Having Archer experience Millar's life through Wycherly—the equivalent of going from first- to third-person and back again—is like looking through a triple layer of safety glass.

A startling disguise is central to the plot of *Wycherly*, a role reversal that (despite foreshadowing and ex post facto explaining) some reviewers found hard to credit. They should have seen a 1955 photo of Millar in Kitchener with his wife and daughter: two "glamour-gals" gussied up for Canadian relatives, looking more like distant sisters than women separated by twenty-four years; Linda started wearing her mother's clothes when she was fifteen. If fiction can be as strange as life, *Wycherly*'s surprise works.

This book went further into what Millar felt was important moral terrain, not in a ponderous way but intimately, conversationally. When sociology student Dolly asks Archer who's to blame for juvenile delinquency, he says, "I think blame is one of the things we have to get rid of. When children blame their parents for what's happened to them, or parents blame their children for what they've done, it's part of the problem, and it makes the problem worse. People should take a close look at themselves." Archer's not arguing for a lack of personal responsibility; he insists on an unflinchingly hard-boiled fate for the book's ultimate villain. It's misplaced guilt he's against. Phoebe's emotional strain stems (like Linda's?) from protecting someone she loves and assuming more blame than she should. Archer's not blindly tolerant of the young, but he offers them help finding their way in a world that can seem alien. "What can you do when they lie to you?" a parent asks Archer. "You can give up lying yourself," he says. It's the adults' job to be honest, moral, caring—and to live by the same rules they lay down for the young. Implicit is a belief that life is sacred. If there's a God, Archer tells Dolly, "He worked in mysterious ways. Like people." He counsels, "Don't stop praying. . . . It keeps the circuits open. Just in case there's ever anybody on the other end of the line." But Archer puts his faith in people, each one of whom is irreplaceable.

When Phoebe asks would it be all right for her to bear the baby she's pregnant with, even though she might pass on a troubled "heredity," Archer unhesitatingly says, "It would be all wrong not to." His words ring like a reaffirmation, on the far side of a good deal of trouble, of the life-affirming decision made in Toronto by Kenneth and Margaret Millar some twenty-one years before.

Jan. 27, 1961

Dear Ivan:

. . . I had a nightmare last night, dreaming that I received one of Alfred's old-style letters in which he savagely announced that *Wycherly Woman* sold a total of 3339 copies. Ora pro nobis.

As always,

Ken

May 29, 1961

Dear Ken:

Just a line to say that we have shipped out six thousand copies of "The Wycherly Woman." . . . I hope all goes well and remain, with my best,

As ever,

Alfred A. Knopf

The publishing matter most preoccupying Millar in 1961 had nothing to do with Lew Archer. It was his quest to get "Coleridge and the Inward Eye" into print, something the author thought vital to establishing his literary reputation (especially in England). After Knopf turned the Coleridge work down as too academic, Millar asked von Auw to submit it to university presses. The agent started at the top, with Harvard University Press, and the response was extremely good. The press's anonymous reader (actually, noted Coleridge scholar Earl Leslie Griggs) praised the book with an enthusiasm rare in such critiques, calling it "admirable," "excellent," "illuminating," and "masterly." "It is a pleasure to recommend Mr. Millar's work," he concluded. "No Coleridge student . . . can afford to ignore it. Indeed, the book should prove of the greatest interest to the general reader as well as the specialist."

Millar was overwhelmed. To have his doctoral work published by Harvard University Press would go a long way toward balancing the unfairness of Harvard's having shut him out of graduate school in 1938. But it was not to be. Twenty years after quashing Millar's Ivy League dream, Harvard did it again. Despite their reader's enthusiasm and their editors' endorsement, the imprint's Board of Syndics turned thumbs down on the book. "The rejection from Harvard was one of the shittiest letters I've ever seen from a publisher in my life," said Dick Lid, who'd had a lot of dealings with university presses. "Earl Leslie Griggs was a brilliant man; you'd have thought his name would have cut enough ice. But their attitude was, 'We can't publish a book by a *mystery* writer!'—even if the mystery writer had a Ph.D."

Nudged by Donald Davie, the English firm of Routledge said they'd print Millar's Coleridge work in the U.K.; but they required a U.S. press to copublish. Von Auw sent the manuscript to Columbia University Press; meanwhile Don Pearce promoted a query from Indiana U.P., where he'd published. Millar preferred his book be done by Columbia, but he told von Auw, "I hardly care what auspices I appear under in this country so long as Routledge does the book in England. I am most anxious for that not to fall through." Adding to his urgency was the knowledge that other Coleridge scholars (including a fellow he'd known at Michigan) were "catching up" to him. When Columbia was slow on the uptake, Millar mailed a manuscript to Indiana—"not wholly without misgivings," he admitted to von Auw, "including the thought that you might think me an ass; but still with a hope that this may settle the problem for us and assure that English publication on which I have set my heart." Millar confessed to having been made gun-shy by Harvard: "I suppose I wince away from the prospect of another such time- and emotion-consuming accident . . . and I feel, perhaps foolishly, safer exposing my love of learning and of my book to a publisher where I am already favorably known through my friends. . . . Well, let's see if Indiana can come up with a reader able and willing to recognize the substantial merits of my book."

The mills of the academic gods ground exceeding slow. Indiana took ten months to tell Millar they hadn't reached a decision. "As at Harvard," Millar wrote von Auw, "they have a pro-report and an anti-report, I gather, and are seeking a third, according to the troika principle." Marshall McLuhan tried to resolve the matter by proposing the manuscript be read for Indiana by a Toronto woman said to be "the greatest living Coleridge scholar." This woman professor agreed to the task but then "rather eccentrically changed her mind," Millar told von Auw, "and I have no interest in trying to change it back." He asked Indiana to return his work so that von Auw could send it to Boston's Beacon Press, where Hugh Kenner (all Millar's academic friends were trying to help) had talked it up. Millar wrote his agent, "I presume at least it won't take them a year, as it did Indiana, to make up their minds."

Meanwhile Millar got on with the writing of the tenth Archer novel, eventually titled *The Zebra-Striped Hearse*. He went to Lake Tahoe to case the scene there, then also for research purposes took a ten-day trip to Aji-jic, Mexico, where John Mersereau, an old writers lunch friend, lived in a sort of expatriate artists colony. Millar invited Maggie, but she stayed home and during his absence got intrigued by the abundant bird life at Chelham Way.

Margaret signed up for a bird-watching course and soon (loaded down with binoculars, sack lunch, and guidebook) was trudging with other birders over mudflats and sandy sloughs. Millar encouraged her new hobby by building bird-feeding stations behind their house and assuming the daily chore of stocking them. Before long he too was an apprentice birder and could ID many species by common and Latin names.

He'd always had a strong affinity with animals, especially dogs. In

Kenneth Millar, about age four,
not long after leaving Vancouver.
(Courtesy of Rhea Kirk)

Kennie with relatives, after a year or
two in Kitchener. His mother, Annie Moyer
Millar, is on the right; to her left is her
mother, Veronica Bowman Moyer.
(Courtesy of Mary V. Carr)

Jack Millar, extreme right, in Kitchener, 1928.
The man in front is Ken's American
architect-artisan uncle, Albert Wood.
(Courtesy of Mari Shaw)

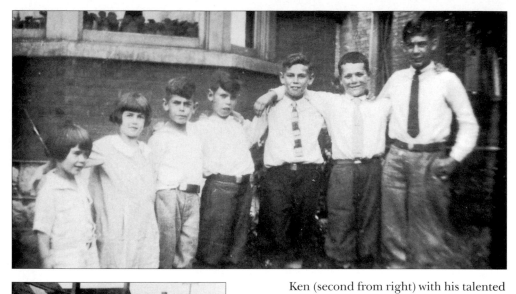

Ken (second from right) with his talented
Wood cousins.
(Courtesy of Mari Shaw)

Eleven years old, in the fall of 1927;
dressed for his trip to Winnipeg.
(Courtesy of Rhea Kirk)

With the Snyder family,
on the Oxbow farm.
(Courtesy of Rhea Kirk)

Kenneth, Margaret, and
Linda Millar, on a visit
to Kitchener in 1948.
The book is Margaret's
The Iron Gates.
(Kitchener-Waterloo
Record Collection of
Photographic Negatives,
Dana Porter Library,
University of Waterloo)

Doctoral candidate Kenneth Millar
at the University of Michigan.
(Bentley Historical Library, University
of Michigan News and Information
Records, Series D Collection)

"John Macdonald" looms
out of the postwar shadows:
The Moving Target, 1949.

Raymond Chandler, photographed by
Alfred Knopf in Los Angeles, 1940.
(Harry Ransom Humanities Research Center,
The University of Texas at Austin)

Kenneth Millar, photographed by
Alfred Knopf in Los Angeles, 1958.
(Harry Ransom Humanities Research Center,
The University of Texas at Austin)

The Millars in Kitchener, April, 1955: just before driving back West in "Honeybug."
(Kitchener-Waterloo Record Collection of Photographic Negatives, Dana Porter Library,
University of Waterloo)

Michael Rennie as Joe Rogers,
the prototype for Lew Archer,
in *Pursuit*'s 1959 dramatization
(with Joan Bennett and the young
Rip Torn) of *Find the Woman*.
(CBS Photo Archive)

Millar in Hollywood, 1959; looking for Linda.
(Regional History Collection, Department of
Special Collections, University Libraries,
University of Southern California)

Ken and Maggie with Alfred Knopf, at the
Santa Barbara Biltmore.
(Hal Boucher)

Paul Newman as Lew Harper, 1966.
(HARPER © 1966 Warner Bros.)

Photo by Alfred Knopf of Millar;
in Knopf's New York office, 1965.
(Harry Ransom Humanities Research Center,
The University of Texas at Austin)

Brian Keith
as NBC's Lew Archer, 1975.
(© NBC/Globe Photos, Inc. 1975)

Ken and Maggie inspect Peter Graves
as Archer, 1974.
(Hal Boucher)

Millar/Macdonald protecting grandson
Jimmie, by the pool at Hope Ranch;
a picture posed for *Esquire*.
(Mike Salisbury)

With Eudora Welty at the
Santa Barbara Writers Conference.
(Virginia Kidd)

The Millars at the new Kitchener Library.
(Kitchener-Waterloo Record Collection, Dana Porter Library, University of Waterloo)

Kenneth and Margaret Millar in December 1980, the week of their interviews
with Diana Cooper-Clark.
(Trevor Clark)

Toronto he'd made friends with neighborhod squirrels and even trained one to take food from his mouth, to his wife's mixed admiration and disgust. "Ken adored all animals," Margaret said. "He wouldn't kill a fly. If there was a fly in the house, he'd get it on his hand and take it outside—where it would promptly come in the other door." Birds had long soared through Millar's books, and now Lew Archer would notice even more of them.

The literary aspect would be a bonus. Millar started watching birds because it was something he and Maggie could share. Marriages needed common interests, he said; he was good at facilitating them. Bird-watching and its attendant tasks were incorporated into the Millars' schedules with typical efficiency. They arranged their routines for maximum productivity. Staples such as wine were bought by the case, to save time. Usually the Millars ate separately and fixed their own meals. Each answered the phone or handled emergencies during the other's shift; writing hours were inviolable. Once Margaret lost her car keys in town; since it happened during his work stint, she managed without calling home.

Millar wrote in his downstairs room, where cheap Picasso and Miró reproductions hung. Sometimes he'd draw the curtains and make the dimly lit chamber even dimmer; he might wear a green plastic visor like an old-time newspaper editor's eyeshade. Sitting in the same big, oft-reupholstered easy chair Margaret had bought him in 1945, a pine board balanced across its arms to hold a spiral-bound notebook and a ballpoint pen, Millar looked like a pilot cocooned in a cockpit, or a navigator sealed in a bathysphere, as he moved his made-up characters in and out of his fiction's mutating light.

Busy as he was, Millar always took time to help friends and colleagues. These included Al Stump, who in 1961 published a book written for and with Ty Cobb: *My Life in Baseball: The True Record*, a sanitized autobiography that (on Cobb's insistence) was anything but wholly truthful about the mean-tempered sports giant's tumultuous years. Before the book came out, Cobb died in an Atlanta hospital room with a Luger pistol and a paper sack stuffed with a million dollars in stocks and bonds. *True* magazine asked Stump to write an honest account of his hair-raising months in Cobb's company. Not only did Stump paint a vivid picture of his bizarre collaboration with the violent and hard-drinking Cobb, he included much of the explosive material Cobb made him leave out of his authorized book, including melodramatic family events that might have been lifted from a Ross Macdonald novel. "Cobb was not sane," Stump said. "The story came to the conclusion that because his mother killed his father when he was seventeen—blew his head off with a shotgun—that he was damaged. The father was a very prominent man: a state senator, publisher of the town newspaper where Cobb grew up. He loved that father immensely; he told me, 'It changed me for the rest of my life.' Well, the conclusion was that he was possibly getting even for his father, winning those games to please old dad, and rules didn't count; if you got in his way, he'd cut you down. Before I mailed the manuscript, I took it to Ken. I knew I had my hands on something unusual here, and he was such a grammarian; he was a master of the language. So he took it home for the weekend, and on Monday he came back to my little studio. He said, 'You've got a helluva good piece here.' He said, 'I made a few suggestions.' So I went through it, and on almost every page he'd made a suggested change; he just wrote it on a side slip, 'cause that's the kind of a guy he was: he wouldn't deface anybody's manuscript. But he liked it so much that I began to realize that maybe I *really* had something here. Anyway the story was such a hit with all the editors, they paid me forty-five hundred or five thousand dollars, the second-highest price they'd ever paid for an article; only Hemingway had been paid more money for a story by Fawcett. Well, it was syndicated all over the country; I made all kinds of money with the damn thing and got a lotta baseball people mad at me because I told the truth—we don't do that in this country about our sports idols. Bob Considine, who was the top authority at that time, called it the best sports story he ever read. It won national first place in the Best American Sport Story contest. Anyway, Ken's help in editing that, in suggesting some changes—the rearrangement of some paragraphs was one thing he suggested—well, I remember when the check came, we all went out and got drunk." Thirty-two years later, Stump's *True* piece was the basis for a hit film in which Robert Wuhl played Al Stump to Tommy Lee Jones's Ty Cobb.

Millar did him other good turns, Stump recalled: "For years Ken recommended an agent named Gideon Kashor, so I wrote to him finally; and Gideon was a wonderful guy. He helped get me started in the *Saturday Evening Post*, which was the hardest market in the country to crack; Gideon was a real loyal guy, he represented me right up until he died. Yeah, Ken helped me on that. He was always doing nice things where I was concerned. He got me a Bantam book, a collection of my sports pieces from the *Post, Collier's, Liberty, True, Esquire;* he says, 'Why don't you put together a conglomeration?' Ken recommended me to one of the Bantam editors, who said fine, but we need it right away to bring it out with the spring list. I'd remarried and was going off to Europe for six months, so I had to grab all the material and notes and sit up at night over there on the bloody Riviera updating these stories. It was called *The Champion Breed,* about athletes who'd succeeded despite handicaps: race, physical, financial, so on. That came about because of Ken."

The dissolution of Al and Claire Stump's marriage saddened the Millars. The end of Don Pearce's long union shocked and angered them. Millar and Pearce, for all the history they shared, saw things from very different points of view.

"I nearly had a nervous breakdown when I had to leave my home and get a divorce and marry somebody else," Pearce said. "I practically collapsed under it. That's not the sort of thing that Ken would tolerate for a moment. He understood life in different terms, I mean: 'you *stay*, through thick and thin. Anyway, no one ever *promised* you a rose garden, you know? If life is difficult, if life is a serious matter at which you must *work*—well, other people may be more fortunate, but if you have a job to do, you *do* it.' I remember him telling me—it fell on my astonished ears, but I tried to believe him because I *always* believed Ken—he told me, 'Sex is not that important. What matters is keeping your word and being on top of temptations to break it or change it. You stay where you're needed, and you don't give in,' and so on. I think had he lived to be a hundred, he still would not have relaxed those things that *he* thought held communities and civilizations and personal relationships together. He said things to me that only my habitual stance of worshipful friendship enabled me to take without buckling. You know, when someone says, 'I think you're a god-damned *jerk*'—clearly, that was changing something. I can't imagine anybody who had been and could always be more useful to me than Ken, for advice or for things he didn't even know he was helping me with. I was like a bloodsucker, drawing various kinds of intellectual and informational strength from him; I must have seemed to him a bit like a child, in comparison. But that's when his usefulness to me ended. His capacity to help me ceased, because he ceased to approve of me. I doubt if he ever mentioned me again."

Millar, in several letters to the Bransons, told his side of the break with Pearce: "No, I didn't turn my back on him. He quit me because I persisted in telling him that he was making a mistake. . . . You misunderstand me if you think I think a man has no right to divorce a wife; but one has to consider the manner and the consequences. Don's course has been destructive. . . . I grieve for him and his family. . . . It makes no sense to me." A quarter-century friendship was over. At the Pearces' divorce trial, Margaret testified as a witness against Don. (Despite Millar's prediction that Pearce's new relationship would last no more than a year, Donald and Dorothy—"a most remarkable person," Pearce attests—have stayed happily married for more than four decades.)

So many of his friends were getting divorced or going into therapy (or both), Millar said, maybe he'd give up watching humans and just watch birds: "They are stupider than people, but not much, and they can fly unassisted."

There was one bright development on the scene, like a hopeful subplot in a Macdonald book: in September 1961, twenty-two-year-old UCLA senior Linda Millar married a twenty-nine-year-old engineering major working as a missile-guidance technician. Millar told von Auw that Lin's fellow was "an excellent man" and she seemed happy. Soon husband and wife were both working (she as a secretary) for the company handling the Saturn space rocket computers. Millar wrote Olding, "All the news from here is good, health-wise, daughter-wise, wisdom-wise?"

The Archer book he mailed to New York in the spring of 1962, *The Zebra-Striped Hearse*, gave him a different sort of satisfaction. "It is, I think, more of a novel and less of an adventure story than anything I've done," the author told von Auw. To Knopf he wrote, "I've tried to give it more of my personal style and tone than any of its predecessors." Millar was pleased with the book (an elegantly designed and typically complex cat's cradle involving painters, surfers, the neurotic rich, and the resentful poor), and he'd stay pleased with it over the years. Looking back a decade later, he'd tell journalist Paul Nelson, "A lot of people think that's my best book. I don't really have an opinion, but I think it *worked;* I think it's well constructed. I take for granted some of the things that I value, like style and so on; but to me, structure is the really difficult thing. It involves a great deal of mental effort, to take this kind of material in its complexity and not just impose a structure on it but find the structure that's inherent in the material; and at the same time obey the rules of the mystery, with your conclusion in your last sentence and your beginning in your first sentence. . . . I think *The Zebra-Striped Hearse* could probably be described as my first book that really comes off in the various ways that I wanted a book to come off; and then it was followed by several other books which did too."

As with *The Wycherly Woman,* Olding sold *The Zebra-Striped Hearse* for abridgment in *Cosmopolitan* magazine, which paid five thousand dollars for such condensations. The author could either cut the book himself or let the magazine do it. ("Well," Margaret Millar said dryly, "some choice.") Millar struggled with the *Zebra* condensation, whittling at his carefully crafted novel. His wife, an old hand at such chores, stepped in to help. "It's difficult to cut a book down to twenty-five thousand words," she said, "unless you really know how to do it, and it just came natural to me. Ken would look la*bor*iously through a chapter, thinking he could *spare* that deft line, *spare* this one. You *can't do* that; you have to cut out the whole shebang. Then, when he learned it, he became very proficient at cutting his own work. That was one little thing I could teach him." When Olding praised the shortened *Zebra,* Millar wrote, "Good bold transitions are the secret and (I cannot tell a lie) Maggie was responsible for many of them. So I just helped her plot her new book."

He dedicated *The Zebra-Striped Hearse* to Harris Seed, who (waiving a fee) had recently handled the formalities to bring Linda Millar's long probation to a quiet end. Millar got Seed to check *Zebra* for errors of jurisprudence or logic, something both Millars regularly asked the lawyer to do for their manuscripts. The only thing Seed recalled ever correcting in any Ken Millar book, he said, was when someone leapt on a car's running board: "This was in the sixties. I said, 'Ken, cars don't have running boards anymore.' "

Dick Lid was someone else Millar asked to read his typescripts. Lid caught a mistake in *Zebra* in time for it to be corrected: a reference to Malibu railroad tracks where none existed. Though Millar took research trips for *Zebra* and other books, he always relied on memory to describe LA, a place he didn't like to visit. He'd depend increasingly on Lid and others to keep him accurate on LA geography.

Betty and Dick Lid knew the Millars pretty well by 1962. "Maggie was very much in control, and she pretty much *presided*," Betty Lid said. "Maggie liked you answering back; you had to assert yourself with Maggie, keep your own sense of self, because she was a very forceful person. Ken, in his quiet way, was different. He had this clear sense of his own power; it was not the power that she had, it was something else. I felt he was invulnerable somehow. Ken never raised his voice. Ken was just calm, always. He was really such a sweet man. I don't think a lot of people knew him very well, because—I don't think he was knowable, in that way. He had this thing around him, this shell. Whatever it was he had, you couldn't penetrate it. He was a very perceptive guy. If you weren't genuine, you just didn't get into his circle. And yet he was never rude. When he didn't like somebody, he wouldn't even bother with them. He just dismissed them as moral human beings. I was complaining about somebody very dramatically once, saying he's this and he's that, making him into a real monster; and Ken said to me, 'Betty—he's not an important person.' Just simply wiped him out!"

Something Millar couldn't dismiss so easily was the 1962 publication in the United States and England of *Raymond Chandler Speaking*, a book that included an edited version of Chandler's 1949 letter to James Sandoe about *The Moving Target*. Readers, critics, and colleagues on two continents could now chuckle at (and quote in print) Chandler knocking the "pretentiousness" of Macdonald's phrasing, Chandler sneering at Macdonald's similes, Chandler calling Macdonald a "literary eunuch." It wounded Millar to be heckled from the grave by a man whose work had once inspired him. Worse than that, it seemed to Millar (who'd learn of other anti-Macdonald letters by Chandler) that the older writer had tried to thwart his career.

"He was very mild about the Chandler business," Dick Lid said, "although it must have hurt. One night he hauled out the exact quotation from that letter of Chandler's, criticizing the simile about the automobile 'acned with rust.' He thought Chandler simply didn't understand how that worked, didn't understand the difference between someone who was writing with a college education and someone who hadn't had one. That was probably defensive, on Ken's part; I'm sure it was. He thought you're writing for an audience that mostly will never know what's gone into a book in terms of erudition or education, anyhow, and that the allusions and all of that are going to pass over that reader—but that's what you should expect in a popular art form; and by and large, at least in talking to me, he was willing to accept that."

What he couldn't ignore was the posthumous wound Chandler had inflicted. Millar sensed it would take years for Ross Macdonald's reputation to recover from *Raymond Chandler Speaking*, and he'd be alert for a chance to defend himself.

Also unignorable was the continued rejection of "Coleridge and the Inward Eye." Millar's dissertation made its disappointing way from Beacon to Duke to Oxford University Press. When no American publisher would commit to the work, England's Routledge cooled on it. Donald Davie suggested Millar's European agent next offer it to the U.K.'s Chatto and Windus. Millar wearied of the struggle. This Coleridge book was his personal albatross. "Patronage seems to be a powerful force in this field, of U. Presses," he wrote von Auw, "and unfortunately I've never kept my academic fences mended. Or fortunately—I prefer open country." He finally accepted the inevitable, Lid said: "He could not get that book published. It was a marvelous case of the academic world just plain shitting on somebody who was a mystery writer: 'You wanna publish? You gotta ask my permission.' Eventually he said, 'I'm not gonna be humiliated anymore; I'm not gonna keep trying to do this.' That was a major shame."

Yet he rolled with the punch. Millar seemed more able now to take disappointments in stride; maybe, as he'd hinted to Olding, he was getting wiser? Anyway, he seemed to be having more fun. He and Maggie, both between books at the same time for a change, took several group birding trips in 1962: to the Santa Barbara islands, to Joshua Tree and Twentynine Palms, to Teton Park and Yellowstone. Millar bought an eight-foot boat he strapped atop the Ford and drove to the beach for sails with Dick Lid or Bob Easton. His new jauntiness was caught in a photograph taken for the sleeve of *The Zebra-Striped Hearse:* standing near the Coral Casino diving boards, wearing his Harris Tweed jacket from Kitchener, a jack-o'-lantern grin on his face, he'd never looked thinner, healthier, happier—a Canadian living in California and damned glad of it. He wrote Anna Branson, "I like it better now than I ever did. What it? It, all of it!" Millar had a new catchphrase: *Writing well is the best revenge.* He was getting good at putting what bothered him into his fiction, and so many things that affected him this year—his best friend's divorce, his disgust with academia, his preoccupation with Coleridge, his anger at Chandler—he'd channel into the next Archer novel, a book he said would have "my most horrible plot yet": a masterpiece-in-the-making that he'd title *The Chill.*

The spirit who bideth by himself
In the land of mist and snow,
He loved the bird that loved the man
Who shot him with his bow.
—S. T. Coleridge, "The Rime of the Ancient Mariner"

In every case, my friend, one principle is to know what the investigation is about.

—Plato, *Phædrus*

A Mess of Shadows was the book's working title, from a line in the Yeats poem "Among School Children." Millar had written a paper about that poem for Cleanth Brooks in 1942; a decade later he spent two hours discussing the same poem with Don Pearce. "He saw 'Among School Children' as a poem about one thing: blocked sexuality, or sexual longing," recalled Pearce. "He said, 'It's about deprived sexuality, and that chestnut tree blossoming at the end is obviously a transmogrified phallic image.'"

At the heart of Macdonald's novel is the blocked and deprived Roy Bradshaw, dean of the college at Pacific Point, an unmarried man of early middle age living with his mother. Millar seems to have taken the framework of Bradshaw's story from a fifties Santa Barbara court case, then added some of his feelings about Don Pearce's personal situation: a "continually developing mess," he wrote Anna Branson, that "shadowed" Millar's year. More than one commentator (including Joyce Carol Oates) guessed Millar also put to fictive use here the private life of Raymond Chandler, who, as soon as his mother died, married a woman twenty years his senior.

Harvard Ph.D. Bradshaw, who wears his formal manner like a suit of armor, represented everything the proletarian-intellectual Millar hated about the academy in general and Harvard in particular. Bradshaw also seems partly modeled on a Harvard-trained Michigan professor Millar despised and went out of his way to avoid, a man with a famously lofty demeanor ("It was like talking to the Matterhorn," Pearce said) and close ties to his mom, who presided at his departmental teas.

Coleridge gave Macdonald the structural and spiritual framework for his novel, a streamlined tale of modern California lashed to the eighteenth-century rigging of "The Rime of the Ancient Mariner" (with a bit of the same poet's "Christabel" thrown in for atmosphere). As it starts, Archer, like the wedding guest narrating "Mariner," looks forward to a pleasant event: a fishing trip to La Paz. But like the wedding guest, Archer's waylaid by a supplicant: the bristly Alex Kincaid, who, like Coleridge's Mariner, seeks someone to hear his sad story. During Kincaid's Pacific Point honeymoon, his bride, Dolly, was visited by a bearded man named McGee (a sometime sailor carrying a load of Mariner-like grief); afterward Dolly disappeared. Archer says he'll look for her. His first stop is the honeymooners' hotel, the Surf House, where he quizzes the photographer, whose heavy camera hangs from his neck "like an albatross": the bird slain by Coleridge's unhappy Mariner (an archer).

Lew sends Kincaid to the nicely named Mariner's Rest Motel, then traces Dolly to the local college. Among those he meets there is Helen Haggerty, a saucy young teacher of modern languages. The provocative Haggerty takes Lew to her apartment and tries to hire him, claiming her life is in danger; but he spurns her. When she's found murdered, Dolly Kincaid is suspected of killing her.

By now *The Chill*'s Coleridge allusions are as common as seagulls on a beach. The eyes of the college's dean of women look like "the beautiful core of an iceberg, all green ice and cold blazing light"—reminding "Mariner" readers of when "ice, mast-high, came floating by, as green as emerald." A pigeon dead on Haggerty's patio stands in for the albatross. For the book's first half, Pacific Point is wrapped in an obscuring fog like the enveloping mist the Mariner encounters "where no living thing was to be seen." The fog lifts, as in the poem, at the rising of the moon, which casts light toward a difficult redemption. On a ship called the *Revenant*, McGee unburdens himself of "his horrible penance," hoping Lew will in effect shrieve his soul ("wash away the Albatross's blood"). Archer does bring about McGee's deliverance from "the Spectre-Woman and her Deathmate," the grotesque "Death and Life-in-Death" pair behind *The Chill*'s modern horrors.

By this point in his career, Ross Macdonald seemed a bit like the Ancient Mariner himself, telling Freudian variations on the same few stories, such as the Oedipus tales so meaningful to Millar (an exile returns, a man "marries" his mother), and the plight of the damaged or endangered daughter. Like the Mariner, whose action begat disaster, Millar did penance by repeating, reimagining, realizing, what happened.

The Chill's Linda figure is Dolly Kincaid. Like Linda, Dolly disappears on a Labor Day weekend. Accused of murder, she's eager to be blamed, saying, "I want to die. I deserve to."

With Dolly "on the verge of a psychotic breakthrough," Archer collaborates with her psychiatrist in having her admitted to a rest home, where a psychiatrist probes Dolly's memory with sodium pentothal.

The psychiatrist is named Godwin: another Coleridge connection. William Godwin, eighteenth-century psychological and social reformer (and father of *Frankenstein*'s creator Mary Shelley), was a Coleridge correspondent; and, as author of the 1794 semimystery *The Adventures of Caleb*

Williams, a sort of great-grandfather of crime fiction. There are other mystery-story allusions in *The Chill,* further linking high art and popular culture: Coleridge's albatross and Spade's black bird. In the book's first scene, Archer's in court testifying in a case involving one Bridget Perrine, whose name splices Brigid O'Shaughnessy and Effie Perrine, the main women in *The Maltese Falcon.* When Lew consults Phyllis and Arnie Walters, his Reno colleagues, we learn they're both (like Hammett) ex-Pinkerton agents. Arnie recalls an old Bay Area case of his that's a droll variation on the Flitcraft story in *Falcon.*

Another mystery writer crucially evoked in *The Chill* is Margaret Millar. Trailing Dolly at the college, Archer remembers "a girl I used to follow home from Junior High. I never did work up enough nerve to ask her for the privilege of carrying her books." This comes on the heels of Lew hearing this exchange between a coed and a varsity man:

> She was explaining something to him, something about Achilles and the tortoise. Achilles was chasing the tortoise, it seemed, but according to Zeno he would never catch it. The space between them was divisible into an infinite number of parts; therefore it would take Achilles an infinite period of time to traverse it. By that time the tortoise would be somewhere else.
>
> The young man nodded. "I see that."
>
> "But it isn't so," the girl cried. "The infinite divisibility of space is merely theoretical. It doesn't affect actual *movement* across space."
>
> "I don't get it, Heidi."

Millar had been prodded into writing for Ontario magazines by John Buchan's account of the race between tortoise and hare. But Margaret Millar won the sprint into hardcover. His wife had written five books by the time Ken sold one; the professional space between them seemed indivisible then, and Millar changed their career metaphor from Buchan's fable to Zeno's conundrum. After Margaret's *Iron Gates* success, Kenneth had told her, "The tortoise will never catch Achilles." But the tortoise kept plodding—and with *The Chill,* his eighteenth book, for the first time drew even.

And in this book he exceeded his past achievements, as he deftly incorporated not only Coleridge but pre-Socratic philosophy into his California fable. Fogbound in a house with a corpse and Dean Bradshaw, Lew uses Zeno's riddle like a Zen koan: "I shut off the violent images with an effort of will and forced myself to think about Zeno, who said that Achilles could never traverse the space between him and the tortoise. It was a soothing thought, if you were a tortoise, or maybe even if you were Achilles."

Poets as well as philosophers inform perception in *The Chill:* Coleridge,

Yeats, Verlaine. Poems are *clues* in this sophisticated mystery in which Macdonald's poetic style is sharper than ever and especially apt. Critic Thomas J. Roberts noted, "Archer, Macdonald's narrator, thinks and sees in one-line poems." Here are some:

> An oval of sunlight from one of the ports, moving reciprocally with the motion of the yacht, fluttered against the bulkhead like a bright and living soul.

> Her graying head was marcelled in neat little waves, all alike, like the sea in old steel engravings.

> A moon like a fallen fruit reversing gravity was hoisting itself above the rooftops.

> An owl flew low over our heads, silent as a traveling piece of fog.

In *The Chill,* Macdonald wrote at the height of his mature style and near the peak of his vision. The book expressed the unity that Millar and Cleanth Brooks and Coleridge thought art should have: a balance in which every element is in sync with all others, with each part pulling its weight. *The Chill*'s characters hum with vitality—such as Helen Haggerty, the racy college teacher. An ash-blonde with a tanned body, stylish clothes, and a fast line of sexy banter, the pouty-mouthed Haggerty prowls Pacific Point with "a restless predatory air"; her scenes have a special sizzle.

Also memorable is Haggerty's father, a retired policeman Archer visits in Illinois after Helen's murder. Lew finds the old cop drinking himself into a stupor, boozily beating himself up over the death of a daughter he helped drive away. In an extended sequence as powerful as anything in Macdonald's oeuvre, Archer tails the ex-cop through a deranged walking tour of the past, a surrealistic journey of dark humor and glaring truth.

Brilliantly conceived and beautifully written, *The Chill* was a Macdonald masterwork. "It is with *The Chill* that he found his own voice," wrote Otto Penzler, "the voice that would prove to influence an entire generation of crime writers." Critic David Lehman put *The Chill* on his 1985 *Newsweek* list of ten favorite crime novels of the twentieth century.

On its release, though, *The Chill* provoked violent dislike in at least one faithful Macdonald reader: Donald Ross Pearce.

Millar's old friend bought the new Lew Archer even though he and its author were no longer speaking. "I guess I was still hooked on Ken in a way," he said. *The Chill* gave him a jolt. In the midst of his marital turmoil, Pearce had seen a psychiatrist who said some things to him that Pearce repeated to Millar. He found these statements transposed into dialogue spoken by Dean Bradshaw. "I gradually saw that I was in a way sort of being partly the model for that character," Pearce said. More disturbingly, Pearce perceived his second wife "caricatured and parodied" in the book. "At that time," he said, "it was quite a blow."

Don Pearce did with *The Chill* what Lew Archer does in that book when he finds a lurid newspaper story about Dolly Kincaid: "I read half of it and threw it in the trash."

The once omnipresent private eye has dwindled almost into obscurity. From glut they have become collectors' items. The routine snarl and snap of Brett Halliday's Mike Shayne is not to be taken seriously, but there is a genuine snap to the inquiries of Joe Puma and Brock (The Rock) Callahan as William Campbell Gault reports them.

—James Sandoe, *Library Journal*, 1963

THE ZEBRA-STRIPED HEARSE, by Ross Macdonald (Knopf). This is Mr. Macdonald's twelfth performance in the manner that Dashiell Hammett invented, that Raymond Chandler elaborated, and that he himself has refined, and it is a model of his excellence. That is to say, it has character, statement and style.

—*The New Yorker*, 1963

The Hollywood Knickerbocker was a hotel full of history. Dashiell Hammett (who died in 1961) was staying at the Knickerbocker in 1931 when he hooked up with a twenty-year-old script reader from Metro named Lillian Florence Hellman Kober. Raymond Chandler's Philip Marlowe, who had his office in the fictitious Cahuenga Building, ate at the coffee shop at the "Mansion House Hotel"—a Knickerbocker pseudonym. William Faulkner lived in the Knickerbocker in the 1930s; D. W. Griffith died there in 1948. Maggie Millar roomed at the Knickerbocker during her wartime Warners stint; and Millar stayed there in June of 1959, when "the mystery of the missing coed" was on every front page in town.

Millar returned to the Hollywood Knickerbocker on the night of Friday, April 19, 1963, for the southern California chapter of the Mystery Writers of America's Edgar Allan Poe Awards dinner (held simultaneously with the main event at New York's Hotel Astor). Ross Macdonald's *The Zebra-Striped Hearse* was one of six books nominated for the MWA's Best Novel Edgar Award. Millar thought he had a decent shot at winning, but he'd thought that last year too, with his first-ever Edgar nomination for *The Wycherly Woman*, and *Wycherly* lost to a book by England's John Creasey. He'd tried taking that loss lightly: "I felt I *deserved* to win," he explained to *Wycherly* dedicatee Dorothy Olding, "having a high opinion of my work (except when I am writing it, when it seems uniformly and interminably hopeless and un-pull-out-able), but I didn't *expect* to. . . . Giving it to Britishers (last year: Julian Symons) tends to avoid civil war within the organization. He said philosophically." (If the MWA was so worried about hurting people's feelings, Olding responded, why give awards at all?)

Millar was only cautiously optimistic about his *Zebra* prospects for the Edgar, though he made his agents the Poe-like promise "I'll keep knocking at that chamber door." Surely though he had a better-than-average chance with *The Zebra-Striped Hearse,* which got not only the by now expected raves from the genre reviewers but impressive notices from more mainstream sources. *Los Angeles Times* book critic Robert Kirsch, giving *Hearse* the same solo treatment he gave "real" novels, said of Macdonald, "He is a master of the lost art of plotting. His characterizations, even the most minor, are superb. And he manages to evoke the Southern California scene in all its special qualities as few novelists can. . . . Then, of course, there is the Macdonald style, which is enough to make writers crawl with envy. Not a word is wasted, not a nuance thrown away." Roger Sale in the *Hudson Review* praised Macdonald's vision of the "lives of quiet bourgeois desperation that are the legacy of California's passionate belief in unreality . . . [T]he real news about California [is] coming via private eye."

Gerald Walker had broken Macdonald out of the mystery-roundup ghetto first, with a review of *The Wycherly Woman* on the book page of the *New York Post.* There were also the first nods of recognition from the academy; UCLA doctoral candidate Carolyn See cited Macdonald works in her dissertation on "the Hollywood novel."

There was a growing awareness that Macdonald was reshaping the private-detective story, putting his personal stamp on the form as distinctively as had Hammett and Chandler. Robert F. Jones wrote the first feature article on Ross Macdonald ("A New Raymond Chandler?") for *Los Angeles* magazine in 1963. "I'd been in the navy in Long Beach but mainly at sea, so I was looking at LA and its environs pretty much with a fresh eye," said Jones, later a suspense novelist. "I'd been an avid reader of Chandler in the Midwest when I grew up, and—well, looking around LA as a *Time* reporter, I didn't recognize the Los Angeles that Raymond Chandler had written about. But when I started reading Macdonald, I saw LA. That just sort of indicates how rapidly Los Angeles was evolving. I found him much more on the money with the way things were, much more in keeping with the spirit of that particular period. He knew the town, he knew the California feel."

Jones talked with Millar at the Coral Casino and then at Chelham Way. "He was a very pleasant, very outgoing man," Jones found, "articulate and smart as hell." Puffing a filter-tipped cigarette, Millar told Jones, "I've tried to write honest social history as best I could. So did Chandler, and Hammett before him. But the Hollywood Chandler wrote about has exploded. It's not there anymore, if it ever was. The mobsters and toughs are gone too, or changed into something less noticeable. In my earlier books, Archer was really hard-boiled, iconoclastic, and dealt with these people. But lately, Archer is turning out more like me. . . . I'm not a hard-boiled guy. Archer is much less the big cheese than Marlowe was. What I'm interested in is other people, and Archer is a means to examine them. My main theme, I really think, is the possibility of communication between men and women, and the tragedy that occurs when that communication breaks down. Failure of communication is built right into the form of the detective novel. Everybody's holding back, and at best you get only a salutation. That's what all the mystery is about."

However much Millar wanted Archer not to be "the big cheese," but only a sort of ironic Greek chorus to the action, readers clearly found Lew Archer interesting in his own right. As Gerald Walker wrote in the *New York Post*, "Macdonald's detective, Lew Archer, is no 'eye'; he's a whole man. You even feel he exists between books, a little bleakly perhaps, but he lives nonetheless. He is someone with a sorrow in his past, a bad marriage, and the sour memory of his lost blond wife will assail him in his most vulnerable moments."

Appreciation of Macdonald beyond the mystery field was pioneered by Anthony Boucher, who'd been calling him a serious novelist for over a decade. Boucher had been crucial to Millar's career from the night they met in San Francisco in 1945, when Boucher inspired him to write his first private-eye stories; Boucher's public and private encouragement had buoyed him ever since. "Tony really *made* Ken Millar," said mystery writer Dorothy B. Hughes, herself an important reviewer. "He used to praise him so much, I said to him one time, 'Tony, I think you're in *love* with Ken Millar.' He took me seriously! He took it as a homosexual reference; his cheeks turned absolutely bright red, and he said, 'No—that's not true! That's not true!' " In 1951, Millar told Boucher, "I write for you more than any one single person (even Maggie who tough though she is is tough in a feminine way and just a leetle repelled by the masculine sort)." Through letters and visits, the Millars befriended the Bouchers. Once upon a time Linda Millar thought of one Boucher son as her boyfriend.

How long ago that all seemed in 1963, when Linda gave birth (on April 1) to a boy named James, making the Millars grandparents, something that seemed to give them a new lease on life, or at least new pleasure in it. "Gramps is fine," Millar wrote the Bransons, ". . . in fact so fine that I keep my fingers crossed in fear of fate. . . . Grandma is fine, too, and reveling in the role, dividing her time between the birds and the books." As for the grandson: "He's one of the lights of our life." The Millars enlivened their own home with a boisterous German shepherd pup, Brandy; and they continued their birding trips in 1963, one of which took them to Monterey for the western Audubon Convention, where Coleridge scholar Millar saw his first albatross.

How nice it would be for Ross Macdonald to win the Edgar in this good year—especially since Maggie already had one of those clay busts of Poe. His books were getting more popular; "Mr. Macdonald writes mysteries that even appeal to people who don't ordinarily read mysteries," *Publishers Weekly* said, adding that there were nearly 2 million Ross Macdonald Bantams in print. (For perspective: 1962 MWA president John D. MacDonald, published almost exclusively in softcover, had sold 25 million paperbacks.)

But sales didn't cut any ice with MWA voters; also there was that English bias to contend with, and half the six Edgar finalists this year were British.

Millar trekked to the Hollywood Knickerbocker for the Edgar dinner anyway, joining such colleagues as Thomas B. Dewey, Charlotte Armstrong (who'd won an Edgar the year after Maggie), and Dorothy B. Hughes. Also present was Elizabeth Linington, aka Dell Shannon, another nominee this year. Ned Guymon came from San Diego. Anthony Boucher emceed.

Though the Best Novel Edgar went to English writer Ellis Peters, Millar got to go to the podium anyhow to accept his "scroll" (a glorified sheet of paper) for *Zebra*'s nomination. He'd come prepared, win or lose, with something to recite. True-crime writer Edward D. Radin's book on Lizzie Borden (which maintained her innocence of the ax murders of her father and stepmother and criticized a 1937 Edmund Pearson work exonerating a suspect named Bridget) prompted many revisionist stanzas of the "Lizzie Borden took an ax" jingle. Millar wrote his own:

> While Lizzie Borden was no saint,
> A murderer Radin proves she ain't.
> Let Pearson in his coffin fidget:
> The bloody dress belonged to Bridget . . .
>
> In old blood Pearson dipped his quill
> And proved that Bridget did not kill.
> She was too young to be his mother:
> He must have been her long-lost brother.

Millar's lines brought down the house, and he left the dais on a high note. "By God, I believe I'll win *next* year," he told Dorothy Hughes, knowing what a strong contender he had in *The Chill*. "Maybe you will," the competitive Hughes genially answered. "*I* don't *have* a book coming out."

MYSTERY OF THE MISSING SCROLL

Ross Macdonald was given a Scroll at the Edgar Awards dinner but went home empty-handed. It seems someone inadvertently carried it off with them, possibly stuck in a program.
—*The March of Crime,* Southern California MWA

In a purely personal opinion, *The Chill* is the finest of Mr. Macdonald's prestige works.
—Dorothy B. Hughes, *New York Herald Tribune*

More people are saying the right things about your work, and I begin to wonder when their views will really filter through to the general public.
—Alfred Knopf to Ken Millar, 1964

If he thought something worth doing, Millar did it with complete commitment, be it writing a novel, learning to high dive, critiquing a manuscript, or making a marriage. He brought the same intensity to bird-watching, which he pursued with a scholar's zeal and a trustee's sense of responsibility. He got involved. With Maggie, Ken Millar helped found the Audubon's Santa Barbara chapter and took part in the Christmas bird count in which cities competed to spot the most species. Millar even made bird-watching athletic: "On one occasion," Margaret wrote of a Christmas count, "when sea birds were blanketed by a deep fog, Ken swam three-quarters of a mile in a fifty-two degree ocean to get us a pair of horned grebes for our list."

That sort of commitment drew Millar in 1964 into a political fight to stop a proposed ridge road along the Sierra Madre, near the Los Padres National Forest; experts said the road threatened one of the few remaining habitats of a bird as rare as the Maltese Falcon. Ken Millar turned the matter into a moral battle.

At stake was the California condor, the largest land bird in North America and perhaps the world. The condor vulture, with its ten-foot wingspan and soaring flight, had an awesome beauty. Only forty or fifty of these Ice Age descendants were left, and they used the mountains north of Santa Barbara as an unofficial sanctuary. The Forest Service proposed opening that area to the general public. More human traffic would mean a bigger fire hazard, Millar said, and greater chance of condors being shot. (Though condors were protected by law, people killed them anyway.) Condors were easily spooked into abandoning the few eggs they laid. If this road was allowed, Millar and other Santa Barbarans including Bob Easton feared, the condor might become extinct.

Forest Service officials treated these citizens' concerns as a joke, which infuriated Millar. The condor was an underdog, and he fought for underdogs. "Anyone, anything, being victimized reminded Ken of his own painful experience," Easton said, "and was apt to rouse a fiercely personal response." Millar began stirring up publicity. Through the bird-watchers network, the Millars met Brooks Atkinson, former *New York Times* drama critic turned roving *Times* columnist. Millar thought him one of the finest men he'd ever met: "a wonderful madman," he told Olding, "much better on nature and stuff than he ever was on plays." During Atkinson's January 1964 Santa Barbara stay, Millar arranged a trip on which the *Times* man saw ten condors; Atkinson wrote several columns on the birds' plight.

Once Millar got the Sierra Club and the National Audubon Society involved on the condors' behalf, the U.S. Forest Service agreed to hold a Santa Barbara hearing and let people speak for and against the road. On February 27, before an overflow crowd of more than a hundred at the Municipal Recreation Center, Millar (Information Officer, Santa Barbara Audubon Society) read a forceful speech. "Do we have to reveal ourselves as pleasure-greedy and frivolous and shortsighted," he asked, "with no thought for generations later than ourselves or forms of life other than our own? Basically, there is no form of life other than our own, and wherever we threaten life, be it only the life of an albatross or a condor, we threaten ourselves. . . . Some few things are so rare and ancient and valuable that they can't be improved by development, so fragile that they can't be carelessly exposed. Let us leave the condor alone."

Those in favor of the road included a fellow who suggested these condor lovers simply shoot and stuff the birds and view them at leisure. ("This one made even the Regional Forester look uncomfortable," Millar wrote.) At the end of the meeting, the Forest Service official decreed that since there were "extremists" on both sides, he'd make a decision somewhere in the middle. "Which seemed to imply," thought Millar, "that he would decide to ruin the wilderness just a little, for the present, and permit the condor to survive for a few more years, perhaps."

Largely thanks to Millar, this Santa Barbara meeting was covered by the *San Francisco Chronicle* and the *New York Times* and prompted editorials in the *Washington Post* and the *Washington Star.* Millar himself wrote a first-person article for *Sports Illustrated,* "A Death Road for the Condor," which was as tautly ironic as a Lew Archer short story; it was read into the *Congressional Record.* The regional forester postponed a decision on the road pending further study. Millar and company kept up the pressure.

Brooks Atkinson learned that *New York Times* man Robert Phelps and his wife, an avid birder, were planning a West Coast vacation; he urged they contact Millar, who invited the Phelpses for lunch at the Coral Casino. Phelps, later the *Times*'s Washington bureau editor, recalled their initial exchange: "When I sat down with him, he said, 'Do you know who I am?' I felt a little embarrassed, although Brooks Atkinson had described him to me as a fine writer. I said, 'Well, I know you write mystery stories.' He says, 'No. I'm a *novelist*, who writes with a mystery *theme*.' "

Millar guided the Phelpses to Ian "Ike" McMillan's ranch in Shandon, near San Luis Obispo, where the Phelpses sighted the California condor. Phelps got permission from *Times* national editor Harrison Salisbury to do a piece on the endangered birds, in which Millar was quoted for three paragraphs. Not a passive interviewee, Millar read the piece beforehand and critiqued it, Phelps said: "He suggested I change a verb here, a paragraph there."

Millar gave money as well as time to the condor cause. When Olding wired in April asking if it was okay to sell *Cosmopolitan* condensation rights to the new Archer novel *The Far Side of the Dollar* (the fourth Macdonald in a row bought by *Cosmo*) he telegraphed back: OF COURSE PLEASE ACCEPT RAPID COSMO OFFER FOR FAR SIDE OF DOLLAR AND KEEP CONDORS FLYING LOVE KEN. Millar had backed his beliefs with cash even in times when he couldn't afford to, Margaret said: "I remember one Christmas when we were really *strapped* for dough, and we had a little girl, and there just wasn't any money. Nobody was going to get a present. And just at the last minute I got five hundred dollars from my agent in New York. Well, Ken took a hundred dollars and gave it to CARE! I was mad as hell. But afterwards it occurred to me this was a good thing to do, very good; so I was proud of him. But even though I'm not known to be stingy, I don't think I'd have done that."

Millar was also generous with help to fellow writers, such as Bob Easton, whose cowritten book on the condors he unofficially edited and then got Brooks Atkinson to write a preface for. Millar vetted all Easton's manuscripts for years with an unselfishness his friend marveled at: "It was rather strange to me when I first knew him because he was extremely hard-pressed for time, and yet he was giving me a lot of the very meager time he had. He was terribly stressed really to produce an Alfred Knopf–quality book every year—and he *had* to produce one a year to live on, so his time was carefully measured. And his health was never very good, so his strength was limited too."

Others who received Millar's frequent editorial help included Wilbur H. "Ping" Ferry, a former corporation PR man who'd looked up Millar at Alfred Knopf's urging when he moved to Santa Barbara to work for a think tank called the Center for the Study of Democratic Institutions. An intellectual provocateur in the Swiftian tradition, Ferry once suggested a way to avoid atomic war: have the U.S. president and the Soviet premier agree to murder fifty children from each other's country before pushing the button. A poker-faced gadfly with a wardrobe that ran to pink shirts and yellow polka-dot bow ties, Ferry found the low-key Millar "about as colorful as a window shade"; yet they got along famously.

"We were good friends; I saw quite a lot of him," said Ferry, adding quickly (like most of Millar's friends), "I never got to know him. He was quite a private man. I don't think he had any really close friends. Except his wife, maybe. He was a sort of loner. He had no social life at all that I know of. He and Maggie never went out after dark; Maggie I think was afraid of the dark in some curious way. I don't recall they ever accepted a dinner invitation. It was a very curious couple you're dealing with. He was vastly amused by Maggie, and she was vastly taken by Ken; they were very much drawn together. I went out for dinner with Ken a few times when he wanted to see a movie, but those were his only after-dark excursions, I believe. He liked those writers' lunches every other Wednesday, which I attended, at the restaurant downtown; but he didn't contribute much there except his presence. He just looked, and listened. He and Barnaby Conrad were the stars of the table. Barnaby talked a lot, but Ken would never say anything; he just kind of sat there sphinxlike. Ken was the icon. He was the successful writer. He was the man who, without making a lot of fuss about it, kept writing those books and getting those very good reviews."

Millar's silence didn't make him poor company, Ferry insisted: "Despite his withdrawnness, he was very pleasant to be with. It allowed one to talk, to talk loud, to spread himself before a very sympathetic listener. He was a very warm friend." Ferry, author of a constant stream of speeches and papers, asked Millar early on to read something he'd written: "I said, 'Look, I'd like you to go over this, both the ideas and the language.' In a couple of days he called and asked me to stop by; he handed it back, and in this very spidery and light writing were these rather diffident but very cogent suggestions. It was a very good editing job, and he improved my prose a great deal. He started being a sort of advisory editor to me. He was a marvelous critic. Gradually I got better and better. So I owed him a lot.

"He asked me to do the same thing for him, but—as Alfred Knopf told me, 'You know, we'd never need to have any editors in this shop if every author was like Ken Millar. We never have to touch a word of his; no question is ever raised. This is the ideal author, from a publisher's point of view.' Alfred was as complimentary as could be. I remember only one substantial correction I made in anything of Ken's: it had to do with the position of the tollbooth on the San Francisco bridge; he had it at the wrong end. And he was delighted I'd found that!"

Ferry's center hosted talks and panels with such figures as Alfred Knopf, Alex Comfort, and Linus Pauling. Millar went to the hilltop center a few times but didn't take to the crowd there, Easton recalled: "He regarded them as misguided academics dreaming quite literally in the clouds and looking down their noses at ordinary life and people including perhaps himself. I once attended a meeting with him at the Center, a kind of symposium they were sponsoring. We were escorted through hushed rooms, dined in a hall fit for ambassadors. One woman came up to Ken and asked effusively, 'What do you do?' 'I'm a novelist,' he replied dryly. 'Oh,' she said, giving him a queer look, 'one of those!' At any rate, when Ken became famous and some of the academics and Center people warmed toward him, Ken had the satisfaction of maintaining his coolness."

Millar found more pragmatic ways of being useful: writing letters to the *News-Press* on local or national issues, attending state Democratic conventions, campaigning for candidates he believed in, matching writer friends with agents, and editing colleagues' manuscripts (in 1964 he edited Hank Branson's Civil War novel by mail). "I think Ken regarded public and artistic service as a moral duty," Easton said. "He felt it was a real moral imperative. That's how he gave back, you see. He had no organized religion that I know of. But I think this was a deep aspect of his personal belief: to give back, in full measure. And he really did it."

Their bird-watching took the Millars to Alberta and British Columbia in spring 1964 for a journey that came to seem like one of Lew Archer's forays into a suspect's or victim's history: those counterclockwise loops in time in which the more the past is penetrated the faster the future approaches, until the two fuse abruptly in the present. In Medicine Hat, Millar visited his aunt Laura, fifty when he lived with her for his fourteenth year, eighty-five now "and still reading"—Laura, whose late husband, Fred, had assembled the leading collection of beetles in western Canada, which he left to the University of Alberta. Millar was moved when he visited scenes from his youth such as the South Saskatchewan riverbank he'd hiked. The coincidences began in Edmonton, where the Millars stayed at the Macdonald Hotel. They met an Edmonton bird-club member whose husband worked at the university; it turned out he curated Uncle Fred's beetle collection. Better yet, the woman herself had attended the University of Western Ontario, as had her older sister—who'd been in Western's production of *Twelfth Night* with Millar. In Vancouver, Millar chanced to speak on the airport bus with an Australian grad student attending Alberta; did he know the professor who curated Uncle Fred's beetle collection? Millar asked. Yes, the professor was supervising his doctoral studies. "Life is very interwoven, is it not," Millar marveled.

The journey had other highlights: harlequin ducks on the Athabasca River, the pileated woodpecker at Elk Island, Edmonton nighthawks. The Millars met an English teacher near Edmonton who showed them around his own eighty-acre bird and wildlife sanctuary. A Canadian National Railroad conductor guided them into some nearly untouched country on the CNR line. Millar found the trip thrilling and would happily have extended it, but (although she liked it too) Margaret found it wearing; they returned to Santa Barbara "early as usual," ten days sooner than planned.

Travel with Margaret was always a challenge; and mishaps (a lost purse, a wasp sting necessitating a five-hundred-mile dash to "the first competent doctor," a sudden "flu") often cut journeys short. "M. is rather allergic to travel," Millar concluded. He catered to her whims, maximizing the couple's opportunities to do things together. After Kennedy's death reminded them both of their mortality, the Millars together gave up smoking: life was so enjoyable now that they hoped to prolong it. Both were doting grandparents ("Perhaps I could believe you were really a grandfather if I could see you being grandfatherly," Olding wrote Millar). They shared a love of good popular music, from Broadway to Brubeck to (later) the Beatles to (always) Ellington. When Margaret took up cycling on a collapsible bike, Ken did too, reporting to Alfred Knopf, "My good wife . . . has covered 500 miles on that vehicle in the past three months, and has an odometer to prove it." (Knopf responded, "Margaret on a bicycle simply staggers me.") In correspondence Millar spoke of his wife with pride, humor, resignation, and admiration. He coined pet names for her, some with comic bite: "my shricking violet," "the Bird Lady of Chelham Way," "my lemon" (a play on the Old English endearment "my leman").

He was aware that his career had in some ways overtaken hers. Maggie was paid about the same hardcover advance money as he, their backlists were in equal demand in Europe, they both sold regularly to *Cosmo,* and each got excellent reviews (Boucher said Margaret's latest, *The Fiend,* was "something extraordinary . . . even by Mrs. Millar's high standards"). But Maggie's novels didn't always make it to paperback (her lack of a series hero hurt her), and ideas for her one-of-a-kind tales were occurring less often: a two-year gap between books was now common. With *The Far Side of the Dollar* Millar again drew even with his wife: each of them had nineteen published books. Millar was childishly excited about this, like an Ontario boy in a swimming race; but he was old enough to know it was the competition that was fun, not the winning. He didn't want Margaret lagging far behind.

Their Hollywood representation had become a sensitive matter. After her early *Iron Gates* success, nothing happened for Margaret at the studios except the television assignments she'd pursued (though recently Swanson had sold two of her books to TV anthology shows for about four thousand dollars each). Millar was still anxious to get something going with Archer in Hollywood, but he didn't want to hurt his wife's chances or pride. "It seems a healthy thing for me and M. to have separate Hollywood agents," he wrote von Auw. Keeping his and her dealings apart led Millar in and out of complicated entanglements, one of which cost him dearly when his (and Archer's) long-awaited Hollywood ship came in.

All this was made more complex by the bicoastal communication (or lack of it) between Ober in New York and Swanson in LA, and by Millar's vacillations. With Margaret's Hollywood interests being newly handled in early 1964 by Evarts Ziegler, her husband wrote Olding, "One question which I'd like to get the answer to straight. Swanee is handling *The Chill,* isn't he? If so, I want to write and urge him to do a selling job, since it would make a hell of a movie or something." Knopf was promoting *The Chill* with a quarter-page ad in the *New York Times,* and the author was keen to capitalize on the stir it might create. Yes, Olding wrote Millar, Swanee was handling *The Chill* and would continue to, "unless you want us to withdraw it from him. . . . By all means urge him to do a selling job because the book damn well deserves it." But after phoning Swanson, Millar told her,

"He didn't know he was representing *The Chill*. I told him he was. It would be untidy to take it from him now. I hope he has copies. He said he had 'stopped work' on it. Oh well."

The Chill was creating its own interest: a producing team at Twentieth approached both Ober and Swanson about buying rights for fifteen thousand dollars. Millar, and Swanson, thought that too low; as Millar pointed out to von Auw: "*Ferguson* sold for $16,500 cash. *Chill* is a very much better story, and I am very much better recognized now, and am due for even more recognition." But author and agent kept the Twentieth channel open. Meanwhile Swanson talked with some Paramount people about a possible Archer TV series, while another would-be producer asked about rights to *The Zebra-Striped Hearse*.

The most promising nibble seemed the one from Paramount producer Gordon Carroll and his partner George Axelrod, currently making the feature *How to Murder Your Wife*. Carroll suggested maybe Millar/Macdonald could write an Archer pilot script based on *The Barbarous Coast*. Millar, bearing a typed copy of *The Far Side of the Dollar*, drove to Hollywood in the spring of 1964 to meet Carroll. He later wrote this no-names-please account for *Show* magazine:

> A producer who last year was toying with the idea of making a television series featuring my private detective Lew Archer asked me over lunch at Perino's if Archer was based on any actual person. "Yes," I said. "Myself." He gave me a semi-pitying Hollywood look. I tried to explain that while I had known some excellent detectives and watched them work, Archer was created from the inside out. I wasn't Archer, exactly, but Archer was me.
>
> The conversation went downhill from there, as if I had made a damaging admission.

Carroll pled difficulties with his movie project and backed away from Archer. The producers sniffing at *The Chill* begged off for lack of funds. Millar claimed to von Auw not to be greatly let down: "I suppose because I'm well satisfied with the way my writing career is going and there is a sense in which you *pay* for money, I believe." To Olding he was more sour: "Nothing good ever happens in Hollywood anyway."

But Hollywood still seemed intrigued with Archer. The next expression of interest came from some independent producers at Universal regarding *Zebra*. So far so good, Millar told Olding, but "of course I had to turn the negotiation over to Swanee and that is probably the end of that. His 'cash-on-the-drum' (I quote) method doesn't seem to work too well with the delicate independents." Millar asked Olding to recommend a new Hollywood agent for *The Far Side of the Dollar*. A few days later, though, the author was seeing things Swanee's way: the fellows who wanted *Zebra* were after a free six-months' option, and Millar (and Swanson) didn't want to give them one. Meanwhile Margaret had broken with Evarts Ziegler, and Millar asked Olding to suggest another good (non-Swanson) agent for her, "though God knows it's no responsibility of yours." He took a different tack after her *The Fiend* got excellent reviews, writing Olding, "If there should be any movie interest I assume your office can handle it without getting entangled with Hollywood." (Olding noted resignedly to her partner, "Ivan—Here we go again.")

Nothing happened with *The Fiend* in Hollywood, though, and things got quiet on the Archer front—until near the end of 1964, when Swanson told Millar one of the would-be producers formerly chasing *The Zebra-Striped Hearse* was now offering five hundred dollars against a purchase price of ten thousand dollars for a six-month option on (of all books) *The Moving Target*. Swanson said unless a better bid was made, "we can forget this cat." But Millar, as he wrote von Auw, admired this suitor's persistence (the man came to Santa Barbara to see him) and wanted to take a chance: "*The Moving Target* is not exactly a sought-after property. Most important, I'd like to see something done in the movies with my work, and it has to start somewhere. I don't really see what I can lose by going along with this on an old book." Millar stunned his New York agents by stating he was sticking with Swanee for the time being, mainly because Margaret *wasn't* with Swanson; and would they please send Swanee copies of *Far Side* to show at the studios?

Von Auw wrote back quickly to say he and Olding thought Millar had definitely decided to go with Evarts Ziegler—and Ziegler had been working on *Far Side* in Hollywood for four months! Fair enough, said Millar—he knew Ziegler was a good agent—but, "do you tell Swanee or do I? If you do, please make it clear that I haven't been playing a double game with him." And the *Target* deal already in the works belonged to Swanee, he emphasized. Unless his New York and Hollywood agents told him it was *very* wrong, Millar intended to okay the *Target* option. Von Auw voiced no objection, and Swanson seemed agreeable, negotiating the purchase price to $12,500 and telling Millar, "We hope we'll be able to get you a decent and proper contract on this." That was that.

The ocean was where Millar washed away everyday mental grime. He was at peace in the sea, as if he belonged there. Memories of his childhood were inextricably a part of this: wading on the Vancouver beach with his mother, sailing with his dad. Millar had a swimming style all his own, his ex-friend Don Pearce saw: "He had a *long* stroke: first the left hand would go over and down and into the water very deliberately like a paddle wheel, with his body and shoulders sort of rotating—then the other arm would come up and over and down. He'd *roll* through the water with this graceless but seemingly tireless stroke, a stroke so slow that if I swam in rhythm to it I'd sink. But somehow he stayed afloat with this long stroke; it was a puzzle. And he'd go for great distances. He always looked happy in the water—not exactly with a smile on his face, but happy. I asked him once how he kept from being bored when swimming, and he said, 'Oh, that's frequently when I get my best ideas for books. I often write whole paragraphs, swimming in the ocean.' " Millar swam in most weather and almost all temperatures. In the summer of 1964, with the sea warm, he got his 105-pound German shepherd, Brandy, to do his daily half-mile in the ocean with him: "It's all I can do to keep up with him," he told Knopf.

Millar was waiting for Maggie to join him in the surf off the Coral Casino at two-thirty on a September Tuesday when a beach-club lifeguard waved him in. Margaret had gotten word there was a fire on Coyote Road, about half a mile from Chelham Way.

Wildfires in the mountains behind Santa Barbara were a constant threat to those who lived in the hills and canyons. The last bad fire had been in 1955. Years of near drought since had left vast brush areas tinder dry. Conditions were especially dangerous on days when the hot Santa Ana winds blew over the mountains from the Mojave. Today was such a day.

The Millars drove home quickly. Several airplanes, including World War II B-17s, were bombarding the neighborhood with fire-retardant chemicals. Hundreds of firemen were pitching camp at Westmont College up the road. Helicopters hovered, monitoring the flames. This Coyote blaze was moving fast. When the Millars looked out their living-room window, they saw homes burning on nearby Mountain Drive.

The winds died down, and by evening the fire seemed under control. But at 9 P.M. the Santa Anas returned, and Coyote roared to life. Flames fifty to a hundred feet high jumped from canyon to canyon. At midnight, Chelham Way residents were told to evacuate. Millar kissed Maggie goodbye and saw her and the dogs off by car to Ping and Jo Ferry's; he stayed to save the house if he could. After checking by phone on friends like the Lids and the Eastons, who also lived in canyons, he went up on the roof with a garden hose to douse embers that dropped onto the eaves and into the yard. At one point the fire reached the head of Chelham Way, two hundred yards from the Millar place; but at 2:30 A.M. the wind shifted, and Chelham Way was spared.

Margaret returned at noon Wednesday, when Coyote seemed licked. Forty-five-mile-an-hour winds revived it, though, and by evening Chelham Way was again in danger. Once more Margaret and the dogs evacuated. Millar loaded his brother-in-law's truck with five shelves from the literal ton of books in the house. The floorboards shook with the fire's force as he picked out volumes to save: the *Walden* his father had left him, the Beardsley-illustrated Baudelaire bought for two bucks in Toronto, Leacock's *Sunshine Sketches of a Little Town*, a set of Proust, a well-marked Freud, books by Faulkner, Fitzgerald, Algren, Coleridge, Poe, Davie, Kenner, Dickens, Hammett, Chandler, Dante, Mencken, Welty, Kafka, Plato, Millar, Millar, Macdonald.

He stayed on the roof a second night as the Santa Anas whipped Coyote's flames as high as two hundred feet. Again the fire roared to the head of the canyon, and again the wind shifted and saved Chelham Way. Others weren't so lucky. A hundred families (thirty of whom the Millars knew) lost homes to Coyote, which burned eighty thousand acres. The fire wasn't contained for nine days. Millar wrote von Auw, "I won't try to describe a forest fire but will save it as background for a novel."

His rooftop vigil was valiant but not unique; many others did as much or more. Bob Easton and a bunch of his City College students physically fought Coyote when it came within thirty paces of them, Easton said: "We were able to start a tiny backfire that moved up the hill a bit and pretty well stopped the main attack; then, with garden hoses and wet sacks and buckets, and shouting like a bunch of wildmen, we charged the fire! Your blood gets up, and you fight it, just like you fight an active enemy. We kept it from getting into Mission Canyon." But Millar showed an imperturbability that seemed remarkable. Betty Lid never forgot a brief telephone exchange she and Millar had during her moment of truth with Coyote. Her husband was away from Santa Barbara the night the wildfire rushed the canyon where the Lid house perched. It was early morning when the flames approached. Betty, asleep, was wakened by the light and heat: her room was bright as day, and she was soaked in sweat. All neighbors for two blocks around had fled. She phoned Millar and told him frantically, "Ken, the fire's coming down the canyon, Dick's gone, and I'm all alone here!" Millar responded with a calm that chilled her. "Betty," he said, "you're always alone."

Mail Forwarding Dept.
Alfred A. Knopf, Inc.
501 Madison Ave.
New York, N.Y.

Dear Sirs:
   You're still sending my mail to: 2136 Cliff Drive, San Barbara, Calif. There is no San Barbara, and I haven't lived on Cliff Drive since 1956. A friend of ours lives there but is now moving so I appeal once again to you to change my listing, though it does provide my life with a kind of goofy continuity (I've moved three times since 1956).

                                    Yours peripatetically,
                                    Kenneth Millar
                                    (Ross Macdonald)

Miss Patricia Powell
Harold Ober Associates
40 E. 49th St.
New York 17, N.Y.

Dear Miss Powell:
   Thank you so much for your prompt reply to my query, which was prompted more by chronic anxiety than by any unusual delay. When I have nothing else to worry about, my wife claims, I worry about the depletion of shellfish in Chesapeake Bay. If there is something within your awareness that needs worrying about, please let me know and I will worry about it.

                                    Sincerely,
                                    Kenneth Millar

If writing well was the best revenge, as Millar said, he had a double portion in January 1965 with the simultaneous publication of his highly praised novel *The Far Side of the Dollar* and an essay in *Show* magazine, "The Writer as Detective Hero," in which Ross Macdonald (ostensibly surveying the history of crime fiction) convincingly argued the superiority of his own work to Raymond Chandler's.

   He began by giving Chandler his due: "The Chandler-Marlowe prose is a highly charged blend of laconic wit and imagistic poetry set to breakneck rhythms . . . an overheard democratic prose which is one of the most effective narrative instruments in our recent literature." But compared to Hammett's realistic Sam Spade, Macdonald said, Chandler's Marlowe—

the lonely knight-errant in the corrupt city—was a middle-aged author's fantasy, "a backward step in the direction of sentimental romance."

The author then contrasted his and Chandler's approach to plot: "Chandler described a good plot as one that made for good scenes, as if the parts were greater than the whole. I see plot as a vehicle of meaning. It should be as complex as contemporary life, but balanced enough to say true things about it. The surprise with which a detective novel concludes should set up tragic vibrations which run backward through the entire structure. Which means that the structure must be single, and *intended*." Another difference was their use of language, Macdonald said: "Marlowe's voice is limited by his role as the hardboiled hero. He must speak within his limits as a character, and these limits are quite narrowly conceived. Chandler tried to relax them in *The Long Goodbye*, but he was old and the language failed to respond. He was trapped like the late Hemingway in an unnecessarily limiting idea of self, hero, and language."

His Archer, Macdonald made clear, was not Chandleresque: "He is less a doer than a questioner, a consciousness in which the meanings of other lives emerge. This gradually developed conception of the detective hero as the mind of the novel is not wholly new, but it is probably my main contribution to this special branch of fiction. Some such refinement of the conception of the detective hero was needed to bring this kind of novel closer to the purpose and range of the mainstream novel."

Subtle attack, effective defense, artful polemic: Macdonald's essay was all of that, plus an effective self-advertisement, for which he was paid six hundred dollars! He'd wanted to get this off his chest since reading Chandler's letter about *The Moving Target*. Now he'd more or less evened the score; in a final aside to Olding, he said of his predecessor, "He had a great talent but was, just between you and me, a poseur with a second-rate mind."

The article was perfectly timed to stir interest in *The Far Side of the Dollar*, and several reviewers took cues from the essay in crafting raves for the Archer book. "Without in the least abating my admiration for Dashiell Hammett and Raymond Chandler," wrote Boucher in the *New York Times Book Review*, "I should like to venture the heretical suggestion that Ross Macdonald is a better novelist than either of them." Walter O'Hearn of the *Montreal Star* reviewed *Far Side* together with a scholarly biographical study of Chandler (Philip Durham's *Down These Mean Streets a Man Must Go*) and concluded, "Mr. Macdonald, like Chandler, has a descriptive gift. But he is realer. . . . The surprises are genuine. Mr. Macdonald plays no tricks. He is interested in character and the effect of character and destiny. He is also interested in plot, which Raymond Chandler wasn't." The *LA Times*'s Robert Kirsch elaborated on Macdonald's notion of Archer as Greek chorus: "Ross Macdonald's *The Far Side of the Dollar* has the power and dimension of a Greek tragedy but the reader is not blackjacked into realizing it, which is at once more compatible with modern taste and perhaps the reason that this estimable author does not receive the total recognition to which he is entitled. . . . This may well be the best book which Macdonald has written to date. (I know I always say that about Macdonald. But I can't very well help it. He is simply one of those rare writers who grows from book to book.)"

Also growing was Macdonald's recognition by reviewers outside the mystery ghetto, and the realization that Macdonald was more than a master of the crime story or a worthy successor to Chandler. Clifford A. Ridley of the *National Observer* said Macdonald bore study "by anyone engaged in sculpting the English language. . . . Mr. Macdonald is dealing with nothing less than a literal search for personal identity." William Hogan told his *San Francisco Chronicle* readers, "I think that Ross Macdonald is an important American novelist."

While Macdonald's MWA colleagues still refused him an Edgar (or even a nomination for *The Chill*), they did elect him their president for 1965, an honor that filled him "with foolish joy," he confessed, especially since his wife had received it ten years ago. (Margaret's *The Fiend* was nominated for an Edgar.) He told Olding, "Now I have just enough success to experience the small poignant sadness that accompanies it, like post-coital tristesse. I hope in the next ten or fifteen years to accomplish some one notable thing, but have no assurance that I shall. (I will, tho.) Anyway, I got a good agent!"

And from England came word the British Crime Writers Association was giving Macdonald "a runner-up award" (their Silver Dagger) for *The Chill*. Millar was tempted to fly to London for the CWA's April dinner but decided he didn't want to spend the money or take time from an Archer novel he was in the final throes of; the new book needed his attention "more than that old one," he said.

His wife, much to Millar's relief, was at work "with enormous gusto" on a new book too—not a mystery but a nonfiction account of the bird-watching life. Margaret had gotten stuck recently on a fiction manuscript; this birding book, which she'd been thinking about for years, was a logjam-breaker for her. Millar took pains, with and without her knowledge, to keep Maggie and her manuscript on track.

Like Margaret, Millar would be fifty this year. With his wife productive, his daughter and family back from a year in Japan, and his own career in satisfying shape, it seemed maybe his life had turned toward good luck. In spite or because of that, he kept his fingers crossed.

He'd earned what he'd gotten by sticking with his genre, perfecting his craft, and improving his style. Millar had outlasted most other private-eye writers of his generation—including William Campbell Gault, who'd given up mysteries for the juvenile fiction market. Gault was a mainstay at the alternate-Wednesday writers' lunches, where his boisterous manner often bumped against Millar's less gregarious facade. "Oh, they'd have clashes," said Bob Easton. "There was one occasion when Ken was holding forth a bit, pontificating on something, and Gault, who could be very abrupt and down-to-earth, said, 'Oh, for Christ's sakes, Ken, come off it!' and just got up and left the table. Ken called him up next day and said he was sorry. 'Sway Ken would do. He was terribly sensitive, and terribly aware of his own real or imagined shortcomings."

Despite their bristlings, Millar and Gault had much in common. Both were serious-fiction readers (Gault liked Bellow, Beckett, and Fitzgerald), and each in his way was a good writer. That was important to Millar, said Dennis Lynds, who started going to the lunches in 1965: "Ken never forgave bad writers, and that's the truth."

A case in point, said Lynds, was Davis Dresser, who, as Brett Halliday, had been churning out books about private-eye Michael Shayne ("that reckless, redheaded Irishman") since 1939. Dresser, raised in Texas, was another Santa Barbara writers' lunch fixture. "Ken didn't like his writing," Lynds said, "and he didn't like Dave either particularly. Dave was loud, crass, and too commercial. But you know Dave thought he was Dostoyevsky, and he meant it; he wasn't kidding. Dave was crusty, assertive, very sure of himself." Gault's assessment was pithy: "Dresser was a shit." Millar kept Dresser at arm's length with puckish humor. "He said the other day at lunch that he didn't know how he could write so fast, 'the words just came to him,'" Millar wrote Olding (who'd met and disliked Dresser). "I said they picked on him." Lynds recalled, "When Dave wrote his fiftieth Mike Shayne book, it was a big deal. The publisher did a gold cover and all, and Dave got testimonial quotes from everybody: he had Gault, he had Easton, I think he got everyone he knew—except Ken. Ken refused. He wouldn't give him a testimonial, 'cause he couldn't. And that made Dave pretty mad." On the other hand, Millar privately tried (and failed) to get the MWA to honor Dresser with a career achievement award.

If Dresser and Gault were the old guard of mystery writers, Lynds was the new wave. Forty-one when he moved to Santa Barbara from New York in 1965, freelance-writer Lynds would soon start publishing mysteries under a number of pseudonyms (mainly Michael Collins); for now he paid the rent with monthly twenty-thousand-word novelettes for *Michael Shayne's Mystery Magazine*, stories printed under Brett Halliday's byline (another reason for Millar not to think much of Dresser). Six foot three, with horn-rimmed glasses and a Dickensian nose, Lynds got Millar's attention immediately. "We took to each other quite a lot," Lynds said. "We used to walk up and down State after the lunches and talk. He'd have this big dog with him, Brandy, or the dog would be in the car. Sometimes we'd meet at the Coral Casino, and he'd have Brandy, and we'd walk on the beach. He liked to talk one-on-one I think. Mostly we'd discuss literature: good magazines, writers, stories that we liked; 'Have you read this one? Have you read that one?' He would question me a lot; I was the New One, so he'd want to know where I'd published and what I thought about. I went to his house once on Chelham Way, a little street off Sycamore Canyon: the lower-middle-class section of Montecito, if you will. And there was Brandy, this monster dog; you could hardly get out of the car until Ken came and called him off. I don't like big dogs much—others were bothered by Brandy—so I didn't visit often. Ken came to my house once when he still drank a bit. My then wife asked if he'd have something, and he said, 'Half a can of beer.' She served him the full can, and he drank precisely half; he left the rest. She wasn't fond of Ken. He'd ignore her, keep her out of the conversation. He was always very polite—but he made it very clear if he wasn't interested in talking to you."

Millar liked talking with Jackie Coulette, wife of poet Henri (Hank) Coulette, or at least liked listening to her (he praised her sense of irony); but all the same he made her uncomfortable. "He was a charming man," she said, "but I find people as quiet as Ken very difficult to be around; I feel I should be up on a tabletop dancing or something to entertain them, to bring them out. One afternoon he came over to the beach house; Hank had gone into town and wasn't back yet. So here we were in the living room waiting—and he just *sat* there. And it really *got* to me. And it lasted about twenty minutes! I was beginning to think, well, what can I *do?* What can I *say?* It just *bothered* me. And I think to some extent it was deliberate, I think part of it was for fun: to see how uncomfortable he could make you!"

Hank Coulette, a Cal State LA instructor who was thirty-eight in 1965, first got in touch with Millar to offer him that school's visiting writer professorship, held in the recent past by Christopher Isherwood and Dorothy Parker. Millar reluctantly declined (he'd lose time from a book) but asked Coulette for freeway directions to Cal State: Lew Archer needed to go there. "They talked for a while on the phone," Jackie Coulette said, "and my husband, who was very shy with people he didn't know, told him what an admirer he was of his work. And Ken, who was also shy with strangers, said, 'Well, when you come up to Santa Barbara, look me up, I'd like to meet you.' We were in Santa Barbara the next summer; Edgar Bowers, a dear friend who's a professor at UCSB and a poet, has a house in Montecito we'd rent. And it took Hank about two weeks before he got up enough courage to call Ken—with my prodding him every day. Ken invited him to one of the writers' luncheons, and that's how they met. One of the things that I think drew the two of them together: Ken was the only person Hank ever met who'd lived in more different houses by the age of eighteen than Hank; I think Hank had lived in thirty-nine places by the time he was eighteen, and Ken beat him. And they really seemed to be on the same wavelength when it came to writing and writers; they admired the same people, like Auden. Ken admired the poet above all other writers; he felt they were the *true* writers. I think one of the reasons each admired the other was they had both tried the other's métier. Hank, who was so used to making everything as succinct as possible, packing everything into only a few words, couldn't understand how *anybody* could write a novel; and Ken couldn't see how Hank could put so much into a poem." Coulette, who'd win a Lamont

Tom Nolan

Prize and a Guggenheim Fellowship, borrowed a phrase from *The Ferguson Affair* ("prime rib of unicorn, or breast of phoenix") for his poem "The Blue-Eyed Precinct Worker." Ross Macdonald's final novel would take its title from a Coulette line. "While I have good poets with me," Millar once wrote to himself, "to hell with the academics."

Mystery Writers of America president Kenneth Millar went to New York alone in April 1965 for the MWA annual dinner. Though Margaret's book *The Fiend* was an Edgar nominee, it seemed unlikely to win over John le Carré's best-selling *The Spy Who Came In from the Cold;* she stayed home to work on her bird book. ("Kick le Carré in the pants for me, right?" she said.)

Millar's MWA duties mostly consisted of attending the Edgars. The rest of his ten-day stay was spent doing radio and press interviews and meeting with editors. Dorothy Olding was out of the country, so Millar and Ivan von Auw attended to business. Ross Macdonald's novel *Black Money* was formally accepted for publication at Knopf, and *Cosmopolitan* bought first serial rights to it. Bantam was also eager for another Archer: after Millar met with the firm's Allan Barnard and Marcia Nasatir (Saul David had left Bantam for Hollywood), the paperback house bid seventy-five hundred dollars to reprint *The Far Side of the Dollar,* a big increase over the forty-five hundred paid for *The Chill.*

But there was bad news too from Bantam: it was letting rights lapse to four earlier Macdonalds, including three *(The Galton Case, The Barbarous Coast, The Doomsters)* Millar thought among his best; von Auw would have to shop those elsewhere. Bantam's decision had to do with market trends. English spy thrillers by le Carré, Fleming, Deighton, Hall, and Ambler were the rage; movie and TV screens were filled with James Bond imitators. Softcover publishers ran with the craze; even the Edgars followed suit. Few authors wrote about private eyes anymore. Macdonald was the leader of a passé form, the best of a dying breed. Bantam's artwork for recent Macdonald books hid the fact that they featured a licensed detective; the cover and jacket copy of their edition of *The Zebra-Striped Hearse* didn't mention Lew Archer at all. While their blurbs hailed Macdonald as an "old master" of mystery, Bantam was phasing his old masterpieces out of print.

Yet Millar knew he had a growing campus readership; college students wrote him fan letters, even came to Santa Barbara to meet him. And these were the sort of readers (or he the sort of writer) who, after they read one Macdonald book, wanted to read them all. It was crucial, he felt, that all books stay available. How else could he (and his publishers) benefit from twenty years of hard work and growing literary excellence?

It was the literary aspect of crime fiction that Macdonald stressed during his MWA presidency, emphasizing the mystery's connection to the mainstream. In interviews he'd carefully cite Yeats or Ibsen, not Stout or

255

Doyle. Accepting his *Chill* Silver Dagger from Julian Symons at the Edgar dinner, he quoted Shakespeare: "Is this a dagger which I see before me, the handle toward my hand? Come, let me clutch thee." (And he did.)

The nineteenth annual Edgar Allan Poe Awards ceremony on Friday, April 30, drew three hundred fifty MWA members and guests to the Versailles Room of the Hotel Astor. President Millar/Macdonald sat at the Knopf table with Ashbel Green and Harding Lemay and their wives, Knopf author George Harmon Coxe, Ivan von Auw, and (by Millar's arrangement) Hank and Anna Branson, in New York for Dutton's publication of Branson's Civil War novel, *Salisbury Plain.* Millar seated Branson next to him and made a point of introducing H.C. to all who came by, including English publisher Victor Gollancz (flamboyant in a green velvet dinner jacket). Gollancz published Margaret Millar in Britain, also John le Carré (who did win the Edgar this year). By the end of the evening, staunch friend Millar had Gollancz and von Auw (Branson's agent) huddled together in the Astor bar making terms for an English edition of *Salisbury Plain.*

Millar took advantage of his presidential prerogative to critique the Edgars dinner in a letter to Michael Avallone, editor of the MWA newsletter:

> Brilliant as it was, and highly successful, it ran too long—in Victor Gollancz' opinion, about twice too long. The old pathologist right on top of eating was unfortunate, to put it mildly, and shouldn't have been asked. The opening remarks could and should have been speeded up (with all due love and respect for Henry Klinger *et al.*) and so by all means should Rex Stout's presentation remarks. Nobody really wants or needs jokes and manufactured suspense on these occasions. On the other hand, Stout's opening statement on the copyright law was forceful and pertinent—for me the height of the evening. Thanks to Harold Masur, who said he'd resign if we had a folksinger, we didn't have a folksinger. But how could such an idea even come up? Who makes these suggestions and decisions? Who picked the Hotel Astor, one of the notoriously bad hotels of New York, as was proved for example by the wholly inadequate drinking arrangements? I admit the food was passable. But we're not a Broadway crowd. Why should we use a lousy Broadway hotel? We're not a bunch of ghouls or funeral directors, either, and the emphasis on pathology and the like should really be alleviated a little. *We're a literary crowd.* Our featured speaker, if any, should be chosen for literary prowess, wit, and brevity. As the temporary titular leader of the brightest group of writers in the world, I suggest we stop presenting a mediocre image, especially on our biggest night of the year.

There was nothing mediocre about visiting author Julian Symons. As well as being a highly regarded crime-fiction writer, Symons was a biographer, poet, editor, social historian, and critic (whose *TLS* mystery reviews had done much to enhance Macdonald's British reputation). He was a man of letters, and he and Millar had immediate rapport. "Other people have said they found it difficult to get more than fifty words out of Ken," said Symons, "but I never found him reticent. We got on extremely well." Their only touchy moment came when Symons assumed Millar wouldn't catch a literary reference: "I said somebody was published by 'an English firm called Faber and Faber, I don't suppose you've heard of them,' and he said, 'Not heard of *Faber* and *Faber?* I would have you know that I was *taught* by W. H. Auden.' He was rather annoyed! I daresay it may have been the way I said it; he thought it was an example maybe of English snottiness. It later became a running joke rather; when we saw each other, the name of Faber and Faber would certainly crop up." Symons and Millar lunched the day after the Edgars and went to the Guggenheim to view paintings by Francis Bacon. "He was so overwhelmed by them," Symons said, "that he didn't really want to look at anything else—which is not to say that he loved them exactly, but he was very strongly moved by them. I was not so much moved."

Paintings and plays were what Millar wanted from New York, not shoptalk with mystery writers. Roped into a Saturday-night party with other MWA members at Harper and Row editor Joan Kahn's apartment, Millar ducked out early by getting agent Bob Lescher (whom he'd befriended at a 1958 Seattle writers' conference) to show up and give him an excuse to leave. Lescher and Millar took a long walk south from East Thirty-sixth Street nearly to the Bowery. "Ken was very observant during this walk," Lescher noted, "and there was a compassion that almost emanated from him. We'd come upon somebody who was maybe shivering in the cold; I don't know that they called them homeless in those days, but some person having trouble and looking for a handout, and Ken would not only stop and do that but would *inquire* of that person. It wasn't condescending and it wasn't some kind of performance, it was simply the act of a man who seemed to have a connection with all kinds of people from all walks of life; and this was the quality in Ken that I found it possible to commune with. I liked him immensely."

As usual Millar had insomnia in Manhattan. A Knopf publicity woman assured him it wasn't apparent when he did a radio interview at WNBC: "Your weariness came over the air as relaxation." Millar at nearly fifty was in excellent physical trim. (Anna Branson wrote him, "We were talking with the girls about how well you looked and [twenty-four-year-old] Annie's comment was 'Yum, yum,' which says a hell of a lot more than just saying you look fit.") He'd come to terms with himself and with his career. Years ago, hard-pressed to pay bills, he'd resented those who earned fortunes writing trash; but his envy had faded. He was happy making a living writing what he liked, and he felt on the brink of a new stage in his fiction. "I think somebody said Yeats was an old man mad about writing," Millar told the *New York Post*'s Martha MacGregor over a Miller High Life at the Algonquin. "That's what I hope to grow up into eventually. Everything else falls away, people, everything. It's like a tontine, a moral and imaginative tontine. You have to live through three generations of yourself before you inherit the wealth."

He took special pleasure from his enduring relationship with Alfred Knopf, who at seventy-three was easing away from his duties at the firm he'd founded in the year of Millar's birth. By Knopf's decree, Ross Macdonald became editor Ash Green's "client" now, though Macdonald had never needed an editor: it was always just Alfred, in itself a compliment. Knopf too seemed pleased with Macdonald's career, though he fretted over Millar's election as president of the Mystery Writers of America: "Quite obviously this nails you down even tighter in the category of writers that you have for so long been trying to escape, efforts that I have whole-heartedly aided and abetted." Knopf told his well-reviewed author, "Someday I hope sales will catch up with the critics." But he thought the firm had pushed Macdonald to a plateau of at least moderate respectability (around seven thousand). He liked *The Far Side of the Dollar* so much he delayed its publication six months so as to include it in Knopf's high-profile fiftieth-anniversary list; Millar responded by dedicating the book "to Alfred," a gesture the old man said pleased and touched him.

Knopf and Millar lunched together Monday, May 3, and walked back to Alfred's office, where Knopf inscribed a copy of H. L. Mencken's *American Scene* to Ken Millar, "an old friend." While Millar sat across from him, Knopf picked up his Leica and snapped several pictures, one of which (at Millar's insistence) would be the author photo for Ross Macdonald's next six books. It was among the best likenesses he'd ever captured, Knopf later said: Millar, half-smiling, head tipped at a confident but not arrogant angle, affection in his unblinking gaze; it's a glance that asks for attention and gets it. He looked like a proud son.

Edward read two books he had already read. He didn't remember that he had read them until he reached the last page of each. Then he read four paperback mysteries by Ross Macdonald. They were excellent.

—Donald Barthelme, "Edward and Pia,"
The New Yorker, September 1965

I read *Black Money* over the weekend and think it is a very fine job indeed. It would be hard to improve on the plotting or characterizations. You know I represented Raymond Chandler all of his writing life and I'm sincere in saying that you have explored even farther into that mysterious twilight of suspense.

—H. N. Swanson to Ken Millar, September 1965

Lew Archer, with his office on the Sunset Strip, had many dealings in Hollywood; he counted movie people among his friends, clients, enemies, and romances. The motion pictures he'd seen as a kid (specifically, the "Inspector Fate of Limehouse" series) helped decide him to be first a cop and then a private detective. He still went to movies (continuing a "lover's quarrel" with them, as Macdonald put it), as shown by a wisecrack in *The Doomsters:* "I'm trying to sell the movie rights to my life. Somebody down here hates me." The joke referred to a 1956 film, *Somebody Up There Likes Me,* in which young Paul Newman played boxer Rocky Graziano.

William Goldman, born in Chicago and schooled in New York, probably chuckled over Lew's joke in 1959 when *The Doomsters* came out in paperback. Goldman mostly read Macdonald in softcover, he wrote: "I had been a lunatic Archer fan since 1950, when I picked up John Macdonald's *The Moving Target* from a crummy book rack in the equally crummy bus station in Elyria, Ohio." Goldman was hooked on Macdonald and other hard-boiled writers when he served in a Pentagon-based army unit in the last months of the Korean War. "I was a big big reader in those days," he said, "and it seemed to me that Hammett and Chandler were extraordinary novelists; but they weren't in those days *thought* of as such. They were thought of as wonderful writers 'in that tradition.' But I remember thinking I didn't see why they weren't in it with the *other* people, working the same side of the street. I thought *The Maltese Falcon* was the best of *anything.* Except I thought Chandler was the much better writer. And then I thought Macdonald was the best of them all."

One other man in Goldman's army unit shared his tastes: a Michigan fellow named R. W. Lid, who was also reading a lot of hard-boiled fiction then. The two soldiers regularly loaded up on Chandler, Hammett, and Macdonald paperbacks from the post library. Dick Lid later went into teaching, which took him in time to Santa Barbara, where he became friends with Millar/Macdonald, who in 1964 dedicated *The Chill* to him, a book Goldman would declare "one of the best novels of the twentieth century."

By 1964, Goldman was a popular novelist himself, whose books *(Boys and Girls Together)* sold a great many Bantam paperbacks. New Yorker Goldman now wanted to write movies and was talking possible projects with producer Elliott Kastner. "Kastner had just seen a movie called *The Professionals*," Goldman said, "a western with Burt Lancaster and Lee Marvin. He said, 'I want to do a picture like that, I want to do a picture with *balls*.' I said, 'Read some Ross Macdonald.' He said, 'I'll read some over the weekend.' He called me Monday and said, 'I love it, I want to do one.' I said, 'Okay, I'll find one, and you option it.' Like an idiot I started with whatever the current one was"—*The Chill*—"and reread them all going back, and of course coming to the first one, *The Moving Target*, which was the *most* cinematic, if you will; he got less cinematic as he went on. And I thought, 'Maybe I could make a movie of this.' I was very new at screenwriting—like, totally new. So Kastner optioned *The Moving Target*, and I wrote the screenplay. And my memory is that he took it first to Frank Sinatra, and Sinatra passed. Then he heard that Newman was interested." Paul Newman in 1964 was one of the world's most bankable film stars. "Newman was in Europe making a not very successful costume movie called *Lady L,*" Goldman went on. "Kastner went over for a meeting, and eventually Newman agreed to do it. I met with him in Connecticut when he was done with *Lady L,* and then at some point I went to California."

The first Millar learned of any of this was the night of May 13, 1965, a week after his New York trip. He got a phone call from the fellow who'd optioned *Target* months ago through H. N. Swanson, informing him that Warner Bros. was about to begin making a big-budget film of the Archer book, starring Paul Newman. Lew Archer's wry eight-year-old joke had come true.

Millar was quick to seize the moment. The next day he dashed off a letter to von Auw urging the agent use this news to make Bantam change its mind about dropping all those Archer titles: "This should strengthen our bargaining position, don't you think?" The author's eventual goal was to have all his books with the same paperback house, making it easier for all concerned to get the most out of Macdonald: "I have observed that the writers in my field e.g. Brett Halliday who do well in paperback generally stay with one house. I realize this isn't always possible, but it is what I aim at, and I'm not getting any younger." He insisted, "I believe my backlist is absolutely certain to appreciate with time." Millar suggested von Auw contact Marcia Nasatir, the Bantam editor "who seems to understand that I'm not just an Erle Stanley Gardner who failed to make the grade."

But a hitch developed at Warners. The studio people were already so high on this unmade project they were thinking of doing a series of Lew Archer movies, as United Artists had done with the James Bond films.

Before making *Target*, they wanted to secure exclusive rights to Archer. Millar wasn't giving those away; he thought fifty thousand dollars was a fair asking sum—and he was adamant, he told von Auw: "I'd much rather see the deal fall through than risk having Archer lost in the clutches of the Warners octopus. . . . I say nuts." Warners wasn't willing to pay Millar's price. The studio's solution: use the book Kastner owned but not its title, and change the detective's name. Goldman was asked to rename the hero. "I came up with 'Harper,' " he said, "because it was almost the same: Lew Harper, Lew Archer." Thus the film became *Harper.* Newman's wife, Joanne Woodward, later claimed on the *Tonight Show* that Archer's name was changed because Newman had had two hits *(Hud, The Hustler)* with H titles. Goldman's response: "If you know anything about the movie business, you know it's all bullshit."

Blessings are always mixed, Millar mused. He was disappointed by the name change, but he saw the bright side: if the movie was successful, it was bound to help his novel sales. This film would come out right after *Black Money.* "It's my best book," he wrote Olding, "and the timing couldn't be better." He suggested that Pocket Books (who were reissuing *their* five Macdonald titles, including *The Moving Target*) be reminded to capitalize on the movie; maybe his English publisher, Collins, might want to do something special with *Target* too.

Millar stepped up his letter-writing in July when he heard from Goldman how well shooting was going in Burbank. Bantam's decision to drop half its Archers seemed especially shortsighted now, and Millar didn't even know Pocket Books' plans. "Knopf never tells me anything about reprint deals," he complained to Olding, "although they are obviously central to my living." With von Auw on vacation in North Africa, Millar took the unprecedented step of broaching business directly to Alfred Knopf. His career was at a turning point, author wrote publisher, and Bantam had made a mistake; couldn't Knopf's people get them to fix it? "If Bantam drop half their Archers and I have to go to a third house, I shall be permanently fragmented indeed, just when I should have a reasonable expectation of making some money for myself and everyone concerned." While he was at it, Millar asked Knopf for "what I would most like to see, in the twentieth year of our partnership": an omnibus (like ones Knopf had done of Hammett, Chandler, and others) of Archer novels "which got scant attention and fairly scanter sales when they first came out." For inclusion he nominated *The Moving Target, The Ivory Grin,* "and either *The Galton Case* or *The Way Some People Die*," all four of which, the writer said, "are classics in the *genre* and known as such."

Again Millar wrote Olding to complain of Bantam's "sour" decision. Here Pocket Books was about to reprint its early Macdonalds for the *fourth* time, while Bantam was dropping much more recent titles after only *one* reprint: "I sometimes wonder if anyone at Bantam has *read* the books." What troubled him most was the prospect of having his work scattered among three paperback houses, which would "effectively and permanently limit" his softcover sales just when (thanks to this movie) they should become his "main source of income." With his ship at last about to come in, Millar didn't want it crashing into the pier. He told Olding, "Like the Century Plant, some writers have a sudden late flowering and then die. I trust I won't be one of them."

His campaign was a success: Bantam made new contracts for the books it had dropped. The writer was pleased no end, he told Knopf's William Koshland. Without missing a beat, he began lobbying Koshland for that Archer omnibus.

Millar was profoundly humble and could be amusingly self-deprecating. (He signed one letter to Olding this month "Erle Stanley Millar.") But when the chips were down, as they were now, he wasn't shy about stating his worth. "I believe we should be ready for what looks like a positive upturn, and even to assist it," Millar told Koshland. "My twenty-year-run is, I suppose, the most sustained performance in the history of the American detective story, and quite a few people are beginning to realize it."

The author bet big on his future this autumn. Using ten years' savings (*not* "movie money," he made sure to tell Knopf), he and Maggie put a down payment on a hilltop home with swimming pool in the exact middle of Hope Ranch Park, Santa Barbara's most desirable residential area. With the large house came four lush acres in a secluded greenbelt a mile's walk from the beach. "They paid ninety thousand," Bob Easton said. "That was a whole lotta money in those days. Ken said one reason he did it was, 'I knew I'd really have to work like hell to pay for it.' "

The Millars moved into 4420 Via Esperanza on September 10. "We wonder at our good fortune and/or daring," Millar wrote Olding. "My dear wife is very happy in this 'new' house," he told von Auw, "which means that I am, too." In fact he'd never seen Maggie happier, he said, in work or in life. "Pressing merrily ahead" with her bird book, she'd learned she'd be named one of 1965's twelve Women of the Year by the *Los Angeles Times*. Millar busied himself with a new regimen of chores at Via Esperanza, including much of the gardening on the four-acre lot. Linda and her husband lived in Canoga Park now and often came to Santa Barbara with two-and-a-half-year-old Jimmy: "a living doll," in his grandfather's considered opinion. Millar turned fifty this December. In some ways it seemed his life was just beginning.

**Paul
Newman
is "Harper"**
Bad guys hate Harper.
They punch his nose.
They kick his head.
See bad guys punch
and kick Harper.
See Harper punch and
kick bad guys.
See Harper.
—Newspaper advertisement,
April 1966

It was another of those loops in time Lew Archer often made: those circles that Macdonald, and Millar, liked to close. Here was Ken Millar on a Friday in January 1966, in a musty screening room on Warners' Burbank lot, the same studio where Margaret Millar had twenty years earlier written her script for *The Iron Gates* while her husband, on naval duty in the Pacific, invented his "successor to Marlowe." The lot was still here, Jack Warner was still here—and maybe this room, with its faded Hearst Castle draperies, was the very one where Margaret in 1945 viewed *The Big Sleep*, Warners' not-yet-released film of Raymond Chandler's first novel, starring Humphrey Bogart (as Marlowe) and newcomer Lauren Bacall.

Now Millar was here to see what Warners had done with *his* first private-eye novel. With Millar was Dick Lid, *Harper* screenwriter Bill Goldman's army buddy from the days when they stocked up on hard-boiled books at the post library: another circle closed.

The Warners connection was no coincidence. Kastner's team brought *Target* here intentionally with the idea of re-creating the spirit of Warners' private-eye films of the forties. Some of *Harper*'s scenes had been shot on the same stages as *The Big Sleep*, using some of the same crew. And playing Harper's client was *Big Sleep* costar (and Bogart widow) Lauren Bacall.

Lid and Millar, alone in the screening room, watched a scratchy work print with no music or titles. Even in rough cut the movie looked good. Paul Newman played Lew Harper, the "new style" private detective, with gum-chewing insouciance. "I thought Newman was terrific," Goldman said later. "The car Harper drove"—a beat-up Porsche—"was Newman's idea. The fact that he wore short-sleeve shirts was Newman's choice; he felt that was right for the character." Newman said he modeled Harper's "almost inattentive" manner on Robert Kennedy's: "While you're talking, you can see him preparing his rebuttal. . . . I thought that was a nice bit of business for a private detective." The actor told Goldman he'd enjoyed playing Harper more than anything else he'd ever done.

Directed by Jack Smight, *Harper* seemed brash and "with it": a "*movie-movie*" that both celebrated and winked at the tough-guy ethic. At one point a character played by Robert Wagner did an impression of Jimmy Cagney. Then Harper did an impression of Newman playing Rocky Graziano: an in-joke with added meaning for Millar. The film flaunted an extraordinary supporting cast; filling minor roles with major talent was a fad *Harper* started. Julie Harris as the jazz pianist, Wagner as the millionaire's pilot, Shelly Winters as the aging movie queen, Arthur Hill as the love-struck lawyer, Pamela Tiffin as the missing man's daughter, Janet Leigh as Harper's about-to-be-ex-wife, Sue (who didn't appear in the novel), gave a strength in the batting order that made this film feel like an event.

Good locations added to the visual appeal: a "Santa Theresa [*sic*]" mansion, ghostly oil derricks, a rusting freighter at the San Pedro dock. The guru's Temple of the Clouds was a Hollywood Hills place called Moonfire. The Bel-Air Hotel, where Millar had once talked things out with Alfred Knopf, played itself. *Harper* had its hard-boiled cake and ate it too, undercutting the private-eye code ("All I can do is do the dirty job all the way down the line") with an ambiguous freeze-frame ending (soon to be another Hollywood fad).

As Millar watched *Harper*, it wasn't love at first sight. Goldman's script, and Newman's performance, took a 1949 story and coated it with a smart-alecky sixties veneer. Millar got a better impression of the film when he saw it later in a movie house filled with noisy ticket-buyers. Paul Newman wasn't Lew Archer, Millar said eventually, but he made a great Harper.

The Warners screening included a cameo appearance by Millar's Hollywood agent. "Swanson came in midway," Dick Lid said. "Made his entrance, said hello, and left. I gathered we were meant to feel tremendously flattered. Ken was not." Seven months ago, Millar had pronounced himself well rid of H. N. Swanson, writing to New York, "One advantage of the twenty-year Swanee episode was that his stupendous inability to see my work leaves me virtually pristine when I want to be." Millar had sold the *Target* option thinking it was for a low-budget, independent film and was irked to learn the contract Swanson negotiated made no provision for greater payment should the book become a major studio movie. Despite *Harper*'s $2 million budget, all Millar got was $12,500. Yet in one of those turnarounds that seemed to have as much to do with Margaret's sensitivities as Millar's good judgment, he'd recently announced to von Auw that he and Maggie were returning to Swanson's fold: "Swanee presents his problems, but at least after twenty years we know what they are."

He and Swanson were in sync on one thing, Millar wrote von Auw: "Swanee and I saw *Harper* last Friday and agree it will be a commercial smash. It's also pretty good." Warners was keen for a sequel, and Goldman would soon start writing one based on *The Chill*.

As *Harper* neared release, *Black Money* was published to fine reviews. Bennett Cerf called Millar from New York and said many people told him the new Archer novel was Macdonald's best yet. (Millar of course agreed.) The author intended to take a brief rest and enjoy his new house, do a little reading, stir some plots. But he barely had time to savor *Black Money*'s notices. The word was out on *Harper,* and producers were eager for Macdonald's services. No one this month was giving Millar any semipitying Hollywood looks.

At Swanson's behest, Millar met with TV's Lee Rich and discussed a possible series, *The Hunters,* about a husband-and-wife detective team (partly inspired by the Girolas); Millar committed to write a "presentation" and a pilot synopsis. A few days later he accepted another assignment from Seven Arts Productions ("the maddest of all," he told Knopf) to concoct a plot for a movie scheduled to film soon with George Segal in Hong Kong; his fee was ten thousand dollars. "It's all rather fun for a change, after twenty-five years chained to a desk," he wrote Knopf. But Millar asked Harris Seed to review these agreements. Seed also took on the task of renegotiating the *Harper* contract; matters regarding rights to Archer had to be resolved before Millar agreed to sell Warners *The Chill.* Involving his lawyer was costly, Millar told von Auw, but he'd found it cost him more not to: "You will excuse my continuing to push. I've been underground a long time, and this is unquestionably the big breakthrough."

Hollywood interest in Macdonald increased in February, when industry trade papers judged *Harper* a probable smash. The *Hollywood Reporter*'s literate critic James Powers wrote, "At a time when too many producers are stumbling over themselves to do takeoffs on the Bond character, *Harper* leaps right back over all those limp bodies to take up the pure American character of the private eye, approximately where Dashiell Hammett left him a generation ago." Kastner and his partner wanted a long-term deal for the Archer novels, and Swanson was eager to get this for "the boys." Millar, counseled by Seed, held back. "Let the boys make a picture with *Archer* and then I will possibly feel inclined to do business with them," Millar scrawled in a memo to Swanson; he was in no rush to tie up his books. "In the case of a *great* series, the writer is *the* or *a* star. This takes a while to sink in!" He added in gleeful postscript: "Meanwhile Maggie can always support me!"

Millar labored on the Hollywood projects at home, then brought his pages to Hollywood for thirteen-hour meeting days, spending more time in LA in two months than he had in the last twenty years. Millar liked working with director Alexander MacKendrick on the Seven Arts project, but *The Hunters* sessions were stressful. "A presentation is a pretty mixed art form," he noted; TV "creation" sent his blood pressure soaring. Margaret grew concerned for his health and warned him not to get too involved with Hollywood. He thanked her for her concern, in notes left next to the teapot, and apologized for the disruption his comings and goings were causing her; but he felt obliged to make the most of these opportunities.

Hollywood was a headache, though. Seed and an LA colleague advised

Millar that his recent Swanson-made contracts were bad ones. Millar got out of the Seven Arts project, taking five thousand dollars. Seed started restructuring the Mirisch-Rich deal, which seemed to violate Writers Guild rules. Meanwhile Swanson urged more agreements on Millar, who refused them. "Turned down $35,000 for *Chill*," he wrote an Ober agent, "because they wouldn't use the name, Archer. I agree 35 is low, but I had a hell of a time getting Swanee up that high; he said it was 'high.' All Swanee wants to do is make deals."

Harper opened nationwide in April. Critics' verdicts were mixed: the *Herald Tribune*'s Judith Crist wrote it a mash note; Pauline Kael, in *McCall's*, was scathing. In general the reviews were fine, and Ross Macdonald was mentioned in nearly all of them. Newman's hero was cheered as a relief from gadget-toting, womanizing screen spies—the return of the classic American private eye. What had been thought derivative in 1949 was a nostalgic asset in 1966: "*Harper* even starts out like Raymond Chandler," enthused the *LA Times*'s Philip K. Scheur.

Millar was more interested in receipts. He asked von Auw to send him information on box-office takings in time for Seed's negotiations over *The Chill*. The news was good: according to *Weekly Variety*, *Harper* was the fourth-highest-grossing film in the country (behind *Dr. Zhivago*, *The Singing Nun*, and *The Sound of Music*).

Harris Seed and his LA associate went to the Warners lot on April 18 to meet personally with Jack Warner and the studio's general counsel. The Santa Barbara lawyer found a film mogul's timetable took precedence over scheduled appointments. "I remember waiting two hours in Mr. Warner's office while his two male secretaries twittered about," said Seed. "It turned out he was watching a screening. I didn't know it at the time or I'd have been even more angry. My associate counsel from Hollywood was trying to tell me this was normal, and I'm thinking, 'I don't *like* it.' " Once begun, the talks went well, Seed said: "Contrary to most events down there, price wasn't the only object for us; price was secondary to legal rights. To them, I guess, price was paramount and legal rights secondary. That's how come we got together." Seed wanted a *Chill* contract that would retroactively correct the *Target* deal. It was a unique concept, said Seed, but they went for it: "It ended with Warner Bros. keeping Harper and Ken retaining ownership of Archer, which was the big thing."

Millar was pleased his books and services were in demand, but these negotiations felt like a constant battle. He blamed most of the problems on contracts Swanson urged him to sign and the New York agents okayed. On April 27, Millar sent von Auw a strong letter terminating (finally) his connection with Swanson and, "with regret," cutting off Ober from any share of his movie or TV money: "I wish for the present to remain unrepresented by any agent in Hollywood, so that my attorneys can complete the Augean task of disentangling my affairs from the mess in which they've been plunged by abominable contracts. . . . My three attorneys are doing this hard expensive work, and I can't afford to be tithed additionally merely to avoid rocking the boat. (The boat nearly sank.)"

Almost overlooked during this hectic period were events that in any other year would have been milestones. The Mystery Writers of America's outgoing president got his third Edgar nomination, for *The Far Side of the Dollar*, and the English Crime Writers Association honored a Macdonald work for the second year in a row, this time with its top prize: *The Far Side of the Dollar* took the Gold Dagger Award as best crime novel of 1965.

In June, *Harper* opened in England, where (as a goodwill gesture by Warners to Millar and Seed) it was titled *The Moving Target*. (In another gesture, second-stage U.S. ads for *Harper* included this boxed notice: "Based on the sensational best selling Novel 'The Moving Target' by Ross Macdonald, America's No. 1 master of suspense and intrigue.") The movie was a U.K. hit ("the best of Hollywood in many months . . . wrapped up in an irresistible package," *Queen* magazine), with Macdonald cited in all reviews.

Black Money meanwhile was doing better in the United States than any previous Macdonald hardcover. Knopf printed eleven thousand copies of the book, and by March (*before Harper*'s release) nearly ten thousand had sold. Alfred personally ordered a three-column "profile ad" of Macdonald, *Black Money*, and the Archer series in the *New York Times*.

Both Macdonald's paperback publishers did new editions of Archer novels this year. Pocket Books' movie tie-in edition of *The Moving Target* solved the problem of how to connect an old title with a new film very simply: by arbitrarily renaming the book *Harper* and slapping Paul Newman's picture on its cover. (No one named Harper of course appeared in the text.) Millar was furious at Pocket's "little trick," done without required permission from Knopf. For good measure, Pocket misspelled his pseudonym as "MacDonald" on the book's cover, title page, and spine (as it did on four other Macdonald Pocket Books this year). Three hundred thousand of these *Harper* paperbacks were printed.

Bantam was proud of its new Macdonalds: three older Archers and *The Far Side of the Dollar*. After hiding the detective in recent seasons, Bantam brought him front and center this year of the *Harper* in photographic tableaux of a gun-toting male nuzzled by half-naked women, with the proud legend "Lew Archer—the Hardest of the Hard-Boiled Dicks." By year's end Bantam had 3 million Archers in print.

Sweating through April and May over story synopses, Millar came to hate his *Hunters* assignment. People who wrote for TV, he concluded, "live in a world of mental slavery." In a note written during or after one story conference, he admitted, "This really is not my line."

"It has to be frustrating," Seed thought, "for a writer who's used to having nothing in his work changed, not even a *comma,* to be in a situation where people are telling him to change *everything*." Seed's objections to *The Hunters* deal were financial: "I thought it was a horrible contract. I finally said to Ken, it's *no damn good*. You're not getting paid enough, it's frustrating to you—go back to doing what you do: being a novelist."

Millar took Seed's advice and in June cut his losses, accepting a flat fee for what he'd already done on *The Hunters* (though he'd be paid additionally should a series be made). He'd worked all winter and spring on Hollywood projects and had little to show for it. When he quit, his blood pressure dropped twenty points. Millar vowed to write nothing but books from now on.

Three of his old ones (*The Moving Target, The Way Some People Die,* and *The Barbarous Coast*) were being collected by Knopf (with the Doubleday Mystery Guild) in the Archer anthology Millar had proposed, under his title, *Archer in Hollywood*. At his own suggestion Millar wrote a foreword, an autobiographical piece that tantalizingly balanced his urge to reveal with his need to conceal. It concluded, "We writers, as we work our way deeper into our craft, learn to drop more and more personal clues. Like burglars who secretly wish to be caught, we leave our fingerprints on the broken locks, our voiceprints in the bugged room, our footprints in the wet concrete and the blowing sand."

As readers might work to glean facts from his fiction, so Millar's friends sifted his smiling silences for nuggets of speech. His manner was unnaturally formal and reticent; no wonder he found Hollywood's jostle unbearable. Even during this year of success, Millar kept cool. "Ken had an aura of great strength about him," said Jerre Lloyd, a young Tulane law professor who met him in Santa Barbara in the summer of 1966. "Physical strength for one thing, but there was a matching strength in the way he processed things mentally. That's why it was sometimes hard to have a conversation with Ken. He made these strong declarative statements, and they were so well thought out that it usually wasn't possible to add anything useful to them. Everything he said was almost an aphorism." ("Style is structure on a small scale.") "You'd *hang* on what he was saying; it was really *good*. But you didn't have small talk with Ken; that was just not possible. He couldn't be casual about anything, with anybody. There was nothing easy about Ken. Nothing. He was friendly, but I don't think he was naturally gregarious. At the same time he went out of his way to be with people, so it was kind of strange."

Lloyd and Millar shared an interest in public affairs and policy; Lloyd had been active in Louisiana state politics and the civil rights movement. But Lloyd was more eager to talk with Millar about literature. "He was absolutely brilliant about that," Lloyd said. "I've never known anybody that was a greater student and analyzer of books and writers. That was his long suit, as far as I'm concerned. He had a great knowledge of literary tradition. I was attempting to write novels in those days, and I was very much *anti*-tradition; and he would say, 'Well, you know, *that*'s a tradition too.' "

During his summer in Santa Barbara (he'd soon move there), Lloyd met with Millar in late afternoon, after writing hours, either at the Hope Ranch house or at Lloyd's run-down residence hotel on lower State. "Ken loved to come there and watch all these old types in the lobby," Lloyd said, "hoping he'd see something he could use in one of his books." Lloyd's shabby hotel found its way into the novel Millar started in 1966 *(The Instant Enemy)*. "Casing a scene" is what the author called such reconnaissance trips. When he and Dick Lid went to the Bay Area once, Millar insisted they stay at a dilapidated San Francisco hotel, Lid said: "One of these fleabags, you know, in a room on the third or fourth or fifth floor, where the tap was all stained and the water would barely trickle out, and you couldn't get hot water up there; you knew you weren't gonna be able to have a shower. Green chenille bedspreads on these old twin beds—oh, God, it was ugly. Ken deliberately wanted to stay there to soak up some atmosphere."

In August of 1966, Millar got the Lids' permission to case their San Fernando Valley house, an angular, modern place cantilevered above a golf course, as a setting for his next book. He came to Northridge with Linda and her three-year-old son, who were visiting from Phoenix where Linda's husband now worked. The Lids were pleased at how good Linda looked. The last time they'd seen her was in 1959, when they'd driven her to an appointment with her UCLA psychiatrist; on their way back to Santa Barbara, she'd had them stop at the beach, where she'd swum so far out they'd become alarmed. There was nothing alarming about Linda today as she stood in the kitchen talking about marriage and motherhood. The Lids were relieved she'd found her way to some measure of happiness. Millar was relieved too. "Perhaps I'll never work as hard, quite, as I have in the last ten years, paying off the bloody medical bills," he wrote Anna Branson this September. "Lin's in good shape now."

So were he and Margaret, he thought. His wife finished the bird-watching book on which she'd worked so diligently for two years; Millar edited her manuscript and airmailed it to the agents on the last day of September. By then Harris Seed was nailing final riders onto Warners' contract for *The Chill*, with the studio to pay Millar fifty thousand dollars for movie rights to the novel; Warners took trade-paper ads announcing the project for 1967, with Paul Newman billed again to play Harper.

It had been an exhausting if exhilarating twelve months. "The changes of the past year or so have been hard for me to handle," Millar admitted to Knopf (who visited Santa Barbara this autumn, after the death of wife Blanche), "what might be called the dubious rewards of 'late success'—but they're under control now, I think. . . . I'm working my way back into fiction and beginning to get glimmerings of the next decade as opposed to echoes of the last one." Rains came to Santa Barbara in November, and with them the best part of the year for him: a cold sea that gleamed as gray as gunmetal, a beach empty of all but the hardiest swimmers, a sky full of Cooper's hawks. Good working weather. Millar had a book going, and he hoped to surprise the customers.

February 16, 1966

Editor, *News-Press:* Ever since my service as a naval officer in far Pacific waters in the forties, I have been haunted by the thought of American young men dying in Asia, and others having to garrison that thankless continent's shores and hinterland. We are beginning now to take on just that bleak and unrewarding task—a task which could eventually bleed us dry, as it bled France and England. For God's sake and our own, let us somehow avoid that open-ended, bottomless mantrap.

—Kenneth Millar
4420 Via Esperanza

Their new residence in Hope Ranch Park, the lush enclave above Santa Barbara, was a long way from Mrs. Funk's boardinghouse where Millar slept as a kid, and from the home where Mayor Sturm's daughter lived within whiff of the tanning factory. The Millars' Via Esperanza perch, up where the big birds nested, gave them a different social perspective.

Jackie and Henri Coulette visited them there soon after the Millars moved in, Jackie recalled: "Hank had just been invited to have his entry in *Who's Who in America,* so he rather diffidently but proudly told them. Maggie said, 'Oh, ho! No kidding! There are seven of us in this *block* in *Who's Who!*' How's that for deflating you? And of course she had her *own* entry. That was the last time Hank attempted to brag in front of them."

The Millars' neighbors in this elevated zone included founders of such major corporations as Northrop and TRW: some of the wealthiest people in the country. (The actor Fess Parker was also a neighbor, allowing Millar to tell people, "I live next door to Davy Crockett.") Millar felt uneasy about his new location, he later told critic-journalist John Leonard: "I kept wondering what am I doing in a place like this, and what will a place like this do to me?" Hope Ranch residents raised eyebrows at these newcomers, with their old Ford covered with pro-ecology and antiwar bumper stickers; the Millars felt their Republican neighbors perhaps didn't much like them. More bothersome, after a birding vacation in Texas, the Millars came home to find someone had broken in through a window and taken fifty dollars, a bracelet, and six bottles of beer. "A burglary, even *in absentia,* leaves a funny feeling in a place," Millar told Knopf. Almost as bad was the treatment they received from "the stupidest deputy sheriffs in the world," Millar wrote von Auw. "One deputy's theory was that we had broken the window in a quarrel and had then gone away and left it hoping that it would appear to be a burglary. No kidding." In time their affluent neighbors seemed to accept the Millars as benign Bohemians ("Oh, they're *writers*"), two of Hope Ranch's "token Democrats."

In any case, Hope Ranch didn't change the Millars. Except for enjoying their swimming pool and a lot more floor space, they lived about as simply up here as they had in the forties down on Bath Street where the Union Pacific rumbled by. "The house in Hope Ranch was quite spacious," Jackie Coulette said, "but there was certainly nothing grand about it, or in it. The furniture was minimal, utilitarian. They had three or four dogs, and the dogs had the run of the place. I don't think they ever entertained. Maggie might throw a bag of chips out on the table and a boxa cookies and say, 'Well, if anybody's hungry . . .' Maybe a soft drink. Ken liked beer. Food was always very simple fare, and modest amounts. I guess what a lot of people think of as the niceties of living, the 'comforts,' didn't seem important to either Ken or Maggie."

And Maggie Millar went her separate way, Jackie noticed. "She had very little time for a lot of people Ken thought of as his friends; she didn't pay much attention to or have very much interest in these people he sort of collected; they weren't part of *her* world. I think she rather liked me. I had thought she liked Hank—she was always certainly cordial—but I have a first cousin who worked at the Coral Casino, and Maggie indicated to my cousin that she didn't think much of Hank!"

"Maggie scoffed at everything," said Jerre Lloyd, who moved to Santa Barbara in 1967 and visited Millar weekly at Via Esperanza. Lloyd would have liked to spend time in Margaret's company but wasn't "allowed" to, he said: "She'd be watching television in the family room whenever I came over; she'd say hi and all that, and then, 'Ken's in the study.' Every Tuesday when I went over there, for *years,* he would not be in the living room with Maggie—because I was supposed to meet him in the study. Which was not oppressive or anything, but it *was* kind of weird. There was a curious lack of casualness in Ken; everything had to be formalized. I really didn't understand Ken, and he really didn't understand me. We spent a lot of time together for two people who didn't understand one another."

Sometimes Lloyd and Millar took one of the dogs for a walk. Other times they'd sit and talk in Millar's study. "It was a small workroom with some nondescript paneling and shelves of books everywhere," Lloyd said. "Right outside his study was a large closet, I think it had been a coat closet. He opened the door one day, and it was kind of startling: it was completely filled with paperback books, mostly his own in various editions. We'd talk about literature. I was very much influenced by the Black Humorists of the day"—Heller, Friedman—"and as he'd often say, that wasn't his cup of tea, but he read them anyway! He read everything. He was always pulling things off a shelf for me to read. Occasionally I'd find something he didn't know about, which was hard to do."

Millar encouraged Lloyd's efforts at novel-writing and tried to get his manuscripts published. "He did tremendous favors," said Lloyd. "He'd have people read my stuff that I *never* could have gotten to read it. He did a lot of that at the luncheons: try to put people in contact with other people. And there wasn't anything selfish in it; he kept quiet about it. But I can't emphasize too much the amount of good that he did. I think the reason was that he'd been so badly treated himself by Raymond Chandler. Not that he had any malice towards Chandler, or anyone else for that matter. But he thought Chandler had been gratuitously negative, and he was anxious not to do that to anyone else. I've never known anyone who spent the time to help people that Ken did. He certainly considered himself a professional writer, and he considered it a profession that had ethics and rules. And it was more than that. The way he thought, there was kind of a sacredness to it too."

Millar helped Dennis Lynds significantly in 1967, writing a letter to his old Dodd, Mead editor Ray Bond recommending Lynds's *Act of Fear,* a private-eye novel written under the name Michael Collins. Bond bought the book, and Ross Macdonald wrote a blurb for its jacket. Later Millar helped get Dorothy Olding to be Lynds's agent.

Herb Harker, Millar's former adult-ed student, still hoped to write fiction professionally. While working as a geological draftsman, a cartographer, and in advertising, Harker went often for friendship and advice to Millar's house. "He didn't mind giving his time as long as he felt it was being spent well," Harker said. "He guarded his energy carefully, to be sure he had what he needed to do his own work; but he was very generous. One time he said to me, 'Sometimes I wish I wasn't a writer almost as much as you wish you were.' He never explained that; I suppose he was referring to the fact that the writer is a lonely soul. If you're serious about it, it's very restrictive; it kind of dictates your life. But he seemed very content to go day to day; he had his routine and he followed it.

"I felt Ken was one of the finest people I ever knew, quite apart from his gifts as a writer, just in his attitude toward his fellow man and the approach he had to life. He didn't need a lotta possessions to fulfill him; he was content with his work, and the chance to get in the ocean every day, and walk his dogs. That's what we'd do when I'd go over in the evening. For quite a while he had four dogs, and we'd take a couple and just walk around in Hope Ranch. We talked about politics; I think we had sympathetic views. We'd talk about movies and entertainment; he was a jazz fan. And of course problems regarding the environment. He was very concerned about the condors. I was concerned, but he went out and *did* something. We talked about writing: what works, what doesn't work. One of the things that always impressed me: I could mention a story he hadn't read for twenty years, something by D. H. Lawrence or something, and he knew the story in detail and could talk about it; his memory was amazing. If I was having some problems with the family or wondering what to do with one of my kids, we'd talk about that. I felt like he was a wise man as well as a good one, and I went to him a lot for counsel. I felt he was a vulnerable man, like he'd experienced great pain in his life. But maybe that was one of the things that made it possible for him to write the stories he did: the fact that he knew what it was like to be hurt."

Some of that hurt went into *The Instant Enemy,* which Millar took extra time with because of *Harper*'s and *Black Money*'s success. With more attention on Macdonald, Millar felt this book should be better than the last one. He airmailed it to New York on June 3, 1967; Ash Green formally accepted it June 7. The "majestic instancy" of this dazzled Millar—but not so much that he didn't ask for a raise in advance from *Black Money*'s twenty-five hundred to four thousand dollars; given greatly improved sales, he felt that was fair. Knopf agreed. The firm also okayed a change in division of the paperback advance (now eighty-five hundred dollars) from a fifty-fifty split to sixty-forty in Millar's favor.

Things weren't running so smoothly in Hollywood. This autumn Millar and Seed learned that Warners' plan to film *The Chill* was on indefinite hold. They attributed this to changes in studio management. William Goldman, paid to write *The Chill*'s script, knew differently: "The director, Jack Smight, had come to me and said he'd do a sequel if I would, and somehow I got the notion Newman was interested in *The Chill.* So I wrote *The Chill,* which of course is a phenomenally complicated story, and made the script as simple as I could. I was as adroit as I could be in getting rid of some of those twists and still keeping enough so the movie worked. I went with it to Newman—and he didn't like it because it was too complicated. I said, 'But it's amazingly much less complicated than the book!' Well, Newman hadn't read the book. I said, 'Then why did you want me to *do* it?' Then I was told Newman never read the book of stuff he was gonna do because he felt, quite rightly, that sometimes you got seduced by the book and carried over some of its quality into your reading of the screenplay. I was shocked. I had thought Newman wanted me to do *The Chill.* Of course without his involvement, this screenplay was worthless." It's also possible that Newman (as he told Millar when the two met at the Center for the Study of Democratic Institutions) simply didn't want to play Harper again for fear of being typecast.

Millar got his Warners money (as did Goldman), but Macdonald's promising post-*Harper* prospects seemed dried up. His and Seed's relationship with a post-Swanson agent foundered over the man's insistence on trying to sell Archer to TV against Millar's wishes. The author didn't want a quick cashing-in. What he had in mind was a long-term, multibook deal with substantial payments and a good chance at quality results; he was willing to wait out the current Hollywood bear market rather than sell himself and his life's work short. By the end of the year, the Millars were living on savings again and on whatever money their books brought in.

It was the books that were important, Millar felt, and interest in his was growing. Macdonald's work was the subject of its first master's thesis in 1967, by Ohio State graduate student Steven Carter; Millar wrote Carter several long letters about the novels' content and construction. ("Technique is poetic justice seen from below, and not only in fiction.") The Millars' friend John E. Smith, now librarian at the University of California at

Irvine, created the Kenneth and Margaret Millar Collection of books and manuscripts. And in December 1967 the *Los Angeles Times* Sunday magazine, *West*, published a substantial feature article on Ross Macdonald.

The *West* piece was written by Dick Adler, who spent a day in Santa Barbara interviewing Millar ("a lean, sun-browned man of 52 with the dry, reserved manner of a Vermont farmer giving directions to a tourist"). "I met him for breakfast down by the ocean," Adler recalled. "Then I went back up to his house, met Margaret, chatted. He showed me his workroom." Adler got Millar to talk somewhat revealingly of his reckless adolescence and about the "sad and angry" letter he'd once written Knopf about Pocket Books' meddling, but Millar wouldn't discuss Linda. "The whole idea of his daughter, he didn't really want to talk about," Adler said. "We spoke about why is it always a child—a child in jeopardy, a child in crime? He said, 'Let me just say that it's based on things that really happened to me, or to people in my family.' I had about five, six hours with him, and then—this happened to me with J. B. Priestley too—at a certain time a taxi arrived that had been preordered. They obviously decided they were going to limit the time. Which is only sensible, if you arrive on foot; you're at their disposal. So either he or she arranged to have the cab come. It was a nice amount of time I had, but it wasn't going to be the 'man who came to dinner.' They had to work." Precisely.

The number of mystery writers who may also be called "novelists"—that is, who traffic more than perfunctorily in such matters
as character and social comment—may still, unhappily, be
counted on the fingers of one hand. Ross Macdonald, Georges
Simenon, and . . . ?

       —Clifford A. Ridley, *National Observer*, 1968

I have a passion for Dickens and for memoirs of the era of 30 or 40
years ago—the Strachey epoch. I love Jane Austen, a book you can
move straight into the middle of. I like the California school of mystery—Dashiell Hammett, Raymond Chandler, Ross Macdonald.

       —Elizabeth Bowen, *Washington Post*, 1968

Millar was convinced that his literary ancestor Coleridge, so wise to
the trends of his own and later times, had to have been "some
sort of a seer." Millar himself seemed to have a touch of the
prophet: after traveling to Europe in 1936, he was sure the world was due
for war. A few years later, doing naval service off Formosa in the global
conflict he'd predicted, he glimpsed another awful possibility, as he
recalled to Ping Ferry: "I foresaw with a sudden pang the danger of American garrisons on the Asian mainland, and started talking about it." He'd
talk a lot more in the late sixties and early seventies, as Lyndon Johnson
and Richard Nixon sent the United States down a jungle path to a bloody
war that Millar thought "an unmitigated disaster."

The war began affecting Millar's civic life in 1965, when he told
Dorothy Olding, "I'm in a bitter struggle for the future of the Democratic
Party here (liberal or Vietnam)." (His forceful arguments caused one member of Santa Barbara's Democratic League to resign angrily from that
body.) At the end of 1965, when it seemed there was a chance for peace in
Asia, Millar wrote Ivan von Auw, "If they really do suspend hostilities in
Vietnam I won't be able to think of *anything* to complain about." That did-
n't happen, though; and on his next birthday he told Alfred Knopf, "I
have a book going"—*The Instant Enemy*—"and feel fine personally, but not
too darn good about the country."

In 1967, Ross Macdonald started getting fan mail from GIs in Vietnam,
and from wounded servicemen in stateside hospitals. "It feels to me like a season of apocalypse," Millar worried to Olding, "perhaps the one that will make
or break us if we're not already broken." To the Bransons he said, "The country is going to hell as I was always afraid it was going to." The violent clamp-
down on antiwar demonstrators reminded him of scenes he'd witnessed in
fascist Europe. "I'm a bit scared of 1968," he confessed to Michael Avallone.
"I don't expect to live forever, but I hope the republic will."

Millar made his views known through letters to the local paper and at the writers' luncheons, which were attended by several *News-Press* staff. As the war escalated, the Millars took their concern to the Santa Barbara streets, marching with hundreds of others in peace rallies, cheering speakers like Dr. Benjamin Spock. Millar often kept silent afternoon vigil with a few other mute protesters on a downtown street corner. As more dissenters felt the crack of police batons, his outrage smoldered. "It got to the point," he said later, "where people who were opposed to the most terrible and useless war in our history were considered war criminals, instead of the people who were doing it. And yet, there it was. People were being put in jail for protesting. They were even being shot, as at Kent State. You couldn't even stand on the corner down in front of the Art Museum as some of us did, periodically, for a number of years during that war, without having your picture taken every week or so by the CIA." One day a cherry bomb blew up the Millars' mailbox: no way to know if it was because of Ken Millar's frequent protest letters to the *News-Press,* which printed them with his address.

Vietnam clouded what were otherwise sunny years for Millar, but he made sure it didn't jeopardize friendships. He and Bob Easton had an unspoken understanding they wouldn't discuss the war. And Millar appreciated the complex issues and options Vietnam forced on young people. "I won't say I'm sorry that you're planning to enlist," he wrote a college-age correspondent in 1968. "My sorrow is for the war in all its meanings. But it's possible to feel pride in the conduct of other men in relation to a war which one abhors." (A few years later though he wrote the same correspondent, "It makes me angry to think of what good young men have suffered for bad old men.")

Macdonald was a sympathetic figure to many young readers during these times. The author whose Archer dealt squarely with troubled young folk seemed likely to be understanding in real life. Herb Harker said Millar was often called on for counsel by friends' teens: "He was so completely down-to-earth and genuine that the toughest kid couldn't talk to him without knowing this guy was giving him the straight goods."

Even at the Coral Casino pool, Millar paid close attention to youngsters and was quick to give aid. *People* magazine writer Brad Darrach witnessed this episode:

> A small, anxious boy is pushing with all his might at the door of a cabana in an exclusive Santa Barbara beach club. Inside the cabana, two larger boys are holding the door shut. On his way to the pool, Millar pauses.
>
> "Please let me in! Please!" the outsider wails. His tormentors giggle.
>
> Millar leans against the cabana door. With a cry of relief, the boy darts in. Millar rolls his eyes at the other two. "I thought there must be six boys in here!" he says.

The compliment softens it, but the rebuke is felt. As Millar leaves, the three boys begin to play together quietly.

"Why did you do that?" Millar is asked.

"That boy needs help," he answers with flat force. "I've known him since he was born."

Ross Macdonald seemed one of those writers J. D. Salinger's Holden Caulfield spoke of, the kind you want to be friends with, once you've read their books. Many readers (generally young, usually male) wrote Macdonald and even telephoned him during the sixties and seventies. One was New York journalist Paul Nelson:

> Close to explosion in the winter of 1970, I had just finished the latest Ross Macdonald book in print. Perhaps that's why I committed an act of no small desperation and guilt. I reached out for at least the shadows of answers from the creator of private investigator Lew Archer, who, like Jean Renoir, knows that the real tragedy in life is that everyone has his reasons. My own existence was certainly a mystery in which the psychic murders seemed to keep piling up. I guess I felt like somebody in one of Millar's novels—those books to which, with hope, I clung—and badly needed a share of the understanding and compassion he'd shown his characters.

Other contacts began less dramatically. William Ruehlmann wrote Millar a fan letter from Washington, D.C., in 1965. "As a teenager, I discovered him in used Bantam paperbacks," Ruehlmann said. "I think the first one I read—I was attracted by the title—was *The Doomsters*. And of course once you start reading him, you say, 'Well, now, this is not only on the thriller level; there's something else here.' Even as a teenager I knew that: it was the wonderful craft of his prose. I was interested I suppose because his books were of the hard-boiled school, which I found stylistically fascinating; but also because in books like *The Galton Case* he seemed to understand troubled teenagers, and I fell into that category. I think every American kid does at one time or another. When I got to college, I wrote and told him I liked his work a lot. Lo and behold he sent me a letter in return, and it was the basis of a long correspondence."

In the summer of 1968, the twenty-three-year-old Ruehlmann, after driving across the country with his army enlistee brother, paid a call on Millar. All his good perceptions about Macdonald were confirmed, Ruehlmann said:

> I met Ken in the morning. As was his custom, he took me on one of those long walks. We went down to the botanical gardens there, with his German shepherd dog Brandy, whom he called Lew. Like Ken, Brandy was

proud and loyal: gentle but dangerous to cross. Ken seemed on the surface shy, but one to one he was very open. He was sweet and kind, but he was so withdrawing in many ways; he was more interested in the other person than he was in asserting himself. He must have been a wonderful teacher. There was no generation gap with Ken. The unnerving quality was that he would *think* before he spoke; and when he did speak, no matter how casually, it was as if the words had been crafted and written and he was reading them to you. The precision of his language, the unaffected grace of it—it made one say to oneself, "Gee, I oughta think more about what I say."

He had the amiability of a man who'd made terms with life and wasn't afraid of it—and wasn't taking out any particular kind of revenge on it, who really was inclined to conserve it. I remember standing beside the aviary there in Santa Barbara; there were these wild birds inside the cage, rare creatures. Ken turned to me and said, "You know, I know the keeper here; I know these birds are very well taken care of. But if it were up to me, I'd let them all go." What interested me about Ken was that he was a scholarly man who believed in the act of life. He was a democratic man with his sensibilities inclined towards the underdog, because he'd been one and he understood them. He hadn't been crushed and spoiled and turned cynical by it; he'd surmounted it. Ken had plenty of problems, but he managed them. And for that reason he was always on the side of whoever was on the outs.

He was a stubbornly ethical man. He believed strongly in personal integrity. The thing about it, though: he knew the limitations of Hemingway, and he wasn't that kind of a fellow. That's the difference. Archer may throw a punch, but with some diffidence afterwards: perhaps it wasn't the right thing. Other people's heroes will throw a punch and have a damn good time doing it. Archer was more complex. Ken was more complex; his work was more complex.

He was quite convinced he was doing important work, and that it counted. One of the things he said to me on the beach that I well remember—it was an offhand statement, it wasn't a brag—he simply said, "I know my work will be read in a hundred years." And indeed it will. He had the confidence of knowing that his work was good; he didn't have to worry about anyone's particular opinion, although he was gratified to get good ones now and then.

I was very aware this was a working writer who was very disciplined, serious about his schedule; so was Margaret. But I was with one or both of them from the moment I entered their house until the end of the day. After lunch at the Copper Coffee Pot, we went back to their house and talked. I remember the sun going down, and we're sitting there talking in the *dark* in their living room, about everything from—'68 was a tumultuous political year—everything from Norman Mailer to H. L. Mencken's *American Language*. It was a heady experience for me. I suspect Ken was not in favor of the war, but because at the time there were a lot of entangling matters, rather than give offense Ken would simply not talk about it.

There was no meanness in him, and there was an instinctive sympathy. I saw it at work. I never heard an unkind word said about Ken from anyone; nor have I read any. I regarded him as a kind of father figure, no question. I never got along with my own father as well as I got along with Ken, as remote as he was physically. I think there may have been a lot of things: Ken never had a son, and I think I kind of fit into that role at a time when it just seemed suitable. I like to think he was as fond of me as I was of him. Certainly gave me every evidence that he was. I kind of felt he and Margaret were loving parents, once removed.

They were two extraordinary people: affectionate, mutually caring, bright. Their conversation was sharp, full of wit and the kind of understanding that goes with a couple that knows each other so well they probably know what the other one's thinking and can get a friendly dig in. It was cocktail hour. "Oh, you want one of *those*," she'd say. "Is it time for one of *those?*" Ken said, "Absolutely." And she walked over to the refrigerator and brought out: a Fudgsicle. This was Ken's "one of *those*."

I suspect Margaret might have been even tougher than Ken, in many ways; her work can be tougher. These were enormously clever, well-read people. They didn't take each other for granted, and they didn't take their world for granted. There was nothing wishy-washy about their goodness. They gave you something to shoot for, it seemed to me. So I traveled back across the country with a kind of cemented feeling that all the instincts I'd had about the caliber of this man went beyond his work and were absolutely true. The ethical element in the morality plays he wrote, the hard-boiled school he tempered, was very much a part of his rather courtly manner and way of life. Ken was his work, his work was Ken. He was such a wonderful man, quite aside from the fact that he was a wonderful writer. He was a wonderful man.

Despite disturbing events at home and abroad and the threat of more to come ("Did you know," Millar asked Olding, "that the government is planning atomic power plants every twenty miles along the California coast from San Diego to 100 miles north of Santa Barbara?"), so many good things were happening for Millar/Macdonald in 1968 that he confessed to feeling unusually sanguine. He wished the war were over, he wrote Olding, but, "still these are precious days." In a summer filled with fiction writing, ocean swimming, and court-watching with Maggie (five "classic" murder trials running simultaneously), Millar told von Auw, "I've slowed down enough to look back once or twice and realize what an incredibly lucky life I've been leading."

Macdonald's *The Instant Enemy* got splendid reviews (including one by Clare Boothe Luce in *New York* magazine, and one in the daily *New York*

Times) and sold over ten thousand copies. Margaret Millar's nonfiction work about bird-watching went into a third printing. "We are living on the income from books alone again," Millar told Harris Seed, "comparatively poor but absolutely happy."

He thought Lew Archer ("my only assured source of income") was "now at the peak of his earning power, however modest." Archer's international profile rose interestingly in 1968: *The Barbarous Coast* was published in Romania (as was Margaret's *Vanish in an Instant*), there was a Czech edition of *The Zebra-Striped Hearse,* and Macdonald was interviewed for Swedish radio. There were also encouraging developments closer to home. Professor Matthew J. Bruccoli, rising scholar of American literature, started compiling a Ross Macdonald bibliographical checklist similar to one he'd recently done on Raymond Chandler. The chancellor of UC Irvine offered Millar a one-week Regents' Lectureship, which pleased him greatly (though he declined in order to finish a book). And Macdonald was asked to work on a script for Alfred Hitchcock.

The Hitchcock bid (which Millar also declined) may have come about in part through Anthony Boucher: "Hitch" was said to be a regular reader of Boucher's column and couldn't have missed the critic's annual raves about Macdonald. In early 1968, for instance, Boucher hailed *The Instant Enemy* as "an extraordinary performance." A month after writing that, the fifty-six-year-old Boucher, a longtime pipe smoker, died of lung cancer. When Millar phoned Boucher's widow, Phyllis White, he said something that impressed and comforted her: "There are a couple of hundred of us working in the ambience that he created."

Millar was establishing his own supportive ambience, through his unpublicized editorial and promotional work on behalf of several younger writers. One of these, Dennis Lynds, this spring won the Edgar Award for Best First Novel with *Act of Fear,* the book Millar had recommended to Dodd, Mead.

A future Edgar winner, Joe Gores, said he'd been inspired by Macdonald's 1955 book *The Name Is Archer* to become first a private detective and then a crime writer. In mid-1968, Joe Gores induced Millar to attend a San Francisco meeting of the northern California MWA chapter, where Millar read aloud a just-written essay, "A Preface to *The Galton Case.*" (The commissioning of this piece for a book in which Macdonald kept company with mainstream authors including Reynolds Price, Truman Capote, Wright Morris, and John Fowles was another benchmark in his career, he felt.)

If Macdonald's talent was beginning to be acknowledged outside his genre, his reputation within the detective-fiction world at this time was formidable, said Gores: "Close to godhead, among people who liked hard-boiled. Certainly on the steps of the pantheon." Gores found Millar in person to be extremely self-contained: "He *watched.* You know how he had that philosophy about Archer—that he should be thin as a sheet of paper and that if he turned sideways you wouldn't see him? *He* sorta went through life that way—no leather patches on the elbows, you know?" Phyllis White recalled watching Millar answer audience questions at a later Bay Area MWA meet: "I felt that Ken was very hard to know, that he was always standing a long way back from the facade. I said something to Joe Gores about that, and Joe said to me, 'He's a Chinese box!' "

During his 1968 Bay Area trip, Millar had Gores drive him to the bird-banding station above Point Bolinas where, though they'd never met him, the personnel greeted Millar warmly; they knew all about him: not as a fiction writer, but for his work on behalf of condors. On the drive back, Millar returned to Ross Macdonald mode, quizzing Gores about auto "repo" men as material for a new Archer novel.

The Goodbye Look would be that new book's name, and Millar had a very good feeling about it. "I seem to be moving further in the direction of the 'mainstream novel,' " he wrote Ash Green, "a development which is deeply satisfying to me." Even though he thought Archer now at the peak of his earning power, Millar the sometime seer had a sort of premonition there might be more exciting things in store. He told Alfred Knopf, "I feel as if I'm turning a corner but don't know the name of the street. I like it, though." Done with *The Goodbye Look* in September, Millar informed Green with modest pride and prescience, "I'm keen on this book, and venture to think it's my largest effort yet—certainly the one least likely to have been written by anyone else. If your firm agrees, *this* would be the book on which to make a somewhat more ambitious presentation, I believe."

Naturally the front page of the *New York Times Book Review,* if it is given over to a very enthusiastic notice of a reasonably good book, does influence sales, but I have seen favorable reviews printed there of books for which we have not in the following week received orders for thirty copies.

—Alfred Knopf, *Atlantic Monthly,* 1957

However skeptical Millar had once been about Santa Barbara's cultural climate, he'd always loved its physical beauty—especially the mind-calming, soul-cleansing sea. The introduction in the late 1950s of oil-well platforms off the Santa Barbara coast had so dismayed and angered Millar and his like-minded writers' lunch friends that this El Cielito bunch had concocted a half-serious plan for some not-so-civil disobedience. "We'd all been in the service," said Al Stump. "One guy was an expert on explosives, another was a machine gunner from the Italian campaign; I'd been on a navy carrier, gunnery. And Ken Millar knew his way around things. So in a drunken moment we conceived the idea of going out at night and blowing one of those wells out of the water. Be easy to do: just slap some plastique on a couple of the legs and get outta there. That would be a message to the oil companies, that they weren't gonna ruin *our* beach. But then we got sober and, reconsidering it, came to the conclusion that we'd kill some people if we did it. It turned out there were night watchmen aboard these damn wells."

Those first offshore structures were grudgingly accepted by the natives. But at the end of the sixties, federal and local authorities allowed construction of a lot more wells, five miles out but clearly visible from the Coral Casino. At first citizens objected to this new derrick invasion on aesthetic grounds; they hated the sight of the things, which stood about twenty stories tall. Before long there was much more to complain about than a spoiled view.

On a January Tuesday in 1969, an underwater well blew out and ran wild at Union Oil's Platform A, spewing oil and gas up from the ocean floor with tremendous force. The well's casing was inadequate to stop the boiling black ooze. One scientist guessed twenty thousand barrels of oil were floating offshore. Ken and Margaret Millar, like thousands of other townsfolk, were sickened and outraged, not only about coastal damage but about danger to diving birds. Within days a citizens group called GOO (Get Oil Out) had formed. The Millars joined GOO's vocal ranks at a weekend protest rally at East Beach.

Five days after the blowout, with the leak still uncontrolled, Secretary of the Interior Walter Hickel came to town to look things over—and decided to let the oil companies keep drilling. By now oil was coming in on Santa Barbara's beaches. "It lay so thick on the water," Millar wrote, "that the waves were unformed; they made a squishing sound." The hulls of all the harbor boats were coated with the black tide, and so were a lot of birds. Condor expert Ian McMillan told the Millars he thought about twelve hundred square miles along the coast were polluted, and that hundreds or thousands of birds were dying at sea.

Bob Phelps from the *New York Times* telephoned Millar for pointers on how to cover the story; Millar suggested he find out how former interior secretary Stewart Udall came to grant oil-drilling leases after promising local leaders he'd protect the Santa Barbara Channel. Millar concluded that the federal government needed the oil companies' millions to help pay for the Vietnam War, and that Santa Barbara's leaders hadn't been able to resist the combined pressures of Uncle Sam and Union Oil. He cut his Union Oil credit card in two and mailed the pieces to the company's president to signal his separation from the polluters.

Soon he had a chance to express his displeasure in person. When California senator Alan Cranston brought Democratic Party leader Senator Ed Muskie to view the spill, the Millars were among those at the airport to greet them with homemade protest signs; Margaret's read "Ban the Blob." The citizens got a bonus target for their anger when a Union Oil jet landed and disgorged the company president. "Many of us booed him," Millar wrote later, "not so much for ruining our coast as for treating us like natives who could be quieted by the techniques of public relations." Maggie Millar was especially vociferous, said Ping Ferry: "Margaret was always in the forefront of these demonstrators, shouting the strongest possible language—things like 'You criminals!' " She was photographed shaking her "Ban the Blob" sign in the oil executive's face, in a picture reproduced in newspapers and magazines around the country. The Union Oil man, trailed by reporters, for some reason marched up to Millar and demanded to know who he was. "My name is Kenneth Millar," the writer said, adding for the newsmen's benefit, "and I happen to be secretary of the Scenic Shoreline Preservation Conference." ("No one ever could intimidate Ken," Margaret proudly recalled. "Nobody!") "That was quite a speech," the oilman huffed, stalking off. This moment too was reported nationally. When Millar wondered why the exec had singled him out, Maggie said the man was obviously accident-prone.

In the wake of Democrat Muskie's visit, Republican president Richard Nixon came to see the oil spill, landing on the beach in a helicopter. The sign-wielding Millars were there to greet him also. Oil kept washing ashore, uniting all sorts of Santa Barbarans: conservatives, liberals, students, fishermen, housewives, professors, artists, construction workers. "This thing radicalized the entire city," Ping Ferry said.

Millar, agreeing to write a piece on the spill for *Sports Illustrated,* rented a twin-engine plane and went up with Margaret, Bob Easton, and some naturalists to inspect the damage. Fifty miles of coastline were smeared with oil. Birds and wildlife were clearly endangered on and near the Channel Islands.

As the weeks wore on, the oil kept oozing, despite the oil people's assurance that everything was okay. Stearn's Wharf became a focus of protest. The old city-owned structure, previously a favored spot for shops and tourists, was now a service facility for the offshore wells; big oil trucks rattled its creaky timbers. The Millars were among a group of a thousand who gathered at Stearn's Wharf on Easter for a mass meeting where speakers argued for an environmental rights movement to parallel the civil rights struggle. At rally's end, several hundred (including the Millars) took nonviolent possession of the wharf. When a truck loaded with oil casings tried to drive onto the pier, Ken and Maggie and others sat down to block it. The driver hopped out wielding a tire iron; local police stepped in to defuse things. "We took it seriously," Maggie Millar said, "because we loved that wharf."

Millar loved the whole town, he'd discovered. Santa Barbara, he wrote Olding, was "the objective correlative of my mental life." He and Maggie and about seventy other protesters picketed Stearn's Wharf for fifteen days, this time with Millar holding the "Ban the Blob" sign and having his picture printed all over the country. When construction of a new oil platform was approved within half a mile of the faulty one, Millar was among those who took to sea in a quixotic flotilla of launches and sailboats that tried (unsuccessfully) to block its assembly.

With Easton, Millar did a second article about the spill for the *New York Times Magazine*. He saw writing these pieces as his civic duty. (Easton found, though, that Millar's concern to protect the environment was matched by an equally strong urge to protect his prose. Writing with the prickly Millar, Easton said, was like "collaborating with a porcupine.") The *Times* story used as its title an "eleventh commandment" articulated by local historian Roderick Nash: "Thou shalt not abuse the earth."

Easton and Millar became prime movers of Santa Barbara Citizens for Environmental Defense, a group that brought an ACLU-aided class-action lawsuit against the oil companies. The writers hoped to take advantage of the Santa Barbara spill to warn of more such dangers and maybe head them off. "We've got to convert this horror to positive good," Millar quoted Easton. "Perhaps we can use it as a pivot to turn the country around before we completely wreck our living space." The activists saw their hopes realized. Within a year of the spill, Earth Day was proclaimed an annual event; and a new ecology movement pressed for legislation to protect the nation's resources and quality of life. As for stopping Channel oil drilling, success was mixed: safeguards were improved, but new wells went in.

Typically, Millar had responded to the problem on several levels: intellectually, viscerally, socially, personally, aesthetically—and morally. Considered by his strict standards, the oil spill was "an ecological crime," and in due course Lew Archer would pursue such criminals.

* * *

In the midst of these rallies and protests, another set of events began in the spring of 1969 that had bigger consequences for Millar's life and Ross Macdonald's career. In late April, John Leonard, assistant editor of the *New York Times Book Review,* came to Santa Barbara to interview Ross Macdonald. The *Book Review,* Leonard said, was planning to take "special notice" of *The Goodbye Look* in May.

Millar knew he'd acquired a core following of smart young readers around the country. Some even came West to visit or interview him—for instance a young fellow from the *Harvard Crimson,* who turned out to be a prodigious quoter of Archer novels ("knew my books better than I do," Millar told Green). From such fans Millar learned there were Macdonald "campus cults" at Harvard, Princeton, and Yale. While Millar had spent two decades writing "Alfred Knopf–quality" hardcover books, a generation of bright youngsters had discovered him for the most part in Bantam paperbacks.

One such devotee was the *Times*'s John Leonard, who described himself "haunting the paperback stores rooting out broken-spined editions" of Macdonald novels. But Leonard got hooked initially by a hardback. "I have a tactile memory of reading *The Chill* in hardcover," he said. "I was living up in Brighton, Massachusetts, I was working the antipoverty program, I was reading a lot of mysteries, and that one just blew me away. I remember thinking, 'Oh my *God.*' I grew up in southern California, and I was immediately taken with the way it combined the deep, dark Freudian family secret with all the great California landscape and mores. I got everything else by him that was available." Leonard hailed from Long Beach (Archer's hometown), and he thought Macdonald captured the California experience as well as any writer: "Page by page and chapter by chapter, this was family life as it seemed to me out there: the fast, fluid culture, the reinvention of the self, a kind of dread in the sun. You learn about how the money operates, and you get wonderful things about surfers and the like, and of course there's the family secret; it comes up over and over again in his writing. The older I get, the truer and shrewder that seems."

As a New York writer, Leonard discovered other Macdonald fanatics, such as Ray Sokolov, a young *Newsweek* critic. In February of 1969, Leonard wrote, he and Sokolov hatched a benign "literary conspiracy" on Macdonald's behalf over gin and tonics in an Eighth Avenue bar: "We dilated on the thesis that Ross Macdonald had, quite consciously, married Freud to the detective story; that this was a worthy union; that not enough people were aware of it—his books sold modestly in hardcover and were only sporadically available in paperback—and attention should be paid. As a new Lew Archer novel, *The Goodbye Look,* was to be published in May, it was up to us to seize the moment."

In charge of making fiction assignments at the *New York Times Book Review,* Leonard was well placed to get the ball rolling. And the Knopf people, primed by Millar, were ready to get behind *The Goodbye Look* in creative ways. The book's jacket drew attention to both novel and author with an enlarged and distorted rendering of Alfred Knopf's photograph of Macdonald, somewhat in the fish-eye style of the Beatles' *Rubber Soul* album cover. Twenty years ago Knopf had launched Lew Archer with jacket art showing a trench-coated Macdonald looming in silhouette as if he himself were "the moving target." Now Archer/Macdonald ruefully cast "the goodbye look" from a book that would say hello to a great many new readers.

Coincidentally, Macdonald's *Times* benefactor had been acquainted with Millar's previous *Times* champion: Leonard knew Anthony Boucher in the early sixties at KPFA, the Pacifica radio station in Berkeley. They never discussed mystery fiction, though, Leonard said: "I was not at that time a mystery reader at all. I was director of drama-literature programming; Tony Boucher did an opera program called *Golden Voices*, and then I talked him into doing a science fiction review program. I just got to know him as this strange, delightful cultural maverick."

Leonard was a bit of a cultural maverick himself, and when he showed up in Santa Barbara, he felt Millar was initially on guard: "This must have been close to the first time there was a sort of mainstream literary interest expressed, so he was maybe wary of what my motives were. He was a very shy man, so it was a little difficult to talk to him; easier to talk to Margaret. But he was clearly very serious about his writing. What he didn't want to talk about was his daughter and any of that material, which I'd heard about in a fuzzy way from the editor at Knopf, so I just didn't push. I'm no crack reporter, and I wasn't out there to do that; it was clear whenever I tried to ask something about it that that was painful and unnecessary, and it was not something I needed. Much more he just wanted to talk about the oil slick and the dead birds in Santa Barbara, and about writing. He gave me some of the essays he'd written, and I brought those back to quote from. I was impressed with how seriously he responded to craft questions. I thought I was going out to get a sort of pleasant sidebar; I came back with something much more substantial."

Leonard wanted *The Goodbye Look* to receive serious *Book Review* coverage—a piece as long as the weekly would do on a worthy mainstream novel, written by someone appreciative of Macdonald's oeuvre—but first he had to convince fellow assistant editor Walter Clemons that Macdonald deserved it, so that the two of them could present a united front to editor in chief Francis Brown. Clemons had never read Ross Macdonald, though an old Princeton classmate for years had urged him to. After quickly reading eleven Macdonald novels, Clemons agreed to help Leonard. Together they talked Francis Brown into giving *The Goodbye Look* a long solo review. To write it, Clemons chose that Princeton friend of his who'd been raving to him about Macdonald for years: *Harper* screenwriter William Goldman.

What happened next took even the conspirators by surprise. "I had no idea that we would play this so big," said Leonard. "The *Times* didn't usually do long interviews with anybody except dying mandarin modernists. It just happened that, through a combination of some of the responses Millar gave me and the fact that Goldman was so enthusiastic *and* the fact there was not a lot to *compete* that week at the *Book Review*, we parlayed all this space. It was startling."

On Sunday, June 1, the front page of the *New York Times Book Review* was given over entirely to William Goldman writing about Ross Macdonald's *The Goodbye Look*. Page two was also all about Macdonald: the conclusion of Goldman's review led seamlessly into Leonard's interview essay (with photograph), which jumped to another half-page. It was an extraordinary package, presenting Ross Macdonald as an author of serious purpose and achievement. "The finest detective novels ever written by an American" was the headline over Goldman's fifteen-hundred-word review, in which he wrote, "Macdonald's work in the last decade has nothing remotely to do with hard-boiled detective novels. He is writing novels of character about people with ghosts. . . . Like any first-rate writer, he has created and peopled his own world. Nobody writes southern California like Macdonald writes it. . . . I've been reading him for 20 years and he has yet to disappoint. Classify him how you will, he is one of the best American novelists now operating, and all he does is keep on getting better."

Leonard's even longer profile-essay picked up where Goldman's review left off: "Ten years ago, while nobody was watching—or, rather, while everyone was looking in the wrong direction—a writer of detective stories turned into a major American novelist. Ross Macdonald said goodbye to Raymond Chandler in *The Doomsters* (1958). He pledged himself to 'extracting a vision of the self from internal darkness—a self dying into fiction as it comes to birth.' Ever since he has been producing books as complex and as pertinent as any we have, and better written than most of what we have. Those books explore guilt, justice, mercy, exile, new beginnings, the 'closed circuit' of time, the 'family romance' (as in Freud: the fantasy you use to rationalize your relationship with your family and yourself), the tension between causality and revolt (you are compelled in your actions, but still responsible for them), and, crucially, the spider web of consequences spun from the abdomen of Oedipus. . . . Macdonald's moral vision, his interest in psychology and sociology, his concern for the continuities of family life, his willingness to risk more of himself in his stories, his clean spare style ('beware the inflated rhetorical'), combined to move the detective novel—'democratic, accessible to everyone, respecting unities and form, almost Elizabethan'—into the mainstream of American fiction."

A terrific notice on the front page of the *New York Times Book Review* was about the best coverage an American author could want in 1969: an unbeatable combination of cultural validation and the sort of publicity money couldn't buy. Such reviews made writers famous overnight and boosted books onto best-seller lists. That had happened earlier this year when the *Book Review* led with Kurt Vonnegut's sixth novel, *Slaughterhouse-*

Five. But the *Times*'s recognition of Macdonald was more unexpected and hence caused an even greater stir, said John Leonard: "Vonnegut was known quite specifically in New York, and everybody in the publishing world had been waiting for that breakout book, which *Slaughterhouse-Five* was clearly going to be; that was all geared up and ready to go. With Macdonald it was more the opposite: a *lot* of enthusiasm for a writer who— though obviously everyone who took mystery fiction seriously knew him very well—had not up to that time gotten that *kind* of attention."

June 1, publication date of the *Book Review* featuring *The Goodbye Look,* was the day before Ken and Margaret Millar's thirty-first wedding anniversary, and the day before Lew Archer's birthday. This June 1, the Sunday of the Memorial Day weekend, was also the tenth anniversary of Linda Millar's disappearance from UC Davis.

Several New Yorkers sent Millar advance copies of the *Book Review.* He wrote Ash Green, "I told Maggie I could prove I was a real pro only by working every day this week, including Memorial Day. Well, it appears I'm a real pro. Fortunately so is John Leonard, whose idea this apparently was." To Matt Bruccoli, at work on a Macdonald bibliography, Millar said, "My publishers are agog, which is the way I like to see publishers."

The author recognized this signal career event and took advantage of it to state a pressing grievance. Recently he'd had a frank exchange of letters with Bantam's Marc Jaffe about that house's "lowest-common multiple" approach to his books: the sexual suggestiveness of Bantam's covers, and their current tagging of Archer as "The Loner with the Lethal Gun." (If they *had* to have such a tag line, Millar proposed instead "The Coolest Man in Crime"). After okaying Bantam's bid of $12,500 for *The Goodbye Look,* made in the instant wake of the *Times* coverage, Millar told von Auw, "Booksellers and readers are constantly complaining to me that my paperbacks are not kept available. The fact is they are very hard to find, whereas competitors like John D MacDonald and Rex Stout (Stout is published by Bantam) are all over the place. One bookseller told me this week, much to my distress, that Bantam seem 'indifferent' to my work. $12,500 tells me otherwise, but the truth is, sales of my older books are not as good as they should be, because they are not available, and Bantam should be told this. Twenty years of work on Archer have created a situation where the paperback publishers should have strong and continuing sales for the *next* twenty years, if they will try for them. I mean this complaint, which is a genuine one and not just an author's gripe—the readers and booksellers are griping to me—I mean it to be a positive statement, not a negative one. I've had experiences with several of the major paperback publishers, as you know—Dell, Pocket Books—and think Bantam is the best of them. I also feel we've climbed over a major watershed this time."

Giving Macdonald and Archer an extra push forward on Sunday, June 8, was a page-one review of *The Goodbye Look* by Ray Bradbury in the *Los Angeles Times*'s Calendar section. Like Goldman's piece, Bradbury's copy praised Macdonald's body of work: "In these books, bruised women run away from too many men who did all the wrong things, while the men run away from themselves, not knowing what they did or how or for what secret reasons. The reasons, if found, must be buried, if uncovered must be gunshot and buried again, by earth or by bottle. Murder here is the last gasp of despair and outrage. And the worst crime of all is not to be discovered, not to be punished, ever. When was the last time you hurried into a bookstore with any great relish, any huge longing to read a fine new book, or even a good one? Here's your chance to examine, simultaneously, the output of one of our best writers. Buy both the *Instant Enemy*, and *The Goodbye Look*. Make your own comparison of Ross Macdonald, excellent and good-to-excellent. Argue me. I could be wrong. Out of 15 of his books I have read, 13 have been very fine. That's a fantastic average. And his end is nowhere in sight." The Bradbury piece was assigned by book editor Digby Diehl and given top placement by arts editor Charles Champlin, unofficial West Coast members of the Macdonald conspiracy.

Ross Macdonald's oldest coconspirator, Alfred Knopf, reached into the past for a way to put his own stamp on the moment. The publisher revived a gimmick first used by reviewer Heywood Broun in 1920, when Sinclair Lewis's novel *Main Street* was all the rage. "Heywood Broun had a considerable following," Knopf said. "Indeed, I remember that when we published Floyd Dell's first novel, *Moon-Calf*, it sold very modestly until Broun printed something like—I can't remember the precise words, but this is about what he said: 'Read *Moon-Calf* by Floyd Dell; yes, even *Main Street* can wait.' And *Moon-Calf* was on its way." Now, with Vladimir Nabokov's *Ada* climbing booksellers' lists, Knopf personally drafted a bold third-of-a-page ad to run in the *New York Times* this lucky Friday the thirteenth; it read:

The *New York Times*
has just called the novels of
Ross Macdonald
"the finest detective novels
ever written by an American."

His new one is
**The Goodbye
Look.**

It has just arrived
at bookstores all over the
country. Price $4.95.
Buy it now. (*Ada* can wait.)

Millar thought Knopf's ad "absolutely perfect." Its hidden reference to Sinclair Lewis, whom the Millars had once met, made him feel, he said, "in a light way, like a member of literary history." Millar admitted to Green,

"I'm getting an enormous charge out of the various favorable developments."

The next happy jolt came on June 27, in a telegram from Green: YOU ARE NUMBER TEN ON NEW YORK TIMES BEST SELLER LIST JULY 6 WE THINK ITS TERRIFIC. *Publishers Weekly* put the book number nine on its fiction list. Knopf ordered a second printing of *The Goodbye Look,* with Goldman's quotable claim ("The finest detective novels ever written by an American") stamped right on its jacket; a third printing in July brought copies to twenty-two thousand—"It's more than I'd hoped for," Millar told Green. He thought the book might last another week or two on the charts at best, but *The Goodbye Look* wouldn't leave. By the end of July it had sold twenty-two thousand, usually not enough to make a best-seller, Green said, but the lists were skewed by sales in New York and LA, where *Look* did especially well. Bradbury's rave had been as important in its way as Goldman's.

Novels above *The Goodbye Look* on this summer's best-seller list included Jacqueline Susann's *The Love Machine,* Philip Roth's *Portnoy's Complaint,* Mario Puzo's *The Godfather,* Nabokov's *Ada,* Michael Crichton's *The Andromeda Strain* (also a Knopf title), and Vonnegut's *Slaughterhouse-Five.* The first week in August, its fifth week on the *Times* list, Macdonald's novel went to eight, slipping past Vonnegut; it was six on *Publishers Weekly*'s chart. "Well," Millar understated to Green, "these are interesting times."

With his writers' lunch cronies he was modestly low-key, murmuring, "Pretty good for an old mystery writer." In letters to the agents he let his happiness show, telling Olding, "I've decided to postpone writing [a new book] until the excitement dies down. I mean *my* excitement about the current breakthrough which I've always hoped for, and, indeed, expected." To von Auw he marveled, "Eighth place on the *Time* magazine best-seller list. Who'd have believed it?"

Time magazine's own unnamed reviewer had trouble accepting Macdonald's new status and lambasted Goldman and Macdonald while trashing *The Goodbye Look.* Bruce Cook in a *National Observer* column ("Can 'Fun' Be 'Serious'?") summarized the controversy: "What Mr. Goldman is saying, basically, is that a piece of fiction written in a form usually taken as entertainment can nevertheless be taken seriously as art and judged by the same standards used to judge all fiction. The anonymous *Time* reviewer, on the other hand, is saying that such genre fiction cannot be art and that those who write it had darned well better remember that, rather than cluttering up their entertainments with a lot of pretentious superfluities." For his part, Cook argued that genre fiction was usually more interesting, intelligent, and better crafted than "real" novels: "It is usually those who care least about art who talk most about it and are determined to uphold its standards."

Millar didn't at all mind the brouhaha and thought it could only help sales. In fact his book went up to seven on *Time*'s own list; in mid-August it was also seven on the *New York Times* chart. "I do want to tell you how absolutely delighted, though by no means surprised, I am by the extraordinary success of *The Goodbye Look*," Alfred Knopf wrote Millar. "I can think of no one who deserves success more than you." Knopf ordered two more printings in August. The waves Macdonald was making in the States caused ripples in remote corners of the globe. From Czechoslovakia came a request to print an eighty-thousand-copy edition of *The Ivory Grin*. Millar's agents got wind of an unauthorized Greek newspaper serialization of *The Goodbye Look*—good news despite being illegal, an Ober rep noted: "The Greeks only pirate first-class stuff."

In the United States, the Doubleday Mystery Guild agreed to do a second Macdonald anthology, *Archer at Large* (*The Galton Case, The Chill, Black Money*), for which Millar wrote another discreetly autobiographical preface. And Bantam came through for Macdonald in a big way, with successful negotiations that brought ten more books (including the Dodd, Mead spy thrillers) into Bantam's catalog. Thanks to this good backlog news and the current book's sales, Millar wrote UC Irvine librarian John Smith, "We have ceased wondering what we'll live on in our old age, if any."

The Goodbye Look had a solid run of fourteen weeks on the *New York Times* top ten, slipping off the best-seller list in mid-October after eight pressings and forty-five thousand copies in print. (The *Washington Post* and *Publishers Weekly* listed the novel until November.) Millar honestly didn't mind seeing his book leave the lists: its "comparative obscurity" as an ex-best-seller would make it easier for him to write the next novel, he told Green. Much as he enjoyed the rush of business, *The Goodbye Look*'s three and a half months in the spotlight had drawn attention to its author in ways he wasn't used to and didn't like. Millar turned down a request to be on Dick Cavett's prime-time ABC-TV show (which he watched). "I really can't," he apologized to Bantam's publicity people and to von Auw, saying it had to do with "the externalization of the self and a writer's loss of keen interest in his work when he's over-exposed. I prefer to err in the direction of under-exposure." (It was hard to imagine Millar, with his long pauses and careful responses, adapting comfortably to the give-and-take of a talk show. Perhaps he also realized he couldn't deflect unwanted personal questions on live TV as he could with sympathetic print journalists.)

And, though he was briefly tempted, Millar said no to two bids for Macdonald to cover the grisly Sharon Tate murders: one from *Life* magazine, the second a Harcourt book offer with a fifty-thousand-dollar advance. "To cover it even adequately would take a year's work by a skilled investigative reporter," he explained, "which I am not. Besides that, I'd have to cover several trials, probably stretching out indefinitely, and would have to live in L.A. to cover them. I have no desire to do so. Nor would I have any assurance of a successful book." Better to stay in Santa Barbara, he decided, where he had another Archer under way by year's end and where his wife was finishing a book of her own (*Beyond This Point Are Monsters*—his title).

Millar took special care of Maggie's feelings during his season of sudden good fortune. He left loving notes for her around the house ("Good morning, heartmate!" read one, a sweet variation on Billie Holiday's "Good Morning Heartache"), went with her on out-of-state bird-watching trips or sent her cheerfully off without him, kept guard over her career with private letters to the agents ("Don't bother answering this item," he wrote Olding in November after learning that Maggie's *The Birds and the Beasts Were There* had been allowed to lapse out of print, "she's happily at work on a new book, and I don't want her depressed by Random House again").

Writing books was the important thing, Millar felt, and he wouldn't let his and Margaret's routines be derailed. ("Each of us likes to begin just as the other finishes," he told Green in a homely metaphor, "so there's one up front in the shop while the other cobbles away in the back.") "Success" was pleasant, but he kept it in perspective. When Collin Wilcox, a new mystery-writer friend, asked cheekily of the Hope Ranch place, "So this is the house that Knopf bought, eh?" without a pause Millar replied, "No, this is the house that Bantam bought."

Her enthusiasms are varied. Besides the books neatly arranged by author (Faulkner, Elizabeth Bowen, Virginia Woolf) in the living-room shelves, there are others in stacks of twos and threes on tables and on an upright piano in the corner: C. M. Bowra's *Memories, 1898–1939, The Collected Stories of Peter Taylor,* Dwight Macdonald's *Parodies* anthology. And mysteries, which she reads late at night. She likes Dick Francis and Andrew Garve. Ross Macdonald? "Oh, yes! I've read all his books. I think I once wrote Ross Macdonald a fan letter, but I never mailed it. I was afraid he'd think it—icky."

—Walter Clemons, "Meeting Miss Welty," *New York Times Book Review,* April 1970

K nowing young people were a big part of Macdonald's readership, Millar kept them in mind as he wrote new Archer stories. "Part of the enormous excitement of writing for popular audiences is that relationship with your audience," he told some Santa Barbara City College students who interviewed him. "You have to catch it and you have to hold it." But he didn't court readers' favor with a with-it style or the sort of opinionated asides that peppered John D. Macdonald's Travis McGee tales. "I'm a bit of an environmentalist myself" was about the most the author allowed Archer on political or social matters. Lew knew reality was complex; "like a good novelist," as Millar said approvingly of journalist J. Anthony Lukas, "he comes to no pat conclusions."

Young readers, though, sensed that Archer (and Macdonald) was honest and sympathetic: he knew the ropes, told the truth, and tried to help. Individuals were what mattered most to him, not politics or taste in music. While he didn't excuse wrong behavior, he knew how hard it was for kids to grow up; and he was on their side.

The country in 1970 was split by a generation gap, with adults railing against irresponsible youth and postadolescents saying don't trust anyone over thirty. Several issues dividing the generations burst into expression in Santa Barbara this year in what the *LA Times* would call "one of the high points in radical, youthful violence in America." Events centered at UCSB and in Isla Vista, the square-mile enclave ten miles outside the city, a sort of ghetto for university students. ("Santa Barbara's not nearly as careful about its children as it is its palm trees," Ping Ferry wryly said.)

Campus resentment brewed over lots of things: the firing of a popular assistant professor, the escalating Vietnam War, arrests of young people in Isla Vista. Rallies and demonstrations often drew as many as five thousand. Bombings and arson fires occurred at school. The February arrest by sheriff's deputies of a student on campus led to rock-throwing.

The afternoon after that arrest, activist lawyer William Kunstler (an attorney for the 1968 Democratic National Convention's "Chicago Seven") spoke to a crowd (including Ken Millar) in the campus stadium. Afterward, young people milled into Isla Vista, where police in riot gear patrolled. The arrest of an ex-student for public drinking caused more rock-throwing. As evening came, a fire was set in a trash bin outside a Bank of America, and a police car was torched. Cops responded with tear gas but had to withdraw, and by midnight the bank was destroyed. The riot went on until 2:30 A.M.

The next day a 6 P.M. curfew was imposed in Isla Vista. Governor Ronald Reagan (who hadn't seen fit to inspect the Santa Barbara oil spill) came to town and declared a state of emergency. A hundred twenty-two students were arrested, and the National Guard was put on alert.

There was more rioting in April. A UCSB student trying to protect the bank from further arson was shot dead by a policeman. Again in June people ran riot through Isla Vista, prompting another curfew and more arrests. The community (students included) was divided on how to respond. Millar, in an impassioned letter to the *News-Press,* urged restraint:

> It is neither natural nor necessary for older citizens and younger citizens to be divided into warring camps. Even if it were possible for us older citizens to win such a war, what would we be doing beating out the brains of our own posterity? The American democracy, which seemed so hopeful and promising just a few years ago, has not yet become the sow that eats her own farrow.

He joined forty-five other Santa Barbarans (including lawyers, teachers, doctors, a retired army major general, and an Episcopal priest) in a self-appointed Citizens Commission on Civil Disorders to hold two months of hearings (with 150 witnesses) in hopes of airing and understanding the issues and calming the city down.

At the same time, eleven young people were indicted in Santa Barbara Superior Court on forty-five charges relating to the bank burning. Their sixteen-week criminal trial, with helmeted sheriff's deputies guarding the courthouse corridors, was the longest to date in Santa Barbara County history. Millar attended nearly every day of it. The presiding judge was John A. Westwick, Linda's former lawyer.

"Westwick was pretty fair in our case," said Bob Langfelder, one of the eleven Isla Vista defendants. Langfelder, twenty-six at the time, became acquainted with Millar. "He told me Westwick would call and tell him whenever there was some juicy case coming up. Our trial received a lot of attention, since the Bank of America had put up twenty-five thousand dollars reward. I got a crash education in the legal system. And Ken and his wife came there every day to watch. I think it was material for him, and a bit of a hobby. He was a very astute observer, detached, very reserved; you

couldn't get an opinion out of him. Somewhere in that time I started reading his books. I knew a sociology prof at UCSB who was very familiar with
his work, a social psychologist fascinated with those plots of his that go
back twenty, thirty years. I was at his house, and he had Macdonald's complete works there, and that was a sort of eye-opener—and made it, you
know, *okay*. You're talking political? And then Archer's so down-to-earth,
and the realism appealed to me. I guess I was in a period of realism then,
and Archer's hardly your touched-up romantic." Millar himself was hard
to know, Langfelder found: "He wasn't an engaging conversationalist. I
kept being critical of the system and trying to draw him out on the police,
but he wouldn't lend himself to easy explanations. He doesn't have Archer
as the brilliant private eye versus the dumb police; he's not into such simple stereotypes. I was trying to make this point how the police in our case
weren't even as good as he gives them credit for in his books. I mean the
police and the DA made some crucial errors in our trial; they just brushed
aside the standards of evidence, and I was trying to blame them. It's funny,
he wasn't critical of them in that sense; he just listened."

During the same weeks he went to the bank-burning trial, Millar attended
the Citizens Commission meetings, where witnesses ranged from the vice-
chancellor of the university to a reformed drug addict. "My sympathies are
not with violence," he wrote Bill Ruehlmann (now teaching in Arizona), "but
to a degree with the students, faced as they feel themselves to be with a
futureless kind of future." To a journalist, he said, "I put my hope in the intelligence of young people, but I feel also that drugs have been a major misfortune. They have ruined a lot of people. Hard drugs, overall, are a
terrible national menace. At the same time it's unfortunate that kids caught
with pot are treated as hardened criminals. Kids looking for reality who can't
get it from their parents will do drastic things to find it."

The commission's work ended with the public distribution of a carefully
written and informative report. "It came out somewhat more liberal than
I'd dared to hope," Millar told John Smith, ". . . but I don't suppose the
kids will like it much."

The jury in the Isla Vista bank-burning trial surprised Judge Westwick
and most courtroom spectators by acquitting most of the eleven defendants. Langfelder, though, was convicted. "I was facing arson charges," he
said, "and expecting to do time in the Santa Barbara County jail. But I did
a lot of detective work; we had to defend our case, we dug up a lotta stuff."
Langfelder's defense people used the services of a private investigator.
Millar, who knew few actual detectives, happened to know Langfelder's.
This idealistic young PI called Millar before the Isla Vista troubles and
came to his house for a talk. Macdonald later wrote:

> I remembered his name. A few years before, as a local university student,
> he had joined the campus branch of the John Birch Society in order to
> expose its purposes. Since then, he told me in my study, he had carved

out a career as a private detective . . . in the Bay area [and] apprehended some fifty criminals. I was surprised by his reason for coming to me. He wanted to establish a code of ethics for private detectives, and thought my Archer stories might serve as a starting point. Nothing came of that. Events carried him away, as they tend to do with young men of action. I saw him once more, in Superior Court, when he was gathering evidence for the defendants in the Isla Vista trial. Then he went underground on another case.

In another blurring of art and life, Macdonald's description of this man could serve as a thumbnail sketch of Lew Archer, or a self-portrait of Ken Millar:

> He is built like a middleweight. . . . His style could be that of a graduate student or an artist, or possibly a young lawyer for the defense. But he is more diffident than self-assertive. He watches and listens, and talks just enough to hold up his end of the conversation. For all his goodwill and energy, there is a touch of sadness in his expression, as if there had been some trouble in his life, a fracture in his world which all his investigative efforts had failed to mend.

Many people meeting Millar were struck by his fundamental sadness: "not a bitterness or gloom or resignation," wrote Matt Bruccoli, "but a tranquil sadness—perhaps even a cheerful sadness." Bruccoli, at work in 1970 on his Ross Macdonald bibliographical checklist, visited Millar in Santa Barbara and later said, "I had the feeling when I was with Ken that I was in the presence of a man who had had great troubles. There was a quietness and a reserve about him that seemed to come from some source I couldn't quite identify. He was not ebullient; he was not spontaneous. But neither was he unfriendly! He was a very private man, and I didn't ask probing questions; I was just happy to spend three hours with him, talking books. I thought Ken was one of the best American writers of his time, and I still do. And I didn't say 'mystery writer'—I said *writer.*"

When Bruccoli visited, Millar was finishing a book that put the 1964 Coyote fire to fictional use. Written with the working title *Digger* (a country name for death), it was published as *The Underground Man*. Millar dedicated this sixteenth Archer novel to Macdonald's bibliographer.

The author thought it important that the novel after *The Goodbye Look* be as good or better than that best-seller. "There is always moral pain involved in following a great success," he told Ash Green, "and I never worked so hard on a book in my life." The result was as much a suspense novel as a detective story, and its author was cautiously pleased. "The main thing," he told Green, "is that it's different from the others, from all the others indeed, and not a self-imitation. Looking over it in some coolness, I think it may get me some new readers. . . . Not," he was quick to add, "that I expect a further breakthrough in sales." Millar told Olding he could use a larger advance from Knopf, but he worried about upping his rate unduly: "Certainly I don't want to strain the situation or interfere with their promotion of the book, which in the case of *Goodbye Look* was generous and effective. What do you think about asking for $7500.00?" Green, enthusiastic about *The Underground Man*, swiftly agreed to the sum, which seems modest even by 1970 standards for an author whose last book had ridden the *New York Times* top ten list for three and a half months.

As he worked on his novel, went to Citizens Commission meetings, and attended trials, Millar had also found time in this busy year to help friends. When Herb Harker after years of spare-time writing finished a novel-length manuscript, the first thing he did was bring it to Millar on a Thursday night. "That same weekend," Harker said, "we moved into a different house. I mentioned to Ken the street we were moving to. He said, 'Well, Lew Archer can find you.' On Sunday we were ready to leave for church when who do I see at the door but Ken. He said, 'I just wanted to stop by and tell you that I really like your book. I want to finish it in the next couple of days, then we'll talk about it.' So we got together and talked about it at length. He'd made a lot of notations, of course. Then I went back to work on it. He made a lot of wonderful suggestions as to what I might do to improve it; and finally he said, 'Well, I think you should send it off.' " Millar got Dorothy Olding to read the manuscript, and she agreed to represent it. Though she couldn't sell that novel, Harker wrote another in the meantime, which Olding placed with Random House.

Millar also arranged in 1970 that Olding read *Black Tide*, Bob Easton's history of oil drilling in the Santa Barbara Channel, which the agent sold to Delacorte; Ross Macdonald wrote its foreword. Millar was delighted when things worked out so well. "I'm like you," he told Olding, "love to see nice things happen to my friends."

He went out of his artistic way for strangers too. By 1970, Macdonald was a prime source of quotes for jackets of books (usually novels) sent by agents or editors. He wouldn't praise a book he didn't like, but when he thought well of something, he'd often send not only a solid blurb but a detailed critique for the author's benefit. (And he corrected typos as a matter of course.)

Sometimes authors showed up in person to thank him. "Leonard Gardner, who wrote *Fat City*"—an acclaimed novel about boxers in central California—"came by yesterday evening," Millar wrote Green, "tall and thin and melancholy and humorous, and I liked him just as well as I liked his book, which made him the current California white hope. He's messing around, as he said, with a movie script for his novel which Ray Stark bought. I have some movie action going, too. . . . Some good people are getting ready to make *The Chill*, I'm told."

Those people included director Sam Peckinpah, whose recent western

The Wild Bunch was a critical and box-office smash. Peckinpah signed with *Harper* producer Elliott Kastner to film *The Chill,* and it seemed Bette Davis might play the key female role. "Here we have a chance for a good one," Millar wrote Olding. The project's financing fell through, though, and *The Chill* was once more put on ice.

But other good things were happening for Macdonald. Academic recognition increased: George Grella of the University of Rochester published a strong essay ("Murder and the Mean Streets: The Hard-Boiled Detective Novel") on the fiction of Hammett, Chandler, and Macdonald; at Boston University, doctoral candidate Robert Brown Parker (later author of several thrillers with a detective named Spenser) submitted as his dissertation "The Violent Hero, Wilderness Heritage and Urban Reality: A Study of the Private Eye in the Novels of Dashiell Hammett, Raymond Chandler and Ross Macdonald."

The *New York Times*'s Harrison Salisbury gave Millar an assignment for a thousand-word piece on California's "national, social, political and economic tendencies" for the *Times*'s new "opposite editorial" page; though Millar later begged off writing this op-ed piece (it needed more research than he'd realized), he was flattered to be asked. *Cosmo* bought *The Underground Man* for condensation (the first Macdonald they'd taken in five years); the author wired Olding he was "delighted"—but this time, he added, "Let them cut it." He noted with pleasure "carom shots" where Ross Macdonald was mentioned in reviews of other California authors such as Joan Didion and Joseph Hansen: indications that Macdonald was becoming an established part of the literary landscape. Bay Area educational filmmaker Art Kaye got Millar's cooperation in making a short documentary on Macdonald ("It will help to get my name around in the schools," Millar explained to Olding); Kaye started filming in Santa Barbara in October.

If Millar and Kaye succeeded in expanding Macdonald's campus audience, Bantam Books was ready to meet the demand with style. The paperback house came up with a great graphic look for its latest Macdonald repackaging: each book had title and author's name in shadowed "three-dimensional" typeface above striking rectangular-boxed photo art, with William Goldman's now-famous quote at the top of the covers. "I'm told that Bantam is going to put out batches of five in boxes for Christmas," Millar wrote Olding. "It's either feast or famine, as we used to say." Critic Gene Shalit displayed the new Bantams coast-to-coast on NBC-TV's *Today* show and called Ross Macdonald "America's best mystery novelist."

But the most exciting thing of all for Millar was a remark made by Mississippi author Eudora Welty in the *New York Times Book Review.* She'd once nearly sent Ross Macdonald a fan letter, she said: "I never mailed it. I was afraid he'd think it—icky." Millar didn't hesitate to send *her* a letter, along with his second Knopf omnibus, *Archer at Large.* Welty replied with a "warm . . . most pleasant and (naturally) intelligent letter," Millar eagerly informed Knopf; the highly regarded Welty said she'd been following

Archer for years. Millar had read Welty for a long time too, ever since her first stories in the *Southern Review,* a little thirties magazine coedited by Cleanth Brooks. Though Millar and Welty had Brooks in common (Brooks having taught that 1942 Michigan course), the two authors otherwise almost dwelt in separate literary hemispheres. "To receive such a letter from such a writer," Millar wrote Knopf, "seemed to me about the nicest thing that had happened to me since you accepted *Blue City.*" He volleyed another letter to Welty, and a long correspondence began.

"So much luck as I've had makes one superstitious," Millar confided to Olding. Inside the successful California writer was a poor Canadian boy who'd learned life was a cruel game of snakes-and-ladders. As a character in a Macdonald book said, "Your good luck and your bad luck balance out; the whole thing works like clockwork."

Millar's happiness and uneasiness increased on Sunday, November 1, when his daughter and her family came for a day's visit from Inglewood, a hundred miles south. Linda was thirty-one now and seemed in better shape than she had in years, though her father could see there were scars on her psyche. She'd been hospitalized in 1968 for a circulatory disorder that caused a slight stroke; recently she'd given up a medical assistant's job when she couldn't keep up the pace. But Linda was a good mother to her seven-year-old. She was in fine spirits this sparkling autumn Sunday. Three generations of Millars had a whale of a good time at the Natural History Museum, where Linda had spent many happy days as a youngster. Millar saw his guests back to the highway in late afternoon. As their car drove out of sight, Linda smiled and waved. Millar went home to work on the proofs of *The Underground Man,* needed in New York by November 10. He wrote Ash Green a letter that evening about Linda's visit and said, "Life is so very good on certain days that one almost lives in fear of having to pay for it in full. But life is by definition a free gift."

Four days later, on a Thursday morning, he learned that his only child had died in her sleep. The cause was at first said to be the circulatory disorder that had troubled her in the past. Millar subsequently told people his daughter died of "a cerebral incident."

He could hardly bear to speak for days. Each hour was a burden, and talking to other people only made it heavier. Linda would be cremated and her ashes placed in Santa Barbara Cemetery on Saturday, November 7. The Millars told almost no one.

Dick Lid in Woodland Hills got a terse call from Millar that Saturday morning: "Ken said, 'Linda is dead.' That was it, just—long silence. I said, 'When's the funeral, I'll be there.' He said, 'In an hour, you can't make it.' And hung up. He had arranged the call so I *couldn't* be there."

"Somehow Ken and Maggie both felt responsible for Linda's death, I'm sure," Ping Ferry said, "even though that wasn't the case; she was an adult." After the funeral, Linda's survivors went to the Millars' Hope Ranch house.

Margaret years later told journalist Paul Nelson how the family coped: "[Linda's husband] Joe was with us, and Jimmy, and we just didn't know what to *do*. I mean it was just one of those *terrible* situations. And I said to Joe that the Beatles movie *A Hard Day's Night* was going to be on television, and he said, 'I'd like to see it because Linda and I watched it together in Japan.' They lived in Japan for a while, and they watched it in Japanese. And we watched it that night, and somehow—it got us *through* the night. I *loved* it, I just simply *loved* it. There's certain movies I could just watch over and over, and *have*, and that's *one* of them. I'll tell you, there's something very *poignant* about that film; I always manage to *bawl* at the end of it."

That night and on Sunday, Millar wrote letters to friends expressing feelings he couldn't put into speech. To John Smith, who'd known Linda, he said, "You will understand me when I say that she was a valiant girl, one of the great moral forces in my life and after Margaret my dearest love. . . . There is some relief in the knowledge that Linda made a great effort and succeeded in it, though she died young." He wrote Olding, "She died young, aged 31, but her short life was as full as many others. The people who knew her best, including her husband and me, felt that she was in almost unaccountable ways a great person. In spite of emotional illness she raised a fine boy with loving care to the age of seven, and in spite of physical illness she worked as a nurse's aide and more recently as a medical assistant. Like my mother, her great ambition was to look after the sick, and in fact she was looking for work in that field the day she died. Her ashes are being placed in Santa Barbara Cemetery above the beach where she took her first swim in the Pacific. She was a strong swimmer in her day. . . . Linda is at peace."

"I presume he was an atheist," said Millar's friend Herb Harker, a Mormon, "which doesn't in the least diminish him in my view, because I never knew a man more concerned about other people; and to me that's the most important thing. He never learned much about my religion, and I never learned much about his. It was kind of off-limits. I only remember one time where we really kind of got into it. As I remember, Ken said he did not think there was an afterlife. And I said, 'Well, we know that anything physical can't be destroyed. You watch a log burn, you think it's gone, but it isn't, it still exists; there's smoke and ashes, there's heat—all it does is change.' I said, 'It's difficult for me to see why, if you can't destroy matter, you can destroy life and have it suddenly end.' And Ken said to me, 'Does that give you comfort?' And I felt like what he said was kind of harsh; it really offended me. I was hurt, mostly, because it seemed to trivialize the feeling I had: as though I believed this because I'm afraid not to."

Asked (a few years after Linda's death) by interviewer Paul Nelson if he was religious, Millar replied, "In a sense. But I don't know that I can define the sense." Nelson persisted: Was he an atheist? "Oh, I believe in human values," Millar said. "I don't have any direct contact with the divine world. If I did have, I'd be afraid of it. I don't know whether that makes me an atheist or not. I think I live in sufficient fear and trembling to qualify as a believer. But I don't want to know the source of my fear and trembling too intimately."

Fear and Trembling was a Kierkegaard work that influenced Millar greatly. In another place, Kierkegaard wrote, "Sin is despair," and conversely, "Despair is sin." Millar didn't despair after Linda's death. And he did have his own sort of beliefs, as he'd tell Nelson: "We're all members of a single body, to degrees that we have no *idea* except in moments of what might be called revelation. Oh, I believe it. Yes. And the idea of all of us being members of a single body, so to speak, has a religious connection. I think it's literally true: we live or die together. And the influences just of one person on another—any two people who know each other—are absolutely staggering, if you trace them. It's the essence of our lives, that interrelationship." It was the essence of Macdonald's fiction too. After Linda's death it became some essence of what kept Millar going. He continued for one thing for the sake of his grandson, who needed him, and whom the Millars needed.

"Jim is a fine boy, with his mother's eyes," Millar told Steven Carter, the Ohio graduate student, one of several correspondents for whom Millar (exemplifying those interconnections) was a long-distance surrogate father, "and we are learning through him one of the most profound mysteries: the persistence and continuity of personality from one generation to another; which is something a good deal more certain (and satisfying) than a life after death. But Jim is being raised as a Roman Catholic, like his daddy, and will have the satisfactions of both. Anyway, I'm glad he's as old as he is—past the age when a boy can't grow without a mother. All of which doesn't quite succeed in silencing my mind in the night watches, or lightening my visits to the cemetery."

Millar continued the business and habits of life. On November 7, he airmailed corrected proofs of *The Underground Man* to New York. And he showed up at the first writers' lunch after Linda's death. "It shocked people a little bit," Jerre Lloyd said, "that he could do that." On November 25, Millar wrote Olding, "Our son-in-law and grandson come up every weekend, and the day before yesterday we went for a bike hike on the waterfront, all four of us—no mean undertaking, and no mean success." The Millars spent as much time outdoors as possible and by the end of December were starting to feel human again. Jim and his dad came to Hope Ranch for Christmas, and Millar reported to Green, "Well, our little family got through the holiday season in decent shape, I believe." But he added, "At the end of the worst and best of years, I'll be content if next year touches neither extreme." There were undreamt of extremes ahead.

As if our fortunes were being carefully meted out to us, so often we
get the best and the worst almost on top of each other, and seldom
know joy without the taste of sorrow.

—Ken Millar to Herb Harker

I had a nice letter from Eudora Welty explaining that she was out
of town when the *N.Y.T.B.R.* asked her, by wire, to review *Underground Man,* and otherwise she'd have been happy to do it. Too
bad—an earlier letter from her is the best account of my intent I've
ever seen.

—Ken Millar to Ash Green

J ohn Leonard, who'd brought Ross Macdonald's *The Goodbye Look* so
dramatically to the attention of *New York Times* readers, cooked up an
even more spectacular debut for *The Underground Man.*
　　Leonard was editor of the *Times Book Review* by 1971. He was also on
the board of New Hampshire's MacDowell Colony, an artists' retreat where
he had occasion to lunch with Eudora Welty, another MacDowell member.
Welty mentioned having read Leonard's interview with Macdonald; she
said she too was an Archer fan. "I was flabbergasted that she was a reader
of Ross Macdonald's," Leonard said. He wrote, "That a Southern lady of
letters had a crush on a California private eye is the sort of datum editors
are paid to memorize." When the next Macdonald crossed his desk, he
sent it to Welty for review.
　　The assignment nearly didn't happen. Welty was out of town when the
bid arrived, and it seemed she wouldn't have time to accept. But she said,
"I just *had* to do that. I remember going to the Western Union office in the
dead of night, to try to set things so I could."
　　Welty, of Jackson, Mississippi, was one of the nation's most admired
writers; her long-awaited 1970 novel, *Losing Battles,* was a best-seller, and
in 1971 she'd be elected to the American Academy of Arts and Letters.
She'd been corresponding with Millar for nine months, since he saw her
remark that she'd once nearly sent him a letter. "So then I had a letter
from Ken," she recalled, "saying, 'This is the first fan letter *I've* ever written to an author about a book, but if you keep writing books like *Losing
Battles* or whatever it was, it won't be my last.' He wrote a very interesting
letter about what he called the North American Language: he thinks the
whole continent speaks a form of the same language, that we're not so isolated as everybody says. So he wrote all kinds of things, and we began writing letters to each other." Their correspondence covered the period of
Linda's death. "He wrote to me after a long silence and said, 'You never

knew my daughter Linda, but perhaps you would want to be told'—and so he told me that she had died. And I'm sure that that just was almost the end of everything, for both of them. It seemed like he had everything terrible visited upon him that anybody could have."

Welty took pains with her *Underground* piece, she said: "I cared a lot about it. And it was important to him too, because it was gonna be a front-page review. I tried to be that responsive to it, 'cause I think it's so good; and I didn't want to be content with just saying what an expert he is, and so on, which everybody knows." Welty (whose past critical subjects included Virginia Woolf, William Faulkner, and S. J. Perelman) delivered a four-thousand-word review: rather longer than what the *Times* had asked for. "She dealt with Walter Clemons at the *Book Review*," Leonard recalled. "Walter is an old friend of hers. And I handed this essay to him and said, 'Wal-ter: it's very, very, very long!' And they did a bit of taffy-pulling."

"I also did something I ought not to," Welty admitted. "After I wrote it, I was so anxious for it to be right that I sent a copy to Ken before I sent it in to the paper, to pass it by him, because I didn't want to mess it up. I knew I shouldn't have done that; it was bad newspaper ethics. But I could not risk making a mess of it. You know, reviewing a mystery is different from reviewing another kind of book. I've reviewed books all my life, but I didn't want to do anything I shouldn't have done; I just wanted to be sure." (Millar himself sometimes extended such courtesies.) And Millar's response? Welty laughed: "He said it was okay."

Millar wrote her, "Your review filled me with joy. . . . You have given me the fullest and most explicit reading I've ever had, or that I ever expected. I exist, as a writer, more completely, thanks to you."

In great excitement, Millar told close associates of Welty's upcoming piece. "It's an enormous blockbuster of a review," he wrote Green, "completely favorable. . . . It strikes me as more important than the 1969 front-page review of *Goodbye Look*. . . . Nothing quite like this has happened to any mystery writer before, I doubt." To Olding: "It's going to be a great help to the book, as well as to my literary reputation—certainly the most satisfying response I've ever had. She's an enormously generous woman." To Alfred Knopf: "Heaping blessings on my head, she sent me a carbon of the first draft in case I wanted to make any suggestions for change. I didn't. Her review . . . is a marvellous act of sympathetic identification with my work, and will certainly be the most important statement that has ever been made about it. I'm overwhelmed by her generosity." Millar sent copies of Welty's carbon to Green, Knopf, Olding, and Hollywood agent Lee Rosenberg. Knopf wrote back, "I am absolutely bowled over by Miss Welty's review. Do you remember the old days when you were anxious to be taken as a serious novelist and we were battling so hard but so vainly to prevent the label of the detective story from being fastened to you? Well, you've certainly got what you wished for now."

Welty's essay was published on the front page of the *Times Book Review* of Sunday, February 14: aptly enough Valentine's Day (as Bill Hogan noted in the *San Francisco Chronicle*). Surely few authors ever received a more heartfelt bouquet. Welty wrote in her first paragraph that *The Underground Man* "comes to stunning achievement." She conveyed well the book's drama and urgency:

> "I don't believe in coincidences," Archer says, as the investigation leads him into a backward direction, and he sees the case take on a premonitory symmetry. And it is not coincidence indeed, or anything so simple, but a sort of spiral of time that he goes hurtling into, with an answer lying 15 years deep.

The missing six-year-old child was "the real kernel of the book, its heart and soul," wrote Welty: "Ronny is the tender embodiment of everything Archer is by nature bound to protect, infinitely worthy of rescue." As the boy makes the case meaningful to Archer, Welty said, so it's Archer who makes all Macdonald's novels matter to the reader:

> As a detective and as a man he takes the human situation with full seriousness. He cares. And good and evil both are real to him. . . . He is at heart a champion, but a self-questioning, often a self-deriding champion. He is of today, one of ours. *The Underground Man* is written so close to the nerve of today as to expose most of the apprehensions we live with.
>
> In our day it is for such a novel as *The Underground Man* that the detective form exists. . . . What gives me special satisfaction about this novel is that no one but a good writer—*this* good writer—could have possibly brought it off. *The Underground Man* is Mr. Macdonald's best book yet, I think. It is not only exhilaratingly well done; it is also very moving.

Welty went on to praise Macdonald's style ("one of delicacy and tension, very tightly made, with a spring in it"), his "spare, controlled" narrative ("an almost unbroken series of sparkling pictures"), and his "beautiful and audacious similes," which serve both as interpretive descriptions and as running evidence gathered by Archer, as when: "The door of Fritz's room was ajar. One of his moist eyes appeared at the crack like the eye of a fish in an underwater crevice. His mother, at the other door, was watching him like a shark."

This extraordinary tribute, thirty-two hundred words long, caused an enormous stir in the Manhattan book world. Knopf quickly printed another ten thousand copies of *Underground* for a total of thirty-five thousand prepublication copies ("pretty good going," thought von Auw) and took a half-page ad in the daily *Times* headlined with Welty's proclamation: "THE UNDERGROUND MAN is Ross Macdonald's best book yet!" Bantam went back to press for fifty thousand more copies each of the several

Macdonalds scheduled for imminent reprint, and a major new paperback campaign was planned. "We are expecting a very enthusiastic reception from storekeepers," Bantam's Marc Jaffe said.

Ordinarily Millar took good fortune in stride. With friends he'd make a point of putting things in perspective. "Everything that happened for him was something that had happened before to someone else," Jerre Lloyd said, "and he could tell you *when*. He was realistic too. During this period when he was in the ascendancy and at the top, he had no illusion about it; he expected the decline to come rather quickly. He just figured everyone had a time when he was popular or critically acclaimed and then it ebbed away. This was just 'his time,' he said, and he wasn't changed fifty milligrams by all that acclaim."

But Welty's essay was something else again. "The one time I ever saw him really flattered and pleased about anything," Lloyd said, "was when Eudora Welty wrote that review. That a writer like that would be so turned on by his books and get in and explore them to that degree really excited him. And why not! He was just like a little kid over that; and it wasn't obnoxious, it was fun to see. I didn't think he could get excited about *anything!*"

The *New York Times* wasn't done with Macdonald. On Friday, February 19, Walter Clemons's review of *The Underground Man* was printed in the daily *Times*. Like Welty, Clemons not only reviewed the new book ("Ross Macdonald has never written better") but commented on the author's entire oeuvre. He concluded, "Mr. Macdonald's career is one of the most honorable I know. His later books are better than his early ones, but I haven't read one that I'd advise against." Clemons said *Underground* was "one of Ross Macdonald's two best books" (the other being *The Chill*). "Read it. Read *The Chill*. Read also *The Zebra-Striped Hearse* and *The Far Side of the Dollar.* You can find most of these in paperback. Get busy!"

Millar's intimates were thrilled by what was happening. "Not only is it a very astute appraisal of your work," said von Auw of the Clemons column, "but it's one of the most powerful selling reviews I have ever seen." Millar told Green he was "quite overwhelmed." Several other long reviews of *The Underground Man* were printed in the next few weeks (Judith Rascoe's in *Life*, William Hogan's in the *San Francisco Chronicle*, Clifford A. Ridley's in the *National Observer*), and a significant movie deal seemed almost certain to happen soon for Macdonald. "In the professional line, external department," a satisfied Millar wrote Olding, "there isn't much more I could look forward to."

But he got more. *Newsweek*'s Ray Sokolov, Leonard's original partner in the Macdonald conspiracy, announced he was coming to Santa Barbara to prepare a major feature—possibly, it was implied, a *Newsweek* cover piece. This was remarkable: such things rarely happened to mystery writers (though scholar Millar remembered that Craig Rice, author of *Home Sweet Homicide*, had been on *Time*'s cover in 1946). It would be great publicity for

The Underground Man, but it also presented problems. A probing news-magazine profile, unlike articles so far done on Macdonald, might explore aspects of Millar's personal life that he'd previously managed to keep out of print. Behind the Millars' Hope Ranch facade, within reach of any journalist, was the painful story of their only child. It was a subdued and wary Millar who welcomed Ray Sokolov to Santa Barbara.

Sokolov had first heard of Macdonald's work in the early sixties from Tim Hunter, later a successful movie director. "I knew Tim in Cambridge, Massachusetts, when he was a budding star of the Harvard film scene," Sokolov recalled. "He said to me, 'You know, the *best* detective novel is by Ross Macdonald'—I think he said it was *The Chill.* It stuck in my mind, and when I noticed another Macdonald novel was coming out, I read it and really liked it; and I couldn't figure out why this author was not better known than he was." It wasn't until near the end of his five-year stay at *Newsweek* that the magazine, reassured by the *Times*'s coverage of *The Goodbye Look* and *The Underground Man,* agreed to let Sokolov do a Macdonald story.

But Millar posed a challenge. "He was hard going, Ken," said Sokolov. "Very friendly, very forthcoming, but the mental weather there was pretty thick; I mean, he just wasn't a cheerful, amusing person. Smart. Almost self-effacing in the intellectual area: he'd say things like, 'Oh, John Leonard is much smarter than I am'—but it was the kind of concession of someone who was clearly quite vain about being bright, you know? He was a very cooled-out person. After a while it was a little nerve-racking. Margaret Millar was really a much easier person to get along with: kind of warmer, livelier, but a little more epigrammatic. She was just sort of lolling around drinking Gatorade, being foxy and amusing. She was extremely spry and intelligent—I mean, she was the light in *that* house, without a doubt; I really liked her. Isn't there a Perelman story about them? One works in the morning, one works in the afternoon, therefore they never see each other? That's exactly what was going on there: essentially they were in the same house, but completely out of contact."

Sokolov's second day in Santa Barbara began with an unforgettable jolt: an earthquake, 6.7 on the Richter scale, centered near Los Angeles but felt sharply enough ninety miles north to shake a New York visitor out of his motel bed. The quake seemed to shake things loose in Millar too: memories of the "seismic disturbances" in his past that he'd only obliquely alluded to in print. When he met Sokolov for their next talk, his cool front melted. "The unrecorded highlight of this interview is that he really broke down in tears when we discussed his daughter," Sokolov said. "She'd died only a few months before; she's really the one that all those novels are about. They had had this terrible tragedy, and they were still upset. He did ask me not to mention any of it in the piece; I think it was a condition of his talking about it, that I wouldn't go into it. What they didn't want was that this quite sensitive child, the grandchild, should have to read about his mother, because they had kept all that from him."

Millar's nearly eight-year-old grandson was dear to him: a legacy of
Linda, a symbol of the future. He taught the boy to swim and wrote
proudly to Olding that Jim could now do the fifty-meter length of the
Coral Casino pool. He read to Jimmy (*Robinson Crusoe*, Roald Dahl's children's books), and Jimmy read to him. The boy would probably be an
engineer, Millar thought, like his dad. "I remember Ken said he had dogs
so that he wouldn't become the overly doting grandfather," Jackie
Coulette recalled; but Millar fooled no one. "Ken *loved* that boy," said Peter
Wolfe, a St. Louis scholar writing a book about Macdonald's work and who
saw Millar with Jim in 1971. The Millars' grandson spent nearly every
weekend in Santa Barbara for many months after his mother's death. Millar sketched Jimmy into *The Underground Man* as six-year-old Ronny, the
boy Welty said was "the real kernel of the book, its heart and soul . . . good
and brave and smart . . . the tender embodiment of everything Archer is by
nature bound to protect, infinitely worthy of rescue." Part of protecting
Jimmy was to spare him the knowledge of his mother's problems.

Sokolov hadn't the heart not to help. "I did agree that I wouldn't discuss
the criminal aspect of it, or the mental breakdown," he said. "It probably
was an error, but we just suppressed all that. We played his game, at
Newsweek; just about everybody else did too, in not really broadcasting the
full details of that family episode. I think we made some kind of compromise; it wasn't false, but it wasn't a full account." (Sokolov's piece said, "The
Millars lead an extremely quiet life, and it has been even quieter since their
only child, Linda, died of a cerebral accident at 31, late last year.")

Millar kept Ray Sokolov's favor a secret. When Dick Lid commented on
the absence of anything potentially embarrassing in the *Newsweek* piece ("I
think I said to Ken, 'How great—but that sounds like the picture *you*
wanted to give' "), Millar said of Sokolov, "Well, he was a sweet young man,
but—he didn't *know* anything."

Ross Macdonald was *Newsweek*'s cover subject for March 22, 1971. The
magazine bore a close-up color photograph of Millar, one eye enlarged by
a Sherlockian magnifiying lens. The *Newsweek* issue caused as much talk in
Manhattan and elsewhere as had Welty's *Times* review. "I can't tell you how
proud and delighted I was to read the piece in *Newsweek*," Bantam president Oscar Dystel wrote Millar. "Everyone in New York is buzzing about
it." Millar, with his listed telephone number, got an unusual number of
long-distance calls this month: sometimes fourteen a day. "I'll be interested to see what the *Newsweek* coverage does for the current book," he
wrote von Auw. To Green he observed: "There seems to be a general feeling that this should be the big one. Well, we'll see."

He hadn't long to wait. Knopf's first printing sold out before publication. The book jumped onto *Publishers Weekly*'s fiction list in fourth place;
a week later it was number two (above Irwin Shaw's *Rich Man, Poor Man*,
Hemingway's posthumous *Islands in the Stream*, and Erich Segal's *Love*

Story), and the trade journal noted, "Many stores tell us this is their best-selling novel." In early April, *Underground* was five on the *New York Times* list; on the *PW* chart (known to the trade as a more accurate indicator) it held at two, "selling 4500 copies a week." Millar seemed quietly dazzled. "I am frankly delighted to be on the big board again," he admitted to Matt Bruccoli, "and especially in second place." *Time* magazine put *Underground* number three on April 5. Green informed him, "We passed 43,000 on Monday. The book moves to no. 4 on the *Times* list on April 18, displacing Allen Drury." To von Auw, Millar wrote, "Well, this is a long-awaited consummation, and a somewhat larger one than I ever looked for." As the book continued to do "ridiculously well," the author said he found it all "incredible, but am too old to be spoiled by it."

Macdonald's new novel was the book of the hour, and his allies and champions did all they could to signal the occasion. *LA Times* columnist Art Seidenbaum wrote a piece ("very friendly," Millar said, "and, I think, perceptive") connecting the stuff of Macdonald's fiction to the Southland's displaced citizens and transient illusions: "Macdonald's books are full of the wandering hungers of California people, the men who embezzle dreams and then keep running, the women who fade toward old-age still thinking about 40-foot pools in San Marino. . . . The secret reality of sadness is more important than the fantasy of murder." At the end of a major Sunday review, *LA Times* critic Robert Kirsch, a longtime Macdonald appreciator, allowed himself a pat on the back for his West Coast perceptiveness: "Critics should not blow their own horns. But perhaps I may be permitted a small peep, for I recognized early the value of Macdonald as a novelist transcending the genre in which he appeared to work. . . . He is a man of sensitivity, sensibility and wisdom, a gifted writer. It is restoring to know that the New York establishment has recognized that something good can come out of California. Many readers out here have known this about Ross Macdonald for years."

The Underground Man was a runaway best-seller—"the first runaway mystery in many years," according to syndicated columnist John Barkham—almost the popular-fiction equivalent of a hit rock LP. If Macdonald seemed like a private-eye version of the Beatles this season, the *New York Times Book Review* was his *Rolling Stone* magazine, with almost every issue in the spring and summer of '71 having a new example of his ubiquitous presence in the moment. Macdonald himself wrote important reviews for the *Times* supplement in April (J. Anthony Lukas's *Don't Shoot— We Are Your Children!* which he praised highly) and May (*A Catalogue of Crime*, a critical compendium by Jacques Barzun and Wendell H. Taylor, which he gently rebuked). In June the *Book Review* ran a Macdonald parody ("The Underground Bye-bye": off-target but indicative of his new celebrity). *The Underground Man* was included in the *Book Review*'s June "Selection of Recent Titles": the weekly's pick of the year's best books so far.

Even Macdonald's ads in the *Book Review* were exciting. Millar thought

Knopf's bold April *Underground* full-pager "*stunning.*" Bantam splashed the covers of ten of its classy new Macdonalds on an April spread quoting Clemons's February blurb ("Who needs a copywriter—with a review like this"): "Read *The Chill.* Read also *The Zebra-Striped Hearse* and *The Far Side of the Dollar.* You can find most of these in paperback. Get busy." Bantam paid sixty-five thousand dollars for reprint rights to *Underground* and several other books. On the West Coast, Harris Seed and agent Lee Rosenberg were negotiating a deal for the new novel with Filmways and producer Marty Ransohoff ("I'd like to see a *good* movie made," Millar told Olding); Filmways felt it had enough of a stake in Archer to supplement Knopf's *Underground* ad budget. Since the novel was an alternate selection of the Book-of-the-Month Club, BOMC ads showed it prominently. *Archer at Large,* the new omnibus, was featured in Mystery Guild layouts. All the while *The Underground Man* rode the charts: in early May, as Millar prepared to go to New York for four days, it was number four on both the *Times*'s and *Time* magazine's top ten, number three in *PW,* and number two on the Western Bestsellers list.

The occasion for his trip was an award from the Women's Advertising Council of New York, which annually honored practitioners of "the seven lively arts." Other 1971 recipients included playwright Edward Albee, singer Beverly Sills, poet May Sarton, and TV's Dick Cavett; last year's honorees in Macdonald's category were historians Will and Ariel Durant. "I'm in more distinguished company than I'm used to," Millar wrote Olding. "I decided I better get my suit pressed."

Millar purposely scheduled a short trip; he could never sleep in Manhattan. Margaret was supposed to come too, but she used the excuse of a lingering cold to drop out. She'd join him later in the week in Toronto; together they'd go to Kitchener, where a reception in their honor was scheduled at their old town's new library.

Millar's thoughts turned often to Canada in this season of great success. Bubbling briefly beneath *The Underground Man* on the *Times* best-seller list was the novel *Fifth Business,* by Canadian Robertson Davies, Millar's old "Passing Show" column-mate at Toronto *Saturday Night,* the man who had edited the quips Millar wrote on his Ann Arbor weekends. Davies had written several books, but *Fifth Business* was his American breakthrough. Millar read it the month it was published. With its plot of murder, obsessive revenge, concealed identity, and violence whose repercussions ripple through decades, *Fifth Business* had some of the twists and pleasures of a Lew Archer novel; in fact the *New York Review of Books* called Davies "a Jungian Ross Macdonald." It was *Fifth Business*'s Canadian scenes that most affected Millar, sequences set in the early years of the century in the fictional Ontario town of Deptford, based on Davies's boyhood Thamesville, which was not far from Kitchener as the Canada goose flies. Millar thought *Fifth Business* remarkably original; "I don't know of anything else that conveys the 'nineteenth-century Russian' quality of twentieth-century Canadian life," he wrote Bill Ruehlmann; he told Peter Wolfe the book "drives so deep into Canadian experience that it's making me dream." One of his waking dreams was a plot, germinating in notebooks, that would draw on his own Winnipeg boyhood and might even involve Archer.

But for the present, *The Underground Man* demanded his attention. The new book gave Millar much to be happy about when he got to New York on Sunday, May 16. His novel was still number four on the *PW* list, with fifty-nine thousand copies in print. Shops such as the Village Brentano's had full window displays of the Macdonald best-seller. Bantam's stylish Ross Macdonald paperbacks were on sale all over town, even in the littlest stationery stores. These were heady times. "It's been a great spring for me," Millar acknowledged to a *PW* writer, one of four journalists who interviewed him in four days.

A lot of the nice things happening were thanks to his East Coast benefactors Leonard, Sokolov, and Clemons. The coconspirators worked another good deed while Millar was in New York. They knew Eudora Welty was also here this week—staying in fact, though not for much longer, at the same Algonquin Hotel as Millar—and they thought it would be fine for the two writers to meet. Through Knopf's publicity people they tracked down Millar on Monday afternoon and told him to rush to the Algonquin, where Welty was about to check out.

"As I came into the lobby and got my key and went for the elevator," Welty recalled, "a man came across the lobby and said, 'Miss Welty? Kenneth Millar.' I just couldn't believe it! He had registered at the Algonquin the day before, from Santa Barbara. Isn't this just like a Ken story? You know how he used to say, there's no such thing as coincidence? So I just saddown in the lobby and threw my coat down and we started talking, and we just didn't stop for I don't know how long. We got to be well acquainted, in a couple of days. I put off a trip I was supposed to take, so we could have some more time to talk."

Alfred Knopf and his sccond wife, Helen, were giving a cocktail party for Ross Macdonald on Tuesday at five. When Millar arrived at the Knopfs' place at 24 West Fifty-fifth Street, he had Welty with him. "It was a nice, big old-fashioned city apartment," Welty said, "right off Fifth Avenue. I was delighted to be there. I don't go to many parties like that, but—it was in the *home* of the Knopfs, and he really just threw his house open in honor of Ken." Sokolov and Clemons were there, and Ivan von Auw (Dorothy Olding was out of town), and (at Millar's request) Margaret Millar's Random House editor, Lee Wright. Film producer Marty Ransohoff was a late arrival; he'd recently bought movie rights to *The Underground Man* and was in negotiations with Harris Seed to enlarge the deal. "Ken was happy about the party," said Welty. "He said, 'I think it really meant something to Alfred.' They'd had such a long relationship, and things had turned out well all around."

Earlier Knopf had warmly written to Millar, "I need scarcely say how delighted I am by the success of the new book. You seem to be well established now as a master of your craft and a novelist to be taken seriously." Later Millar would write the Knopfs, "Your party was and will remain one of the high points of my life. It gave me particular pleasure, if I may speak of such things, to spend a little time afterwards with you and feel the happiness that you share. And when Helen put her arms around my good angel Eudora and invited her to come and stay a week, I thought I was in a company of angels, and wasn't wrong in my thought."

After the party Millar and Welty went for dinner and then walked around New York, not getting back to the Algonquin until after midnight. "I took him down Broadway," she remembered, "and he just came to life. He said, 'Now *this* is where it *is*.' The side streets had been sort of genteel, but here everything was going on. There was a cop chasing a man, shooting; the fire department was whizzing by. In fact I was kind of scared, with people running through the streets. But Ken just said, 'Oh, my.' He knew what all that was about. I said, 'I've never seen a man chase another man in public with a gun before.' He said that was an old story to him. And all this time he was so calm, and rather formal and everything; but he was all eyes and ears. He had a great inner calm, supposedly, but I think actually he was pretty emotional. But he had such control: the most controlled person I ever saw. And he was very patient, although I think inwardly impatient. And he would *listen*. He didn't miss anything anyone said. And he thought about it before he answered; that was just his habit. He respected other people, in a very grave way, and he would wait for them to speak.

"I think the thing about Ken was, he had thought about everything himself, probably early in life, about the way things should be. Maybe because he was so poor and had to shift for himself and really educate himself. I had the feeling, from what he's written and so forth, that he just sat down and weighed the situation: what I can do, what I can't do, what I may hope to do, and the way to do it. And the answer to everything was to study it and try to master it. I think he applied that to so many other things; that was just a feeling I had. He *knew* what he had to work with, and it was *pretty good*. His mind was just splendid, and he knew it; and he made the most use of it that he could. And at the same time he was very ready in his feelings, and very responsive. I can imagine when he was very young that he could be pretty explosive; I don't know. But one way to solve that was to be so good physically, to do everything: you know, high dive, swim, sail boats; I believe he wrote somewhere that he was a wrestler, back in school. He just decided what he most needed to do, and what would be the most sensible way to go about it, and then he would do it; all very quietly, to himself. He was very private.

"He had a real core of gentleness and sweetness. Really supportive of people: his friends, or strangers. Very supportive of young people. You get that from his books: he cared so much about the young; I'm sure he could see himself, in lots of difficult situations. And he was able to use all of that, in the detective story. And it made him unique, among novelists of all kinds. It was so remarkable, what he did with his life."

Millar was only in Canada a week this spring of 1971, but he loved almost every minute there and looked for reasons to return. He and Margaret had a grand time at the three-hour Kitchener library reception in their honor: librarian Dorothy Shoemaker (Margaret's old Sunday school teacher) presided as dozens of Kitchenerites and other Ontarians lined up to say hi to the local boy and girl made good. "We spent one day driving a 300-mile circuit through the hardscrabble Scots settlements where my father's people came from," Millar wrote the Knopfs: "Wiarton, Walkerton, and a bulge in the road named Millarton which hasn't changed since I was a small boy. Nostalgia hung like a cloud on the horizon, but the emotional atmosphere remained dry. We had lived away long enough and *had* enough not to belong there any more, to see it with affection but without need." The only thing that marred their trip was when Margaret walked into a plate-glass door; she passed out in Millar's arms and had to be taken to the hospital. It wasn't a bad accident (she was okay in a few hours), but, he wrote Peter Wolfe, "the death of Linda, less than a year ago, invested it with terror."

The Millars came back to rainy weather in Santa Barbara but sunny news: Marty Ransohoff was offering $1.35 million to film *Underground Man* and any other six Macdonald books of his choosing, plus twenty years' exclusive movie and TV rights to Lew Archer.

This was exactly the sort of long-term arrangement Millar had held out for: "Such an overall sale of Archer was necessary before anything large-scale could be done with him," he told Green. Millar accepted. Terms were complex, with twenty years' retriggered rights and exercised options; nailing down the details took months. The author sweated the deal all summer, but he put complete trust in Harris Seed, to whom he apologized, "I'm sorry that you should be involved on my behalf with people who seem to have little concern for cooperation or courtesy—qualities in which you yourself are so strong."

Millar's attorney remembered with pleasure the last night of reckoning: "I was in Hollywood, in the agent's office, negotiating with Filmways; and we had reached an impasse on several points that I thought were quite important. I felt strongly about Ken's side of the argument, and apparently the Filmways people felt very strongly about their side as well. But I knew one thing that they didn't know, and that was that Filmways had taken out a full-page ad the prior Sunday in the *New York Times* saying they'd bought the book and were gonna make a picture out of it. So at that point, I got that ad out, and I tacked it to the wall in the agent's office and said, '*You* explain to your client why you didn't make the deal—'cause I don't *have* to, and I'm *not* gonna do it. And I'm gonna stand in that doorway until you agree; and if you don't, I'm goin' in the other direction, which is home to Santa Barbara.' One of those incidents you'd love to live forever." Millar congratulated his lawyer on a finished agreement the client termed "nothing short of historic."

While these events were highly satisfying, Millar seemed to take equal pleasure in friends' achievements, as when Herb Harker telephoned from Calgary in June and said Olding had sold his book *Goldenrod* to Random House. "Of all the good news I've had this year, this is the best," Millar wrote Olding. "I'm deeply grateful to you for my friend, and for myself. It will mean a new life for him."

Millar kept in touch with his friends mostly by mail. Nineteen seventy-one, a year when many people wanted to congratulate or do business with Macdonald or make his acquaintance, found Millar "drowning in correspondence." He wrote his novels in his bedroom, seated in the old stuffed chair; but letter-writing was done at a rolltop desk in the den. Harker said, "I remember one night he patted this big pile of envelopes and said, 'This is my correspondence, that I work away at when I can, in the evening.' I know he wrote a lotta letters to all kinds of people." In 1971 these included Eudora Welty, Julian Symons, Donald Davie, Dorothy Olding and Ivan von Auw (as well as other Ober people), Alfred A. Knopf, Ash Green, Hank and Anna Branson, old Ann Arbor friend Nolan Miller (now teaching at Antioch), Jeff Ring (a northern California junior high student), Peter Wolfe (the young Missouri professor writing a book on Macdonald's fiction), Steven Carter (who'd done his master's thesis on the concept of justice in the Archer books), Ralph Sipper (a Bay Area bookseller keenly interested in Ross Macdonald's work), Matt Bruccoli, MWA colleagues Michael Avallone and Edward D. Hoch, and (after a seven-year silence they coincidentally both broke in the same week) Robert Ford, Canada's ambassador to Russia. "The letters I get from young people, ranging in age from fifteen up, are the ones that for some reason mean most to me," Millar told Nolan Miller, "and the ones I answer first."

Some new correspondents in 1971 included top people from Millar's English hardcover house, Collins, including Sir William Collins himself, who urged that Macdonald come to London in October for the British publication of *The Underground Man*. Collins promised a major publicity campaign to boost Macdonald's U.K. profile and sales. "I don't think there is a chance in this world of Ken going to England," Ivan von Auw wrote an overseas colleague. "He stays pretty much a hermit in Santa Barbara." But Millar could still surprise people. Gratified by how well the New York trip had gone, he made up his mind to try London—and got Maggie to say she'd go too. "We're very glad to have the opportunity after all these years," he told Olding.

Once decided on London, the Millars began expanding their proposed itinerary. It would be nice to get out in the English countryside, they agreed. Scotland beckoned too: Ken and Maggie each had Scots ancestry. Bantam's Marc Jaffe, in Santa Barbara in July, stirred them up about the

Frankfurt Book Fair in October, and they said they'd try to attend; both Millars sold well in Germany. And shouldn't they go to Switzerland to meet their good mutual publisher there? Another Santa Barbara visitor, a publicity woman from the French house Hachette, suggested Millar go to Paris for the October publication of *L'homme clandestin*. What about—Millar was serious—Moscow, where Bob Ford could arrange a fine welcome? "Hell, I may never come back," he told Wolfe. Informed of an eighty-thousand-copy Czech edition of one of his books, he astonished an Ober agent by saying, "I hope to visit Czechoslovakia some time in the next few years." She quipped to a colleague about the pause-prone Millar, "Do you think he's going to become the U.S.'s most silent roving ambassador?"

But there were limits, he knew. To Julian Symons, who'd suggested during a 1969 trip with wife Kathleen and daughter Sarah that the Millars visit England, Millar now wrote, "If I was dubious, when you were here, about our ever being able to come to England, it had to do with Margaret's difficulty in travelling and doing other things that people ordinarily and quite easily do. Well, I have got her up to the point of abandoning, for a week or two, this continent. But there are still severe limitations on our movements. I am being brutally frank with you and Kathleen because you will understand me. It would be difficult for Margaret to meet any number of people at your house. . . . She asks if we could have lunch together, perhaps at a pub, instead? M. *thrives* on informality, as you may have noticed." He felt he'd expressed himself poorly and wrote Symons again: "I'm not so night-bound as Margaret is and I'd dearly love to visit your house and if possible meet some of your friends, while Margaret will be content, she says, to stay by herself. . . . This self-disinvited guest doesn't seem to know how to handle his social mistake without making the further gaffe of reinviting himself. Conceivably—I blunder on—we might manage to meet at your house and eat somewhere afterward, with or without dear M. . . . I hope this note hasn't further muddied the waters and made Kathleen and you give up on us. That would *really* make me feel badly."

The Millars dropped Frankfurt from their plans when it conflicted with other events, and Millar gave up Moscow when Ford was unexpectedly recalled to Ottawa for a month. Still their schedule was ambitious: five days in Paris, four in Geneva, three in Edinburgh, three in Yorkshire, ten in London. "It's a little late for us, perhaps," the fifty-five-year-old Millar wrote Harker, "but better late than never." He said to Green, "I'm at the same time keen and a little frightened, as if I might run into my own young prewar ghost." He told Wolfe his anxiety had as much to do with his wife as himself: "I'm poised at the intersection of fear and expectation. It's a long time since I've crossed an ocean, but I'm not afraid of that as much as of the sheer unexpected, like my wife's walking into a plate-glass door and falling unconscious into my arms. . . . We humans have so little, and we set such store by it, as indeed we must."

Despite elaborate preparations, the Millars' trip threw them some curves. They landed in France on the first day of a subway strike that flooded the capital with what seemed like "every car in Paris"; their cab took three hours to crawl from airport to hotel. Millar found the odyssey "strange and exciting"; Maggie complained about the exhaust fumes. Anyway they both liked the bird-watching in a courtyard behind the Hotel George V. Millar lunched with half a dozen journalists, some of whom wrote about him for their papers; and he was greatly taken with his French publisher, Alex Grall. Switzerland was less of a success. After visiting Byron's Castle of Chillon, the Millars took a cable car twelve thousand feet up Mount Blanc; Margaret hadn't dressed warmly enough and caught cold, forcing them to cancel Scotland and northern England. They went straight to London, where Collins people scrambled to find them hotel rooms.

Collins scheduled a lunch for the Millars on Tuesday, October 19, with the important English crime reviewers. About fifteen people (including Symons, Matthew Coady, Billy Collins, and H. R. F. Keating) came to the meal at the Collins offices in a rambling house in St. James's Place off Piccadilly. "We were there at a big oval table in a boardroom up at the top," recalled Keating, then the London *Times*'s mystery critic. "Ken and I sat next to each other, and I was a little embarrassed because I'd written a very short and not altogether enthusiastic review about his book before, in which I'd said he was something like a third-generation descendant of playwrights like Webster. I was implying that the books had about them a certain derivative element, but he took it as more of a compliment than it was meant to be. He thought, here's this British critic saying I'm comparable to Webster, which, indeed, you know, it's something one could easily think; he was pleased with this comparison. And I think I rather attempted not to talk about books, and his books, and talked about his reaction to England or whatever. So, yes, that was a little embarrassing, as a lunch."

The next day, Symons and a radio producer came to the Millars' suite at Duke's Hotel across from the Collins building, to tape remarks for a BBC program. Symons wrote:

> He talked with characteristic gentle candor about the background of his own books, and their quality for him as an attempt to come to terms with his own childhood. The producer Robin Brightwell intervened once, twice, three times, suggesting questions of a more direct kind that he thought I might put. At length Ken broke off and, without raising his voice or showing any sign of annoyance, said—I am giving the gist of what was said, not exact words—"Mr. Brightwell, I understood I was being interviewed by Mr. Symons. I should have been told in advance if I was to be interviewed by you, and perhaps I might not have agreed to it." It was one of the most effective put-downs I have heard, the more so because of its perfect politeness.

"And the producer squashed," Symons remembered, "and said, 'Oh, yes, yes, of course, Mr. Macdonald, of course!' " Afterward Symons lunched with the Millars: "I was intending to take them to a French restaurant; but I just said casually, 'Well, now, what kind of food would you like?' Margaret said, 'Well, what we *don't* want is any of that filthy *French* food!' So I thought, 'Oh, well, farewell to that restaurant.' I took them to a pub in London, a very pretty pub called the Salisbury in St. Martin's Lane. Ken was perfectly happy. And I said to Margaret, 'What would you like to drink?' And she said, 'Well, I'd like a cup of tea.' And I said, 'Margaret, I'm afraid this is a pub, and I'm afraid I can't get tea for you.' And she said, 'What! You're telling me this is an English pub, and tea is a great English drink, and I can't get tea here?' I said, 'No, I am telling you that, I'm afraid.' So she settled for, I don't know what, something like cider."

The main event of Macdonald's visit was a party given him at the St. James's Place building on October 20 by Sir William and Lady Collins. About two hundred authors, publishers, critics, journalists, booksellers, and others attended, including the Millars' friend Nolan Miller, in London this fall with a group of Antioch students. "I never thought I could enjoy such a party but simply did," Millar admitted to Wolfe. "After it was all over I had my first Scotch-and-water of the trip." Millar went alone to dinner at the Symonses' Battersea home, where he hit it off well with journalist Matthew Coady. But a BBC interview done without Symons's assistance was "a complete bust," he wrote Wolfe: "The interviewer told me as he began that his only knowledge of me came from his reading of my *Who's Who* entry and his opening question was: 'I understand you're both a Ph.D. and an M.A. Isn't your writing detective stories rather a waste?' It went downhill from there."

As for print reporters, Millar told Olding, "Got along very well with the journalists, or so it seemed." Philip Oakes in the London Sunday *Times,* Bill Foster from the Edinburgh *Scotsman,* and Mike Fearn of London Express Features all did long, positive pieces; but the *Guardian*'s Peter Preston poked fun at Millar's "shuffling modesty" and mockingly contrasted Archer's supposed image ("Flip, maudlin, and black as the bleakest hangover") with Millar's reality: "Adlai Stevenson meets James Stewart, played by Henry Fonda. . . . Blandly humane; generous; kind; and jetting home to Santa Barbara tomorrow in case any goddam factories were thinking of moving in to sully the literary peace."

The Millars attended to business in England: he signed a Serbo-Croat contract for *The Underground Man;* her publisher Gollancz arranged to reissue three books in hardcover. London was generally successful, Millar judged, and probably necessary; though he shrugged to Olding: "It'll be interesting to see if it helps the book, or indeed if books are helpable or simply live their own lives." As for the city itself, the Millars found it comfortable ("Canadians seem to feel at home in London," he told Harker) but a disappointment; it struck them, Millar wrote Ruehlmann, "as a rather large damp Toronto, littered with the loot and monuments of Empire, populated by the world's most polite people, who seem rather sad and uncertain at this moment in history. But who isn't?"

Unexpectedly, the long flight home was the most interesting part of the journey for Millar. Headwinds over the North Atlantic kept their 747 so low that land was visible. Millar gazed with awe at the icy coasts of Greenland, the frozen floes of Hudson Bay, and Lake Athabasca where his parents had lived before he was born. "Those sights," he wrote Harker, "and not Switzerland and not Paris and not London, were the real culmination of the trip." His thoughts were recurring more and more these days to Canada and especially to Winnipeg, site of that story he planned. He'd been wanting to go back there—and now this 747, needing to refuel, by pure luck landed in Winnipeg, where Millar hadn't been for forty years: "so once again I made a loop in my life," he wrote Knopf. The place hadn't changed much, he told Symons: "There are many more tall buildings but the prairie is still absolutely flat as if rolled." For Millar, and Macdonald, the bittersweet past was forever alive in the present, so long as memory served.

His genre are exciting plots—in the tradition of Dashiell Hammett, a well-known American communist writer. . . . It is characteristic of Kenneth Millar to give a social portrait of a modern American society with all its vices, to show the almighty power of money and the way powerful capitalist syndicates merge frankly with gangsters' syndicates nowadays, and the way organized crime gets closely interwoven with politics.

—Introductory note to *Blue City, Znamya* (USSR), 1972

The critical backlash against Ross Macdonald (which Millar claimed to have expected) began about half a year after Welty's review. In a piece in the *Catholic World,* Bruce Cook conceded "Archer is a masterful creation" and Macdonald "an extremely able and resourceful writer, one who understands the uses of metaphor and can coax more out of mood and setting than most practitioners of the mystery story manage to get from plot and character"; but Cook chided Macdonald for his recurring themes ("He seems to be rewriting the same novel over and over again"), his recent "terribly involuted and complicated" and "incredible" plots, his supposed resentment of his genre's restrictions, and for "mangling" the mystery form. Cook deemed *The Underground Man* "a failure," Macdonald's "worst novel to date."

Richard Schickel, in a *Commentary* essay, was less generous. While claiming "one does not really [*sic*] begrudge Ross Macdonald his recent success," *Life*'s movie critic said Macdonald's "great defect as a novelist" was his "failure to evoke a milieu [i.e., southern California] and the related failure to develop a wide range of memorable characters to populate it." Schickel regretted that Archer didn't talk more like Chandler's Marlowe, "whose marvelous, wisecracking style—cynicism partially masking idealism—was one of the great delights of modern detective fiction." Schickel suggested "Macdonald's present eminence does not depend on the literary quality of his work but on the fact that he is our only writer of generation-gap mysteries at a moment when that gap is much on everyone's mind." Schickel judged Macdonald "a writer of severely limited capabilities."

Yet Macdonald's readership grew. After *The Underground Man*'s strong hardcover showing (45,000 sold for Knopf and another 50,000 for the Book-of-the-Month Club), Bantam upped its print run; in January 1972, Marc Jaffe reported 445,000 *Underground* paperbacks published—which meant over forty thousand dollars in author royalties, as Millar calculated by hand. "What interests me most about our current strong sale of THE UNDERGROUND MAN," Jaffe wrote, "is that it's priced at $1.25. In a curious kind of way this is a breakthrough if you consider the novel to be a 'mystery.' I don't think there's ever been a $1.25 mystery. You are therefore leading the pack." Bantam now had over 8 million copies of thirteen Macdonald titles in print; their new in-store Macdonald promotion program included a forty-five-copy, prepacked floor display. As a sort of investment in his future, Millar bought (for $10,694.50) seven hundred shares of Bantam stock in late 1971 and early 1972. He could afford a flier: he was getting paid for his Filmways deal in quarterly $30,000 chunks. With royalties on the rise, Millar would gross about $137,000 in 1972.

Bantam's big edition of *The Underground Man* introduced the book and Macdonald to many new readers and brought Millar an increased amount of fan mail. A letter from UCLA's Meteorology Department chairman complimented the accuracy of the novel's fire-weather description: "It is fascinating to see the interplay of Santa Ana and sea breeze. The growing intensity of the fire naturally tends to accelerate the sea breeze; so the fire, like your other characters, is working toward its own destruction."

Another interesting letter came from Bob Langfelder, the Isla Vista trial defendant, who wrote:

> A reader only rarely has to justify why he is reading a particular book, but in this case I had to. I was sitting alone in my apartment reading your book. I was about half way through and really into it and not wanting to be disturbed when a local, Isla Vista radical friend stopped by to give me sympathy about going to jail in a week. At the moment, I didn't need any sympathy and wanted to go on with the book, but I stopped to talk to Barry. (One has to take sympathy when they can get it.)
>
> However, his words were not sympathetic but hostile. He saw the book I was reading and wanted to know why I was reading that "crap" right before I was going to jail. Barry had in his hand a copy of a novel by George Orwell.
>
> "What do you think I should be reading right before I go to jail?" was my counter. "Do you think I should be reading Orwell or Solzhenitsyn's *The First Circle* or *One Day in the Life of Ivan Denisovich*?"
>
> "Yes, something like or George Jackson's *Prison Letters*," was Barry's reply.
>
> To defend my radical integrity, I told him that I just finished reading Solzhenitzyn and it was "heavy," but Russia and even Soledad seem so far away and abstract. I thought that I would read a book that takes place right here in the county. I thought it might give me a better sense of the area I live in.

Langfelder analyzed *Underground*'s psychological characterizations (which he found credible), criticized its ideology ("for my beliefs you overdo the Freudian determinism [e.g. the lost father theme] that accounts for the breakdown of the family which in turn leads to crime. . . . I would have had Brian Kilpatrick commit the murder out of jealousy [possessiveness] and then consciously or unconsciously start the forest fire with the cigarillo in order to collect fire insurance on his waning real estate investments. So he would be the jealous, mentally ill land exploiter who destroys his family, the environment, and himself not so much out of guilt but as the natural evolution of such a mentality. [Would that sound too forced?]"), and praised Macdonald's prose: " 'He pointed to the offshore islands which lay on the horizon like *blue whales*,' p. 110—Beautiful image."

The Underground Man brought several unexpected contacts. New York filmmaker Craig Gilbert, seeking a suitable California household as subjects for an ambitious TV documentary ("It had to be California. The American culture is fashioned on California"), read *Underground* and found it "described with absolute accuracy the kind of family I was looking for." He called Millar in Santa Barbara, he said: "He invited me out. He had a lot of newspaper people over from the *Santa Barbara News-Press* and we talked." Soon the director found his subjects (the Louds of Montecito) and began seven months' shooting on *An American Family,* a twelve-hour series that got a lot of attention when shown on PBS in 1973. More *Underground* feedback ("That book continues to surprise me," Millar told Bruccoli) came from Osvaldo Soriano, a twenty-nine-year-old Argentine literary critic, who sent Millar his full-page review of the novel from the newspaper *La Opinión*. Soriano himself was writing a novel, he said, set in Los Angeles (a city he'd never been to) and featuring Philip Marlowe, with a cameo appearance by Lew Archer. This book, *Triste, solitario y final* (from a phrase in Chandler's *El largo adiós*), would be the first of six for Soriano, who'd become internationally known as one of several Argentinians using the hard-boiled form to confront Latin American issues.

Macdonald's work reached more remote corners. From Moscow, Bob Ford wrote that *Blue City* (the book dedicated to Ford) would be serialized in the Russian literary review *Znamya* and *The Goodbye Look* published in a hundred-thousand-copy edition (Macdonald's largest printing anywhere). Ford thought Ross Macdonald was the first American detective-story writer to be translated into Russian since Dashiell Hammett. Macdonald's English visit was paying dividends: *Underground Man* sold well there; Matt Bruccoli, back from the U.K., reported that Fontana's new Ross Macdonald paperbacks were attracting great attention in London. They drew grateful notice from best-selling writer *(The Savage God)* and poetry critic A. Alvarez, who told the London *Observer*'s readers, "My private literary event this year has been my belated discovery of the novels of Ross Macdonald. I rate him higher than Raymond Chandler, the best in the American thriller genre since Dashiell Hammett. His view of the world is sombre, his prose lucid and restrained. My favourite so far is *The Chill*, but I am still avidly researching the subject."

Macdonald had been linked to Hammett and Chandler in the States for years, but now after his two best-sellers, he was connected to them in a new way: as the contemporary master giving book-jacket imprimaturs to his deceased predecessors. Surely the irony (two or three shades) wasn't lost on Millar as he provided a blurb for a batch of Chandler paperbacks ("He wrote like a slumming angel and invested the sun-blinded streets of Los Angeles with a romantic presence") and a hardcover omnibus ("Raymond Chandler wrote with wonderful gusto and imaginative flair"). With considerably more enthusiasm ("I take seriously my membership in the School of Hammett"), Millar sent Green several lines on Hammett for paperback use: "As a novelist of realistic intrigue, Hammett was unsurpassed in his own or any time." Macdonald also let his name be used to promote a first novel from Knopf, *The Friends of Eddie Coyle,* by a Massachusetts assistant U.S. attorney, George V. Higgins.

He did much more in order to help launch another first novel: Herb Harker's *Goldenrod.* Harker's wife died before it was published (she lived to see her name on its dedication page). Millar wrote Olding, "We'll try to keep Herb's book from going unnoticed." He asked the *New York Times* if he could cover *Goldenrod,* and John Leonard said yes. Macdonald's nine-hundred-word piece in the *Book Review* showed Harker's work about an aging rodeo rider (busted up by a horse named Sundown) and his two sons in as beguiling a light as any novelist might wish for; its last two lines summed up not only the book but its author, the former adult-ed student Millar fourteen years earlier had said should be a writer: "Since a work of fiction is, among other things, a record of the whole experience of creating it, *Goldenrod* can be read as a version of the author's struggle to become a modern man and an artist. In a wider arena than the Calgary Stampede he has ridden a more difficult horse than Sundown—the one with wings—and though it nearly threw him once or twice, Harker stayed on." The book didn't go unnoticed. It got other good reviews ("Enormously moving . . . the reader feels like cheering"—*Publishers Weekly*), was a Book-of-the-Month Club alternate, and got bought for filming. "Few husbands have been able to set such a marker on the graves of their wives," Millar told Harker. He was glad Herb was doing more writing: "It's a useful recourse, and an endless one. . . . It feeds on memory and pain: I don't have to explain that to the author of *Goldenrod.*"

Millar was feeding some painful memory of his own into a new manuscript in 1972, one that had a lot to do with his daughter, Linda; but he made time to accommodate a number of visitors. Dorothy Olding came to Santa Barbara twice this year; the agent had a growing roster of West Coast clients (thanks mostly to Millar) including Harker, Bob Easton, and Dennis Lynds. Jon Carroll arrived from the Bay Area to do a feature on Macdonald for *Esquire.* "He was soft-spoken, formal, courteous," said Carroll. "We talked in a very dark room which was his study. Margaret Millar was out *there* somewhere, doing something with plants. He was extremely forthcoming, but it occurred to me about halfway through that I should have known a shitload more about Freudian analysis before I began, because I did get the sense he was leaving little clues for the interviewer: literary antecedents, mostly. It was never going to be a piece about his personal life, and he certainly gave me no sense of bonhomie, as though we could have *boomed* at each other in a manly way and gone catching the big fish together; that didn't seem to be in the cards." Carroll's article showed Millar's knack at making connections between any two literary points:

> "Have you thought much," the reporter asked, "about the antecedents of the private detective? Does he go back to"—words failed him and he sought the bookcase for examples—"to, uh, Don Quixote or Samuel Johnson or who?"
>
> Millar smiled. "I don't know that he goes back to either of those, although Johnson was a moralist who wrote moral stories, and the detective story is *par excellence* a morality story. That's true of Don Quixote too. And in Don Quixote you get the relationship betwen Don Quixote and Sancho Panza, which is something like the relationship between Sherlock Holmes and Dr. Watson. In other words, you have a great, somewhat comic figure and a lesser, somewhat comic figure, who holds him down to earth and connects him with ordinary reality."

Another interviewer, Toronto journalist Jerry Tutunjian, gave Millar dramatic proof of the surprising reach of Macdonald's work. "I'm Armenian, originally from Jerusalem," Tutunjian said. "I'd been in Canada for a couple years in the midsixties when I went back to Jerusalem in 1967 to see my parents. It was the beginning of summer; I was bored. A friend told me, 'Read this book'—it was *The Chill*. I'd never heard the name Ross Macdonald; I was not a mystery reader. I took the book home, and a few days later the Six-Day War started. They were shooting, you know: planes blasting, and missiles. Jerusalem is an old city, and the house my parents lived in was on a sort of a hill; at the bottom of the slope was a natural cave. All of us hid in the cave, about thirty or forty of us, cooped up for a couple days while the war was going on; and I was reading *The Chill*. It was a good diversion. I was sitting at the mouth of the cave so I could have sunlight to read by. There were babies crying, and women. Eventually I had to leave the cave because the women were Moslem, and they didn't want guys around. I didn't care; I was reading the book. So I got hooked on Ross Macdonald. When I came back to Canada, I read everything by him I could get my hands on."

Sam Grogg made his way to Santa Barbara from Ohio's Bowling Green University, where he was writing his doctoral dissertation on Macdonald, and interviewed Millar for the *Journal of Popular Culture*. "I showed up at this beach club, all dressed up to meet this guy who'd written all these books I was in love with," Grogg said, "and he comes out in a pair of swimming trunks: 'Hi, how are you.' I'm not in a tuxedo or anything, but clearly I'm not dressed for the situation. And he said, 'Come on, I don't have any trunks that'd fit you, but here, I'll lend you a pair.' I put on these big, baggy swimming trunks, we swam a few laps together, and then we came back and popped my tape recorder down and began to talk. I mean, he immediately made me feel at home. He paid attention to me, unlike the other people I was interviewing on that trip like Irving Stone and Irving Wallace. He was a serious man, a very calm man, a man who had literally an aura around him. You could come in as fractured and frantic and youthful and exuberant as you were—and you felt like you were sitting next to a mythical Socrates. I mean, the guy had these blue eyes, and—there was a peacefulness about him, and a wisdom, an understanding, that I think came from his willingness to embrace the nightmarish side of human behavior.

"On the one hand, he was a guy who could recite Shakespeare and talk about all of American literature and was very interested in architecture and conservation—I remember his gazing out at the ocean, at the offshore oil derricks out there, and there was a *look* in his eyes: he really did see those derricks as being like the handles of daggers that were stabbing into the ocean floor—all that, on the one hand; and on the other hand, he could also give you some very practical insights. For instance: having come to southern California for the first time, you immediately want to get on the phone and say to your wife, 'Pack up all your belongings and come on out, 'cause I'm staying *here!*' Particularly if you're in Santa Barbara. And he gave me some very practical advice; he said, in essence, 'Don't be a fool.' We were walking around outside the Biltmore Hotel, and he said, 'You see that cabana right over there? A double murder occurred there just a few weeks ago. And in the cabana over behind that tree, there was a recent suicide.' Brought me right back down to earth. He was saying, 'You may think you're in the Garden, but the snake is in the garden too.'

"I think another reason probably why he and I got along was because we didn't have any political differences. He was certainly intolerant of the conservative mentality, and my background was liberal to the extreme: my dad was a labor organizer in the thirties; Stevenson was a real hero around our house. So there might have been these intangible things that connected me to Macdonald. Maybe he was the replacement father, for a while. I think Ken Millar functioned as the surrogate father to probably hundreds of people. Great communicator. I remember I said I was thinking about coming out and teaching at the University of California at Santa Barbara; they were developing a film and popular-culture program. And he looked at me and said, 'You don't want to go over there with those guys.' It was like Dad—if you have a good relationship with your dad—saying, 'Don't do that.'

"I always felt like the dissertation I wrote about him was fairly inadequate, because I was a little bit mesmerized by him. I kept not wanting to scratch beneath the surface of the books because then I would have to divulge things about his personal life—and I just didn't want to do it. The privacy of the guy— In many ways he was very accessible, but you didn't want in any way to break what was a kind of an understanding. He was such a—these words are so sentimental, but—he was such a gentle soul that I just didn't wanna fuck with it. I just wanted him to be okay, even in the short time that I knew him. If I thought in any way at any point I had done anything to make him feel bad, I would have suffered for the rest of my life."

Grogg (who went into film and later was associated with such movies as *Trip to Bountiful* and *Kiss of the Spider Woman*) was in the advance guard of an academic movement to recognize genre fiction as capable of being literature. But even at Bowling Green, where he was part of Ray B. Browne's popular-culture-studies division, Grogg's activities were viewed with alarm, he said: "I was considered to be *destroying* everything that centuries had built up! Two Victorian scholars in the English Department, Virginia and Lowell Leland, were horrified at what graduate students like me were doing. I was getting a Ph.D. for reading *detective* novels? Their worst tenured nightmares come true."

Still the academy was beginning to take notice of detective novels in the early 1970s, even at the best Ivy League schools. "I can just about put my finger on when that began," said Max Byrd, in 1972 an assistant professor of English at Yale, "because Ken Millar was involved in that. I got my Ph.D. at Harvard in 1970, and then I taught at Yale for six years before coming out to California. And while I was teaching at Yale, a wonderful professor named Alvin Kernan and another one named Peter Brooks started an experimental course called 'Literature X.' One of the things they did was the mystery story as a model for plots; and one of the books we read was *The Chill,* which I think alternated with *The Galton Case.* We read those along with *Oedipus Rex,* Dostoyevsky, Sherlock Holmes, and various others, talking about how the mystery story really was connected at its basic plot level and thematic concerns with these other 'higher' literatures, and that there was a continuity. I don't think anyone had ever done that before in an academic environment. These were very high-powered people giving this course at Yale, and what went on at Yale had its reverberation throughout the whole business. Macdonald's books were the ones that they went to because they're so classic: the crime is always uncovering an earlier crime and a still earlier one, and of course there was Macdonald's avowed oedipal interest. So when they introduced Ross Macdonald into 'Literature X' right after Sophocles, that was a pretty daring thing to do, because of the strong distinction then between lowbrow and highbrow. But of course that was about the time when Eudora Welty did her famous book review; and at Yale, anything that comes out of the *New York Times* rather staggers them! They were busy rethinking that. It was rather daring, that 'Literature X' course, and very successful."

Byrd, married to a Santa Barbara woman, met Macdonald around 1972. "We would come out to Santa Barbara for part of the summer," Byrd said. "My in-laws knew Ken Millar from the Coral Casino. I went several times to the every-other-Wednesday writers' lunches. Then I spent a few evenings over at Ken Millar's house just chatting, sometimes quite late into the night. Great talker. I was absolutely of no interest I would have thought to anybody, just a beginning teacher; I didn't see why he would take the time. The thing I remember most was how interested he was in academics. When he found out I did my Ph.D. at Harvard, he was eager to talk about academic literary criticism. His Coleridge dissertation had been turned down by a Harvard reader who became my thesis adviser, a dear friend; Ken said he'd never forgotten that. He brought that up often. He said he still kept up with Coleridge criticism.

"I also remember his extremely deliberate manner of talking. He kind of set the pace: slowed it down. He was a very observing man. The feeling I had was that he watched very carefully, and that one reason he talked so slowly was to let other people carry on. He really had a dignity about him. You felt you were in the presence of someone extremely serious, and of real stature. Actually my impression was of a very bookish and donnish man; his study was like a professor's: he just had books all around him. His wife would bring in coffee or a beer from time to time, but she didn't join in; I don't know *yet* what I think about that. We talked about writers, including mystery writers he admired. He said how much he liked Chandler, what a literary kind of writer Chandler was, the stylishness of his books."

Byrd, encouraged by the success of Harvard friend Michael Crichton, later wrote several thrillers himself. "Millar as a writer was a very literary man," said Byrd, "very conscious of putting together something in an artistic way—everything from his style to his sense of the layers of his plot. He was a real craftsman. Other writers, their stories are clearly about figuring out who did it, or having the hero be somehow the dominant figure; but I don't think of Macdonald's stories as being about detection so much as narration: how you tell the story. That probably goes back to my feeling that he was a very bookish man, very literary. Archer's is a much quieter voice, but with a lot of the melancholy that Millar gave off—although other people talked about his being a much more melancholy person than I ever saw him be. But again, I think those talks of ours were quite happy conversations for him; I think he simply liked the idea of scholarly chat. Well, he never really left the university, in some way. We used to talk at Yale how professors so often turned out to be the villains in his books!"

As the academic and mainstream worlds paid more attention to Macdonald, his crime-fiction colleagues seemed perversely to ignore the achievements of the former Mystery Writers of America president. In 1965, when the MWA gave *The Spy Who Came In from the Cold* a best-novel Edgar, its newsletter cheered, "One of the few mysteries of our time to land on the best-seller lists, THE SPY was a popular choice since it showed that 'it can be done.'" After *The Goodbye Look*'s 1969 success, though, the MWA's Hillary Waugh said Edgar choices shouldn't be influenced by mere popularity. Michael Avallone, much involved with the MWA, wrote Millar in

1969, "Ed Hoch mentioned about a month ago how sorry he is (and ashamed) that Ross Macdonald has never won an Edgar." Two years later, Avallone told Millar, "I've got a ten dollar bet that MWA will give you an Edgar this year for THE UNDERGROUND MAN—a scroll [nomination] is a *cinch*." Avallone lost his bet. No Macdonald novel after 1965's *The Far Side of the Dollar* was even nominated for an Edgar.

"It is sort of odd," Ed Hoch said later, "especially since he did win both the Gold Dagger and the Silver Dagger from the Crime Writers Association of England. At that time especially, if you were writing about a series character—and I write about several, in short stories, so I know what I'm talking about—it seemed the Edgar committee always wanted either a new character or something entirely different. In the sixties and seventies, Ross Macdonald was writing some of his best books; but they probably said, 'Well, it's just another Lew Archer.' I'm speculating; I was never on the novel committees then. But if that's what happened, it was a big mistake."

Perhaps envy and resentment played their parts. Collin Wilcox told Millar about hearing a panel of detective writers at a fan convention agreeing Ross Macdonald now "had it made." When Ray Sokolov and John Leonard appeared as guest speakers in 1971 at a New York MWA chapter meeting where Art Kaye's documentary was shown, they were unexpectedly harangued during a question period by an audience member. "Some woman really got pissed off at the two of us for suppressing the real story about his daughter," Sokolov recalled. "Thought we'd really been bad journalists. She may actually be right I guess by some standard, since the crucial incident in his life was being genteelly suppressed over and over. It really wasn't a service to the reading public in a certain way, and I did feel a little embarrassed about it, but—it seemed right at the time. I never knew who this woman was; it was nobody I could identify, and I certainly didn't try! I just wanted to get out of there."

Millar was dismayed at how few MWA colleagues saw fit to congratulate him on what he'd accomplished in recent years. Maybe they simply didn't understand what he was about, he mused; after rereading the serious piece he'd done on Hammett for the *1964 Mystery Writers' Annual,* he wrote Olding, "No wonder I puzzle MWA." In 1972, the Mystery Writers of America gave their Grandmaster Award not to Ross Macdonald but to his exact contemporary John D. MacDonald.

At least Margaret Millar didn't go unrecognized: her *Beyond This Point Are Monsters* got a 1971 Edgar nomination. The question of Margaret's career was a somewhat delicate one, with her once ascendant star now standing still while her husband's soared. Most people who telephoned the house these days were seeking Ross Macdonald; if Maggie answered, some addressed her as Mrs. Macdonald—or maybe she was Mr. Macdonald's secretary? Margaret was better known now in other countries such as Germany, where she'd had recent good-sellers, than she was in the States. Jackie Coulette said, "I remember how impressed I was when Hank and I were walking down the street in Lund, Sweden, and there was a window display of Maggie's work in a bookstore; I didn't realize she was that big a name." Millar made a point of mentioning his wife's achievements to all who interviewed him. "He was very protective of her," Sam Grogg said, "and she was very mothering of him. There was going to be a new paperback series of all her works"—Avon paid fifteen hundred dollars apiece to reissue ten titles—"and he talked a lot about that; he was very proud of her. And very deferential, in wanting me to acknowledge her: 'Don't forget that Margaret here is *another* writer!' They were a great couple."

Still, there could be an edge to Maggie's attitude. Dennis Lynds was at a 1972 screening she attended of Kaye's film at Santa Barbara's Anacapa Theatre in a week when Millar was out of town. "She sniped through the whole thing," he said. "Little remarks here and there: 'Oh, *there's* the Great Man.' 'There's this,' 'there's that'—it was quite something. I don't know if she was being jocular, but—there was an undercurrent."

The urge to commit a book struck Margaret less and less often. Given Millar's income, she didn't need to write; and increasingly, she didn't *want* to. With bird-watching, gardening, swimming, and now distance bicycling (which Millar joined her in), Margaret found plenty to do. She'd had her say as a writer, she told people; she was retired.

Ross Macdonald meanwhile continued to permeate the scene. "What gives me particular pleasure," Millar confessed to Knopf, "being a wordman, is that I'm following Hammett and Chandler into the current language. In last month's *Esquire,* in an article on Joe Bonnano, Gay Talese referred to a Ross-Macdonald-like situation, and there are similar references in the current *TV Guide* and the L.A. Times *West* magazine. Today I had lunch with a young Harvard teacher who will be teaching a couple of my books next fall; two weeks ago I had lunch with a Yale professor who taught *Zebra-Striped Hearse* last year. There are several books underway, one at U. of Missouri and one at U. of Chicago (the latter a doctoral dissertation), and Matthew Bruccoli's lavishly illustrated checklist."

Especially gratifying was the University of Michigan's bestowing on Dr. Kenneth Millar its Outstanding Achievement Award for distinguished alumni. Millar traveled alone (Maggie canceled at the last minute) to the U of M campus in November 1972 to accept the honor. He was apprehensive but ended up having a good time. Things had changed at Michigan: the English Department people seemed more sympathetic now to popular art in general and crime fiction in particular. Macdonald enjoyed a lot of adulation from faculty and students at the grad school where once upon a time Millar's fiction-writing was viewed with barely veiled contempt. Millar closed another one of those circles he loved to round off.

"Life is beginning to taste good again," he wrote Bruccoli, "after a couple of years which were ruined by the alternations of good and bad fortune." What was most pleasing to him—more than the awards, the academic recognition, the journalist pilgrims (all of which he liked)—was knowing that in this hectic year he'd written another novel; and not just any book, but one in which he'd distilled (in typically concealed and revealing fashion) a lot of his painful feelings about the good and bad fortune of all his years. *Sleeping Beauty* was its title, and Millar called it "the book which is most important to me."

> It is interesting that children rather noticeably understand irony.
> They get it from fairy tales.
> —Eudora Welty, "And They All Lived Happily Ever After,"
> *New York Times Book Review,* 1963

> "Look, I'm telling you my family secrets."
> —Ross Macdonald, *Sleeping Beauty*

A seventeenth-century fairy tale by Charles Perrault provided the phantom underpinning for Macdonald's seventeenth Archer novel, in which Millar through fiction paired the most distressing event in Santa Barbara's recent history with the most tragic fact of his private life.

In Perrault's tale, a spiteful curse fates a princess to pierce herself fatally with a spindle at fifteen. A good fairy alters the curse so the princess will instead fall into deep sleep for a hundred years, then be wakened by a king's son who'll marry her.

In Macdonald's book, a young woman named Laurel Lennox suffered the effects of a misadventure when she was fifteen: she and a teenaged boy ("who may have a kind of hex on her") ran off to Las Vegas, pretended she was kidnapped, and got a thousand-dollar ransom. The boy was jailed and Laurel exonerated, but she's never really recovered. Separated from a husband who "treats her as if she were a fairy princess," Laurel gobbles Seconals and sometimes longs "to go to sleep and never wake up." During a visit to Archer's apartment, she steals some Nembutal and leaves abruptly, perhaps bent on suicide.

Hired to find the missing woman by her husband, Archer becomes a sort of surrogate prince, looking for Laurel in Pacific Point, whose citizens are transfixed by communal catastrophe: an oil leak that seeps up from the ocean bed and spreads ashore like an evil spell.

The slick, caused by an ill-advised oil platform stuck in the seafloor "like the metal handle of a dagger that had stabbed the world and made it spill black blood," is an "ecological crime" to match the forest fire in *The Underground Man.* But where *Underground* danced along like wildfire, *Beauty* oozes like the black tide, slow and inexorable. The huge slick spreads from sea to shore "like premature night," turning beach sand to pitch, smearing windows, fouling air, killing birds. Clumps of people silently watch the oil's progress, spellbound like the servants in Perrault's tale, "as if they were waiting for the end of the world, or as if the end had come and they would never move again."

In the wake of this unnatural act, the laws of physics seem suspended, as if the world's turned upside down. An owl flies across the night sky "as silently as a fish under water." A lake resembles a chunk of sky spattered on the ground. The moon floats low to the earth like a target balloon. Seagulls seem made out of white plastic. An old woman who looks like an aging boy drinks water "as if it was hemlock."

Human nature is awry. Parents reject their roles in word and deed ("Could you possibly not call me Mother, dear?"). Couples who hate one another are held together by anger and guilty knowledge; lovers are driven apart by inexplicable tensions. Some marriages fracture over pride and sexual greed; others are held together by lust and the love of money.

Time stretches, or speeds up, trapping the unwary in traumas of fifteen or twenty years past. Houses become enchanted keeps, holding occupants in thrall to things that happened there: a man raises his son in the home where the mother was murdered; the son makes it his own disenchanted wedding cottage. People in this bewitched place are but dimly aware of the trances they're in; years go by like weeks, minutes stretch for hours.

Archer himself starts perceiving the world as distorted. Returning to his apartment after thirty hours, it seems to him years have passed: "There was a drabness in the light, a sourness in the air. It gave me a shock to realize that the change was not in the apartment but in me." When he comes to a lookout tower, Archer has the odd feeling the tower's watching him, though inside he finds nothing "but a drift of sand marked with footprints": a visual echo of the "beautifully shaped prints" Laurel's "narrow feet" had made in the beach sand when Lew met her.

In Laurel Lennox, Macdonald showed his last picture of Linda Millar, altering her image through the looking glass of fiction. Laurel's a rich girl with emotional problems, haunted by an adolescent folly for which someone else took the brunt of the blame. Fearful and unhappy (but with "a real sweetness underneath it all"), troubled by everyday cruelty, Laurel resists bringing a child into the world. Seemingly damaged by some forgotten event, latently suicidal, she's sought help from psychiatrists. "She has so much empathy," her grandmother says, "it's virtually psychotic." Yet the grandmother adds, "This may seem a strange thing to say about a girl who has suffered as much as Laurel and made so many mistakes. But I don't think she wants to be any different. And of course she's had her good times."

Lew had only a brief encounter with Laurel, but she made a deep impression on him, he says: "Dark and troubled . . . At the same time quite strong, in her way, and valuable, even beautiful. I never met a girl who cared so much."

Like a father, Lew feels responsible for Laurel. "I shouldn't have let her get away from me," he says. "I knew she needed help, but I didn't want to admit it to myself. I wasn't prepared to give it, I suppose." But he worries that his paternal motives are impure: "I caught an oblique glimpse of myself as a middle-aged man on the make." After consummating one of his few seductions (with the Lennox girl's aunt, in the Lennox girl's room), Archer experiences semi-incestuous shame: "I dreamed I was sleeping with Laurel, and woke up guilty and sweating in her bed." In an instant he moves from sex to guilt to death: there's an oil-soaked corpse floating in the sea outside—a grotesque double to the oil-damaged bird Laurel had held when Lew met her.

Sleeping Beauty sustains an involving tension. There are recurring reminders that time is finite. An earth slide leaning against a cliff looks to Archer "like sand in the bottom of an hourglass which had almost run out." In the empty room of someone else who's disappeared, Lew notes an alarm clock that isn't ticking: "It had stopped a few minutes short of midnight, or of noon." But the same signs that signal something ending could also cue renewal. An hourglass can be turned right side up. The clock could as easily mark the start of a new day as the end of an old one.

There's a tenderness at the book's core, emanating from Archer's looking for Laurel. His task reminds us of his pursuit of the missing boy in *The Underground Man,* but here the quest is even more involving. Laurel seems more vulnerable because she's damaged, like the oil-soaked bird she tried to save. Perhaps, like the bird, Laurel's hurt beyond repair.

That "black bird" again brings to mind the Maltese Falcon, an object Millar said could symbolize the absence of the Holy Ghost. *Beauty*'s sharp-beaked bird and the girl who holds it augur the loss, through greed and pride, of nature and of life itself, in the form of a single grebe or an only child.

In *Sleeping Beauty* Macdonald developed characteristic themes with skill. The family romance, with its attractions and compulsions, is exemplified among others by Laurel and husband Tom Russo: both united and threatened by common memories of a lost childhood paradise ("In flight from the past," Millar wrote in a notebook, "Laurel runs directly into the past"). Parents groom children to repeat their own mistakes, then punish them. Children shoulder the guilt for grown-ups' actions. Lies are repeated enough they seem true. People suppressing the awful past are compelled to make a terrible present. Guilt is a cause of mutual enchantment, freezing time and crippling the will.

Adding another dimension to the work is its fairy-tale motif, developed all the way to the end: the main villain's demise occurs with a fall through the air and a swirl of smoke worthy of a witch dispatched by the Brothers Grimm. Like a fairy tale, the book can be read over and over for instruction, irony, pity, terror.

Through Macdonald's art, Millar did the impossible: turned life's hourglass upside down, retraced those "elegant footprints" along the shore. This time the story came out right: the princess is found, the pills thrown away, the victim rescued, the wicked punished, the scapegoat set free. The hero succeeds. The spell is broken. The daughter lives.

As a man gets older, if he knows what is good for him, the women he likes are getting older, too. The trouble is that most of them are married.

—Ross Macdonald, *The Zebra-Striped Hearse*

Charlotte Capers: I would like to ask you about Kenneth Millar, whose pseudonym is Ross Macdonald. He is a celebrated detective story writer, or writer, and is a friend of yours, and I'm interested in how you two met.

Eudora Welty: We met because he wrote me a letter after I had said, in an interview published in the *New York Times* with Walter Clemons, that I admired his work. . . . Then I reviewed a book of his, *The Underground Man,* and we got to be friends again. . . . I think so much of his work, and he's such a nice man. Then, in a typical Ross Macdonald fashion, we, unknown to each other, turned up at the same time in the same hotel in adjoining rooms in New York. . . . At the Algonquin—and met then, and had some good conversations, and walked, and talked, and so on, and got to be good friends. So, I felt that he was almost like an old friend, especially after he dedicated his new book to me, so I invited him to come to this wonderful occasion for me, and he came, which I think was just wonderful—from Santa Barbara. I was sorry his wife couldn't come. She had planned to.

Capers: What's the title of his new book?

Welty: *Sleeping Beauty.*

Capers: I'm his fan, too, I can't wait to read it.

Welty: Oh! I know it! I'm going out today to try to buy some copies. Rosie wanted to take my inscribed copy home on the plane, but I wouldn't let her.

Capers: I don't blame you. Well, I thought he was a most attractive man, and I'm delighted that he came.

—Charlotte Capers, "An Interview with Eudora Welty, 8 May 1973"

"It is certain to become the third straight bestseller by the author of *The Goodbye Look* and *The Underground Man*—the incomparable novelist whose books the *New York Times* has called 'the best series of detective novels ever written by an American' ": so Knopf trumpeted *Sleeping Beauty* in a full-page ad in the *Times Book Review* in the spring of 1973. Millar had tried to make the novel a worthy follow-up to its best-selling predecessors, but *Sleeping Beauty* was also a highly personal work—"more of my lifetime images came in on that oily tide than ever before," he told Peter Wolfe; and he sent a typescript to his most valued reader, Eudora Welty, for her prepublication reaction. Millar dedicated the book to Welty, not only from gratitude for her *Underground* review but because he felt they'd become good friends. Welty liked *Sleeping Beauty,* Millar wrote Ash Green: "She gave me such a reading as authors dream of."

Eudora Welty was Macdonald's best-known literary champion, but he had other notable fans, including Welty confidants Reynolds Price and Elizabeth Bowen. ("She was crazy about him," Welty said of Irish writer Bowen. "She used to carry around paperbacks when she was doing lecture tours in America, and when I would give her one of his to read—I told Ken this, I think it embarrassed him—she would say, 'Oh, *beloved* Ross Macdonald!' ") Along with the younger Joan Didion and the older Wallace Stegner, Macdonald was among the most highly regarded writers in California by 1973: roughly comparable in career terms to where Raymond Chandler had been a quarter century earlier when Macdonald launched the Archer series. The memory of Chandler's behavior toward the first Archer still stung Millar; he'd made a conscious effort to repay Chandler's nastiness with his own kindness to young writers. Early in 1973 he read a book that "challenged" his achievement the way *Target* had challenged Chandler's; Millar reacted with a generosity that helped launch its author's career.

Yale Drama School grad Roger Simon had published two novels before he wrote *The Big Fix*, a breezy private-eye tale with young, political, pot-smoking LA detective Moses Wine. *The Big Fix* would be published by Straight Arrow, the book division of *Rolling Stone* magazine. Simon was friends with a colleague of Dick Lid's at Cal State Northridge, and Lid agreed to show Millar a manuscript copy of *The Big Fix*.

"He responded with the most wonderful, warm, generous letter to me," recalled Simon, who lived in Los Angeles. "He *really* liked the book. I think what he liked was it hadn't been done before: that it took the form and moved it forward and had a different sensibility; and he liked the literary style. He felt I was deficient in plotting; I still am, although I'm better now. I was sort of bowled over, but practical: I wrote back saying thank you, thank you, thank you—and my publisher would *love* for you to give a quote! And he did, he gave me a great quote. He also invited me to have lunch with him up there in Santa Barbara at the writers' luncheon."

Simon drove up to a Wednesday gathering at El Cielito in March of 1973, he said: "Of course I didn't know exactly what he looked like; I guess he must have realized who I was, 'cause he knew I'd be coming at a certain hour and I'd look confused, right? And I looked fairly hippie at the time: I had long hair and a beard. He had a very quiet, wry, puckish sense of humor. The way he identified himself was, he picked up this straw panama hat and put it on, like Lew Archer, and stood up and looked at me, and *smiled!*

"He did have this sort of mannered way; he seemed almost out of time. But he was *really* shy. Part of it may have been that there were so many years between us; I was twenty-nine. He was the obvious heavyweight of that luncheon gathering; on the other hand, he wouldn't impose himself. I've been around a lot of people particularly in the movie business who are powerful, interesting artists; and I would say of the fine artists I have known, without exception he was the most modest. He was extraordinarily generous with other writers, almost in a gurulike way; he wanted to mentor people he liked. I learned from him it was a good thing to be like that—if not good for your work, at least good for the soul."

Simon saw Millar often in the next two years, he said: "I must have gone up there maybe a dozen times to the Coral Casino and the writers' luncheons. I swam with Ken a few times; he was a really powerful swimmer." Like others, Simon felt Millar's essence elusive: "I think now I never really got to know him. I think he was an essentially private person, and a human being of tremendous pain; you could just see it in his body, and in his eyes. I was loath to talk to him about the personal tragedies of his life, which were so reflected in his fiction; I was so much younger, I think I was too shy. I would confine conversation to literary chitchat or events of the day or films. All I remember is a kind of tension around the family; being introduced, but not a real feeling of what was going on, and I couldn't ask.

"I was so transfixed by Ken, so enamored of him as a human, as a writer. My feeling is that by the midseventies he was the most respected writer in California, on a serious level. I was fascinated with Ken because he was to me a serious artist. And I think part of the reason I've only written six of these detective novels is I have this ambivalence around detective fiction—that it's not really *serious*. And *he* was so clearly serious as a writer that it made *me* feel okay about it.

"You could tell what interested him was people who were trying to do something different with the detective form, trying to push it forward. He was really a true literary personality, in that he didn't like a lot of those detective novels that were merely imitating the past; but he was not the kind of person that would bad-mouth people—a unique thing among writers, I think. *I'm* pretty willing to do it. He just didn't. Rather than say 'Boring' or 'What crap,' his way was to politely bypass something."

Millar touted Simon's work in ways that exactly counterpointed the bad turns Chandler had done Macdonald. Chandler knocked *The Moving Target* to James Sandoe; Millar praised *The Big Fix* to Matt Bruccoli and to Julian Symons in England, where Simon's book got fine reviews and won a Crime Writers Association award. Chandler bad-mouthed Macdonald to an important Chicago bookseller; Millar praised Simon to Ralph Sipper, his Bay Area bookman friend. "Oh, he was a big booster," Simon said. "It was a tremendous generosity."

Simon sold *The Big Fix* to Hollywood and then wrote its screenplay. In coming years he alternated Moses Wine books with movie scripts, and he sensed the Hollywood work caused a change in his and Millar's relationship: "When *The Big Fix* was made into a movie, I think in an odd way he was really impressed, simply because I had written the script myself and negotiated shoals he hadn't been able to. Part of the reason was that he was such a withdrawn person; he wasn't comfortable taking his gloves off in the Hollywood environment. It was a weird feeling I would have, because I considered him such a superior writer I couldn't understand why he'd be impressed. He wanted to do it, I know. Everybody who puts down Hollywood is also mesmerized by it; I knew he in his own way was mesmerized by it, Ken. As I became more successful working as a screenwriter, he would seek my counsel about the ways of Hollywood. He had an inflated sense of my connections; he assumed I had great entrée into this mysterious world of the cinema! He would play the faux naïf a little bit: 'You know all about these producers; what do they really want? They're just making monkeys of us poor intellectuals.' I never believed it. Because first of all, I don't think there's anything too complicated about greed.

"He'd ask what I thought about certain producers or executives; did I know so-and-so, because so-and-so was calling him up. I'd give my opinion, but it always made me feel slightly tarnished in an odd sort of way—like I was the Grub Street author and he was up there in sylvan Santa Barbara staying on the narrow path, writing book after book after book. I felt sometimes like I was his conduit to hipness, and he was my conduit to quality! I saw him as a devoted person; and if I was going off in one of my other directions, I was embarrassed to be around him because then I'd have to explain to him—and to *me*—why I hadn't been doing the detective fiction. I felt a little embarrassed because I felt like I'd failed him, and myself. That's why I didn't see him that much in the late seventies."

When Simon first went to Santa Barbara in the spring of 1973, many Americans (including Millar and Simon) were transfixed by the Senate's televised Watergate hearings in which the unseemly doings of Richard Nixon's Committee to Reelect the President (CREEP) were exposed: break-ins, dirty tricks, enemies list, payoffs. "Those are the cosmic criminals of our times," Simon wrote Millar of all the president's men, "and the question is how to write them without it coming out propaganda or a turgid rehash of the television news." Millar told Bob Ford in Moscow, "We sit in front of the television set spellbound by the stories of the reign of Richard the Terrible."

Some saw similarities between Washington's alleged high crimes and misdemeanors and the doings in a Ross Macdonald book. The *New York Times* asked Macdonald to write an op-ed piece on "Watergate as 'caper' or 'whodunit.'" Millar turned the assignment down, but he had plenty of Watergate thoughts. "There is some kind of general family history," he wrote Bill Ruehlmann, "based on my own, that I write of—the history of my lifetime told in family terms—and I must say recent events support my long suspicion that there is something very much wrong. Now we're headed for the rapids, I'm afraid, betrayed by a philosophy that began to take over with the second war, but I think we'll come out on the other side." The whole affair, he said, only went to show "the essential meaning-lessness of evil."

Nixon was a prime source of his own trouble, Millar told journalist Jeff Sweet: "He's almost infallibly wrong in his choice of help. He picked all of those people, and they picked him, too. . . . He magnetized the elements of . . . a thoroughly corrupt administration. He's always behaved in the same manner. I've followed him ever since my own activities in the Helen Gahagan Douglas campaign, which he won by making her out to be a Communist. He's always operated by the same principles. It's no secret to anybody." Millar analyzed the president as deftly as he'd sketch a witness in the box at the Santa Barbara courthouse: "I think that Nixon has divided values and he's never been able to make them jibe. On the one hand, you know, he comes from a very strict religious family. And on the other hand, he grew up in a tradition or a feeling where you've got to make it big. And the two things, between them, have been the upper and nether grindstones, and they've destroyed him."

Millar could comprehend Nixon, but he couldn't abide what he'd done. "You see," he told Sweet, "that's the mistake people like Nixon make. They think that understanding power and all the various faculties and abilities a man has are intended for his own self-aggrandizement and to do things to other people. It's not true." Nothing made Millar angrier than abuse of power. Easton said, "He could be extremely violent in likes and dislikes where his own feelings and principles were involved. He made me feel he fero-ciously hated Reagan, Nixon, what they stood and stand for, likewise the big oil-company executives who directed development in the Santa Barbara Channel." The Skylab space module was going to crash to earth during the Watergate hearings; most hoped it would destroy itself in some barren desert, but Millar wrote Ruehlmann *he* knew what to do with Skylab: "You've heard of the Florida White House? and the California White House? Well."

While Washington staged Watergate, Jackson, Mississippi ("cradle of the Confederacy"), prepared a more cheerful happening: a six-day "Eudora Welty Celebration," part of the tenth annual Mississippi Arts Festival. Eudora Welty Day, a state-proclaimed holiday, would be May 2, two weeks after Welty's sixty-fourth birthday.

"I've lived here all my life in Jackson," Welty said, recalling the event. "Everybody knows me, and they wanted to give me a party. They said, 'Now we want to bring all of your closest, best friends, no matter where they live; bring 'em to Jackson, we'll put 'em up at a hotel'—I'm afraid they didn't *pay* for it, but anyway—'we've planned everything nice, for three or four days.' I said, 'How can I ever *choose,* and besides, they all live far away and it might not be possible.' They said, 'That's not for you to worry about; just make a list of the people you'd most like to have.'

"So that's what I did. And I put Ken on it. And Margaret too. And they accepted. But Margaret—on again, off again—at the last, she didn't come. But all my oldest friends, in New York and around Santa Fe, they all came. And I'm so happy now, because so many of them are gone; and that was a time that everybody got to meet one another. It was wonderful that Ken came. And my agent, Diarmuid Russell, an Irishman, from Dublin, he was my dear friend and agent, and he liked Ken's work." Russell, Welty's agent for thirty-three years, and dying of cancer, had never been to her home-town. "They met at my house," she said of Russell and Millar, "and after-wards Diarmuid said to me he'd so much enjoyed meeting Ken. He said, 'He's a man with a great deal of tenderness in him.' Which is true; it was so apparent to somebody like Diarmuid, who has a good deal of tenderness in him too.

"Everybody got to be close to each other. It was an incredible experi-ence. Everybody was invited to someone's house for a luncheon, for about six of them, all over town. And at night, the New Stage Theatre, which is a small regional professional theater—they put on a play made from one of my stories, which had been on Broadway: *The Ponder Heart*. They did it just for the guests, you know. And then we had a big party afterwards. It was just lovely.

"I was remembering the things that Ken brought. He brought an alarm clock! But that's what you needed. And binoculars, to see the birds. And notebooks and things. He walked all around, he really *found out* about the place. He investigated things on foot."

"It was a very pleasant three or four days of hanging out in Jackson in the springtime and going to lots of parties, and then to a reading Eudora gave," said Reynolds Price, of North Carolina, another guest for the cele-bration, which was organized and run by a committee of a thousand (mostly women) volunteers. "I certainly had a sense that this was not Ken's world at all; at times he did seem like a kind of retired detective trapped in a ladies' tea or something! But he certainly kept his dignity, although I very much had the sense of a very powerful man whose top could blow off and one wouldn't want to be near."

But Millar declared later to Ash Green, "Mississippi *was* a lot of fun, and a moving experience, too—not unlike visiting the birthplace of a saint in her own lifetime. I was very glad to be asked, and glad I went." Millar had never been deep in Dixie to speak of and thought he'd hate it, but didn't. "We all had a splendid time immersed in the vast differences of the south," he wrote Julian Symons, "which is an oral agrarian culture floating still on a quiet ominous sea of blacks." To Green, he admitted, "Except or but for the blacks, omnipresent and rather quiet, I became almost sorry we won the civil war." In the Old State Capitol (now a museum), he viewed Jeffer-son Davis's books and weapons and lingered at an exhibit of photos (many by Welty) of poor country folk, then spent hours in a room filled with Welty correspondence and memorabilia. Past and present seemed to merge in

Welty, of whom Millar wrote Ruehlmann: "She is one of the world's gentlest minds, at the same time one of its keenest."

"The nation's foremost lady of letters" and "a woman of quiet dignity and charm" was how Mississippi governor William Waller described her to a crowd of five hundred in the Old Capitol's Hall of Representatives, as he proclaimed Eudora Welty Day. Nona Balakian described the scene for the *New York Times Book Review:* "Amid the clatter of radio and television equipment, photographers and such, Miss Welty in a pink dress sat quietly, obviously pleased, her blue eyes as unguarded as a young girl's. Later, in grateful response to the Governor's words and a standing ovation, she expressed wonder at the whole event: 'If anything like this has ever been done to another author,' she quipped, 'then I think we can beat them.'"

Millar, in a letter to Symons, described what happened next: "Eudora boldly read aloud, in that same chamber where secession was first declared, and in the presence of the current governor, a passage from *Losing Battles* celebrating the sexual life." Asked about this later, Welty said, "Well, it was not *chosen* for that reason. I read the part at the end of the big family reunion, and it had things that I feel about reunions: 'Don't leave anybody out,' one of those things. But all the time they're talking, the wife and husband are being reunited after two or three years, so they're in each other's arms. I suppose it could be called 'erotic,' but—I was trying to draw us all into one circle, which I felt we had done."

The main private events of the week for Millar were a party at Welty's house Tuesday night and a smaller dinner there Thursday, after which guests talked until midnight. "In those days I had a screen porch here, just outside," Welty remembered later, sitting in her Jackson living room, "which a hurricane tore away. This was all open then, all these rooms; so people were all over and could move around. I had food in there; that's my mailing room now, but it used to be the dining room. So it was a nice evening in May, the time of the little, fresh Louisiana strawberries about this big, along with the drinks and everything."

"Altogether a lovely experience," Millar wrote Symons. In a sentence that hinted how deeply he'd come to feel about Welty, he said this "demi-week" in Jackson was for him nearly "the biggest week since a week in June 1938 when M. and I got married."

Millar was a bit more candid during long talks in Jackson with Reynolds Price. "He and I had these two rooms side by side in the Sun and Sand Motel," Price recalled. "We sort of followed each other around that particular set of days, and we would meet in the evenings and have a nightcap and talk about things." Price, forty in 1973, was often referred to as Welty's protégé. He and Millar had begun a correspondence, at Price's instigation; Millar was surprised and touched when Price thanked him for the pleasure and instruction of Ross Macdonald's work. (Asked in a 1972 interview who his favorite novelists were, Price said, "Eudora Welty is the living writer that I admire most. . . . I very much respect a number of living people—Bernard Malamud, Saul Bellow, some of the early work of John Updike, some of the work of William Styron, the detective novels of Ross Macdonald . . . the sort of people that most everybody else likes who reads much fiction.") Millar tucked a Reynolds Price reference into *Sleeping Beauty:* going through Laurel's things, Archer finds a book of stories called *Permanent Errors,* a 1970 Price collection.

"One night he and I had a few drinks and were sitting in the motel in Jackson," Price said, "when this one particular very memorable moment occurred. We were talking about Eudora and what a wonderful person she was; and I went on you know about how important she'd been to me, and how I'd met her when I was a senior in college—Eudora's twenty-four years older than me—and we talked on in that way. And Ken stopped me and said, 'No, you don't understand.' He says, 'I'm saying I love her as a woman.' And I'll take a Bible oath that he said that to me, and it kind of practically blew me out of the chair. And I don't know—at that point I didn't feel I knew him well enough, or hadn't gathered my wits about me enough, to pursue that in any way, and nothing more was ever said by him or me about it, but—he obviously was not a man who used words of that sort lightly. Of course he was the soul of taciturnity, but I think there was a lot of power in that relationship. I think that for both of them this was an emotional relationship of *great* importance, in both their lives.

"She took great delight in him too. Eudora's always been this tremendous mystery fan, and she's also been a great fan of men in her life. She really loves the company of men, and I think there were just all sorts of ways in which they hit it off together at the particular time they met. It wasn't news to me. I mean, as a well-wishing sort of younger friend of both of them, I'd thought that's what I'd seen developing, just from hearing her talk about the times they met and the fact that they corresponded voluminously. I think she was a great romance of Ken's life, at the end of his life. And Kenneth Millar was of great importance to Eudora Welty; I think it ran very deep for her. My own sense is that they were in love with one another. And it was late in both their lives."

Recalling that week in May, Welty said, "I never did get to see Ken by himself; not till I took him to the airport when he left did we really get to be by ourselves. He had a good time, I think. He said he did. He's so shy, and quiet. And it didn't matter at *all.*"

Home from Jackson, Millar read in the newspaper that Welty had won the Pulitzer Prize for fiction for her 1972 novel, *The Optimist's Daughter* (which, like *Sleeping Beauty,* has a title character named Laurel). *Sleeping Beauty's* first reviews were printed that same week. *Newsweek's,* by Peter S. Prescott, was a rave; the critic said Macdonald's classic motifs were elegantly developed in this new novel: "the search for the lost child; the idea that family determines fate; the need to restore order to the past as well as to the present; the balance between natural and moral disaster; scattered images suggesting the imminent end of man and his endeavors; and a harmony of structure: the bird that is washed up from the oil-slicked ocean at the book's beginning is paired a little later with a man who is similarly oiled and destroyed. Most interesting of all is the pairing that Macdonald has made uniquely his own: that of the victim, who is immobilized by her consciousness of the world's violence and cruelty, with Lew Archer—'thief catcher, corpse finder, ear to anyone,' as he says of himself—the competent man." *Time*'s review, on the other hand, was nasty: "*Sleeping Beauty* is a blurry effort," claimed John Skow, "far less vivid than *The Underground Man*, the Archer thriller whose appearance two years ago caused the world of belles-lettres to proclaim the discovery of a new Dostoevsky. . . . At best, the writing is rechewed Macdonald. At worst, the words might have been bought by the carload from the Erle Stanley Gardner estate. The world of belles-lettres is subject to cyclical hysteria, some of it fairly predictable, and it seems likely that Ross Macdonald (whose new novel carries a wistfully belletristic dedication to Eudora Welty) will be sent back to the cellar, where nature has ordained that detective-story writers should work." The book sold briskly ("in spite of *Time*," Millar wrote Harker, "or maybe because of it") and hopped onto *Time*'s own best-seller list, where it went to number three.

Other solidly supportive reviews came from Clifford A. Ridley in the *National Observer* and Robert Kirsch in the *LA Times*. But it was the *New York Times* that counted most, and Crawford Woods in that paper's Sunday book section gave *"The [sic] Sleeping Beauty"* what Millar called "a preposterously bad review." It began: "This detective story carries a dedication to Eudora Welty—a gracious and appropriate gesture, but one that suggests, as the book suggests, that the author has fallen prey to the exuberance of his critics and is now writing in the shadow of a self-regard that tends to play his talent false." It was a tricky case Woods tried to make: that *Sleeping Beauty* was both "a largely satisfying mystery" that "cracks along vividly enough," and a work hampered by "bad prose and ponderous philosophizing." The new novel, he contended, was "a book more built than written, a methodical account framed in language generally too dim to call for much praise." To support his assertions, Woods quoted Archer saying of an elevator descent that he felt "as if I were going down to the bottom of things" (not mentioning that this particular elevator went to the morgue) and misquoted a line he was offering as an example of "half-chewed California Zen." At least Woods's piece was buried on an inner *Book Review* page. The daily *Times* also went after Macdonald with a review by notorious put-down artist Anatole Broyard (who also incorrectly called the novel *"The Sleeping Beauty"*). "Occasionally, the author writes a thoughtful line," Broyard allowed, "but it doesn't seem enough to justify the paroxysms of praise that greet his works." Macdonald's good moments, he wrote, "are not enough to disguise the fact that there are no people in Mr. Macdonald's books—only a few types with two cents' worth of Freudian psychology to set them in motion."

The widely reviewed *Sleeping Beauty* drew other raves (*Playboy:* "every bit as good as *The Underground Man* . . . No other mystery writer probes so deeply into the convoluted sources of violence"; the *Chicago Tribune:* "consummate skill . . . a masterpiece of *trompe l'oeil*") and further slams (the *New Republic:* "One of the stranger mysteries in the chronicle of American letters is the process by which Ross MacDonald [*sic*] . . . virtually overnight became the nation's seasonal darling"; the *Massachusetts Review:* "This novel is a disgrace in every respect"); but it was Woods's piece that stuck in Millar's mind. He hadn't felt so bad about a review since his mixed notices for *The Three Roads*. He tried to ignore Woods, he told the *Times*'s Nona Balakian (met in Mississippi), "But the subject wouldn't leave me alone, and I finally decided that I had an obligation to stand up for my book." Millar and Balakian coincidentally had talked of what a mistake it was for authors to answer reviewers in print (as Joyce Carol Oates had recently done); but, stinging from Woods's attack, Millar wrote Ash Green, "There is no reason why carefully composed books should be killed off by irresponsible reviews, at least not in silence." Macdonald penned a 350-word letter to the *New York Times Book Review,* taking Woods to task for his "grotesque distortions" and "thimblerigged quotation." Such author replies were rare in 1973; this one looked like sour grapes when it was printed in August. "It was justified," Welty said, "but it would have been better if someone else had done it. I told Ken I would have replied to that, but I couldn't do it—since that book was dedicated to me! I remember getting very upset; I was so infuriated. It was a very *stupid* review."

Sleeping Beauty stayed on the major best-seller lists for six weeks, reaching nine on the *New York Times* chart and seven on *Publishers Weekly*'s. The novel sold about forty-five thousand copies: not as good as *The Underground Man,* Millar admitted to Ping Ferry, "but satisfactory, and I prefer *this* book." As *Beauty* slipped off top-ten lists in July, Millar told Matt Bruccoli: "I'm eager to get into a new one."

But not that eager. There were tempting distractions, and Millar succumbed. The Book-of-the-Month Club proposed that Ross Macdonald edit a Knopf-published suspense anthology. Millar took on the task with enthusiasm, enlisting bookseller Ralph Sipper's aid in obtaining works by likely authors (Maugham, Simenon, John D. MacDonald, Daphne du Maurier) and soliciting suggestions from friends and colleagues like Julian Symons. Another matter occupying him was the Popular Culture Association's vote to award Ross Macdonald its first Merit Award, which Millar agreed to accept in person at a PCA event in Chicago in December.

The PCA was affiliated with Ray B. Browne's Center for the Study of Popular Culture at Bowling Green. Browne and his wife and colleague, Pat, visited Santa Barbara this summer. "Browne is quiet and unassuming and very sharp," Millar reported to Ferry. "So is his wife." Browne found

Millar "extraordinarily human and humble" during a lunch at the Coral Casino, he said: "He was very very solicitous of our young daughter. She stepped out one time and got reasonably close to the swimming pool, and he was up on his feet and bounding out to be sure she was all right. After lunch he said he had to excuse himself and go out and walk his blind dog that he had in the back of the car. I walked out with him and he put the dog on a leash and walked him around in the park, then came back and reinstituted our conversation. I thought he was an extraordinarily tender, caring kind of person. But he had his other side: he did not always suffer fools, I guess I would say pretentious fools, easily."

Browne, acquainted with Millar's peers in the popular-culture field, was struck by an unexpected ambivalence in this author: "I had the feeling that although he was a man of great accomplishment, he really was not a man of great self-confidence. He volunteered about his little run-in with John D. MacDonald. The two of them were such different personalities; John D. was a big, old commanding macho personality, but really sensitive underneath. I once asked John D. about his run-in with Ross over the use of the name, but he refused to talk about it. Ross on the contrary was a little bit humbled, a little bit frightened by it, and I thought backed off far too quickly. I thought he'd had just as much right to 'John' as John D. did, and I said that to Ross; he backed off again. I think Ross never did quite achieve or manifest the security that he ought to have had. I believe he was a little bit intimidated by his wife—I never met Margaret; she was always out watching birds when I was around—maybe intimidated by both of their lives, and I know terribly terribly undercut by the death of their daughter. I thought their grasp of life, which should have been so pure and firm and complete, was really rather tenuous.

"I think more than any writer I know—this is going to sound a bit condescending—I sorta felt sympathy for him; I felt, 'We need to *understand* Ross.' God knows, he was quite capable of standing on his own feet, you know; but he was so gentle, and kind, and helpful. I believe that he was so thin-skinned that negative reviews—that for people not to understand him was in fact to wound him, to cut him. When we were at the club, all the personnel there knew him—'Hello, Mr. Millar'—and he *glowed* in their attention, but it struck me that he was not quite sure he deserved it. I'm back to that ambivalent personality. I may be making too much out of that, but—I *know* that had he been in the presence of John D. MacDonald, he would have deferred to him. At the same time— When the literary critic of the *LA Times*, Robert Kirsch, whom I knew from grad school, was there at the writers' lunch sort of huffing and puffing and being important, Ross did not say, 'Yes, Bob'—he sort of kept Bob in his place. So I'm back to that ambivalence; an ambivalent character.

"There was about the man a kind of vulnerability, a sensitive vulnerability, which made everybody warm up to him and sort of protect him. Despite his skill, his thoughts, and his heroic nature, he didn't really stand tall. I always had the feeling that, dammit, people didn't give Macdonald all the credit he deserved; he was so nice and gentle and vulnerable that he didn't demand it. I guess I'm always thinking of him in comparison with John D. If you didn't respect John D. MacDonald, he'd kick you in the butt. If you didn't respect Ross Macdonald, he would sorta say, 'Well, that's the way it goes; that's life.' "

The writers' lunch Browne visited was by now a local institution, held every other Wednesday at noon at Harry's (later Josie's) El Cielito. The restaurant's name meant "little heaven," Millar liked to point out; and the luncheon was a sort of haven for Millar. "We drank a bit, but not a lot," said Roger Simon. "My memory is that Ken would have a beer, and he would do it in a way, like, he was with the *guys* here at lunch, and we should have a *drink!*"

Millar assumed responsibility for alerting regulars when it was time to reassemble. "The Sunday night before," Herb Harker said, "you could know you were gonna get a call from Ken reminding you of the luncheon on Wednesday. He called the whole roster and dropped a reminder so the fellows wouldn't forget; he was that dedicated to it." Millar divided these calls over two or three nights, since the luncheon corps was now about fifty. Newsman Bill Downey said, "When Ken called to remind you about the meetings, you could feel the shyness at the other end." Dennis Lynds said, "*You* had to do most of the talking, because Ken was very slow-spoken— and very hard to get off the phone, because there'd be long silences! You'd want to say, 'Ken, are you *there?*' In the period between '68 through '73, I didn't go very often. One reason was because you *did* drink, and if I have three beers for lunch, I can't work in the afternoon. But Ken would call to remind me anyhow, every other Monday."

There was no agenda at the lunch, Lynds said: "Everybody had an individual check; everyone drifted in at different times. Nobody was very self-conscious. You could bring guests, but you'd introduce them only to whoever was sitting nearby. No one had a regular seat; it was catch-as-catch-can, and I liked that. If Ken brought somebody, he'd try to sit with them, but that might not even be possible; by the time he got there, there probably wouldn't be three seats together. So you'd sit down wherever there was an empty seat, and you talked to whoever was around you. And you got to know people that way."

Harker agreed: "You'd sit by one person one time, another person the next; it was wonderful, the most informal thing you can imagine. There was no chairman, no introductions, no anything. It was usually a rowdy occasion. Once in a while there'd be somebody saying something with everyone listening, but mostly you'd have several conversations going on." They had a great group, Harker thought: "Dennis was there a lot, and Bob Easton. Paul Lazarus, a motion picture producer; he taught a screenwriting course at UCSB. Bill Gault. Larry Pidgeon, who was in charge of the editorial page at the *News-Press,* a wonderful guy; I can remember some discussions we had about Vietnam: Larry supported our government, and that wasn't true of everybody at the table; we'd get some fairly warm conversations going. Chet Holcomb, who was also with the newspaper. For a while Jack Schaefer, who wrote *Shane,* moved here from Santa Fe. Willard Temple, a short-story writer for the *Saturday Evening Post;* a great fellow. Don Freeman, who wrote children's books. Clifton Fadiman, an interesting guy. Artie Shaw was there several times; he's a wonderful storyteller. Ken said one time how much he enjoyed that lunch; he said, 'This is better than a university course in writing.' You'd get some terrific conversations going."

Bill Gault recalled this exchange: "One day Ken and I were discussing a writer we both admire, F. Scott Fitzgerald. A publisher got into what had been a dialogue by saying, 'I have never been able to understand why he is so admired; I didn't like *The Great Gatsby.*' Ken gave him his nonconcerned stare and said, 'Two writers have agreed on the man. It really doesn't matter what a publisher thinks of the book.' "

During the luncheons' heyday, Ralph Sipper (who moved to Santa Barbara in the midseventies) wrote, "Though he would deny it, Macdonald is clearly the dominant, if restrained force at the gatherings—'our leader,' as local novelist Bill Gault jokingly refers to him." Sipper said, "*Everybody* wanted to sit next to Ken."

Gault was the liveliest participant, according to Jerre Lloyd: "He was real garrulous and brought everybody out; if somebody wasn't talking, he'd ask them a question." But it was Macdonald who drew outsiders to the lunches, Lloyd said: "*Dozens* of people came through Santa Barbara to see Ken, and he was always accessible. He was sort of a guru of literature, and I can't help but think that he influenced a lot of people."

The lunches filled a need in Millar for the sort of camaraderie he'd experienced years ago with Pearce, Ford, and Lee at the University of Western Ontario. To keep the collegial clubhouse feel, he insisted the lunches be for men only. "Barny Conrad and Paul Lazarus wanted to invite women to join," Harker recalled, "and Ken was absolutely opposed! He said, 'That's fine; if you want to have a group of men and women, that's fine—but leave *this* group alone!' He said, 'You bring women in, you just change the whole thing.' He gave an example: One day we went to lunch and here were a couple of women at our table; they said they'd heard about this writers' lunch and wanted to check it out. Ken said afterwards, 'You see? What'd I tell you?' He talked about one of the guys there; he said, 'He made an absolute *fool* of himself in front of those women; he talked differently, and it just changed everything!' So he vetoed that as long as he had anything to do with it, and I think the veto pretty well stuck."

There was no shortage of males to fill seats. Ted Clymer, who wrote educational textbooks and lived across the road from the Millars, was a regular; as was Irving Townsend, the Columbia Records executive turned writer. Poets Hank Coulette and Phil Levine attended in summer. William

ROSS MACDONALD

Saroyan and William Eastlake were occasional visitors. "Normally we met in a room over on the right, at a table for maybe thirty," said Lynds. "But everybody tried to come to the lunch before Christmas, and you'd get a horde then of sixty or sixty-five. Then we went into a big back room where there were two long banquet tables, with probably thirty at each. Enormous. The whole back room of El Cielito would be full of writers: tons of people from the university, the poets, the *News-Press* guys, and writers from all around town."

"Those were fun gatherings," Lloyd said. "I was a trust officer in a bank, and everyone at the luncheon was interested in that because not too many others worked in the outside world; they were always asking me questions. I said to Ken, 'Since I'm the only one who has a real job, I'm like a spy at the luncheon.' He said, 'If you're a spy, I'm a double agent.'"

QUESTIONS
1. Ross Macdonald's novels have, in the 1960's and '70s, come increasingly to be praised as quality literature. Basing your comments on this section from *The Far Side of the Dollar* and any other works by Macdonald you may have read, show what aspects of his work might make him superior to other writers of detective fiction. You might refer to George Grella's discussion of Macdonald's work (see "Theories" section of this book).

—*Detective Fiction: Crime and Compromise*, edited by Dick Allen and David Chacko, 1974

Paul, Joanne to Costar in 'Pool'
That attractive study in contrasts, azure-eyed Paul Newman and his avocado-eyed wife, Joanne Woodward, together again in a film? . . . The project is "The Drowning Pool," Lorenzo Semple's adaptation of an early mystery by best seller Ross Macdonald (whence "Harper," earlier). With Paul as the private eye—and wouldn't you like to have that guy focus his eyes on you?

—Joyce Haber, *Los Angeles Times*, July 4, 1974

"**D**ouble agents," "burglars who secretly wish to be caught," "shoplifters who see their own furtive images in a scanning mirror"—the guilty metaphors Millar applied to Macdonald and his crime-fiction colleagues were humorously appropriate to the genre, but they were also clues to the lawless life Millar had avoided; like most Macdonald images, they did double duty.

Millar minted another one like this, saying he was breaking into the academy by the back door or maybe the second story, through being given the left-of-mainstream Popular Culture Association's Award of Merit. At the ceremony, four scholars would read papers on his work. "This will be embarrassing, heady, and rather frightening," Millar wrote Matt Bruccoli, "particularly since I'm expected to respond. Well, it can't be worse than my orals were."

He needn't have worried. The five to six hundred academics packing Chicago's Palmer House ballroom the last Friday night in 1973 (two weeks after Millar's fifty-eighth birthday) were all Macdonald fans. Moderator John Cawelti of the University of Chicago, a pioneer in popular-culture studies, told those assembled, "We conceived of this award about a year ago because we thought that it would be valuable to dramatize the idea that there were writers and other creators working in popular traditions who were we felt achieving very significant and important art; and it was interesting to me that when we had the idea for the award and we thought

347

about who should be the first one to get it, there was absolutely no doubt in anyone's mind that Ross Macdonald was the appropriate recipient. I don't think any other candidate came anywhere near in our estimation of the person who most symbolized the qualities that we were trying to dramatize in the award."

All four papers were good; the first one, George Grella's, Millar thought "quite brilliant." In his eighteen-minute talk (reprinted in the *New Republic*), Grella, a young professor at the University of Rochester, pinpointed recurring patterns in Macdonald's plots, which in their "richly exfoliating complexity" he said more resembled Dickens's and Faulkner's than Hammett's or Chandler's. Grella listed thematic statements the plots expressed: "All men are guilty and all human actions are connected. The past is never past. The child is father to the man. True reality resides in dreams. And most of all, everyone gets what he deserves, but no one deserves what he gets." Sam Grogg gave a paper adapted from his Macdonald dissertation. ("I was a little flustered," said Grogg, "because not only was I saying some words about him in front of him, in public, I was saying the words *to* him, not to all those other people. And I sat back down after I'd given my little speech, and Ken kinda leaned over and patted my leg, and he said, 'Thanks.' I still remember that!") Chicago State University grad student Johnnine Hazard, who'd also done a Macdonald dissertation, read a paper placing Lew Archer in the tradition of realistic "plain" detectives ("courageous, honest, persevering, daring, modest, clever, selfless, successful in a very unromantic world"). She closed on a personal note that got a laugh with its Watergate allusion: "Graduate students rarely have the pleasure of meeting the subject of their thesis, and I'm very grateful to have the opportunity of meeting Mr. Macdonald; but I wouldn't be candid if I didn't add that I have a few tremors too. And when I get done hearing Mr. Macdonald speak, or answer questions, I may decide, as they do in Washington these days, that what I said here is inoperative." Finally Sheldon Sacks, a University of Chicago professor whose usual field was the theory of eighteenth-century literature, explored Archer's ethos in a half-hour talk that ended: "Ross Macdonald has allowed me the great privilege of following Lew Archer, detective, through the end of the maze, to permanent human significance, even in the most grotesque brutalities of riddles in time."

After ninety minutes of scholars' praise, an emotional Macdonald stood to deliver his own essay. It took him a few sentences and several throat-clearings to get the tears from his voice. "I'm really quite overwhelmed," he said, "and deeply honored, that four such eloquent papers should have been prepared about my work, and that so many of you should have turned out to hear them and listened to them with such appreciation. I—I really can't tell you how—how joyous an occasion this is, for me. And really quite unexpected when, twenty or twenty-five years ago, I started on the Archer trail."

His talk, "Down These Streets a Mean Man Must Go" (playing on a famous phrase of Chandler's), traced Millar's lifelong involvement with "serious" and "popular" literature and suggested how the two were intertwined. "His paper was extremely good, a terrific job," George Grella said. "I remember certain things vividly; they've stuck with me. He talked about his childhood, and it's just heartbreaking to think of the things that happened. He said he was about sixteen and went into this pool hall kind of place and picked up a book on a rack there, and it was a Hammett book, and he started reading it and he said he had this extraordinary feeling that he was finally reading a book about the life that was happening all around him. I thought that was stunning. The other thing was how he'd wanted to complete Coleridge's 'Christabel,' and I find that very very telling: because in a way he's always writing these sort of dark romances, pervaded by medieval ideas and some sense of perversion, which is all in that unfinished poem of Coleridge's."

At the end of his talk ("if you can believe this of an academic meeting," Millar wrote Peter Wolfe), the five or six hundred in the Palmer House ballroom gave Macdonald a standing ovation. "Those people just *revered* this man," Grogg said. Millar sat down then to sign books and speak with all who approached him, exercising what Grogg called "that amazing gift he had to put this *hand* over you." As Ross Macdonald, Millar could transcend his own insecurities and become the wise father figure people expected Lew Archer's creator to be.

Frank MacShane saw Ken Millar undergo a different sort of transformation in Santa Barbara in 1974. MacShane, chairman of Columbia University's writing division, was in California researching an authorized biography of Raymond Chandler; he looked up Millar at the suggestion of Eudora Welty. Nattily dressed in academic tweeds, MacShane was startled by Millar's appearance and manner at the Coral Casino: "He came out dressed like a parody of a certain sort of American on vacation, in this kind of Hawaiian shirt, Bermuda shorts, and a straw hat: he looked rather ridiculous. But exceedingly courtly at the same time. So courtly and so—weird. It was very stiff, to say the least. We went into this building, and he was so very formal: '*Well*, Professor MacShane, *what* would you *like* to *eat?*' I got rattled, and I pointed at what I thought was a salad—it was this enormous pile of lettuce. And so it was on my plate. We went upstairs to eat. I hadn't even read his stuff; probably I seemed like a total dumbbell. Anyway I kept asking him questions about Chandler, and he would answer in monosyllables; it was hard to get him to say anything. And all the while I'm stuffing down this 'salad.' It was getting pretty dreary. I didn't know if he was like that normally, or whether I'd done something wrong."

No doubt his reticence had to do with MacShane's project. Chandler was still a sore topic for Millar, who'd recently turned down a publisher's suggestion that *he* write a Chandler biography. When a *New York Times Magazine* editor phoned and asked him to pen an appreciation of Chandler, Millar exploded, "If Chandler had wanted to be kindly remembered, he shouldn't have tried to do me in!" (He recommended Julian Symons for the assignment.)

The sudden appearance of Margaret Millar rescued MacShane's meeting: "His wife changed everything in one second: she was full of fun and vitality, and it became human again. Still he was very formal and not very forthcoming. I was a bit disappointed, 'cause I'd come all the way up there to see him. He said, '*Well,* Mr. MacShane, have we finished our *business?*' I said I guess so, but you mentioned a bookshop; maybe we could go see that. 'Very *well.* Let us go *downstairs* and see what we can *do.*' He had just got a puppy, who was tied down below"—MacDuff, a replacement for Brandy, who'd died—"and so he got the dog, put it in the back of the car, and off we went. Then he said, '*Tell* me, Professor MacShane, you have written *other* books, have you?' I said, yes, I had. 'What was that?' 'Well, I wrote a book on Ford Madox Ford.'

" 'Ford Madox *Ford?*'

"He suddenly *changed!* 'Well, now!' he said. 'I know his daughter, she lives right around the corner, we must go see her.' We must do this, we must do that; it was incredible! He turned into a most lively and amusing character and insisted on taking me to see the university. Then he said, 'Now you must come up to the house.' By now I'd sort of recovered from the shift of gears! And he couldn't have been nicer and more friendly, and such a contrast with the terrible, frosty beginning. He was most eager to talk about Wystan Auden, whom I knew as it happened, and who had been at Columbia. And he was very enthusiastic then about Chandler and what he'd done; he thought he was a wonderful writer. And he was a great enthusiast of Ford. I hadn't realized how literary he was in that sense, that he'd read so much. That's where his heart was, in a way."

But when Brad Darrach spent a week in early 1974 observing Millar for a *People* magazine story, the mask seemed firmly back in place. "He was a very controlled man, facially," Darrach said. "It wasn't that he was consciously trying to hide; I think he was pretty open. I think decisions had been made long, long ago that a lot of impulses had to be cemented solid, so they wouldn't get loose.

"I had the feeling he was *manacled* to his wife, and maybe she to him. I was aware of the ravine in their marriage: something very fundamental had happened between them, and I felt it had reached the point where there was barely civility. It was a really arid home atmosphere when I was there. From things he said, I got the impression she was a person who had either taken a terrible blow or made a decision that she was massively aggrieved: the whole abandonment of her writing, for one thing. I had a feeling as in certain earthquakes: you know how the bottom will fall out of an area, like a limestone sink? It was as though the bottom had fallen out of her in some way, and she had to reestablish her whole life; and I had a feeling she had decided to do it in some way without him. And it all centered around the daughter, I'm sure.

"He talked a great deal about his daughter; it was much on his mind. I remember him talking about the daughter taking cough medicine and drinking it when she was small: that should have been a *clue* to them, but it wasn't. He was intending to write a book about all of that. Of course the theme of the disappearing daughter occurs all through his books, but I think he meant to write something very direct about that whole experience. What happened during that period between him and his wife I think was an area that was sheathed in some kind of silence.

"When he and his wife were together, there was a numbness. She was almost surly. In fact I would say she *was* surly. I didn't see it a lot, 'cause they weren't together a lot in my presence. But it was like, 'Leave me *out* of this; I don't want to be *involved* in this.' " Darrach's story recorded this vignette:

One day in the beach club pool, Margaret is asked teasingly, "How does it feel to be married to a great man?"

"Haa!" she yelps. "Ask Mrs. Nixon!" Whirling, she splashes water in her husband's face. "And how does it feel to be married to a great woman?"

"Uuuhhh!" he groans. "I can't say it's like climbing Everest—but maybe Annapurna."

"Yet when she had me to herself," Darrach said, "she was very pleasant and sweet. I think she was a woman comfortable talking about subjects in which she was interested, and not comfortable talking about herself. She was clearly not going to talk about anything personal; we certainly didn't talk about the daughter. She was like a person who had accepted a mold: 'Okay, this is it, this is who I am, this is what I'm gonna do—and that's *all* I'm gonna do, and you can't have any more of me.' She was not a woman with many friends, I think.

"There was some similarity between them, in that sense of accepting limitations. But in her case, it was resentful; in his case, it was more fear-based, like, 'I *have* to set limits or I might explode, or my life would fly apart, or there's an abyss I might fall into.' You felt he was a more endangered person. She felt self-secure in ways that he did not; there was something about him that was clinging to her.

"He accepted that role in the relationship; I have a feeling it must have gone back before this terrible thing happened with the daughter. Because it's like his wife had the eephus on him, you know? And he couldn't shake it.

"I think he chose constriction, in his writing and in his marriage. I do admire his books. In my opinion they're not 'great works of art,' but they're remarkable; there's artistic and emotional power in them, and an unusual amount of it. He's certainly up there with the most interesting masters of that form. But for him to write through Archer is *such* a constriction of the man he was. He was like a tree trying to grow up through a rock or something: he *struggled*. He had certain glittering talents, like his verbal flash, but they really weren't his best ones. He told me he'd felt he had no clear subject to write about; and so he accepted and used, obviously to great advantage, this mystery form, and he sort of wedged himself into it—like those square pears growing in a box, you know? He was constricted; he *chose* to be constricted—almost as though he were afraid of his own life force, of the things he might do if he didn't corset himself.

"I liked him. I felt he was a really valuable being. Every generation there must be a thousand Shakespeares around, you know? But getting through is another matter. I keep thinking of him in terms of things that grow; and he got blocked. Had to crawl up a wall rather than blossom in the open air. He was a bigger man than he ever got to be.

"I have an image of him in my mind, based on something he told me of him as a little boy in a little room, looking out a window, solitary, alone. Northern childhoods, you know? The bleakness, the barrenness, the grimness. I seem to remember a sense of waiting to live. And I had a feeling that went on to the end of his life, that waiting to live. It's sad. That was an important soul."

Margaret could be more than surly to Millar when no journalists were around. "I felt sometimes she was very cruel to him," said one friend who asked to remain nameless. "Sometimes if he was late for an appointment with her, he'd become very upset; he would. Because he *knew* he was in for trouble: she would shout at him, you know. But those were isolated incidents. For the most part she and he were very congenial with each other, and good friends. But I was disgusted with her sometimes. And she was disgusted with me sometimes, so we worked out even. But I felt like Ken was kind of on edge a lot. When I would phone to see whether I could come over some evening, he would almost always check with Maggie to see how she was feeling and if it would be all right, even though I would just be seeing him in his study. Frequently the answer would be no, it was not convenient. Of course that's her privilege; that was her home.

"It seems like there must have been some rivalry there. For years she was kind of the star of the family; and then gradually, gradually, he came along and kind of overtook her. I don't know whether that created any problem or not. Maggie's an original; she's not like anybody else, and I had great admiration for her. But I think she'd be difficult to live with. And I felt like Ken was a vulnerable person, and I felt bad for him sometimes."

To a New York friend going through a rough marital patch, Millar confided, "Margaret's and my marriage has been very close to the edge at times, though not in recent years. I am glad now that we held on, gradually changing from lovers to friends, loving friends. I guess I don't believe in endings." When Julian Symons asked in 1974 if the couple might come to a planned World Crime Writers Conference in England, Millar replied, "It's very doubtful that Margaret will attend . . . since she stopped writing crime fiction some four years ago. I hope she comes back to writing eventually, but at the present time she's just beginning to *read* again. Our daughter Linda's death, which occurred some four years ago, was a blow to Margaret. But her pleasure in life and nature is reviving, though I don't think to the point where she would be ready for the big trip once again. I brought her home in poor shape from the last one." To Bill Ruehlmann, Millar said he had "to limit my time away from home, where our life is slow and quiet and demanding and intricate, and has to be paid attention to."

Despite such demands, Millar was grateful. "I must say I enjoy the variety of this later life," he told Ruchlmann. One diversion he and Margaret both enjoyed was watching some of the filming of a TV movie based on *The Underground Man.* The first project from Millar's elaborate Filmways deal, this Paramount television feature starred Peter Graves (fresh from the long-running *Mission: Impossible*) as Lew Archer and was also the pilot for a possible Archer series.

Millar approved of Graves ("a serious and very pleasant man") as his detective; in fact, he told *LA Times* columnist Cecil Smith, he'd had a sort of premonition about the actor: "In thirty years of writing about Lew Archer, I never thought much about how he looked. Except that he was Californian, tanned, athletic. Then one night a few years ago, I saw Peter on *Mission: Impossible* and thought, 'That's Lew Archer; that's the way he looks.' It was really quite eerie when I was told Peter was playing Lew, because I had nothing at all to do with the casting. Even stranger was the casting of Dame Judith [Anderson] as Mrs. Snow. All the way through the writing of the book, the image I had in mind for Mrs. Snow was Judith Anderson, who is a neighbor of ours in Santa Barbara. It gives you the feeling of having had it all happen before." Another thing Millar noted with surprise was how much he identified with his fictional character: whenever one of the actors in a scene addressed "Archer," Millar looked up.

After seeing a few days' filming at the Santa Barbara courthouse, he and Margaret went by limo to LA (the first drive there for either of them in years) to see interior scenes shot. Millar made another unexpected connection: the Benedict Canyon location house was the former home of early film cowboy Fred Thompson, a celluloid hero of Millar's Wiarton youth. In his quiet way, Millar seemed to be having a ball. "Rather fun discussing characterizations with Dame Judith and Peter Graves," he wrote Wolfe. Cecil Smith described the Millars watching the action "as intently as any star-struck tourists." Judith Anderson told *People* magazine, "The director was always saying, 'Judy baby, Judy baby.' Finally Mr. Macdonald couldn't control himself and he said very softly and gently, 'We in Santa Barbara wouldn't ever call her that.' The director asked, 'Well, why not? What would you call her?' And Mr. Macdonald said, 'We'd call her Dame

Judy baby.' " A cameraman took a still shot of the Millars with Graves: Millar, head cocked, gives the actor an up-from-under glance and a quizzical smile, as if asking, "Is that you, Lew?" Margaret Millar favors Graves with a pleased grin. "These are good days," Millar wrote Bruccoli, "and Margaret agrees."

There was something else to be happy about in 1974: the Mystery Writers of America, on the twenty-fifth anniversary of the first Archer book, was at last honoring Ross Macdonald—not with a best-novel Edgar but with the organization's Grandmaster Award for distinction in the mystery genre. New Awards chairman Ed Hoch had a lot to do with the MWA's ex-president getting this special Edgar, whose previous recipients included Agatha Christie, Rex Stout, Ellery Queen, Erle Stanley Gardner, Georges Simenon, James M. Cain, Alfred Hitchcock—and (in 1972) John D. MacDonald. "That was one of the points I made," said Hoch. "I said, 'Hey, how come you've al*ready* honored John *D.* MacDonald, and you've never honored *Ross* Macdonald?'—who, to my mind at least, was a much better writer." Millar was delighted with the honor: "a kind of longevity award," he described it to his teenage correspondent Jeff Ring. "A number of nice things have happened to me," Millar told Mike Avallone, "but nothing (except my wife) nicer than this." To Peter Wolfe, he wrote, "I'll finally have an Edgar."

As usual he went to New York alone, and stayed at the Algonquin. Glad as he was to receive his honor, Millar didn't want any special publicity fuss made; he nixed Bantam's bid to arrange TV appearances. "He seemed to be a very shy man, or at least he wanted to stay out of the limelight," said Hoch, who met Millar at the Essex House for the Edgar dinner on Friday, May 3. "My wife and I greeted him, and there were a certain number of press people who wanted to interview him—and we saw him at one point sneaking out around the back of a curtain, to avoid being trapped by the press!" Roger Simon, also at the dinner, said, "I remember him being treated like a real celebrity there. I have a visceral memory of him in the Essex House lounge, with everyone grouped around him, and a very confused look on his face. I think he realized he was a good writer, and quite clearly he took it seriously; but I think at a certain point his fame took off in a way beyond what he expected. And he wasn't the kind of man who'd court that, in the way that people in the movies court the press and expect it. With Ken, given his inherent shyness, I think it came from over his shoulder; it sneaked up on him. I think this was a man who received more accolades than he ever expected."

The dinner in the Essex House Colonnades had five hundred guests. Millar sat at a table with Dorothy Olding, Ash Green, and other Knopf people. "The most touching moment of the evening," reported the MWA newsletter, "came when Ross Macdonald in his shy, quiet voice, as he received the Grandmaster Award said, 'We have one Edgar in our home on the fireplace,' referring to that won by his wife, Margaret Millar, for her

Beast in View. 'And sometimes late at night we hear the sound of crying. But now,' holding up *his* Edgar, 'he won't be lonely. Thank you.' " Millar wrote Bruccoli, "They finally decided to accept this rude westerner as one of their own."

Photographer Jill Krementz chronicled Macdonald's Manhattan visit for *People,* taking pictures at the Edgar dinner and at the Knopf and Ober offices. (She also photographed Millar in Santa Barbara.) His last day in New York, a Saturday, Millar lunched with Krementz and her companion, Kurt Vonnegut ("most pleasant, and seems to serve *in loco parentis* to a whole group of younger writers," Millar noted approvingly). That day Krementz took a classic picture of Ross Macdonald: a haunting head shot of the author in his forties-style fedora, staring with sober compassion straight in the lens, looking for all the world like Lew Archer. This indelible image would loom from the back jacket of what would be Ross Macdonald's last novel, completing a passage begun with the noir silhouette on the first Archer book: in a quarter century, author had merged with creation. Macdonald became Archer, or Archer became him.

The same couldn't be said of Peter Graves, playing Archer in the two-hour TV feature *The Underground Man.* Graves did his stolid best in the film, which had its "world premiere" on *NBC Monday Night at the Movies* May 6, but the odds were against him. The novel's plot had been truncated and Archer's persona fiddled with. This TV Archer lived in the past, watching reruns of forties movies, stocking his booze in a safe lined with a W. C. Fields poster, playing bland pseudo-jazz on his car's eight-track. His "office" was a café-bar run by a former cop; barkeep and Archer played a running trivia game with old songs, plays, and films. But the PI was with-it enough to swap slang with a seedy hippie: "Lay something new on me." Despite a good supporting cast and some nice Santa Barbara locations, the movie was lackluster and tedious.

"I'm sorry it didn't turn out better," Millar wrote Peter Wolfe, "but it did present a structural problem, and, even in cut-down form, there was too much material for the script-writer to handle. I enjoyed it in parts, however, especially the scenes between Graves and [Jack] Klugman, and thought that Graves was appealing in the rôle." When Matt Bruccoli said he'd viewed *The Underground Man* in company with F. Scott Fitzgerald's daughter Scottie, Millar told him, "I would rather watch her than it. Paramount spent a lot of money on it, and hired some good actors, but the script seemed rather obscure and hysterical. You can't say that about Scottie Fitzgerald."

Even before the film aired, NBC turned thumbs-down on an Archer series. That was fine by him, Millar wrote Wolfe: "a constant interest in a TV series—and who can avoid such interest . . . could become a real problem." But the network changed its mind after *The Underground Man* drew well over 12 million viewers despite a minimum of promotion. Quick plans were made to film an Archer series for the coming winter. At first it was said Jackie Cooper would play Archer (no more peculiar a choice than Dick Powell as Marlowe), but when the ink was dry it was Brian Keith signed to star in thirteen hour-long episodes of a series that would replace the eight-year-old *Ironside*. Millar would receive $2,000 an episode in royalty and consultant fees; if the series was successful, Paramount would likely protect its "exclusivity rights" by paying Millar a further $150,000.

Out of vogue a dozen years ago, private eyes were back in fashion. Recent TV detectives included Mannix, Cannon, and Barnaby Jones. They were joined in 1974 by Harry-O and Jim Rockford of *The Rockford Files*. Millar traced this screen wave of private eyes directly to the 1966 success of *Harper*. The trend achieved its aesthetic peak with the 1974 film *Chinatown,* in which Jack Nicholson played a PI in 1930s Los Angeles; *LA Times* reviewer Charles Champlin called Robert Towne's *Chinatown* script an "homage à trois" to Hammett, Chandler, and Macdonald: "As in Ross Macdonald . . . the present villainies have blood ties to the buried past."

Several more big-screen detective stories went into production in the wake of *Chinatown*'s release, among them another movie of a Macdonald book: Paul Newman agreed to star with wife, Joanne Woodward, in a feature based on *The Drowning Pool,* to be produced for Twentieth Century–Fox by the men who had made *Harper*. Warners would release the film, which would shoot in Louisiana in October; the story's locale was switched from southern California to Lake Charles and New Orleans (Woodward's old stomping grounds). It seemed at first the tangle of contracts governing all the Macdonald projects would force this film's detective to assume yet another identity; the movie for a while was titled *Ryan's the Name*. But an arrangement was made enabling Newman's character to be called Lew Harper, with the movie's title *The Drowning Pool*.

There were other film projects based on Macdonald and Millar books: Viacom optioned *The Ferguson Affair* for a television feature; a Canadian producer bought rights to *The Three Roads*. Millar was receiving TV and movie money regularly: thirty thousand dollars here, sixty thousand dollars there. *The Drowning Pool* deal was especially good, giving Macdonald an eventual one hundred thousand dollars plus 5 percent of net profits. Millar told Hank Coulette (not to boast but as fact) that these deals would make Macdonald a millionaire. Naturally such projects were gratifying, but they were also distracting for a man who felt it his duty to write books. As Millar also told Coulette, he had to do his main work before he was sixty: that's as long as he could trust his health, given a family history of strokes and other illness. In 1974 he'd turn fifty-nine. "Too many awards," he worried to Bruccoli, "not enough books."

Writing, his defense against the world, had become his world. The scenes he made up while sitting in a darkened room seemed more real to Millar than his own life. Yet he had less energy for creation these days; it seemed to demand more concentration. Critical or nonfiction prose came especially hard: doing the three-thousand-word introduction to his suspense anthology took him six weeks. He begged off writing a foreword for the trade publication of Bill Ruehlmann's groundbreaking dissertation, *Saint with a Gun: The Unlawful American Private Eye*, though he was proud of his young friend's achievement: "Time, which I used to have nothing but of, is now in short supply."

When Millar started sneaking up on a novel this spring, his blood pressure climbed steeply. It took two months of preparation before a breakthrough into actual writing, he told Wolfe; yet when summer came, his attention wandered. "Authors get weary of their own work and sometimes like to forget about it," Millar told Jeff Ring. "At the moment I am forgetting my authorial pains in the pleasure of owning a new pup." This was Skye, a German shepherd, his second new dog since Brandy's death. He found other distractions: he wrote a poem (his first in years), enjoyed another visit from Dorothy Olding, wrote Bantam's Marc Jaffe about paperback sales. ("The Macdonald books go on and on," Jaffe reported, "with SLEEPING BEAUTY off to a strong start. We have 432,000 copies in print at the moment.")

Millar went to New York a second time in 1974, to publicize the Macdonald-edited *Great Stories of Suspense*. He even agreed to some television interviews: "Am slated to appear on TV yoked with [Watergate figure] E. Howard Hunt," he told Wolfe, "(who started with an early book as a Knopf author). Strange bedfellows, life makes." The Hunt appearance fell through, but Millar enjoyed himself in Manhattan: lunching with Ping Ferry and wife at the Yale Club, going to Michael's Pub to hear pianist Marian McPartland, and having such a good time in general that he felt he'd overcome his long-standing East Coast dread.

Back in Santa Barbara, his manuscript waited. Millar was at work on it as another birthday approached. He had a striking way of announcing the onset of a new book: "The rats are stirring again," he'd say. Some scurried out of his poor Canadian past, but he put them through their paces in privileged California, a place filled with people (like him) who'd come here from elsewhere to reinvent themselves.

"Santa Barbara was an elephant burial ground," Jerre Lloyd said. "People migrated there after acquiring a pile somewhere else, and you were always curious about how they'd gotten it. The 'new money' people were always careful not to talk about its origins. I felt the reason these people didn't like to speak about their past was that they didn't want to remind themselves of where they came from; but many of them were *so* secretive, it couldn't help but pique your curiosity. I'm sure this phenomenon affected Ken as much as anyone." When Lloyd asked what the central idea of *The Underground Man* was, Millar said, "Money stolen during the war, blown up on the bull market: that's where a lot of these people got it."

He often felt like an outsider in California, and especially in Hope Ranch. But when Ken and Margaret Millar dressed for Sunday brunch at the Coral Casino or the Biltmore, they blended in with the visiting corporate execs and with other Hope Ranch dwellers; and they seemed proud of the niche they'd earned on their own terms in the Santa Barbara scheme of things. "They waited and waited over a period of years," Jackie Coulette said, "and finally got *the number one* cabana at the Coral Casino beach club. It wasn't anything special—just a bare little three-sided room with a few lounge chairs in it—but they felt they had truly arrived! It did have a wonderful view of the ocean, and of the pool and the other cabanas. It was the best lookout." Maggie was an especially gleeful observer of the club goings-on, journalist Sally Ogle Davis wrote: "From the Millars' cabana number 22 in the favored upper tier, she had a bird's eye view of the human comedy. 'Look at her,' Maggie would declare, pointing out a grande dame of Santa Barbara society. 'Everything's been lifted but her morals!' "

But the longer he lived in California, the more Millar's thoughts turned to Canada. He said a Canadian found himself by going elsewhere. Millar had found himself as Ross Macdonald, California novelist: watching the natives with an outsider's eye, in the tradition of such archetypal California writers as Frank Norris and Raymond Chandler of Illinois, and Dashiell Hammett and James M. Cain of Maryland, not to mention such resident and visiting aliens as England's Christopher Isherwood and Evelyn Waugh. Having earned his California identity, Millar was tantalized by the idea of disinterring his Canadian past; he was also scared of it. He wrote Julian Symons in 1972, "As I get older and look forward and back, I wonder if I can undertake the kind of family and personal history that I could, and probably should, write for Ontario. It's too soon yet though, to embrace all that old sadness, the substance of my mother, the shadow of my father." In 1974, Millar wrote Symons, "I hope I live long enough to write my own biography, as I have long intended to do. But not yet. There's still more living to do now, before I come full circle to my Pacific Coast beginnings." What he would try to do first, he said, was round off the Archer saga in some satisfying way: "The book I am working up now is last but one, I think, though it could serve as the last if it had to." Time, Millar knew, was his enemy: the foe that defeated all Archers. As Macdonald told some Santa Barbara college kids who interviewed him, "I started out aiming at posterity. Now I'm just aiming at the present."

First confession of the day: I have never read any of Ross Macdonald's private-eye fictions. Second confession: After watching the
first episode of NBC's *Archer,* a new weekly series exploiting the
character created by Mr. Macdonald, I doubt I will ever read any of
his private-eye fictions.

> —John J. O'Connor, *New York Times,* January 1975

The Drowning Pool (Warner Bros.) . . . This one was made from a
novel by Ross Macdonald that I haven't read, but he's generally
been better than he's made to look here. Before three minutes
are up you know you're in for a lot of sententious imitation Chandler: a private eye getting into a situation that is supposed to evoke
moral resonances for our time. But it doesn't have the usual tight
beginning of suspense films that usually come unglued; this one
begins unglued.

> —Stanley Kauffmann, *The New Republic,* July 1975

Millar was at last well into a new manuscript by early 1975, a book
he meant to be the next-to-last Archer—or the last, if need be. It
was linked in a roundabout way to the series' first book, dealing
as it did with the disappearance of a once-famous artist, an idea that grew
from the missing-author plot that had been the seed of *The Moving Target.*
Millar made Archer's "target" a kidnapped oilman and kept the vanished
author in reserve; as he reworked the plot over time, the missing author
became a vanished painter. In choosing this tale for the penultimate
Archer, Millar traced a long circle through his spiral-bound notebooks
back to Archer's origins.

He liked his manuscript and the name he'd found for it, *The Blue Hammer,* a reference to the human pulse-vein, from a line in a poem by Hank
Coulette. Millar kept his working title a secret, making puns on it that only
he got: "I'm busy on another Archer novel," he wrote Bruccoli, "for which
I have a smashing but secret title"; he told Sipper, "All I have to do is jack
it up and put a good book under it."

He struggled with the book, though, in ways new to him. "My style
seems to be changing," he said with surprise to Peter Wolfe. "Style is really
quite involuntary, at least in these later stages." Friend and neighbor Ted
Clymer said, "Ken spoke of working mightily to bring the parts and pieces
of his book together; it just seemed that that task was becoming increasingly difficult. He told me once that he found that a modest amount of
alcohol was a helpful stimulant to getting things started."

Meanwhile TV took another shot at Lew Archer, with a one-hour series
starting January 30 on NBC. The results were poor. *LA Times* columnist

Cecil Smith wrote, "To all Lew Archer fans, I must regretfully report this ain't him." The *New York Times*'s "Cyclops" also thought the series violated the spirit and content of Macdonald: "*Archer* is merely a confusion of head-lines and the going paranoia."

Series star Brian Keith had plans to pull the show farther away from Macdonald; he told the *LA Times* if the show was picked up for a second season, he'd insist it be filmed in Hawaii: "I've got it in writing. I've even worked out how Archer would operate in the islands. I figure he'd proba-bly live on a boat." Keith (a Hawaii resident) seemed to be confusing Archer with Travis McGee, John D. MacDonald's character, whose address was a Florida houseboat. Cecil Smith mused, "You wonder how Ken Millar . . . would take to an Hawaiian Archer."

Millar's disappointment was apparent in a laconic letter written to Jeff Ring the day after *Archer*'s first episode: "You may wish to be told that Archer so-called is appearing on TV these next twelve weeks, Thursday nights, in the person of Brian Keith. He's an accomplished actor, and about the right age. I have nothing to do with the scripts, except that I read them." Soon he was spared even that. In early February, after only two broadcasts, NBC canceled *Archer* in what *Daily Variety* called "one of the speediest executions on record." The network cited poor ratings and bad reviews as its reasons. Actually ratings were good: a 24 Nielsen share, nearly 10.5 million viewers. But killing the series saved NBC a costly move to Hawaii, and Paramount wouldn't have to pay Millar $150,000 "exclusiv-ity rights."

Another film project gave Millar a pretext to get away from his novel in April and go to Toronto, where he told Bob Ford, "*The Three Roads* is, if all goes well, to be shot as a movie for its sins." The author's visit was appar-ently meant to attract financial backing. Millar appeared on some TV shows and gave newspaper interviews, then went to Kitchener to visit Mar-garet's father (now ninety), something he almost always did when travel-ing East. From Kitchener he went to Manhattan and the Mystery Writers of America annual dinner at the New York Hilton, where Ed Hoch tapped Macdonald at the last minute to present Eric Ambler with this year's Grandmaster Award.

Back in Santa Barbara, Millar soon had another occasion with which to distract himself: the Santa Barbara Writers Conference, an affair that had grown in a few years from a small event with a couple dozen attendees to a weeklong gathering that drew people from all over the Coast. The confer-ence in a way was an outgrowth of the writers' lunch, and Ross Macdonald had taken part in every one so far. Barnaby Conrad, the main organizer, had gotten Joan Didion to participate in 1974. This year Millar arranged for Eudora Welty to attend.

"I don't do those things much, but I wanted to do that," Welty said. "It meant I could spend a week in Santa Barbara. When I got there, it was late in the evening, like ten-thirty. Ken met my plane, and he said, 'Now I thought maybe the first thing you'd like to do would be to sort of get your bearings; I wanted to show you where the ocean is.' Well, that's exactly what I would like, you know: I had reached there, and I wanted to know how I was located. So he drove me around, in that soft California dark; and we got out of the car, and we walked down to the ocean, someplace where the road goes down to a beach house or something. So he had thought of everything to show me, and I just loved it; I had a wonderful time."

Welty stayed at the Miramar, where the conference was held. "Ken drove me all over the place," she said. "He showed me everything that he loved about Santa Barbara. He really gave me a sort of look at what his life was like. One of the things that he took me to see was the courthouse, to sit in on some trial, which he and Margaret did all the time. And I could see them at their cabana and everything. We were sitting looking off at some view once and all of a sudden this man flew out, just like a miracle of some kind; I'd never seen anybody hang-glide before. But the best times I had in Santa Barbara were the long rides we took in the car, when Ken took and showed me everything."

Millar's feelings for Welty were as strong as ever. When Jill Krementz sent him a print of a photograph she'd taken of Welty in her Jackson garden, he described the qualities he saw in it: "Pathos, gentleness, courage, feminine fluorescence and iron discipline, the blessed light at the windows. Your picture goes to the heart, as its subject does, and I am going to have to hang it on my wall." Welty's admiration for Millar was also undimmed. "A supremely moral writer" who "cares about the welfare of each human soul in his novels" is what Welty called Ross Macdonald when she introduced him at the Writers Conference—at the same time noting the "basic absurdity" of her presenting this author in a region he'd made his own. She likened it to someone "on a first visit to the Mediterranean Sea, introducing to it the Rock of Gibraltar."

Macdonald was probably known on Gibraltar too. His work was finding admirers in ever more remote corners. From Moscow, Bob Ford wrote and asked would Millar send an inscribed copy of one of his novels for the poet Andrey Voznesensky, protégé of Boris Pasternak: Voznesensky, Ford said, had been reading Macdonald with great pleasure in both English and Russian. Millar was overwhelmed. "He is the most eminent poet I ever heard from," he told Ford, "and I still haven't gotten over it."

Adding a bit to Macdonald's American fame was *The Drowning Pool* film with Paul Newman as Lew Harper, released in the United States in the summer of 1975. "Harper days are here again!" claimed its ads, but this movie had none of *Harper*'s style. Some critics were harsh ("The film is poor," Penelope Gilliatt, the *New Yorker*) and some tolerant ("Just enjoy it for the intelligent escapism it is," Vincent Canby, the *New York Times*). Millar found the film violent and unpleasant, as when Harper rebuffs a teenager's sexual advance by slapping her and saying, "Sorry about that." "No, you're not," she taunts. "You're right," Harper admits, "I'm not." Jokes about hitting kids weren't funny to Millar. "You didn't miss a thing with the *Drowning Pool,*" he wrote Ping Ferry. "I finally saw it last week and considered it a poor amoral movie, I'm sorry to say." He was starting to think that if he wanted a decent film made from one of his books, he'd have to write it himself. Other movies meanwhile were siphoning off some of Macdonald's feel and material. *Night Moves,* said by reviewers to show a Macdonald influence, seemed to draw on Millar's biography for the character of its private eye, "driven to search out his own father, who had long ago abandoned him."

As Macdonald's presence on the popular-culture scene grew, envy of his success seemed to increase. Jane S. Bakerman, a professor of English from Indiana State University, said, "The first time I went to Bouchercon," an annual gathering of mystery authors and readers begun in 1970 in honor of Anthony Boucher, "a bunch of younger hard-boiled writers were sitting around on a panel talking about how out-of-date Ross Macdonald was. And I was getting madder and madder, thinking, 'You guys should be grateful for his keeping the genre alive so you could all eventually get published.' What they were really saying was *they* wanted to be as famous as Ross Macdonald, and right *now.*"

Though some of Macdonald's "colleagues" felt he had it made, Millar worked as hard as ever on his new manuscript all through 1975. It was turning into his longest book yet, and for some reason the hardest to write. "I seem to be getting wordier," he told Ferry. After having been in love for so long with his *Blue Hammer* title, he now had doubts about it and asked what Ferry thought of *Portrait of the Artist as a Dead Man.* When he mailed his typescript to New York in September, it was officially called *The Tarantula Hawk.* A few weeks later, he dropped that for *The Silent Hammer,* from a variant line in the same Coulette poem. Finally Millar went back to *The Blue Hammer.*

A similar uncertainty seemed reflected in the text. "When I read the manuscript of *The Blue Hammer* before it was submitted, I sensed a change, a softening, not only in tone but in diction," Bob Easton wrote. "I mentioned this to Ken as part of my usual criticism. He said it was deliberate. He said he wanted to be deliberately a little mellower, a little gentler, a little more tolerant. But I sensed also a lessening of tension, a loosening of overall grip. . . . I was a bit shocked and startled at what appeared to be lapses such as I'd never seen." Easton advised several word changes and even some structural revision. Millar surprised him again by not bristling at the suggestions but simply following them. He made other changes suggested by Ralph Sipper.

Millar complained mildly that everything took him longer these days, and that there was less time to do it in. "My life seems to be spaced out by endless delays," he told Steven Carter. Some were of his own making. He agreed to go to England alone for three weeks in October to attend a crime writers' conference and get out in the countryside he and Margaret had missed seeing on their truncated 1971 trip. His ticket was bought and his hotel booked, but the day before he was due to leave, he canceled. "Margaret had a cancer removed from her face the other day," he explained to Ferry, "and while they got it all (all the way down to the bone) it's been causing her distress both physical and emotional, and she's not in the best shape to be left alone." On the plus side, Margaret had recently begun writing a mystery: her first manuscript since Linda's death five years ago, and another reason for Millar not to upset her equilibrium. (Maggie's plot, which she'd first tried to get Ken to use, involved a woman shackled to a husband whose mind veers in and out of awareness, causing him to confuse past with present.)

Millar used the weeks of his canceled trip to make still more revisions on *The Blue Hammer*. Working every day of October, he came up with another five thousand words: an entirely new last chapter. On November 5 he mailed this latest typescript to Knopf, who scheduled the book's publication for June 1976. It might not be the best Archer, Millar told friends, but it was certainly the longest—and his first in three years.

Knopf was quick to let booksellers know about it, listing it with other titles in an ad on the front cover of *Publishers Weekly* in December: "**Ross Macdonald.** His new Lew Archer novel, **THE BLUE HAMMER,** is certain to be yet another bestseller. June, $7.95." In Sarasota, Florida, Millar's old colleague John D. MacDonald, whose Travis McGee books had color-coded titles (*The Deep Blue Goodby, Nightmare in Pink,* etc.) glimpsed this line and saw red; he typed a two-page, single-spaced letter to Millar that reached him a few days after his sixtieth birthday. MacDonald was "bemused and depressed" about the new Archer title, he wrote, for it was sure to cause confusion with his McGee books:

> I will assume that neither you nor anyone at Knopf had the slightest idea of any meretricious opportunism in going with a color title at this stage. Let me even assume that you and Knopf will feel outraged and insulted that I should imply that there was anything deliberate about it.
>
> I am willing to believe you.
>
> But there is a big sleazy commercial world out there, to which such hitch-hiking is a way of life. Dozens of dim little talents have come out with bad books with color titles since McGee became successful. Regardless of your and Knopf's innocence on all counts, people are not going to believe that you and Knopf have no knowledge of the McGee books, the color titles, the public acceptance etc. People are going to chuckle, nod wisely and accuse you of a deliberate opportunism.

I really think it is a pretty dumb thing to do. . . . I feel that if it is not too late to alter that title, it would be a wise move.

There was a symmetry here, if Millar cared to see it: MacDonald's two out-of-the-blue letters a quarter century apart, the first concerning Archer's debut, the second about what might or might not be his farewell. But this time Millar didn't bother to respond. Life seemed too short.

The big guns of the Beat Generation, if their half of this fascinating anthology provides a fair sampling, are manned by culturally underprivileged poets and their critical mentors, and a mixed group of fiction writers who share an embarrassed distrust of traditional human relationships. . . . Broyard, significantly the only beat humorist, does very much better work.
—Kenneth Millar, "Passengers on a Cable Car Named Despair,"
San Francisco Chronicle, 1958

People have been telling me about Margaret Millar for years and now I am glad I didn't listen to them. Now that I have finally read one of her books, I have 21 more to look forward to.
—Anatole Broyard, "Ay, Ay, Ay, Margaret Millar," *New York Times*, 1976

I n a way it was like the good old days: she working away on a book, he about to have one published. But while Maggie was fired with creative energy at the start of 1976, Millar was worn out from wandering a year and a half in a forest of words called *The Blue Hammer*. When it was time to read the novel's proof, he called on fellow Fitzgerald-lover Bill Gault for help.

"We met in the parking lot of a country club near his home," Gault said. "Maggie's there with him. The day is dark, gloomy, windy. He hands me the proofs, and Maggie says, 'You guys look like a couple of secret agents, exchanging documents!' She was a funny woman; didn't take herself that seriously. He said, 'Look, this book—I'm havin' a little trouble, maybe you could check it.' I thought, 'Well, what do I know about this intellectual prose?' So I took it home and read it, and some of the things—I just couldn't get the connection. I said, 'Ken, I liked this, but this part here I didn't like.' Certain things I didn't understand. Well, he didn't say anything. But when the book came out, the stuff I'd suggested he take out was sorta taken out. So he must have listened to me, you know: the peasant, the paisan." Millar dedicated *The Blue Hammer* to Gault.

Without resting, Millar took on the writing of a first-draft screenplay of *The Instant Enemy* for a novice producer. Since film rights to Archer were tied up, he changed the story's detective's name to Lou Darnell. He didn't do the job for the money (though he was paid Writers Guild scale and was allowed to join the union health plan); he did it in hopes it would lead to a good movie. Millar wanted to see one first-rate film made from a Ross Macdonald book: something as good as *The Big Sleep* or *The Maltese Falcon* or *Chinatown*. Completing this rough-draft treatment on top of *Hammer* left him mentally exhausted. For the first time in thirty-five years Millar had no definite writing plans.

"I said, 'Well, what are you going to do now?'" recalled Frank Mac-Shane, who saw Ken Millar in New York City in April 1976. "And he said, 'How do *I* know? I'm going to relax and have some fun.'"

MacShane, who'd just published his Chandler biography (which Millar thought excellent), saw Millar at a small cocktail party thrown for Ross Macdonald by Knopf in the library of the St. Regis Hotel, which the aging Knopf attended with wife Helen. MacShane was present by Millar's request; others Millar made sure were invited were Michael Avallone, Nona Balakian, Ray Sokolov, Walter Clemons, Joan Kahn, Lee Wright, and John Leonard.

MacShane saw more of Millar during his visit. On a Thursday afternoon, Millar guest-conducted a session of MacShane's graduate nonfiction workshop at Columbia. "In the class he was wonderful," MacShane said. "He was very responsible, and I suppose a little bit nervous because I think he found it awkward to speak off-the-cuff, so he had these notes; and he talked about his childhood, and how he and his wife had grown up together in that village in Canada, and how they'd got started. And it was very *interesting!*" MacShane especially wanted him to read the work of student Jane Bernstein (later a novelist), a great Macdonald admirer.

"I had started to read mysteries with my husband," Bernstein remembered, "and we'd read everything that Macdonald had ever written; we really loved him. I think of myself primarily as a fiction writer, but who knows these days. And in that nonfiction class I wrote for the first time about my sister's murder. My sister was murdered in 1966 in Tempe, Arizona, by somebody she'd never met. After ten or eleven years, I was really just at a point where I was ready to think about it in any way. So I wrote about that, and Ken was a visitor to this—I guess they called them master classes in those days. He was running the workshop the day I handed in that piece, and he was very affected by it. So it was kind of a nice moment for me, to be admired by somebody I admired very greatly." Bernstein's story seemed to remind Millar of his own late daughter, she said: "He was extremely moved by it. Now, hearing about Linda, I think part of what really attracted him in some way was the story about a troubled young woman; I think that's what must have connected in such a strange way for him." To Bernstein, Millar seemed extremely shy: "Very very quiet, very uncomfortable, very uneasy with himself. It felt as if he was kind of a stranger in his own body."

She and Millar corresponded. In his first letter, he told her, "To a writer who has been at it for quite a while, nearly forty years, and especially to one who has been a teacher, too, it means a great deal to have been of interest or use to a writer from a succeeding generation. You throw something—a horseshoe?—into the air, and if you're lucky you'll later hear a clang. Your letter was a clang." Of her work in progress, he volunteered, "I'd be glad to help in any way I can, at whatever stage."

MacShane saw Millar again during his April trip, at a National Book

Critics Circle panel MacShane moderated. Nona Balakian, secretary of the year-old NBCC, had asked Ross Macdonald to be part of the group's first symposium on criticism, held at Columbia's Low Library. Other panelists included novelists Hortense Calisher and Wilfrid Sheed, book editors Tom Congdon and Richard Seaver, and critics Maurice Dolbier and Anatole Broyard. They were all to talk about "the state of book reviewing in the country today from various perspectives." Millar spoke first and argued for a gently civilized approach by reviewers: "Even when they're faced with fairly worthless books, such as some of my early books were, one thing that the critics should do, I think, is avoid unnecessary punishment. 'Cause I really think it's possible for an extremely unfriendly review to silence a man, sometimes permanently." In an analogy that seemed as much a Millaresque formula for a happy home life as a critical method, he said, "The relationship between author and critic is really, and should be, a very intimate one: almost like a marriage, or a brotherhood. Each should be willing to listen to the other—and I think the closest to silence the transaction can become, the better."

The panel's other reviewers disagreed, especially Anatole Broyard, the waspish *Times* man who'd savaged *Sleeping Beauty*. Broyard said, "Mr. Macdonald says a bad review might silence certain novelists. I've tried as hard as I can! A publisher told me that the sales of a certain well-known writer, a best-seller, have fallen off appreciably—he flattered me—he said as a result of my review. . . . I said in that review that a well-established reputation is the hardest thing in the world to lose. And I think it's the critic's job to shake a few of these well-established reputations." The Louisiana-born Broyard was an interesting case. Supposedly at work for years on an unseen piece of fiction (in introducing him, Balakian referred to his "forthcoming novel," which never did come forth), he was thin and strikingly handsome, so fair-skinned that most assumed he was Caucasian; few knew Broyard was African-American. He might have been a character from a Macdonald novel, one of those people who move to another state and discard an unwanted past. (In fact in plot notebooks, Millar often considered the idea of a black person "passing" for white.) Like Anthony Boucher, whose initials he shared, Broyard won fame reviewing fiction for the *New York Times*. Unlike Boucher, Broyard seemed gleeful at his *Times*-given power to wound. Millar, with a novel coming out soon, might have been wise to ignore Broyard's provocative statements ("On a given day of the week, there's only one book perhaps that's reviewable. . . . I can remember taking up a book and saying, 'This is the only reviewable book that I have in front of me, and it's not good' "), but they went too much against his grain. He told Broyard, "I don't accept your premise that there are just good books and bad books; most books are somewhere in between." Other panelists took courage and spoke back to Broyard too. "I don't think I said that," the reviewer countered, "but I'll let it go." Ross Macdonald would hear from Anatole Broyard later this year.

As usual Millar was in New York alone; Maggie still refused to go there. But she joined him later in Ontario, where they visited relatives, including her father, now in a Kitchener home for the blind. They also spent time in Toronto and Peterborough (where Hugh Kenner and Robertson Davies hailed from). In Peterborough, Millar called twenty-one-year-old university student Linwood Barclay, a new correspondent who'd sent him a novel manuscript, and invited him to dinner with Margaret's Peterborough kin.

"We talked a bit about his roots," said Barclay, later an editor at the *Toronto Star.* "He seemed very interested in me, and I think he must have been that way with most people. He seemed to pay such attention, as opposed to so many people who are waiting for a lull so that they can start talking. He was very open, very quiet, very gentle: almost fatherly, I guess, in a sort of way. I'd lost my father when I was sixteen, and I felt drawn towards other figures who were about my father's age at the time; and he seemed like a particularly nice one. I was so impressed at the time he took to answer my letters! Here I am just some young college student, and he spent so much energy reading these manuscripts I had written and commenting on them—which really I guess amazed me. I started reading him when I was in high school, probably with *The Chill.* You can't imagine the thrill that it was to have someone whom you just *revered* call you up and be so kind and show that sort of attention. I was walking on clouds for days." Barclay noticed something odd though during his hours with Millar: "A couple of times in the evening he seemed somewhat confused, almost like he couldn't figure out the floor plan of the house; he couldn't find the right door a couple of times."

Returning to Santa Barbara, Millar still felt worn out. He answered piled-up correspondence and made an effort to catch up on his reading ("as if I ever could"), enjoyed the presence of his thirteen-year-old grandson (now a novice surfer), who spent the summer with the Millars, and (encouraged by Julian Symons) made plans for another trip to England and Switzerland in September, this time with Margaret: "We're both past sixty and had better seize the day." Maggie seemed in fine fettle, having sold her first novel in six years (*Ask for Me Tomorrow*) to Random House (for thirty-five hundred dollars) and already at work on another. Millar was content to keep resting.

In June he was visited by Otto Penzler, an enterprising young editor-publisher who'd asked to do a collection of Millar's old *San Francisco Chronicle* book reviews. "He was very shy," Penzler recalled, "and so was I basically. It was difficult to maintain a conversation. So we sat in that cabana all day, looking over the beach, seeing the oil rigs out there. I guess it was about five in the afternoon when he finally said, 'Well, let's talk about the book. What do you want in it?' I don't know what made me say this, but I answered, 'What I'd *really* like to do would be a book of the complete Lew Archer short stories.' I'd just started my company, it was a very small press, I wouldn't have *dreamed* of asking him to let me publish a book like that; it would have been rude and presumptuous. But I blurted that out, and he said, 'Why, that would be all right.' I said, 'Oh, I don't think we should make that kind of an agreement here, I'm sure the people at Knopf would resent it terribly.' 'Well, no,' he said, 'I don't think they'll mind. Why, they've never asked me. And you have. And I'd like you to do the book.' I couldn't believe it was that simple! All you had to do was *ask*, and he said yes?" The volume Penzler produced a year later, *Lew Archer: Private Investigator,* went through four printings in twelve months, was selected by the Detective Book Club, and helped launch Penzler's Mysterious Press as an important crime-fiction imprint.

The fourth annual Santa Barbara Writers Conference in June 1976 gave Millar another reason not to resume writing just yet. For the second year in a row, Eudora Welty came from Mississippi to take part in the eight-day event. "Fortunately for the town and us, she seems to love it," Millar wrote Peter Wolfe, "and her presence simply elevates the atmosphere. . . . And Eudora took no money and paid her own hotel bill! That's dedication." Millar took Welty to a writers' lunch, which raised some eyebrows given his usual adamant stance against women there; and he brought her to the Hope Ranch house, which irritated his wife.

"It seems that Margaret had said she didn't ever want anybody to come to their house," Welty said. "This should just be *their* house." ("Our home is a special island away from society," Margaret Millar told a journalist in 1975. "We don't encourage guests.") "So there I was. She was nice to me, when she saw me there. On the other hand when she got mad, there wasn't anywhere to *go*. It could be pretty explosive; it could be anything. I used to get very upset inside, nothing I could do about it, when she would have a temper tantrum without any cause and just blast Ken to the devil, right in public. And slam doors, she was good at that. Everybody knew it, because she did it in public all the time. But Ken would say, 'Well, in a house with any two people, *any* two people, it can be like this.'

"I was there in Ken's house when one of the fellows who had enrolled in the Writers Conference came by with a manuscript. This was a man who was making his living in San Francisco and trying to be a writer on the side; and the whole time the man was in town he would see Ken privately and talk to him, which no one would know about except I just happened to be there. And Margaret is saying, 'He's *trash*, why do you want to fool with him?' You know. Another time he'd told one of these people to meet him at their beach club, and Margaret was furious: 'Why are you bringing that *crumb* in here?' And every time, Ken would just back off, impervious in a way, and make whatever change it was she wanted. Well, what else could you do?

"We were standing out in front of this restaurant they liked after dinner once, while Ken was fixing to bring the car: checking the trunk, this and that; and she just hated that he was taking so much time, that he wouldn't just *do* it. She said, 'Well, if we ever *split*, you'll know why.' Who cared? What was the big deal? But that was her way.

"For no reason at all once she said to me, 'When Ken is away, of course I open your letters to him, but only to see if there's anything in them he needs to be informed about.' I don't know why she told me that, but—I don't think she'd ever have found anything in any of them to give her pause."

Millar's participation in the conference (for which he and other workshop leaders were paid a token hundred dollars) was typically thorough and committed. Welty watched him conduct his session: "He took a manuscript that had been sent him and just went through it carefully for the benefit of the class, to show what was good and what was a mistake. It was a very patient examination, just like an editor would give. A lot of people were bored in the audience, because they—you know, they wanted somethin' else, I don't know what. But it was so good of him to do that, and he made a thorough study of it."

Millar singled out conference participant Fred Zackel for special attention. When Ross Macdonald publicly "waxed enthusiastic" over Zackel's "hard-boiled detective novel" in progress, it got written up in the *LA Times*. Millar helped Zackel greatly in the next few years, coaching and encouraging him to complete his manuscript, promoting it to Ash Green and to Harper and Row's Joan Kahn, putting Zackel together with Dorothy Olding, and finally giving a jacket quote when *Cocaine and Blue Eyes* was published in 1978. (The book was eventually made into a film starring football-player-turned-actor O. J. Simpson.) Zackel (who later earned a Ph.D. and became a university professor) wrote Millar, "I went to that first Santa Barbara Writers Conference 2½ years ago because I needed someone to tell me to quit trying to be a writer, to stop kidding myself, to say that my dream was worse than silly. I needed someone to tell me the dream had died. . . . And I thank you for stooping to help me. For knowing and caring about me. Your courtesy and gentleness and generosity were rare and strange to me. You gave a reason to me to go on. You gave me hope. Now you say I made it, that my book is a major accomplishment, that you're delighted with me. . . . God, how many times can I say thank you? Not nearly enough. Nowhere near enough. Thank you."

Millar was critiquing manuscripts at the 1976 conference when his own twenty-fourth novel (the eighteenth Archer) was published. *The Blue Hammer* was the most widely reviewed Macdonald book yet, covered by many midsize-city newspapers as well as the major New York and LA dailies and magazines. From one-sentence squibs to full-page essays, most reviews were positive, and many were raves: "brilliantly conceived and woven . . . very possibly his best" (John Seagraves, *Washington Star*), "he has seldom been in better form" (*The New Yorker*), "an excellent addition to the Archer canon" (Elmer R. Pry, *Chicago Tribune Book World*), "one of his best" (Walter Clemons, *Newsweek*), "perfect blend of style and action . . . as good as the more relentlessly 'serious' American novelists . . . and better than most" (William McPherson, *Washington Post Book World*).

Several critics perceived a maturing in Archer's outlook. Robert Kirsch wrote in the *LA Times:* "Lew Archer has changed. . . . He has become mellower, more involved with other people, vulnerable to autumnal romance, even concerned now with long-range balances." Kirsch picked up on those elements that softly echoed the first Archer book, *The Moving Target.* In *Target,* Archer fought a thug to his drowning death; faced with a similar chance in *Hammer,* Archer instead takes his prey into custody:

> For some reason, it became important to me that Rico shouldn't make it into the black water. . . . As I marched Rico back to my car and got him safely inside of it, I understood one source of my satisfaction. Twenty-odd years ago, near an oil-stained pier like this, I had fought in the water with a man named Puddler and drowned him.
>
> Rico, whatever his sins, had served as an equalizer for one of mine.

The affection between Archer and a younger woman reporter ("a level-eyed brunette of about thirty . . . well-shaped but rather awkward in her movements, as if she weren't quite at home in the world") delicately balanced the loss of his wife, Sue, first mentioned in *Target.* These subtle closures were what made Millar say *The Blue Hammer* could stand as the last Archer, "if it had to." Kirsch read the book as a possible precursor of things to come: "*The Blue Hammer* may be the bridge between the older Archer novels and some new shoreline of fiction. If so, Macdonald is the writer to do it . . . a master in his own right who's ready to explore new terrain."

The sour note in a near-universal chorus of praise was sounded by Anatole Broyard, who seemed to be exercising his avowed pleasure in trying to shake an established reputation. In his long *Times* review (in which he gave away most of the mystery's surprises), he said:

> Some time ago, a critic writing in *The New York Times* called Mr. Macdonald the author of "the best detective novels ever written by an American," and several of his books have been national best sellers. If I were to hazard an explanation of this phenomenon, I would suggest that this author is more popular than most because his mysteries are more mysterious than most. Perhaps his considerable audience is tired of the tyranny of causation. Here again is the arbitrariness and freedom of the fairy tale. Here is a prelogical world in which the grinding of fate's wheels is wholly unpredictable. . . . Mr. Macdonald's motto seems to be: Give them enough rope, and they will knot it. This does not, however, have the effect of making his people complex: They resemble, rather, a group of birds—parrots, perhaps—mindlessly beating their wings against the cage of his plot.

The Broyard slam was more or less countered by Michael Woods's favorable assessment in the *Times*'s Sunday *Book Review* ("Archer tracks the past more obsessively than ever, and the result is the best work Macdonald has done in a number of years"), and this time Millar kept his displeasure private. He really couldn't complain, he wrote Wolfe: "All the reviews have been favorable, with one notable exception which was almost laughably *contra*." Actually he was surprised at how good the book's notices were, he told Ping Ferry: "better than I expected in view of the difficulty I had finishing it."

The responses of bright readers often meant more to him than newspaper assessments. Chandler biographer Frank MacShane wrote Millar of *The Blue Hammer:* "It seems to me a perfect example of the power and potential of the murder story—the way in which the violence of our lives so often reveals the concessions and lies (and complete subversions of reality) we try unsuccessfully to repress. The violence shows that we cannot do it. The theme of living a lie under the illusion that somehow it is a way of survival is also poignantly revealed in your book, and I could not help but think of [Ford Madox Ford's] *The Good Soldier.* Apart from that, the novel is beautifully paced and is vivid without being picturesque, and that I think is one of your strengths (rather unlike Chandler's line). . . . And it seems to me you have solved at least for this story the problem of involvement that Chandler wrote of when he said that the detective could never get involved with the characters."

Jan La Rue, a member of the music faculty at New York University, responded enthusiastically to the tempo of Macdonald's prose: "It seems to me that the control of sentence rhythms has increased in *Blue Hammer*. . . . The slowing down in this sentence of yours, for example, hit me like a Weingartner retard: 'I sat behind a long red light and watched the spoor of oil smoke dissipating, mixing with the general smog that overlay this part of the city.' The counterpoint of images in the last paragraph of Chapter 9—gaunt trees and masts; reflecting candlelight—gives a marvelous effect, contrapuntal emotionally, too, since the word *gaunt* reminds the reader of the hollowness of this ménage, despite its seeming richness. Here's another beautiful sentence: 'A flock of starlings flew in a twittering cloud, and the first shadow of evening followed them across the sky.' There are many more."

Julian Symons said, "I thought *The Blue Hammer* was your best book for a long time, and one of the very best you've written." In the *Times Literary Supplement*, Symons would note how the opening of *Hammer*, "which casually mentions 'the towers of the mission and the courthouse half submerged in smog,' most delicately suggests the mists and confusions through which Archer will look for the truth about Richard Chantry's missing painting"; Symons judged this novel "in some ways the peak of Macdonald's achievement." His colleague H. R. F. Keating, including *The Blue Hammer* in 1987's *Crime & Mystery: The 100 Best Books*, echoed Symons in thinking it a peak achievement for Macdonald: "a paean of praise to life, to the continuing future, even to its farthest romantic reach of defying death for ever," and a work of "exceptional strength."

Hammer review coverage was supplemented by feature interviews with Macdonald in the *Chicago Sun Times,* the *Houston Chronicle,* and the *National Observer.* John Leonard spotlighted the novel in a "Critic's Notebook" piece for the daily *New York Times.* Knopf did a 35,000-copy first printing of the book, which was an alternate selection of the Literary Guild; by publication day, 33,518 books had sold. Another three press runs brought copies to 48,000. Although it didn't crack the *New York Times* top ten list (thanks in part perhaps to what Green described to Millar as "your fellow panelist Broyard's piece of dementia"), *Hammer* did make the charts of the *Los Angeles Times,* the *Chicago Tribune,* and *Time* magazine. "Am all for writing a short lighter book now," a still-fatigued Millar informed Ferry, "and only hope I can."

Instead he agreed to participate in another time-consuming activity: a summerlong series of near-daily interviews with journalist Paul Nelson, who'd made first contact by telephone a few years earlier. Millar and Nelson had met in New York in April; now Nelson, who specialized in stories on artists (usually singer-songwriters) he admired, had an assignment to profile Ross Macdonald for *Rolling Stone* magazine.

Millar was eager to reach *Rolling Stone*'s young audience but was firm about not allowing mention of his only child's troubles in Nelson's piece. In the past he had trusted sympathetic journalists not to write about Linda; but given the in-depth sort of story Nelson and his magazine specialized in, Millar felt he needed more than an implicit promise. With help from Harris Seed's office, he drafted a letter of agreement for Nelson and *Stone* publisher Jann Wenner (a Writers Conference participant) to sign ("After having given the matter much thought, I have decided that I can only consent to an interview with 'The Rolling Stone' on the express conditions that . . . any material to be published by 'The Rolling Stone' will be submitted to me in advance of publication for my approval of all biographical material pertaining to my family, and that 'The Rolling Stone' will not publish any such material not approved by me"). "This sheet of paper," Nelson recalled, "basically said he could get an injunction and stop the presses if there was anything about the daughter in the piece; this was mostly for the sake of the husband and the grandson." Nelson and Wenner signed, and the interviews began: forty-five hours of taped conversations at the Coral Casino cabana and in Millar's Hope Ranch study.

"He was an *extremely* tough interview at first," said Nelson, a dry, soft-spoken man who quizzed Millar on scores of subjects from the biographically specific to the aesthetically abstract. "He couldn't make small talk at all; he'd just smile at you. It was maddening. It took about an hour to get used to this. When you asked him a question, he'd examine its logic: take it apart phrase by phrase. Very scholarly, very exact; it wasn't a put-down. I don't think he was quite aware how uneasy people were around him. It was like taking a college course and having a final exam every day: you had to go in with a hundred and fifty or two hundred questions, because he could not just wing it. And if he didn't like a question, he'd say, 'Rephrase your question.' Sometimes he'd pause for up to a minute; you'd think he was finished talking, but he wasn't. That took adjusting to. He really was one of the most intelligent people I'd ever met; he'd read *everything*, and he knew where it all fit into American literature, or the detective genre. But there was a constant problem I had: One day he'd say his books were totally autobiographical, the next day he'd say they weren't at all. And when I'd try to get him to talk personally instead of about themes, that was territory he did *not* want to be in. In fact it got him *extremely* angry. 'Why do you keep trying to *do* this?' he'd say. He wanted to tell the truth, but he didn't want to go into too much depth. And the daughter was just *not* a subject you brought up with him. He came on very quiet and scholarly, but underneath he was really one of the toughest people I'd ever known. Like iron. And if there was a line he didn't want you to cross, there was no way in hell you'd cross it. Lot of contradictions in the man. Deep-set strength beneath this incredible kindness and gentleness, and then it would come roaring out. And he was so quiet and so meek as a rule that when he *did* get angry, it was more frightening than a maniac."

Nelson roused Millar's ire one day with a discussion of Raymond Chandler. "He said he preferred Chandler's first books to *The Long Goodbye*, which was my favorite," Nelson said. "And I kept trying to explain what I thought was so good about *Goodbye,* and finally he just exploded. He said, 'To hell with Chandler! Chandler tried to kill me!' He had me stop the tape then and insisted I erase that part, and he explained to me all about what Chandler had done: writing negative letters to people about Macdonald's first book and so on. And we began taping again, and then he spoke quite calmly about Chandler and said how he'd aped him at first and how Chandler was a great writer and all that. But I could tell that I'd talked a little bit too much about Raymond Chandler."

Nelson introduced Millar to another avid Macdonald fan: singer-songwriter Warren Zevon, whose highly praised eponymous Asylum album was released in 1976. Nelson had met Zevon and wife Crystal recently in New York, where (he later wrote) they brushed aside questions about Warren's work to ask about Ross Macdonald: "They'd read all his books and could quote passages verbatim. I was impressed. 'Provided it's all right with Millar,' I said, 'I'll take you with me to visit him for a day or two.' It was as if I'd invited them to meet God."

Zevon recalled years later getting hooked on Macdonald while living in Spain: "My ex-wife Crystal and I started reading him based on a review somewhere of *The Underground Man* and maybe on the movie *Harper*—two reasons the literary community would not want to admit that people are ever drawn to read authors. I did not come to Ross Macdonald, like people imagined, through Chandler and Hammett; I was not a mystery fan. Through the sixties I read John Updike and John Fowles and of course Mailer, that's who I liked. Crystal and I thought Macdonald was a great great writer. And that, combined with the Los Angeles stuff—the fact that we were abroad and he was so evocative of Los Angeles—caused us to read one book of his after another."

There were personal reasons for Zevon to respond deeply to Macdonald's work: his biography straddled cultural and psychological fault lines not unlike the splits in Millar's. The Chicago-born son of a Russian-immigrant boxer-gambler and a quiet Scots-Welsh Mormon woman, Zevon grew up in half a dozen different cities (Fresno, San Pedro, San Francisco, Los Angeles), with his often-absent father looked down on by his mother's family. Like Millar, he had a powerful maternal grandmother, he told Nelson: "My grandmother is very senatorial—a big lady in every way. She ran the family." His childhood sounded like something out of a Macdonald novel (*The Galton Case*, say): "I grew up with a painting of an uncle, Warren, who looked just like me. He was a military man, a golden boy, an artist. He'd been killed in action. Uncle Warren was sort of the dead figurehead of the family." His ideal as a child, Zevon said, was "a dead man—with my name, looks, and career intentions." As a teen, Zevon struggled with conflicts similar to ones that had formed Millar: studying classical music and seeking out Stravinsky, and at the same time playing folk and rock and being an avid surfer ("I *was* that kid in *The Zebra-Striped Hearse*," he told writer Grover Lewis).

Primed as he was to meet his idol, Zevon wasn't ready for Millar's cool facade. The budding rock star's exuberance collided with the author's imperturbable presence. "Zevon came bouncing into the cabana around noon," Nelson remembered, "and his opening line was 'I just had the Lew Archer Special downtown at the Copper Coffee Pot!' Macdonald didn't say anything. Zevon blurted out something else. Still nothing from Macdonald. Finally Zevon shrank back in a chair, and a bit later he slunk outside again; it just destroyed him." But Zevon recovered. Two years later, he'd tell a journalist Ross Macdonald was his favorite writer: "Macdonald has still not let me down. A nice balance between blood-and-guts and human-itarianism, with just the right acceptable amount of formal poetry. He's my ideal. I got the opportunity to meet him: he's a pro*found*ly kind, gentle, nice, intelligent man."

Nelson grew fond of Millar too. "I liked the man extremely," he said. "He felt like he didn't belong anywhere: sort of a citizen of nowhere. I suspect he lived for books and learning. A very shy man, and I gather his life as a child had been so terribly tough that the social graces were almost beyond him. He could talk one-on-one nicely, but— They chose not to go to people's houses, Ken and Margaret; he was not at ease that way. Both of them were somehow Midwestern, like they were living in the past; their values were from the forties and fifties. But educated to the teeth, both of them. It was an odd marriage, I'm sure; I don't know what kind it was, but it wasn't a normal one."

Nelson found Millar's wife harder to deal with, he said. "Margaret was impossible: *the* most highly strung person I've ever met in my life. If she went twenty miles out of Santa Barbara, she flipped out. There seemed to be a lot of repressed little kid in her; I think she was scared to death. The kind of person who had to have her whole life planned in advance: know that she was going to have a Spanish class on Monday at ten, things like that. I never knew what her reaction might be when I showed up at the house: sometimes she'd give me a big hello, maybe offer me cookies; other times she'd stare at me, say nothing, and leave the room. All summer she promised to sit down and talk for an interview, but she'd keep putting it off. Finally it was the day before I had to leave. She said, 'Okay, we'll do it tomorrow morning at eight.' The next morning, Macdonald called me at six. He was *seething;* he'd gotten up and found a note from Margaret saying she'd gone out birding and he should call and cancel her interview. So he said to come over anyway and *we'd* talk instead. And eventually, later in the day, Margaret showed up and started chatting, and he just slipped away and left us. She spoke with this kind of naive openness about their courtship and all, as if they were still sixteen years old and he was carrying her schoolbooks. But she seemed psychologically incapable of digging any deeper than that. It was great while it lasted; then she changed gears again, and that was that."

Margaret was prone to changing gears. In September, she and Millar were about to go to England and Switzerland to meet press and publishers (both had books coming out in Europe) and see some sights. At the last moment Margaret, at work on another novel, canceled. "The basic truth," Millar wrote Ferry, "is that both of us, and M. in particular, are not good at staying away from home for very long. Indeed our last and only previous visit to England was cut short by Margaret's illness, which I'd hate to see a repetition of."

So he went "Margaretless" to London, where tragic news greeted him: a letter from Julian Symons told of the death by accidental pill overdose of the Symonses' daughter Sarah (whom the Millars had met in Santa Barbara). "You of all people will know how we feel," Symons wrote. "We're deeply sorry that at present we're not fit for any company. . . . Our hearts are full of grief." Millar respected his privacy; he wrote Symons later: "My feeling when Linda died was simply that the days were burdens to be lifted and that other people, no matter how close, tended to add to the burden. . . . Even on me the effect of your loss—my loss, too—was to turn me away from people and their pleasures so that, apart from business-related meetings, I spent my time in London quite alone. I walked a great deal through the city, with you and your wife and family much on my mind." Millar did enjoy a meeting with his English publisher, Sir William Collins. In his late seventies and in seemingly good health, Sir William took the stairs two at a time when Millar saw him greeting a Bible group led by Malcolm Muggeridge. Two days later, Billy Collins dropped dead, putting a melancholy closing bracket to Millar's London stay.

From England, Millar went to Zurich. He didn't much care for that stuffy-seeming city ("overhung by the unfriendliness of the small ungenerous rich"), but he very much liked his agent there, Ruth Liepman, and his German publisher, Daniel Keel, a cultured and amusing man who reminded him of the young Alfred Knopf. It turned out Keel had taken Margaret Millar's latest novel for publication without knowing she was married to Ross Macdonald: "Such are the occasional pleasures of writing books," Millar told Wolfe.

On his own in Europe, maybe for the last time, on the spur of the moment Millar went to Venice and surprised himself by greatly liking that canal-riddled city, "in all its beautiful broken down strangeness." He wrote Wolfe, "I seem to be crazy about places surrounded or indeed half inundated by the sea (like the Vancouver of my earliest memories?)." While he was at it, he went to Amsterdam ("I like the watery places," he told Symons) before flying home via New York City, where he caught a glimpse of Frank MacShane getting into a taxi, a chance sighting that made him oddly happy.

In Santa Barbara again after his lonely European odyssey, the sixty-year-old Millar found his thoughts returning once again to the land of his youth. "More and more my mind bends back toward Canada," he wrote Ferry; "indeed, I am planning a book about somebody's childhood there, not exactly mine." But he put off starting it.

He took pleasure in his wife's renewed career, which made Maggie boisterous. "Here is proof positive," she inscribed her twenty-second book, "that reports of my retirement have been greatly exaggerated, mostly by me." *Ask for Me Tomorrow* got good reviews, the most surprising being Anatole Broyard's long notice in the *New York Times;* possibly Ross Macdonald's harshest critic was perversely drawn to this suspense tale by its having been written by Mrs. Kenneth Millar. Broyard found it full of "character, atmosphere, wit, passion—the same things, in fact, that I read serious novels for."

Millar's standards were high too. That was why he postponed starting a book, he confided to Jane Bernstein in the fall of 1976: "I'm unable to write for long periods, or perhaps I should say unwilling because I hate to write badly. So I wait. Right now I'm waiting, somewhat washed up in feeling, and conscious that I may never write again as well as I once did. But then I may. Even age has its compensations, and you become more intelligent, like a light in a cellar, as your energy fails." Not the most hopeful simile.

Some are born Canadian, some achieve Canadianness, and others
have Canadianness thrust upon them.

—Margaret Atwood

You thought the national flag was about a leaf, didn't you? Look
harder. It's where someone got axed in the snow.

—Margaret Atwood

Macdonald may have been the best-known writer in his field by the late 1970s, but Millar didn't take it for granted he'd be recognized in person, even by someone who'd traveled halfway across the country to see him. When he met Jane S. Bakerman, a young Indiana academic come to interview him for *Writer's Yearbook,* he carried a copy of *The Blue Hammer* as photo ID, holding Jill Krementz's somber portrait of the artist up next to his real-life smiling face.

"Isn't that nice?" Bakerman asked later. "I was touched. The day was full of pleasant gestures like that. I'd stayed at a motel where he'd made a reservation for me, and he said he thought I would like it because Julian Symons had stayed there. That was a test, sort of: Did I register ten on the Richter scale? I did recognize Julian Symons's name, of course. He was kind of sly and playful in little ways like that.

"We did the interview in his cabana at the beach club. I was struck by the symbolism that you could see an oil derrick outside the window. I didn't know what I was doing, I had never done one of these before; I went out very well prepared but the way a scholar would prepare. And he *knew* how to conduct an interview. Oh, he was *won*derful. He thought carefully about what he said. I did not feel he was holding back at all. He was ex*treme*ly patient with me; I was kind of shy. He didn't volunteer oodles of personal information. He spoke of the pleasure they took in their grandson. I don't think he was a smoker, and that was painful for me; there was no ashtray in the cabana. We had lunch there; he sat quietly at table, with his hands folded. Margaret came by briefly in the afternoon; I was struck by how pretty she was. And he dropped me off at the airport."

Millar's manner with young women was often gentlemanly protective. Such females seemed to remind him of his daughter or of the girl he'd married or of roads taken and turnings missed. In his most mannered style he wrote Jane Bernstein: "My epistolary ennui is dissipated by such a clear and honest prose as your letter commends, and the fact that you wish to mention your concerns to me, and perhaps the fact that my late daughter's middle name was Jane and I may imagine beneath the top level of consciousness that I have swum, or could, back up to the top of Niagara Falls."

Whether acting fatherly or like a smitten teen, Millar was noticeably affected by females. "He was somewhere between a spectator and the kind of man who would dance attendance," said Brad Darrach. "I don't think he could see through women: I think there was a sort of sheen over them that he could not penetrate. He wasn't childish in any way about it, but he was not behaving like a male as sophisticated as he had every right to be, given his intelligence and the range of his experience."

A young woman journalist who preferred not to be named had a mildly unsettling experience in Santa Barbara with the ambiguously appreciative Millar. "He was not an easy interview," she said. "Then he drove me around to see the sights up in through the mountains. I then went back to the hotel across from the beach club; and as I was getting ready to go into the dining room to have dinner alone, the phone rang. It was Ken. He spoke very slowly; he said, 'Hel-lo. . . . This is Ken   Millar . . . speaking. I just . . . want . . . to tell you . . . how much . . . I enjoyed our day . . . and how much . . . you meant to me.' It was a little too nervous and heartfelt; it seemed like a boyish-crush thing to me. So I said in my best Mary Tyler Moore voice, trying to short-circuit this, 'Oh, Ken, and it meant *so much* to me too! And I enjoyed it *so much*!' And just parroted his words back at him. And in the middle of this, there was a huge clatter on the line, like a crash of something—like he was interrupted or something fell or he dropped the phone—and then it hung up. And I sat there, waiting, not knowing what to do. I was afraid if I went into the dining room, he might come over; if he came over to the *hotel,* I was in big trouble. And I had certainly felt he and his wife were definitely a solid couple, so I was totally stunned by what seemed to be this sort of declaration of affection. About twenty minutes later, the phone rang again. And—it was the strangest experience—he said, 'Hel-lo. . . . This is Ken . . . Millar . . . speaking.' And he repeated exactly the same words as before, so slowly and deliberately. I don't know if he was *reading* them, but—'I just . . . want to tell you . . . how much I enjoyed . . . our day.' Again I tried to say the same thing right back to him, although by this time my chipper Mary Tyler Moore voice was sort of fading on me. It was quite bizarre. But I went into the dining room, and he didn't come over. The next day they both arrived before I left for the airport, and nothing was said about those calls; it was as if they had never happened."

Millar's awkward social manner could be disquieting at the best of times, and it added to the sense of his being ill at ease and out of place. (Clifford Ridley, of the *National Observer,* wrote, "In a gray suit, a gray tie, and a white Stetson, nearly the size of a beach umbrella, he suggested an actor who had just auditioned for two roles at once. Neither of them current at the Coral Casino.") After thirty years in southern California, Millar seemed to many visitors and residents to be still unsure of himself and his place in the sunshine.

It was a perception he seemed to share. Richard Moore, who made a 1977 educational-TV film about Macdonald, said, "I had a feeling he was somehow *astonished* at finding himself in such surroundings, given his beginnings, and that he felt it was likely to evaporate at any moment."

Despite what he'd achieved, Millar still didn't feel he belonged in this beautiful city. Canada was bred in the bone; he stayed an uneasy exile in California, waiting for the other snowshoe to drop. "Canada seems to hang like a glacier slowly moving down on me from its notch," he wrote. "I expect it to overtake me before I die, reminding me with its chill and weight that I belong to the north after all."

Much of Millar's manner and mental weather—his love of silence, his modesty, his "cheerful sadness," his lack of interest in creature comforts, his cautious pessimism ("We'll see"), his dry humor (more Leacock finally than Chandler)—becomes more understandable when he's seen as a Canadian: something he more and more saw himself as. Canada (said Canadians) thrived on self-effacement, insecurity, and anxiety.

"How did Canada get that way?" asked Don Pearce, Millar's Ontario contemporary. "We talked about that once, Ken and I. He was praising to me all the virtues of the United States when we were graduate students in Ann Arbor. He was on a high, having rediscovered his native land, America, and become emancipated from the land of his imprisonment, Canada. Ken was explaining to me that there were men like Lincoln in the United States, and he named others, who walked around as public figures knowing that they were going to be shot at any moment of any day: walked around, conducted their affairs, and carried themselves with pride. And he said, '*That* has irradiated the sense of life and the sense of heroism and purpose in this country. Things can be *done* here, because a few men showed people how to do them!' He said, 'Nobody ever did that for Canada. Nobody ever put their arm in the fire for that nation, or for any cause or purpose of public importance there. And that's why it'll never be a *nation*, but only a country of clerks.'

"It's a nation of strangers, Canada. It's all a mass of divisions. People are kind of alone and without a self-image that is clear and definite. Add to that the fact that there is this great thing called the North, which expands just like forever up to the Arctic Circle. All Canadians are aware of it. It's *cold* in Canada; it's barren, up there. It has chilled its national culture to the bone. Silence, and space, enter into the Canadian psyche in a way they don't into any other. And I have a feeling you can find a lot of that in Ken. A lot of that in his writing too: Archer can be very laconic.

" 'Who am I? What am I?' Canadians are always in quest of the self. And this *invades* Ken. His work is to a large extent a quest for himself. The author who is holding the pen is in search of the person who is behind the man holding the pen: a ghost. This is entirely Canadian.

"The other thing that functions in the Canadian psyche is the notion of colonialism: in other words, 'I am powerless.' It's impossible to be a colonial and not have an inferiority complex, a humility, a self-embarrassment of some kind. So, being a Canadian is really a tough job.

Tom Nolan

"But out of all these oppositions and strains, you get diversity and range and a great variety; you get multiperspectival types. Marshall McLuhan, say; Northrop Frye, Ken Millar, Glenn Gould, Hugh Kenner—to take just five who come to mind—all in the same generation, all conspicuous for their ability to see things in enormous diversity and to codify them in interesting ways. And to become, all of them, extremely interesting to Americans.

"The man from the provinces, even though he's a country bumpkin in some ways, can see what's going on in the capital better than the people who are in it. So there's that aspect to Ken. If he read or caught the pulse of American life, it was because he came from outside it. He told me once— he was so happy about a few good reviews of *The Ivory Grin* or *The Doomsters* or another of the early good books—he said, 'I believe that I have taken the pulse of this country,' after about six books. A provincial can do that."

The detour-filled route Millar found to creative expression—from Ontario high school teacher to Michigan grad student to California detective novelist—could be seen as typically Canadian. Having in mind Robertson Davies (educated at Oxford, an actor in London, and a southern Ontario newspaper editor before becoming a significant Canadian novelist), Millar exclaimed to Peter Wolfe, "What infinitely complicated stratagems the heavy suppressive night of the Canadian self-hating culture imposed on those of its sons who wished to write fiction." Most other would-be Canadian novelists of their generation did what the Millars had: left Canada. Margaret Laurence, after years in Africa, wrote her first Manitoba novels in England, where Mordecai Richler wrote his Montreal books. Mavis Gallant moved to Paris in 1950. Herb Harker came to Santa Barbara to write of Alberta. "Canadians become Canadians by going elsewhere," Millar wrote poet-ambassador Robert Ford in Moscow (who certainly proved his point).

"I really think that Lew Archer is a Canadian-American type," Millar told a surprised CBC radio interviewer in 1975. "I think his psychological and ethical makeup is predominantly Canadian, rather than American. What he sees with his Canadian eyes is American life." As Macdonald described him in Richard Moore's 1977 film, Archer was certainly a different figure from the detectives created by Chandler or Hammett: "Archer is a life-size hero. . . . I tried to write about a fairly good man, though. He embodies values and puts them into action. You don't have to be a hero to do that. Perhaps that's what we need, though: a democratic kind of hero. A man who doesn't blow his own horn, but just goes and does his job right and treats other people fairly well." In other words, a good Canadian.

Robertson Davies, in a talk given in the States in the spring of 1977, ventured the notion that the ordinary Canadian, unencumbered by strong national identity, was well suited to be a particularly contemporary champion: "a new kind of hero, a hero of conscience and spirit in the great drama of modern man." Davies proposed such a hero explore not his continent's wild landscape but the "desperate wilderness behind the eyes" (paraphrasing Canadian poet Douglas LePan, and unknowingly para-phrasing a line from an unpublished 1950s poem by Kenneth Millar to Margaret). Davies said, "The Canadian voyage, I truly believe, is this per-ilous voyage into the dark interior . . . a voyage in which many are lost for-ever, and some wander in circles, but it is the heroic voyage of our time"—and one that Archer and Macdonald, cloaked in genre, had been taking for three decades.

The emergence of Davies and other writers signaled a new stage in Canadian letters. "Canada is coming alive," Millar wrote Donald Davie in the midseventies. From his Santa Barbara study, Millar the armchair liter-ary detective traced these newcomers' origins. "Robertson Davies is still writing under the influence of Stephen Leacock," he told Jerry Tutunjian. "You can make a direct connection, and I'm sure he would, between *Sun-shine Sketches of a Little Town* and *Fifth Business.*"

Millar was keenly interested in the new Canadian fiction. He had Knopf (her American publisher) send him works by the critically well-regarded Margaret Laurence. (Unknown to Millar, the interest was mutual. Linwood Barclay met Laurence when she was a writer in residence at Trent Univer-sity and found that "she was a terrific fan of Ross Macdonald's. I was regu-larly feeding his books to her; she thought they were just wonderful.") Reading Alice Munro's story "The Beggar Maid" in the *New Yorker* in June 1977, Millar correctly deduced Munro was once a student at the University of Western Ontario; he wrote her, "I have never before read a story which so piercingly and succinctly examined the terrors and hopes through which the intellectual and emotional life of Canada apparently must still, forty years after my graduation from UWO, find its way. Your story filled me with joy and the kind of hopeful excitement that only the truth, and the promise of further truth, can evoke."

As Millar became aware of these new voices, Canadian litterateurs were discovering Ross Macdonald. Published in Canada by Random House since 1962, Macdonald was hardly a best-seller there: the Canadian hard-cover of *Sleeping Beauty* sold a scant fourteen hundred copies. But in the years of heightened national pride and scholarly activity before and after the hundredth anniversary in 1967 of the country's confederation, Canada claimed Macdonald as one of its own. John Leonard recalled, "I spoke at the MLA in Montreal and went to a bookstore that had all Cana-dian writers' books; they wouldn't allow any U.S. writers on their shelves. But there was Ross Macdonald—and Saul Bellow, because he'd been born in Canada; they counted as Canadians."

In Macdonald's case at least, the claim seemed valid. In two intriguing essays, Russell M. Brown, of Scarborough College, University of Toronto, argued convincingly that Macdonald's mysteries "have many qualities about them which are demonstrably Canadian, that in fact the very quali-ties which have distinguished Millar's novels from other American myster-ies turn out to link him with many contemporary Canadian novelists."

Brown thought Macdonald's use of landscape as "a kind of presence" was typical of Canadian writing; that his "sense of a past which, if understood, would explain the present" was similar to that of novelists such as Laurence, Davies, and Leonard Cohen; that his concern with the topic of individual responsibility could be seen in such writers as Davies and Richler; that his preoccupation with the search for the lost father was also a recurrent motif for Hugh MacLennan and Margaret Atwood; that in "developing complex causal chains leading from past to present," Macdonald, like other Canadian novelists, "is able to show his readers all the ways in which cause and effect intertwine": as Davies showed the expanding consequences of a child throwing a snowball in *Fifth Business,* so Macdonald traced the source of a huge brush fire back to a single dropped cigarillo, the result of a violent crime "with its own sources to be probed," in *The Underground Man.* Many of Macdonald's novels were like Davies's and Laurence's in being "investigations of inheritance both literal and symbolic," Brown said. And the critic thought Macdonald showed another Canadian characteristic in his break with the good-and-evil dichotomy of traditional American hard-boiled fiction, "replacing this vision with one of a world not so much of moral ambiguities as a world where a single deed may turn out to be both good and evil and in which guilt and innocence are virtually indistinguishable," with blame shared by many in a complex web. Brown concluded, "Macdonald has done more than merely reinvigorate the American mystery. He has also Canadianized it."

Millar felt himself further Canadianized when a first cousin, Dr. Gordon MacDonald, of Riverside, California, came to visit for the first time in the mid-1970s. Dr. MacDonald had grown up in Nyssa, Oregon, where he'd known Millar's father's father, John Millar, who'd died there. His cousin's surname, variant spelling and all, made Millar feel even more justified in his choice of pseudonym. His old memories jostled, he became "entranced" with Canada and wanted to mine his northern past more explicitly.

He could imagine an ambitious nonfiction work, a multigenerational memoir telling his family's story and a good chunk of Canada's: how his grandfather left Scotland near the time of the American Civil War and founded an Ontario newspaper, how his father crossed the continent and founded a paper in British Columbia, before going to sea; then how John Macdonald Millar's son fared, in Canada and the States. It could be the book of a lifetime, if Millar brought it off: a Canadian *Roots,* or a work like Christopher Isherwood's account of his parents, *Kathleen and Frank.* He should try to do it, Millar thought. Yet he dreaded exploring his painful history: "all that old sadness," as he told Julian Symons, "the substance of my mother, the shadow of my father," the ghost of his daughter.

At other times, from 1973, he worked at a novel set in and near Winnipeg in the 1920s. "With it," he wrote Gerald Walker, "I think I want to go further, and further back, into Canada. The 'natural situation' "—the objective correlative of the story, like the fire in *The Underground Man* and the oil spill in *Sleeping Beauty*—"will be extreme frigidity, I think. Deep concealing snow."

As the seventies unspooled, Millar thought more about Lew Archer in relation to his author's Canadian past. In 1977 he noted, "Ultimately my novels may be attempts to put together *Wiarton again.*" Archer's following threads of consequence back to before things went awry was a way perhaps for Millar to return psychologically to where he'd last felt safe as a child. Russell Brown saw that too in Millar's books: that "the mid-west and Canada" often represented for Macdonald's characters "the Eden which exists no more—the place of now-lost innocence and unattainable sanctuary."

Millar tried to start another book in 1977, though he had no financial need. Good money was coming in: $45,000 in *Drowning Pool* percentage payments, between $67,000 and $100,000 from Bantam for *The Blue Hammer.* Toting up assets, Millar figured he and Margaret had over half a million in cash, savings, and real estate.

Taking him away from his writing briefly was the making of Richard Moore's half-hour film on Macdonald for a PBS-TV series, *The Originals: The Writer in America,* whose other subjects included Wright Morris, Janet Flanner, John Gardner, Toni Morrison, and Eudora Welty. Another diversion was the screenplay Millar agreed to write of *The Instant Enemy,* based on his own treatment from the year before.

An alarming 1977 distraction was Margaret's lung-cancer operation. Doctors removed an entire lobe and with it, apparently, all the cancer. "Ken was wonderful through my illness," Margaret told Canadian journalist Beverly Slopen, "the nurses wanted to know where I found such a man. When I had been home from the hospital for three days, I was lying on the sofa, still totally helpless. . . . Ken said the most touching thing to me. He was there with the dogs, tending to everything, and he said, 'You know, I'd be happy to end my days this way.' " Within two months, Margaret was back to her routine of swimming, biking, and writing—though she didn't feel up to a trip to Ontario for the funeral of her ninety-two-year-old father.

With his wife on the mend and his screenplay on automatic pilot, Millar made another try at getting a novel started. Near the end of the year, still stuck "in the planning stage," he was forced to acknowledge writing came a lot harder now; and nonfiction seemed nearly impossible. Millar puzzled over why he was having such problems. Was he trying to probe areas his subconscious felt it dangerous to enter? Was his mind throwing up obstacles to long-suppressed facts? If so, he had to dismantle those roadblocks; he'd done it before. "A man can't fight these wars without some help," he knew from experience. In October he started sessions with a Santa Barbara psychiatrist, the same man who'd helped him and Margaret and Linda through their worst weeks of 1956.

Asked for his views on the future of the mystery, Mr. Macdonald, a quiet-spoken, thoughtful man, said that getting into paperback was more difficult for younger writers these days than it had been for him. . . . Still, he had no doubt that the genre has a future—certainly the hardboiled detective story in the Chandler-Hammett-Cain, and now Macdonald, tradition. . . . As for Ross Macdonald's future, he's going to keep writing Lew Archers "as long as my hands are able."

—Richard R. Lingeman, "Book Ends,"
New York Times Book Review, April 1978

It almost seemed an unwritten rule with shy Ken Millar: when going to meet a smart young woman, bring a book. He'd given his first college girlfriend, Gretchen Kalbfleisch, a book (*Oil for the Lamps of China*) for her eighteenth birthday. Margaret Sturm had been translating a book of Greek history when he saw her in the London, Ontario, library and recognized his fate. Millar displayed Macdonald's *The Blue Hammer* to Jane Bakerman. And when *Newsweek*'s Diane K. Shah met him in the lobby of New York's Algonquin Hotel in March 1978, he was holding a copy of a work he'd been reading for half a century.

"It was 'The Rime of the Ancient Mariner,' " Shah remembered, "not the kind of book you expect to see somebody carrying around; I said, 'Oh, *tell* me about that.' I got the feeling it was a prop, that he had sort of planned this, to have something to open the conversation with."

Shah interviewed Macdonald at the Second International Congress of Crime Writers, a high-profile gathering that saw New York mayor Ed Koch declare March 12 through 18 "I Love a Mystery Week." "When I encountered him," Shah said, "he seemed very frail, a little shaky. He was quite tall, and pretty shy. But he was terrific, he really was." Shah, who later wrote several mystery novels, was a Macdonald fan: "I must have read all of his books three times and underlined. He's just the best."

Millar at first thought he wouldn't go East this year. As he'd explained to Nolan Miller in January, extricating himself from a promise to address Miller's Antioch students, "The fact is that Margaret, while making a decent physical recovery from her lung operation, has not recovered emotionally and lives in considerable fear. . . . I now see that I can't leave her alone here with the responsibilities of this house, any time in the next year. The psychic wound, if I had stopped to figure it out . . . would have appeared to me what it is: harder to live down than the physical wound. And Margaret is as vulnerable as a violin."

But his wife recouped her spirits enough for Millar to go to New York in March. He was one of 275 American and European authors gathering at the Biltmore Hotel for the heavily promoted congress, which was linked to several tie-in events around the city (a Mystery Writers Stakes race at Aqueduct, tours of police and crime labs, publishing-industry panels and parties, and the MWA's annual Edgar Awards).

Ross Macdonald did his part to publicize the goings-on. He was interviewed by *Newsweek*, the *New York Daily News*, the *New York Times Book Review*, National Public Radio, and BBC television; and he wrote material for a special *Publishers Weekly* issue. "The Mystery Writers were very very pleased to have him there," said Julian Symons. The congress was Symons's idea, to promote and celebrate the mystery story. There were surely things worth celebrating. New interest in the genre had been stirred recently, some thanks to *Murder Ink*, a popular tribute volume edited by Dilys Winn (awarded a special Edgar this week). Stores devoted exclusively to crime fiction were opening all over the country. Courses in the mystery were offered in many schools here and abroad. Crime and suspense novels now made up about a third of U.S. fiction best-sellers (something Macdonald's breakthrough helped bring about). The mystery story seemed lots better off than in 1946, when the MWA was founded with the motto "Crime does not pay—enough!"

But in other ways, the genre was in trouble. Though readership was growing, there still weren't enough readers to satisfy publishers, several of whom were cutting back on mysteries. As conglomerates gobbled up the independent houses, "bottom-line" thinking replaced traditional practices from the era of Knopf, Cerf, and Scribner. Until recently publishers had been happy with the six or seven thousand copies they could count on selling (mostly to libraries) of a given mystery; but fewer houses now bothered with such modest numbers. "Publishers are getting greedy," MWA member Harold Q. Masur told a radio interviewer during "I Love a Mystery Week." "They don't want to fool around with a bunch of smaller books; they want to publish the big one. The profits are there, the big money is there; it's less work for them."

For genre writers with "crossover" books, the rewards could be huge. After scoring a best-seller with her first novel, *Where Are the Children?*, suspense writer Mary Higgins Clark (a congress attendee) got half a million dollars from her hardcover publisher and a million from her paperback house for 1978's *A Stranger Is Watching*—sums comparable to those being paid "blockbuster" mainstream authors like E. L. Doctorow *(Ragtime)* and Colleen McCullough *(The Thorn Birds)*. Garden-variety mystery writers were feeling the squeeze, though. Beginners had a harder time getting into paperback or even hardcover. It seemed unlikely young writers could still do what the Millars had: make a frugal living through mysteries while improving skills and working toward greater success.

All this saddened Millar, who'd often urged would-be novelists such as Jerre Lloyd to try detective fiction "in the meantime," as Millar had. More disheartening was the decline in quality as books were aimed at bigger markets and lower common denominators. When the merely popular drove out the serious, there'd be nothing to buy but Ian Fleming and Mickey Spillane. "Is it possible that a form of fiction can be too successful for its own good, attracting writers whose sole qualification is the possession of a typewriter and readers who would be better off at the movies?" asked Macdonald rhetorically in *Publishers Weekly.* "Somehow the wild laws of the market take care of the bad writers, paying some of them like idiot princes."

Ross Macdonald, the philosopher king of detective novelists, was a star attraction at the Second International Congress of Crime Writers. Alfred A. Knopf and Bantam Books jointly sponsored a Ross Macdonald Luncheon on Thursday, March 16, where the author read an untitled speech written for the occasion, a serviceable reshuffling of remarks about himself and the Gothic tradition that he'd made several times before. It wasn't a difficult talk, yet Millar had trouble with it. "Every sentence made sense," recalled Julian Symons, "but it wasn't fully coherent. He jumped from one thing to another without apparently understanding that he was doing so. For about the first five minutes, he really was tremendously hazy." Millar regained his footing, though, to give what Symons described in the London Sunday *Times Magazine* as "the most interesting speech of the congress."

Fred Klein, Bantam Books' vice president of promotion and advertising, noticed a big change in Macdonald, though, when he said hello to him at the luncheon: "It was like he was in left field. It was sad to see what I'd always considered a very sharp, sensitive man, who was now almost absentminded. He was very close to the vest that day; it was almost like he wouldn't even admit that he was Ross Macdonald. That may have been protective coloration, I suppose. But he was like an old, old man."

Symons also noted a certain blurriness, as well as a bit of odd behavior: "My wife and I had a long talk with him that evening; he was staying at the Algonquin, and we were staying at a very much cheaper hotel almost opposite, called the Royalton. And he said, 'I'll see you tomorrow morning, about eleven.' So we said, yes, fine, very good. Well, it was about eight-thirty in the morning, there came a knock on our door—and there was Ken, fully dressed and with his hat on and smiling, saying, 'We have a date for breakfast, haven't we?' Well, we just put it down to confusion, that we got the times wrong. But there was a general sort of absentmindedness in his manner: he didn't always answer precisely what you were saying; his mind seemed to stray onto something else."

Once back in Santa Barbara, Millar felt there weren't enough hours to do the things that *had* to be done, let alone new projects. The *Instant Enemy* screenplay still took nearly all his creative energy in 1978. When New Orleans writer Jerry Speir asked for input on a book he was doing on deadline about Macdonald's fiction, Millar limited participation to a one-hour telephone call, apologizing, "I'm sorry I can't offer you more time, but I am running short of that commodity."

Millar used what writing strength was left after script chores to answer correspondents, including Eudora Welty. His friendship with Welty, Millar wrote Donald Davie, was "one of the best things that have ever happened to me . . . an opening of the heart." Welty and Millar hadn't seen each other for a while, but they were linked in a way this spring by both being a part of Richard Moore's series on American writers shown on PBS-TV. And in April, Eudora Welty's *The Eye of the Story: Selected Essays and Reviews* was published with the dedication "To Kenneth Millar."

He stopped seeing his Santa Barbara psychiatrist in June 1978, apparently concluding his problems weren't psychological but merely "the encroachments of age." Happily his wife stayed productive: despite painful shingles, Margaret finished writing a comic mystery (*The Murder of Miranda*), about which Millar was typically enthusiastic ("Parts of it remind me of Evelyn Waugh!"). Margaret had eye trouble late in 1978, prompting three trips to a retinal clinic in Palo Alto; but she seemed feisty as ever. A few years later she'd tell a Mystery Writers of America meeting, "In 1978 we had quite a severe earthquake in Santa Barbara. They're never *quite* so bad, though, that the insurance companies have to pay off the deductible. But the house was a mess. Ken was missing—because, as every woman in this audience knows, men have some intuitive, built-in warning system that enables them to get out when an emergency is about to occur. So he was at the beach with the three dogs. Meanwhile, the house was a shambles: every drawer and cupboard was open, including the refrigerator, with the contents spilling out; gallons of water had spilled out of the swimming pool and the toilets—which was a new experience to me; all the books had fallen out of the bookcases. So I began to clean up. A few minutes later Ken appeared and surveyed the damage, saying, 'What are you doing?' I said, 'I'm having an orgy, why don't you join me?' and handed him a mop."

Millar finished his *Instant Enemy* script, "for good or ill," in November and turned it over to another writer, much to his and everyone else's relief. "It did have the virtue of being hard to write," he told Davie. "Soon I can get back to my knitting."

Still he didn't begin a book. Bantam had printed eight hundred thousand paperbacks of *The Blue Hammer;* Macdonald's income was a comfortable $136,000 in 1978. (Margaret earned $14,000 this year.) Millar savored the pleasures of later life. These included visits from grandson Jim, now an energetic high school student in Irvine. "He's genuinely good," Millar told Davie in December. "What more can I say for him? And not a piss-willie either. This week he's off in his new car (a secondhand VW most of which he earned himself) to go skiing in Utah." Millar shared the affectionate company of a new dog, Star, a Newfoundland he claimed was the smartest animal he'd ever had: "as clever as a cop who knows where all the exits are and who controls them, and how, and would follow the stock market if I were to teach him to read."

Millar found this Santa Barbara winter "deep and slow and golden" and seemed almost to dread the effort of starting a novel. When two producers from England's Royal Shakespeare Company proposed putting together a Lew Archer play, the author asked Dorothy Olding what she thought of his collaborating with them; his agent answered, "I can only say that it has been a long time between books."

Millar knew that. The play was only a daydream, he said, to take his mind off "high local pressures": his wife's intermittent illnesses, his own declining strength. "After our incredible long romantic youths, and even more romantic middle-ages," he wrote Davie alarmingly on the eve of his sixty-third birthday, "our foreheads come up against vertical stone. Well, I'll write my name on it, with whatever relevant facts I can bring to mind."

At the lowest point in my life, the doorbell rang. And there, quite literally, was Lew Archer, on a compassionate mission, come to save my life.

—Warren Zevon to Paul Nelson, *Rolling Stone*

Lacking a Ross Macdonald novel to publish, Knopf hoped to keep the author's momentum going in 1979 with a third Lew Archer anthology. After much discussion, Millar and Ash Green agreed on the novels to include in it: *The Doomsters, The Zebra-Striped Hearse,* and *The Instant Enemy.* The novels' author wrote Olding the first week in March, "I've been rereading parts of the three books, not with unmitigated pleasure, but on the whole with some satisfaction. My excuse is that I have to write an introduction to them. They are violent and sad books, as intended." Millar had done this sort of guardedly autobiographical preface before, and well; but this one gave him trouble. He turned down a request from the *New Republic* to review Shana Alexander's book on Patty Hearst (the kidnapped California heiress-turned-bank-robber whose story seemed to many as if it might have come from a Ross Macdonald novel) in order to bear down on the task. He had difficulty organizing his thoughts and even his handwriting: certain words and letters came out wrong and had to be retraced. "My own personal tides are not as strong and dependable as I would like them to be," Millar wrote Jane Bernstein in April, "but one can't have everything forever." This anthology was titled *Archer in Jeopardy,* but Millar seemed the one in peril. May found him still laboring over his foreword: "Not easy," he told Olding, "but I hope to say something that hasn't been said before." The shortest such foreword he'd ever written, it avoided direct reference to the novels at hand but conveyed poignantly how Millar's early life had affected Macdonald's fiction:

> I hope my books echo (but not too plainly) the feelings which moved my kin when they were alive, the things they were ready to die for, money and music, paintings and each other, fear of God, and their fundamental wish to be remembered, if possible loved.
>
> I love them better now than I did then, and through my stories I understand them better. Sometimes I feel that the stories were written by them to me, asking me to communicate their sorrows and explain their dreams.

Considering the effort it cost him, the little preface seemed a big achievement. Millar was grateful for Olding's assurance the piece was okay. He seized the quick chance to write another more revealing such fragment about himself and his poetry-writing sea-captain father, for a small-press edition of fourteen Millar/Macdonald book reviews. Each assignment he completed now seemed like a victory. This one ended:

> The last time I saw my father's living eyes, I was a high school boy in Southern Ontario. He was a patient in a metropolitan hospital in Toronto. He had entirely lost the power of speech, but he could still write.
>
> He wrote me a few lines in a book on his knee.
>
> I wish I could tell you what he wrote to me that day. His writing was so shaky that I couldn't make out the words. But I could see that it was written in rhymed couplets.

"Are you working on a book?" Olding asked pointedly in June. Millar felt it necessary to reassure her, "I am not retiring from fiction. But I had reached a point where I had to gather my forces and intentions, and refresh myself with a change. I haven't told anyone that I had stopped writing because in fact I hadn't—that film script was the toughest job I ever undertook—and of course I didn't want that kind of publicity. So I will ask you to keep it to yourself."

His wife had a book out this season: her tale of high jinks and low morals at a beach club, *The Murder of Miranda*, which got good notices such as this one from the *New York Times Book Review*'s Newgate Callendar: "In many respects it is a novel of manners, written in sophisticated prose with a leavening of humor. . . . She is a virtuoso." Meanwhile half a dozen older Macdonald works, from *Find a Victim* to *Sleeping Beauty*, were available in new editions from his paperback house, which bragged, "Ross Macdonald has 13,400,000 books in Bantam print!"

"Believe me," Bantam's Fred Klein said two decades later, when million-copy press runs were common, "the number of copies we put out for Ross Macdonald in those days were nothing to what they would certainly be today. And there came a time when we decided we were going to package Macdonald's books as 'A Lew Archer Novel,' sort of subtly making the transition from mystery to novel. Again, today that's much more prevalent, but there never was such an idea back in the sixties, maybe into the seventies. Yet it was happening: certain kinds of mysteries had become more sophisticated and better written; they were *novels* that *dealt* with mysteries or whatever. Certainly the public recognized it quickly. And I really think it was Ken who began it all."

Millar was anxious to begin another book, but his attentions were needed elsewhere. Margaret's eye trouble was getting worse. She had laser surgery to repair retinal damage; the Millars hoped for the best. Ken Millar's preoccupation seemed to express itself in atypical sloppiness about business matters: he misplaced correspondence, failed to initial agreements, forgot to mail contracts. When someone at Ober wrote to say a reprint house that had already arranged for a hardcover edition of *The Moving Target* now also wanted to do *The Dark Tunnel,* Millar misread the letter and replied he "would be glad to see *The Moving Target* back in hardcover."

Mostly he kept his troubles to himself or emphasized the positive. To Julian Symons he wrote in athletic metaphor, "We skate along, having to avoid the places where the ice is thin, but able to stand upright most of the time." When it seemed that Margaret had "just about completely regained her health," he finally confided to Olding, "It will come as no surprise to you that I have been having a fairly difficult year—I'd have mentioned it earlier if it would have served any purpose." Things were nearly normal again, he assured Olding in August, and he looked forward to "getting back into full working fettle." With this August letter, Millar returned a foreign contract his agent had sent for his signature—a contract Olding had to mail back again: he'd forgotten to sign it.

Despite his own problems, Millar took time to help friends, acquaintances, and total strangers—Dr. Edwin C. Peck Jr., for instance, an Irvine, California, psychoanalyst who sought Ross Macdonald's creative input in treating a patient in 1979. "I had a homicide detective in psychoanalysis," remembered Dr. Peck, "which is a kind of personality structure that almost never gets into analysis for a variety of reasons. This fella was a complicated individual, with a lot of depression and anxiety. So as sometimes happens in the field, you get fired up about your patient's area of specialty. I dug into the works of Millar and a lot of detective writers, and then I wrote to several of them. And Millar was particularly thoughtful and responsive. We exchanged letters, and then I spoke with him on the telephone.

"At first he started off real humble about what he did not know, and how he was a writer of stories rather than a student of the behavior of homicide detectives. But interestingly, he could really grasp the character of this analysand of mine who had done outstanding work running a city department and kind of intensely identified with the role of hero. So, humble though Ross Macdonald was, he was effective in correctly estimating the cadence of the guy's psychology, for instance the role of the family life: he seemed to be in touch with that. It was this combination of humility, availability, and that he could use his imagination to effectively estimate what the actual homicide detective would be like, correctly—even though he said he couldn't! Yeah, he made quite a contribution. In fact the analysis turned out to be successful. The guy came in immobilized—serious depression, anxiety, radically out of touch with his family—and, working at the analysis, he became deeply aware of his love for his children, got a better position in his department, and more secure work than he'd ever had in his life. So, yeah, Macdonald gave me a *lot,* in two letters and one talk on the phone. Others cooperated, but no one else was as helpful. He was just one of those rare characters."

Paul Nelson asked Millar for a more direct sort of intervention in 1979. The *Rolling Stone* writer came to Santa Barbara to see Warren Zevon, who'd moved with his wife to Montecito a year earlier. "One way or another," Zevon recalled, "I think we were prompted to buy a house in Santa Barbara 'cause it was Ross Macdonald Land to us; that was reason enough back then to make, you know, moves around the world." The singer-songwriter and his wife were apart this season, though. Zevon had just checked out of Pinecrest, a Santa Barbara facility he'd entered for the second time (with Nelson's help) to fight drinking and other problems.

"Zevon was in bad, bad, bad shape," Nelson said. "I had to go back to New York. People had been trying to get him to return to the drug center, and the only way I could see his actually doing it was if Ken Millar came and told him: somebody he *really* respected, a major father figure. So I said to Millar, 'I know this guy just reveres you, he looks up to you like a god; would you be willing to go and talk to him,' 'cause I know it would mean more coming from you.' Margaret said, 'Good luck, it's a fine thing you're trying to do, but face it: the guy's chances of straightening out are about zip.' But Ken said, 'Sure, if you think it'll do any good, I'll go.' I went back to Zevon's house. Zevon didn't know he was coming. The doorbell rings, Zevon goes to the door, and it's Ken Millar. I went off and left them alone and came back after Ken was gone. For Zevon, he said, it was like right out of one of Macdonald's books: 'I went to the door and Lew Archer was there, come to save my life.' It never dawned on me that's how he'd take it: there was Lew Archer, trying to straighten out this troubled kid who happened to be Zevon."

Years later, Zevon remembered the day: "I was right out of detox, in a time when the attitude towards drug and alcohol renunciation had a lot more to do with medallion-wearing therapists than it did with twelve-step programs. So I was sitting in my palatial shithouse in Montecito, in terrible Valium withdrawal, with instructions not to miss therapy the next day. I was in real bad shape. And I remember him coming to the door. Ken was wearing some kind of plaid fedora, like a private eye. And I said something to him like, 'This is a little scary for me.' And he said, 'Nobody's scared of old Ken,' and walked in and spent the afternoon.

"He was a very comforting presence; you know, Valium withdrawal involves considerable fear and trembling. Everything he said was informed by a tremendous amount of compassion: like the books, like what we love about his books on *that* plane. I remember a couple of things he said to me. There was a big book about Stravinsky on my coffee table; I'd known Stravinsky. I said, 'Here's a guy that lived to be eighty-eight. Worked up to his last day, *never* had problems with alcohol or drugs.' He said one word: 'Lucky.' Of course, that word stayed with me all my life—coming from someone who really didn't have anything to do with the world of rehabilitation or Recovery Nation, but could just say a word: 'Lucky.'

"We walked around my backyard, and he was telling me the *names* of things! I said, 'Look, you know, I got this great big house, I don't *like* it, I don't know what any of these *plants* are, this all just makes me un*comfort*able, what's *wrong* with me?' He said, 'How old are you?' I said, 'Thirty.' He said, 'You feel guilty. Writers are overcompensated, in our culture.' And I thought that was also profound. Now when journalists ask me aren't I bitter about I guess presumably not being Bryan Adams, I think, 'Bitter about not being overcompensated, I guess they mean.'

"In the context of the same discussion, I said to him, 'I dun*no*, I read about Fitzgerald drinkin' gin, and I figured if you drank gin, maybe you could write like Fitzgerald. I gotta worry now because writing has stopped being fun.' He said, *'Fun?'* So I remember that too all the time, when writing's hard—as we know it's always hard, and it's always horrible—*'Fun?'* And that was the last time I saw him."

Zevon wrote to thank Millar, saying, "You're not only the finest novelist but the personification of the noblest qualities of your work." The record artist dedicated his 1980 album, *Bad Luck Streak in Dancing School*, "For Ken Millar *il migliore fabbro*." Reminded sixteen years after his thank-you letter that he'd quoted *The Doomsters* to Millar to describe the author's compassionate visit, Zevon recited the line verbatim: "Was it: 'It was one of those times when you have to decide between your own inconvenience and the unknown quantity of another man's troubles'? Well—he meant that stuff. Obviously. He *was* that *guy*."

In September 1979, Millar made a concerted effort to write some fiction. The results were not encouraging. "I've been back at my desk for a short time, not making very much progress or very much noise," he reported to Green. "I seem to have been touched by the encroachments of age, which I suppose might naturally enough show themselves in the late months of my sixty-fourth year. The trouble seems to be lifting—even though no doctor could give it a name more searching than high blood pressure and the like—and while I can't certainly predict the future, it will surely allow me further writing."

Macdonald didn't *have* to do another book, of course. Millar could afford to retire. (He learned this autumn that Knopf was holding more than $170,000 for him in its coffers, money he hadn't even known he had coming.) But writing was more or less what Millar lived for, writing and reading. And he yearned to complete the thirty-year Archer saga in some satisfying way.

An exciting idea occurred to him after he conferred, at his psychiatrist friend's referral, with a Stanford Center expert on memory organization. Millar penned these spidery lines in a notebook: "Archer discovers his own early—perhaps pre-memory—life in Wiarton. The Wiarton story is pre-memory, emerging at the end as Archer's own pre-memory life. Archer goes all the way back and finds himself."

Here was an audacious way to combine autobiography and fiction, the present and the past. Lew Archer—a man in but not of California, the life-long loner obsessed with excavating the causes of others' trauma—would find the buried roots of his own alienation in Ken Millar's Canada. The door leading out of the Archery was the door through which it was entered. The end of the story was in its beginning, and the biggest circle of all would close: "It's all one case."

Like Archer nearing the end of a mystery, Millar felt himself in a race with time, and with his own diminishing abilities. He seemed to need something extra to spur him to the finish line. Millar had always been opposed to freelance writers (in whose ranks he proudly included himself) accepting book advances; cash up front made you beholden to publishers, he warned aspiring authors, and you became an employee instead of an artist. But in December 1979 ("almost as a goad to himself," Green thought), Millar did what he'd never done before in thirty-five years as a novelist: had his agent arrange a contract for a book that wasn't yet written. The house of Knopf agreed to pay Ross Macdonald an advance of forty thousand dollars (half on signing, half on delivery) for an untitled mystery novel due December 1, 1981.

Lew Archer remembers.
—George Grella

Archer is a life-size hero. He's got a better memory than most.
—Ken Millar to Richard Moore

Macular degeneration was the cause of Margaret Millar's eye trouble, and there was no cure. Operations slowed its progress but couldn't stop it. (Of her four laser surgeries, Maggie said, "I might as well have phoned them in.") Though left with peripheral vision, Margaret was legally blind. "I don't know why," she said later, "but blindness has sort of followed me around all my life. Unless I'm just acutely conscious of it. I had two blind dogs. My father was blind when he died at ninety-three. I wrote a *book* about blindness. And it just seems to have— Oh, I don't know, I guess I got a little superstitious about it: almost as if I were asking for it, right? Nope. Not right. I'm not religious."

Margaret Millar's plight troubled her husband greatly, said Bob Easton: "When Margaret's health deteriorated, first with the cancer operation on her lung, this distressed Ken terribly because he felt so totally responsible for her in a very gallant way. When her eyesight began to go, that *really* put an extra burden on Ken and just concerned him so much. He was always very caretaking, very thoughtful of her."

Maggie's attitude was good, and she stuck to her routine: swimming, lunching at the club, attending trials with Millar, and even bicycling around Hope Ranch. With the help of magnifying equipment, she resumed writing. "We've had some recent trouble in our lives," Millar wrote Olding stoically, "but . . . I think we can claim we are riding out the storm, and Margaret riding out the storm of blindness." To keep her informed of local events ("a writer has to know something *special*," Margaret emphasized), Millar read her the newspaper daily, as he'd done years ago for his blind professor Mueschke at Ann Arbor. Maggie's mind was as sharp as ever, and her husband marveled at how much she remembered—Kitchener, for instance: "Margaret has the whole town in her mind, street by street. Her memory is fantastic."

Memory was on Millar's mind a lot. His own had always been remarkable. In college he could recall whole books, including their page numbers. At Michigan, Margaret said, he tested so well in memorization he was urged to switch his major to math: "This was in a memory course, and one of the tests was to multiply a four-figure number by a four-figure number in your head in five minutes, then do it over again with another number. The idea was to test tiredness in relationship to memory: Did you become less proficient, did it take longer, et cetera. I don't know what the conclusion was, but I do know that he got a big kick out of it: which is *my* idea of a nonhobby."

All his life Millar recited poetry from memory, and he seemed to have total recall of his own prose. Betty Phelps got corrected by him once: "In his book *Black Money*, there's a sentence around page twelve that I liked very much, and I told him what it was: 'A little pale moon hung in a corner of the sky, faint as a thumbprint on a window.' He said, 'No: "windowpane." ' And of course it has to be *windowpane* or the rhythm is wrong: 'A little pale moon hung in a corner of the sky, faint as a thumbprint on a windowpane.' "

His memory served Millar well in engineering plots so intricate they might have been concocted by a math whiz. Memories were at the core of Lew Archer's job: they were what he sought, what he recovered. Memory was at least half of fiction-writing, Millar told Jerry Tutunjian: "It's the interplay of memory and intellect together that make imaginative work."

It was triply alarming then when Millar sensed his memory faltering. This began as early as 1971, with occasional mistakes in months and days: writing *March* for *May*. Revising *Sleeping Beauty* in 1972, he confused its chronology by putting *Monday* for *Tuesday*, *Tuesday* for *Wednesday*, and so on; the error was caught at Knopf before the book went to press. ("It's great to be backstopped by you people," he thanked Ash Green.)

In May of 1972, Millar misquoted his own 1952 line about Dashiell Hammett as "We all came out from under Hammett's overcoat." His original quip, a play on Dostoyevsky's remark that all modern Russian writers came out from under Gogol's short story "The Overcoat," was "We all came out from under Hammett's black mask."

By 1974 he was forgetting which of his books were due to be reissued by Bantam. He confessed that year to a correspondent, "I am so prone to getting lost when I go anywhere by car, that I've practically given up out-of-town driving. The road seems to change every year or so in Southern California, but the map in my mind remains the same, ten years out of date." When Julian Symons responded to his confiding that he hoped to bring the Archer cycle to closure, Millar forgot he'd already told Symons that and wrote, "I was struck by your suggestion that I 'round off the Archer saga,' because that is precisely what I am working towards."

He was repeating himself in letters by 1976. ("Thank you for your interest," then three sentences later, "Thank you for your interest." He told Linwood Barclay his fiction manuscript brought "back Canada palpably to me," then a paragraph later said the work "brought Canada palpably back to me.")

The week *The Blue Hammer* was published, a New York City high school teacher wrote Knopf a letter pointing out two mistakes: Lew Archer having dinner at 8 P.M., then buying a meal around midnight because "I hadn't eaten since breakfast"; a body "buried" in the desert then later "found" there. Small errors (and unnoticed by Knopf's proofreader, Millar's editor, and several others) but unusual for the meticulous Ross Macdonald.

(Millar thanked this attentive reader and asked quite seriously if he'd proofread Macdonald's next book.)

More significant mistakes were occurring by late 1976. Millar "worked hard" on his introduction to Otto Penzler's edition of the Archer short stories; nonetheless it contained "a serious inaccuracy" that Penzler called to his attention: "You state that 'the other stories in this volume, with two exceptions, were written for EQMM.' As I'm sure you will recall, only two were written for EQMM, but four were written for MANHUNT. I think you will want to rewrite that line."

His ability to speak in perfectly shaped paragraphs had impressed people since college, but by 1976, Millar was sometimes finding speech elusive. Jane Bakerman quoted him saying, "A lot of the so-called literary material that young writers produce . . . The sentence finishes itself." During his 1976 interviews with Paul Nelson, Millar couldn't recall such familiar names as John O'Hara and Wilkie Collins. In Dick Moore's 1977 film, he took verbal detours to avoid proper names and titles—referring for instance to "my book about the oil spill" instead of *Sleeping Beauty.*

He had trouble signing contracts by early 1978 and was leaving crucial information out of correspondence: bringing a book to someone's attention by title but neglecting to mention its author; stating the month and weekdays of an upcoming trip but not its dates. He repeated words in handwritten sentences ("Have I mentioned that that your reviews seem to me to grow in amplitude and ease?") or omitted them ("At the moment we have the pleasant duty of looking after our fifteen-and-a-half grandson James. Or is he looking after us?"). Making a list of those to be sent complimentary copies of *Archer in Jeopardy,* Millar included Eudora Welty's name twice and wrote "John Simon," a New York critic he didn't know: surely he meant John Leonard? By the end of 1979, Millar was having difficulty reading books, and he wondered, "Can I be slowing down?"

In this fraying mental state, with his wife's situation weighing on him, he tried to write a novel. "The less delightful people with whom I consort in fiction are slow to come to my bidding, but they're coming," he insisted to Ash Green in early 1980. "I have some tentative ideas, and underlying them some new approaches, I think to the Archer story. You will forgive me if I say no more: my later books have been slow to bring in but I trust worth the carriage."

It grieved him that the genre he'd given his life to had changed he thought for the worse, due to the blockbuster mentality in publishing and the trend toward more violently sensational and less realistically serious thrillers. "They ruined the book market in that area," he told *San Francisco Chronicle* writer Mickey Friedman. "It used to be a respectable form, but not any more. . . . The form is aimed in the wrong direction and being done in a way that does it no good. . . . Throughout Europe, it's a highly respected form. It's respected in every country except this one. That's a great disappointment to me."

Changes in the writing world were sadly evident during Ross Macdonald's last appearance at the Santa Barbara Writers Conference, where the author was confronted not by the idealistic young people of previous summers, who'd seemed willing to make sacrifices in the service of their authorial dreams, but by would-be dealmakers who apparently viewed the writing game chiefly as a vehicle to five- or six-figure incomes. "Ken Millar was a very vulnerable-looking figure in this *Day of the Locust*–type scene," said Jim Pepper, a Santa Barbara bookman. "He was bombarded with very invasive questions hurled at him, like 'How much money do you make?' 'How much do you pay your agent?' 'What did you get for paperback rights to *The Blue Hammer*?' He was hesitant, taking more than his time to respond—but he was responding, carefully, thoughtfully. It was a real Nathanael West–like situation."

Millar had more than a deteriorating cultural scene to worry about. He spoke to Friedman of coming to terms with aging: "It's not just an idle thing. You're fighting for your life. . . . You begin to realize things you hadn't thought of before—like, you're not invulnerable."

Foreign editions of Macdonald's California books were being printed all the time now in such far-off places as Israel, Czechoslovakia, Poland, and Russia (Bob Ford alerted Millar to the unauthorized publication of *The Far Side of the Dollar*, under the translated title *Path Leads to El Rancho*, in *Ogonek*, the most popular weekly magazine in the U.S.S.R.). Interviewers wrote or called on Millar (on Margaret too) from all over the country and around the world; in 1980, Macdonald was contacted by writers from Finland, Denmark, Sweden, and Japan. Those journalists who Millar saw in 1980 were saddened and alarmed by the man they encountered.

John Milton, editor of the *South Dakota Review*, found Millar friendly but distracted when he met him for lunch at the Coral Casino in May 1980. After they ordered, Millar forgot and started to order a second time. When Milton tried to give him a list of questions to answer by mail, Millar said, "No, I can't do that."

Between spring and fall of 1980, he got worse. In August he could still compose a letter, but his penmanship was erratic. Concerned for Dorothy Olding, whose blood pressure was high, Millar wrote, "I hope you will give yourself steady and serious care. You are a valuable person in my life—in all our lives—and we love you." A word got snarled in his pen; above its illegible scrawl he printed "VALUABLE."

Jane Bernstein, last in touch with Millar in March 1979, wrote and then telephoned in September 1980 to ask for a letter of recommendation supporting her Guggenheim application. "Frank MacShane suggested it," she said. "I find asking for those things about the hardest thing in the world, but I took a deep breath and called him. And at first he didn't seem to remember who I was, which was painful. Then he said no, he couldn't do it, which was even more painful. And then he told me his wife was sick."

Wall Street Journal writer Rich Jaroslovsky was warned in advance, "almost nonchalantly," of Margaret's blindness when he telephoned for an interview with Macdonald in late 1980. The journalist expected an awkward scene with the Millars, he wrote: "And yet at lunch, they—and especially she—kept up a lively stream of comments, questions and stories. Their devotion to each other was obvious and touching." But Jaroslovky's time with Millar was difficult. "While Mr. Millar didn't declare his writing career over," the *Journal* man later wrote, "he considered his best days to be behind him." Surprised and depressed, Jaroslovsky spiked his Macdonald story.

By now Margaret was aware of his problems. As he warned visitors of her blindness, so she tried to prepare people for his behavior.

"She said several times that he hadn't been well," recalled Diana Cooper-Clark, a teacher at Toronto's York University who arrived in Santa Barbara in December 1980 to interview both Millars for a book of dialogues with mystery writers. "As she put it, his memory wasn't as good as it once was, and he forgot things, right? But I thought, it's the way wives talk sometimes; that's how I took it." Cooper-Clark had already interviewed such crime-fiction writers as Patricia Highsmith, Julian Symons, Ruth Rendell, and Janwillem van de Wetering; she was especially eager to talk with Ross Macdonald. "There was something about his writing that just grabbed me in the heart. I loved his beautiful sentences and the way he put words together, but also the psychological aspect long before people were really doing that. And he was so gracious in his language and metaphors and all of that; I thought he was wonderful. And the excessive patterns, I loved! And even when he wrote essays or did other interviews, I was so fascinated by everything he said and how he said it: there was always such beauty in his articulation. I read *everything* by him; he was marvelous."

Cooper-Clark didn't notice anything untoward in Millar's manner when she and her husband had dinner with the Millars. "He was what I had expected him to be," she said, "quiet, and sort of shy, but very *giving* in his shyness and silences. I didn't feel him aloof at all, I thought he was lovely. Maggie was very voluble, and they told us wonderful stories. Maggie's hilarious. And Ken was very much the straight man. She'd say, 'Ken, do you remember when . . . ?' And Ken was adding to it. She had him telling us the story of this radio quiz show called *Quiz Kids*, in the States? With all these little genius children, who'd ask famous people to come on this show. So when W. H. Auden was on it in Michigan, the Millars were in the audience for support. And Auden came on wearing this mortarboard, right, with the tassel flopping in his face? And the kids read out a line and asked, 'Who wrote that?' And he was guessing: 'Yeats? Kipling? T. S. Eliot!' And the kids said, 'No! *You* said it!' So they told us these hilarious stories. I realized later, as long as the four of us were together, we absorbed any problems Ken might be having, because the three of us were talkers and Margaret would *feed* him lines; she would be taking *care* of him."

The next day, interviewing Millar alone at the Coral Casino shortly after his sixty-fifth birthday, Cooper-Clark understood what Margaret had been hinting at. "This was supposed to be my dream interview," she said. "And before we started, he too said to me, 'My memory isn't what it used to be.' He knew. And within five minutes it was absolutely clear something awful was happening. He could not cope." Questions that would have been easy a year or two earlier ("How would you define tragedy?") had him groping for words; he had to be prompted on names like Dickens; he lost the thread of his thoughts. "It was very disjointed. He was going all over the place. At the same time we kept pushing on, and he did give me some marvelous things. There was no tension or anxiety in him; it wasn't making him agitated. Even though he found my questions difficult, he was quite serene actually. I was the one who was upset, not him. I had tears in my eyes a lot of the time; well, I didn't want him to notice that, so I had my head down a lot, looking up at him, that kinda thing. After about half an hour, I knew this was it: I knew he'd never give another interview. Probably never write again.

"I was awfully upset. And it went on like that for about three hours; it was a *long* interview. I'd done enough of these by now to know this one was a disaster. But he wanted to keep going; when I'd suggest taking a break or meeting the next day, he did not want to stop. It was almost as if he *had* to do it then, because he'd gotten up for it that day, and every day he'd slip a little more. . . . Yes, there was a real compulsion to continue; I mean, he really was doing the best that he could. And it was horrible to watch, because he was such a dignified man. It's like the musician going deaf, the painter going blind. I was thinking like crazy: I'm going to have to do something to save this; needless to say, it was a massive editing job. Near the end of the interview, I said to him—this was not exactly the truth, but I said—'Sometimes writers like to, you know, blend some of the interview with things they've said in the past.' I said, 'Do you want to do that?' He said, 'Oh, sure, if I've said it, use it.' Certainly I didn't take anything whole cloth, but sometimes the odd sentence from something he'd written would fit. It was the only thing I could do for him, because I wasn't going to have him stammering and stuttering all over the page; he was so dignified, and he had so much pride.

"And at the end of these three hours, I was so upset, I asked him, 'Are you working on another book?' And then I felt terrible. But I didn't want to treat him as though he had no possibility left. And he didn't react as though it were a painful question." Millar answered with good humor, irony, and literal truth: "I'll write another book, if I can."

> . . . the whole current of his recollections ran back to old times, and what a crowd of emotions were wakened up in his breast . . . a poor houseless, wandering boy without a friend to help him, or a roof to shelter his head.
>
> —Charles Dickens, *Oliver Twist*

Millar didn't say much to people about his troubles. "I think he might not have said *anything* to *anyone*, if he didn't have to," guessed Ralph Sipper. Millar only told Bob Easton what was happening when Easton asked him to vet his latest manuscript, as Millar had done for twenty years. " 'I'd better not,' he said in his customary unblinking fashion," Easton wrote. " 'I'm losing my memory.' . . . But he made no claim for sympathy, no protest against fate." It was the same when Millar broke the news to him, Sipper said: "He was very reserved, stoical, unemotional about this terrible thing that was happening to him. He didn't wear his heart on his sleeve."

Sipper had already sensed that something was amiss. He'd agreed in late 1980 to edit a collection of autobiographical Macdonald pieces, *Self-Portrait,* to be published by Noel Young's Capra Press. When Sipper asked Ken to clarify personal details in them, Millar couldn't: he no longer remembered those things.

But that wasn't why Millar brought up the subject. He wanted Sipper to deal with his correspondents, let them know Ken couldn't answer letters anymore. What should he tell them, Sipper asked. "Use your good judgment," Millar said.

It was a while before the writers' lunch people even realized anything was wrong. They thought Millar was simply being his quiet self, only more so, until he started acting strangely. "After the meeting one day," Bill Gault recalled, "he said, 'Wait for me outside, will you?' I said, 'Sure.' So I wait. And I wait, and I wait. Finally Ken comes out and he says, 'What are *you* waiting for?' "

The Millars pulled together, once more a team. "I saw them once in the supermarket," said Gayle Lynds, "and they were the most tender people to one another. She was half-blind and couldn't get quite around, and he was losing his—sensibilities; and they were like one person. Together they were whole, and it was quite beautiful. There was a lot of tenderness and compassion between them, and respect. All the good things that can happen with a long marriage. When they got to the checkstand she basically told him what to do, and he paid while she talked to the checker. The bag kid helped 'em, and they were able to maneuver it. They had a lotta dignity."

Collin Wilcox was also impressed by the Millars' mutual affection when he saw them at the Coral Casino in early 1981. "I came away inspired, really," he said, "because I'd never got the impression of them as a warm and loving couple. I'm not saying they *weren't,* but they didn't put those things on display. But now they had this very quiet way of being so supportive of each other." Millar told Wilcox about an operation he was going to have in May to alleviate his concentration problems. "As I understand it," Wilcox said, "they were to put a plastic tube from his brain down into his stomach, to drain off fluid. He described it all sort of academically; he seemed to think it was really interesting, that they'd perform an operation like that."

Easton said, "It had something to do with spinal fluid and opening up the brainpan and taking pressure off the brain—oh, a very complex thing. Margaret of course knew all the details and was very up on those things. She elected to have that happen and hoped it would help. But it didn't help. And that upset her tremendously."

After the operation his doctors decided what Millar actually had was "premature senility," or, as it was now starting to be called, Alzheimer's disease. There wasn't any treatment. Julian Symons visited Santa Barbara in 1981 and sat through a painful lunch with Millar, who seemed, Symons wrote, "a kind of smiling shell." He didn't think Millar knew who he was.

Ross Macdonald's *Self-Portrait: Ceaselessly into the Past* was published at the end of 1981, with an afterword by Ralph Sipper and a foreword by Eudora Welty. Some reviewers complained the collection's twenty-one pieces were repetitious and didn't reveal enough, but others thought the book had permanent worth. Charles Champlin in the *LA Times Book Review* said it gave "as perceptive, elegantly written and illuminating an analysis of the detective story, its history, technique and value, as can be found anywhere." In the *National Review,* Terry Teachout called *Self-Portrait* "a valuable and fascinating addition to the output of one of this country's most consistently undervalued literary artists."

Margaret had a book out too, the novel *Mermaid,* written on her special equipment in four and a half months. When it was published, she was at work on another, *Banshee.* "Writing keeps me sane," she told the *LA Times*'s Wayne Warga in early 1982, adding with a laugh, "or as sane as I am. I'm making no great claims."

Warga's *Times* piece publicly broke the news of Millar's plight. The journalist saw the Millars at the Coral Casino, where they still went every day. As Millar sat placidly, Margaret told Warga of the semi–non sequiturs in which they now communicated. (She: "Have you noticed how much friskier the dogs are in the morning?" He: "Yes. Currier and Ives did some of their best painting as young men.") Warga said later, "Her attitude was wonderful; it was, 'I'm going to get through this.' There was about her a sense of an absolute survivor. She just kept going, no matter what. She was obviously the strength in the marriage." Maggie was being helped with Ken by a Brooks Institute photography student, who drove Millar to the writers' lunch and took him for daily swims. "He was very gracious, that young man," said Warga. "One thing that amazed me about Ken: here was a man in his late sixties who had the body of a forty-year-old. He was in such good physical condition. He went out there and he swam those laps and he swam those laps, until finally it got so that somebody had to get in the pool and stay with him; but he did it. And he had this incredible build. He wasn't muscular or anything; just the most healthy-looking man I've ever seen."

Margaret told Warga, "Here we are, two people who live by books. What has happened has taken ninety percent of our lives away. I keep reminding myself of what we have left. I can't get out of it anyway. I've faced my own problem pretty well. I haven't faced his well, at least not as well as I think I should. . . . I lose my temper and then I go on guilt trips. The trips aren't as big as they used to be, but the temper remains the same."

Years later Margaret described the "nutsy" sort of thing that made her lose patience: "I would try to get him to put on his shoes, to get him dressed. I'd say, 'Okay, go and put on your shoes.' I'd point to his feet, and grab his feet, and then the shoe. So one day he went in to put on his shoes, and he was gone a long, long time, and I began to get a little *suspic*ious. I went in, and he had taken all of his shoes—he had a weakness for shoes, always bought the same kind, very inexpensive Hush Puppies, and he always bought them too big, he had to have lots of room—and he had tied knots in all of the shoelaces. I mean, *navy* knots! Oh, *my*. And there was just no way of dealing with that, except by getting the screaming meemies."

After a while Margaret was sure Millar no longer knew who she was: "Hadn't the faintest." Bill Ruehlmann (one of many who wrote or called or visited when they learned of Millar's condition) said, "Margaret told me of one conversation where she sat down at his bedside and asked him, 'Who am I?' and Ken looked at her and smiled and said, 'The boss.' Well, at once that's marvelously clever and marvelously sad. And marvelously true: she had taken his life over." Yet certain ingrained impulses remained, Margaret said: "Whenever a woman would enter a room, he would always get up; and he'd always say 'please' and 'thank you.' It was instinctually part of his nature, to be kind and gentle. And it was extraordinary: I could start a line of poetry, and he could recite the rest."

As Margaret wrote on her latest novel, Ken went through work motions too. One day he found a page of an old Archer short story typescript and scrawled random words on it: "and tumbled tumbled free air into brook broken broken Trembling." He couldn't read books anymore, but he still liked to handle them, moving volumes from one shelf to another, rearranging by size and color. "John Ball told me," said Ray Browne, "Margaret told him she would much rather Ross were dead than that his whole mental life consist of putting blue books with blue books and red books with red books: a sad, sort of terrifying comment." Margaret let him open the mail for a while, until he lost some checks and contracts. Other days he puttered in the yard. "Looking after an Alzheimer's patient is very very difficult," Margaret said, "because you never know what the *hell* they're gonna do next." One afternoon Millar wandered away from the house with one of the dogs. A policeman found them downtown and brought them home. Ken Millar didn't seem to know where he was: he walked up to his wife and asked, "What is your name? And would you have a bed tonight where I could sleep?"

"What hurts the most," said Eudora Welty, "is that Ken *knew* what was happening to him, I mean he had to face that; 'cause he had a brilliant mind, and this just slowly came about. It started with not being able to remember things. I had some letters from him saying, 'It scares me, my hands can't write, what happened?' And how he must have suffered with all of that, and all inside. There wasn't any way to comfort him. He was unable to write eventually. I wrote to him anyway, and Margaret said he was glad to get my letters, that he'd put 'em in his shirt pocket. I don't know."

Welty, half a continent away, agonized over Millar's fate. Reynolds Price said, "I know she felt very intense grief and deeply miserable from the time she first heard Ken would not be in touch anymore. Eudora found it very difficult to believe that he really had Alzheimer's. I think her feeling was that the illness might be a kind of reaction to domestic unhappiness, some kind of depressive withdrawal. And her sense was that she was being prevented from getting *through* to him, that in some sense Margaret was kind of barring the door so that Eudora could not go out there and see Ken and at least satisfy her own mind that he really was irretrievable."

"I wanted to go back and see him," Welty said, "but people told me he wouldn't know me or anything. One fellow I saw in New York, who'd been to Santa Barbara, said, 'Oh, what's the point, he didn't even know who I *was*'—kind of a brush-off, you know? That hurt me; that kind of *got* me. Because, how do *we* know? There might have been one moment when Ken recognized or knew him that would have given Ken some pleasure."

"She asked me if I thought she should go to see him," said Price, who was teaching at Duke. "And I said, 'Well, I don't think you'll ever be satisfied until you do.' But she seemed sort of reluctant. Finally, whenever the Knoxville, Tennessee, World's Fair was, Eudora and I went there on opening day to be on the *Today* show, and she was so deeply distressed about Ken, I just said, 'Well, I'll go out with you, if that'll help.' And Eudora and I made a sort of pact that we were going out together to see him. And then suddenly a little while later, in the middle of the semester, she called me and said, 'There's this opening for me to go out there.' Some occasion had presented itself, and she felt that if she didn't go *right then,* that she never could go. And I couldn't get away from school, so she went out on her own."

The occasion was the third annual *Los Angeles Times* Book Prizes, where Ross Macdonald would be given the Robert Kirsch Award for a distinguished body of work. Kirsch, an early champion of Macdonald's fiction, had died in 1980; the two previous Kirsch Award recipients were Wallace Stegner and Wright Morris. Macdonald wouldn't attend the November 19, 1982, ceremony in LA, but Margaret would. And, thanks to Ralph Sipper, so would Welty; Sipper arranged for her to spend the week of the *Times* event in Santa Barbara.

The seventy-three-year-old Welty came unaccompanied from Jackson, Mississippi, to Santa Barbara by plane, lugging her bag between terminals when she changed flights in Denver. "She paid her own way, stayed at the Miramar Hotel, had dinner with us at night," said Sipper. "Her whole purpose during this four- or five-day visit was to just talk to Ken."

"They were so sweet to me," Welty said of Sipper and his wife. "I couldn't have gone if Ralph and Carol hadn't sort of sponsored me. I felt that I had Margaret's permission to come out. They made it all possible, they met me and took me everywhere. You know, we felt the same way about Ken."

Welty found Millar sadly disabled, Margaret at the end of her rope, and Maggie's sister aiding Millar with tenderness. "He was helpless as far as things that your hands know what to do," Welty said. "Didn't very well handle a knife and fork, someone else had to cut his meat up. That disease, that's the way it leaves you: without knowledge of how to do anything, button something. And Margaret's sister was so sweet, I mean, she would just quietly do this. He would go swimming, and she'd help him with his clothes. The situation was easy, since they all knew each other so well, and she was a nurse.

"He could still swim. He remembered how to swim, and he had someone to go swimming with him every day in the pool there at the club. He swam well, and it did him good. When he got out of the pool, he seemed so much more alert, you know; he would say, 'When did you come?' to somebody, or 'I'm glad to see you, I'm gonna eat lunch,' or somethin' definite. Then it would sort of trail off. He took care always to have a good physical condition, and he had a wonderful swimmer's body; in his bathing suit, he just looked wonderful, right at the last. All of that, it did him no good."

Welty sat through a "horrible" lunch at the Coral Casino, she said, as Maggie blurted things Welty found appalling. "Margaret said, 'Well, of course I had to poison the dogs.' They had three dogs when I was there earlier, two German shepherds and one little mongrel that Ken found on the beach and brought home, a real sweet little kind of female terrier. 'I didn't have any time left to attend to those dogs,' she says, 'so they're all gone now.' She tells this to Ken. You know: the loves of his heart. Whether it was true or not, I don't know. It doesn't matter whether it was true or not, it was just—telling him that: that she had to poison 'em. I don't understand that, I mean she just— *Punishing* him all the time. *She* loved those dogs too. It was terribly difficult, the whole situation of course, just terrible. No telling what she did go through. She was probably at her wits' end about everything and just flew out with that, I don't know why. I couldn't see into her mind, at all.

"Same with their grandson, a charming young man. He called to ask if he should visit, and Margaret said, 'Oh, I told him if he wanted to come, fine, if not, don't bother, do what he pleased.' Said that in front of Ken. You imagined this man sitting there, seeing everything he cared about slipping away from him. There was so much shut up inside him. Well, there is in everybody, but— It just seems to me especially cruel; the things that happened to him.

"Like Ken said . . . He looked at me and he said, 'I can't write.' And he looked at his hands.

"It was the cruelest thing of course that could happen to anyone, but especially to Ken, I think. Just the very cruelest that could have come over him."

Maggie told Welty she would soon put Millar in a nursing home. When Welty only looked away, she added, "Well, he's not going to get any better, you know, it's just going to get worse. He'll be just like a vegetable."

"I mustn't judge her," Welty said later, "she had a hard time. Putting him in a nursing home, to me that seemed so awful. Of course I can see now that probably was the only way they could handle his physical needs. Because he began to take falls, without warning. He fell several times with all of his weight, this big six-foot man who weighed a hundred and eighty pounds or whatever he was. To fall, without catching himself, and people couldn't even lift him, he was bigger than they were. That would take him by surprise, you see."

Welty was glad she went to Santa Barbara. "It turned out *fine,*" she said, "because he *did* know me." Sipper agreed. "She could reach him," he said. "Ken would have these moments of lucidity, and when she was around, he had more of them as far as I could see. He didn't just sit silently and gaze off into the distance as much. He responded to her."

Welty spent most of her visit simply talking to Millar. "I told him about a trip I'd made on that crack transcontinental Canadian train that goes from Montreal out to Vancouver," she said. "I told him I'd thought of him so often, crossing Ontario and all those places, and that when I'd get off sometimes between trains, for instance in Winnipeg, I'd remember he'd written about a school he'd been to there, so I thought, 'This is where Ken was, this is where he would be, this is what he would see.' And his eyes just lit up at the place names, he knew *exactly* what I was talking about, and he would join in with some things.

"I told him that at one part of the trip they stopped the train because of an earth slide in front of us, and its sister train that starts at the Vancouver end had to stop for the same reason. So what they did was take everybody off each train and switch 'em, and the trains just went back where they'd come from! This kind of appealed to him, I think. And I said, 'So that was the best part of the trip, 'cause we went on a bus into Medicine Hat.' And he knew the name of the bus: he said, 'Moose Mountain bus.' Yes! It's what it was. And I said, 'We saw elks running along,' and he, he could just see, he could just *see* that road! And he was just so alive to it all, and he remembered. So I remembered as *much* as I could, because everything I could tell him was something that rang a bell. It was amazing. But I was thrilled, because it turned out that we could really talk, just like we're talking now. You know it both broke your heart, and—you realized how much would go through his mind, even fleetingly, and clue him in on something, and he *knew* it. And I know so much of his boyhood was with him all the time, and he could call on it if he needed to."

One day Welty and Millar sat alone in the beach club cabana. "You could look out into the harbor there," she said, "and see those oil platforms that had always upset Ken so, that he wrote that mystery about, with the oil spill and everything. And he didn't know what they were. But he looked out there and he said, 'There's something *wrong* about those. . . .' He said, 'They don't belong there, do they?' "

As I hope my books make clear, there's no retreat from the "California experience," as visiting critics call it. It's like a furnace which uses you up, leaving nothing at the end but a spoonful of fine ash and the record of enormous fantasies.

— Ken Millar to Dorothy Olding, 1968

And the   Oh! dream of joy! Is this indeed
Ancient   The light-house top I see?
Mariner   Is this the hill? Is this the kirk?
beholdeth his   Is this mine own countree?
native country.

— S. T. Coleridge

The day after his sixty-seventh birthday, Millar moved into Cliff View Terrace, a private rest home on the Santa Barbara mesa: perhaps the eighty-fifth place he'd lived in. "It was a nice home," said Bob Easton, "down on Cliff Drive oddly enough, maybe half a mile from where Ken and Maggie once lived." Another Archeresque circle closed. "I'd go and see him there," Easton said, "and Margaret would, and Ralph Sipper, and others. He'd recognize you in a sense, but in a sense he didn't know you were there. He'd talk almost like we're talking here for a time—and then just wander right off it. But he never got violent, the way some Alzheimers do. And he didn't give the impression of being unhappy, of being penned up against his will. You'd say, 'Well, Ken, I'll see you later.' He'd say, 'I'll see you later.' "

"The romantic image of it is to say that he withdrew into himself like a monk," said Bill Ruehlmann, some of whose family also had Alzheimer's disease, "like Ken slowly closing the door. Actually the brain cells are going away, and you're becoming catatonic."

Herb Harker went to visit Millar at Cliff View, where he watched his friend try to sip water from a flower vase and heard him speak sentences that didn't add up ("I think I'll go and wash out the tugget. I can't spend my life at this"). "I could have wept," Harker wrote. "In all ways, in his countenance, his dress, his posture, his quiet demeanor, his controlled speech and action, his gentleness—in all of these, he was scarcely discernible from the man I had known. But the towering thing about him, his mind, had left him. And it was hard to watch him grope for something to pull against. He was like a lone fisherman in a heavy sea, who has lost his oars."

Near the anniversary of his daughter's birthday on June 18 (Linda would have been forty-four), Millar had "a cerebrovascular accident" and was admitted to Cottage Hospital for three days. On June 23 he was transferred to Pinecrest, where Warren Zevon once spent time. "I told them I wouldn't authorize any steps to extend his life artificially in hospital," Margaret Millar said. "That was what we had agreed a long time ago to do for the other if a decision like that had to be made." Kenneth Millar, aged sixty-seven, died on Monday, July 11, 1983.

He was mourned under two names from Santa Barbara to Moscow. The wide appeal of his books could be gauged by the range of publications carrying news of his death: the *New York Times, Daily Variety,* the *Times* of London, *Rolling Stone.* Ross Macdonald's passing made the front page of the *Wall Street Journal.* Dailies around the country printed critical appreciations: the *Los Angeles Times* (by Charles Champlin), the *Detroit News* (Clifford A. Ridley), the *Virginian-Pilot* and the *Ledger-Star* (William Ruehlmann), the *Los Angeles Herald-Examiner* (Mikal Gilmore). The *Washington Post* paid tribute in an editorial.

Several people wrote personal reminiscences. *Wall Street Journal* staffer Rich Jaroslovsky did the story he couldn't bring himself to file while Millar was alive. Frank MacShane (later an Alzheimer's sufferer) remembered Millar for the *New York Times Book Review.* Paul Nelson, never able to craft a Macdonald profile without mentioning things he'd promised not to, instead wrote a memoir of Millar for *Rolling Stone.* Santa Barbara cartoonist Charles Schulz drew a *Peanuts* comic strip in which Lucy asked would-be author Snoopy: "You want your book to sell, don't you? You know what they always put on the covers of books they want to sell? 'In the tradition of Hammett, Chandler and Macdonald.' "

There were obituaries in English, German, and Swiss newspapers. BBC radio broadcast a ten-minute discussion of his work. Julian Symons wrote pieces for the Sunday *Times* and for *London* magazine. Many would clearly miss not only the books but the man behind them. "It's sad that we have to lose at the same moment a character like Lew Archer from American fiction and a writer as intelligent and decent as Ross Macdonald," CBC producer Robert Weaver told the *Toronto Star.* Macdonald meant a great deal now in Canada, where writers like Howard Engel, Ted Wood, and Eric Wright were finally creating an indigenous mystery fiction, forty years after Margaret Millar's Ontario books and twenty-four years after Archer went north in *The Galton Case.* Macdonald was commemorated by the *Toronto Star,* the *Toronto Globe and Mail,* the *Kitchener-Waterloo Record,* and the *Montreal Star.*

In his adopted town of Santa Barbara, the alternative paper *News & Review* put Ross Macdonald on its cover. Here Millar was recalled as much for his civic activism as for his books. James G. Mills wrote the *News-Press,* "Several years back, on the death of *News-Press* artist-writer Dick Smith, [Millar] praised Dick for having tried to keep alive the birds, plants and animals . . . stating that the whole living county was his monument. We could say the same of Ken Millar."

The Foundation for Santa Barbara City College, for whom Millar had taught a night class a quarter century earlier, started a Macdonald memorial fund; and Millar was given a posthumous award. A writing group was named for him; this Millar-commemorating group held classes at Linda Millar's old grade school, across from the Millars' first Santa Barbara home at 2124 Bath. "It was so strange," said Margaret. "We had been living in the house *right* across the street when he wrote his first [Macdonald] book. And that he should get an award there for the body of his work . . . It was a *nice* irony for a change."

It was Macdonald's year for prizes. Within a month of his getting the Robert Kirsch Award, the Private Eye Writers of America voted him its first Life Achievement Award ("The Eye").

Detective fiction, Millar sometimes said, was his "accommodation"—to the need for a form to channel his talent, and to his vow to make a living through fiction. But the private-eye tale was much more to Millar than a blueprint and a meal ticket. In his books he wrestled with the worst and better angels of his nature. Knowledgeable critics felt he achieved things with the mystery that had never before been done. Geoffrey O'Brien, author of *Hardboiled America*, wrote, "Macdonald's narratives are beautifully built machines in which the constructional genius of an Agatha Christie is wedded to a gift for writing about flesh-and-blood people in real and contemporary places. This particular combination of talents had not often, if ever, occurred in the mystery field (earlier on, it was declared an impossibility by Raymond Chandler . . .)." John McAleer, Rex Stout's biographer, said Millar did what Chandler couldn't: "In his last major novel, *The Long Goodbye*, [Chandler] tried to reconcile the hard-boiled detective story with the novel of manners, which he now recognized as the true matrix of the detective story. His principal disciple, Ross Macdonald, completed this reconciliation after Chandler's death." Julian Symons thought it pointless to compare the mature Macdonald with Chandler or Hammett: "Macdonald's achievement is wholly individual, unique in the modern crime story."

Several literary commentators felt Macdonald's achievement extended significantly beyond the crime genre. "Ross Macdonald is one of the central authors of his time and place," wrote George Grella. "Finally, his novels may be the truest of any, in his lifetime, in America." Matthew Bruccoli stated, "The twelve novels from *The Galton Case* to *The Blue Hammer* constitute a quest cycle; taken together, they form one of the splendid achievements in American fiction." Frank MacShane called Macdonald simply "one of the best writers of his generation."

Millar thought the future of mystery fiction was to merge with the novel—to return to where it began, in the realistic imaginings of Charles Dickens and Wilkie Collins (completing another circle). In the years since his death, the blurring of genres that began when *The Goodbye Look* made the front page of the *New York Times Book Review* accelerated, with literary authors (Norman Mailer, Gabriel Garcia Marquez, Umberto Eco) writing metamysteries, and new thriller writers (Scott Turow, Ruth Rendell, Peter

Hoeg) displaying styles worthy of any Knopf or Faber and Faber novelist. Surely Ross Macdonald spurred some of this cross-genre traffic, if only by showing how seriously crime fiction could be written and taken.

All sorts of authors admired him: Iris Murdoch, Thomas Berger, John Fowles, Charles Portis, David Hare, Stephen Sondheim, Joyce Carol Oates. The writer who was never at home in any country wrote books that were read all over the world. After his death, Macdonald's southern California novels continued to be published in England, France, Spain, Portugal, Israel, Germany, Italy, Sweden, Denmark, Switzerland, Finland, Poland, Hungary, Czechoslovakia, Brazil, Argentina, Greece, Japan. Lawrence Block, an MWA Grandmaster, wrote how he and his wife once found themselves in West Africa for three weeks with nothing to read: "Then, in our hotel in Lomé, the capital of Togo, I discovered five Lew Archers, secondhand paperbacks that had been badly printed in India. The newsdealer wanted an extortionary ten dollars apiece for them, and I paid it willingly. They sustained us all the way back to JFK. Of course we had read them all before, some of them two or three times. It didn't matter. . . . Wonderful books." Macdonald was one of the writers Japanese novelist Haruki Murakami (*Norwegian Wood, A Wild Sheep Chase, Hardboiled Wonderland and the End of the World*) gorged himself on as a teen in Kobe in the middle 1960s: "I go to the used-book stores and buy a dozen very cheap Ross Macdonald, Dashiell Hammett, Ray Bradbury . . . Raymond Chandler."

Macdonald's appeal was universal because his themes were timeless: "The point of the stories wasn't death," said the *Washington Post*, "but the consequences of death revealing history and intention. The crime that chiefly attracted his interest was betrayal of trust—between husbands and wives, between children and parents, sometimes of patients by doctors. It was all set in a California landscape evoked with accuracy and force." His style set him apart too. As critic Thomas J. Roberts said, "Archer, Macdonald's narrator, thinks and sees in one-line poems." Or as Don Pearce put it, "The colors he would dab in are always done with minimal, strong subtlety. It's like making a drink, you know: *just* enough lime, a drop or two. *Just* enough dry vermouth, or you'll wreck the taste. He knew how to do that to a text; he's exquisitely subtle. It's fragrance that he adds, a little bit of exquisite flavor that makes all the difference."

He learned from Romantic poets and Victorian novelists as well as hard-boiled writers, and his books were built to last. They could be enjoyed on many levels: as detective stories, family chronicles, regional histories. Donald Davie said, "I don't reread those books now for the story, I reread them for what they tell me about the California I knew: not just the coast, not just Orange County, not just Palo Alto, but various interesting places—I mean the Central Valley, and the edges of the Mojave. I think they're wonderful from that point of view." For some, Macdonald made a lifelong impression with a single sentence. Betty Phelps can still quote: "'A little pale moon hung in a corner of the sky, faint as a thumbprint on a windowpane.' Once or twice a month my husband and I see it in the sky, and we say, 'Oh, there's the little pale moon'—to us that means Ken Millar."

It was as a writer of mystery fiction of course that Macdonald would be best remembered. In that field, he became sui generis. Symons wrote, "With him a particular kind of crime story ended." But a profusion of new sorts began, and Macdonald seemed to have influenced most of them, either directly or as a standard of excellence.

Joseph Hansen bristled at the "weak-willed middle-aged little-theater types" in *The Drowning Pool*, but its author was one of those who spurred him to write his own detective books, he said: "Not until I chanced on Dashiell Hammett, Raymond Chandler, Ross Macdonald, did it occur to me that writing a mystery might, after all, be a fine thing to do. These men were real writers." Hansen's homosexual investigator Dave Brandstetter opened the door for a host of other writers' gay and lesbian sleuths.

Women started writing books about female private eyes in the 1970s and 1980s, a nearly unprecedented thing in mystery fiction. Macdonald was often their inspiration. Marcia Muller, whose first Sharon McCone book was published in 1977, told *Publishers Weekly* how she came to the genre: "I picked up a Ross Macdonald mystery and I fell in love with his work. . . . I had finally found the form I wanted to write." Sara Paretsky, whose V. I. Warshawski debuted in 1982, also read Macdonald (and put his name in one of her books). The best-known woman PI was Sue Grafton's Kinsey Millhone. Like Millar (whom she met), Grafton lived in Santa Barbara; in tribute to Macdonald she based Millhone in Santa Teresa, the fictionalized Santa Barbara where Archer so often worked.

The eighties saw crime fiction exploring the psychological and sexual abuse of children, with Jonathan Kellerman's 1985 Edgar-winning *When the Bough Breaks* proving a watershed book. Ross Macdonald inspired him to write that novel, says Kellerman, an LA clinical psychologist at the time: "I was driving on Sunset Boulevard, and I saw an antique store going out of business. I stopped in, and they had some used books including *The Underground Man*. I'd heard of Ross Macdonald, but I had never read him; I hadn't read mysteries for years. But the jacket notes sounded intriguing, and I bought it for a dime. I loved the way the man wrote. Something clicked. I said, 'This man's a great writer, and he's writing about family psychopathology, and that's something I know from my work.' Also it gave me a focus on the whole southern California thing, what I call the malignance behind the palm trees: where you have the beautiful weather and ambience but there's always a sinister evil lurking." In 1990, Kellerman wrote, "Let's be honest: Ross Macdonald remains *the* grandmaster, taking the crime novel to new heights by imbuing it with psychological resonance, complexity of story, and richness of style that remain awe-inspiring. Those of us in his wake owe a debt that can never be paid."

Other crime writers were equally grateful. Robert B. Parker, author of the popular Spenser series, wrote, "I owe him, as does every one of us who step, albeit less gracefully, to the same drumbeat. For in his craft and his integrity, he made the detective form a vehicle for high seriousness. It was not that others hadn't tried, it was that he succeeded. . . . Lew Archer *is* the form." James Ellroy (who dedicated a 1984 novel "In Memory of KENNETH MILLAR") told an interviewer, "Ross Macdonald—on an emotional level—for me is the great teacher." In Spain, Catalan writer Jaume Fuster created detective Lluis Arquer, who owed his very name to Lew Archer. Peer admiration of Macdonald wasn't confined to private-eye writers. Asked in 1986 to name her favorite mystery authors, England's P. D. James answered, "Among the Americans, I particularly admire the hard-boiled school. I don't often reread them—they're very different books from mine—but I think that Dashiell Hammett, Raymond Chandler, and Ross Macdonald in particular—I do like Ross Macdonald—are marvelous writers."

Kenneth Millar, humble but proud, thought Ross Macdonald's novels would still be read in a hundred years. It seems certain the books will stay in print into the twenty-first century. One professional dream of Millar's went unfulfilled: despite films of *Blue City*, *The Three Roads*, and *The Ferguson Affair*, no movie (the entertaining *Harper* aside) has yet effectively translated Macdonald's prose to the screen. But in 1996 something happened that might have pleased Millar nearly as much: Santa Monica's KCRW-FM produced a seven-and-a-half-hour, full-cast adaptation of *Sleeping Beauty*, heard on many National Public Radio stations. Lew Archer (played by Harris Yulin, the show's director) was at last brought to decent dramatic life not through movies or television but on radio, the medium that first sparked Millar's love of popular culture when he was seven years old in Wiarton.

Margaret Millar remained active after Macdonald's death, in some ways more active than when Millar was alive. Accompanied by her sister, she took several trips: to New York, to Canada, to England. The first such was in April 1983, two months before her husband died: Margaret went to Manhattan to receive a Grandmaster Award from the Mystery Writers of America. "I don't know whether I deserve this award," she said at the Edgar dinner, "but I do know I worked like hell for forty-three years to get it. I wish my husband were here with me right now."

Maggie moved out of the Hope Ranch house and put it up for sale as soon as Millar was in Cliff View Terrace. "I couldn't bear to live in the house anymore," she told writer Ed Gorman. "Any more than I can bear to put on any of the tapes that he made or anything like that, or hear any of the music. I hardly ever play music for that reason. It reminds me of Ken and it makes me just too damn sad." She moved into a condo apartment in the Bonnymede-Montecito Shores complex near the Coral Casino. (Another irony: Millar and others were chased by a bulldozer while protesting the 1973 development of this site.)

Margaret lunched daily at the Coral Casino, raised a new dog in her apartment, watched *Jeopardy* nightly with binoculars on a forty-six-inch TV screen (and rooted for the women). She wrote (but didn't sell) a twenty-seventh book. And she endured what Millar was spared: the 1989 death of their twenty-six-year-old grandson, James, of a drug overdose in Las Vegas, a city Millar hated and always wrote of as evil. It was bleak testament to the power of Millar's art that this third-generation sorrow seemed like something from a Ross Macdonald story.

Margaret Sturm Millar came from hardy stock: Hen Sturm lived to be ninety-two. Maggie had no intention of sticking around through years of illness, though; she spoke approvingly of "assisted-suicide" activist Jack Kevorkian. Before a scheduled trip to Toronto in 1992 to be honored at the twenty-third Bouchercon, Margaret broke a hip. An earlier operation that removed one lung had put a strain on her heart and weakened it. Margaret Millar died March 26, 1994, at the age of seventy-nine. As with Ken Millar, there was no memorial service, official or unofficial. "I wish other people would get as sensible about funerals and stuff as Ken and I were," Margaret had told Ed Gorman. "Cremation and ashes and that's that. No making your friends suffer through a funeral."

Denied a memorial service, his friends and admirers remembered Ken Millar in their own ways. The poets (Donald Davie, Reynolds Price, Diane Wakoski) wrote poems. Davie said, "I thought he was a brave man, very brave. I think he had a very curious and unhappy life. Born into an extraordinarily dislocated situation: Californian, lost his father, raised as a poor relation in Canada, then going to Michigan . . . Nah, he'd started with most of the strikes against him. That he managed to put it all together and *get steadily better* for a long time—I thought it was wonderful. I'm very proud to have known him and to have been his friend, very proud."

Millar predicted he'd die before Maggie, and in the 1970s he arranged that his cremated ashes would be scattered in the Santa Barbara Channel, "where, in the destructive element immersed, I have spent the best hours of my best days." He'd always seemed happiest in the sea, where his dog Brandy kept him company. After Brandy's death, a certain seal waited for Millar each day and swam with him. The Pacific was the one constant in his life, Ken Millar said: the ocean at Santa Barbara was the same ocean his father had taken him sailing on in Vancouver. He swam in that sea even after his memory went, and the sea took his ashes. "In the end as in the beginning," Robert Easton wrote, "the victim was Ken." And the hero.

ACKNOWLEDGMENTS

INTERVIEWS

I am grateful to the many who agreed to be interviewed in person or by telephone.

Margaret Millar was not only good enough to speak with me for several hours but allowed me unrestricted access to the Millar Collection at UC Irvine and to whatever other Millar-related material I was able to find.

Donald Ross Pearce, a friend of the Millars' for thirty years, generously spent many weeks giving me what amounted to a graduate seminar in the personality of Kenneth Millar and the artistry of Ross Macdonald.

Mari Shaw, Bertram Wood, Gardner Wood, Moyer Wood, Paul W. Wood, Maybelle Leeman, Mary Carr, Ruth Gress, Meta Faryon, and Dr. Gordon MacDonald provided much useful information on the family backgrounds of Kenneth and Margaret Millar.

Clay Hall, Mr. and Mrs. Sandy Baird, Margaret (Gretchen) Kalbfleisch Kingsley, Mrs. Sheldon Brubacher, Mr. and Mrs. Cully Schmidt, Stan Stuebing, Sid McLennan and family, Alex Duncan, Warnock Macmillan, Howard Duench, Dorothy Shoemaker, Aleda Snyder Whittemore, Rhea Snyder Kirk, Margaret Jaimet Dobson, Wilbert Hiller, and Mr. and Mrs. Ed Devitt illuminated Ken and Margaret Millar's Kitchener years.

R. A. D. Ford and Mary Lee recalled Ken Millar's undergraduate career at the University of Western Ontario.

Anna and Annie Branson, Marianne Meisel, Ralph Raimi, Charlie Miller, Nolan Miller, Georgia Haugh, Warner G. Rice, Donald A. Yates, Laurence Goldstein, Carlton Wells, and Cleanth Brooks each had things of interest to say about the Millars' stays in Michigan.

Robert Easton, Donald Davie, Hugh Kenner, Al Stump, Claire Stump, Harris Seed, Eleanor Van Cott, Lydia Freeman, Lucille Smith, Herb Harker, Jerre Lloyd, Ted Clymer, Corinne McLuhan, Dick Lid, Betty Lid, Robert Langfelder, Matthew J. Bruccoli, Geoffrey Aggeler, Dennis Lynds, Gayle Lynds, Jackie Coulette, James Pepper, Ralph Sipper, Clifton Fadiman, Bob Phelps, Betty Phelps, Marsha Neville, W. H. "Ping" Ferry, Warren Zevon, and William Campbell Gault all shed light on the Millars' decades in Santa Barbara.

Ash Green, Harding Lemay, Stanley Kauffmann, and Pat Knopf spoke of Ross Macdonald's dealings with the house of Knopf. Saul David, Oscar Dystel, Marc Jaffe, Fred Klein, Esther Margolis, Alan Barnard, Marcia Nasatir, Len Leone, and Lew Satz told of Macdonald's association with Bantam Books.

Eudora Welty spoke at generous length about Ken Millar over a four-day period in Jackson, Mississippi.

Reynolds Price recalled when he met Ken Millar in Jackson.

Ed Hoch, Michael Avallone, Joe Gores, Roger Simon, Collin Wilcox, Howard Engel, Michael Z. Lewin, Otto Penzler, Dorothy B. Hughes, Robert Wade, Jane Guymon, Pauline (Mrs. James) Fox, Jonathan Kellerman, and Phyllis White (Mrs. Anthony Boucher) described the place Ross Macdonald held among his mystery-writing peers.

Gerald Walker, William Hogan, John Milton, and Digby Diehl spoke as men who had edited or published Millar or Macdonald pieces. Jerry Speir and Peter Wolfe recalled how it was to write books about Macdonald's fiction. Richard Moore and Arthur Kaye talked of their documentary films about Ross Macdonald. William Goldman told of writing two scripts from Macdonald novels. David Karp discussed the *Archer* TV series.

Paul Nelson, John Leonard, Ray Sokolov, Dick Adler, Brad Darrach, Charles Champlin, Jerry Tutunjian, Wayne Warga, Trevor Meldal-Johnsen, Robert F. Jones, Dick Lochte, Susan Sheehan, Diane K. Shah, Jon Carrol, Bill Melton, Burt Prelutsky, Mickey Friedman, Bob Gottlieb, Diana Cooper-Clark, Sam Grogg, Jane S. Bakerman, Frances Ring, and Beverly Slopen shared memories of interviewing Ross Macdonald.

Frank MacShane, Jane Bernstein, Nona Balakian, Walter Clemons, and Robert Lescher talked, among other things, about Ken Millar's visits to New York.

Steven Carter, Linwood Barclay, and William Ruehlmann described their epistolary friendships (and visits) with Ken Millar.

Dr. Ed Peck recounted how Millar/Macdonald lent insight by proxy to an analysand.

Ray B. Browne, George Grella, and Max Byrd addressed the acceptance of Ross Macdonald's work by the academy.

Julian Symons, H. R. F. Keating, and Matthew Coady remembered the Millars' visit to England.

Charles Kelley, Jerry Bauer, Star Black, Hal Boucher, Jill Krementz, and Mike Salisbury recalled Ross Macdonald from the photographer's perspective.

Robertson Davies, Kitty Carlisle Hart, and E. Howard Hunt each responded to a written question.

In addition, several of those named either sent copies of letters from Ken Millar or made it possible to obtain copies of his letters from their archives.

Alice Munro allowed Millar items to be copied from her papers at the University of Calgary.

ACKNOWLEDGMENTS

Osvaldo Soriano of Argentina mailed me articles and reviews he'd written in Spanish about Macdonald, which Don Yates was nice enough to paraphrase in English.

Maynard MacDonald allowed access to correspondence between John D. MacDonald and Kenneth Millar.

Others who answered questions of one sort or another included Robert Weaver, Jonathan Kirsch, Patti Seidenbaum, and Stan Chambers (KTLA).

INSTITUTIONS

The chief repository of Ross Macdonald source material is the Kenneth and Margaret Millar Collection, in the Department of Special Collections of the University Library at the University of California, Irvine. There this biographer spent many engrossing months examining thousands of letters, notebooks, and other documents written by, sent to, or concerning the Millars. Over a four-year period, I was given extraordinary assistance by the Special Collections staff, particularly by then Head of Special Collections Roger Berry, a person without whom this book could not have been written. I was privileged to receive Mr. Berry's assistance even after his retirement, as he came in regularly to facilitate my full use of the Millar Collection. Other Special Collections people whose aid I depended upon included Sylvester Klinicke, Irene Wechselberg, and Eddie Yeghiayan. Mr. Berry's successor, Jackie Dooley, also extended me several courtesies. My very great thanks to all of them, and also to the Friends of the Library, especially Margo Allen.

Ken Millar's extensive correspondence with the Harold Ober Agency is housed in the Ober Archives, Department of Rare Books and Special Collections, Princeton University Libraries, Princeton University. Thanks to the staff there for facilitating access to this material. I am also grateful to Pat Powell at the Ober Agency in New York.

Millar's letters to Alfred Knopf and others at the Knopf firm are housed in the Harry Ransom Humanities Research Center of the University of Texas at Austin. My thanks to Cathy Henderson there.

Letters from Ken Millar to Anthony Boucher (William A. P. White) are in the Anthony Boucher collection at the Lilly Library of Indiana University, where Saundra Taylor was of great assistance.

The University of Michigan holds much material of interest to the Macdonald scholar. Among those guiding me to it were Kathryn L. Beam, in the Special Collections Library of the Harlan Hatcher Graduate Library; Marjorie Barrett, Nancy A. Bartlett, Marilyn McNitt, and Brian A. Williams at the University's Bentley Historical Library; Larry Goldstein at the *Michigan Quarterly Review;* and Tom Hubbard at campus radio station WUOM.

Others who located significant Millar items included Margaret R. Goostray, at Special Collections in the Mugar Memorial Library at Boston

University; Howard Prouty at the Margaret Herrick Library of the Academy of Motion Picture Arts and Sciences (Beverly Hills, California); Carmen R. Hurff, curator, Rare Books & Manuscripts, University of Florida Libraries; Bernard R. Crystal at the Rare Book and Manuscript Library of Butler Library at Columbia University; Rita A. Christensen of Special Collections at the Harold B. Lee Library at Brigham Young University; Jean Geist of the Popular Culture Library of the Jerome Library at Bowling Green State University; and staff at the Department of Special Collections, University Research Library, UCLA.

In Oregon, Mrs. Louise Hill of the Malheur County Historical Society located and sent information regarding the McDonalds and the Millars of Nyssa, Oregon; as did staff at the Malheur County Library.

Other American libraries and archives to whom I am indebted include the Shasta County (California) Historical Society; the El Dorado (California) County Library; the Woodland (California) Public Library; the Santa Barbara Public Library; the Santa Barbara Historical Museum; the Library and Special Collections at the University of California, Santa Barbara; the Los Angeles Public Library; the Pasadena Public Library; the Burbank Public Library; the Glendale Public Library; the Santa Monica Public Library; the Chicago Public Library; the Enoch Pratt Library of Baltimore; the Occidental College Library (California); the New York Public Library; the San Jose State University Library; the Warner Bros. Archive at the School of Cinema and Television at the University of Southern California; the Regional History Center, Department of Special Collections at USC; and the Library of Congress.

Thanks also to Georgia Jones-Davis, then at the *Los Angeles Times Book Review*.

Sandra Burrows, at the National Library of Canada in Ottawa, was extremely helpful in tracing and verifying John Macdonald Millar's peripatetic newspaper career; she provided invaluable documentation and suggested further useful avenues of inquiry. Others who found proof of John Millar's varied activities included Catherine Myhr at the Glenbow Museum in Calgary, Marilyn Mol at the Athabasca Archives, and staff at the Legislature Library in Alberta, the British Columbia Archives & Records Service, the Chilliwack Museum & Historical Society, the Nicola Valley Archives Association, and the Vancouver Public Library.

Dale Wilson, of Walkerton, Ontario, provided much useful information regarding Millar family activities in that town.

Pablo Machetzki, at the Waterloo County Board of Education, assembled wonderfully notated information about Ken Millar's school attendance and residences in Kitchener.

Ryan Taylor, Susan J. Hoffman, and other staff at the Kitchener Public Library gave generous assistance.

Documentation of Ken Millar's attendance at various schools was given by the Medicine Hat Public Schools of Alberta, the Suddaby Public School

ACKNOWLEDGMENTS

in Kitchener, the Kitchener-Waterloo Collegiate and Vocational School, and by St. John's–Ravenscourt School's alumni association and Mr. M. H. Ainley.

Other Canadian libraries and archives that provided aid or resources included the United Church of Canada Archives; Victoria University Archives, Victoria University in the University of Toronto; the University of Western Ontario's D. B. Weldon Library; the National Library of Canada; the National Archives of Canada; the City of Winnipeg Archives and Records Center; the Winnipeg Public Library; the London (Ontario) Public Libraries; the Bruce County (Ontario) Public Library; the Bruce County (Ontario) Museum & Archives; the Vancouver Maritime Museum; the Manitoba Culture, Heritage and Citizenship Provincial Archives; the Archives of Ontario, the University of Toronto Libraries; the McMasters (University) Library; the University of Waterloo Library and Special Collections; Wilfrid Laurier University; the Canadian Library Association; the Metropolitan Toronto Reference Library; and the Whyte Museum of the Canadian Rockies.

And thank you to Penny Coates, at the *Kitchener-Waterloo Record*.

INDIVIDUALS

My greatest thanks go to the resourceful and effective Mary Rousson, who provided excellent research assistance throughout this project.

The late Lee Goerner believed in this biography and enabled it to begin and to continue.

He learned of its possibility through Loretta Weingel-Fidel, surely the smartest and nicest literary agent ever.

Jane Rosenman at Scribner proved to be a superb and very supportive editor.

Her assistant, Caroline Kim, made the hectic times much less so.

Harris W. Seed and Eleanor Van Cott, cotrustees of the Kenneth and Margaret Millar Trusts, were extremely helpful and encouraging over the course of a long project. Their successor, Norman Colavincenzo, saw us safely into print.

Ralph B. Sipper extended many courtesies in my research.

Davis Dutton, of Dutton's Books North Hollywood, proved time and again to be a fine bookman and a true gentleman.

Others giving much appreciated help or encouragement included Larry Dietz, Karen Stabiner, Carol Bruce, Clancy Sigal, and Steven Bach.

My wife, Mary, gave me unfailing strength and support.

A journey of a thousand miles, and a dozen years, begins with a single question. A special thank-you then to Dick Lochte, who in 1984 asked, "Why don't *you* write a book about him?"

PERMISSIONS

Permissions continued from the copyright page.

The extracts (approximately 173 words, pages 107 and 114) from *Selected Letters of Raymond Chandler*, edited by Frank MacShane, are reproduced in North America with kind permission from Grove/Atlantic Inc. © 1981; in the U.K. and Commonwealth countries (excluding Canada) with kind permission of Penguin Books Ltd. (from *Selected Letters of Raymond Chandler*, edited by Frank MacShane, for publication by Hamish Hamilton, 2000), letters of Raymond Chandler copyright © 1981 College Trustees Ltd.; and in non–English language countries with kind permission from College Trustees Ltd. © 1981.

The extracts from Raymond Chandler's "The King in Yellow" and *The Little Sister* are reprinted in the United States with kind permission from Alfred A. Knopf; and in the U.K. and Commonwealth countries and in the rest of the world with kind permission from College Trustees Ltd. © 1938 and © 1949.

The extract from *Letters: Raymond Chandler and James M. Fox* is reprinted throughout the world with kind permission from College Trustees Ltd. © 1978.

Permission to quote from unpublished letters written to Kenneth Millar or others was graciously given by Michael Avallone, Allegra Branson Hoxter (for Anna Branson), Hugh Kenner, Robert Langfelder, Jan la Rue, Maynard MacDonald (for John D. Mac-Donald), Nicholas MacShane (for Frank MacShane), Otto Penzler, Sam Sandoe (for James Sandoe), Tom Shanks (for H. N. Swanson), Roger Simon, Kathleen Symons (for Julian Symons), Phyllis White (for Anthony Boucher), Morton G. Wurtele, Fred Zackel, and Warren Zevon.

Sentences from an unpublished manuscript by Herb Harker are used by kind permission of Herb Harker.

Correspondence from Saul David, Oscar Dystel, and Marc Jaffe is quoted by kind permission of Bantam Books.

Correspondence from Isabelle Taylor is quoted by kind permission of Doubleday.

Correspondence from Ivan von Auw, Dorothy Olding, and others is quoted by kind permission of Harold Ober Associates.

Excerpts from correspondence with the Harold Ober Agency is published with kind permission of the Princeton University Library.

Correspondence and memos from Alfred A. Knopf, Ash Green, and others at the house of Knopf is quoted by kind permission of the firm of Alfred A. Knopf.

Permissions to quote cited materials from various archives, collections, and libraries has been granted by the University of California, Irvine; University of California, Los Angeles; Boston University; the University of Michigan; Indiana University; Columbia University; the University of Texas at Austin; Princeton University' the University of Florida; and Brigham Young University.

NOTES

These previously published books about Ross Macdonald have proved useful and interesting:

Dreamers Who Live Their Dreams: The World of Ross Macdonald's Novels, Peter Wolfe (Bowling Green University Popular Press, 1976).

Ross Macdonald, Jerry Speir (Ungar, 1978).

Ross Macdonald/Kenneth Millar: A Descriptive Bibliography, Matthew J. Bruccoli (University of Pittsburgh Press, 1983).

Inward Journey: Ross Macdonald, edited by Ralph B. Sipper (Cordelia Editions, 1984; Mysterious Press, 1987).

Ross Macdonald, Matthew J. Bruccoli (Harcourt Brace Jovanovich, 1984).

Ross Macdonald, Bernard A. Schopen (Twayne, 1990).

Certain sources have been abbreviated in the notes:

Many letters to and from Kenneth Millar, unpublished manuscripts by Kenneth Millar, and other documents and material pertaining to Kenneth Millar are contained in the Kenneth Millar Papers in the Department of Special Collections of the UCI Libraries at the University of California, Irvine; referred to in the notes as UCI.

Letters by Kenneth Millar to Matthew J. Bruccoli are in the Matthew J. Bruccoli Collection on Kenneth Millar/Ross Macdonald in the Department of Special Collections of the UCI Libraries at the University of California, Irvine; referred to in the notes as MJB Collection, UCI.

Correspondence between Kenneth Millar and Alfred A. Knopf and others at the Knopf firm (excepting Ash Green) are collected at the Harry Ransom Humanities Research Center, the University of Texas at Austin; referred to in the notes as HRHRC.

Millar's correspondence with Ivan von Auw, Dorothy Olding, and others at the Ober Agency is contained in the Harold Ober Agency Archives, Manuscript Division, Department of Rare Books and Special Collections, Princeton University Library; referred to in the notes as Princeton.

Millar's letters to Anthony Boucher and to Ralph Sipper are in the Lilly Library at Indiana University; referred to in the notes as Indiana.

Millar's correspondence to R. A. D. Ford are in the R. A. D. Ford fonds, Literary Manuscript Collection, National Library of Canada; referred to in the notes as National Library of Canada.

Millar's correspondence with H. N. Swanson is in the H. N. Swanson Collection of the Margaret Herrick Library at the Academy of Motion Picture Arts and Sciences (Beverly Hills, California); referred to in the notes as Margaret Herrick Library.

11 " 'Ten years ago' ": John Leonard, "Ross Macdonald, his Lew Archer and other secret selves," *New York Times Book Review,* June 1, 1969.

11 " '. . . the Archer books' ": William Goldman, "The finest detective novels ever written by an American," *New York Times Book Review,* June 1, 1969.

12 "Yet he believed in the writing of candid biography": "The more truth we learn about a man, no matter how damaging in a sense, the better we can love him," Millar to Matthew Bruccoli, September 12, 1975, MJB Collection, UCI.

12 "He valued works that made connections between a novelist's life and his fiction": "I have been fascinated most of my adult life by the connections between imaginative work and the author's life both secret and overt," Millar to Daniel Halpern, March 26, 1976, typed copy, UCI.

12 "much material that proved helpful in explicating the books of Ross Macdonald": "I can think of few more complex critical enterprises than disentangling the mind and life of a first-person detective story writer from the mask of his detective-narrator," Ross Macdonald, "Down These Streets a Mean Man Must Go," *Antaeus,* Spring/Summer 1977; reprinted in *Self-Portrait: Ceaselessly Into the Past* (Capra Press, 1981).

12 " 'like burglars who secretly wish to be caught' ": Macdonald, preface to *Archer in Hollywood* (Knopf, 1967).

13 " 'I'm amazed at some of the chances I took as a boy' ": Millar to Peter Wolfe, September 19, 1972, UCI: "As for the spiritual risks, the ones with people, I remember with pleasure and some nostalgia and pride the chances I took in my youth, the like of which now would probably kill me."

13 " 'I don't have to be violent . . . my books are' ": Millar interview with Paul Nelson, UCI.

13 " 'long conspiracies of silent pain' ": Ross Macdonald, foreword to *A Collection of Reviews* (Lord John Press, 1979); included in *Self-Portrait* (Capra Press, 1981).

15 " 'I stood beside him in the offshore light' ": Ibid.

16 " 'fatal predisposition to words' ": Macdonald, introduction to *Kenneth Millar/Ross Macdonald—A Checklist* (Gale Research Co., 1971).

17 "a huge black lifeguard kept watch like Neptune": Millar to Paul Nelson, UCI; Millar fiction fragment, notebook, UCI.
      The lifeguard was Joe Fortes, a well-known figure from early Vancouver history. See for example *Vancouver's First Century: A City Album 1860–1960* (Vancouver, Canada: J. J. Douglas Ltd., 1977).

17 "a body spread-eagled in the alley below": Millar interview with Arthur Kaye, UCI; Millar interview with Paul Nelson, UCI.

18 "he blamed himself ": Millar interview with Paul Nelson, UCI.

19 " 'I must be the only American crime novelist' ": Macdonald, "Down These Streets"; reprinted in *Self-Portrait.*

19 " 'My original sin, so to speak' ": Millar interview with Paul Nelson, UCI.

20 "Sometimes she took Ken into the street and begged for food": "Ken remembered begging for money and food on the streets at the age of six," Robert Easton, "A Quiet Man," in *Inward Journey* (Cordelia Editions, 1984; Mysterious Press, 1987).

20 "she brought the six-year-old to an orphanage": Ibid.

21 " 'Most of the detective work that accomplishes anything' ": "No More Crime Films, Producers Promise: Portrayal of Crimes in the Movies Distinctly Menace the Future of Youth," *Canadian Echo,* September 20, 1922.

21 " 'The Mystery of the Silver Dagger' ": Advertisement, *Canadian Echo,* 1922.

22 "Kenneth bullied younger classmates": Details of Millar's youth from Millar notebook "Notes of a Son and Father," UCI.

24 "He devoured the adventure serials": Millar interview with Arthur Kaye, UCI. Regarding *Tarzan* and *Oliver Twist,* see also Millar interview with Paul Nelson, UCI.

Millar speaks extensively to Kaye and to Nelson of his boyhood travels among his relatives; see also Jerry Tutunjian, "A Conversation with Ross Macdonald," *Tamarack Review,* 1974. The more intimate details in this section are revealed in Millar's "Notes of a Son and Father."

25 "sons of well-to-do merchants and ministers": Millar interview with Arthur Kaye, UCI.

25 "Ken Millar liked stories of heroes who worked outside the law": Ibid. For extended reference to Falcon Swift, see Macdonald preface to *Lew Archer, Private Investigator* (Mysterious Press, 1977).

25 "a 'sophisticated' woman who smoked cigarettes and drove an automobile": Dr. Gordon MacDonald interview with TN.

25 "Aunt Margaret had worked as a Detroit bookkeeper": Douglas McDonald (cousin of Millar's) to Millar, June 21, 1938, UCI.

25 "Her party guests were active on the stock and grain exchanges": Millar interview with Arthur Kaye, UCI.

26 "There were odd things about his aunt's household": Millar spoke of his uncle with the handgun in the Packard to Arthur Kaye, Paul Nelson, and other interviewers, and in his preface to *Archer in Jeopardy* (Knopf, 1979).

26 " 'smiled like a lioness' ": Millar notebook, UCI.

26 "He got into fistfights": Personal details from Millar, "Notes of a Son and Father," UCI.

26 " 'An *excellent scholar*' ": W. Burman (headmaster), St. John's College School midsummer term 1928 report, UCI.

26 " 'Be kind, industrious and independent' ": John Macdonald Millar to Millar, July 1, 1928, UCI.

26 " 'Throughout my life' ": Macdonald, introduction to *A Collection of Reviews* (Lord John Press, 1979); reprinted in *Self-Portrait.*

27 " 'A most promising young Scholar' ": W. Burman (headmaster), St. John's College School midsummer term 1929 report, UCI.

28 "an after-school job as stockboy and handyman in a 'groceteria' ": Millar interview with Arthur Kaye, UCI; also Millar short-story manuscript, UCI.

29 "Brubacher said Kenneth's poems reminded him of early work by Byron and Shelley": Millar interview with Arthur Kaye, UCI; Jerry Tutunjian, "A Conversation with Ross Macdonald," *Tamarack Review,* 1974.

30 "hunted in secondhand-book stores for back issues": Millar to Alfred Knopf, August 10, 1971, HRHRC.

30 " 'I had read all of *Crime and Punishment*' ": Kenneth Millar, "Murder in the Library," *Mystery Writers of America Annual,* 1965.

30 "She submitted a Maugham-like tale": M. Sturm, "Impromptu," *The Grumbler,* 1931; reprinted in *Early Millar: The First Stories of Ross Macdonald & Margaret Millar* (Cordelia Editions, 1982).

30 "a sketch of his own": Ken Miller [*sic*], "The South Sea Soup Co.," *The Grumbler,* 1931; reprinted in *Early Millar.*

31 " 'Mint machines' ": Millar the budding social critic worked a reference to "mint machines" into his Sherlock Holmes parody for *The Grumbler.*

31 "a kind of conspiracy of silence": Millar interview with Arthur Kaye, UCI.

32 " 'As I stood there absorbing Hammett's novel' ": Macdonald, "Down These Streets"; reprinted in *Self-Portrait.* Asked by Arthur Kaye in 1970 which Hammett book he'd read that day in McCallum's, Millar said, "I think it was probably *The Glass Key.*" In later years, when his memory was less reliable, Millar began saying it was *The Maltese Falcon.* Surely *The Glass Key* is more likely to have induced Millar's profound reaction; its first scene is set in a billiard room where men are gambling and making political deals: a place rather like McCallum's.

NOTES

32 "Millar dropped this junk down a manhole": Donald Pearce interview with TN.

33 " 'Form News' ": These two items may well have been written by Kenneth Millar, the *Grumbler*'s literary editor.

33 " 'Someday I'm going to marry that girl' ": Margaret Millar interview with TN.

34 "Millar didn't want to work in an office": Millar interview with Arthur Kaye, UCI.

34 "he counted the number of rooms he'd lived in": "The year I graduated, 1932, I counted the rooms I had lived in during my first sixteen years, and got a total of fifty." Macdonald, introduction to *Kenneth Millar/Ross Macdonald;* reprinted in *Self-Portrait.*

34 "reading Schopenhauer and Kierkegaard into the night": Millar interview with Arthur Kaye, UCI.

34 " 'Hell lies at the bottom of the human heart' ": Millar notebook, UCI.

34 " 'His writing was so shaky' ": Macdonald, introduction to *A Collection of Reviews;* reprinted in *Self-Portrait.*

35 " 'The best of his talents were wasted' ": Millar, "Notes of a Son and Father," UCI.

36 " 'Thou sad-voiced sky-born Fury' ": Kenneth Millar, "Wild Goose," *The College Cord,* February 3, 1934.

36 " 'Ken Millar has a reflection' ": "Discords," *The College Cord,* April 13, 1934.

36 "a smart scholarship student who found him intense": Margaret Gretchen Kalbfleisch Kingsley interview with TN.

36 "someday Esquire *would* publish his work": Millar to Matthew Bruccoli, April 27, 1968, MJB Collection, UCI.

37 "Craving sex": Millar, "Notes of a Son and Father," UCI.

37 "He'd struggle for years with her memory": Ibid.

37 " 'roars of laughter' ": Don Herron, "Players' Club Spring Play Well Presented Last Night," *University of Western Ontario Gazette,* April 3, 1936.

37 "he saw Emlyn Williams's *Night Must Fall*": Millar to Nolan Miller, January 4, 1977, the Nolan Miller Papers, Special Collections Library, University of Michigan; also, typed copy, UCI.

37 "marching in an antifascist demonstration": Millar to Julian Symons, courtesy of Julian Symons.

    Other details of Millar's European trip from Millar interviews with Arthur Kaye, Paul Nelson, and others; and from Donald Pearce interview with TN.

38 "he made good Munich contacts": Millar interview with Arthur Kaye, UCI.

38 "an affair with a melancholy German girl": R. A. D. Ford letter to TN, November 12, 1991; Millar, "Notes of a Son and Father," UCI.

38 "he'd shaken the worst of his depression": Millar, "Notes of a Son and Father," UCI.

39 " 'Millar Speaks of Recent Journey' ": "Millar Speaks of Recent Journey: Large Gathering at Hesperian Club Hears Talks by Kenneth Millar and Donald Herron," *University of Western Ontario Gazette,* March 5, 1937.

39 " 'I came after Armageddon' ": Unsigned Kenneth Millar essay, "Dog Eats Dog," *The Gazette Literary Supplement, University of Western Ontario Gazette,* December 17, 1937.

39 " 'I thought he was not only sort of sinister' ": Donald Pearce interview with TN.

44 " 'Sin is despair' ": Søren Kierkegaard, *The Sickness Unto Death: A Christian Psychological Exposition for Edification and Awakening,* trans. Alastair Hannay (Penguin, 1989).

44 " 'There is a force' ": Millar, "Notes of a Son and Father," UCI.

44 " 'rich on the heritage of the Christian West' ": Ibid.

44 " 'He was *always* serious' ": Margaret Millar interview with TN.

44 "had a 'nervous breakdown' ": Details of Margaret Sturm's history from Millar, "Notes of a Son and Father," UCI.

44 " 'He knew his fate when he saw it' ": Ibid.

44 " 'a true Kierkegaardian view' ": Ibid.
45 " 'bitter choice' ": Ibid.
45 " 'Dear Mr. J_____ ' ": Handwritten copy, UCI.
45 " 'Will meet you in the lobby' ": Letter, UCI.
46 "the teetotaling sister of alcoholic brothers": Margaret Millar interview with TN.
47 " 'If light were dark' ": Kenneth Millar, "If Light Were Dark," Toronto *Saturday Night,* May 4, 1940.
47 " 'The King in Yellow' ": Raymond Chandler, "The King in Yellow," *Dime Detective,* March 1938; collected in *Five Sinister Characters* (Avon, 1945), et al.
47 "They were too young": Millar to Steven Carter, July 2, 1971, courtesy of Steven Carter.
47 " 'When the boat came back for us' ": Margaret Millar interview with TN.
47 " 'A woman feels funny' ": Ibid.
47 " 'Would you like a little divorce?' ": Anna Branson interview with TN. Also unpublished Kenneth Millar manuscript, circa 1939, UCI.
47 "The newlyweds slept in separate rooms": This and other details of the Millars' married life and parenthood from Millar, "Notes of a Son and Father," UCI.
47 "a lot of drillwork he found distasteful": Millar interview with Arthur Kaye, UCI.
48 "They couldn't afford movies": Margaret Millar interview with TN.
48 "In bed late one Saturday morning": Donald Pearce interview with TN.
48 "Millar went to hear a high school commencement address": Macdonald, introduction to *Archer at Large;* reprinted in *Self-Portrait.*
48 "A radio quiz announced": Ibid.; also Donald Pearce interview with TN.
48 "he wrote dozens of stories, sketches, and poems": Manuscripts, Millar Collection, UCI.
48 " 'Morley Callaghan was the one' ": Jerry Tutunjian, "A Conversation with Ross Macdonald," *Tamarack Review,* 1974. Millar continued, "He wasn't exactly a crime writer, or what you might call a member of the hard-boiled school, but his style belonged in that category. I think it had a great influence on me. I still have an enormous admiration for his work."
49 " 'That's when you really feel the entrapment' ": Margaret Millar interview with TN.
49 "the half dozen stories he wrote for 'the Sunday School papers' ": TN located these four: "Abernethy the Squirrel," *Explorer,* November 5, 1939; "That Thy Days May Be Long in the Land," *Onward,* January 7, 1940; "Alexander the Great," *The Canadian Boy,* March 17, 1940; "Nora of the Cliffs," *The Canadian Girl,* April 28, 1940.
49 "a comic verse taken by *Saturday Night*": Kenneth Millar, "Fatal Facility," Toronto *Saturday Night,* July 29, 1939.
49 "including 'The Yellow Dusters' ": Kenneth Millar, "The Yellow Dusters," Toronto *Saturday Night,* November 4, 1939.
49 " '*Saturday Night* came out on Saturday morning' ": Ross Macdonald, introduction to *Kenneth Millar/Ross Macdonald;* reprinted in *Self-Portrait.*
49 " 'He was a *born* teacher' ": Margaret Millar interview with TN.
50 "thought he spoke above most students' level": Warnock Macmillan interview with TN.
50 " 'Mother knows best' ": Millar, "Notes of a Son and Father," UCI.
50 "She wanted to be a writer": Apparently Margaret Sturm also sold stories to "the Sunday School papers," unlocated.
50 " 'Probably just nerves' ": Margaret Millar interview with TN.
51 " 'I was brought up with mysteries' ": Ibid.
51 "Nearly three hundred mystery novels came out in the United States in 1940": "The market in the United States absorbs about one new mystery book every working day in the year," in L. H. Robbins, "They Get Away with Murder," *New*

York Times Magazine, November 17, 1940; "Two hundred and eighty-two crime novels passed under the portals of *The Criminal Record* during the calendar year," in Judge Lynch, "Come, Sweet Death," *Saturday Review of Literature,* December 7, 1940.

51 "a murder mystery with a high school setting": Millar notebook, circa 1940, UCI.

51 " 'I had to do something to get out of that bed' ": Margaret Millar interview with Paul Nelson, UCI.

52 " 'We both almost had a conniption fit' ": Stanley Handman, "Murder for Fun and Profit," *Weekend Magazine* 8, no. 28 (1958).

52 "Doubleday's contract listed Margaret and Kenneth Millar as coauthors": Doubleday contract, UCI.

53 *"Today's Poets":* Chad Walsh, *Today's Poets: American and British Poetry Since the 1930's* (Charles Scribner's Sons, 1964).

53 "the only American crime writer to receive early ethical training in a Canadian Mennonite Sunday school": Macdonald, "Down These Streets"; reprinted in *Self-Portrait.*

53 "Millar dubbed Auden": Donald Pearce interview with TN.

54 "Millar attended Auden's Friday-evening student 'at-homes' ": Margaret Millar interview with TN.

54 " 'It was strange' ": Ibid.

54 " 'this certain scene I'd written' ": Ibid. The scene is in Margaret Millar's *Wall of Eyes* (Random House, 1943).

54 " 'With so many fine books to read' ": Edmund Wilson, "Who Cares Who Killed Roger Ackroyd?" *New Yorker,* January 20, 1945.

54 "used Auden as the model for his fictional detective": Julian Symons, *Bloody Murder: From the Detective Story to the Crime Novel* (Mysterious Press, 1993).

54 " 'a remarkable kind of saint' ": Millar to Charles Miller, February 17, 1978, the Charles H. Miller Papers, Special Collections Library, University of Michigan.

54 "Millar had 'really loved him' ": Millar to Charles Miller, undated, the Charles H. Miller Papers, Special Collections Library, University of Michigan.

55 "feel guilt at 'betraying' ": Millar notebook, UCI.

55 "partly because Millar didn't care to go . . . more because he didn't think it a good idea": Robert Easton letter to Matthew J. Bruccoli, September 22, 1982, courtesy of Robert Easton.

56 " 'The man in the black shirt' ": Raymond Chandler, *The Little Sister* (Houghton Mifflin, 1949).

56 "no doubt her husband was a genius": Donald Pearce interview with TN.

56 "it was suggested he might wish to change his major": Ibid.; Margaret Millar interview with TN.

56 "that way (Millar guessed)": Millar interview with Paul Nelson; Millar discreetly didn't mention Davies by name. He wrote Peter Wolfe of Davies: "For some time we sort of collaborated at a distance on a column of smart cracks but—by this time I was in Ann Arbor—I never met him" (January 20, 1973). Millar told his bibliographer Matthew J. Bruccoli that for much of 1941 "The Passing Show" was written "mostly, but not entirely" by him; Bruccoli, *Ross Macdonald/Kenneth Millar: A Descriptive Bibliography* (University of Pittsburgh Press, 1983).

Judith Skelton Grant's *Robertson Davies: Man of Myth* (Viking, 1994), written with Davies's cooperation, does not mention Millar in saying that Davies "wrote much of 'The Passing Show,' the *(Saturday Night)* page-three column of wisecracks, rhymes and whimsies."

57 "The *Bat* contract": Doubleday contract, UCI.

57 "A Michigan newspaper piece": unidentified publication, Margaret Millar folder, Kitchener Public Library.

57 " 'commendable' ": *Saturday Review of Literature,* July 19, 1941.

57   "its sound plot": "Briefly Noted," *New Yorker,* July 19, 1941.

57   " 'a mystery find of considerable voltage' ": Will Cuppy, "Mystery and Adventure," *New York Herald Tribune Books,* July 20, 1941.

57   " 'Margaret Millar is a humdinger' ": Will Cuppy, "Mystery and Adventure," *New York Herald Tribune Books,* February 22, 1942.

57   " 'Ken was very impressive' ": Georgia Haugh interview with TN.

57   " 'They both at that time' ": Marianne Meisel to TN.

57   "a novel published by Scribner's": Marianne Roane, *Years Before the Flood* (Charles Scribner's Sons, 1945).

58   " 'For God's sake be quiet' ": Marianne Meisel interview with TN.

58   "She rescinded her ban": Margaret Millar interview with TN.

59   "Millar was often cheerfully physical": Anna Branson interview with TN.

59   " 'You never knew when' ": Donald Pearce interview with TN.

60   " 'There was a lot of fighting' ": Marianne Meisel interview with TN.

60   "Millar contributed to Linda's repertoire": Donald Pearce interview with TN,

62   " 'For what is the sensibility of our age?' ": Cleanth Brooks, *The Well Wrought Urn: Studies in the Structure of Poetry* (1947).

62   " 'the private detective employed by your parents' ": Chad Walsh, *Campus Gods on Trial* (Macmillan, 1953, 1962).

62   " 'To me' ": Donald Pearce interview with TN.

63   " 'We were talking' ": Ibid.

63   "Alone with his wife": Millar, "Notes of a Son and Father," UCI.

63   "Once she threw an egg at him": Shelly Lowenkopf, "Santa Barbara Mystery Writers," *Santa Barbara News & Review,* August 29, 1985. ("Yes, it was a three-minute egg. He ducked and it splattered on the wall. I was so piqued with him that I let it stay for some time.")

63   "Another time she dropped a typewriter from a second-story window": "I once threw a typewriter out a second-story window": Margaret Millar quoted in "Margaret Millar and the Greatest Opening Lines Since 'In the Beginning . . . ,' " in Dilys Winn, *Murderess Ink: The Better Half of the Mystery* (Workman Publishing, 1979).

63   "Talking late one night": Donald Pearce interview with TN.

63   " 'She was always nervous' ": Marianne Meisel interview with TN.

63   " 'I really think' ": Anna Branson interview with TN.

64   " 'Margaret was talking' ": Donald Pearce interview with TN.

65   " 'And Margaret Millar' ": University of Michigan English Department Newsletter, September 7, 1943, Bentley Historical Library, University of Michigan (FImu C26 Eng.); used by permission.

65   "the *Toronto Star* paid": Millar notebooks, UCI.

65   " 'a definite reputation and standing in mystery fiction' ": Isabelle Taylor to Margaret Millar, January 21, 1943, UCI.

65   " 'It doesn't come off' ": Ibid.

65   "She'd begun corresponding": Margaret Millar interview with TN. Margaret Millar's *Do Evil in Return* (Random House, 1950) is dedicated to Faith Baldwin.

65   "an advance of five hundred dollars": Random House contract, UCI.

66   "Things weren't good": Millar, "Notes of a Son and Father," UCI.

66   " 'While we were very very proud of each other' ": Margaret Millar interview with TN.

67   "Millar hastened to the Ann Arbor rental library": Millar interview with Paul Nelson, UCI.

67   " 'He was rather smug and pleased' ": Marianne Meisel to TN.

68   *"New York Times Book Review"*: "New Books for Christmas: MYSTERIES," *New York Times Book Review,* December 5, 1943. Among ten other mysteries selected were Dorothy B. Hughes's *The Blackbirder* and Raymond Chandler's *The Lady in the Lake.*

69 " 'Everyone else looks pretty shoddy to me' ": Margaret to Kenneth Millar, May 13, 1945, UCI.

69 " 'The waiter just brought me' ": Kenneth to Margaret Millar, July 8, 1944, UCI.

69 "he managed to master Morse code in fifteen minutes": Kenneth to Margaret Millar, June 29, 1944, UCI.

69 "in the rented house of Listerine manufacturer Gerard Lambert": Millar interview with Paul Nelson, UCI; Millar to Matthew J. Bruccoli, September 12, 1975, MJB Collection, UCI.

 Millar was pleased to read in Bruccoli's 1975 biography of John O'Hara that O'Hara had dined at this same Lambert house in the fall of 1949.

69 *"New York Times":* Isaac Anderson, "Crime Corner," *New York Times Book Review,* October 1, 1944.

69 *"Chicago Sun":* Elizabeth Bullock, "Sleuths and Slayers: There Are Real Ideas in 'The Dark Tunnel,' " *Chicago Sun Book Week,* October 8, 1944.

69 *"New Republic":* E.H. (unidentified), "Crime and Punishment," *New Republic,* October 16, 1944.

69 *"Saturday Review"*'s mystery critic": Judge Lynch, ". . . let him die!" *Saturday Review,* January 6, 1945.

70 " 'The only place I imagine with automatic ease' ": Kenneth to Margaret Millar, March 12, 1945, UCI.

70 " 'really first-class' ": Kenneth to Margaret Millar, March 4, 1945, UCI.

70 " '*good,* though not so good' ": Kenneth to Margaret Millar, March 30, 1945, UCI.

70 " 'It's going to be a strange book' ": Kenneth to Margaret Millar, April 12, 1945, UCI.

71 " 'Please don't tell me' ": Kenneth to Margaret Millar, April 14, 1945, UCI.

71 " 'It does sound Chandlerish of course' ": Margaret to Kenneth Millar, April 19, 1945, UCI.

71 " 'Just did it so I could report to you' ": Margaret to Kenneth Millar, March 5, 1945, UCI.

71 " 'slinging crap' ": Margaret to Kenneth Millar, February 25, 1945, UCI.

71 " 'you will *not* have to' ": Ibid.

71 " 'I think it's excellent' ": Kenneth to Margaret Millar, March 30, 1945, UCI.

71 "Dorothy B. Hughes": Dorothy B. Hughes, *Albuquerque* (New Mexico) *Tribune,* May 11, 1945.

71 " 'There are mountains and the sea' ": Margaret to Kenneth Millar, April 13, 1945, UCI.

72 " 'Sweet, darling *Gates*' ": Margaret to Kenneth Millar, April 15, 1945, UCI.

73 " 'Chandler is undoubtedly one of the best' ": D. C. Russell, "Raymond Chandler, and the Future of Whodunits," *New York Times Book Review,* June 17, 1945.

 The essayist was Diarmuid Russell, Eudora Welty's lifelong literary agent.

73 " 'Now a publisher' ": James Sandoe, "Dagger of the Mind," *Poetry: A Magazine of Verse,* April–September 1946.

73 "the studios were especially impressed by books that were well promoted by publishers": "Movie Companies Look to Detective Story Writers for the New 'Psychological' Film," *Publishers Weekly,* March 9, 1946.

73 " 'I am excited, scared and miss you like hell' ": Margaret to Kenneth Millar, June 12, 1945, UCI.

74 " 'I know you won't go Hollywood' ": Kenneth to Margaret Millar, June 22, 1945, UCI.

74 "No city had ever looked better to him": Millar interview with Arthur Kaye, UCI.

74 " 'Hello my darling' ": Margaret to Kenneth Millar, July 27, 1945, UCI.

74 " 'All writers lunch together' ": Margaret to Kenneth Millar, July 30, 1945, UCI.

74 " 'He was perfectly charming' ": Margaret to Kenneth Millar, August 3, 1945, UCI.

74 "great admiration for Melville": Millar to Fred Dannay, November 25, 1946, Fred-

eric Dannay Papers, Rare Book and Manuscript Library, Columbia University.

74 " 'It's *not* good' ": Margaret to Kenneth Millar, August 1, 1945, UCI.

74 " 'WE ALL had to listen' ": Margaret to Kenneth Millar, August 3, 1945, UCI.

75 " 'I'm so busy' ": Margaret to Kenneth Millar, July 30, 1945, UCI.

75 " 'He said, "Good God" ' ": Margaret to Kenneth Millar, August 1, 1945, UCI.

75 " 'Tall [very]' ": Ibid.

75 " 'Encourage me in this' ": Margaret to Kenneth Millar, July 30, 1945, UCI.

75 Details of August 14 events from Margaret Millar interview with TN; also Millar to the Bransons, October 7, 1945, UCI.

76 " 'I don't know how she got stuck with *him*' ": Margaret Millar interview with TN.

76 "his concern for a foaling mare": Margaret and Kenneth Millar, prefatory note to Faulkner story ("The Hound") in the Mystery Writers of America anthology *Murder by Experts* (Ziff Davis, 1947).

  The Millars were responsible for this anthology's title, submitting it with other possibilities to the book's editor, Fred Dannay (one-half of "Ellery Queen"), in a letter of November 25, 1946 (Columbia University). In 1949, the title *Murder by Experts* was licensed for an MWA-approved radio series, which ran for two and a half years on the Mutual network.

76 " 'He has a knack' ": Kenneth to Margaret Millar, June 20, 1945, UCI.

77 " 'I liked Boucher' ": Kenneth to Margaret Millar, October 15, 1945, UCI.

77 " 'I really *enjoyed* writing' ": Kenneth to Margaret Millar, November 4, 1945, UCI.

77 " 'I'm developing a detective' ": Kenneth to Margaret Millar, October 15, 1945, UCI.

  In obvious jest, Millar wrote "Christopher Marlowe," then lightly lined out "Christopher" so as to leave it clearly visible. The "successor to Marlowe" part was no joke, though.

77 " 'Give me another twenty years, baby' ": Kenneth to Margaret Millar, June 16, 1945, UCI.

77 " 'marvellous' ": Margaret to Kenneth Millar, November 22, 1945, UCI.

77 "a $300 fourth prize": Second prize went to a William Faulkner entry (one of his "Uncle" Gavin mystery tales), first prize to Manley Wade Wellman.

78 " 'The dandified esthete' ": Herbert Marshall McLuhan, "Footprints in the Sands of Crime," *Sewanee Review,* October-December 1946.

78 " 'I make a point' ": Kenneth Millar, "Find the Woman," *Ellery Queen's Mystery Magazine,* June 1946.

78 "The couple's 1945 income": Millar notebook, UCI.

78 " 'It's your own business' ": Kenneth to Margaret Millar, July 14, 1945, UCI.

78 " 'You stated quite bluntly' ": Kenneth to Margaret Millar, January 3, 1946, UCI.

79 " 'I've been trying' ": Kenneth to Margaret Millar, February 8, 1946, UCI.

80 " 'If we live here' ": Margaret to Kenneth Millar, February 22, 1946, UCI.

80 " '. . . We could make more money' ": Kenneth Millar, *Trouble Follows Me* (Dodd, Mead, 1946).

80 " 'The Stateside Blues' ": Kenneth to Margaret Millar, April 4, 1945, UCI. Other manuscripts written aboard the *Shipley Bay* are at UCI.

81 " 'That is because' ": Kenneth to Margaret Millar, December 20, 1945, UCI.

81 " 'The main cause' ": Kenneth to Margaret Millar, January 19, 1946, UCI.

81 " 'That wild strange marvellous night we had together' ": Kenneth to Margaret Millar, February 6, 1946, UCI.

  This paragraph links quotes from several letters from Kenneth to Margaret Millar: "we had a lovemaking . . . I worship you," February 7, 1946; "The way other people believe in god [*sic*]," January 20, 1946; "The sweet and powerful language of your body . . . beyond everything else," January 19, 1946; "I cling desperately," January 12, 1946; all UCI.

81 " 'merely to cohabit' ": Kenneth to Margaret Millar, December 3, 1945, UCI.

81 " 'I'll be resuming' ": Kenneth to Margaret Millar, December 27, 1945, UCI.
81 " 'Those hours' ": Kenneth to Margaret Millar, March 11, 1946, UCI.
81 " 'There's something' ": Ibid.
82 " 'Can't get enough of jazz' ": Ibid.
82 " *best I ever heard'* ": Kenneth to Margaret Millar, March 12, 1946, UCI.
83 " 'Between the mountains and the sea' ": Francis Fisher Browne, "Santa Barbara," from *Volunteer Grain* (1897).
83 " 'When I was a boy' ": Marshall Bond Jr., "Around the Upper East," from *Adventures with Peons, Princes & Tycoons* (Star Rover Press, 1983).
     I owe these two quotes to their inclusion in *Tales of Santa Barbara: From Native Storytellers to Sue Grafton,* selected by Steven Gilbar and Dean Stewart (John Daniel & Co., 1994), which also nicely juxtaposes Ross Macdonald's fictional brush fire in *The Underground Man* with Margaret Millar's nonfiction account of the Coyote fire in *The Birds and the Beasts Were There.*
83 "a magical place where the light came from": Jerry Tutunjian interview with TN.
83 " 'he couldn't help thinking of himself' ": Kenneth Millar, "Chapter IV," *The Three Roads,* typed manuscript, UCI; passage cut from published version (Knopf, 1948).
84 " 'a very manly room' ": John Ross Macdonald, *The Drowning Pool* (Knopf, 1950).
84 "the situation had its advantages": Details of the Millars' postwar ménage from Millar, "Notes of a Son and Father," UCI.
84 " 'No writee, no eatee' ": Margaret Millar interview with TN.
84 "He gave himself a year": Millar interview with Arthur Kaye, UCI.
84 " 'a tough mystery in the Hammett tradition' ": Millar to the Bransons, May 12, 1946, UCI.
84 "crossed with the wide-open Jacksonville, Florida": Macdonald interview with Arthur Kaye, UCI. Millar's naval duties took him briefly to Jacksonville.
84 "much taken with *Really the Blues":* Macdonald interview with Paul Nelson, UCI.
84 " 'It was the brotherhood of man!' ": Donald Pearce interview with TN.
84 "The ideal image for an artist was jazz variations": Millar interview with Paul Nelson, UCI.
85 " 'They really *spoke* to me, directly' ": Ibid.
85 "Nelson Algren's *Never Come Morning":* Ibid.
85 " 'a substitute for a postwar nervous breakdown' ": Dick Adler, "Will the Real Ross Macdonald Please Keep Writing?" *Los Angeles Times West Magazine,* December 10, 1967.
85 " 'I loved writing dialogue' ": Margaret Millar interview with TN.
85 "The town didn't have or need traffic lights": Macdonald, "Black Tide," in *Self-Portrait.*
86 " 'When you grew up in Kitchener' ": Sally Ogle Davis, "Murder, fatalistic humor and a three-Edgar family," *Toronto Globe and Mail,* July 16, 1983.
86 "Ellington's 'C Jam Blues' ": Donald Pearce interview with TN.
86 " 'to rise through mysteries to the serious novel' ": Millar to the Bransons, October 7, 1945, UCI.
86 " 'the first book of mine I'm not ashamed of' ": Millar to Henry Branson, July 6, 1946, UCI.
86 " 'literate and exciting' ": *New Republic,* September 9, 1946.
86 " 'a God-given ability to write' ": Anthony Boucher, "Murder, They Say!" *San Francisco Chronicle,* September 1, 1946.
87 " 'I owned a house before I owned a car' ": Margaret Millar interview with TN.
88 " 'Just what is your business?' ": Kenneth Millar, "The Bearded Lady," *American,* October 1948.
88 " 'Whenever I am asked' ": Quoted in Elmore Leonard's introduction to H. N. Swanson's *Sprinkled with Ruby Dust: A Literary and Hollywood Memoir* (Warner Books, 1989).

NOTES

88 " 'I'm having my fling' ": Millar to Anthony Boucher, September 12, 1947, Indiana.

88 " 'like something left over from a sad and dingy past' ": Millar, *Winter Solstice* note-books and typescripts, UCI.

88 " 'I was much intrigued' ": Alfred Knopf to Millar, March 28, 1947, HRHRC.

89 " 'I prize your imprint' ": Millar to Alfred Knopf, April 3, 1947, HRHRC.

89 " 'If you should decide' ": Millar to Knopf, July 8, 1947, HRHRC.

89 " 'Very, very tough' ": unsigned review, "Mystery and Crime," *New Yorker*, August 23, 1947.

89 " 'Raw meat' ": "The Criminal Record," *Saturday Review*, August 16, 1947.

89 " 'Routine enough' ": Anthony Boucher, "Murder They Say," *San Francisco Chronicle*, August 17, 1947.

89 " 'the poet laureate of sexual psychopathy' ": Millar to Richard C. Boys, December 29, 1952, the Richard C. Boys Correspondence, Special Collections Library, University of Michigan.

89 " 'a good deal less offensive' ": James Sandoe, "Suspense," *Chicago Sun Book Week*, August 17, 1947.

89 " '*Blue City* retains its own pattern' ": Nelson Algren, "Johnny Comes Marching Home," *Philadelphia Inquirer*, August 17, 1947.

89 " 'Unless one or two things like that happen' ": Millar interview with Paul Nelson, UCI.

90 " 'ten thousand good words' ": Millar to von Auw, September 4, 1948, HRHRC.

90 " 'I am not delighted with this sale' ": Knopf to Millar, October 1, 1947, HRHRC.

90 "Their combined earnings in 1947": Millar notebooks and tax forms, UCI.

90 "a fifteen-page critique": Appended to letter from Curtiz secretary to Margaret Millar, March 25, 1947, UCI.

90 " 'I feel we can get a much better setup elsewhere' ": Swanson to Millar, September 4, 1947, UCI.

90 " 'As far as the job situation is concerned' ": Ibid.

90 " 'By God I'll fall back on my thrillers' ": Millar to Branson, August 4, 1946, UCI.

91 " 'Man chases hit-run slayer' ": Millar notebooks, UCI.

91 "eighteen pages of a tale called *Hit and Run*": Millar notebooks, UCI.

91 "four pages of notes for *The Snatch*": Ibid.

91 "Millar had it in mind to do a series of books with this detective": Millar interview with Paul Nelson, UCI.

91 " 'What Bowman launched thee forth?' ": Kenneth Millar, "Wild Goose," *The College Cord*, February 3, 1934.

92 " 'I'm not Archer, exactly' ": Macdonald, "The Writer as Detective Hero," *Show*, January 1965: "I wasn't Archer, exactly, but Archer was me." Paraphrased by Millar elsewhere.

92 " 'Lew Archer was actually named' ": Chuck Thegze, "Behind Lew Archer: Interview with Ross Macdonald," *Village Voice*, February 10, 1975.

92 "a few blocks east on the Strip": Technically, the unincorporated Sunset Strip area was not in Los Angeles.

92 " 'I did it to prove to myself' ": Millar to Branson, May 10, 1948, UCI.

93 " 'I'm the new-type detective' ": John Macdonald, *The Moving Target* (Knopf, 1949).

93 "Millar subscribed to Wyndham Lewis's idea": Donald Pearce interview with TN. See Millar's 1953 Ann Arbor lecture, "The Scene of the Crime," published in *Inward Journey* (Cordelia Editions, 1984; Mysterious Press, 1987).

95 " 'Life is full . . .' ": Geoffrey T. Hellman, "Publisher: II—Flair Is the Word," *New Yorker*, November 27, 1948.

95 " '*Son* of a bitch!' ": Anna Branson interview with TN.

95 " 'Beside the Santa Barbara Biltmore's Olympic Pool' ": Bennett Cerf, "Trade Winds," *Saturday Review*, May 1, 1948.

95 "As of May 31": Millar notebooks, UCI.

96 "the dedicatee of *Blue City*": *The Dark Tunnel* was dedicated to the memory of John Lee, *Trouble Follows Me* to Donald Pearce, *The Three Roads* to Margaret. The pseudonymous *The Moving Target* would have no dedicatee.

96 " 'He was off the sauce that whole summer' ": Margaret Millar interview with TN.

96 " 'Their talent?' ": Barnaby Conrad, *Fun While It Lasted* (Random House, 1969).

96 " 'In the past week' ": Margaret Millar, *The Cannibal Heart* (Random House, 1949).

97 " 'He would go up there' ": Donald Pearce interview with TN.

97 "To conquer his fear of it": Millar notebooks, UCI.

97 " 'He was a great man for testing himself' ": Hugh Kenner interview with TN.

97 " 'highly recommended' ": unsigned review, "Mystery and Crime," *New Yorker,* June 5, 1948.

97 " 'distinguished' ": "The Criminal Record," *Saturday Review,* June 26, 1948.

97 " 'an astonishing stride beyond' ": James Sandoe, *Chicago Sun,* June 11, 1948.

97 " 'from overmuch psychiatry' ": Howard Haycraft, "Speaking of Crime," *Ellery Queen's Mystery Magazine,* October 1948.

97 " 'the Hitchcock fork' ": Helen B. Parker, "Companions for Vacation Hammocks," *New York Times Book Review,* July 25, 1948.

97 " 'It took me months to make it bad enough' ": Millar to the Bransons, July 2, 1948, UCI.

98 "In Toronto, Random House of Canada gave Margaret Millar a luncheon": "The Millars From Kitchener Succeed as Mystery Writers," *Toronto Globe and Mail,* July 17, 1948.

98 "Millar considered her the more naturally gifted writer": Donald Pearce interview with TN.

99 " 'Cut it any way you like' ": Knopf to Millar, September 2, 1948, HRHRC.

99 " 'I have a serious novel on the fire' ": Millar to von Auw, September 4, 1948, HRHRC.

99 " 'George Harmon Coxe . . . Ray Chandler' ": Coxe was a veteran Knopf whodunit writer. Chandler hadn't published a novel since 1943.

100 " 'bitterly disappointed' ": Quoted by Kenneth to Margaret Millar, September 11, 1948, UCI.

100 " 'Son of a bitch!' ": Anna Branson interview with TN.

100 " 'Crossing from California' ": Kenneth to Margaret Millar, September 9, 1948, UCI.

100 " 'My drive across the country got me nowhere' ": Millar to Blanche Knopf, October 24, 1948, HRHRC.

100 " 'I love you better than I love myself' ": Kenneth to Margaret Millar, September 19, 1948, UCI.

100 " 'You're everything I want' ": Margaret to Kenneth Millar, September 13, 1948, UCI.

101 "In a letter thanking Millar": Knopf to Millar, September 17, 1948, HRHRC.

101 " 'Why not?' ": Kenneth to Margaret Millar, September 20, 1948, UCI.

101 "stiff terms": Knopf to von Auw, September 20, 1948, HRHRC; von Auw to Knopf, September 23, 1948, HRHRC.

101 "the first entry": When the Mystery Writers of America in 1956 updated "the Haycraft-Queen Definitive Library of Detective-Crime-Mystery Fiction" (a respected compilation of "cornerstone" titles) to include essential works published since 1948, *The Moving Target* was one of only twelve books added.

101 " 'It's weak of me' ": Kenneth to Margaret Millar, September 30, 1948, UCI.

101 " 'I could never stand another separation' ": Margaret to Kenneth Millar, October 1, 1948, UCI.

101 " 'I feel like weeping' ": Kenneth to Margaret Millar, October 7, 1948, UCI.

101 " 'There's no one I feel completely at home with but you' ": Kenneth to Margaret Millar, September 30, 1948, UCI.

101 " 'I love you awfully!' ": Margaret to Kenneth Millar, October 4, 1948, UCI.
101 " 'The only advantage of living in Ann Arbor' ": Kenneth to Margaret Millar, September 23, 1948, UCI.
101 " 'Knopf is at once Olympian and dressy' ": Geoffrey T. Hellman, "Publisher: I—A Very Dignified Pavane," *New Yorker,* November 20, 1948.
102 " 'While I hesitate to disagree with you' ": Millar to Blanche Knopf, December 5, 1948, HRHRC.
102 " 'It's a specter' ": Donald Pearce interview with TN.
103 " 'The next chapter' ": Millar, "The Inward Eye," dissertation typescript, UCI.
103 " 'Even theses end' ": Millar to Blanche Knopf, November 22, 1948, HRHRC.
103 "This would be one of their *good* years": Kenneth to Margaret Millar, UCI.
103 "twenty-one cases of empty beer bottles": Anna Branson interview with TN.
103 " 'We had a copy of the Berlioz Requiem' ": Ibid.
103 " 'I figured he ought to hear something' ": Donald Pearce interview with TN.
105 " 'All she needs' ": Margaret to Kenneth Millar, UCI.
105 " 'almost innocently' ": Millar, "Notes of a Son and Father," UCI.
105 " 'Her candor has always been lovely' ": Ibid.
105 " 'Linda was a terror' ": Anna Branson interview with TN.
105 "a book she later wrote": Margaret Millar, *Vanish in an Instant* (Random House, 1952).
105 " 'strange misspelt tales' ": Millar to Knopf, October 18, 1949, HRHRC.
105 " 'Boy, this is really gruesome' ": Margaret to Kenneth Millar, October 5, 1948, UCI.
105 "A couple of things happened to Linda and Margaret Millar": Ann Arbor details from Millar's "Notes of a Son and Father," UCI.
106 "Millar had earlier tipped Boucher that he'd done a pseudonymous book for Knopf": "I'm publishing a book in April, pseudonymously," Millar Christmas card to Boucher, December 1948, Indiana.
106 " 'Just at the time that the tough genre in fiction needs revitalizing' ": Anthony Boucher, "Criminals at Large," *New York Times Book Review,* April 3, 1949.
106 "Millar hand-carried a copy of the *American Mercury*": Phyllis White (Mrs. Anthony Boucher) interview with TN.
107 " 'You can write like a son of a bitch' ": Boucher to Millar, March 12, 1949, Indiana.
107 " 'I fell in with the plan' ": Millar to Boucher, March 14, 1949, Indiana.
107 "a summer *Times* roundup": Anthony Boucher, "Chillers for the Warm Months," *New York Times Book Review,* June 19, 1949.
107 " 'the high point of recent American books' ": Anthony Boucher, "Speaking of Crime," *Ellery Queen's Mystery Magazine,* August 1949. Boucher listed *The Moving Target* as one of "The Best Mystery Books of 1949" in his "Speaking of Crime" column for the February 1950 issue of *EQMM.*
107 " 'You can put this on your Hammett-Chandler shelf; it won't be at all out of place in that company' ": This compliment is also a veiled reference to James Sandoe's umbrage at *Blue City* ads linking Millar's name with Hammett's and Chandler's—hence, a subtle clue to Macdonald's identity.
107 " 'An astonishing book has come from Knopf' ": James Sandoe to Raymond Chandler, March 20, 1949, Department of Special Collections, University Research Library, UCLA.
107 " 'pretentiousness' ": Chandler to Sandoe, April 14, 1949, Department of Special Collections, University Research Library, UCLA; excerpt printed in *Raymond Chandler Speaking* (Houghton Mifflin, 1962); entire letter printed in *Selected Letters of Raymond Chandler* (Columbia University Press, 1981).
108 " 'the most creditable [Chandler] imitation' ": James Sandoe, "Week's Best Novels of Mystery and Suspense," "Book Day," *Chicago Sun-Times,* April 29, 1949.

NOTES

109 " 'All I really want' ": Millar to Blanche Knopf, November 22, 1948, HRHRC.
109 " 'The picaresque or something like it' ": Millar to Pat Knopf, February 23, 1950, HRHRC.
109 " 'Even my mother bought a copy' ": John D. MacDonald to Harold Ober, September 2, 1949, HRHRC.
109 "What he *would* do, he told Ober": Ober to MacDonald, September 15, 1949, HRHRC.
109 " 'Please thank Mr. Millar for me' ": MacDonald to Ober, September 19, 1949, HRHRC.
109 " 'I wanted to write as well as I possibly could' ": Millar, "The Scene of the Crime," Ann Arbor lecture, 1953.
110 "all but ruined once": Millar notebook, UCI.
110 "Margaret's kin had suffered from": Millar, "Notes of a Son and Father," UCI.
110 " 'I took the confession of murder by someone I knew' ": Beverly Slopen, "The Most Private Eye," *The Canadian,* August 20, 1977.
110 " 'In *Ontario*' ": Jerry Tutunjian, "A Conversation with Ross Macdonald," *Tamarack Review,* 1974.
110 " 'Montecito was a hotbed of hard drinking' ": Al Stump interview with TN.
110 " 'the kind of play that only a mother or an actor could love' ": John Ross Macdonald, *The Drowning Pool* (Knopf, 1950).
112 "Linda seemed more out of place in Santa Barbara": Details about Linda from Millar's "Notes of a Son and Father," UCI.
113 " 'the spectacle of a prose writer of high attainments' ": Anthony Boucher, "Chandler, Revalued," *New York Times Book Review,* September 25, 1949.
113 " 'Human compassion and literary skill' ": Anthony Boucher, "Best Mysteries of 1949," *New York Times Book Review,* December 4, 1949.
113 " 'I have an idea' ": Millar to Knopf, February 20, 1950, HRHRC.
113 " 'Chandler's last was just as well written as ever' ": Knopf to Millar, February 27, 1950, HRHRC.
113 " 'He was one of the few authors' ": Pat Knopf letter to TN, October 1994.
113 "I . . . quite agree": Knopf to Millar, February 27, 1950, HRHRC.
114 " 'You haven't let me down at all' ": Boucher to Millar, September 8, 1950, Indiana.
114 " 'You seem to have committed yourself' ": Chandler to James M. Fox, January 4, 1951, from *Letters: Raymond Chandler and James M. Fox* (Neville + Yellin, 1978).
114 " 'Anything that fantasy can invent' ": Millar to Knopf, February 20, 1950, HRHRC.
114 "he'd insert expressionist sketches of Zanuck into a couple of Archer short stories": See descriptions of Angel Funk and his Palm Springs estate in "Gone Girl" in *The Name Is Archer* (Bantam, 1955), first published February 1953 as "The Imaginary Blonde" (also known as "The Singing Pigeon"). See also description of Edward Illman in "The Suicide" in the same collection, first published October 1953 as "The Beat-Up Sister": "In a white terry-cloth bathrobe, he had the shape and bulk of a Kodiak bear. The top of his head was as bald as an ostrich egg. He carried a chip on each shoulder, like epaulets. . . . He was a suave old fox." A Twentieth Century–Fox.
115 " 'A fierce old man sits sputtering in the witness box' ": Brad Darrach, "The Man Behind the Mysteries," *People,* July 8, 1974.
115 " 'He and Margaret sat through the big ones' ": Harris Seed interview with TN.
115 " 'It's rather fun' ": Millar to Pat Knopf, February 23, 1950, HRHRC.
115 " 'pseudonymous books written, too quickly' ": Millar to Professor Thorpe, December 11, 1950, Bentley Historical Library, University of Michigan.
115 "the UCSB English faculty": Santa Barbara's university campus was initially known as Santa Barbara College; when its affiliation with the UC system was

strengthened, it became known formally as the University of California, Santa Barbara (or UCSB).

115 " 'I grew up in a part of southern Ontario he knew' ": Hugh Kenner interview with TN.

116 " 'Ken was quietly persuasive' ": Kenner, "Learning," in *Inward Journey* (Cordelia Editions, 1984; Mysterious Press, 1987).

116 " 'He was immensely valuable to me' ": Kenner interview with TN.

116 " 'You will write the *Ulysses* of the tecs yet' ": Kenner to Millar, date not given, cited in "JOSEPH THE PROVIDER/BOOKS: Catalogue Fifty-Seven" (1995).

116 " 'Ken's working quota' ": Kenner interview with TN.

116 " 'We never talked a lot about writing' ": Al Stump interview with TN.

118 "This head dodge would help Lew Archer": e.g., Macdonald, *The Chill* (Knopf, 1963): "He threw a punch at my face. I shifted my head. His fist crunched into the plaster wall."

118 " 'a more human book than either of the others' ": Millar to Boucher, September 18, 1950, Indiana.

119 " 'As it's a long time since Hammett' ": James Sandoe (uncredited), "Mystery," *Chicago Sun-Times*, September 12, 1950.

119 " 'He told me he was a best-seller in France' ": Kenner interview with TN.

119 "the Millars' total combined income": tax forms, UCI.

119 " 'Being a woman and less responsible economically' ": Millar to Thorpe, December 11, 1950, Bentley Historical Library, University of Michigan.

120 "and took notes of the guest speaker": Millar notebook, UCI.

120 "'Linda's 'maladjustment' ": School counselor's report cited in Superior Court documents, *The People of the State of California vs. Linda Jane Millar*, "Application for Probation," August 27, 1956.

120 " 'he thought it was normal' ": Ibid.

120 " 'The clothes, without Jessie in them' ": Margaret Millar, *The Cannibal Heart* (Random House, 1949).

120 "Linda asked if she could go to Michigan too": Millar, "Notes of a Son and Father," UCI.

121 *"The Saturday Review"*: Kathleen Sproul, "The Criminal Record," *Saturday Review*, August 25, 1951.

121 " 'The problem is the age-old one' ": Millar to Knopf, August 28, 1951, HRHRC.

121 " 'The chairman of the graduate committee' ": Donald Pearce interview with TN.

121 "Millar joked to Boucher": Millar to Boucher, July 9, 1951, Indiana.

121 "not wanting to be like the men on his doctoral committee": Millar to Bruccoli, January 10, 1970, MJB Collection, UCI.

122 " 'in crisp black funeral silks' ": Macdonald, *The Way Some People Die* (Knopf, 1951).

124 " 'Macdonald can write really well' ": James Sandoe, "Mystery and Suspense," *New York Herald Tribune*, August 19, 1951.

124 " 'The tough ones don't come any better than this' ": Lenore Glen Offord, "The Gory Road," *San Francisco Chronicle*, August 5, 1951.

124 " 'Macdonald has the makings' ": Anthony Boucher, "Criminals at Large," *New York Times Book Review*, August 5, 1951.

124 " 'An element of smugness enters in' ": Millar to Boucher, July 9, 1951, Indiana.

124 "done under the conscious influence of Nelson Algren's *The Man with the Golden Arm*": Millar interview with Paul Nelson, UCI.

124 " 'He spent quite a bit of time explaining to me' ": Pearce interview with TN.

126 "might break his back": Millar to Thorpe, December 13, 1952, Bentley Historical Library, University of Michigan: "I haven't told you, or anyone else but M., but last year the combined strain of my novel (THE IVORY GRIN) and my dissertation almost broke my back."

126 " '1000 pages longhand' ": Millar to Knopf, July 25, 1951, HRHRC.

126 "a Santa Barbara household in turmoil": Details from "Notes of a Son and Father," UCI.

127 " 'Please don't worry about me going to pieces' ": Margaret to Kenneth Millar, June 18, 1951, UCI.

127 " 'The accident was pretty ghastly and mysterious' ": Margaret to Kenneth Millar, July 30, 1951, UCI.

127 " 'We're getting bloody sick of each other' ": Ibid.

127 " 'attempted suicide' ": Millar, "Notes of a Son and Father," UCI.

127 " 'Grant's words were much in his mind' ": Ibid.

127 "escaped hospitalization by the skin of his teeth": "I myself escaped hospitalization by the skin of my teeth," Millar to Steven Carter, April 24, 1968, courtesy of Steven Carter.

127 " 'he saw the necessity' ": Millar, "Notes of a Son and Father," UCI.

128 " 'happily rusticating' ": Millar to Boucher, August 27, 1951, Indiana.

128 " 'He was sitting in a chair' ": Hugh Kenner interview with TN.

128 " 'Archer never in the book' ": Knopf to Millar, July 15, 1951, HRHRC.

128 " 'I am quite as eager' ": Millar to Knopf, July 25, 1951, HRHRC.

128 " 'With all due respect' ": Millar to Dave Herrmann, September 10, 1951, HRHRC.

128 " 'Is the hardboiled mystery on the way out . . . ?' ": Millar to Boucher, August 27, 1951, Indiana.

128 "prodded Knopf": von Auw to Knopf, August 24, 1951, HRHRC.

130 " 'After the first ten books' ": Millar to Thorpe, December 13, 1952, Bentley Historical Library, University of Michigan.

130 " 'He had a mansion' ": Robert Wade interview with TN.

130 "Some traveled long distances": *The Third Degree*, MWA newsletter, 1952.

130 " 'God, they got black guys, servants, all around' ": William Campbell Gault interview with TN.

131 " 'Between us we've had about the best critical receptions of the year' ": Millar to H. N. Swanson, Margaret Herrick Library.

131 " 'He wasn't *keen* on my doing it' ": Margaret Millar interview with TN.

131 " 'To many Santa Barbarans' ": Verne Linderman, "Good Mysteries Demand Characterization Based on Sound Psychology, Say Millars of Cliff Drive," *Santa Barbara News-Press*, March 30, 1952.

132 " 'It's a long wait' ": Millar to Henry Branson, August 8, 1952, UCI.

132 "an Archer short story ('The Guilty Ones') structured like a TV play": Published in *Manhunt*, May 1953; later rewritten extensively for inclusion in *The Name Is Archer.*

132 " 'If it makes the splash I expect it to' ": Millar to H. N. Swanson, April 18, 1952, Margaret Herrick Library.

132 " 'I like it immensely' ": Knopf to Millar, August 5, 1952, HRHRC.

133 "Knopf quoted the Pocket Books honcho": Knopf to Millar, August 21, 1952, HRHRC.

133 " 'Do you think the book needs rewriting?' ": Millar to Knopf, August 28, 1952, HRHRC. The lines quoted are from the letter Millar actually sent Knopf. A slightly different draft (UCI) was printed as "Farewell to Chandler" in *Inward Journey*.

135 " 'I am all for the writer' ": Knopf to Millar, September 3, 1952, HRHRC.

135 " 'And good luck to all of us' ": Knopf to Millar, October 16, 1952, HRHRC.

135 " 'We talked about all the current issues' ": Harris Seed interview with TN.

135 " 'Margaret and I always had a very guarded relationship' ": Hugh Kenner interview with TN.

136 " 'She would *roll* her cigarette holder' ": Pearce interview with TN.

136 " 'My God that guy has crust' ": Margaret to Kenneth Millar, July 15, 1951, UCI.

136 " 'I flunked sewing' ": Claire Stump interview with TN.

136 " 'M. J. [Mary Jo], who is seven months pregnant' ": Kenner to Pearce, November 1, 1952, courtesy of Donald Pearce.

136 " 'We saw a civilization taking shape' ": Millar to Adlai Stevenson, November 6, 1954, handwritten copy, UCI.

136 " 'I see the mystery in all its varying degrees' ": Millar to Richard C. Boys, December 29, 1952, the Richard C. Boys Correspondence, Special Collections Library, University of Michigan.

136 " 'to impart first-class standards' ": Millar to Thorpe, December 13, 1952, Bentley Historical Library, University of Michigan.

138 " 'U.S. Removes Library Books' ": Associated Press story, June 23, 1953.

138 " 'In response to numerous inquiries' ": *The Third Degree*, Mystery Writers of America, Inc., August 1951.

138 " 'He was a hot number right then' ": Pearce interview with TN.

138 " 'Ace Writer of Mysteries Talks Today' ": Becky Conrad, *Michigan Daily*, July 1, 1953.

138 " 'I'll do my damnedest' ": Millar to Boys, January 11, 1953, the Richard C. Boys Correspondence, Special Collections Library, University of Michigan.

138 " 'The last occasion I had' ": Kenneth Millar, "The Scene of the Crime: Social Meanings of the Detective Story," lecture given at Auditorium A, Angell Hall, University of Michigan. Transcribed from a recording, University of Michigan. Later, Millar rewrote and expanded his remarks as an essay ("The Scene of the Crime"), eventually printed in *Inward Journey*.

140 " 'He was awfully pleased' ": Pearce interview with TN.

140 " 'Ken was proud of the fact' ": Kenner interview with TN.

141 " 'No, I haven't been drinking, much' ": Margaret Millar, *Do Evil in Return* (Random House, 1950).

141 " 'Mussey was my darling' ": Margaret Millar interview with TN.

141 " 'But I don't mean sexual love' ": Millar to Branson, July 8, 1953, UCI.

142 " 'I should like to see [the mystery's] philosophic possibilities explored' ": Millar, "The Scene of the Crime."

142 " 'the present state of the fiction market' ": Knopf to Millar, June 3, 1953, HRHRC.

143 " 'THROUGH HAROLD OBER IN 1949' ": MacDonald to Max Wilkinson, Western Union form (undated), Rare Books and Manuscripts, University of Florida Libraries.

143 " 'An "agreement" to which Mr. MacDonald refers' ": Millar to von Auw, March 16, 1953, typed copy, University of Florida.

143 " 'Could you have mistaken . . . ?' ": Millar to MacDonald, August 31, 1953, University of Florida.

144 " 'I was not implying' ": MacDonald to Millar, September 5, 1953, UCI.

144 "Saul David, a fan of Millar's since reading *Blue City*": Saul David interview with TN.

145 " 'I'm sure you can understand' ": Knopf to Millar, October 30, 1953, HRHRC.

145 " 'I expect to write a mystery novel every year' ": Millar to Knopf, November 2, 1953, HRHRC.

145 " 'If we like them, we will show them to Bantam' ": Knopf to Millar, October 30, 1953, HRHRC.

145 " 'I leaned over backwards a bit' ": Millar to Knopf, November 2, 1953, HRHRC.

145 " 'We're in a somewhat awkward three-cornered situation now' ": Knopf to Millar, November 9, 1953, HRHRC.

145 " 'We'd like to see Kerrigan beaten up' ": Saul David to Millar, November 24, 1953, UCI.

146 " 'I'd like to say how pleased we are' ": Ibid.

146 " 'a crowning stupidity' ": Millar to Branson, November 15, 1953, UCI.

146 " 'like hell' ": Millar to Boucher, December 6, 1953, Indiana.
146 " 'in a way I regret that I was ever persuaded to leave you' ": Chandler to Knopf, July 16, 1953; in *Selected Letters of Raymond Chandler,* ed. Frank MacShane (Columbia University Press, 1981).
146 " 'I'd like to ditch that character' ": Millar to Branson, November 28, 1953, UCI.
146 " 'partly because there were so many Kenneth and Margaret Millar titles on the market' ": "Kenneth Millar/'John Ross Macdonald,' " *Wilson Library Bulletin,* December 1953.
146 " 'I don't suppose any harm has been done' ": Knopf to von Auw, December 4, 1953, HRHRC.
147 " 'I wouldn't have redone the book' ": Millar to Knopf, January 5, 1954, HRHRC.
147 " 'I think this sort of thing should not appear' ": Knopf to Millar, January 15, 1954, HRHRC.
147 " 'I've no wish to offend anyone' ": Millar to Knopf, January 23, 1954, HRHRC.
147 " 'Mr. John Ross Macdonald must be ranked high' ": Julian Symons (unsigned), "Criminal Practices," (London) *Times Literary Supplement,* November 20, 1953.
148 " 'Reasonable Facsimile' ": Unsigned review, "Reasonable Fascsimile," *Time,* July 26, 1954.
148 " 'Annual Event' ": Unsigned review, "Annual Event," *Newsweek,* September 6, 1954.
148 " 'Linda was an interesting girl' ": Kenner interview with TN.
148 "One woman complained": *People vs. Linda Jane Millar,* Santa Barbara Probation Department report.
149 " 'I think she was mainly interested in experiencing life' ": Geoff Aggeler interview with TN.
150 " 'Most of his acting ability is in his fists' ": Quoted in Tim Brooks and Earle Marsh, *The Complete Directory to Prime Time Network TV Shows 1946–Present,* 4th ed. (Ballantine Books, 1979).
150 "the Millars got a joint payment of seven hundred dollars": Millar notebooks and tax forms, UCI; correspondence with Swanson, Margaret Herrick Library.
150 " 'As far as the future is concerned' ": Knopf internal memo, January 11, 1954, HRHRC.
150 " 'probably the handsomest and smartest' ": von Auw to Knopf, June 1, 1954, HRHRC.
150 " 'My best thanks' ": Knopf to von Auw, June 4, 1954, HRHRC.
150 " 'Falls somewhat below his best work' ": Lenore Glen Offord, "The Gory Road," *San Francisco Chronicle,* August 29, 1954.
150 " 'A long haul here' ": *Kirkus Reviews,* June 1, 1954.
151 " 'the best yet' ": Anthony Boucher, "Criminals at Large," *New York Times Book Review,* August 1, 1954.
151 " 'I had difficulties with publishers' ": Millar to Boucher, August 9, 1954, Indiana.
151 "*New York Times* best-of-the-year list": Anthony Boucher, "Boucher's Choices: The Best Mysteries of 1954," *New York Times Book Review,* December 5, 1954.
151 " 'Bantam at least seems solidly behind me' ": Millar to Boucher, August 9, 1954, Indiana.
151 " 'vastly enthusiastic' ": David to Millar, August 16, 1954, UCI.
151 " 'grand' ": David to Millar, September 26, 1954, UCI.
152 " 'One of the great turning points in my life' ": Joe Gores interview with TN.
152 "Bill Pronzini . . . ranked Macdonald's anthology": In Bill Pronzini and Marcia Muller, *1001 Midnights: The Aficionado's Guide to Mystery and Detective Fiction* (Arbor House, 1986). Pronzini's ranking was for *Lew Archer, Private Investigator* (Mysterious Press, 1977), the expanded version of *The Name Is Archer.*
152 "Douglas G. Greene went further": Douglas G. Greene, "The Fifteen Greatest Detective Short Story Volumes Since Poe," included in *The Fine Art of Murder: The*

NOTES

Mystery Reader's Indispensable Companion, eds. Ed Gorman, Martin H. Greenberg, Larry Segriff, with Jon L. Breen (Carroll & Graf, 1993).

152 " 'the joint conclusion—believe it or not' ": Millar to the Bransons, June 5, 1954, UCI.

152 "a Gore Vidal play based on the same subject": Gore Vidal, *Dark Possession*, performed February 15, 1954, on *Studio One* (CBS). This was the first of several original plays Vidal wrote for live TV.

152 " 'Every sound was a threat' ": Margaret Millar, introduction to International Polygonics, Ltd. paperback edition of *Beast in View* (Random House, 1955), 1983.

154 " 'We had to pioneer a novel land' ": Millar, "To M.," notebook, UCI.

154 " 'a place where our cultural conflicts are worked out' ": Millar, "Notes of a Son and Father," UCI.

155 " 'the somatic expression of a spiritual malaise' ": Millar to Henry Branson, February 18, 1955, UCI.

155 " '3 were killed' ": Linda to Kenneth Millar, March 25, 1955, UCI.

156 "sat for a newspaper photographer". "Former KCI Teacher Urges New Library/Wife With Him," *Kitchener-Waterloo Record*, April 7, 1955.

156 " 'Linda is usually a cheerful soul' ": Millar to Sandoe, April 25, 1955, the James Sandoe Collection, Special Collections and Manuscripts, Brigham Young University.

156 " 'first rate' ": Knopf to Millar, October 10, 1955, HRHRC.

156 " '. . . I want you to take me seriously, Lew' ": Ross Macdonald, *The Barbarous Coast* (Knopf, 1956).

157 "The Millars' late friend M. M. Musselman": Author of several books and screenplays, Musselman was a boyhood friend and sparring partner of Ernest Hemingway's; in 1920, the two budding men of letters collaborated on *Hokum: A Play in Three Acts* (Wellesley Hills: Sans Souci Press, 1978).

157 " 'I do find myself wondering' ": Knopf to Millar, October 10, 1955, HRHRC.

158 "he'd gross nearly fourteen thousand five hundred dollars": Millar tax forms, UCI.

158 " 'thoughtful and friendly warning' ": Millar to Knopf, October 15, 1955, HRHRC.

158 " 'If [the new book] has enough success' ": Millar to von Auw, January 13, 1956, Princeton.

158 " 'stupidity' ": Ray Bond to Millar, December 28, 1955, UCI.

158 "Someone at the firm made a list": "Suggested titles for THE DYING ANIMAL, John Ross MacDonald [*sic*]," Knopf in-house communiqué, November 22, 1955, HRHRC.

158 " 'wit, impact, and the all-important element of class' ": Millar to Knopf, December 9, 1955, HRHRC.

158 " 'Agreed' ": Knopf to Millar, December 14, 1955, HRHRC. The *Cosmopolitan* magazine condensation of this book, though, was published as *The Dying Animal* (March 1956).

159 " 'the dissolution of my marriage of inconvenience' ": Millar to von Auw, February 20, 1956, Princeton.

160 " 'My imaginative identification' ": Notes for "Confessions of a Constant Reader," February 1956, Santa Barbara Library talk, Millar notebook, UCI.

160 " 'That made me think of a half-built life' ": Linda Millar, Rorschach test reaction, March 7, 1956, quoted in documents appended to *People vs. Linda Jane Millar*, "Application for Probation."

160 "he caught Linda smoking": This and other details of Linda's behavior from documents attached to probation application, ibid.

160 " 'We knew what Linda was up to' ": Stump interview with TN.

160 " 'to be loved on any terms, by anyone' ": Millar, "Notes of a Son and Father," UCI.

161   " 'the fairly normal incestuous content' ": Ibid.

161   "Linda's big and little problems": Ibid.

163   " 'It isn't true . . .' ": Kenneth Millar, "Find the Woman."

163   " 'I have only one daughter, Mr. Archer . . .' ": "Gone Girl," first published as "The Imaginary Blonde," *Manhunt*, February 1953.

163   "At 5:30 P.M. Thursday, February 23": Details of Linda's activities and other events from *People vs. Linda Jane Millar* and *Santa Barbara News-Press* stories.

164   " 'Police Have Suspect Car' ": *Santa Barbara News-Press,* February 24, 1956.

164   " 'Expert Examining Hit-Run Vehicle' ": *Santa Barbara News-Press,* February 25, 1956.

165   " 'Girl, 16, Faces Arrest' ": *Santa Barbara News-Press,* February 26, 1956.

166   " 'She had been planning to go to a girlfriend's house' ": *People vs. Linda Jane Millar,* psychiatrist's report.

166   " 'we are filled with grief' ": "Girl, 16, Faces Charges in Hit-and-Run Death," *Santa Barbara Star,* March 1, 1956.

166   " 'We look to the future without fear' ": Millar to von Auw, March 5, 1956, Princeton.

166   " 'One-fifth gallon in an hour' ": Millar, "Notes of a Son and Father," UCI.

167   " 'Nothing seemed to matter' ": *People vs. Linda Jane Millar,* Probation Department report.

167   " 'Ironies' ": Margaret Millar interview with TN.

167   " 'Artists are people who voluntarily undergo' ": Donald Pearce interview with TN.

168   " 'As a man writes his fiction' ": Ross Macdonald, preface to *Lew Archer, Private Investigator;* reprinted in *Self-Portrait.*

168   " 'Life seems to come in tidal waves' ": Millar to von Auw, May 4, 1956, Princeton.

168   "Her parents wept": "Linda Millar Faces Adult Court Trial," *Santa Barbara News-Press,* May 10, 1956.

168   " 'I am prompted by the moral and practical necessity' ": Millar to von Auw, May 11, 1956, Princeton.

169   " 'to move immediately to get for Linda' ": Millar to von Auw, May 18, 1956, Princeton.

169   " 'Happily it's no snake pit' ": Millar to von Auw, June 13, 1956, Princeton.

169   " 'Maggie's a grief-stricken woman' ": Millar to von Auw, June 3, 1956, Princeton.

169   "all three Millars were summoned": *People vs. Linda Jane Millar,* grand jury testimony.

169   " 'One of my children' ": Claire Stump interview with TN.

169   " 'He was determined that Linda should go through with whatever the law demanded' ": Lydia Freeman interview with TN.

171   " 'Nice person' ": Millar, "Notes of a Son and Father," UCI.

171   " 'It was just a ghastly experience' ": Claire Stump interview with TN.

171   " 'I was at the Catholic high school' ": Aggeler interview with TN.

172   " 'no rational enthusiast' ": Anthony Boucher, "Report on Criminals at Large," *New York Times Book Review,* June 24, 1956.

172   " 'an admirable, thoroughly absorbing piece of work' ": James Sandoe, "Mystery and Suspense," *New York Herald Tribune,* July 15, 1956.

172   " 'Macdonald's masterpiece!' ": Knopf ad, *New York Times Book Review,* July 8, 1956.

172   " 'You know how much I like THE BARBAROUS COAST' ": Knopf to Millar, July 11, 1956, HRHRC.

173   "After five months' controversy": "Linda Millar Guilty in Hit, Run Fatality: Judge Wagner Raps Lack of Co-operation by Defense," *Santa Barbara News-Press,* July 11, 1956.

NOTES

173 " 'After I had dinner' ": *People vs. Linda Jane Millar,* Linda's handwritten statement.
175 "the evening's *News-Press":* "Probation in Hit-Run Case: Linda Millar Is Granted 8-Year Suspension by Judge," *Santa Barbara News-Press,* August 27, 1956.
175 " 'Many of the callers' ": "Judge Is Threatened for Millar Decision: Linda and Parents Leave Town, Plan Fresh Start," *Santa Barbara Star,* August 30, 1956.
175 "Juicy excerpts": Ibid.
176 " 'She was a headstrong young lady' ": Harris Seed interview with TN.
177 " 'When there's trouble in a family' ": Ross Macdonald, *Sleeping Beauty* (Knopf, 1973).
177 " 'On the eve of Memorial Day' ": Millar, "Memorial Day," notebook, UCI.
177 *"Clearing a space":* Millar to von Auw, November 15, 1956, Princeton.
177 " 'Things are working out better' ": Millar to Mrs. Clara Lon Gould, Harold Ober Associates, September 5, 1956, Princeton.
178 " 'a watershed event' ": Millar interview with Paul Nelson, UCI.
178 " 'get the genie back into the bottle' ": Millar to Michael Avallone, October 19, 1975, UCI.
178 "The very hardest thing for him to face": Millar interview with Paul Nelson, UCI.
178 " 'I asked him about the accusation' ": Jerry Tutunjian interview with TN.
179 "an unpublished Archer novelette ('The Angry Man')": manuscript, UCI.
179 "his 'diary of psychic progress' ": Millar to Dorothy Olding, May 27, 1957, Princeton.
179 " 'I was dreaming about a hairless ape' ": Ross Macdonald, *The Doomsters* (Knopf, 1958).
182 " *'The Doomsters,* by Ross Macdonald' ": Millar to von Auw, May 27, 1957, Princeton.
182 " 'I like the fact that it runs close to 100,000 words' ": Millar later amicably trimmed his manuscript.
183 " 'Things look green after the drought' ": Ibid.
185 " 'Ever since the days of Francis Galton' ": Margaret Millar, *The Invisible Worm* (Doubleday, Doran, 1941).
185 " 'It looks like an interesting decade coming up' ": Millar to Knopf, August 26, 1957, HRHRC.
185 " 'Hostility toward life apparently including me' ": Robert Easton, "A Tribute," in *Dictionary of Literary Biography Yearbook: 1983* (A Bruccoli Clark Book/Gale Research Company, 1983).
185 " 'He could maintain long silences' ": Shelly Lowenkopf, "Santa Barbara Mystery Writers," *Santa Barbara News & Review,* August 29, 1985.
186 " 'Ken was an unusually *controlled* person' ": Donald Davie interview with TN.
186 " 'M. is more chipper' ": Millar to von Auw, September 24, 1957, Princeton.
187 "the best winter of his life": Millar interview with Arthur Kaye, UCI.
187 " 'Sometimes he would read aloud a short story' ": Herb Harker interview with TN.
188 " 'I'll never know how he achieved that' ": Noel Young, "Writer as Teacher," *Santa Barbara News & Review,* July 21, 1983.
188 " 'The hiss-and-boo villain died in the nineteenth century' ": Jon Carrol, "Ross Macdonald in Raw California," *Esquire,* June 1972.
188 " 'what we both desire' ": Millar to Boucher, March 2, 1958, Indiana.
188 " 'the hardboiled private detective story can become literature' ": Anthony Boucher, "Criminals at Large," *New York Times Book Review,* February 23, 1958.
188 " 'a milieu evoked' ": James Sandoe, "Mystery and Suspense," *New York Herald Tribune Book Review,* February 16, 1958.
188 " 'snake-pit' ": Sergeant Cuff, "The Criminal Record," *Saturday Review,* June 14, 1958.

188 " 'kind of homesick' ": Lenore Glen Offord, "The Gory Road," *San Francisco Chronicle*, March 16, 1958.
189 " 'generally unpleasant personnel' ": Sergeant Cuff, "Criminal Record."
189 " 'I am worried and distressed' ": Knopf to Millar, February 28, 1958, UCI.
189 " 'He writes like an angel' ": Dave Herrmann to Knopf, February 26, 1959, HRHRC; quoted by Knopf to Millar, February 28, 1959, HRHRC, UCI.
189 " 'Dear Alfred' ": Millar to Knopf, March 9, 1958, HRHRC.
190 " 'Don't, for heaven's sake' ": Knopf to Millar, March 13, 1958, UCI.
190 " 'This is a fine Archer' ": Quoted by Knopf to von Auw, May 21, 1958, Princeton.
190 " 'with great enjoyment' ": Knopf to Millar, July 2, 1958, HRHRC.
191 " 'She was madly in love with him' ": Margaret Millar interview with TN.
191 " 'major contribution to the form' ": Loren D. Estleman, "Off the Record/Plus Expenses: The Private Eye as Great American Hero," *Alfred Hitchcock's Mystery Magazine*, September 1983.
192 " 'I'm afraid my son had a *nostalgie de la boue*' ": Ross Macdonald, *The Galton Case* (Knopf, 1959).
192 "The poem offered in evidence, 'Luna' ": "I wrote that when I was 19 and in college. That is probably as good a poem as I ever wrote. Poets who don't develop past the age of 19 ought to give up and I did." From "An Interview with Ross Macdonald," *Concept Twelve* (1971), "the literary magazine of Santa Barbara City College," printed by Noel Young.
192 "where Rexroth chanted poems a bit abashedly": Donald Pearce interview with TN.
192 " 'Passengers on a Cable Car Named Despair' ": Kenneth Millar, *San Francisco Chronicle*, June 29, 1958.
193 " 'An intellectual is someone who's smart and insists on it' ": Jerre Lloyd interview with TN.
193 "for Millar, the novel's central events": Millar interview with Paul Nelson, UCI. See also Macdonald, "A Preface to *The Galton Case*," in *Afterwords*, ed. Thomas McCormack (Harper & Row, 1968); printed as "Writing the Galton Case," in Ross Macdonald, *On Crime Writing* (Capra Press, 1973) and in *Self-Portrait*.
195 " 'Now let's see if I can write a better book' ": Millar to Knopf, October 16, 1958, HRHRC.
196 "Ross Macdonald was now Bantam's number one mystery writer": Millar to Knopf, September 29, 1958, HRHRC.
197 " 'It appears that the market is there' ": Ibid.
197 " 'Pocket Books didn't care' ": David to Millar, March 3, 1959, UCI.
197 " 'I've always believed there was mileage in my work' ": Millar to Knopf, November 15, 1958, HRHRC.
197 " 'I have the ambition' ": Millar to Knopf, January 5, 1958, HRHRC.
198 " 'All agreed with Ken's hopes' ": Robert Easton letter to TN, March 7, 1991.
198 " 'It's not a book that will make money' ": Millar to von Auw, January 31, 1959, Princeton.
198 " 'It's not a case of now or never' ": Millar to Knopf, September 29, 1958, HRHRC.
198 " 'The 99 Best Crime Stories' ": Julian Symons, "From Buchan to Bond" (part two of three parts), (London) *Sunday Times*, December 7, 1958.
198 " 'While we talked about the idea' ": Julian Symons, "The Case of Raymond Chandler," *New York Times Magazine*, December 23, 1973.
198 " 'Less surprisingly,' Millar modestly noted to von Auw": Millar to von Auw, Princeton.
199 " 'a dagger behind every velvet curtain' ": Claire Stump interview with TN.
199 " 'Oh, *sure*,' Mudrick said sarcastically": Donald Pearce interview with TN.

NOTES

199 " 'Not having much money' ": Dick Lid interview with TN.
200 " 'Material things never mattered to them' ": Betty Lid interview with TN.
201 " 'he thinks that this is the most imaginative character' ": Agency memo, March 10, 1959, Princeton.
201 " 'There has been a singularly involving excitement' ": James Sandoe, "Mystery and Suspense," *New York Herald Tribune Book Review,* March 29, 1959.
202 " 'For the jacket of Ross Macdonald's new novel' ": Anthony Boucher, "Criminals at Large," *New York Times Book* Review, March 29, 1959.
202 " 'For some reason' ": Millar to von Auw, March 29, 1959, Princeton.
202 " 'One way and another' ": Ibid.
202 " 'Lin's doing extremely well' ": Ibid.
203 " 'What is man?' ": Kenneth Millar, "The New Books—Contributions to the Theory of Tragedy," *San Francisco Chronicle,* July 19, 1959.
203 " 'To paraphrase an old line' ": von Auw to Millar, July 23, 1959, UCI.
203 " 'I can assure you that's the last time' ": Linda to Kenneth and Margaret Millar, November 12, 1957, UCI.
    Details of Linda's behavior at UC Davis from documents appended to *People vs. Linda Jane Millar,* "Report Concerning Violation of Terms and Conditions of Probation," July 6, 1959.
204 "which the *News-Press* reported": "Linda Millar Sought for Probation Violation," *Santa Barbara News-Press,* June 3, 1959.
204 "On Wednesday, Ken Millar took a United flight": Details of Millar's activities in Sacramento, Stateline, LA, etc., from Millar address-book diary jottings, UCI; from items appended to court documents; from newspaper stories (see below).
204 " 'S.B. police should forward full teletype' ": Millar, address book/diary, UCI.
204 " 'good and gentle' ": Ross Macdonald, introduction to *Lew Archer, Private Investigator;* reprinted in *Self-Portrait.*
205 " 'He was a short broad man' ": Macdonald, *The Zebra-Striped Hearse* (Knopf, 1962); Walters, along with his partner-wife, is in *The Chill* (Knopf, 1964) as well.
    Girola also inspired the character of Joe Quinn in Margaret Millar's *How Like an Angel* (Random House, 1962), she said: "He was based on a real-life private detective Ken and I knew from Reno. We were both very much taken with the man and we both used him in our work." (Quoted by Shelly Lowenkopf, "Santa Barbara Mystery Writers," *Santa Barbara News & Review,* August 1985.)
205 " 'Mr. Millar (missing girl's father)' ": *People vs. Linda Jane Millar,* "Supplementary Investigation Report," June 6, 1959.
206 " 'a brief piece for his Sunday paper' ": "Writers' Daughter Vanishes," *Woodland Democrat,* June 7, 1959.
206 " 'He said, "Look" ' ": William Hogan interview with TN.
207 " 'Linda is not a runaway from college' ": Millar address book/diary, UCI; quoted in newspaper stories.
207 " 'Mystery Writer's Toughest Case—Daughter Vanishes' ": *New York Post,* June 8, 1959, with photo.
    Many newspapers printed stories about Linda Millar's disappearance. This is a partial list in addition to articles already cited:

NEW YORK POST

"Mystery Writer Has Only One Clue: His Daughter's $10 Check," June 10, 1959.

SANTA BARBARA NEWS-PRESS

"Hit Run Driver Still Missing," June 5, 1959.
"Linda Still Missing; Foul Play Feared," June 8, 1959.

NOTES

"Father Begs Linda to Return, After She Is Reported in L.A.," June 9, 1959, with AP photo.
"No Word Yet of Missing Linda Millar," June 10, 1959.
"Linda Millar Back Home with Family," June 11, 1959, with photo.

RENO EVENING GAZETTE

"Police Seek Missing Girl," June 5, 1959.
"Missing Coed Located by Reno Private Eyes," June 11, 1959, with UPI photo.
"Coed Admitted to Hospital," June 13, 1959.

SACRAMENTO UNION

"Father Joins Hunt for Missing Coed," June 8, 1959, with photo.
"Missing Davis Student Meets Father in Reno," June 11, 1959.

SACRAMENTO BEE

"Coed from UC at Davis Disappears," June 6, 1959.
"2 Will Be Queried About Davis Coed Missing 10 Days," June 8, 1959, with UPI photo.
"Search for Davis Coed Moves to LA," June 9, 1959.
"Warrant Seeks Missing Coed for Protection," June 10, 1959.
"Missing Coed Is Found Safe in Reno," June 11, 1959.

SACRAMENTO UNION

"Father Joins Hunt for Missing Coed," June 8, 1959, with photo.
"Coed's Father Flies South in His Search," June 9, 1959.
"We Love You, Father Calls to Lost Coed," June 10, 1959, with AP photo.
"Missing Davis Student Meets Father in Reno," June 11, 1959.
"Davis U. Coed Now Resting at Her Home," June 12, 1959.
"Linda Millar Put in Care of Psychiatrist," June 14, 1959.

WOODLAND DAILY DEMOCRAT

"Davis Coed Disappears," June 8, 1959, with photo.
"Hunt for Missing Coed Shifts to L.A.," June 9, 1959, with *Democrat* photo.
"Davis Coed's Dad Writes Frantic Plea," June 10, 1959.
"Missing Cal Aggie Coed Found Wandering in Reno," June 11, 1959.

NEW YORK HERALD TRIBUNE

"Mystery Writers' Daughter Vanishes at Nevada Casino," June 8, 1959.
"Calif. Girl, 19, Missing 11 Days, Returns Home," June 12, 1959, with UPI photo.

LOS ANGELES TIMES

"Daughter of Detective Story Writer Missing," June 8, 1959, with UPI photo.
"Missing Coed Seen in Market in Hollywood," June 9, 1959.
"Father Pleads for UC Coed Daughter Return," June 10, 1959, with *Times* photo.
"Coed Missing 10 Days Reported on Way Home," June 11, 1959.
"Coed, Missing for 11 Days, Returns Home," June 12, 1959.
"Report Filed in Coed Case," July 3, 1959.
"Coed Receives Continuance of Probation," July 7, 1959.

(HOLLYWOOD) CITIZEN-NEWS

"Mystery Writers' Daughter Missing: Officers of Two States Hunt for Missing Girl, 19," June 8, 1959, with UPI photo.

NOTES

"Daughter of Mystery Novel Writer Missing," June 8, 1959, with UPI photo.
"Hunted Girl in Hollywood," June 9, 1959.
"Hunt for Missing Girl in Hollywood," "Father Pleads for Daughter to 'Come Home,' " June 9, 1959, with two *Citizen-News* photos.
"Dad's Plea to Missing Girl," June 9, 1959, final, with two *Citizen-News* photos.
"Father of Missing Girl Leaves Hotel," June 10, 1959.
"Missing Girl Returns Home," June 11, 1959.

LOS ANGELES HERALD & EXPRESS

"Mystery Writer Dad in Plea to Missing Co-ed," June 9, 1959, with two *Herald-Express* photos.
"Cal. Co-ed's 10 Days of Wandering Told," June 11, 1959.

(LOS ANGELES) MIRROR NEWS

"Hunt Lost Coed in Hollywood," June 9, 1959, with *Mirror News* photo.
"Linda Found, Heads Home," June 11, 1959.

SAN FRANCISCO CHRONICLE

"Mystery at Tahoe—UC Coed Lost 8 Days," June 8, 1959, with UPI photo.
" 'Missing Coed in L.A.,' " June 9, 1959.
"Coed Mystery Deepens—Warrant for Her Arrest," June 10, 1959.
" 'Lost' Coed Home After Reno Trip," June 11, 1959.
"Missing Coed Found Safe, Going Home," June 11, 1959, final.
" 'Lost' Coed Home After Reno Trip," June 12, 1959.
"The Worrier," This World section, June 14, 1959.
"Judge Spares 'Vanishing' UC Coed," July 7, 1959.

207 " 'She could be anyplace in the United States' ": "Davis Coed Disappears," *Woodland Daily Democrat*, June 8, 1959.
208 " 'You know,' he told Slayman": "Hunt for Missing Coed Shifts to L.A.," *Woodland Daily Democrat*, June 9, 1959.
208 " 'Come home, dear' ": Quoted in whole or in part in several newspapers.
208 " 'I had to teach the next day' ": Lid to TN.
209 " 'He was almost out of his mind' ": Stump interview with TN.
209 " 'I'm afraid she is trying to sink out of sight' ": June 10, 1959, unidentified LA paper, *Los Angeles Examiner* clip file archive, Regional History Center, USC library.
210 "Millar scrawled on the back of a Channel 5 logsheet": Logsheet dated June 9, 1959, UCI.
210 " 'Mystery Writer Disappears' ": (Los Angeles) *Mirror News*, June 10, 1959.
210 " 'The answer of course is yes' ": Lid to TN.
211 " 'some kind of psychic break' ": "Linda Millar Back Home with Family," *Santa Barbara News-Press*, June 11, 1959.
211 " 'I do know I tried my hardest to get back' ": *People vs. Linda Jane Millar*, Linda Millar handwritten statement.
213 " 'I personally don't believe Linda called home' ": Lid to TN.
213 " 'on the spur of a rather desperate moment' ": Millar to von Auw, July 24, 1959, Princeton.
214 " 'I have to make some money' ": Millar to von Auw, July 12, 1959, Princeton.
215 *"Mystery"*: Gene Davidson and John Knoerle, "Ross Macdonald Interview," *Mystery*, November/December 1979.
215 *"New Yorker"*: unsigned review, "Mystery and Crime," *New Yorker*, August 13, 1960.
215 " 'the wrong side of the tracts' ": Ross Macdonald, *The Ferguson Affair* (Knopf, 1960).

217 " 'I am now one of those health bugs' ": Millar to Knopf, October 26, 1959, HRHRC.

217 " 'This may seem like an odd simile' ": Olding to Millar, July 15, 1960, UCI.

218 "a rave in the *New York Times Book Review*": Anthony Boucher, "Criminals at Large," *New York Times Book Review,* July 24, 1960.

218 " 'Happy Day!' ": Millar to von Auw, January 8, 1961, Princeton.

218 " 'rather staggering' ": Von Auw to Millar, August 15, 1960, Princeton.

218 " 'almost laughably good' ": Millar to von Auw, September 3, 1960, Princeton.

219 " 'as if England had joined the European Community' ": Millar to Knopf, June 21, 1960, HRHRC.

219 " 'Talk about togetherness!' ": Maurice Dolbier, "About the Millars of Santa Barbara," *New York Herald Tribune,* November 13, 1960.

219 " 'The Millars do not collaborate' ": *Publishers Weekly,* November, 1960.

219 " 'I don't think I write escape fiction' ": Martha MacGregor, "The Art of Writing About Murder," *New York Post,* November 27, 1960.

219 "a comical *New Yorker* sketch": S. J. Perelman, "Oh, I Am a Cook and a Houseboy Bland," *New Yorker,* February 18, 1961; included in *The Rising Gorge* (Simon and Schuster, 1961).

219 " 'Maggie's a hard girl to keep away from home' ": Millar to von Auw, November 8, 1960, Princeton.

219 " 'We'll have a man in the White House' ": Margaret Millar to Sandoe, November 9, 1960, the James Sandoe Collection, Special Collections and Manuscripts, Brigham Young University.

220 " 'as a token of affection' ": Millar to Olding, December 6, 1960, Princeton.

220 " 'Ken and I would talk about Alfred' ": Harding Lemay interview with TN.

221 "They should have seen a 1955 photo": illustrating "Former KCI Teacher Urges New Library."

223 " 'Dear Ivan' ": Millar to von Auw, January 27, 1961, Princeton.

223 " 'Dear Ken' ": Knopf to Millar, May 29, 1961, HRHRC.

223 " 'admirable,' " " 'excellent,' " " 'illuminating' ": Unsigned reader's report on "Coleridge and the Inward Eye," sent with letter from Mark Saxton to Ivan von Auw, December 10, 1959, UCI.

223 "Millar was overwhelmed": Millar to von Auw, December 26, 1959, Princeton.

224 " 'I hardly care what auspices' ": Millar to von Auw, January 8, 1961, Princeton.

224 " 'not wholly without misgivings' ": Millar to von Auw, January 21, 1961, Princeton.

224 " 'As at Harvard' ": Millar to von Auw, November 25, 1961, Princeton.

224 " 'rather eccentrically changed her mind' ": Millar to von Auw, February 7, 1962, Princeton.

224 " 'I presume at least' ": Millar to von Auw, March 17, 1962, Princeton.

225 " 'Ken adored all animals' ": Margaret Millar interview with TN.

225 "she managed without calling home": Margaret Millar, *The Birds and the Beasts Were There* (Random House, 1967).

227 "in several letters to the Bransons": Millar to Anna Branson, June 15, 1962, UCI; Millar to the Bransons, October 27, 1962, UCI; Millar to Branson, August 19, 1963, UCI.

227 " 'They are stupider than people' ": Millar to Olding, March 22, 1962, Princeton.

227 " 'an excellent man' ": Millar to von Auw, September 18, 1961, Princeton.

227 " 'All the news from here is good' ": Millar to Olding, March 22, 1962, Princeton.

227 " 'It is, I think, more of a novel' ": Millar to von Auw, March 1, 1962, Princeton.

228 " 'I've tried to give it more of my personal style' ": Millar to Knopf, April 2, 1962, HRHRC.

228 " 'A lot of people think that's my best book' ": Millar interview with Paul Nelson, UCI.

228 " 'Well . . . some choice' ": Margaret Millar interview with TN.

228 " 'It's difficult to cut a book down to twenty-five thousand words' ": Ibid.

228 " 'Good bold transitions are the secret' ": Millar to Olding, Princeton.

228 " 'This was in the sixties' ": Seed interview with TN.

229 *"Raymond Chandler Speaking"*: eds. Dorothy Gardiner and Kathrine Sorley Walker (Houghton Mifflin, 1962).

230 " 'Patronage seems to be a powerful force' ": Millar to von Auw, March 9, 1962, Princeton.

230 " 'I like it better now' ": Millar to Anna Branson, December 7, 1962, UCI.

230 " 'my most horrible plot yet' ": Millar to Olding, August 4, 1962, Princeton.

231 "Plato, *Phaedrus"*: Jonathan Barnes, *Early Greek Philosophy* (Penguin Books, 1987).

231 " 'continually developing mess' ": Millar to Anna Branson, June 15, 1962, UCI.

231 "More than one commentator": e.g., T. R. Steiner, "The Mind of the Hardboiled: Ross Macdonald and the Roles of Criticism," *South Dakota Review*, Spring 1986; Joyce Carol Oates, "The Simple Art of Murder," *New York Review of Books*, December 21, 1995.

232 " 'like an albatross' ": Ross Macdonald, *The Chill* (Knopf, 1964).

233 " 'The tortoise will never catch Achilles' ": Kenneth to Margaret Millar, March 30, 1945, UCI.

234 " 'Archer, Macdonald's narrator' ": Thomas J. Roberts, *An Aesthetics of Junk Fiction* (University of Georgia Press, 1990).

234 " 'It is with *The Chill* that he found his own voice": Otto Penzler, *The Crown Crime Companion* (Crown Trade Paperbacks, 1995).

234 "1985 *Newsweek* list": David Lehman, "A Sleuth's Hall of Fame," *Newsweek*, April 22, 1985.

236 " 'The once omnipresent private eye' ": James Sandoe, "Mystery—Detective—Suspense," *Library Journal*, June 1, 1963.

236 " 'THE ZEBRA-STRIPED HEARSE' ": Unsigned review, *New Yorker*, January 12, 1963.

236 " 'I felt I *deserved* to win' ": Millar to Olding, April 18, 1962, Princeton.

236 "why give awards at all?": Olding to Millar, April 24, 1962, UCI.

237 " 'He is a master of the lost art of plotting' ": Robert R. Kirsch, "Notes from the Crime File: Mystery Writer in Groove," *Los Angeles Times*, October 25, 1962.

237 " 'lives of quiet bourgeois desperation' ": Roger Sale, "Gossips and Storytellers," *Hudson Review*, Spring 1963.

237 "a review of *The Wycherly Woman* on the book page of the *New York Post"*: Gerald Walker, "Mystery Man," *New York Post*, May 21, 1961, courtesy of Gerald Walker.

237 "Carolyn See cited Macdonald": *The Drowning Pool* and *The Barbarous Coast* are quoted in "The Hollywood Novel: An Historical and Critical Study"—"A dissertation submitted in partial satisfaction of the requirements for the degree Doctor of Philosophy in English by Carolyn Penelope See," September 1963, UCLA.

237 "the first feature article on Ross Macdonald": Robert F. Jones, "A New Raymond Chandler?" *Los Angeles*, March 1963.

237 " 'I'd been in the navy in Long Beach' ": Robert F. Jones interview with TN.

238 " 'Macdonald's detective, Lew Archer, is no "eye" ' ": Walker, "Mystery Man."

238 " 'Tony really *made* Ken Millar' ": Dorothy B. Hughes interview with TN.

238 " 'I write for you more than any one single person' ": Millar to Boucher, July 9, 1951, Indiana.

238 " 'Gramps is fine' ": Millar to the Bransons, May 17, 1963, UCI.

238 " 'He's one of the lights of our life' ": Millar to Bransons, August 19, 1963, UCI.

238 " 'Mr. Macdonald writes mysteries' " *Publishers Weekly*, November 26, 1962.

NOTES

239　" 'While Lizzie Borden was no saint' ": Millar, "Ode to Lizzie," Millar notebook, UCI.

240　"Mystery of the Missing Scroll": "Mystery of the Missing Scroll," *The March of Crime* (Southern California MWA newsletter), May 1963.

240　" 'In a purely personal opinion' ": Dorothy B. Hughes, "Mystery & Suspense," *Sunday* (New York) *Herald Tribune Book Week,* March 22, 1964.

240　" 'More people are saying the right things' ": Knopf to Millar, January 17, 1964, HRHRC.

240　" 'On one occasion' ": Margaret Millar, *The Birds and the Beasts Were There.*

241　" 'Anyone, anything, being victimized' ": Robert Easton, "A Tribute," *Dictionary of Literary Biography Yearbook: 1983* (A Bruccoli Clark Book/Gale Research Company, 1983).

241　" 'a wonderful madman' ": Millar to Olding, December 12, 1964, Princeton.

241　"Atkinson wrote several columns": Brooks Atkinson, "Sometimes It's Not Too Easy to Get a Good Look at a California Condor," *New York Times,* January 28, 1964; Brooks Atkinson, "The Vanishing California Condor Is Today More Preyed Upon Than Preying," *New York Times,* June 19, 1964 (Millar cited).

241　" 'Do we have to reveal ourselves as pleasure-greedy' ": Millar, "Remarks of Kenneth Millar, Information Officer, Santa Barbara Audubon Society, prepared for meeting called by Forest Service, February 27, 1964," typescript, UCI; also HRHRC.

241　" 'This one made even the Regional Forester look uncomfortable' ": Ross Macdonald, "A Death Road for the Condor," *Sports Illustrated,* April 6, 1964; included in *Self-Portrait.*

241　" 'Which seemed to imply' ": Ibid.

241　"Largely thanks to Millar": Unsigned story, "Fate of Condors Debated on Coast," *New York Times,* March 3, 1964 (Millar quoted); unsigned story, "The Road That Might Doom Our Unique Bird," *San Francisco Chronicle,* February 28, 1964 (Millar quoted); Robert S. Brodey, "California Condor Menaced," Letters to the *Times, New York Times,* June 15, 1964. *Washington Post* and *Washington Star* editorials unlocated but cited by Millar to Knopf (March 8, 1964, HRHRC).

241　" 'A Death Road for the Condor' ": Macdonald, "A Death Road for the Condor."

241　" 'When I sat down with him' ": Robert Phelps interview with TN.

242　"in which Millar was quoted": Robert H. Phelps, "Volunteer Force to Guard Condors in California," *New York Times,* May 17, 1964.

242　"OF COURSE PLEASE ACCEPT": Millar to Olding, April 28, 1964, Princeton.

242　" 'I remember one Christmas' ": Margaret Millar interview with TN.

242　" 'It was rather strange to me' ": Easton interview with TN.

242　" 'about as colorful as a window shade' ": Ping Ferry interview with TN.

243　" 'He regarded them as misguided academics' ": Easton to Matthew Bruccoli, October 10, 1982, courtesy of Robert Easton.

244　" 'a moral duty' ": Easton interview with TN.

244　" 'Life is very interwoven' ": Millar to Knopf, June 9, 1964, HRHRC.

245　" 'Perhaps I could believe you' ": Olding to Millar, UCI.

245　" 'My good wife' ": Millar to Knopf, April 25, 1964, HRHRC.

245　" 'Margaret on a bicycle' ": Knopf to Millar, April 28, 1964, HRHRC.

245　" 'something extraordinary' ": Anthony Boucher, "A Roundup of Criminals at Large," *New York Times Book Review,* June 21, 1964.

245　" 'It seems a healthy thing' ": Millar to von Auw, November 9, 1964, Princeton.

245　" 'One question' ": Millar to Olding, January 3, 1964, Princeton.

245　" 'unless you want us to withdraw it' ": Olding to Millar, January 7, 1964, Princeton.

246　" 'He didn't know' ": Millar to Olding, January 18, 1964, Princeton.

246　" '*Ferguson* sold for $16,500 cash' ": Millar to von Auw, March 23, 1964, Princeton.

246 " 'A producer who last year was toying with the idea' ": Ross Macdonald, "The Writer as Detective Hero," *Show,* January 1965; reprinted in *Self-Portrait.*

246 " 'I suppose because I'm well satisfied' ": Millar to von Auw, May 8, 1964, Princeton.

246 " 'Nothing good ever happens in Hollywood' ": Millar to Olding, June 26, 1964, Princeton.

246 " 'of course I had to turn the negotiation over' ": Ibid.

247 " 'though God knows' ": Millar to Olding, June 30, 1964, Princeton.

247 " 'If there should be any movie interest' ": Millar to Olding, July 21, 1964, Princeton.

247 " 'Ivan—Here we go again' ": Ibid., margin note.

247 " 'we can forget this cat' ": Swanson to Millar, November 4, 1964, UCI.

247 " 'not exactly a sought-after property' ": Millar (quoting what he's written Swanson) to von Auw, November 9, 1964, Princeton.

247 "Von Auw wrote back quickly": von Auw to Millar, November 13, 1964, Princeton.

247 " 'do you tell Swanee or do I?' ": Millar to von Auw, November 16, 1964, Princeton.

247 " 'We hope we'll be able to get you a decent and proper contract' ": Swanson to Millar, November 23, 1964, UCI.

248 " 'It's all I can do to keep up with him' ": Millar to Knopf, July 5, 1964.

248 "a fire on Coyote Road": The Coyote fire is described superbly in Margaret Millar's *The Birds and the Beasts Were There.* See also Raymond Ford Jr., *Santa Barbara Wildfires: Fire on the Hills* (McNally & Loftin, 1991).

248 "he picked out volumes to save": List of books imagined by TN, based on Millar mentions of volumes important to him. Certainly Millar would have included his and his wife's works, some hardcover copies of which were all but impossible to replace.

249 " 'I won't try to describe a forest fire' ": Millar to von Auw, September 27, 1964, Princeton.

249 " 'We were able to start a tiny backfire' ": Easton interview with TN.

249 "Betty Lid never forgot a brief telephone exchange": Betty Lid interview with TN.

250 " 'You're still sending my mail to' ": Millar to Knopf Mail Forwarding Dept., September 10, 1964, HRHRC.

250 " 'Thank you so much for your prompt reply' ": Millar to Pat Powell, October 11, 1965, Princeton.

251 " 'He had a great talent' ": Millar to Olding, December 12, 1964, Princeton.

251 " 'Without in the least abating my admiration' ": Anthony Boucher, "Criminals at Large," *New York Times Book Review,* January 24, 1965.

251 " 'Mr. Macdonald, like Chandler' ": Walter O'Hearn, "Chandler Tradition," *Montreal Star,* February 13, 1965.

251 " 'the power and dimension of a Greek tragedy' ": Robert R. Kirsch, "*Far Side of the Dollar* Has Power of Greek Tragedy," *Los Angeles Times,* January 12, 1965.

252 " 'nothing less than a literal search for personal identity' ": Clifford A. Ridley, "Murder Takes On New Dimension in Macdonald Story," *National Observer,* January 18, 1965.

252 " 'an important American novelist' ": William Hogan, "The Far Side of Ross Macdonald," *San Francisco Chronicle,* February 18, 1965.

252 " 'with foolish joy' ": Millar to Knopf, November 8, 1964, HRHRC.

252 " 'Now I have just enough success' ": Millar to Olding, January 20, 1965, Princeton.

252 " 'with enormous gusto' ": Millar to Olding, March 29, 1965, Princeton.

252 "a logjam-breaker for her": Ibid.

252 " 'Oh, they'd have clashes' ": Easton interview with TN.

253 " 'Ken never forgave bad writers' ": Dennis Lynds interview with TN.

253 " 'Dresser was a shit' ": Gault interview with TN.

253 " 'He said the other day at lunch' ": Millar to Olding, April 2, 1962, Princeton.

254 " 'He was a charming man' ": Jackie Coulette interview with TN.

255 " 'While I have good poets with me' ": Millar note, UCI. Millar once wrote Julian Symons (among other things, a poet), "We prose writers secretly write for the poets and secretly yearn to be noticed by you" (January 20, 1973; courtesy of Julian Symons). To Ash Green (October 20, 1969, UCI) Millar admitted, "More heartening than almost anything is the good opinion of good poets like [Donald] Davie and Henri Coulette."

255 " 'Kick le Carré in the pants for me' ": Margaret to Kenneth Millar, April 28, 1965, UCI.

256 " 'Is this a dagger which I see before me' ": "Prizes and Awards," *Publishers Weekly*, May 10, 1965.

256 "The nineteenth annual Edgar Allan Poe Awards ceremony": Details from "The Third Degree," MWA newsletter, 1965.

256 " 'Brilliant as it was' ": Millar to Michael Avallone, May 11, 1965, from the Avallone Collection, Department of Special Collections, Boston University.

257 " 'Other people have said they found it difficult' ": Julian Symons interview with TN.

257 " 'Ken was very observant' ": Robert Lescher interview with TN.

257 " 'Your weariness came over the air as relaxation' ": Amy O'Leary to Millar, May 28, 1965, HRHRC.

257 " 'We were talking with the girls' ": Anna Branson to Millar, July 30, 1965, UCI.

257 " 'I think somebody said Yeats was an old man mad about writing' ": Martha Mac-Gregor, "The Week in Books," *New York Post*, May 9, 1965.

258 " 'Quite obviously this nails you down even tighter' ": Knopf to Millar, February 16, 1965, HRHRC.

258 " 'Someday I hope sales will catch up with the critics' ": Knopf to Millar, January 22, 1965, HRHRC.

258 "pleased and touched": Knopf to Millar, January 10, 1964, HRHRC.

258 "among the best likenesses he'd ever captured": Alfred A. Knopf, *Sixty Photographs* (Knopf, 1975). Note that Knopf made at least two exposures of Millar this day; the one reproduced in his book is different from that used on several of Macdonald's.

259 *"New Yorker":* Donald Barthelme, "Edward and Pia," *New Yorker,* September 25, 1965.

259 " 'I read *Black Money*' ": Swanson to Millar, September 13, 1965, UCI.

259 "The motion pictures he'd seen as a kid": The Inspector Fate films are mentioned by Archer in chapter ten of *The Barbarous Coast.* Their objective correlative in Millar's life, perhaps, are the Falcon Swift stories he read as a boy and recalled in his preface to *Lew Archer, Private Investigator* (see *Self-Portrait*).

259 " 'lover's quarrel' ": "My lover's quarrel with Hollywood began at the age of seven": from the introduction to *Archer in Hollywood* (Knopf, 1967).

259 " 'I had been a lunatic Archer fan since 1950' ": William Goldman, "The Macdonald Conspiracy," in *Inward Journey.*

259 " 'I was a big big reader in those days' ": William Goldman interview with TN.

260 " 'one of the best novels of the twentieth century' ": Ibid.

260 " 'This should strengthen our bargaining position' ": Millar to von Auw, May 14, 1965, Princeton.

260 " 'I have observed that the writers in my field' ": Millar to Olding, July 15, 1965, Princeton.

260 " 'I believe my backlist' ": Ibid.

260 " 'who seems to understand' ": Millar to von Auw, May 14, 1965, Princeton.

261 " 'I'd much rather see the deal fall through' ": Millar to von Auw, June 2, 1965, Princeton.

261 " 'I came up with "Harper" ' ": Goldman interview with TN.

261 " 'If you know anything about the movie business' ": Ibid.

261 "It's my best book": Millar to Olding, June 22, 1965, Princeton.

261 " 'Knopf never tells me anything' ": Millar to Olding, July 15, 1965, Princeton.

261 " 'If Bantam drop half their Archers' ": Millar to Knopf, July 18, 1965, HRHRC.

261 " 'I sometimes wonder' ": Millar to Olding, July 20, 1965, Princeton.

262 "The writer was pleased no end": Millar to Koshland, July 30, 1965, HRHRC.

262 " 'Erle Stanley Millar' ": Millar to Olding, July 10, 1965, Princeton.

262 " 'I believe we should be ready' ": Millar to Koshland, July 30, 1965, HRHRC.

262 *"not* 'movie money' ": Millar to Knopf, September 15, 1965, HRHRC.

262 " 'They paid ninety thousand' ": Easton interview with TN.

262 " 'We wonder at our good fortune' ": Millar to Olding, September 20, 1965, Princeton.

262 " 'My dear wife is very happy' ": Millar to von Auw, September 20, 1965, Princeton.

262 "one of 1965's twelve Women of the Year": Jack Jones, "Writer Keeps One Eye on Novel, Other on Sparrow," *Los Angeles Times,* January 4, 1966. See also Pat Dayton, "Writer Aware of Her Fame but Respects Predecessors," *Santa Barbara News-Press,* December 17, 1965.

262 " 'a living doll' ": Millar to the Bransons, October 28, 1964, UCI.

263 "shot on the same stages as *The Big Sleep"*: Philip Oakes, (London) *Sunday Times Magazine,* June 5, 1966.

263 " 'I thought Newman was terrific' ": Goldman interview with TN.

263 " 'While you're talking' ": Paul Newman interview, *Playboy,* July 1968.

264 "The actor told Goldman": Millar to von Auw, January 17, 1966, Princeton.

264 " 'One advantage of the twenty-year Swanee episode' ": Millar to Jim Riesman (Ober agency), June 12, 1965, Princeton.

264 " 'Swanee presents his problems' ": Millar to von Auw, September 4, 1965, Princeton.

265 " 'Swanee and I saw *Harper*' ": Millar to von Auw, January 17, 1966, Princeton.

265 "Bennett Cerf called Millar from New York": Millar to Knopf, February 12, 1966, HRHRC; Millar to von Auw, February 12, 1966, Princeton.

265 " 'the maddest of all' ": Millar to Knopf, February 9, 1966, HRHRC.

265 " 'It's all rather fun for a change' ": Ibid.

265 " 'You will excuse my continuing to push' ": Millar to von Auw, February 12, 1966, Princeton.

265 " 'At a time when too many producers are stumbling' ": James Powers, " 'Harper' Shapes Up as a Smash Hit: Funny, Exciting, Offbeat Love Story," *Hollywood Reporter,* February 10, 1966.

265 " 'Let the boys make a picture with *Archer*' ": Millar note (unsent) with Swanson letter to Millar, February 11, 1966, UCI; also Millar to von Auw, February 17, 1966, Princeton.

265 " 'A presentation is a pretty mixed art form' ": Millar to Knopf, February 9, 1966.

265 " 'notes left next to the teapot' ": Kenneth to Margaret Millar, UCI.

266 " 'Turned down $35,000' ": Millar to Jim Riesman (Ober agency), March 24, 1966, Princeton.

266 "Judith Crist wrote it a mash note": Judith Crist, "Return of the Pre-Bond Man," *New York Herald Tribune,* April 3, 1966.
    Millar to von Auw, April 12, 1966, Princeton: "I wish it were a better movie, but if Judith Crist likes it I don't have to."

266 "Pauline Kael, in *McCall's,* was scathing": Pauline Kael, "At the Movies," *McCall's,* April 1966.

266 " '*Harper* even starts out like Raymond Chandler' ": Philip K. Scheur, "Newman Versatile in Playing 'Harper,' " *Los Angeles Times,* February 23, 1966.

266 "the fourth-highest-grossing film in the country": von Auw to Millar, April 14, 1966, Princeton.

266   " 'I remember waiting two hours in Mr. Warner's office' ": Harris Seed interview with TN.

266   " 'I wish for the present to remain unrepresented by any agent in Hollywood' ": Millar to von Auw, April 27, 1966, Princeton.

267   " 'the best of Hollywood in many months' ": *Queen,* June 8, 1966.

267   " 'live in a world of mental slavery' ": Millar to Bill Koshland, June 10, 1966, HRHRC.

267   " 'not my line' ": Millar note, UCI.

268   "his blood pressure dropped twenty points": Millar to von Auw, June 17, 1966, Princeton.

268   " 'We writers' ": Introduction to *Archer in Hollywood;* reprinted in *Self-Portrait.*

268   " 'Ken had an aura of great strength' ": Jerre Lloyd interview with TN.

269   " 'Perhaps I'll never work as hard, quite' ": Millar to Anna Branson, September 2, 1966, UCI.

269   " 'The changes of the past year or so' ": Millar to Knopf, December 30, 1966, HRHRC.

269   "the best part of the year for him": Millar to Knopf, November 16, 1966, HRHRC.

269   "hoped to surprise the customers": Millar to Harding Lemay, December 4, 1966, HRHRC.

270   " 'I kept wondering' ": John Leonard, "Ross Macdonald, His Lew Archer and Other Secret Selves," *New York Times Book Review,* June 1, 1969.

270   "their old Ford": Raymond A. Sokolov, "The Art of Murder," *Newsweek,* March 22, 1971.

270   " 'A burglary, even *in absentia*' ": Millar to Knopf, May 2, 1966, HRHRC.

270   " 'the stupidest deputy sheriffs in the world' ": Millar to von Auw, April 8, 1966, Princeton.

273   " 'majestic instancy' ": Millar to von Auw, June 9, 1967, Princeton.

273   " 'The director, Jack Smight' ": William Goldman interview with TN.

273   " 'Technique is poetic justice seen from below' ": Millar to Steven Carter, October 23, 1967, courtesy of Steven Carter.

274   " 'a lean, sun-browned man of 52' ": Dick Adler, "Will the Real Ross Macdonald Please Keep Writing?" *West* magazine, *Los Angeles Times,* December 10, 1967.

274   " 'I met him for breakfast' ": Dick Adler interview with TN.

275   " 'The number of mystery writers' ": Clifford A. Ridley, "Surveying the Current Whodunit Offerings," *National Observer,* January 6, 1968.

275   " 'I have a passion for Dickens' ": Charles Monaghan interview with Elizabeth Bowen, "Portrait of a Woman Reading," *Washington Post Book World,* November 10, 1968.

275   " 'some sort of a seer' ": Millar interview with Paul Nelson, UCI.

275   " 'I foresaw with a sudden pang' ": Millar to Ping Ferry, May 3, 1973; typed copy, UCI.

275   " 'an unmitigated disaster' ": Macdonald interview with Jeff Sweet, *Gallery,* August 1974.

275   " 'I'm in a bitter struggle' ": Millar to Olding, June 22, 1965, Princeton.

275   " 'If they really do suspend hostilities' ": Millar to von Auw, December 28, 1965, Princeton.

275   " 'I have a book going' ": Millar to Knopf, December 30, 1966, HRHRC.

275   "Macdonald started getting fan mail from GIs": correspondence, UCI.

275   " 'It feels to me like a season of apocalypse' ": Millar to Olding, October 3, 1967, Princeton.

275   " 'The country is going to hell' ": Millar to the Bransons, December 21, 1967, UCI.

275   " 'I'm a bit scared of 1968' ": Millar to Avallone, December 31, 1967, from the Avallone Collection, Department of Special Collections, Boston University.

276 " 'It got to the point' ": Macdonald interview with Trevor Meldal-Johnsen, *Gallery*, March 1976.

276 "a cherry bomb": Millar to Olding, February 2, 1969, Princeton.

276 " 'I won't say I'm sorry' ": Millar to William Ruehlmann, March 23, 1968; typed copy, UCI.

276 " 'It makes me angry' ": Millar to Ruehlmann, October 26, 1972; typed copy, UCI.

276 " 'A small, anxious boy' ": Brad Darrach, "Ross Macdonald: The Man Behind the Mysteries," *People*, July 8, 1974.

277 " 'Close to explosion' ": Paul Nelson, "It's All One Case," in *Inward Journey*.

277 " 'As a teenager' ": William Ruehlmann interview with TN.

277 " 'I met Ken in the morning' ": Ibid.

279 " 'Did you know . . . that the government is planning atomic power plants' ": Millar to Olding, December 9, 1968, Princeton.

279 " 'still these are precious days' ": Millar to Olding, August 3, 1968, Princeton.

279 " 'I've slowed down enough' ": Millar to von Auw, September 28, 1968, Princeton.

279 "one by Clare Booth Luce": *New York*, circa September 1968, unlocated. (Cited by Millar to Green, September 28, 1968, UCI.)

279 "the daily *New York Times*": Thomas Lask, "Homicide à la Carte," "Books of the Times," *New York Times*, July 6, 1968.

280 " 'We are living on the income from books alone' ": Millar to Seed, July 29, 1968, typed copy, UCI.

280 " 'now at the peak of his earning power' ": Millar to Seed, May 1, 1968; typed copy, UCI.

280 " 'an extraordinary performance' ": Anthony Boucher, "Criminals at Large," *New York Times Book Review*, March 3, 1968.

280 " 'There are a couple of hundred of us' ": Phyllis White letter to TN, May 31, 1990.

280 "a book in which Macdonald kept company with mainstream authors": Thomas McCormack, ed., *Afterwords: Novelists on Their Novels* (Harper & Row, 1968).

280 " 'Close to godhead' ": Joe Gores interview with TN.

281 " 'I seem to be moving further in the direction of the "mainstream novel" ' ": Millar to Ash Green, May 6, 1968, UCI.

281 " 'I feel as if I'm turning a corner' ": Millar to Knopf, March 26, 1968, HRHRC.

281 " 'I'm keen on this book' ": Millar to Green, September 28, 1968, UCI.

282 " 'Naturally the front page' ": Alfred A. Knopf, "Book Publishing: The Changes I've Seen," *Atlantic Monthly*, December 1957.

282 " 'We'd all been in the service' ": Stump interview with TN.

283 " 'It lay so thick on the water' ": Ross Macdonald, "Life with the Blob," *Sports Illustrated*, April 21, 1969; included in *Self-Portrait*.

283 "He cut his Union Oil credit card in two": Herb Harker, "A Tribute," *Dictionary of Literary Biography Yearbook: 1983*: "It was not an act he took pleasure in, nor did he express any malice. A snip of the shears tokened his separation from the despoilers."

283 " 'Many of us booed him' ": Macdonald, "Life with the Blob."

283 " 'Margaret was always in the forefront' ": Ping Ferry interview with TN.

283 "in a picture reproduced in newspapers and magazines": E.g., *Business Week*, February 15, 1969; *Sports Illustrated*, April 21, 1969; *Fortune*, April 1969.

283 " 'No one ever could intimidate Ken' ": Barney Brantingham, "Millars mobilized to 'ban the blob,' " *Santa Barbara News-Press*, January 28, 1989.

283 " 'This thing radicalized the entire city' ": Ferry interview with TN.

284 " 'We took it seriously' ": Brantingham, "Millars mobilized."

284 " 'the objective correlative of my mental life' ": Millar to Olding, February 11, 1969, Princeton.

284 "having his picture printed": E.g., "Oil in the Velvet Playground," *Ramparts*, November 1969.

NOTES

284 "a quixotic flotilla of launches and sailboats": See "GOO Fishes In," *Newsweek,* December 8, 1969; also letter from Lt. T. B. Kichline, U.S. Coast Guard, to Millar, December 10, 1969, UCI.

284 "With Easton, Millar did a second article": Ross Macdonald and Robert Easton, "Santa Barbarans Cite an 11th Commandment: 'Thou Shalt Not Abuse the Earth,' " *New York Times Magazine,* October 12, 1969.

284 " 'collaborating with a porcupine' ": Robert Easton, "A Tribute," *Dictionary of Literary Biography Yearbook: 1983.*

284 " 'We've got to convert this horror' ": Macdonald, "Life with the Blob."

285 " 'special notice' ": John Leonard to Millar, March 24, 1969, UCI.

285 " 'knew my books better than I do' ": Millar to Green, January 1, 1969, UCI.

285 " 'I have a tactile memory' ": John Leonard interview with TN.

285 " 'We dilated on the thesis' ": John Leonard, "I Care Who Killed Roger Ackroyd," *Esquire,* August 1975.

286 " 'I was not at that time a mystery reader' ": Leonard interview with TN.

287 " 'Macdonald's work in the last decade' ": William Goldman, "The finest detective novels ever written by an American," *New York Times Book Review,* June 1, 1969.

287 " 'Ten years ago, while nobody was watching' ": John Leonard, "Ross Macdonald, his Lew Archer and other secret selves," *New York Times Book Review,* June 1, 1969.

288 " 'Vonnegut was known quite specifically in New York' ": Leonard interview with TN.

288 " 'I told Maggie' ": Millar to Green, May 30, 1969, UCI.

288 " 'My publishers are agog' ": Millar to Matthew Bruccoli, May 28, 1969, MJB Collection, UCI.

288 " 'The Coolest Man in Crime' ": Millar to Green, January 2, 1969, UCI.

288 " 'Booksellers and readers' ": Millar to von Auw, June 1, 1969, Princeton.

289 " 'In these books, bruised women run away' ": Ray Bradbury, "Macdonald . . . the Sadness of Murder," *Los Angeles Times* Calendar, June 8, 1969.

289 " 'Heywood Broun had a considerable following' ": Alfred A. Knopf, "Publishing's Last 50 Years," *Saturday Review,* November 21, 1964.

289 " 'absolutely perfect' ": Millar to Green, June 23, 1969, UCI.

290 " 'It's more than I'd hoped for' ": Millar to Green, July 14, 1969, UCI.

290 " 'these are interesting times' ": Millar to Green, June 28, 1969, UCI.

290 " 'Pretty good for an old mystery writer' ": Easton to Matthew Bruccoli, September 22, 1982, courtesy of Robert Easton.

290 " 'I've decided to postpone' ": Millar to Olding, July 16, 1969, Princeton.

290 " 'Eighth place' ": Millar to von Auw, July 16, 1969, Princeton.

290 "*Time* magazine's": unsigned review, "Detection Pushed Too Far," *Time,* August 15, 1969.

290 " 'What Mr. Goldman is saying' ": Bruce Cook, "Can 'Fun' Be 'Serious'?" *National Observer,* September 15, 1969.

290 " 'I do want to tell you' ": Knopf to Millar, September 5, 1969, HRHRC.

291 " 'The Greeks only pirate first-class stuff' ": Ober memo, July 1969, Princeton.

291 " 'We have ceased wondering' ": Millar to John Smith, July 15, 1969, UCI.

291 " 'comparative obscurity' ": Millar to Green, October 20, 1969, UCI.

291 " 'I really can't' ": Millar to von Auw, July 17, 1969, Princeton.

291 " 'To cover it even adequately' ": Millar to Olding, December 15, 1969, Princeton.

292 " 'Good morning, heartmate!' ": Kenneth to Margaret Millar, March 1, 1970, UCI.

292 " 'Don't bother answering this item' ": Millar to Olding, received November 20, 1969, Princeton.

292 " 'Each of us likes to begin' ": Millar to Green, June 28, 1969, UCI.

292 "When Collin Wilcox": Collin Wilcox interview with TN.

293 " 'Her enthusiasms are varied' ": Walter Clemons, "Meeting Miss Welty," *New York Times Book Review,* April 12, 1970.

293 " 'Part of the enormous excitement' ": "An Interview with Ross Macdonald," *Concept Twelve*, 1971.

293 " 'I'm a bit of an environmentalist myself' ": Ross Macdonald, *Sleeping Beauty* (Knopf, 1973).

293 " 'like a good novelist' ": Macdonald review of *Don't Shoot—We Are Your Children!*, *New York Times Book Review*.

293 " 'Santa Barbara's not nearly as careful' ": Ping Ferry interview with TN.

294 " 'It is neither natural nor necessary' ": Kenneth Millar, "Disaster Area to Reclaim," "Our Readers' Views," *Santa Barbara News-Press*, June 17, 1970.

294 " 'Westwick was pretty fair' ": Bob Langfelder interview with TN.

295 " 'My sympathies are not with violence' ": Millar to Ruehlmann, March 10, 1970; typed copy, UCI.

295 " 'I put my hope in the intelligence of young people' ": Ed Wilcox, "The Secret Success of Kenneth Millar," *New York Sunday News*, November 21, 1971.

295 "a carefully written and informative report": *Report of the Santa Barbara Citizens Commission on Civil Disorders*, September 15, 1970. Copy at UCI.

295 " 'It came out somewhat more liberal' ": Millar to John Smith, September 20, 1970, UCI.

295 " 'I was facing arson charges' ": Langfelder interview with TN.

295 " 'I remembered his name' ": Macdonald, introduction to *Lew Archer, Private Investigator;* reprinted in *Self-Portrait*.

296 " 'not a bitterness or gloom or resignation' ": Matthew J. Bruccoli, "Kenneth Millar (13 December 1915–11 July 1983)," in *Dictionary of Literary Biography Yearbook: 1983*.

296 " 'I had the feeling when I was with Ken' ": Bruccoli interview with TN.

296 " 'There is always moral pain involved' ": Millar to Green, July 19, 1970, UCI.

297 " 'Certainly I don't want to strain the situation' ": Millar to Olding, July 18, 1970, Princeton.

297 "Ross Macdonald wrote its foreword": Robert Easton, *Black Tide* (Delacorte Press, 1972); Macdonald's foreword was reprinted in *Self-Portrait*.

297 " 'I'm like you . . . love to see nice things happen to my friends' ": Millar to Olding, June 24, 1972, Princeton.

297 " 'Leonard Gardner' ": Millar to Green, October 27, 1969, UCI.

298 " 'Here we have a chance for a good one' ": Millar to Olding, received November 20, 1969, Princeton.

298 "a strong essay": George Grella, "Murder and the Mean Streets: The Hard-Boiled Detective Novel," *Contempora*, March 1970; included in Dick Allan and David Chacko, eds., *Detective Fiction: Crime and Compromise* (Harcourt Brace Jovanovich, 1974); and in Robin W. Winks, ed., *Detective Fiction: A Collection of Critical Essays* (Prentice-Hall, 1980; Foul Play Press, 1988). Millar recommended this essay to his librarian friend John Smith (Millar to Smith, April 23, 1970, UCI).

298 "Harrison Salisbury gave Millar an assignment": Salisbury to Millar, August 27, 1970, UCI.

298 "Millar later begged off ": Millar to Salisbury, 1970, handwritten copy, Princeton.

298 " 'delighted' ": Millar to Olding, September 24, 1970, Princeton.

298 " 'carom shots' ": Millar to Olding, November 1, 1970, Princeton.

298 " 'It will help to get my name around in the schools' ": Millar to Olding, October 4, 1970, Princeton.

298 " 'I'm told that Bantam is going to put out batches' ": Millar to Olding, 1970, Princeton.

298 " 'I never mailed it' ": Clemons, "Meeting Miss Welty."

298 " 'warm' ": Millar to Knopf, May 14, 1970, HRHRC.

299 " 'most pleasant and (naturally) intelligent' ": Millar to Knopf, June 23, 1970, HRHRC.

299 " 'To receive such a letter' ": Ibid.

299 " 'So much luck as I've had' ": Millar to Olding, July 2, 1970, Princeton.

299 " 'Your good luck and your bad luck balance out' ": Ross Macdonald, *The Ferguson Affair* (Knopf, 1960).

299 " 'Life is so very good on certain days' ": Millar to Green, November 1, 1970, UCI.

300 " '[Linda's husband] Joe was with us' ": Margaret Millar interview with Paul Nelson, UCI.

300 " 'You will understand me when I say' ": Millar to John Smith, November 7, 1970, UCI.

300 " 'She died young' ": Millar to Olding, November 8, 1970, Princeton.

300 " 'In a sense' ": Millar interview with Paul Nelson, UCI.

301 " 'Jim is a fine boy' ": Millar to Steven Carter, January 8, 1971, courtesy of Steven Carter.

301 " 'Our son-in-law and grandson come up every weekend' ": Millar to Olding, November 25, 1970, Princeton.

301 " 'Well, our little family got through the holiday season' ": Millar to Green, December 31, 1970, UCI.

302 " 'As if our fortunes' ": Millar to Harker, November 29, 1971, courtesy of Herb Harker.

302 " 'I had a nice letter' ": Millar to Green, December 31, 1970, UCI.

302 " 'I was flabbergasted' ": Leonard interview with TN.

302 " 'That a Southern lady of letters' ": John Leonard, "I Care Who Killed Roger Ackroyd," *Esquire*, August 1975.

302 " 'I just *had* to do that' ": Eudora Welty interview with TN.

303 " 'She dealt with Walter Clemons' ": Leonard interview with TN.

303 " 'Your review filled me with joy' ": Millar to Welty, January 18, 1971; typed copy, UCI. A month later, with coverage of Macdonald escalating, Millar wrote, "I told her [Welty] I have become her Frankenstein monster" (Millar to John Smith, February 24, 1971, UCI).

303 " 'It's an enormous blockbuster' ": Millar to Green, January 18, 1971, UCI.

303 " 'It's going to be a great help' ": Millar to Olding, January 26, 1971, Princeton.

303 " 'Heaping blessings on my head' ": Millar to Knopf, January 23, 1971, HRHRC.

303 " 'I am absolutely bowled over' ": Knopf to Millar, February 4, 1971, HRHRC.

304 "as Bill Hogan noted": William Hogan, "The Artistry of Ross Macdonald," *San Francisco Chronicle*, February 26, 1971.

304 " ' "I don't believe in coincidences," Archer says' ": Eudora Welty, "The Underground Man," *New York Times Book Review*, February 14, 1971; reprinted in *The Eye of the Story: Selected Essays & Reviews* (Random House, 1978).

304 " 'pretty good going' ": von Auw to Millar, February 14, 1971, Princeton.

304 "a half-page ad in the daily *Times*": Knopf ad, *New York Times*, February 22, 1971.

305 " 'We are expecting a very enthusiastic reception' ": Marc Jaffe to Millar, February 18, 1971, UCI.

305 " 'Mr. Macdonald's career is one of the most honorable I know' ": Walter Clemons, "Ross Macdonald at His Best," *New York Times*, February 19, 1971.

305 " 'Not only is it a very astute appraisal' ": von Auw to Millar, February 19, 1971, Princeton.

305 " 'quite overwhelmed' ": Millar to Green, February 22, 1971, UCI.

305 "Judith Rascoe's in *Life*": Judith Rascoe, "A detective of past sins," *Life*, February 26, 1971.

305 "William Hogan's in the *San Francisco Chronicle*": Hogan, "The Artistry of Ross Macdonald."

305 "Clifford A. Ridley's in the *National Observer*": Clifford A. Ridley, "Lew Archer Returns for Another Tour of Macdonald's Sad Cosmos," *National Observer*, March 15, 1971.

305 " 'In the professional line' ": Millar to Olding, February 19, 1971, HRHRC.

306 " 'I knew Tim in Cambridge, Massachusetts' ": Ray Sokolov interview with TN.

307 " 'Ken *loved* that boy' ": Peter Wolfe interview with TN.

307 " 'The Millars lead an extremely quiet life' ": Raymond A. Sokolov, "The Art of Murder," *Newsweek*, March 22, 1971.

307 "Millar said of Sokolov": Dick Lid interview with TN.

307 " 'I can't tell you how proud and delighted I was' ": Oscar Dystel to Millar, March 18, 1971, UCI.

307 " 'I'll be interested to see' ": Millar to von Auw, March 26, 1971, Princeton.

307 " 'There seems to be a general feeling' ": Millar to Green, February 22, 1971, UCI.

308 " 'Many stores tell us' ": "Best Sellers," *Publishers Weekly*, March 15, 1971.

308 " 'I am frankly delighted' ": Millar to Bruccoli, March 19, 1971, MJB Collection, UCI.

308 " 'We passed 43,000' ": Green to Millar, April 14, 1971, UCI.

308 " 'Well, this is a long-awaited consummation' ": Millar to von Auw, February 25, 1971, Princeton.

308 " 'ridiculously well' ": Millar to Nolan Miller, March 22, 1971, the Nolan Miller Papers, Special Collections Library, University of Michigan; typed copy, UCI.

308 " 'incredible, but am too old' ": Ibid.

308 " 'very friendly' ": Millar to Olding, March 25, 1971, Princeton.

308 " 'Macdonald's books are full of the wandering hungers of California people' ": Art Seidenbaum, "Place for Private I," *Los Angeles Times*, March 24, 1971.

308 " 'Critics should not blow their own horns' ": Robert Kirsch, *Los Angeles Times* Calendar, March 14, 1971.

308 " 'the first runaway mystery in many years' ": John Barkham, "Where Writing Is No Mystery," *New York Post*, August 21, 1971.

308 *"Don't Shoot—We Are Your Children!"*: Macdonald, "Don't Shoot—We Are Your Children!" *New York Times Book Review*, April 25, 1971.

308 *"A Catalogue of Crime"*: Ross Macdonald, "A Catalogue of Crime," *New York Times Book Review*, May 16, 1971; reprinted in Macdonald, *A Collection of Reviews* (Lord John Press, 1979).

308 " 'The Underground Bye-bye' ": Richard Lingeman, *New York Times Book Review*, June 6, 1971.

Millar appreciated well-done parodies, even of his own work. One good one of Macdonald (which Millar praised to Anthony Boucher) is Ron Goulart's "The Peppermint-Striped Goodby" in *Best Detective Stories of the Year: 21st Annual Collection* (E. P. Dutton & Co., 1966).

308 "the *Book Review*'s June 'Selection of Recent Titles' ": "A Selection of Recent Titles," *New York Times Book Review*, June 6, 1971. *The Underground Man* was also included in the *Book Review*'s year-end "Selection of Noteworthy Titles" (December 5, 1971).

309 "Knopf's bold April *Underground* full-pager": Knopf ad, *New York Times Book Review*, April 4, 1971.

309 " 'stunning' ": Millar to Green, April 4, 1971, UCI.

309 "an April spread": Bantam Books ad, *New York Times Book Review*, April 4, 1971.

309 " 'I'd like to see a *good* movie made' ": Millar to Olding, April 12, 1971, Princeton.

309 " 'I'm in more distinguished company' ": Millar to Olding, May 10, 1971, Princeton.

309 " 'a Jungian Ross Macdonald' ": Roger Sale, "A Dirty Dean and a Brazen Head," *New York Review of Books*, February 8, 1973.

309 " 'I don't know of anything else' ": Millar to Ruehlmann, March 13, 1971; typed copy, UCI.

310 " 'drives so deep into Canadian experience' ": Millar to Wolfe, March 13, 1971, UCI.

310 " 'It's been a great spring for me' ": Barbara A. Bannon, "Authors & Editors," *Publishers Weekly*, August 9, 1971.

310 "thought it would be fine for the two writers to meet": Leonard, "I Care Who Killed Roger Ackroyd."

310 " 'As I came into the lobby and got my key' ": Eudora Welty interview with TN.

310 " 'I need scarcely say how delighted I am' ": Knopf to Millar, April 20, 1971, HRHRC.

311 " 'Your party was and will remain one of the high points of my life' ": Millar to Alfred and Helen Knopf, May 28, 1971, HRHRC.

312 " 'We spent one day driving a 300-mile circuit' ": Ibid.

312 " 'the death of Linda' ": Millar to Wolfe, September 21, 1971, UCI.

312 " 'Such an overall sale of Archer' ": Millar to Green, May 28, 1971, UCI.

312 " 'I'm sorry' ": Millar to Seed, typed copy, UCI.

312 " 'I was in Hollywood' ": Seed interview with TN.

313 " 'nothing short of historic' ": Millar to Seed, typed copy, UCI.

313 " 'Of all the good news I've had this year' ": Millar to Olding, June 26, 1971, Princeton.

313 " 'drowning in correspondence' ": Millar to Collin Wilcox, June 19, 1971, from the Wilcox Collection, Department of Special Collections, Boston University.

313 " 'The letters I get from young people' ": Millar to Nolan Miller, August 24, 1971, the Nolan Miller Papers, Special Collections Library, University of Michigan; typed copy, UCI.

313 " 'I don't think there is a chance in this world' ": Ober memo, Ivan von Auw, April 8, 1971, Princeton.

313 " 'We're very glad to have the opportunity' ": Millar to Olding, June 26, 1971, Princeton.

314 " 'Hell, I may never come back' ": Millar to Wolfe, July 10, 1971, UCI.

314 " 'I hope to visit Czechoslovakia' ": Ober memo, June 30, 1971, Princeton.

314 " 'Do you think he's going to become' ": Ibid.

314 " 'If I was dubious' ": Millar to Julian Symons, August 4, 1971, courtesy of Julian Symons.

314 " 'I'm not so night-bound' ": Millar to Symons, August 12, 1971, courtesy of Julian Symons.

314 " 'It's a little late for us, perhaps' ": Millar to Harker, August 18, 1971, courtesy of Herb Harker.

314 " 'I'm at the same time keen and a little frightened' ": Millar to Green, September 21, 1971, UCI.

314 " 'I'm poised at the intersection' ": Millar to Wolfe, September 21, 1971, UCI.

315 " 'every car in Paris' ": Millar to Knopf, November 16, 1971, HRHRC.

315 " 'strange and exciting' ": Millar to Wolfe, November 22, 1971, UCI.

315 "Maggie complained about the exhaust fumes": Margaret Millar interview with Paul Nelson, UCI.

315 " 'We were there at a big oval table' ": H. R. F. Keating interview with TN.

315 " 'He talked with characteristic gentle candor' ": Julian Symons, "A Transatlantic Friendship," from *Inward Journey.*

316 " 'And the producer squashed' ": Symons interview with TN.

316 " 'I never thought I could enjoy such a party' ": Millar to Wolfe, November 22, 1971, UCI.

316 " 'The interviewer told me' ": Ibid.

316 " 'Got along very well with the journalists' ": Millar to Olding, October 31, 1971, Princeton.

316 "Philip Oakes in the London Sunday *Times*": Philip Oakes, "In for Life," *Illustrated London News,* (London) Sunday *Times,* October 24, 1971.

316 "Bill Foster from the Edinburgh *Scotsman*": William Foster, (Edinburgh) *Scotsman,* November 20, 1971.

316 "Mike Fearn of London Express Features": Mike Fearn, "Ross Macdonald," London Express Features, copy at UCI.

316 " 'shuffling modesty' ": Peter Preston, "The farther side of the dollar," (London) *Guardian*, October 23, 1971.

316 " 'It'll be interesting to see if it helps the book' ": Millar to Olding, October 31, 1971, Princeton.

316 " 'Canadians seem to feel at home in London' ": Millar to Harker, November 15, 1971, courtesy of Herb Harker.

316 " 'a rather large damp Toronto' ": Millar to Ruehlmann, November 23, 1971; typed copy, UCI.

317 " 'Those sights' ": Millar to Harker, November 15, 1971.

317 " 'so once again I made a loop in my life' ": Millar to Knopf, November 16, 1971, HRHRC.

317 " 'There are many more tall buildings' ": Millar to Symons, November 5, 1971, courtesy of Julian Symons.

318 " 'His genre are exciting plots' ": B. Rodnom Gorode, *Znamya*, no. 2, 1972, typed translation sent by R. A. D. Ford to Millar, November 23, 1972, UCI. Also National Library of Canada.

318 " 'Archer is a masterful creation' ": Bruce Cook, "Ross Macdonald: The Prince in the Poorhouse," *New Catholic World*, October 1971.

318 " 'one does not really' ": Richard Schickel, "Detective Story," *Commentary*, September 1971.

318 " 'What interests me most' ": Jaffe to Millar, February 3, 1972, UCI.

319 " 'It is fascinating to see the interplay' ": Morton G. Wurtele to Macdonald, April 10, 1972, UCI.

319 " 'A reader only rarely has to justify' ": Langfelder to Millar, March 18, 1972, UCI.

320 " 'It had to be California' ": Cecil Smith, "Finding—and Filming—an American Family," *Los Angeles Times*, January 11, 1973.

320 " 'That book continues to surprise me' ": Millar to Bruccoli, November 15, 1972, MJB Collection, UCI.

320 "from Osvaldo Soriano": Soriano to Millar, November 8, 1972, UCI.

320 "*La Opinión*": Osvaldo Soriano, "*Una novela de Ross Macdonald desnuda la crisis de la sociedad norteamericana*" (review of *El hombre enterrado*), *La Opinión*, December 14, 1971.

320 "since Dashiell Hammett": R. A. D. Ford to Millar, November 23, 1972, UCI.

320 " 'attracting great attention in London' ": Bruccoli to Millar, July 12, 1972, UCI.

320 " 'My private literary event this year' ": A. Alvarez, "Books of the Year," *Observer Review*, December 17, 1972.

321 " 'He wrote like a slumming angel' ": This quote, taken from Macdonald's preface to Matthew Bruccoli's *Kenneth Millar/Ross Macdonald—A Checklist* (Gale Research Co., 1971), which appeared initially on several Chandler books published by Ballantine in 1972, was used on other publishers' Chandler editions into the 1990s.

321 " 'Raymond Chandler wrote with wonderful gusto' ": Used in advertisements for *The Midnight Raymond Chandler* (Houghton Mifflin, 1971).

321 " 'I take seriously my membership in the School of Hammett' ": Millar to Green, May 29, 1972, UCI.

321 " 'As a novelist of realistic intrigue' ": This line was printed on several Hammett books reprinted by Vintage in 1972 and would be used on other Hammett reissues into the nineties.

321 " 'Since a work of fiction is, among other things' ": Ross Macdonald, "A Western story that is playing for keeps," review of *Goldenrod* (Random House, 1972), *New York Times Book Review*, June 11, 1972.

321 " 'Few husbands have been able to set such a marker' ": Millar to Harker, February 11, 1972, courtesy of Herb Harker.

321 " 'It's a useful recourse' ": Ibid.

321 " 'He was soft-spoken, formal, courteous' ": Jon Carroll interview with TN.

322 " 'Have you thought much' ": Jon Carroll, "Ross Macdonald in Raw California: Geography as Motive," *Esquire,* June 1972.

322 " 'I'm Armenian' ": Jerry Tutunjian interview with TN.

322 " 'I showed up at this beach club' ": Sam Grogg interview with TN.

324 " 'I can just about put my finger on when' ": Max Byrd interview with TN.

325 " 'One of the few mysteries of our time to land on the best-seller lists' ": "The Edgars That Came in from the Cold," *The Third Degree,* May 1965.

325 "the MWA's Hillary Waugh said Edgar choices shouldn't be influenced by mere popularity": Hillary Waugh, "Edgars, Anyone," *The Third Degree,* May 1969: "But the Edgar is not being awarded for the most popular book, or the biggest seller, or the one that brings the greatest financial reward to its author. It says to the recipient, 'We, your peers, agree that yours is the best job done in our field this year. You are the pro of pros.' "

326 " 'Ed Hoch mentioned about a month ago' ": Avallone to Millar, March 2, 1969, UCI.

326 " 'I've got a ten dollar bet' ": Avallone to Millar, June 21, 1971, UCI.

326 " 'It is sort of odd' ": Edward D. Hoch interview with TN.

326 "Collin Wilcox told Millar": Wilcox to Millar, May 30, 1970, UCI.

326 " 'Some woman really got pissed off' ": Sokolov interview with TN.

326 "Millar was dismayed": Referred to by Avallone to Millar, June 21, 1971, UCI.

326 " 'No wonder I puzzle MWA' ": Millar to Olding, June 13, 1972, Princeton.

327 " 'What gives me particular pleasure' ": Millar to Knopf, August 10, 1971, HRHRC.

327 " 'Life is beginning to taste good again' ": Millar to Bruccoli, May 4, 1972, MJB Collection, UCI.

328 " 'the book which is most important to me' ": Millar to Green, January 16, 1973, UCI.

329 " 'It is interesting that children' ": Eudora Welty, "And They All Lived Happily Ever After," *New York Times Book Review,* November 10, 1963.

329 " 'Look, I'm telling you my family secrets' ": Ross Macdonald, *Sleeping Beauty* (Knopf, 1973).

331 " 'In flight from the past' ": Millar notebook, UCI.

333 " 'As a man gets older' ": Ross Macdonald, *The Zebra-Striped Hearse* (Knopf, 1962).

333 "Charlotte Capers, 'An Interview with Eudora Welty: 8 May 1973' ": In Peggy Whitman Prenshaw, ed., *Conversations with Eudora Welty* (University Press of Mississippi, 1984).

333 "a full-page ad": *New York Times Book Review,* May 6, 1973.

333 " 'more of my lifetime images came in on that oily tide' ": Millar to Wolfe, June 1, 1973, UCI.

334 " 'She gave me such a reading as authors dream of' ": Millar to Green, October 21, 1972, UCI. To an Ober agent, Millar wrote, "I'm encouraged by the reactions of one or two writer friends, notably Eudora Welty to whom I'm dedicating it, to think that it may have literary merit of a sort" (Millar to Phyllis, November 6, 1972, Princeton).

334 " 'He responded with the most wonderful, warm, generous letter to me' ": Roger Simon interview with TN.

335 "Millar praised *The Big Fix* to Matt Bruccoli": Millar to Bruccoli, April 29, 1973, MJB Collection, UCI.

335 "and to Julian Symons": Millar to Symons, September 10, 1974, courtesy of Julian Symons.

NOTES

335 "to Ralph Sipper": Millar to Sipper, March 19, 1973, Indiana.

336 " 'Those are the cosmic criminals of our times' ": Simon to Millar, April 24, 1973, UCI.

336 " 'We sit in front of the television set' ": Millar to R. A. D. Ford, July 16, 1973, National Library of Canada.

336 " 'There is some kind of general family history' ": Millar to Ruehlmann, May 15, 1973, courtesy of William Ruehlmann. Also, typed copy, UCI.

337 " 'the essential meaninglessness of evil' ": Millar to Ruehlmann, August 14, 1974; typed copy, UCI.

337 " 'He's almost infallibly wrong' ": Jeff Sweet, Ross Macdonald interview, *Gallery*, August 1974.

    On December 1, 1973, Millar wrote Ping Ferry, "I don't see how Nixon can last, having corrupted everything and everyone he's touched. It was brought home to me this week when Chapin was indicted and his father-in-law H___ , who lives just across the street, put his house up for sale." Typed copy, UCI.

337 " 'He could be extremely violent in likes and dislikes' ": Robert Easton to Matt Bruccoli, September 22, 1982, courtesy of Robert Easton.

337 " 'You've heard of the Florida White House?' ": Millar to Ruehlmann, May 15, 1973, typed copy, UCI.

338 " 'It was a very pleasant three or four days' ": Reynolds Price interview with TN.

338 " 'Mississippi *was* a lot of fun' ": Millar to Green, May 7, 1973, UCI.

338 " 'We all had a splendid time' ": Millar to Symons, May 7, 1973, courtesy of Julian Symons.

338 " 'Except or but for the blacks' ": Millar to Green, May 7, 1973, UCI.

338 " 'She is one of the world's gentlest minds' ": Millar to Ruehlmann, May 15, 1973; typed copy, UCI.

339 " 'Amid the clatter of radio and television equipment' ": Nona Balakian, "A Day of One's Own," *New York Times Book Review*, May 27, 1973.

339 " 'Eudora boldly read aloud' ": Millar to Symons, May 7, 1973.

339 " 'Well, it was not *chosen* for that reason' ": Welty interview with TN.

339 " 'Altogether a lovely experience' ": Millar to Symons, May 7, 1973.

339 " 'Eudora Welty is the living writer that I admire most' ": Ariel, "An Interview with Reynolds Price," 1972, included in Jefferson Humphries, ed., *Conversations with Reynolds Price* (University Press of Mississippi, 1991).

340 " 'the search for the lost child' ": Peter S. Prescott, "The Corpse Finder," *Newsweek*, May 7, 1973.

341 " '*Sleeping Beauty* is a blurry effort' ": John Skow, "More Than 10 Billion Sold," *Time*, May 14, 1973.

341 " 'in spite of *Time*' ": Millar to Harker, June 1, 1973, courtesy of Herb Harker.

341 "Clifford A. Ridley in the *National Observer*": "Macdonald's Back, and Another Case Runs Itself Down," *National Observer*, May 19, 1973.

341 "Robert Kirsch in the *L A Times*": Calendar, May 20, 1973.

341 " 'a preposterously bad review' ": Millar to John Smith, August 18, 1973, UCI.

341 " 'This detective story carries a dedication to Eudora Welty' ": Crawford Woods, "The [*sic*] Sleeping Beauty," *New York Times Book Review*, May 20, 1973.

341 " 'Occasionally, the author writes a thoughtful line' ": Anatole Broyard, "The Case of the Quick Read," *New York Times*, May 21, 1973.

342 " 'every bit as good as *The Underground Man*' ": *Playboy*, July 1973.

342 " 'consummate skill' ": *Chicago Tribune Book World*, June 3, 1973.

342 " 'One of the stranger mysteries' ": *New Republic*, June 2, 1973.

342 " 'This novel is a disgrace' ": *Massachusetts Review*, Autumn 1973.

342 " 'But the subject wouldn't leave me alone' ": Millar to Nona Balakian, July 5, 1973, courtesy of Nona Balakian; typed copy, UCI.

342 " 'There is no reason why' ": Millar to Green, June 11, 1973, UCI.

NOTES

342 "when it was printed in August": Ross Macdonald, "Letters to the Editor," *New York Times Book Review*, August 5, 1973.

342 " 'but satisfactory' ": Millar to Ferry, typed copy, UCI.

342 " 'I'm eager to get into a new one' ": Millar to Bruccoli, July 16, 1973, MJB Collection, UCI.

342 " 'Browne is quiet and unassuming and very sharp' ": Millar to Ferry, typed copy, UCI.

343 " 'extraordinarily human and humble' ": Ray B. Browne interview with TN.

344 " 'When Ken called to remind you about the meetings' ": Shelly Lowenkopf, "Snapshots: The Write Wednesday," unidentified article (probably *Santa Barbara News & Review*), circa 1984.

345 " 'One day Ken and I were discussing a writer' ": William Campbell Gault, "A Tribute," *Dictionary of Literary Biography Yearbook: 1983*.

345 " 'Though he would deny it' ": Ralph Sipper, "Faces of Ross Macdonald," *Santa Barbara Magazine*, Winter 1980.

345 " '*Everybody* wanted to sit next to Ken' ": Ralph Sipper interview with TN.

347 "*Detective Fiction: Crime and Compromise*": Eds. Dick Allen and David Chacko (Harcourt Brace Jovanovich, 1974).

347 " 'burglars' ": Macdonald preface to *Archer in Hollywood;* reprinted in *Self-Portrait*.

347 " 'shoplifters' ": Macdonald, "Down These Streets a Mean Man Must Go"; reprinted in *Self-Portrait*.

347 "breaking into the academy by the back door": Millar to Green, August 4, 1973, UCI.

347 " 'This will be embarrassing' ": Millar to Bruccoli, July 16, 1973, MJB Collection, UCI.

347 " 'We conceived of this award about a year ago' ": Remarks transcribed from tape recording, courtesy of Ray B. Browne.

348 " 'quite brilliant' ": Millar to Wolfe, January 14, 1974, UCI.

348 "reprinted in the *New Republic*": George Grella, "Evil Plots," *New Republic*, July 26, 1975. The best and most succinct analysis of Macdonald's recurring patterns and techniques.

348 " 'I was a little flustered' ": Grogg interview with TN.

348 " 'Down These Streets a Mean Man Must Go' ": Reprinted in *Self-Portrait*.

349 " 'His paper was extremely good' ": George Grella interview with TN.

349 " 'if you can believe this' ": Millar to Wolfe, January 14, 1974, UCI.

349 " 'He came out dressed like a parody' ": Frank MacShane interview with TN.

350 "Millar exploded": Jerre Lloyd interview with TN.

350 " 'He was a very controlled man, facially' ": Brad Darrach interview with TN.

351 " 'One day in the beach club pool' ": Brad Darrach, "Ross Macdonald: The Man Behind the Mysteries," *People*, July 8, 1974.

352 " 'I felt sometimes she was very cruel to him' ": Interview with TN.

352 " 'Margaret's and my marriage has been very close to the edge at times' ": Millar to Gerald Walker, January 6, 1974, courtesy of Gerald Walker; typed copy, UCI.

353 " 'It's very doubtful that Margaret will attend' ": Millar to Symons, September 10, 1974, courtesy of Julian Symons.

353 " 'to limit my time away from home' ": Millar to Ruehlmann, March 27, 1974; typed copy, UCI.

353 " 'a serious and very pleasant man' ": Millar to Wolfe, February 21, 1974, UCI.

353 " 'In thirty years of writing about Lew Archer' ": Cecil Smith, " 'Underground Man' to Surface on TV," *Los Angeles Times*, March 19, 1974.

353 " 'Rather fun discussing characterizations' ": Millar to Wolfe, February 21, 1974, UCI.

353 " 'The director was always saying, "Judy baby, Judy baby" ' ": Michael Small, "Chatter," *People*, June 25, 1984.

354 " 'These are good days' ": Millar to Bruccoli, February 24, 1974, MJB Collection, UCI.

354 " 'a kind of longevity award' ": Millar to Jeff Ring, March 15, 1974; typed copy, UCI.

354 " 'A number of nice things have happened to me' ": Millar to Avallone, February 25, 1974, from the Avallone Collection, Department of Special Collections, Boston University.

354 " 'I'll finally have an Edgar' ": Millar to Wolfe, April 26, 1974, UCI.

354 " 'The most touching moment of the evening' ": *The Third Degree*, June 1974.

355 " 'They finally decided to accept this rude westerner' ": Millar to Bruccoli, MJB Collection, UCI.

355 " 'most pleasant' ": Millar to Wolfe, June 10, 1974, UCI.

355 " 'I'm sorry it didn't turn out better' ": Millar to Wolfe, May 9, 1974, UCI.

355 " 'I would rather watch her than it' ": Millar to Bruccoli, May 18, 1974, MJB Collection, UCI.

355 " 'a constant interest in a TV series' ": Millar to Wolfe, May 9, 1974, UCI.

356 "it was said Jackie Cooper would play Archer": Millar to Wolfe, August 16, 1974, UCI.

356 "Millar would receive $2,000 an episode": Lee Rosenberg (of Adams, Ray & Rosenberg) to Millar, November 18, 1974, UCI.

356 "Millar traced this screen wave of private eyes directly to . . . *Harper*": "It was sort of an irony that the movie *Harper*, which came out ten or eleven years ago, should have helped to start the whole current private eye craze, you know. But they waited to put Archer on television until there were twenty-seven other private eyes in the same season"—Millar to Trevor Meldal-Johnsen, "Ross Macdonald Interview," *Gallery*, March 1976.

"Millar takes particular pride in . . . *Harper*. . . . 'It was the first successful hard-boiled detective movie in the last generation. . . . It is really what started the whole current phase in detective movies,' " Celeste Durant, "Ross Macdonald: After 19th Novel," *Chicago Sun-Times*, July 28, 1976.

356 "an 'homage à trois' ": Charles Champlin, "*Chinatown* Tour de Force," *Los Angeles Times*, June 21, 1974.

356 "Millar told Hank Coulette": Jackie Coulette interview with TN.

356 "As Millar also told Coulette": Ibid.

356 " 'Too many awards' ": Millar to Bruccoli, February 24, 1974, MJB Collection, UCI.

357 " 'Time, which I used to have nothing but of' ": Millar to Ruehlmann, June 28, 1974; typed copy, UCI.

357 " 'Authors get weary of their own work' ": Millar to Jeff Ring, July 17, 1974; typed copy, UCI.

357 " 'The Macdonald books go on and on' ": Jaffe to Millar, June 18, 1974, UCI.

357 " 'Am slated to appear on TV' ": Millar to Wolfe, November 13, 1974, UCI.

357 "The Hunt appearance fell through": E. Howard Hunt letter to TN, May 31, 1995.

357 " 'The rats are stirring again' ": Jerre Lloyd interview with TN.

357 " 'Money stolen during the war' ": Ibid.

358 " 'From the Millars' cabana number 22' ": Sally Ogle Davis, "Murder, They Wrote," *Santa Barbara Magazine*, Summer 1994.

358 "He said a Canadian found himself by going elsewhere": Millar to Ford, February 1971, National Library of Canada.

358 " 'As I get older and look forward and back' ": Millar to Symons, January 19, 1972, courtesy of Julian Symons.

358 " 'I hope I live long enough' ": Millar to Symons, September 10, 1974, courtesy of Julian Symons.

358 " 'The book I am working up now' ": Ibid.

358 " 'I started out aiming at posterity' ": "An interview with Ross Macdonald," *Concept Twelve* (1971).

359 " 'First confession of the day' ": John J. O'Connor, *New York Times,* January 30, 1975.

359 " 'this one begins unglued' ": Stanley Kauffmann, *New Republic,* July 26, 1975.

359 "the next-to-last Archer—or the last, if need be": Millar to Symons, September 10, 1974, courtesy of Julian Symons.

359 "a poem by Hank Coulette": "Confiteor" section of "III. The Blue Hammer," in Donald Justice and Robert Mezey, eds., *The Collected Poems of Henri Coulette* (University of Arkansas Press, 1990).

359 " 'I'm busy' ": Millar to Bruccoli, January 7, 1975, MJB Collection, UCI.

359 " 'All I have to do' ": Millar to Sipper, February 8, 1975, Lilly Library, Indiana University.

359 " 'My style seems to be changing' ": Millar to Wolfe, November 13, 1974, UCI.

359 " 'Ken spoke of working mightily' ": Ted Clymer interview with TN.

360 " 'To all Lew Archer fans' ": Cecil Smith, "A Lew Archer in Name Only," *Los Angeles Times,* January 30, 1975.

360 " '*Archer* is merely a confusion of headlines' ": Cyclops, "Thursday's New Entries Promote Non-Thinking," *New York Times,* February 16, 1975.

360 " 'I've got it in writing' ": Cecil Smith, "Brian Keith's playing Lew Archer—but with Hawaii on his mind," *Los Angeles Times TV Times,* January 26–February 1, 1975.

360 " 'You wonder' ": Ibid.

360 " 'You may wish to be told' ": Millar to Ring, January 31, 1975; typed copy, UCI.

360 " 'one of the speediest executions on record' ": "Fast Ax for 'Archer' Series," *Daily Variety,* February 11, 1975.

360 " '*The Three Roads* is, if all goes well' ": Millar to Ford, March 28, 1975, National Library of Canada.

361 " 'Pathos, gentleness, courage' ": Millar to Jill Krementz, June 11, 1974; typed copy, UCI.

361 " 'A supremely moral writer' ": Welty notes, UCI.

361 " 'in both English and Russian' ": Ford to Millar, December 2, 1974, UCI.
      Ford had earlier informed Millar that Macdonald had a selective readership in English among the Moscow intelligentsia (Ford to Millar, September 22, 1971, UCI).

361 " 'He is the most eminent poet I ever heard from' ": Millar to Ford, March 28, 1975, National Library of Canada.

361 " 'The film is poor' ": Penelope Gilliatt, "How Long Does It Take to *(a)* Fill a Hydrotherapy Chamber, *(b)* Empty Your Head?" *New Yorker,* June 30, 1975.

361 " 'Just enjoy it' ": Vincent Canby, "What to See If You Can't Get into the Hits," *New York Times,* July 6, 1975.

362 " 'You didn't miss a thing' ": Millar to Ferry, August 28, 1975; typed copy, UCI.

362 " 'The first time I went to Bouchercon' ": Jane S. Bakerman interview with TN.

362 " 'I seem to be getting wordier' ": Millar to Ferry, August 7, 1975; typed copy, UCI.

362 "*The Tarantula Hawk*": Millar to Bruccoli, September 12, 1975, MJB Collection, UCI.

362 "*The Silent Hammer*": Otto Penzler, "Interview: Ross Macdonald," *Ellery Queen's Mystery Magazine,* January 1976. ("MACDONALD: . . . My new novel, *The Silent Hammer,* has just gone in to my publisher.")

362 " 'When I read the manuscript' ": Easton to Bruccoli, September 22, 1982, courtesy of Robert Easton.

362 " 'My life seems to be spaced out by endless delays' ": Millar to Carter, September 9, 1975, courtesy of Steven Carter.

363 " 'Margaret had a cancer removed' ": Millar to Ferry, September 30, 1975; typed copy, UCI.

363 "an ad on the front cover of *Publishers Weekly*": December 8, 1975.

363 " 'bemused and depressed' ": MacDonald to Millar, December 16, 1975, Rare Books and Manuscripts, University of Florida Libraries.

365 " 'The big guns of the Beat Generation' ": Millar, "Passengers on a Cable Car Named Despair," *San Francisco Chronicle*, June 29, 1958.

365 " 'People have been telling me' ": Anatole Broyard, "Ay, Ay, Ay, Margaret Millar," *New York Times*, October 13, 1976.

365 " 'We met in the parking lot of a country club' ": Gault interview with TN.

366 " 'I had started to read mysteries' ": Jane Bernstein interview with TN.

366 " 'To a writer who has been at it for quite a while' ": Millar to Bernstein, May 17, 1976, courtesy of Jane Bernstein.

367 " 'Even when they're faced with fairly worthless books' ": Transcribed from audio-tape, courtesy of Nona Balakian. See also *Publishers Weekly* account, May 10, 1976.

367 "Broyard was African-American": See Henry Louis Gates Jr., "White Like Me," *New Yorker*, June 17, 1996. A fictional character apparently inspired by this aspect of Broyard's biography appears in the 1998 mystery novel *A Darker Shade of Crimson*, by African-American writer Pamela Thomas-Graham (Simon & Schuster).

368 " 'We talked a bit about his roots' ": Linwood Barclay interview with TN.

368 " 'as if I ever could' ": Millar to Kuehlmann, May 16, 1976; typed copy, UCI.

368 " 'We're both past sixty' ": Millar to Nona Balakian, May 26, 1976, courtesy of Nona Balakian.

368 " 'He was very shy' ": Otto Penzler interview with TN.

369 " 'Fortunately for the town and us' ": Millar to Wolfe, June 28, 1976, UCI.

369 " 'Our home is a special island' ": Marshall Berges, "Margaret Millar & 'Ross Mac-donald,' " *Home Magazine, Los Angeles Times*, June 29, 1975.

370 " 'waxed enthusiastic' ": Digby Diehl, "Between Lines at Writers Conference," *Los Angeles Times* Calendar, July 4, 1976.

370 " 'I went to that first Santa Barbara Writers Conference' ": Fred Zackel to Millar, October 5, 1977, UCI.

370 " 'brilliantly conceived and woven' ": John Seagraves, "Lew Archer at Mid-Century," *Washington Star*, July 4, 1976.

370 " 'an excellent addition' ": Elmer R. Pry, "Believe it or not, Lew Archer finds love," *Chicago Tribune Book World*.

370 " 'one of his best' ": Walter Clemons, *Newsweek*, June 21, 1976.

370 " 'perfect blend of style and action' ": William McPherson, "Archer with a Deadly Aim," *Washington Post Book World*, June 27, 1976.

371 " 'Lew Archer has changed' ": Robert Kirsch, "The Mellowing of Lew Archer," *Los Angeles Times*, June 15, 1976.

371 " 'Some time ago' ": Anatole Broyard, "Books of the *Times*," *New York Times*, June 11, 1976.

372 " 'Archer tracks the past' ": Michael Woods, *New York Times Book Review*, June 13, 1976.

372 " 'All the reviews have been favorable' ": Millar to Wolfe, June 28, 1976, UCI.

372 " 'better than I expected' ": Millar to Ferry, July 7, 1976; typed copy, UCI.

372 " 'It seems to me a perfect example' ": MacShane to Millar, undated but probably May 16, 1976 ("Gracias a Dios," wrote MacShane, "my [Chandler] biography was reviewed on the front page of the *New York Times Book Review* today"), UCI.

372 " 'It seems to me that the control' ": Jan La Rue to Millar, August 14, 1977, UCI.

372 " 'I thought *The Blue Hammer* was your best book for a long time' ": Symons to Millar, October 30, 1976, UCI.

NOTES

372 " 'which casually mentions "the towers of the mission and the courthouse" ' ": Julian Symons, "In pursuit of the past," *Times Literary Supplement,* April 2, 1982.

373 " 'a paean of praise to life' ": H. R. F. Keating, *Crime & Mystery: The 100 Best Books* (Carroll & Graf, 1987 [U.S.]; Xanadu Publications Limited, 1987 [U.K.]).

373 "in the *Chicago Sun-Times*": Celeste Durant, "Ross Macdonald: After 19th Novel," *Chicago Sun-Times* Living, July 28, 1976.

373 "the *Houston Chronicle*": Susan Wood, "Things aren't what they seem with Macdonald," *Houston Chronicle,* May 9, 1976.

373 "the *National Observer*": Clifford A. Ridley, "Yes, Most of My Chronicles Are Chronicles of Misfortune," *National Observer,* July 31, 1976.

373 "a 'Critic's Notebook' piece": John Leonard, "Critic's Notebook: An Evening with 2 Walking Anachronisms," *New York Times,* May 26, 1976.

373 " 'your fellow panelist Broyard's piece of dementia' ": Green to Millar, June 23, 1976, UCI.

373 " 'Am all for writing a short lighter book now' ": Millar to Ferry, July 7, 1976; typed copy, UCI.

373 " 'After having given the matter much thought' ": Draft letter from Schramm, Raddue & Seed to Millar, June 25, 1976, UCI.

373 " 'This sheet of paper' ": Paul Nelson interview with TN.

374 " 'They'd read all his books' ": Paul Nelson, "Warren Zevon: How He Saved Himself from a Coward's Death," *Rolling Stone,* March 19, 1981.

374 " 'My ex-wife Crystal and I' ": Warren Zevon interview with TN.

375 " 'My grandmother is very senatorial' ": Nelson, "Warren Zevon."

375 " 'I grew up with a painting of an uncle' ": Ibid.

375 " 'I *was* that kid' ": Grover Lewis to TN.

375 " 'Zevon came bouncing into the cabana' ": Nelson interview with TN.

375 " 'Macdonald has still not let me down' ": Zevon interview with TN, 1978.

376 " 'The basic truth' ": Millar to Ferry, July 7, 1976; typed copy, UCI.

376 " 'You of all people will know' ": Symons to Millar, September 13, 1976, UCI.

376 " 'My feeling when Linda died' ": Millar to Symons, October 11, 1976, courtesy of Julian Symons.

377 " 'overhung by the unfriendliness' ": Millar to Wolfe, October 9, 1976, UCI.

377 " 'Such are the occasional pleasures' ": Ibid.

377 " 'in all its beautiful broken down strangeness' ": Millar to Ferry, November 24, 1976; typed copy, UCI.

377 " 'I seem to be crazy about places' ": Millar to Wolfe, October 9, 1976, UCI.

377 " 'I like the watery places' ": Millar to Symons, October 11, 1976, courtesy of Julian Symons.

377 "a glimpse of Frank MacShane": Millar to Jane Bernstein, October 5, 1976, courtesy of Jane Bernstein.

377 " 'More and more my mind bends back' ": Millar to Ferry, September 3, 1976; typed copy, UCI.

377 " 'Here is proof positive' ": Joseph the Provider catalog #53 (1994).

377 " 'character, atmosphere, wit, passion' ": Anatole Broyard, "Ay, Ay, Ay, Margaret Millar," *New York Times,* October 13, 1976.

377 " 'I'm unable to write for long periods' ": Millar to Bernstein, October 5, 1976, courtesy of Jane Bernstein.

378 " 'Some are born Canadian' ": Margaret Atwood, introduction, *The New Oxford Book of Canadian Short Stories in English,* selected by Margaret Atwood and Robert Weaver (Oxford, 1997).

378 " 'You thought the national flag was about a leaf' ": Margaret Atwood, *Strange Things: The Malevolent North in Canadian Literature* (Clarendon Press/Oxford, 1995).

378 "come to interview him for *Writer's Yearbook"*: Jane S. Bakerman, "A Slightly Stylized Conversation with Ross Macdonald," *Writer's Yearbook 1981.*

378 " 'Isn't that nice?' ": Jane S. Bakerman interview with TN.

378 " 'My epistolary ennui' ": Millar to Bernstein, undated, courtesy of Jane Bernstein.

379 " 'He was not an easy interview' ": interview with TN.

379 " 'In a gray suit, a gray tie' ": Clifford A. Ridley, "Yes, Most of My Chronicles Are Chronicles of Misfortune," *National Observer,* July 31, 1976.

379 " 'I had a feeling he was somehow *astonished'* ": Richard Moore interview with TN.

380 " 'Canada seems to hang like a glacier' ": Ross Macdonald, "The Writer's Sense of Place: A Symposium and Commentaries," *South Dakota Review,* Autumn 1975; reprinted in *Self-Portrait.*

381 " 'What infinitely complicated stratagems' ": Millar to Wolfe, January 20, 1973, UCI.

381 " 'Canadians become Canadians' ": Millar to Ford, February 1972, National Library of Canada.

381 " 'I really think that Lew Archer is a Canadian-American type' ": Macdonald radio interview with Michael Enwright, *This Country in the Morning,* Canadian Broadcasting Corporation, January 1, 1975.

381 " 'Archer is a life-size hero' ": *Ross Macdonald* film, part of public-television series *The Originals: The Writer in America,* produced by Richard Moore, first broadcast 1978.

381 " 'a new kind of hero' ": Robertson Davies, "The Canada of Myth and Reality," in *One Half of Robertson Davies* (Viking, 1977).

382 " 'Canada is coming alive' ": Millar to Davie, April 10, 1973, courtesy of Ralph Sipper.

382 " 'Robertson Davies is still writing under the influence of Stephen Leacock' ": Tutunjian, "A Conversation with Ross Macdonald."

382 " 'I have never before read a story which so piercingly and succinctly examined' ": Millar to Alice Munro, June 27, 1977, Alice Munro fonds, Special Collections, MacKimmie Library, University of Calgary.

382 "a scant fourteen hundred copies": Green to Millar, September 16, 1974, UCI.

382 " 'I spoke at the MLA in Montreal' ": Leonard interview with TN.

382 "In two intriguing essays": Russell M. Brown, "In Search of Lost Causes: The Canadian Novelist as Mystery Writer," *Mosaic,* Spring 1978; Russell Brown, "Ross Macdonald as Canadian Mystery Writer," in *Seasoned Authors for a New Season: The Search for Standards in Popular Writing* (Bowling Green University Popular Press, 1980).

383 "Brown thought Macdonald's use of landscape as 'a kind of presence' was typical of Canadian writing": Mystery-fiction publisher-scholar Otto Penzler, in *The Private Lives of Private Eyes, Spies, Crimefighters, & Other Good Guys* (Grosset & Dunlap, 1977), made the keen observation that Lew "Archer is more acutely aware of the environment than any detective since November Joe, 'the detective of the woods' about whom Hesketh Prichard wrote more than half a century ago." Prichard was a Canadian; his November Joe tales, serialized in the Wiarton, Ontario, newspaper, were almost certainly the first mystery stories Kenneth Millar read.

383 " 'all that old sadness' ": Millar to Symons, January 19, 1972, courtesy of Julian Symons.

383 " 'With it . . . I think I want to go further' ": Millar to Walker, March 27, 1973, courtesy of Gerald Walker.

384 " 'Ultimately my novels' ": Millar note, *"WIARTON,"* on back of royalty advance statement ("Received from The Mysterious Press") from Harold Ober Associates to Millar, January 18, 1977, UCI.

384 " 'the mid-west and Canada' ": Brown, "In Search of Lost Causes."
384 " 'Ken was wonderful through my illness' ": Beverly Slopen, "The Most Private Eye," *The Canadian*, August 20, 1977.
384 " 'A man can't fight these wars without some help' ": Millar to Avallone, October 19, 1975, UCI.
384 "he started sessions": Millar expense records, notebook, UCI.
385 " 'Asked for his views on the future of the mystery' ": Richard R. Lingeman, "Book Ends," *New York Times Book Review*, April 2, 1978.
385 " 'It was "The Rime of the Ancient Mariner" ' ": Diane K. Shah interview with TN.
385 " 'The fact is that Margaret' ": Millar to Miller, January 19, 1978, the Nolan Miller Papers, Special Collections Library, University of Michigan Library.
386 "interviewed by *Newsweek*": Diane K. Shah with Margaret Malone, "Murder, They Said," *Newsweek*, March 27, 1978.
386 "*New York Daily News*": Millar's schedule indicates a March 15, 1978, interview with Pete Hamill of the *News*. If an article resulted, it has not been located.
386 "National Public Radio": "Whodunnit?" *Options* series, National Public Radio, 1978.
386 "BBC television": BBC TV, "Crime Writers: What Next?" producer Bernard Adams, 1978.
386 " 'The Mystery Writers were very very pleased' ": Symons interview with TN.
386 " 'Publishers are getting greedy' ": "Whodunnit?" *Options* series.
387 " 'Is it possible' ": "The State of the Art: A Symposium Conducted by Brian Garfield," *Publishers Weekly*, March 10, 1978.
387 " 'the most interesting speech of the congress' ": Julian Symons, "Murder at the Biltmore," (London) Sunday *Times Magazine*, May 21, 1978.
387 " 'It was like he was in left field' ": Fred Klein interview with TN.
387 " 'I'm sorry I can't offer you more time' ": Millar to Speir, April 12, 1978, courtesy of Jerry Speir.
388 " 'one of the best things that have ever happened to me' ": Millar to Davie, December 12, 1978, courtesy Ralph Sipper.
388 "*The Eye of the Story: Selected Essays and Reviews*": Random House, 1978. In his favorable *New York Times* review of this book, Anatole Broyard managed to avoid mentioning it was dedicated to Kenneth Millar or that it included Welty's review of *The Underground Man*.
388 " 'In 1978 we had quite a severe earthquake' ": *The Third Degree*, June/July 1983.
388 " 'It did have the virtue of being hard to write' ": Millar to Davie, December 12, 1978.
388 " 'He's genuinely good' ": Ibid.
388 " 'as clever as a cop' ": Ibid.
388 " 'deep and slow and golden' ": Ibid.
389 " 'I can only say' ": Olding to Millar, December 5, 1978, Princeton.
389 " 'high local pressures' ": Millar to Olding, December 22, 1978, Princeton.
389 " 'After our incredible long romantic youths' ": Millar to Davie, December 12, 1978.
390 " 'At the lowest point in my life' ": Nelson, *Rolling Stone*, March 19, 1981.
390 " 'I've been rereading parts of the three books' ": Millar to Olding, March 5, 1979; typed copy, UCI.
390 " 'My own personal tides' ": Millar to Bernstein, April 9, 1979, courtesy of Jane Bernstein.
390 " 'Not easy' ": Millar to Olding, undated, received May 1, 1979, Princeton.
390 " 'I hope my books echo' ": Macdonald preface to *Archer in Jeopardy;* reprinted in *Self-Portrait*.
391 " 'The last time I saw my father's living eyes' ": Macdonald foreword to *A Collection of Reviews;* reprinted in *Self-Portrait*.

NOTES

391 " 'Are you working on a book?' ": Olding to Millar, June 12, 1979, UCI.

391 " 'I am not retiring from fiction' ": Millar to Olding, June 28, 1979, Princeton.

391 " 'In many respects it is a novel of manners' ": Newgate Callendar, "Crime," *New York Times Book Review*, April 29, 1979.

391 " 'Ross Macdonald has 13,400,000 books in Bantam print!' ": Bantam press release, August 1979, UCI.

391 " 'Believe me' ": Fred Klein interview with TN.

392 " 'would be glad to see *The Moving Target*' ": Millar to Phyllis Westburg (Harold Ober Associates), May 17, 1971, Princeton.

392 " 'We skate along' ": Millar to Symons, June 8, 1979, courtesy of Julian Symons.

392 " 'It will come as no surprise to you' ": Millar to Olding, August 3, 1979, Princeton.

392 " 'I had a homicide detective in psychoanalysis' ": Dr. Edwin C. Peck Jr. interview with TN.

392 " 'One way or another' ": Zevon interview with TN.

393 " 'Zevon was in bad, bad, bad shape' ": Nelson interview with TN.

394 " 'You're not only the finest novelist' ": Zevon to Millar, undated (apparently 1980), UCI.

394 *"Bad Luck Streak in Dancing School"*: Asylum album, February 1980.

394 " 'I've been back at my desk' ": Millar to Green, September 3, 1979, quoted by Green in "A Tribute," *Dictionary of Literary Biography Yearbook: 1983*.

394 " 'Archer discovers his own early—perhaps pre-memory—life in Wiarton' ": Millar notebook, UCI.

395 " 'It's all one case' ": A phrase often uttered by Lew Archer. Paul Nelson used it as the title of his *Rolling Stone* piece on Millar when it was reprinted in *Inward Journey*.

395 " 'almost as a goad to himself' ": Green, "A Tribute."

395 "The house of Knopf agreed to pay": Ober "BOOK CONTRACT" memo, undated, Princeton.

396 " 'Lew Archer remembers' ": Grella, "Evil Plots."

396 " 'Archer is a life-size hero' ": Richard Moore film.

396 " 'I might as well have phoned them in' ": Alex Law, "A moment with Millar," *The (Hamilton, Ontario) Spectator*, June 1988.

396 " 'I don't know why' ": Margaret Millar interview with TN.

396 " 'My father was blind when he died at ninety-three' ": Actually Hen Sturm was ninety-two when he died.

396 " 'When Margaret's health deteriorated' ": Easton interview with TN.

396 " 'We've had some recent trouble' ": Millar to Olding, received August 5, 1980, Princeton; typed copy, UCI.

396 " 'a writer has to know something *special*' ": Mignon T. Marsh, "You can call him Ross—or you can call him John, but this Macdonald is really Kenneth Millar," *NRTA Journal*, March-April 1981.

396 " 'Margaret has the whole town in her mind' ": Mickey Friedman, "The first family of mystery writing," *San Francisco Examiner*, May 19, 1980.

396 " 'This was in a memory course' ": Margaret Millar interview with TN.

397 " 'In his book *Black Money*' ": Betty Phelps interview with TN.

397 " 'It's the interplay of memory and intellect' ": Millar interview with Jerry Tutunjian, courtesy Jerry Tutunjian.

397 " 'It's great to be backstopped by you people' ": Millar to Green, October 21, 1972, UCI.

397 " 'We all came out from under Hammett's overcoat' ": Millar to Green, May 29, 1972, UCI.

397 " 'We all came out from under Hammett's black mask' ": From Millar preface to "Find the Woman" in *Maiden Murders/Mystery Writers of America* (Harper, 1952).

397 " 'I am so prone to getting lost' ": Millar to Jeff Ring, July 17, 1974, typed copy, UCI.

397   " 'I was struck by your suggestion' ": Millar to Symons, September 10, 1974, courtesy of Julian Symons.

397   " 'Thank you for your interest' ": Millar to Linwood Barclay, January 19, 1976; typed copy, UCI.

397   " 'back Canada palpably to me' ": Millar to Barclay, March 18, 1976, courtesy of Linwood Barclay.

397   "a New York City high school teacher": Joseph A. Gisler to Knopf, May 30, 1976, UCI.

398   " 'You state that "the other stories" ' ": Penzler to Millar, June 28, 1977, UCI.

398   " 'A lot of the so-called literary material' ": *Writer's Yearbook 1981*.

398   " 'Have I mentioned that that your reviews' ": Millar to Peter Wolfe, February 14, 1978, UCI.

398   " 'At the moment we have the pleasant duty' ": Millar to Linwood Barclay, August 27, 1978, courtesy of Linwood Barclay.

398   " 'Can I be slowing down?' ": Millar to Jerry Speir, November 27, 1979, courtesy of Jerry Speir.

398   " 'The less delightful people' ": Millar to Green, February 3, 1980. Quoted by Green in "A Tribute."

398   " 'They ruined the book market' ": Friedman, "The first family of mystery writing."

399   " 'Ken Millar was a very vulnerable-looking figure' ": Jim Pepper interview with TN.

399   " 'It's not just an idle thing' ": Friedman, "The first family of mystery writing."

399   "Bob Ford alerted Millar": Ford to Millar, August 24, 1978, UCI.

399   " 'No, I can't do that' ": John Milton, "Coincidentally: A Brief Memoir," *South Dakota Review,* Spring 1986.

399   " 'I hope you will give yourself steady and serious care' ": Millar to Olding, received August 5, 1980, Princeton.

400   " 'And yet at lunch' ": Rich Jaroslovsky, "Ken Millar Alias Ross Macdonald, 1915–1983," *Wall Street Journal,* July 15, 1983.

400   " 'She said several times that he hadn't been well' ": Diana Cooper-Clark interview with TN. An audiotape of the Millar/Cooper-Clark interview is in the Millar Collection.

401   " 'a massive editing job' ": Diana Cooper-Clark, "Interview with Ross Macdonald," *Designs of Darkness: Interviews with Detective Novelists* (Bowling Green State University Popular Press, 1983).

402   " 'I think he might not have said *anything* to *anyone*' ": Ralph Sipper interview with TN.

402   " ' "I'd better not," he said' ": Robert Easton, "A Tribute," *Dictionary of Literary Biography Yearbook: 1983.*

402   " 'He was very reserved' ": Ralph Sipper interview with TN.

402   " 'Use your good judgment' ": Ralph Sipper, "The Last Goodbye," in *Inward Journey.*

402   " 'After the meeting one day' ": Gault interview with TN.

402   " 'I saw them once in the supermarket' ": Gayle Lynds interview with TN.

402   " 'I came away inspired, really' ": Wilcox interview with TN.

403   " 'It had something to do with spinal fluid' ": Easton interview with TN.

403   " 'a kind of smiling shell' ": Julian Symons, (London) Sunday *Times,* July 17, 1983.

403   *"Self-Portrait":* Ross Macdonald, *Self-Portrait: Ceaselessly into the Past,* foreword by Eudora Welty, edited and with an afterword by Ralph B. Sipper (Capra Press, 1981).

403   " 'as perceptive, elegantly written and illuminating an analysis' ": Charles Champlin, "Ross Macdonald: detecting bits and pieces of the self in fiction," *Book Review, Los Angeles Times,* September 6, 1981.

403 " 'a valuable and fascinating addition' ": Terry Teachout, *National Review*, November 26, 1982.

403 " 'Writing keeps me sane' ": Wayne Warga, "The Millars: Tale of Fortitude," *Los Angeles Times*, February 11, 1982.

403 " 'Her attitude was wonderful' ": Wayne Warga interview with TN.

404 " 'I would try to get him to put on his shoes' ": Margaret Millar interview with TN.

404 " 'Margaret told me of one conversation' ": William Ruehlmann interview with TN.

404 " 'Whenever a woman would enter the room' ": Margaret Millar interview with TN.

404 " 'and tumbled tumbled free' ": "MIDNIGHT BLUE by Ross Macdonald" typescript page, UCI.

404 " 'John Ball told me' ": Ray Browne interview with TN.

405 " 'What is your name?' ": Eudora Welty interview with TN.

409 " 'As I hope my books make clear' ": Millar to Olding, February 4, 1968, Princeton.

409 " 'I could have wept' ": Unpublished Harker manuscript, courtesy of Herb Harker.

409 " 'a cerebrovascular accident' ": Steven Dougherty, "Ross Macdonald's Legacy: Lew, a sleuth for all seasons," *Los Angeles Herald-Examiner*, July 13, 1983.

409 " 'I told them I wouldn't authorize any steps' ": Derrick Murdoch, "The mistress of thrillers," *Toronto Globe and Mail*, May 22, 1984.

410 "the front page of the *Wall Street Journal*": "Died," *Wall Street Journal*, July 13, 1983.

410 "the *Los Angeles Times* (by Charles Champlin)": Charles Champlin, "A Loss for Detective Fiction," August 1, 1983.

410 "the *Detroit News* (Clifford A. Ridley)": Clifford A. Ridley, "Ross Macdonald dies; created 'Lew Archer,' " *Detroit News*, July 13, 1983.

410 "the *Virginian-Pilot* and the *Ledger-Star* (William Ruehlmann)": William Ruehlmann, "Mystery master cast light into society's dark alleys," *Virginian-Pilot* and the *Ledger-Star*, August 14, 1983.

410 "the *Los Angeles Herald-Examiner* (Mikal Gilmore)": Mikal Gilmore, "Macdonald raised hard-boiled fiction to the level of literature," *Los Angeles Herald-Examiner*, July 18, 1983.

410 "the *New York Times Book Review*": Frank MacShane, "Meeting Ross Macdonald," *New York Times Book Review*, September 11, 1983.

410 "Paul Nelson . . . *Rolling Stone*": Paul Nelson, "Ross Macdonald December 13th, 1915–July 11th, 1983," *Rolling Stone*, September 1, 1983; reprinted (as "It's All One Case") in *Inward Journey*.

410 "a *Peanuts* comic strip": August 11, 1983.

410 "for the Sunday *Times*": July 17, 1983.

410 "and for *London* magazine": Julian Symons, "A Transatlantic Friendship," *London*, July 1983; reprinted in *Inward Journey*.

410 " 'It's sad that we have to lose at the same moment' ": Richard Young, "Canadian critics mourn mystery writer MacDonald [*sic*]," *Toronto Star*, July 13, 1983.

410 "the *Toronto Globe and Mail*": July 16, 1983. See also July 13, 1983.

410 "the *Kitchener-Waterloo Record*": July 15, 1983. See also July 13 and August 13, 1983.

410 "the alternative paper *News & Review*": Week of July 21–27, 1983.

410 " 'Several years back' ": *Santa Barbara News-Press*, July 18, 1983.

411 " 'It was so strange' ": Margaret Millar interview with TN.

411 "his 'accommodation' ": Jerre Lloyd interview with TN.

411 " 'Macdonald's narratives are beautifully built machines' ": Geoffrey O'Brien, *Hardboiled America: The Lurid Years of Paperbacks* (Van Nostrand Reinhold Company, 1981).

411 " 'In his last major novel, *The Long Goodbye*' ": John McAleer, *Rex Stout: A Biography* (Little, Brown, 1977).

411 " 'Macdonald's achievement is wholly individual' ": Julian Symons, *Bloody Murder: From the Detective Story to the Crime Novel, a History* (Viking, 1985; Mysterious Press, 1992) (earlier title: *Mortal Consequences*).

411 " 'Ross Macdonald is one of the central authors' ": George Grella, Ross Macdonald entry, *Contemporary Novelists: Third Edition* (St. Martin's Press, 1982).

411 " 'one of the splendid achievements in American fiction' ": Matthew J. Bruccoli, "Kenneth Millar (13 December 1915–11 July 1983)," *Dictionary of Literary Biography Yearbook: 1983*.

411 " 'one of the best writers of his generation' ": MacShane, "Meeting Ross Macdonald."

412 "Iris Murdoch": Peter Wolfe to Millar, April 24 1974, UCI.

412 "Thomas Berger": See Thomas Berger, "The Justice of Ross Macdonald's Voice," in *Inward Journey*.

412 "John Fowles": From John Fowles's afterword to Sir Arthur Conan Doyle's *The Hound of the Baskervilles* (John Murray and Jonathan Cape, 1974): "Conan Doyle belongs to the tale-tellers, in the long modern line from Poe to Ross Macdonald. . . ."

412 "Charles Portis": Quoted by Lewis Nichols, "American Notebook," *New York Times Book Review*, September 22, 1968.

412 "David Hare": David Hare to Millar, undated (probably November, 1972), UCI.

412 "Stephen Sondheim": Sondheim, interviewed by Anthony Shaffer, "*Theater;* Of Mystery, Murder and Other Delights," *New York Times*, March 10, 1996: "one of the reasons I like Ross Macdonald so much is that his plots make sense."

412 "Joyce Carol Oates": Joyce Carol Oates, "The Simple Art of Murder," *New York Review of Books*, December 21, 1995. Publication of a two-volume Raymond Chandler set by the Library of America prompted an Oates essay that included these sentences: "Of Chandler's younger contemporaries and heirs, Ross Macdonald (1915–1983) is outstanding. . . . Lew Archer has learned from Philip Marlowe the arresting power of the well-turned simile, but in Archer's voice language is more artfully restrained, less forced and outrageous and inclined to insult. . . . Where Chandler's crammed and confusing mysteries are largely a matter of coincidence, motivated by human greed and rarely plausible when explained, Macdonald's mysteries are thoughtfully plotted family dramas in which a malevolent past erupts into the present. A classically tragic, or a Freudian, determinism is the key to Macdonald's finely honed puzzle-novels, which might be recommended even for readers with a temperamental aversion to the mystery-detective genre."

412 " 'Then, in our hotel in Lomé' ": Lawrence Block, "My Life in Crime," *American Heritage*, July/August 1993.

412 " 'I got to the used-book stores' ": Sarah Wright, "Dancing as Fast as He Can," *Boston Magazine*, January 1994.

412 " 'The point of the stories wasn't death' ": Unsigned editorial, "Ross Macdonald," *Washington Post*, July 16, 1983.

412 " 'Archer, Macdonald's narrator, thinks and sees in one-line poems' ": Thomas J. Roberts, *An Aesthetics of Junk Fiction* (University of Georgia Press, 1990).

412 " 'I don't reread those books now for the story' ": Donald Davie interview with TN.

413 " 'With him a particular kind of crime story ended' ": Julian Symons, "Last of the classic crime-writers," (London) Sunday *Times*, July 17, 1983.

413 " 'Not until I chanced on Dashiell Hammett, Raymond Chandler, Ross Macdonald' ": From Robin W. Winks, ed., *Colloquium on Crime: Eleven Renowned Mystery Writers Discuss Their Work* (Charles Scribner's Sons, 1986).

413 " 'I picked up a Ross Macdonald mystery' ": Dulcy Brainard, "Marcia Muller: 'The Time Was Ripe,' " *Publishers Weekly*, August 8, 1994.

413 "also read Macdonald": "An Interview with Sara Paretsky," *Armchair Detective*, Summer 1991.

413 "put his name in one of her books": Sara Paretsky, *Guardian Angel* (Delacorte Press, 1992), p. 149.

Other novelists who have mentioned Ross Macdonald in their fiction include Stephen Greenleaf *(Book Case)*, Susan Isaacs *(After All These Years)*, Paco Ignacio Taibo II *(Life Itself)*, Peter McCabe *(City of Lies)*, John Dunning *(The Bookman's Wake)*, and George C. Chesbro *(Shadow of a Broken Man)*.

James Ellroy dedicated his 1984 novel, *Blood on the Moon:* "In Memory of KENNETH MILLAR 1915–1983."

413 "in tribute to Macdonald she based Millhone in Santa Teresa": Shelly Lowenkopf, "Santa Barbara Mystery Writers," *Santa Barbara News & Review*, August 29, 1985.

413 " 'I was driving on Sunset Boulevard' ": Jonathan Kellerman interview with TN.

413 " 'Let's be honest' ": Warner Books Macdonald promotional material, 1990.

414 " 'I owe him, as docs every one of us' ": Robert B. Parker, "Heroes and Debts," In *Inward Journey*.

414 " 'Ross Macdonald—on an emotional level—for me is the great teacher' ": James Ellroy interview, "A Matter of Crime, Vol. I."

414 "Catalan writer Jaume Fuster": See Nina King with Robin Winks, *Crimes of the Scene: A Mystery Novel Guide for the International Traveler* (St. Martin's Press, 1997), pp 31–32.

414 " 'Among the Americans' ": P. D. James radio interview, KCRW-FM, Santa Monica, California, 1986.

414 "films of *Blue City, The Three Roads*, and *The Ferguson Affair*":

Blue City: A Paramount Picture, 1986
screenplay by Lukas Heller and Walter Hill
"based on the novel by Ross Macdonald"
produced by William Hayward and Walter Hill
directed by Michelle Manning
starring Judd Nelson and Ally Sheedy

The Three Roads was filmed as
Double Negative (aka *Deadly Companion*): UDO Communications/
    Quadrant Films of Toronto, 1986
screenplay by Thomas Hedley Jr.
produced by Jerome S. Simon, David Main
directed by George Bloomfield
starring Michael Sarrazin and Susan Clark

The Ferguson Affair was filmed for television as
Criminal Behavior: shown on ABC-TV in 1992
starring Farrah Fawcett and A. Martinez

414 "a seven-and-a-half-hour, full-cast adaptation of *Sleeping Beauty*": Commercially available from Audio Editions/The Audio Partners. In 1998, KCRW-FM was producing a similar unabridged adaptation of *The Zebra-Striped Hearse*.

414 " 'I don't know whether I deserve this award' ": "Edgar Days," *The Third Degree*, June/July 1983.

414 " 'I couldn't bear to live in the house anymore' ": Ed Gorman, "Interview: Margaret Millar," *Mystery Scene*, May 1989.

415 "Millar and others were chased by a bulldozer": Millar to Green, January 16, 1973, UCI: "almost got run down by a bulldozer yesterday: four of my companions were knocked over: the driver was arrested! we're not winning but we're not losing either."

See also "Rain fails to stop grading at old Hammond Estate," *Santa Barbara News-Press,* January 16, 1973.

415 "she spoke approvingly of . . . Jack Kevorkian": Margaret Millar interview with TN.

415 " 'I wish other people would get as sensible' ": Gorman, "Interview: Margaret Millar."

415 "The poets . . . wrote poems":

Reynolds Price: "The Core: for Ross Macdonald," in *Inward Journey.*

Donald Davie: "On Hearing About Ross Macdonald," in *Inward Journey*; retitled "Alzheimer's Disease: for Kenneth Millar (Ross Macdonald)," in *Collected Poems* (University of Chicago Press, 1990).

Donald Davie: "A Measured Tread/for Kenneth Millar dead," in *Collected Poems.*

Diane Wakoski: "George Washington and Lew Archer in the Desert," in *Inward Journey.*

415 " 'I thought he was a brave man, very brave' ": Davie interview with TN.

415 " 'where, in the destructive element immersed' ": Millar to Symons, March 6, 1973, courtesy of Julian Symons.

415 "a certain seal waited for Millar": Brad Darrach interview with TN.

415 " 'In the end as in the beginning' ": Robert Easton, "A Tribute," in *Dictionary of Literary Biography Yearbook: 1983.*

INDEX

ABC-TV, 201, 291
Act of Fear (Collins), 272, 280
Ada (Nabokov), 289, 290
Adeline, Aunt, 17, 19, 23, 27, 34, 35
Adler, Dick, 274
Adventures of Caleb Williams, The (Godwin), 232–33
À feu et à sang (Blue City), 119
Aggeler, Geoff, 149, 171
Alcoholics Anonymous, 120
Alexander, Shana, 390
Alfred A. Knopf, 30, 32, 50, 68, 86–87, 88–89, 90, 94, 99–101, 106–7, 112, 113, 119, 133, 144, 145, 146, 150, 156–59, 168–69, 186, 197, 219, 220, 248, 255, 257, 273, 292, 318, 343, 363, 390, 397
  KM anthologies of, 261, 262, 268, 390, 398
  pricing of mysteries by, 189, 218
  promotion by, 202, 218, 245, 267, 286, 289, 304, 308–9
Algonquin Hotel, 310, 333, 354
Algren, Nelson, 12, 85, 89, 98, 124, 130, 187
Alvarez, A., 320
Ambler, Eric, 197, 255, 360
American, 92, 97, 151
American Academy of Arts and Letters, 302
American Language (Mencken), 278
American Mercury, 30, 92, 106
American Scene (Mencken), 258
"Among School Children" (Yeats), 231
An American Family, 320
Anderson, Dame Judith, 117, 353–54
Anderson, Maxwell, 41
Archer (TV series), 355–56, 359–60
Archer, Lew, *see* Lew Archer
Archer, Mr. (teacher), 33, 92
Argosy, 51, 197
Aristotle, 29, 63
Armstrong, Charlotte, 239
Articulate Energy: An Inquiry into the Syntax of English Poetry (Davie), 197

Ask for Me Tomorrow (M. Millar), 368, 377
Atheneum, 219
Atkinson, Brooks, 241–42
Atlantic Monthly, 282
Atwood, Margaret, 378, 383
Auden, W. H., 37, 48, 58, 64, 76, 254, 350, 400
  as detective-story fan, 53–54, 59, 67, 116
  KM encouraged in mystery fiction by, 54
  teaching style of, 53
Avallone, Michael, 256, 275, 313, 325–26, 354, 366
Avon, 327

Bacall, Lauren, 74, 263
Bacon, Francis, 257
Bakerman, Jane S., 362, 378, 385, 398
Balakian, Nona, 339, 342, 366, 367
Baldwin, Faith, 65
Bank of America, 294–95
Banshee (M. Millar), 403
Bantam Books, 144–46, 151–52, 156, 158, 168, 169, 172–73, 196–97, 226, 255, 285, 291, 292, 387, 397
  Archer series decisions of, 255, 260, 261–62
  book promotions of, 309, 319, 333
  KM books repackaged by, 298
  KM's grievance at handling by, 288
  printings of, 238, 267, 357, 388, 391
Barclay, Linwood, 368, 382, 397
Barkham, John, 308
Baudelaire, Charles-Pierre, 40, 119
BBC, 315, 316, 410
Beacon Press, 224, 229
Beast in View (M. Millar), 152–53, 167, 169, 173, 183, 198, 355
Beatles, 245, 300, 308
beatniks, 192, 196
Bellow, Saul, 340, 382
Ben-Hur (Wallace), 92
Berger, Thomas, 12, 412
Bernstein, Jane, 366, 377, 378, 390, 399
Beyond This Point Are Monsters (M. Millar), 291, 326

477

INDEX

Capra Press, 187
Carlisle, Kitty, 114
Carr, John Dickson (Carter Dickson), 116, 197
Carroll, Gordon, 246
Carroll, Jon, 321–22
Carter, Eddie, 213–14
Carter, Steven, 273, 301, 313, 363
Cassell, 147
Castle, The (Kafka), 53
Catalogue of Crime, A (Barzun and Taylor), 308
Catholic World, 318
Catullus, 216
Cavett, Dick, 291, 309
Cawelti, John, 347
CBC, 381, 410
CBS, 197, 201
Center for the Study of Democratic Institutions, 242, 243, 273
Center for the Study of Popular Culture, 342
Cerf, Bennett, 65, 95, 96, 114, 219, 265
Champion Breed, The (Stump), 226
Champlin, Charles, 289, 356, 403, 410
Chandler, Raymond, 8, 11, 12, 47, 50, 54, 56, 67, 70, 71, 73, 77, 87, 88, 89, 90, 91, 92–93, 94, 99, 107–8, 110, 111, 112–13, 114, 119, 125, 128, 130, 131, 133–34, 136, 139, 146, 147, 148, 151, 152, 167, 181, 183, 190, 231, 236, 237, 266, 275, 280, 287, 327, 358, 366, 412
  as critical of KM, 198, 229, 251, 272, 334, 335, 349–50, 374
  death of, 201
  KM's blurb for paperbacks of, 321
  KM's work compared with, 250–51, 252, 259, 318, 411
Charyn, Jerome, 11
Chatto and Windus, 230
Chekhov, Anton, 48
Chesterton, G. K., 30
Chicago Sun, 69, 89, 97
Chicago Sun Times, 107, 119, 373
Chicago Tribune, 342
Chicago Tribune Book World, 370
Chinatown, 356, 365
"Christabel" (Coleridge), 36, 41, 231, 349
Christian Science, 17
Christie, Agatha, 30, 198, 218, 354, 411
Chums, 24
Citizens Commission on Civil Disorders (Santa Barbara), 294, 295, 297

City Detective, 150
Clark, Mary Higgins, 386
Clemons, Walter, 286, 293, 303, 309, 310, 333, 366, 370
Cliff View Terrace, 409
Climax, 158
Clymer, Ted, 345, 359
Coady, Matthew, 315, 316
Cobb, Ty, 225–26
Cocaine and Blue Eyes (Zackel), 370
Cohen, Leonard, 383
Cohen, Mickey, 122
Coleridge, Samuel Taylor, 13, 15, 36, 56, 103, 125, 231–35, 275, 409
College Cord, 36
Collier, John, 74
Collier's, 226
Collins, 218, 261, 313, 315
Collins, Lady, 316
Collins, Michael, *see* Lynds, Dennis
Collins, Sir William, 313, 315, 316, 376
Collins, Wilkie, 11, 110, 398, 411
Colman, Ronald, 117–18
Columbia University Press, 224
Comfort, Alex, 243
Commentary, 318
Committee to Reelect the President (CREEP), 336
Condon, Eddie, 82
Congdon, Tom, 367
Congressional Record, 241
Conrad, Barnaby, 96, 243, 345, 360
Conrad, Joseph, 190
Considine, Bob, 226
Cook, Bruce, 290, 318
Cooper, Jackie, 356
Cooper-Clark, Diana, 400–401
Coral Casino Beach Club, 96–97, 117, 149, 157, 200, 248, 271, 276–77, 282, 343, 349, 378, 379, 403, 415
  KM's acquisition of cabana at, 358
Cornell University, 42, 45
Cosmopolitan, 132, 142–44, 158, 217, 219, 228, 242, 245, 255, 298
Coulette, Henri (Hank), 254–55, 270, 271, 326–27, 345, 356, 359
Coulette, Jackie, 254, 270, 271, 307, 326–27, 358
Coward, Noël, 37
Coxe, George Harmon, 99, 256
Crack-up, The (Fitzgerald), 104
Crane, Stephen, 89
Cranston, Alan, 283
Creasey, John, 236

INDEX

as father, 14, 50, 51–52, 60–61, 66, 105, 149, 154, 155, 156, 160–61, 166–67, 169, 177, 178, 203–4, 351
as father figure, 279, 301, 323, 349, 368, 393
father's relationship with, *see* Millar, John Macdonald "Jack"
father surrogates of, 21, 33, 54–55
film and television royalties of, 356
finances of MM and, 90, 95, 119, 129, 132, 158, 213, 319, 356, 384, 388, 394
first Hollywood visit of, 75–76
first published pieces of, 49
on foreign publicity campaign with MM, 313–17
formal manner of, 268, 271, 278, 279, 295, 311, 325, 334–35, 349–50
grandson of, *see* James
Hammett discovered by, 31–32, 349
health problems of, 66, 90, 119–20, 131, 135, 152, 213, 217, 357
Hollywood agents of, *see* Carter, Eddie; Rosenberg, Lee; Swanson, H. N.
Hollywood as seen by, 76, 149, 201, 246, 335–36
Hollywood projects of, 265–69
as host, 58, 104
identification with Oliver Twist by, 24
on imagery in *Divine Comedy*, 53
intelligence of, 56, 116, 117, 311
on jazz, 81–82, 84–85, 86
as KCI teacher, 49–50, 52
and lecture on history of detective story, 138–40
limelight shunned by, 291, 354
literary agents of, *see* von Auw, Ivan; Green, Ashbel; Harold Ober Agency; Keel, Daniel; Liepman, Ruth; Ober, Harold; Olding, Dorothy
as literary editor of *Grumbler*, 30
"Lizzie Borden" verses of, 239
in London, 37–38
loneliness of, 142, 154
marriage of, *see* Millar, Margaret Sturm
on "Miltonic split," 124–25
moodiness of, 178–79, 185–86
motto of, 230
music and, 103, 245
Navy commission of, 66, 68–82
and parents' separation, 15, 17–18, 19, 20
personal moral code of, 13, 34, 41, 105, 169, 227, 244, 278, 279
physical fitness of, 257, 311, 404, 406
on place in detective genre, 262

poetry and, 29, 36, 154, 179, 254–55
politics of, 135, 136, 219, 244, 275–76, 323, 337
poverty of, 20, 23, 28, 31
primary and secondary education of, 21, 24–34
on private detective in Isla Vista bank burning case, 295–96
pseudonyms of, 100–102, 109, 119, 142–44, 146, 151
in psychoanalysis, 178–79
as public speaker, 138
on purpose of detective novel, 139, 237–38
reaction to fame of, 305, 308
on relationship between critic and writer, 367
religious beliefs of, 300–301
reminiscences of and obituaries for, 410, 415
in revenge on Kitchener Library restrictions, 32
as sailor, 185
and self-blame for parents' problems, 19–20
self-confidence in work shown by, 278
self-containment of, 229, 242–43, 280–81, 295, 296, 311–12, 335, 350, 351–52, 375
self-effacing manner of, 343–44, 349, 366, 379–80
sense of humor of, 40, 59, 67, 334
sense of isolation felt by, 95–96, 101
"serious" writing and, 84, 86, 87–88, 100, 158, 197, 198, 217, 237–38, 258
sexuality of, 13, 22, 37, 47, 50, 81, 161, 227, 231
on shore leave in N.Y.C., 81–82
silences of, 254, 268, 314, 344, 374, 375
as "split" youth and man, 13–14, 31, 33, 127, 343
as successor to Hammett and Chandler, 8, 11, 12, 131, 151, 236, 237, 252, 327
as swimmer, 95, 97, 217, 247–48, 322, 335, 404, 406, 415
taboo subjects in interviews of, 306–7, 326
teaching career sought by, 36, 45, 47–48, 98, 155
UCSB job denied to, 198–99
verbal and mental strength of, 39–40, 269
Vietnam War opposed by, 270, 275–76, 279

INDEX